PAINTING OF THE HIGH RENAISSANCE IN ROME AND FLORENCE

VOLUME I

PAINTING OF THE HIGH RENAISSANCE IN ROME AND FLORENCE

S. J. FREEDBERG

Icon Editions
Harper & Row, Publishers
New York, Evanston, San Francisco, London

This book was first published by Harvard University Press.

First ICON EDITION published 1972.

 For information address Harper & Row, Publishers, Inc., 49 East 33rd Street, New York, N.Y. 10016. Published simultaneously in Canada by Fitzhenry & Whiteside Limited, Toronto.

STANDARD BOOK NUMBER: 06-430013-7

BERNARD BERENSON
IN MEMORIAM

ACKNOWLEDGMENTS

My first thanks, and the acknowledgment of my deepest sense of obligation, go to the Foundations which have made the writing of this book possible. The John Simon Guggenheim Memorial Foundation twice gave me fellowships for work on this project, in 1949–1950 and 1954–1955; the American Council of Learned Societies provided for a year, in 1958–1959, in which the task of writing was completed; the Harvard Foundation for Advanced Study and Research contributed generously toward the purchase of illustrations and to the expense of typing the manuscript. I am not less obliged to my University and to my colleagues in my own department who were willing that I pursue this task at the expense of my accustomed duties with them. Among my colleagues I owe a particular debt for their encouragement to Frederick Deknatel and John Coolidge, and to the late Wilhelm Koehler for his interest.

I owe much to my students in the seminars I have given in and around the subject of this book in recent years; our discussions have made many of my ideas more concrete or sometimes altered them. I have taken up some of their discoveries and suggestions, and have tried to credit them appropriately in the text. I have also acknowledged particularly, in every instance where I can recall my debt, the admirable generosity of Mr. Philip Pouncey in communicating not only to me directly, but to all scholars in this field, his great store of unpublished knowledge of it. I have another obligation that cannot be individually credited: it is obvious that, in a book of this kind, one is building on our whole inheritance of study of the history of art. It is impossible for me to establish where dependence ends and originality, if any is to be found here, may begin; in this respect my obligation is monumental and unspecifiable.

My researches were much facilitated by the cooperation of the late Dr. Bartolommeo Nogara of the Vatican, by the officers of the Florence Soprintendenza, by the personnel of the Gabinetto dei Disegni at the Uffizi, and of the departments of drawings at the Louvre and the British Museum. I owe a continuing debt of gratitude to the staff of the Fogg Museum Library and to Miss E. Louise Lucas and Miss Mary Ward, especially, for patient services of too many kinds to mention. I owe still more to the generous use that, on the occasion of each period of my study in Florence, I was allowed to make of the library of the late Bernard Berenson at I Tatti. My enduring thanks go to Miss Nicky Mariano for her loving help to me in this task. To Mr. Berenson himself I owe a debt, as much personal as scholarly, which is beyond all power to repay. I offered him, and he accepted, the dedication of this book in the last year of his life. Sadly, the dedication must now be made *in memoriam*.

For their help in assembling the large body of photographs that comprise the illustrations of this book I should like to thank the following friends, colleagues, and kindly interested persons: Mlle. Rosaline Bacou, Miss Sally Burrage, Mr. Eugene Carroll, Mrs. Albert TenEyck Gardner, Mrs. Hugh Matthews, Mr. Henry Millon, Mr. Philip Pouncey, Signora Maria Todorow di San Giorgio, Ambassador J. D. Zellerbach, and Prof. Federico Zeri; most particularly I am indebted to Mr. Michael Rinehart. My thanks go also to the responsible officers of the museums who have supplied photographs to me and to the indispensable commercial photographers, among them especially Signore Francesco Brandini of Florence.

Dr. Bernice Davidson watched my plans for this book take their first shape, and when the manuscript was finished she was its first reader. Both her sympathetic response and her criticisms were received with gratitude. Professor Craig Smythe was my second reader, and his kind, patient, and precise corrections of my errors of sense and style have been invaluable to me. Miss Kathleen Weil Garris used her great abilities, suitable to much more important tasks, to help me with the last laborious details of final preparation for the publisher of the manuscript, and I am under deep obligation to her. The typing of the manuscript offered unusual problems, which were overcome by the extraordinary capacities and exertions of Miss Dorothy Dean, now staff secretary of the Harvard Department of Fine Arts. Editing required the exercise of many virtues, and, in particular, an almost heroic patience. I am fortunate to have had the book, at that stage, in the kind and very able hands of Miss Ann Orlov; she in turn had the invaluable help of Miss Blair McElroy.

This book is essentially concerned with the history of that style in the painting of Rome and Florence of the early sixteenth century which, by common consent among historians of art, has come to be called "classic," or "classical." In my text I have preferred the latter form, believing that the term "classic style" should be reserved for the original happenings of this kind, in the Great Age of ancient Greece, and that "classical," with its modifying suffix, is best used to describe the later analogues, or derivations, of that style, not only within Antiquity but in the time we shall be discussing. I trust that what I intend to demonstrate of the living process of becoming, being, undoing, and transformation of this "classical style" of the High Renaissance will become clear enough to the reader; and that so also will the conception I entertain of the relation in this process between particular event and generalization. On this assumption, I shall not burden my reader with a preface. His patience will be taxed sufficiently; and to my reader, for his patience, I also give my thanks.

CONTENTS

I

INTRODUCTION

THE GENESIS OF HIGH RENAISSANCE CLASSICAL STYLE

NOTE

The attention of the reader is called to the fact that there are no footnotes in this book, but that there are superscript numbers in the text which correspond to the illustration numbers in Volume II.

References to the relevant literature on each of the artists and works discussed will be found in the index raisonné beginning on p. 579 of this volume.

The material in the text printed in double columns will be of interest primarily to the specialist reader.

Abbreviations used frequently in the text are as follows:

Frey, *Br.*	Frey, K., *Sammlung ausgewählter Briefe an Michelangniolo* (Berlin, 1899)
Golzio	Golzio, V., *Raffaello nei documenti nelle testimonianze dei contemporanei e nella letteratura del suo secolo* (Città del Vaticano, 1936)
Milanesi, *Corr.*	Milanesi, G., *Les correspondants de Michel-Ange* (Paris, 1890)
Milanesi	—— *Le lettere di Michelangelo Buonarroti* (Florence, 1875)
Pastor	Pastor, L. v., *History of the Popes* (London, 1908–1955)
Vasari	Vasari, G., *Le vite de' più eccellenti pittori, scultori ed architettori* [1568], G. Milanesi, ed. (Florence, 1878–1885, repr. 1906)

NOTE TO THIS EDITION

Technical circumstances have made it impossible to revise this book as I should have liked to do for the readers of this edition. To make up for this in part I have added a section of corrigenda *at the end of this volume. This section supplies the reader with at least the raw material with which a revision would begin, and it will arm him against those places in the text which either more recent researches of others or my own present judgment tells me may no longer be correct. The attention of the reader is directed to these* corrigenda *by asterisks in the margin of the text at each place in question. Certain typographical errors have been corrected in the text, and where changes in the photographic captions have seemed necessary they have been made by printing an amended caption, in smaller type, underneath the original one. The index raisonnée has not been altered, and should be used in conjunction with the* corrigenda.

This book was ten years in the writing: the "mean" date of its gestation is therefore about seventeen years past. I am gratified that the concern of fellow scholars with the High Renaissance since then has produced new truths that make my corrigenda *necessary, but it is also good to realize that so much of this book may still be read without correction. I hope its new readers, like many in the past decade, will find it a useful guide into the splendors and intricacies of this great period of art.*

January 1971

I

INTRODUCTION

THE GENESIS OF HIGH RENAISSANCE CLASSICAL STYLE

THE beginnings of the High Renaissance style in painting belong to Leonardo just as unequivocally as its time of fulfillment, in Central Italy, belongs to Raphael and Michelangelo. The first document for the High Renaissance style is Leonardo's, and from his own beginnings: the first fragmentary work in painting that is universally acknowledged to be his, the head of an angel in the *Baptism of Christ* of Verrocchio (Florence, Uffizi; c. 1476),[1,2] contains the essential idea on which the new style would build. This is not an image of transition between two styles except in a literally surface sense: in it an Early Renaissance preciosity of drawing and of finish coexist with its novelty of underlying form. To that novelty, however, there is no avenue of transition; there is no bridge between the style of this head by Leonardo and that of Verrocchio's portions of the painting. No near-contemporary experiment prepares Leonardo's image, nor is there any evolution toward it we can document in prior work of the young Leonardo himself. Its appearance is more sudden, and less resolvable into the context of art around it, than had been the emergence of the style of Masaccio fifty years before. As in Masaccio, the new identity of Leonardo's image results not merely from the novelty of form that we perceive but from the fact that this form is the manifest projection of a new idea; and this idea depends upon a new conception of the nature of art, and of the role of art in the interpretation of nature and of man.

Behind Leonardo's image lies the whole tradition of the investigation of nature since Masaccio, which has attained, in Leonardo's eye and hand, a culminating subtlety. The concept of the "primitive," still applicable to what Verrocchio has painted in this picture, can no longer be applied to the sophistication of optical and manual experience that appear in Leonardo's angel. In this sense alone Leonardo's image marks a new stage in the development of the Renaissance, but this is a conquest which is here turned toward a profoundly different end. This subtle knowledge is used not merely to describe an actuality but to lend substance, of supreme convincingness, to what is not real: the data of nature — so scrupulously recorded by Verrocchio in the second angel's head — have been altered by Leonardo and recombined into a form unlike any in our actual experience. This new form intends the reconciliation of two nominally conflicting aims: to achieve a harmony of regular, clear, and proportionate relations that is not evident in nature and, at the same time, to assert that this harmony pertains to an existence which is compellingly true. The image, revised into an aspect that is not in nature, nevertheless effectively conveys the look and breath of life. So far in the Renaissance these requirements had been, for the most part, met separately; Leonardo's image is the first in which they have been reconciled in such fashion that we apprehend in one moment, with equal intensity of conviction and without conflict, both the artifice and the actuality of the painted form.

Not only the form but the content of Leonardo's image has been arbitrarily remade from nature: the expression of mind, or of spirit, in the face of Leonardo's angel makes his companion seem, by contrast, as earthbound in feeling as he is in form. Leonardo's angel projects, as a sensible fact, the radiance of spirit — a luminous serenity — for which his halo is only the denatured symbol; and this radiance is charged with the sensation of a strong, slow pulse of life. Like the form in which it resides and from which it emanates, this state of spirit is both harmonious and vital and, also like it, belongs to an order of being higher than that of our accustomed world. Both the form and content of the image have been conceived with an identical ambition and with equal force of meaning: spirit and substance, equally asserted, concord in their mutually perfected vital harmony and, in their concord, merge into a unity. In this, also, Leonardo has achieved a reconciliation of what predecessors and contemporaries of the Renaissance had normally conceived as opposites.

The angel's head was Leonardo's initial exposition of the kernel of his new thought. In it he made the first statement, subsequently to be far more deeply searched and vastly elaborated, of a matured classicism of artistic style. This is the first event in the history of classicism in the Christian world that resembles, in its essence, that of the Great Age of Antiquity. It was not until a half-decade later that Leonardo had the opportunity to demonstrate in an extended form what the multiple consequences of this new idea might be: the *Adoration of the Magi* (Florence, Uffizi; 1481)[3-5] is the vehicle of this demonstration. So much thought went into the conception of the *Adoration* that it is not surprising that there was no energy, or no interest, left for the labor of its execution. The physical completion of the painting must have seemed to Leonardo a problem of much lesser order than its ideation. The new art was by nature an art of ideas and its substance lay, paradoxically, in them. That Leonardo was perhaps undiligent in the *Adoration*, but not mistaken, to record not much more than his ideas was proved by the wonderment his unfinished picture stirred among his contemporaries, and by its long and profound authority of example. Leonardo left, in the *Adoration*, perhaps less a painting than a program, of the ideas with which he and his successors in the new style would later work.

The idea that had first been stated in the angel of the *Baptism* implies its application to much more than the human image, but the development of the *Adoration* from this first idea is most immediately apparent in this very field: in Leonardo's exploration of the further possibilities of an ideal reconstruction of humanity. Among the young knights of the *Adoration* he projects countenances of a more regular and a fuller harmony than in the angel, but each one is subtly different from the other. And he has shaped the head of the only female actor, the Madonna, according to a comparable but softer canon, with a gentler rounding of its form. These perfected countenances of mature youth represent, not individuals, but a category of appearance and personality, deduced from a collective experience that nature offers of a phase of being in which human beauty is at its apogee. The other actors who take roles in the *Adoration* are also deduced from the collective observation of their category of human age: the older actors in particular are evidently representative types. These types are, by nature, less perfectable than those of youth, but they are no less arbitrarily conceived. The formulation of their type does not depend on any merely median experience of nature but on the selection of preferred qualities, of appearance and of moral value also, that their category of person offers. This typological condensation of and selection from nature is in itself an ideal process; but beyond this, the type once established, the heads that embody it are further arbitrarily revised to accommodate each of them, as much as plausibility allows, to specific intentions of ideality of form and expression. Each group of actors, by age, in the *Adoration* is an ideal generalization of a category of humanity; and the identity of each category is relieved in contrast with the others. This process of ideal typifying has, in the *Adoration*, an almost doctrinaire insistence: it is the overstatement not unexpected in the first development of a new idea.

Like the features, the expressions of the actors are — concordantly — conceived in categories. Here the weight of the moral factor in Leonardo's process of selection is quite clear. It is the "best" kind of response that we associate with a given type, as well as the strikingly characteristic, that he describes: the old kings show the gravity and concentration of wise age, the knights deep wonderment and love, the pages a tender excitement. Albertian *convenienza* here acquires a stringency as intellectual principle that, again, tends toward the doctrinaire. However, while within each group expression is categorically alike, it varies from one head to the next in a way more evident than do the features, and with a finer articulation of differences. Within each set of types there is a vibrant play of changing feeling, and through the types from youth to age, a moving crescendo into seriousness and intense concentration. By Leonardo's manipulation of the content of these heads his stringency of generalization is redeemed and his ideal categories of humanity are infused with a compelling emotional vitality.

Where it is visible, the bodily structure of the actors in the *Adoration* has been formed according to the same principles that shape their heads, but with less unrelieved insistence. This is a development beyond the first idea of Leonardo in the early angel (already undertaken, however, in the intervening *Madonna Benois*); the body of the angel showed hardly any symptom of the arbitrary processes at work in its head. In the *Adoration*, the intention to reform the body and its dress into a new harmony is most apparent in the Virgin: her whole figure has been shaped in curves, some sweeping, some slow, but all of smooth melodious effect. No awkward accident of natural appearance is permitted to intrude into the measured, woven pattern into which her body is composed: it makes visual music to give pleasure to the beholder's eye. The Virgin's pose retains an element of gentle preciosity, but there is more of ease in the way in which she turns, with the slightest incipient effect of a contrapposto, on her seat. Her posture instantly connotes a state of physical being that is the consequence not of an action but of a state of mind: the posture of her body illustrates, and its draperies comment and elaborate, a harmonious aliveness. The description of the figure and its affect of pattern concord in meaning, and this meaning is the same as that of the vital harmony of form and content in the Virgin's head. Of the equal and like perfections of form of the head and body, and of the single content that infuses both, a consonant entity of being has been created.

As if ramifying from this core of harmony in the Virgin, other possible, though less perfected, applications of the same ideal principle surround her. The male figures have been shaped in their drapery, and in the little of their bodies that is visible, into regularized and almost invariably curving forms. A few figures, like the terminal ones to either side, are posed at rest; but moving inward from them toward the Virgin there is an accelerating tempo of activity. The crescendo of intensity of feeling in the heads is accompanied by a similar increasing expressive urgency in posture: again outward form and inner state of mind concord. Regardless of the power of impulse of the actor, the bodily expression of his movement is through harmonious shapes. The utmost power of emotion, as Leonardo describes it, assumes the tenor of a harmony: even passion speaks in rounded resonance, different as a power but not different as a mode from the state of feeling of the Virgin. Even contrasts are related in this common ground and, as the wave of adoration grows and breaks upon the serene ease of the Virgin and her Child, it is clear that all these stages and varieties of feeling are gradations of an essential, and more than ordinary human, harmony of spiritual state.

The principle of an arbitrarily formed and mobile harmony is now decisively applied in the *Adoration* beyond the single figures, to their relation in composition. The figures of the picture are disposed, around the central image of the Virgin, in an instantly sensible, containing geometric pattern. This pattern is composed of two main interlocking shapes: the broad-based triangle made between the Madonna and the foremost older men, and the semicircle that embraces all the rest. The semicircle is more explicit in its form than in any earlier painting of the Renaissance, but it is startling to realize that the triangle of the composition, in this most clearly defined shape, is quite unprecedented in the history of painting. The triangle has the affect of an unshakable solidity of shape, but a solidity that contains and controls the implication of a movement: above its base its upper sides converge in equal and balancing directions on each other. The shape of the semicircle, oppositely, first implies movement, which then is contained by the disciplinary clarity and symmetry of the form. These two shapes are complementary demonstrations of the same proposition, and that is the basis of the concept of the figures, too: of forms of ideal harmony, vitally inhabited; here, in this aesthetic geometry, the prescription is in terms more explicit than it is in the figures. The two main motives of design play against each other, at once reinforcing their identity and demonstrating their community of basic kind and, as they interlock, the union between them is flexible and vibrant. The life of the design is of course not merely a function of this geometric framework but of the human images that it contains. Their vitality, literally inhabiting this energy of abstract shape, at once takes from and gives to it.

Within the essentially balancing geometry of the compositional scheme a further new idea has just begun to manifest itself: it is the extension into composition of the conception — also only incipient — of contrapposto that is in the figure of the Virgin. The rigidities of symmetrical design are avoided by a variety of counterpoint in the movement among compositional parts: a shifting of one form is countered by an opposite and complementary movement of another. It is in the figures of the old men closest around the Virgin that this device is most perceptible. The foci made by their opposite and counterbalanced forms expose, also, a further motive in the compositional scheme. Through them, and through the oblique directions implied in the contrapposto of the Virgin (and in her Child, almost an extension of her figure) run two intersecting diagonals: a pattern that suggests movement but at the same time resolves it into balance. These two diagonal motives, like the crossing of a lace, bind together all the elements within the composition, not only in the foreground but in the background; the distance, with its variety of forms — less stringently disciplined as the scene diffuses into space — is bound into and upon the primary schema of design.

The linking of the distance and the foreground space depends, not on a perspective structure, but on the incorporation of the elements of distance into one pattern with that of the foreground — a pattern that, in this instance, is in the main an ordering of the surface of the picture. Within the rearward space there is, certainly, perspective demonstration in abundance; toward the left side of the picture especially perspective lines are extended toward the front. But this extension only makes it more apparent that there is in fact no means of spatial continuity between front and rear; the perspective scheme on which the landscape is constructed is entirely detached from the space occupied by the foreground group. Such a happening is not new in fifteenth-century painting, but in an artist so expert in perspective science as Leonardo the dismissal of perspective consistency is a differently purposeful and differently meaningful act. It indicates his deliberate rejection of what had been, for Leonardo's "realist" predecessors, the authoritative basis of analysis and representation of reality and often, as well, the basis of the organization of pictorial form. Leonardo asserts, in his construction of the *Adoration*, that perspective has no more necessary authority in the making of a picture than do the separate elements of reality that perspective subsumes: perspective may serve within, but may not determine, the order — of more than a reality — which Leonardo invents. It is not irrelevant that the checkerboard rigidities of perspective structure are not, in shape or in affect, consonant with the mobile harmonies of Leonardo's new style.

Not only the relation of near and distant space but the structure of the space of the foreground group itself is not, either primarily or consistently, according to perspective logic. The shape imposed on that group, like the shapes of figures in it, results from the compromise of representational intention with aesthetic choice. The semicircle which includes the foreground figures is a solution so right for its purpose as to seem inevitable: it would seem suitable to fulfill all Leonardo's conceivable requirements: it is an inherently ideal form on which the figures can be organized as an arrangement on the picture surface and, at the same time, within the space. The effect of spatial ordnance is adequate; yet it is also evidently contrived: we sense, and can discern, the artifices with which the figures have been constrained to their adjustment among these requirements that are not, as yet, wholly manipulable in their relation to each other: of place in the superficial order of design, of place in space, and place within the whole controlling, arbitrary, ideal scheme of form. Most marked of all, among these artifices, are the frequent disproportions of the figures in their scale.

It is most conspicuously in the expression of its space that the *Adoration* betrays its character of an experimental beginning; it is the department in which Leonardo's conception of pictorial harmony is still only tentative. The space, whether that inhabited by the figures or as a void, is incompletely felt and incompletely formed. Nevertheless there is in it, as well, the profoundly significant symptom of a new idea: of a space which, while it may employ perspective where it will, is based upon an inversion of the Albertian rule. Leonardo's space begins, not as Alberti prescribes with the perspective grid, which then is populated with the figures, but oppositely, with the figures: their own volume shapes surrounding space. In a large pictorial structure like the *Adoration* the space is a consequence of, and is incidental to, the figures' grouping.

In the *Adoration* Leonardo has sacrificed one kind of logic, that of the perspective-minded Quattrocento, but he has replaced it with another. In no earlier picture are we so aware of the explicit functioning of intellect, or of a comparable range and complexity of ideas. It does not seem to be only an accident of survival that we have, for the *Adoration*, so considerable an evidence of its preparation in drawing, and that these drawings are invariably concerned less with documenting a representation than with the working out of an idea. Not only is the style of the *Adoration* "ideal" in the commonly accepted meaning for us of the word; it is the most ideated picture so far created in the history of art. Later in his career, when Leonardo had fixed his habit of recording his ideas in words as well as in their visual symbols he defined, in his own written language, most of the conceptions on which his new style was based. Often it is not in his explicitly artistic writings that a definition of artistic principle occurs, but in his scientific notes: since, in Leonardo's view, knowledge was indivisible and painting the preferred instrument of its communication, his principles of science were principles of painting too.

Painting, for Leonardo, is "the sole means of reproducing all the known works of nature" which it does "with subtle and philosophic speculation" (*Trattato* I, 4v); ". . . the mind of the painter must transmute itself into the very mind of nature and be the interpreter between it and art, commenting with art the causes of its demonstrations as they are determined by its laws . . ." (*Trattato* I, 24v). None of these words counsels imitation but, instead, the depiction of that truth which intellect may find behind the façade of visible experience. In a scientific context Leonardo defines this prescription more precisely: "This is the true rule how observers of natural effects must proceed: while nature begins with reasons and ends in experience, we must follow the opposite [path], beginning with experience and with that investigating the reasons" (Cod. E 55r). The program is the same as that by which, in painting, Leonardo seeks the typical and general that underlie the evidence of surface observation. In painting it is not sufficient to describe the physical phenomena alone: "A good painter has two chief objects to paint, man and the intention of his soul. The former is easy, the latter hard, because he has to represent it by the attitudes and movements of the limbs" (*Trattato* I, 60v); a "figure is not praiseworthy if there does not appear in it the action that expresses the feeling of its spirit" (Cod. A 109v). It is through substance that spiritual life must be communicated; and this life must be expressed in a concordant vital motion of the body: "The painted movement appropriate to the mental state of the figure should be shown with great liveliness . . . if this is not done, such a figure will be called twice dead, for it is dead because the figure is an imitation, and dead again when it does not display motion, either of the mind or body" (*Trattato* III, 110). And, with arbitrary license: "Where natural vitality is lacking, create an artificial one" (Cod. Atl. 147r). The action of the body, or its cause, "energy, originates in the movement of the spirit . . ." and then inspires the physical form, "running down through the limbs of conscious animals, it expands their muscles . . ." (Cod. Arundel 151r and v). This inspiration is pervasive in the form: in an untranslatable phrase it is "tutta in tutto, e tutta per tutto" in the body where it is caused (Cod. Atl. 302v). In the same definition energy is described as incorporeal and weight corporeal, and immediately redefined as spiritual and material. The contrast is of the two realms that Leonardo unifies, in their interaction, in his painting. To this interaction of spiritual and physical being, harmonious form must be given, since painting depends "on the harmonious proportion of the parts [that] pleases the senses" (*Trattato* I, 11). And this harmony, since it encloses vital forms, must live in itself as music lives harmoniously, in movement: "Music is not to be called anything other than the sister of painting . . . rhythm circumscribes the proportionality of the members of which harmony is composed not otherwise than the circumferential line surrounds the members of which human beauty is generated" (*Trattato* I, 16–16v).

There is not, in Leonardo's writings, any central summarizing definition of his art; the work of art itself is his manifest definition. Yet, each separate verbal definition of a principle proceeds from an identifiable common conceptual core: to see, within the indissoluble unity of being, a functional equilibrium between substance and spirit, and between immediate experience and general law. Leonardo had no collective name by which to call this new doctrine of style; it was Vasari who described it, two generations later, as the beginning of that "third manner which we wish to call the modern" (Vasari IV, 11).

The *Adoration* is an explicit demonstration of Leonardo's own later definitions, but in a form less pure and succinct than the later words themselves, or than the paintings he subsequently would achieve. The place of the *Adoration* at the beginning of an evolution is evident in the elements that are still in it of the accepted mentality of the time in which it was invented: the stress on multiplicity of men and things — Alberti's *copia* — is one of these; so also is the insistent fineness of the drawing and the instances of febrility of feeling — sometimes more than entirely classical principle allows. These elements are not yet wholly reformed into harmony with the essential new idea, but for all their interest and number, these persistences of Quattrocento mind remain a minor fact and the new idea uncontestably the dominant.

It is in the context of other Florentine painting of the time of the *Adoration*, circa 1480, that the relation between old and new, and the significance of the new, in Leonardo's art comes more fully clear. In Florence of this date a variety of artistic modes exists which may be thought of as developments, of different bent and different emphasis, of the central ideas — more easily definable by generalization than from any one concrete example — of the style of the Early Renaissance. Among Leonardo's Florentine contemporaries it is the practice of Domenico Ghirlandaio[6] which is least like his. Too summarily, we may describe Ghirlandaio's art as a development, almost to an extreme degree, of the most objectively comprehensible and the simplest ambitions of the Early Renaissance style: the accurate transcription of the tangible evidence of nature. The achievement of this ambition is prerequisite to Leonardo's style but, beyond this, their art has no connection. Even when Leonardo wishes — as he does in incidents within his paintings — to describe a precise fact of appearance his method surpasses Ghirlandaio's. The realism of Ghirlandaio is derived from what might be described as tactile scrutiny; it is the reality of solids apprehended in their plastic form as tangible loci of perspective space. Leonardo's realisms are not only plastic but optical as well: with a subtlety far more than Ghirlandaio's, he recreates substance in its environment of air and light; even in his acts of exact natural description Leonardo demonstrates a different order of perception. It is more important, however, that Leonardo's perception is part only of a whole process of intellectual apprehension which proceeds far beyond the merely visible stratum of the observed fact, and in this Ghirlandaio does not share. The whole ideal construct in which, in Leonardo, descriptions are immersed, is a world quite separate from that of Ghirlandaio's diligent prose.

Essentially the same distinction separates Leonardo's style from that in painting of his master Verrocchio; the contrast evoked within the *Baptism of Christ*[2] is sufficient documentation of their difference. Like Ghirlandaio's, Verrocchio's rare instances of painting are primarily concerned with the reproduction of tangible reality, and in this Verrocchio exceeds Ghirlandaio in the precision with which he describes complexities of form.

In the *Baptism* Verrocchio's figures are dominantly plastic and, appropriately, sculptural, almost stark within an airless space. Yet, to indicate their more exact appearance they are modelled with a highly differentiated light; in the body of Christ it may be Leonardo's hand that seems, more subtly than elsewhere, to articulate this light. Verrocchio's intimacy of observation and his use, to describe it, of a complex light are certainly among the guiding indications for young Leonardo, but not more. Verrocchio's vision is still of the isolated plastic object: light reveals the substance, but the substance is not unified to its environment of light.

Also precedent to Leonardo's style is what Verrocchio's variety of form and light implies: a conception of a world at least incipiently in movement. In his "proper" medium of sculpture, more than in his painting, Verrocchio's whole figures and compositions are in fact conceived in terms of imminent, or even actual, motion. Where Ghirlandaio's paintings are, mostly, accumulations of static images, rigidified by now old conventions of perspective logic, Verrocchio's works tend to transcribe a reality that is felt as animate. This animation extends at least in part beyond the region of the physical, to the description of psychological states — and it is again in sculpture rather than in painting that this is true — of remarkable immediacy and vitality.

It is in the art of Antonio Pollaiuolo [7] that there is the most persuasive demonstration of the conception, as the Renaissance before Leonardo had evolved it, of a vital world. This vitality is expressed by Pollaiuolo in a vocabulary of realism as extensive and accomplished as Verrocchio's. However, the very vehemence of action of Pollaiuolo's figures is not a precedent but an antithesis for Leonardo's, for whom aliveness must be harmoniously expressed. Also unlike Leonardo is Pollaiuolo's concept of vitality as being dominantly an expression of the physical being: the states of mind of Pollaiuolo's actors are consequent upon their physical activity. Expression of countenance and body may concord as they do in Leonardo, but neither expression is harmonious. The countenance does not convey a generalization of an attitude of spirit but a response, as momentary as the action of the body, of the psychological to the physical mechanism. The emotions that Pollaiuolo describes may be characterized, in an arbitrary verbal distinction, as psychological, but not psychic, states.

In these three contemporary practitioners of Early Renaissance style their primary concern, in spite of differences of emphasis, was with the description of physical reality. Among the great Florentines who, toward 1480, were mature in style, Botticelli represents an artistic attitude significantly different. He had learned, in part from the example of Verrocchio and Pollaiuolo, the most sophisticated techniques for transcription of reality — a reality which, like that of these older painters, was animate. Botticelli's skill in describing nature was equal to that of Verrocchio and Pollaiuolo, and his sensitivity of response to it was even greater. Certain of his pictures, particularly of the earlier seventies,[8] contain parts, and in a few cases are altogether, of a fineness in the record of reality that, until Leonardo, cannot be surpassed. But these descriptions do not seem to be, as such, the primary end of any Botticellian image; it is not the "realization" of a figure or the illustration of its action that is his chief concern. Usually the description of reality is inconsistent or incomplete; distortions, sometimes exquisitely subtle, sometimes blunt, have been imposed upon the forms in order to extract from them an arbitrary ornamental value. Then, dominant above all else in each painting, is its insistent expression of a superphysical state, communicating not "psychological" response but a profound and pervasive condition of the spirit.

Botticelli's art, like Leonardo's, represents a significant historical resolution, of a tradition of spiritual communication older than the Renaissance (but reshaped in contemporary, Neo-Platonic terms) with the Early Renaissance disciplines of representation. In Botticelli of the early seventies a synthesis has been achieved of which the elements are much the same as those which the early art of Leonardo reconciles. In Botticelli, as in Leonardo, adequate physical description coexists with an ornamental and affective value imposed on the form, and further coexists with a profound, generalized, spiritual state of being. But in Botticelli the equilibrium among these elements is precarious and short-lived; as he develops the element of natural description tends increasingly to be displaced by the other two. In a quite opposite way, the development of Leonardo is measurable in terms of the increasing affirmation of equilibrium among the elements of his synthetic style. The spiritual state that Botticelli wishes to express is exquisite and unstable, dominantly and sometimes even morbidly introspective: it is quite distinct from the vitalized generalizations of feeling, synthesized from external stimulus and inward response, that Leonardo's actors show. The reshaping of physical form in both artists is unlike: Botticelli often as not offends against the laws of plausibility, as Leonardo takes care not to do. The shapes in which form is recast in Botticelli tend, as in Leonardo, toward musicality, but Botticelli's musicality is complicated and excitant in rhythm, not measured, proportionate, and consonant. And, in the whole order of the composition Botticelli knows no means of concord between vitality and ideal order, as Leonardo does, but only the alternatives, incommensurable for him, of traditional perspective logic and free improvisation.

The humanity in Botticelli's pictures is, as much as in Leonardo's, a representation of an ideal, and this is a mutual difference in them from their contemporaries. But these two ideals are essentially diverse. In Botticelli's most peculiarly characteristic images, the physical being is tenuously beautiful, spare and even exquisitely refined. The sense of substance of the body is diminished until — Neo-Platonically — we feel the translucence of the spirit through it. Form and spirit concord in fineness, but the form is ultimately not more than the vehicle — the means of visible articulation — of the being it contains. Leonardo's actors are, in contrast, inhabited substantialities: in them bodily presence and its beauty of form are not less meaningful than the body's content of spirit and emotion. Leonardo's ideal humanity is conceived like that of classical Antiquity while Botticelli's ideality remains, for all its aestheticism and sophistication, Christian in its essence.

The whole synthetic structure of Leonardo's art in the *Adoration* functions according to principles that are basically like those which govern Ancient classical style. However, Leonardo's new version of the classical style is not imitative or self-consciously recreative; it is in no sense a neoclassicism. It originated — in a way we shall try to explain — out of an experience of a preexistent and contemporary Christian culture which had acquired, partially and inconsistently, some of the attitudes — some imitated and some self-generated — of a classicism. The *Adoration* constantly betrays — as all art of the High Renaissance will continue subsequently to do — that its classicism was born out of, and lives within, a Christian context. But it remains that the first step in the fulfillment of this classical style that was possible to Christian culture is in Leonardo, and that the multiple meanings of this step are first demonstrated in the *Adoration*. Earlier in the Renaissance there had, of course, been phenomena of style that had not only surface aspects of classicism but, as well, basic elements of classical gestalt. There is a line of accomplishment in Quattrocento art of what may be called (to distinguish it from Leonardo's new act of style) early classicism, which may be traced in Central Italian painting through the pure line of aesthetic descent from Masaccio: its peak is in the style of Piero della Francesca.[8] This early classicism bears, to the style of Leonardo, a relation that (in terms of roughest analogy only) is like that of the Greek art that precedes the Golden Age to the style of that time: Leonardo's style is equally a maturing of potential in his antecedent line. This does not discount the creative power of invention that makes the maturing of the style; the act of maturation is far more than merely reminiscent.

The aesthetic notion "classical" is in origin an appellation of value judgment, signifying "of the highest class"; it implies that the achievement of this class has at its command resources that are not only more, but qualitatively higher, than those of a preceding art. It denotes fulfillment, not only of aesthetic resource but, in the way of older judgments, of intellectual and moral development as well. The *locus classicus* is thus not only preceded by a lesser style (which nevertheless prepares it) but may be followed by a style of which — despite the possibility of still more developed aesthetic resource — the moral and intellectual value may be less. It is such a synthetic junction of fulfillments that the term "classical" implies, and which has come to being in the art of Leonardo. The term "High Renaissance" itself, in its distinction from the term "Early Renaissance," contains the same complex of value judgments and implications of historical process. The association of the terms "High Renaissance" and "classical" is a mutual and multiple reinforcement of meaning, referring at once to the historical situation and the character of this art, and to its analogy, partly willed, in kind and process, to a supreme moment of an inextinguishable tradition.

A comparison with the Early Renaissance antecedents of Leonardo's classicism helps to define the fulfillment he achieved. It is Piero della Francesca, the highest representative of the earlier classicism, who makes the case of his time most clear. In him, intendedly precise natural description coexists effectively with intellectually formulated principles of geometric order. Within each seeming accident of appearance Piero seeks out, or invents, a rationale of form. Whole physical beings, with their multiple excrescences, seem to be constructed by a process of building outward, in successively more minute geometrizing steps, from a central geometric core. Actuality and intellectual analysis are simultaneously satisfied by this process. However, the two ambitions that they represent are absolutely far apart;

despite the relentless step-by-step logic of transition that Piero makes between them, the separateness of their extremes is always sensible. They are not harmonized upon a middle ground, as in Leonardo's method: Piero's process is not synthetic but extensive. That Piero controls the great extent embraced between the poles of his ambition is a consequence of his extreme stringency and logic of procedure, but the austere discipline he achieves thereby is not the harmony of Leonardo.

The geometric character of Piero's structures is that of the perspective system which, in his own hands, became the culminating expression of the pictorial science of the fifteenth century. This system is based upon the reproduction — and the creative reconstruction — of a static world. Its order is of absolute rigidity; each substance in it is immobilized, rooted as it were to the square destined for it on the perspective plan; each form is, further, apprehended in its separate geometric identity within this plan. The sense of clarity and order is, according to Piero's perspective doctrine, absolute; but this is both a static and an additive order. Leonardo's order is, on the other hand, as animate in form as it is in the expression of its human personalities; its unity is achieved not by addition but by synthetic complements of mobile shapes and beings. Piero's mute and immutable creation does not, in fully classical sense, make a harmony; as Leonardo's own definition implies, there is no music without movement.

In the Early Renaissance painting of Florence that is contemporary with the *Adoration* classicizing precedents exist for many separate elements within its style, but nowhere are these elements singly handled as they are by Leonardo, and above all, no other contemporary combines such elements into a comparable whole. Leonardo's invention is an isolated fact, in its moment, and for many years to come. For two decades after 1480 the dominant direction of Florentine painting consisted in the further development of the diversities of Early Renaissance style (which we have earlier described in part). Precisely because it is so conspicuously an isolated act, the causes of Leonardo's invention cannot lie in any circumstance of history external to the artist; a naïve historicism is even less applicable to this case than to others in the history of art. Leonardo's invention is, of course, ultimately an act of personal genius, but to say this is a mystical tautology and not an explanation. But this genius did permit, or cause, Leonardo to confront the situation of art in his time and comprehend it in its varieties of meaning: to recognize the problems that these varieties of meaning posed and work out their solution. Since the artistic problem of the Early Renaissance was, in an exceptionally precise degree, the visible symptom of its more general cultural problem, Leonardo's accomplishment of a solution was of far more than its artistic import.

This problem had been implicit in the art of the Early Renaissance since its invention of a new idea of style; it was the inevitable consequence of the confrontation of invention with tradition. We can, here, indicate the nature of the problem only in terms that are excessively schematic. The proposition made by the innovators of the Early Renaissance was, essentially, twofold: it set forth the validity and interest for art of the world of physical reality, and proposed that this reality demonstrated a rational and objectifiable order. This conception was the nominal antithesis of the concern, inherited from medieval art, with supernatural and generalized religious, spiritual values, and of the medieval modes of subjective and nonrational apprehension. The principal talents of the time and the chief energies of art were devoted to the exploration of the new proposition; however, the same personal and cultural energy that inspired inventive search seems also to have regenerated, in its ambience, the vitality of the older tradition. The intention to make spiritually expressive works of art continued, altered often by contact with the new invention, but not diminished by it. It would not seem that, in the first generation of artists of the Early Renaissance, there was any assumption of a necessary incompatibility between spiritual and physical experience: the point of conflict came rather in the concept — philosophical as well as aesthetic — which was ancillary to each, of rational order on one side and a nonrational mode of apprehension and presentation on the other. Spiritual and physical experience managed to coexist effectively in art — sometimes in a mutually restrained accommodation, more usually by the simple domination of one interest over the other. Occasionally, as in the evolved art of Donatello in particular, inspired acts of artistic violence brought the two worlds powerfully together. When all but the first kind of conjunction occurred, however, the principle of order was at stake, compromised or even wholly sacrificed.

The spiritual values of tradition were already changing, in kind and in aspect, under the pressures exerted on them in this coexistence with the new inventions, but an actual, rather than potential, conflict between realism and spiritual value did not emerge until the new realism had approached its full measure of development. It became evident toward 1460–1470 that the realism of the Quattrocento was a self-sufficient and a separable way of artistic practice and of thought, capable on the one hand of making a work of art out of the data only of physical experience, and on the other hand of translating superphysical sensation entirely into realist terms. In this decade realism not only achieved an apparently complete competence but, further, acquired such authority as to compel the nearly entire submission to its vocabulary and means of the content of human expressiveness of art. Spiritual sensation was now no longer (in the work of most important artists) of the generic, superpersonal kind associated with the ideas of religion; it became instead the property of a precise event and of a highly specified individual form. When expressiveness of this kind was intense it not only violated the rationality of order, as it had done before, but was communicated in a complex description of its physical effects that dispersed the unity of form. Only where expressive content was much diminished or, indeed, where reality alone sufficed, could rationality of form be present too: the art of Ghirlandaio and Perugino would in time demonstrate this in a most obvious degree.

In the moment in which Leonardo was receiving his first artistic education the situation of art in Florence thus contained the matured matter of a conflict of principles. Physical reality could coexist with the expression of spiritual being only by denying its collective nature and its value of general idea, and by translating it into an experience bound to individual personality and form; and, when this conjunction was achieved with any power of content, it could not then be reconciled with aesthetic and ideal requirements of rational order, or with its implication of a harmony. Philosophic thinking, confronting an analogy of this situation in its own sphere, recognized a now mature conflict of principles and faced, with a new sense of urgency, the — for philosophy — eternal problem of the relation between spirit and substance, and of the rationalized justification of their relation. More than it invented, contemporary philosophy recast an old solution, ultimately Christian, in the terms of a modern Neo-Platonism.

Like the philosophers, but, as far as we know without stimulus from them, Leonardo recognized the problem that had matured in the arts. We postulate that Leonardo realized, in the process of his own education and his experience of art outside it, both the resources and the limitations of the current Quattrocento modes and perceived the major elements of conflict of artistic principles which, in different measure, each mode did not reconcile. The problem, grasped by Leonardo in the moment of its maturity as a problem, was to effect this reconciliation of principles. To do this it was first necessary to revise the concepts both of reality and of spiritual value as they appeared within contemporary practice, and at the same time to devise a new embracing principle and new means for their rational concordance. Leonardo refused the thesis of realism, that spiritual expression subserved particular matter, and did not adopt the new — but also archaistic — solution advanced by Neo-Platonism and by its artistic spokesman, Botticelli, that spirit and substance, though coexistent, were separate and incommensurable. Both these conceptions of relation were conjunctive and unequal, and Leonardo sought instead an equal, functional, and synthetic relation of which the governing mode should be its rationality, of ideas and of form. We have already seen the first evidence of the solution Leonardo found.

The character of mind that invented this solution was, like the problem itself, a consequence of a particular historical situation: not only does this mind shape experience but it is itself shaped by the content of experience that is available to it. Requiring solution in synthesis, the historically presented problem predisposes the synthetic response of the intelligence that works with it. This intelligence, with its power, at the level of highest genius, to synthesize data in terms of its consonant functioning, was in its beginnings and in its first decisive acts an intelligence of art. It was this artist's intellect which — in a way not different in essential bent from the whole "realist" tradition of the Early Renaissance — was to extend its shaping, synthesizing power into a vast range of natural science; but the problems of nature with which Leonardo would mostly deal would remain those which were susceptible to the instrument of visual perception, or which were reducible, in the process of analysis or in solution, to the symbols of design.

Leonardo's solution was remarkable not only in its kind but in its time of happening. It is possible for the historical dialectician to believe that a High Renaissance style should have been invented eventually, and that its character should not have been fundamentally different from that given it in the actual invention of Leonardo: this seems in fact to have occurred, but only, at the earliest, a decade and a half after Leonardo's *Adoration*, and two decades after his first proposal of the ideal core of the new style in the angel of the *Baptism*. A historical crisis may precipitate a new solution, but when Leonardo invented his new style there was yet no crisis, but only the recent maturing of the elements out of which a cultural crisis would subsequently grow. Leonardo's genius asserted itself not alone in personal, but in the more significant fact of historical precocity. His departure from Florence in 1481, leaving the unfinished manifesto of the *Adoration* behind him, almost restored the development of art in that city to its normal rhythm. The picture remained to bemuse the minds of Florentines but not to be comprehended wholly until, more than a decade later, the processes of more ordinary artistic history caught up with it.

Leonardo's art was a still more wholly isolated phenomenon in Milan than it was in Florence. This isolation may have been propitious, for in it Leonardo was able to dedicate himself, without the distraction of competing styles, to the further research of his own ideas. The *Virgin of the Rocks* (Paris, Louvre; the version in London, despite the possible reading of the documents, * not by Leonardo),[10,11] contracted for in 1483, is not only a finished exposition of the intimated beauties of the *Adoration* but a more developed exposition of the thesis it contains. Like the *Adoration*, the *Virgin of the Rocks* holds strong persistent evidences of a quattrocentesque fascination with descriptions of reality — here, because they are in finished state, yet more visible: in the painting of the folds of drapery, in the hair, and in the quality of texture of the skin, there is the culmination of a century of realist ambitions. There are, further, ultimately subtle visual records of botanical and geological phenomena. This supreme descriptive fineness is a separable artistic end for Leonardo, but in one aspect of its meaning only; it works within a context that subsumes its simple function of description of reality. The background — from which the picture takes its name — apparently a document of an exact study of geology, indicates how this search for seemingly exact truth proceeds. Accurate in description of detail and plausible as a whole geological formation, the construction into which the rocks are built is nevertheless not an actuality; it is a recombination into ideally dictated form of the results of observation. According to Leonardo's own dictum, his observation is not only of appearances but of their underlying causes. He has acquired more than information of the look of rocks; he understands the laws of statics by which they "work"; he apprehends the observed data in their functional relationship. Thus knowing so precisely the outward form of nature and, so profoundly, its inner mode of working, it is possible for him — more than to imitate — to recreate, to his own aesthetic prescription, a nature that is at the same time arbitrary and plausible. This mode of recreation applies, obviously, to more than those aspects of his works which deal with geology or flora; it is the same kind of functional understanding and consequent power of aesthetic recreation that permits him to reshape humanity.

In this invented background the vibration of form and light, only adumbrated in the *Adoration*, is a subtle and pervasive obbligato to a quality of form and content in the figures that is more tempered than in that picture, and more immediately perceptible as harmonious. This difference is not merely the result of subject matter — a devotional image contrasted with an incident of narrative. The Virgin, central personality in both paintings, is not cast in these two pictures in a very different emotional role, yet the *Virgin of the Rocks* displays a more contained and graver state of mind. The same quality, of more muted, yet not less subtly vibrant spirit, shows in the face of the angel and, differently articulated to befit their age, in the faces of the children. Feeling is less urgent and complex than in the *Adoration*, but it has a deeper resonance. The forms of the actors, in face and body both, and their character of movement, have a concordant deeper harmony: fuller, rounder, more deliberate and slow. Here, further, we can see what the *Adoration* only hints at in its unfinished state and what, as well, was there imperfectly conceived: the remodelling not only of contour, but of the entire plastic form, toward a pattern of full roundness. As the forms acquire this degree of plastic depth — even here not yet consistently expressed — the slow pulse of rhythm that moves through the figures warps, with their movement, within space. The space created by the figures, as well as their design in silhouette, begins to be knit into an animate unity of structure of which the harmony thus becomes at once more various and more substantial. The very disposition of the figures in plan in the *Virgin of the Rocks* affirms this growing intent to achieve a harmony which, literally, is more solidly based: the triangle with its barely suggested spatial differentiation in the *Adoration* here tends, with a conscious emphasis, toward the spatial form of the pyramid.

As subtly and variously as the light has been manipulated in the *Virgin of the Rocks*, it is by no means yet according to Leonardo's developed conception of *sfumato*. The light is still in part a precise searching and descriptive instrument, and the multiplicity and fineness of effects it seeks are almost too many to be reconciled wholly into a harmony. Yet the range of depths and luminosities the light explores is, more explicitly than in the unfinished *Adoration*, new to art; and it asserts a new kind not only of optical, but of pictorial experience. In the *Virgin of the Rocks* the reaches and the powers of the lights and shadows assume a role, and a dimension of aesthetic meaning, not less than that of the forms the light reveals. Light, as chiaroscuro, and form become equal agents in the work of art; and as light extends its role it begins, in this picture, to absorb the aesthetic and descriptive functions which, in most contemporary practice, were filled by color. Color, in the *Virgin of the Rocks* — and in the *Last Supper* which succeeds it — is still a meaningful factor of pictorial effect, but already ancillary to the light. Chiaroscuro — its darks as much as its lights — has begun to infuse the colors, muting them, as in the darkened blue and near-browns of the Virgin's dress and in the red mantle of the angel; or (as in the yellows of the lining of the Virgin's cloak and in the angel's sleeve) chiaroscuro transmutes color, by a power of translucence, into a primary meaning of its light. These last incidents of colored radiance are only episodes within the painting; mostly the chiaroscuro works as if to absorb color, and to replace its effects with its own rich repertory of sensation. The tonality that dominates the *Virgin of the Rocks* is that of its browned, neutral, background, darkly atmospheric, which invades and encompasses the figures.

The primacy of the new chiaroscuro over color and the process, which begins here, of absorption of the one into the other, is at the beginning the consequence of a temperamental choice, but it was a choice which, for more than temperamental reasons, required to be made. An art like Leonardo's, of which the profoundest novelties were of intellectual conception, and in which the observation of sensuous phenomena was ceaselessly accompanied by the working of a generalizing mind, would tend to see in color a secondary aspect of experience; and even within color Leonardo wished to seek the essence, light, of which color was a function. In this art, which sought a harmony, and in which it would increasingly be realized that harmony entailed concession and accommodation, the factor, color, predetermined by the first act of choice to be secondary, would tend to a decreasing role. For the Quattrocento color had served, in one of its most important uses, as an agent of analysis, defining the separate identity of seen things as well as their discrete places in an order of design. In a view that sought a unity of vision and design, this Florentine tradition of the Quattrocento, of "local" color — color as a property of distinct phenomena — could be only an impediment; and to make Leonardo's unity it was necessary that local color be dissolved into an including ambience of light.

This process of domination of color by chiaroscuro, and of sublimation of the color into light, can first be documented so explicitly in the *Virgin of the Rocks*, but it had an earlier, unintendedly more complete and, in Florence, directly influential demonstration in the unfinished *Adoration*: the revelation in that picture of the vast resources of a Leonardesque chiaroscuro would, in time, be reinforced by Leonardo's own later development of a chiaroscuro mode, to make indelible impression on the painting of the Cinquecento within Florence.

The *Virgin of the Rocks* stands so relatively close in the time of its conception to the *Adoration* that the development in style between the two, though evident, is not surprising in degree. The comparison of the *Adoration* with the *Last Supper* (Milan, S. M. delle Grazie; c. 1495–98),[12,13] begun more than a decade later, makes a differently compelling effect: the *Last Supper* belongs to a measurably higher region of artistic being. The impact of this fresco on the spectator, even in its ruined state — and its ruin makes of it a document comparably as "unfinished" as the *Adoration* — is, unlike the *Adoration*, absolutely instantaneous, concentrated and explicit. The character of generalization here is much more broad and clear: the earlier picture seems, in comparison, still to be entangled in its quattrocentesque *copia*. There is no relic in the *Supper*, as there still is in the *Adoration*, of the need to read the parts before the whole comes clear: the fresco comes into the mind and eye of the beholder at once and all at once, in instant unity.

The design which, by its whole effect, creates this instant impact of a unity is formed of elements like those in the *Adoration* but more explicit in their geometry of shape, and their way of combination is simple to the point of boldness. The motives of the composition are deduced in part from the function of the picture as a spatial insert in the wall: its considerable dependence on straight lines derives from the perspective system drawn from the given rectangular frame. However, this perspective does not work as would a Quattrocento scheme; Leonardo's notion of the function of perspective science is now still more arbitrary than in the *Adoration*. Space within the wall is not illusionistic; it is not readable from any point within the actual hall as an extension in perspective of our space. Within the picture, the perspective of the room is adequate as a setting for the persons in the foreground plane, but the space behind is not habitable by the figures and is not connected with them. The station point has been placed much too close to the picture plane so that, while preserving a plausible appearance of constructed space, the effect of the perspective scheme shall not be — in Pieresque fashion — static and additive, but active in the swift convergence of orthogonals. This energized convergence forms a counterpoise of elements in movement. The whole perspective space, thus energized, and closing arbitrarily upon the figures, becomes a vibrating sounding board for them and throws them into greater salience.

The convergence of perspective lines has been more obviously manipulated toward another arbitrary end, simultaneously aesthetic and contentual. The equal energies of the orthogonals converge upon, and find their equilibrium within, the central image of the Christ — the one unmoving, wholly stable human form within the picture. His figure, with its outstretched arms, works like a key: it locks, within its stable core, the counterbalancing energies of composition, and at the same time locks the composition of the surface with the artifice of space; finally, it locks, in an indissoluble identity, the core of form into the core of content. Outward from the image of the Christ the rounded waves of the figure composition swell across the network of converging straight lines. The figures, in their rounded substance, are the complement of the rectangular void of space, and the outward impulse of their energy is counter to, and balances, the framework of convergences. This latter circumstance of structure coincides exactly with the intention of the picture's content as the Apostles, irrevocably bound to the Christ, yet recoil from him in response to his quiet but terribly charged utterance, just spoken.

The new power of generalization does not stop at problems of pictorial form but is equally applied to the humanity that acts the Last Supper. The figures here are drawn in simpler shapes than in the *Adoration*: minor elements of form are quite subsumed in sweeping and powerfully ample curves. The full, even heavy, roundness of shape is applied also to their three-dimensional development of form. The Apostles become a more than ordinary humanity not only by an idealizing revision of appearances but by aggrandizement of mass and sense of scale: they have the aspect of creatures of a hitherto unimaginable grandeur and physical power. The effect in them of an expansion of the dimension of humanity is accentuated by a close massing of the figures, and by an arbitrary violation of all but the aesthetic criteria of scale — a violation perceptible to the spectator, like all of Leonardo's trespasses against reality, only beneath a first impression of entire plausibility.

The heads of the Apostles,[13] like those of the actors of the *Adoration*, are based upon the multiple categories of humanity that nature offers, but this evidence of nature has been more boldly and decisively cast into a mold of typicality. There is less interest than in the *Adoration* to invent subtleties that differentiate or modify ideal appearance, and concordantly there is almost no concern to describe nuances of content in these heads. Expression of face, and of gesture also, is positive and clear, forceful in explicit statement: it emanates a power of spiritual being that has grown in dimension like the body it inhabits. It is according to Leonardo's prescription that the Apostles should feel as they look and look as they feel. This race of beings, their way of acting individually and in concert, and the environment in which they meet belong so perceptibly to a region of superior existence that the onlooker cannot but realize that this world, for all its palpable presence, is meant for his regard but is not meant, in any sense of an illusionistic realism, for him to share. The strip of tablecloth across the front plane of the picture is meant to be a sensible boundary between our actual world and this ideal.

The *Last Supper* is the profound and decisive development of the program laid down in the *Adoration*, more than a decade and a half before. The complexities and the few elements of unclarity in that first extensive statement have now been resolved, and its intellectual principles have been almost dogmatically made clear; but in Milan there was no painter who could, even by devoted acts of imitation, understand them.

The *Last Supper* was finished by 1498, on the threshold of the new century, when Leonardo had been absent from Florence sixteen years. There, rid of Leonardo except for that disturbing and incomprehensible relic, the *Adoration*, painting continued to develop much as if Leonardo did not exist. The process of development was characterized, as in general in the latest phases of a style, by an ever-increasing diversity of modes; single strands of artistic possibility, earlier extracted from the core of the ideas of style of the Early Renaissance, were drawn out farther still, and occasional new recombinations were invented for some old ideas. The cleavage between the opposite extremes of style of circa 1480, represented by the modes of Ghirlandaio and Botticelli, increased to the extent of absolute polarity: in Ghirlandaio by his descent to an artistic prose even more bald than in his early style; in Botticelli by an accelerating access of spirituality, and ultimately even of mysticism in his art. This polarity of artistic style represented the entire evolution, in the 1490's, of the problems of conflict that had first matured in the seventies.

The incipient conflict of cultural attitudes which the different modes of painting symbolized had been, as we observed, partly — only temporarily — resolved in Neo-Platonism. But in the 1490's this conflict, culturally as well as artistically grown to the dimension of full crisis, broke out in the violent cleavage of all of Florentine society. Savonarola was the agent, but the symptom also, of reaction against the "modern" ideas of the Renaissance by that greater part of Florentine society which had, in effect, never participated in it. The culture of the Renaissance belonged essentially to an elite; there were whole orders of the population and of the Church in whom the mentality of the Middle Ages persisted with little or no basic change. The Savonarolesque revolution was only temporarily successful, and it represented a historical reaction rather than a new beginning, but it still performed a function which was related to the inception of a new period of culture and a new style of art. It posed, in drastically present and pervasive terms, the problem of conflict between the physical and supernatural, and reasserted that spirituality was not an abstract fiction of religious experience but a vital and an actual motive force. Finally, it confronted Florentine culture with the need for an urgent consideration of its elements of crisis. The revolution was of the many, but the response in this constructive sense would be, again, by the very few.

About the time when Botticelli began to abandon a relative moderation of his Neo-Platonic resolution of the Florentine dilemma and move instead toward a mystical extreme, another kind of pseudo-resolution appeared in Florentine painting. This was less a resolution than a species of forcible conjunction of the antipodes of late Quattrocento style; the personality who achieved it was Botticelli's pupil, Filippino. In his art spiritual expression became more intimate and specifically personal than in Botticelli but it also became conspicuously less pure: sentimental, nervous, and at times morbid. This exaggerated content was expressed in forms for which there was no fixed and including norm of naturalism but in which — contrasting sharply with the style of Botticelli — there was the utmost stress of physical existence, often turgid, and of precise characterization of realist detail. It was Filippino who finally executed the picture for the altar in S. Donato a Scopeto for which Leonardo's *Adoration* had been intended. Done after careful pondering of Leonardo's painting, and with the evident intention to imitate and rival some of his effects, Filippino's altar (Florence, Uffizi; 1496)[14] is a revelation of the inaccessibility of Leonardo's ideas to a still Quattrocento mind. Precisely on account of the sincerity with which it pursues its disparate artistic ends Filippino's *Adoration* is the antithesis, in its disunity, of Leonardo's.

There is, nevertheless, an element in Filippino's style of which the purpose seems to be that of a binder among its disparities; this element is derived — and as is Filippino's habit, exaggerated — from Botticelli, but it also is related to a principle of Leonardo's art. It consists in the imposition on all the properties of style of a common animation which, however, is of uneven and eccentric temper; it is closest to the suggestion of a unity when it becomes so urgent as to seem to sweep with it the matter it affects. This current of activity, inclusive as it may be, is still not a device of synthesis; and it is not accompanied by any system of accommodation of extremes or of their regulation in a harmony. In the hands of an artist of far different stature, the idea of a pervading urgent animation might have been potential of a significant reshaping of contemporary style, for it, and the other elements of Filippino's art, are those on which a baroque style could be built; not, however, without its own kind of new accomplishment of synthesis. Filippino himself, in some few of his developed works — as in the *Assunta* of S. M. del Popolo in Rome — came as near to an anticipation of baroque style as was possible to a painter of the fifteenth century. His art remains a symptom of dilemma in his time and a document of an attempt, at least in part aware, to solve it.

The style that emerges in the painting of Piero di Cosimo in the nineties is another form of the conjunction of extremes: of eccentric fantasy of content and of the most scrupulous realism of form.[15] In his realism, Florentine system is combined with Flemish expertness in the reproduction of detail. Piero makes no effort in his pictures of the nineties to synthesize these extremes within his art; on the contrary, the deliberate exploitation of their contrast is a major resource for him. The subjects of his best paintings of this period are from the repertory of Antique literature but nothing could be less classical than the interpretation these themes receive in Piero's style.

Piero was an end product of the Quattrocento development of individuality, which in him culminated in personal and artistic eccentricity; his was a mind which delighted in dilemma, not in its resolution.

The nineties in Florence did know a form of classicism which, because it is such, bears a positive relation to the High Renaissance style — though not to its long antecedent act of invention by Leonardo. If Leonardo's accomplishment in the *Adoration* had not existed it would be possible to speak of this late Quattrocento form of classicism as a necessary prerequisite to the emergence of a High Renaissance style; and though it was not necessary to Leonardo, it was in fact an actual historical precondition to the emergence of a High Renaissance classicism in the art of Michelangelo and Raphael. This late Quattrocento classicism was not a new invention but a persistence, or in part a regeneration, of the early classical tradition of Masaccio and Piero della Francesca. The monumental art of Ghirlandaio belonged at least in part within this category. Ghirlandaio's concept of reality was based, in an important aspect of it, on the ideas of a conservative perspective science: the surface expertness of Ghirlandaio's realist practice was not separable from the hard core in it of order which results from the perspective system. The element in Ghirlandaio's style that is relatable to classicism is less a consequence of the choice of an aesthetic principle than a substratum of his technique of realism. Because there is never — or almost never — any emotion in the art of Ghirlandaio that could induce action, and rarely any will to describe even physical mobility of a decided kind, he has no reason to contravene the logic of perspective order that had come to him by inheritance. The cast of classicism that exists in Ghirlandaio's paintings is there by inertia; it is a tired descent of the tradition founded in the Carmine.

Quite clearly willed, on the other hand, is the character of classicism in the style brought from Umbria to Florence in the nineties by Pietro Perugino.[16] This importation was a kind of return to Florence, without interest, of the investment made a half-century before in another Umbrian, Piero della Francesca. Perugino's style had been formed, in its beginnings, on the models of Piero's Quattrocento classicism and then passed through an advanced realist discipline, apparently in Verrocchio's school. The style that Perugino developed fully in the nineties, when he was a half-time resident in Florence, was a precise consequence of this education. Its clarity and its habits of geometric order were based, as were Piero's, on the rationale of the perspective grid; but on these there is imposed a more "modern" mode of transcription of appearances, more flexible and intimate. By contrast with Piero's analysed and crystalline descriptions Perugino's realism seems, and is, a descent towards ordinary experience. Perugino also relaxed the high austerity of Piero's order of pictorial structure: the order of Perugino's pictures is less stringent, and because this is the case, an effect of harmony in them is more readily apparent.

The content of human expression is also more accessible in Perugino; in place of the abstraction of Piero's faces there is an identifiable, if not inspired, content of conventional religious sentiment, perfectly in accord in its slow temper with the calm of the pictorial scheme.

In more respects than can be adduced for any other style in Florence of the nineties, Perugino's approximates the classicism of the High Renaissance. His style contains a developed realism of individual parts, but this realism is chastened by its context of a harmonizing order; it contains an adequate communication of inward states of mind, and these are concordant with the same placid order. Less than most other modes of this time, this one holds few possibilities of internal contradiction and is made of elements that concord, and concord with and within a matrix of rational harmony. Yet this art is not, despite its analogy to High Renaissance classicism, of that style. Its internal components may be in accord but they are not in balance: bodily realism and expression of the spirit in the human image are not equal in their interest, as they are in Leonardo. The accord that is achieved between them is in consequence of a happening which is much at variance with the character of High Renaissance style: it is accomplished by a reduction of vitality, of both motion and emotion, to a nearly minimal level. This is, indeed, the basis of the whole approximation of a harmony in Perugino: his harmony, of structure as well as of persons, is the result of a relaxation. In its most literal sense, this is a style of *détente.* It represents the end of a tradition, not a beginning; it is essentially a vitiation of the early classicism of Piero. Nor does this style have in any way the potential of self-transformation into a High Renaissance classicism: to achieve this transformation would require a significant alteration of emphasis among the component parts of style and, more important, a new functional and synthetic principle of their relation, of which the vital seed could not be generated from *détente.* Raphael worked such a transformation, not at first upon the style of Perugino directly but upon its offshoots; the style of Perugino himself, however, persisted in its former mold well into the sixteenth century, unconcerned and impotent to accomplish its own transformation.

The last decade of the Quattrocento in Florence is, essentially, a decade of dissolution of the Early Renaissance style. Within this dissolution, however, phenomena of style appear which attempt, and in part achieve, some kind of reconstruction of the unity of artistic expression. The degree to which these attempts of reconstitution are, as such, self-aware is doubtful. More than they are the result of precise analysis of the problems offered by the development of Quattrocento art, they would seem in part to be persistences, or recurrences, in the last phase of Early Renaissance style, of attitudes invented earlier; and in part a result of a natural late phenomenon of eclecticism, in most instances not intellectually articulate. Self-conscious or not in origin, the historical fact remains: the appearance in the nineties in Florence of modes based on recombinations of extant elements of style. The elements of recombination inevitably resembled those, derived from the same artistic background, which enter into the new synthesis of the High Renaissance. Florentine painting tended of itself, in the 1490's, toward the end considerably before achieved by Leonardo: the resolution of its own diversity of development. Precisely lacking to the authors of these recombinations was the capacity — the capacity of Leonardo's genius — to comprehend, in terms of exact intellectual concept, the problems of their artistic environment and to formulate, out of the creative resources of personality and mind, a new principle of synthesis. The situation in Florence was now such, however, as to have matured as far as it was possible the dissolution of Early Renaissance style and to require, far more overtly than in the moment of Leonardo's *Adoration*, new resynthesis. The basis was present upon which another personality, of dimension similar to Leonardo's, could operate with comparable effect.

MICHELANGELO

Because the terrain had been thus prepared, Michelangelo's emergence is a less prodigious event of history than Leonardo's. Singularly, it would seem that the precedents Leonardo had left behind in Florence were not, in any way that we can document, a part of Michelangelo's preparation. Though Michelangelo alone in Florence in the 1490's was competent to gather Leonardo's meaning, there is no evidence that Michelangelo, in the period of his first formation, was in any way obliged to Leonardo. This could hardly have been the result of an unlikely accident of inattention; nor is it reasonable that the antipathy of Michelangelo to Leonardo's temperament, as it emerged particularly in the *Adoration*, should have been so soon so marked as to preclude any sympathetic comprehension. The absence of discernible dependence is rather due to the very different nature of the process by which Michelangelo came to the formation of a classical style.

Leonardo's classicism was conceived out of the precise circumstances of its moment, looking only forward from these; it was in essence, though not in all its aspects of appearance, a singularly "modern" act of art. Michelangelo's classicism, while no less than Leonardo's a profound personal invention, was paradoxically generated out of backward historical reference. This "historicism" which enters into Michelangelo's construction of a new style is, however, a result of a realization, as keen as Leonardo's, of the insufficiencies of contemporary art. Michelangelo's research into the past is a phenomenon of complex cause: it implies, among other things, the awareness of the absence of developable potential in the artistic present and the knowledge of the need, in the present, of regeneration, and that one way of regeneration could be a return to the vital sources from which the vitiated present had descended.

Michelangelo's first training in the arts, as a painter, was essentially conservative. It was in Ghirlandaio's shop that he was first indoctrinated with a concern for descriptive accuracy from which he was slow to liberate himself, in his paintings particularly. It was also in this shop, however, that he was first exposed to the relic of an early Quattrocento classicism. Beyond the relic, in the study of the Carmine that was obligatory for all apprentices of the time, he found the source of this tradition. Because there was a temperamental affinity, of grandly stubborn power of personality, between the young Michelangelo and the distant Masaccio, he must have felt those early works not as a noble but superannuated accomplishment — as they were to most students of his generation — but as a vital way of art. On Michelangelo's transfer to Bertoldo's school of sculpture, the authority of Masaccio was reinforced, in still deeper historical excavation, by experience of the Antique sources of the classicism of the Early Renaissance. To his study of Antique sculpture Michelangelo brought not only his artist's mind and eye but a verbal comprehension of Antiquity, acquired in his frequentation of the humanists of the Palazzo Medici.

The same classical education was available to young artists other than Michelangelo in the later 1480's and early nineties, but for most of them, like his friend Granacci, it had no classical effect whatever. In their teacher, Bertoldo, the environment of classicism produced an archaeological mode — more a formalistic imitation than a recreation of an Ancient classical style. Only in Michelangelo was the experience of classical Antiquity an experience of its essence, and only in him did it act as precipitate and basis for a new personal style. This experience must have been, exactly, recreative: even in his early works Michelangelo's comprehension of the nature of classicism exceeds what could have been revealed to him by the Antique objects accessible for him to study. Where no contemporary of Michelangelo's was able to see these objects in a more than philological fashion, he was able to grasp the intimations in a copy or a ruin, and reconstruct their essence.

Michelangelo's classicism was explicitly shaped by his understanding of the Antique, but this very understanding was conditioned by contemporary circumstance: to his contemplation of Antique classicism he brought the problem of art in his own time, as Leonardo brought it to his surrounding Quattrocento art; and Michelangelo's search into, and discovery of, the nature of classical style in Antiquity was guided in part by the solution the contemporary problems sought; reciprocally, Ancient classicism illumined Michelangelo's process of solution.

It must be recalled that, though much in Michelangelo's early education in the arts was classicizing, it was by no means all such, no more than were the other aspects of his formative upbringing. He was early exposed, in the Medici circle, to the mixed, but eventually Christian, doctrine of Neo-Platonism, with sufficient effect so that his verbal thinking in after years almost always bore its impress. To the spiritual incitement of Neo-Platonism there was added the impact — to that depth which Michelangelo's own confession bears witness — of the preachings of Savonarola, whose effective beginnings in Florence coincide precisely with the time of Michelangelo's early art. In the field of Quattrocento accomplishment in art that was most relevant to Michelangelo, sculpture, the most demanding precedent was that of Donatello, whose range of expression had embraced the possible extremes of the Early Renaissance mentality. It would seem that Michelangelo's comprehension of classical example was in no small part promoted — in an only apparent paradox — by the unclassical aspects of his education and contemporary cultural environment. It was from a capacity of intense spiritual being, initially Christian in its form and orientation, and sharpened in the present atmosphere of conflict between reality and superrational, that there emerged Michelangelo's perception that Antique art was spiritually inhabited: that it was not, as it was for some of his contemporaries, merely a repository of recipes for naturalism or, as it was for others, a dictionary of approved humanist quotations. Because Michelangelo was as sensible of the vital and spiritual content of Ancient art as he was of its naturalism — as he was able to supply the content in the deficient documents of Ancient art he knew — he realized that, in this Antique classicism, there was a model for the resolution of the conflicts and disparities of the art of his own time.

The first creators of the Renaissance had had a distinctly similar, though far less profoundly synthetic sense of the nature of Antiquity; it was this analogy, as well as the temperamental affinity of personal greatness, that drew Michelangelo closer to the inventors of the Renaissance than to the models of the masters of his contemporary time. In the habit of elliptical descriptive statement of Masaccio, and yet more of Jacopo della Quercia — in both, a partly medieval residue — there was an element of coincidence with the classical doctrine of generalization; from their example Michelangelo took authority for his tendency to generalize in a truer classical sense. In both these older artists the generalization was of vital spiritual sensation — again, a part persistence of a medieval value — as well as of naturalistic form, and this mutual generalization was the plane of concord on which the two worlds met: in this, too, there was a parallel with Ancient classicism and support for Michelangelo's own incipient intention. The apparatus Michelangelo brought to his view of Antiquity included the new problems of his time and all this time's accumulation of experience, but there is a substratum of his purposes and processes of first classicizing thought which resembles that of his artistic ancestors.

This retrospective character in Michelangelo's early work makes an effect in it of much less decisive novelty than is in the early works — at least those which are safely documented — of Leonardo. In Leonardo's angel of the *Baptism*, in the Benois *Madonna*, and in the *Adoration* the style is instantly perceivable as new, "modern" in its contemporary context. Michelangelo is slower to disentangle a new identity for his style from its partial analogues in the past. However, his process of emergence, though less decisive than Leonardo's, can no more than that be described as a process of transition. Each retrospective reference Michelangelo makes is also a critique, and the critique is made according to the sense of a new intent of style of which the unmistakable evidence is even in his earliest certain work. This, the *Madonna of the Steps* (Florence, Casa Buonarroti; c. 1490–92)[17] makes an almost reactionary reference to precedents in Donatello and at the same time, in heavy dignity of form and clarity of order, depends on Masaccio: the dignity of one model has been employed to correct the intensity of the other. A powerful, but generalized and restrained spiritual content has been synthesized effectively with a massive gravity of substantial form. The concord of idea between form and content is in their mutual grave power, and a positive device for binding them together has been found in the rhythmic mode of the design: a slow-weaving, rounding continuity, pulsing with controlled inner force. Details of description, for all their fineness, are decisively subsumed within the generalization of design. The nascent but already sensibly explicit character of classicism in this relief shows little that may be specifically dependent upon Ancient art, but the sense of a relationship with Antique style is so strong as to have suggested (Justi) the possibility of Michelangelo's knowledge, when he conceived it, of an antique *stele* (perhaps indirectly, in a gem); in any case it is clear that the process of reciprocal illumination between Michelangelo and Antique art had already certainly begun.

The fuller emergence of a classical style in Michelangelo is not merely a matter of his attainment of a personal maturity but of the completion of this process of reciprocal illumination. Michelangelo fulfills his own identity, at first, by submission to the evidence of Antique art, incipiently in that creative paraphrase which is the *Centaurs* relief (Florence, Casa Buonarroti; c. 1492),[18] and decisively in the first work done in Rome, the *Bacchus* (Florence, Bargello; 1496–97).[20] It is possible that the full revelation to Michelangelo of Antique classical style required the experience of more examples of it than he could find in Florence. His response to the experience in Rome is the effective reconstitution, in the *Bacchus*, of an Ancient classical style which is, in the same instant, the absolute constitution of a modern classicism. The *Bacchus* is both recreative and creative, and in the fact of this duality its classicism acquires a different nature, as a phenomenon of art and history, from the classicism of Antiquity. The classical style of Antiquity was an evolutionary consequence of a view of the world, entertained in the instinct as in the mind, as a unity of substance and of spirit. The unity that is achieved in the *Bacchus* has no historical inevitability; it is the product of an act of will, imposed upon a historical situation of conflict between substance and spirit. Michelangelo's act of will responds to an ambition formulated in his society by a limited group even among its culturally functioning elite; it does not and cannot correspond to the wider mentality of the world within which he performed his act. His proposition, made in terms of art, is culturally an artifice, and this is indicative for the whole phenomenon, not only of art but of cultural history in general, which we designate as the High Renaissance.

The unity of human person and personality that, in the *Bacchus*, is accomplished in the mold of Antique form and subject matter is an effective synthesis of what, in Christian culture, had become polarities; it is not the Ancients' original indivisible essence. For all the beauty and idea of worth that is attached to the physical being of the *Bacchus*, it is still a vessel for a separable entity of spirit. There is a subtlety of psychic state in the *Bacchus* — a febrility almost miraculously controlled — which exists in no Ancient precedent. Even in this image of pagan sensuality of form there is a conception of spiritual existence that betrays the artist's heritage of Christianity. The spirit now wonderfully pervades and infuses flesh; they perfectly interpenetrate but, in this very concept of an interpenetration, their original separateness is implied. This reconstitution of a classical unity is not only different in historical origin, and in the fact that it is a reconstitution, from the classicism of Antiquity; it will be distinguished in its own history to come by the intense self-consciousness of effort needed to sustain the artifice it is and which it represents. To this end a generation of genius would devote itself, to attain glory and inevitable defeat.

Because spiritual value continues to be separately identified from outward form, there is no necessary initial conflict between an image of pagan subject like the *Bacchus* and the practice, in other images, of a Christian art; the same conviction of a spiritual presence, obviously different in the meaning it intends, can find a habitation within traditional Christian religious forms. As much as the classical language of Leonardo, Michelangelo's new style can be applied with entire convincingness to the interpretation of religious themes. The *Pietà* of St. Peter's (Rome, St. Peter's; 1498–99)[19] is no less sincerely Christian than the late works of a Savonarolan Botticelli; only its kind of spiritual experience is different. Feeling is not less profound, but it is contained within a discipline of tragic dignity. The Virgin has renounced violence of passion, but not its depth; and from her restraint passion takes on double resonance. Her spirit has a terrible peace: this too is a kind of harmony. As in Leonardo's actors in the *Last Supper*, quite contemporary, there is, in Michelangelo's Virgin, a sense of a dimension of humanity grander than our own, and this grandeur also is not only of a psychic but of a consonant physical presence. This whole physical being is cast in a form of which the affect is one with that of its spiritual content: it is gravely and powerfully moved and, equally, contained. The shape of composition, for the first time in a sculptural group in so clear a fashion, is the broad-based triangle — the resolution of the implication of activity with the certainty of stability — that Leonardo had first used in painting two decades before. Though the sculpture is inevitably less complex than Leonardo's contemporary fresco, it reveals in all essential aspects that Michelangelo has attained a stage in the formation of a High Renaissance classical style that is comparable to Leonardo's. In his decade of development through the accomplishment of the *Pietà* Michelangelo has drawn abreast of Leonardo's development of more than two decades: both artists approach the boundary of the new century with their independently conceived, but effectively equal, new-proved propositions of a classical style.

FRA BARTOLOMMEO

Neither of these highest points to date of the new classical achievement, the *Last Supper* and Michelangelo's *Pietà*, had been attained in Florence, precisely where there were artists who were at least potentially competent to follow their example. That city lacked all but the evidence of the initial steps in the solution of the new style: nevertheless, the very latest years of the Quattrocento saw the formation, in a third artist of great talent, of an incipiently distinguishable High Renaissance style. Baccio della Porta (Fra Bartolommeo only after 1500) in turn helped to move his less gifted and more reluctant associate, Albertinelli, in the same direction.

The important document of Baccio's beginnings in the new style is the fresco *Last Judgment* of S. M. Nuova (Florence, Museo di S. Marco; 1499–1501),[21] designed by Baccio wholly, but of which the upper part is of his execution and the lower part Albertinelli's; largely ruined, it is luckily Baccio's portion which is still legible. Behind this fresco is the visible precedent of the early classical tradition of the Quattrocento: of Ghirlandaio (whose *Coronation of the Virgin* in S. M. Novella is a chronologically near antecedent for its composition) and, still more, of the imported Quattrocento classicism of Perugino. The new classicism that is achieved by Baccio seems to be explicitly prepared by the latent manifestations of comparable kind in late fifteenth-century style. The distinction is at once as visible as the relation. However, unlike Ghirlandaio's or Perugino's static styles, the design of the upper portion of the *Last Judgment* is based upon a geometric shape that moves: a perspective semicircle projected into space. The shape of composition implies movement, however gently, as much as it exemplifies an order; that movement, furthermore, is full and deep. Disposed within this plan are figures of a monumental-seeming scale, heavily proportionate in form. These are not merely fixed beside each other, as in Ghirlandaio's like composition, but are linked by simple curving impulses of drapery or by gestures with which they make discreet communication. The heads are not near-portraits, as in Ghirlandaio, nor Peruginesque masks of conventional sentiment, but those of beings who seem gently animate and, as well, incipiently idealized in appearance and tonality of feeling. The effect of this aerial company is one of monumental breadth and quiet harmony of presence and relation. Unassertively, with neither the decisiveness nor power of Michelangelo or Leonardo, and far less articulately, Baccio's own portion of this fresco seems to speak the language of the new style. The lower portion of the fresco, where Albertinelli has transcribed the design given him by Baccio, seems, on the other hand — as far as we can reconstruct its character — to be still quattrocentesque, in style partly like Perugino and like the contemporary Signorelli also.

The contrast of style within the fresco serves not only to isolate what Bartolommeo has achieved, but to indicate the process of his achievement. It is on the basis of a preexistent classicizing *détente*, of Perugino's and of Ghirlandaio's kind, in itself impotent of development, that Bartolommeo has creatively imposed the changes that can make of it a High Renaissance classical style. Accepting absolutely its prescription of a rational order, he has infused into that order a measure of the animation which it conspicuously did not have. Even the gentle impulses of movement that he had induced in the *Last Judgment* are sufficient seed, not to regenerate a vitiated style, but rather to initiate a new one, based on a different concept of formal and contentual relation. This animation is a function of a will not only to inspire life into a static rationality of order but to give it, in this way, the harmony that moves in music; at the same time it is the symptom of an expansion of the life of spirit which, as it expands, shapes form to new aesthetic resonance, in terms of monumentality, and to new moral dimension, in terms of dignity.

The process of generation of a Cinquecento classical style in Fra Bartolommeo was different from that by which a style, in its elementary respects similar, was generated in his contemporary, Michelangelo. Unlike the historically complex synthesis of Michelangelo, Fra Bartolommeo's new style, far less complex and far less dynamic, proceeds from a simpler, but still creative, reformation of immediately preexistent possibilities of art, in which he himself had been, at the beginning, content to practice. Unlike Michelangelo, or Leonardo, Bartolommeo does not embark on his career with an invention; he comes to it. His new style is so closely related to a major aspect of the style of the latest Quattrocento that it seems almost to be an unforced, almost a natural, next consequence which might be built on that tradition.

More nearly identifiably than was the case with Michelangelo, the expansion of a spiritual dimension which seems to be the motive power of generation in the Frate of the new style may be precisely Christian in its source. Apparently early attracted to Savonarola's teaching, Bartolommeo experienced, in the very course of painting of the *Last Judgment*, a spiritual crisis which caused him to abandon its completion to Albertinelli, and for a while to abandon painting altogether is favor of an entirely monastic existence. The reaction was more drastic in a way than Botticelli's response to Savonarola's inspiration, but until this act of renunciation, fortunately temporary, the Frate's religiosity shows no tendency, within his art, to antirationality or mysticism. His intenser spiritual being is, on the contrary, infused into, and seems to be the agency that transforms, the realist and rational matter of art to which he had been educated to a higher and a different power. At the end of the century Fra Bartolommeo — a little in his temper as in artistic situation — resembles his Dominican ancestor Fra Angelico, but in inverted analogy: not, like the *Beato*, giving the form of orderly nature to Christian spirituality but, instead, regenerating the content of spirituality in this order.

*Unlike Michelangelo, Fra Bartolommeo seems to have studied the models that were left behind by Leonardo before his departure for Milan. The indication of this appears specifically in certain of the heads in the upper range of the *Last Judgment*, where there are evident relationships to actors in the *Adoration*. Not only types, but the character of modelling and handling, may suggest a Leonardesque dependence. Yet, these are the only identifiable results of the study of Leonardo in this, for Bartolommeo, stylistically decisive fresco. It would appear that it is less a case of guidance of Baccio in his process of invention by Leonardo's example than of a personal development which leads him toward a comprehension, but by no means to an imitation, of Leonardo's style. Leonardo's early accomplishment is still without decisive artistic consequence in Florence but now, two decades after its occurrence, it is at last no longer wholly isolated in its native place.

II

FORMATION OF THE CLASSICAL VOCABULARY

(c. 1500–c. 1508)

II

FORMATION OF THE CLASSICAL VOCABULARY (c. 1500-c. 1508)

THE classical style in painting had emerged in Florence in a time of which the political and social actualities were hardly such as to promote, by any character of their own like that of a classicism, any corresponding happenings of art. The last decades of the fifteenth century had begun in relative stability but turned rapidly into a time of commotion more violent than the state had experienced since the mid-Trecento. The first years of the new century in Florence were less violently disturbed but still by no means serene. In Italy in general, of which Florence still remained a sensitive political nexus, there were troubles due to personal ambition, to dynastic conflict, and invasion which perpetuated the previous atmosphere of instability. Generated in a time of conflict, the new classical style continued to develop in a similar historical climate without apparent impediment on that account. We have seen, indeed, that a precondition to the creation of the new style may have lain in the cultural dichotomy from which the worst of Florentine political commotion came, and that the invention of a classicism is in part interpretable as a solution, in the terms of art, to the provocation of cultural disturbance. The life of the new idea in art continued after 1500, as it had before, in a sphere above and apart from the ordinary vicissitudes of actuality; the inventing artists had the power not only to ideate but to realize an ambition that their society could not attain.

The agents who continued the development of the new style in these years in Florence were, initially, the same artistically isolated individuals by whom the style had been invented. Absent from Florence in the time during which they had attained their first fulfillments of expression in a High Renaissance classicism, Leonardo and Michelangelo returned to the city to demonstrate their new achievement there. In their demonstrations, Florence saw the new style for the first time in such explicitly defined form, and with the decisive impress in them of the artists' personal maturity. That those demonstrations were quantitatively few, and at first as isolated as they had been before in the context of contemporary art, was of no matter; they imposed absolutely: by their force of new idea, even though it was as yet imperfectly comprehended and, still more, by their prima facie evidence of genius. Such was the authority of the two repatriated masters, each reinforcing the effect made by the other, that it established an incontrovertible new standard and style of art for Florence. It was not important now to the immediate future of the new style that Fra Bartolommeo, who had so recently achieved a basically similar form, but not a similar plane, of art at home in Florence, should have temporarily retired from painting just at this time.

LEONARDO AND MICHELANGELO

There is contemporary evidence of the great impact made by Leonardo's first public artistic statement after his return to Florence when, in the spring of 1501, he exhibited a version, now lost, of a cartoon for the theme of the *Madonna and Child with St. Anne.* We can deduce with some reasonable certainty what the design of this work was, but to reconstruct something of its effect as an aesthetic object we must depend on the surviving, and chronologically just previous cartoon of the same theme, executed before Leonardo's departure from Milan (London, Royal Academy; c. 1499).[22] The interval of time between these two cartoons is so small that it is reasonable to assume that the Florentine version contained few significant developments in its manner of handling or its technique in detail. In the Milanese cartoon, Leonardo had applied the conclusions just reached in the *Last Supper* to a more compact and limited object, where their effect could be even more concentratedly perceptible. There is the same clear rounding as in the *Last Supper* of massive form, of which the smooth spatial movement is here still more visible, as is the cursive fullness of the folds of drapery. In accord with the character of the subject, dignified and ennobled, but not heroic, the intention in manipulation of the forms is slightly but meaningfully changed from that in the figures of the *Last Supper.*

The curving shapes of the cartoon are richer and slower in movement and more artfully interwoven, and the relations of proportion among the forms are more instantly sensible as harmonious. From the formal qualities alone of the figures of the cartoon, there emerges an effect which is different from, and also more, than what emerges from the intellectual clarity of shapes in the *Last Supper*: here there is a communication of sensuous pleasure to the eye and spirit of the beholder by the qualities of form. Such an intention to convey visual pleasure had existed in some measure in Leonardo's previous paintings, but even as an intention it had been only imperfectly formulated, and it had been subordinate to intellectualizing aesthetic or to moral principles involved in his conception of a harmony. In the Milan cartoon Leonardo indicates that his harmony is now meant not only to impose upon the mind and spirit but to enchant the senses so that the work of art shall, literally, be lovely. Leonardo himself would speak (*Trattato*, I, 5) of "bellezze che . . . innamorino." Among Leonardo's works this is the first where not some portions of a picture, but its entirety, compels the immediate sensation in the spectator of the beautiful. It is an effect more profoundly revolutionary than may at first appear: in joining to the intellectual ideality of form the conception of a sensuous content to be derived from it, Leonardo has achieved what is in effect a recreation of the sense of beauty as classical Antiquity understood and felt it. As far as we can determine, this is a recreation achieved with no more specific reference to Antique models than we can document in any of Leonardo's activity in his past. It would seem to be a consequence, internally generated, of the unfolding of another possibility of his synthetic comprehension of experience: he now embraces, within the vital unity of the work of art, the element of pleasurable sensuous response, which becomes peer to and part of an inseparable texture with the properties of intellect and moral good.

This quality of beauty proceeds in the cartoon, to begin with, from its finer harmony of form, but it arises still more from the sense, more pervasive here than in any of Leonardo's prior works, that this harmony is of subtly mobile relations: a new dimension of aesthetic effectiveness has been assumed in the cartoon by what Leonardo himself might have described as a musicality. Not only the bodily forms and draperies but the heads also indicate this same development of a subtle harmony of rounding form, exquisitely movemented: the heads are of a perfection that recalls Praxitelean models which, in their original loveliness that he recreates, Leonardo could not have known. The faces wear that veiled radiance we first knew in the angel of the *Baptism*,[1] but raised here to a far higher power — stronger, but also more tender, and more vibrantly differentiated in its content of spiritual expression. The emanation that is here of love, in the spirit of the persons and in their loveliness of form, creates a relation between the image and the spectator which is at once an ennoblement and a seduction.

This atmosphere of enchantment in the Milanese cartoon is very different from the dramatic tone and somewhat doctrinaire austerity of form in the *Last Supper*.[12] Yet, beneath this difference of character and intention Leonardo, though less outwardly dogmatic, is no less explicitly intellectual in his process of creating the cartoon. In it there is a self-conscious effort to develop, beyond the standard of the groups of apostles in the fresco, a more cogent integration of compositional form. The higher integrity of design in the cartoon is clear in this comparison, and clearer still by contrast with the Madonna composition from the first year in Milan: the figure elements have now been drawn together into a single absolutely compact whole. The selection of the St. Anne theme, as far as we know in the case of the Milan cartoon undetermined by commission, may have been motivated in part by the way in which it lent itself to this peculiar aesthetic problem which Leonardo seems now to have found most compelling. The form of the compacted group is no longer triangular, but tends to the superior geometric solution of the ellipse: this shape is at once more animated and more compellingly inclusive, and more concordant with the cursive forms which it contains. The drawings (Venice, Louvre, British Museum) that are preparatory to this cartoon indicate the urgency of Leonardo's will to vital compacting of the given forms: they are quick rotary probings of a ball-like shape upon which then, in the cartoon, a corrective and controlling measure is imposed.

The cartoon that Florence saw on public exhibition in the SS. Annunziata in 1501 was a product of Leonardo's sense of a relentless consequence in his pursuit of solution to an artistic problem. The new cartoon revised the design, and in a minor detail — the substitution of a lamb for the St. John — altered the subject of the Milan version; the changes were made with the intention of achieving a still higher state of integration, of content as well as of form. The pallid reflection of the Florentine cartoon in the painting by Andrea del Brescianino (formerly Berlin)[23] enables us to reconstruct a part of Leonardo's intention: in place of the overlapping intersection of the two large forms, still parallel, in the Milan design, the Florence version rather actually includes the Mary — as in a symbol of birth — within the figure of St. Anne; the two main forms are thus even more indissolubly related. By replacing the image of the young St. John with that of the lamb a psychological as well as a formal complication of the essential theme has been eliminated and a more compelling unity of whole meaning has been made possible. By its more nearly perfect unity of structure and of subject matter the conception of the Florentine cartoon must have attained an ideality yet higher than that of the version from Milan. However, to ensure that this effect of ideality should not seem too evidently intellectual, or make the humanity it touched seem too distant and too rare, Leonardo invented a compensating motive of action and of psychological interplay among the figures which conveys the atmosphere almost of an event of genre: the perfection of form and of the state of spirit of the actors, and the extreme artificiality of design in which they are arranged, are presented to us in the terms of a seemingly entire human accessibility. The population of Florence that saw this cartoon could not but be enamored of this unprecedented loveliness that seemed so natural; but surely few among them in 1501, even of the artists, were prepared to see, much less to understand, the mechanism of great artifice from which this appearance grew.

It was Michelangelo, returned to Florence in May 1501, who was most nearly so prepared but now, in actual contact with Leonardo's contemporary art, and in comparison with it, significant differences emerge in Michelangelo's conception of the new style and in his degree of development within it also. Michelangelo seems to have reacted quickly to his own experience of Leonardo's cartoon of 1501; the evidence of it is in his drawing, presumably of the same year, of the St. Anne theme in Oxford (Ashmolean 291).[24] As the drawing shows it, the impress made on Michelangelo by the cartoon was from its aesthetic core of structure — its compact and interwoven vital unity; there is no interest in the drawing in the qualities which complete Leonardo's conception of a harmony, such as his musicality of form or of expression. Michelangelo is now, as not before, prepared to profit by experience of Leonardo, but only from the results achieved by him in his working with the aesthetic substance of classical style; Michelangelo is no more than before prepared to accept the concept of humanity formed by Leonardo's temperament. The *Bruges Madonna* (Bruges, Notre Dame),[25] perhaps conceived and executed circa 1501, may show the influence of Leonardo's cartoon, but only in an attenuated way: the similar unity of elliptical form contains a tonality of content that is wholly different. More ideally reshaped than the Virgin of the Roman *Pietà*, but not in Leonardo's way, the Bruges Virgin does not intend Leonardo's loveliness. She does not enchant; there is an almost masculine power latent in her and she ponders, with profound inwardness, the inevitability of tragedy.

On his return to Florence Michelangelo seems to reattach himself to the Florentine tradition; on the one hand this reinforces his still persistent concern for veracity of detail, and on the other reinforces the intensity, and the traditionally Christian character, of his spiritual expression. No work of this period in Florence is so authentically classical, and certainly not in a recollective sense, as had been the *Bacchus* [20] of the preceding Roman years. In the *David* (Florence, Academy; 1501–04),[26] there is almost an equivocation between the ambitions of the new style and the intentions inherited from Quattrocento art. Almost as much as in the Roman *Pietà* there is the stress, in the *David*, of exact description of anatomy, and in the head there is such a passionate intensity as almost conflicts with the waiting substance of the body. The example of Donatello, of his *St. George* and his *David* combined, and of Verrocchio, compete in this statue with the authority of the Antique. It is the dimension of spiritual idea and its matching dimension of form that finally dominate any elements of conflict in the conception of the *David*, and at the same time subsume the residues of Quattrocento style that are in it.

From the *David*, as from the contemporary or just previous conception of the *Bruges Madonna*, it becomes evident that the community of classical style that Michelangelo shares with Leonardo is not altogether a community of stage in its development. In the Roman *Pietà,*[19] Michelangelo had attained a fulfilled statement of the classical proposition which was effectively equivalent to that made contemporaneously by Leonardo. In both artists, in the *St. Anne* cartoons as in the *David* and the *Bruges Madonna*, there is an immediate further development upon their prior first fulfillments. But the direction of development is distinct, impelled by the difference of the two personalities and by their very different relation to tradition. Leonardo, of more naturally collected disposition, and rigorous in intellectual pursuit of a sequence of ideas, proceeds immediately toward the formulation of a more embracingly synthetic harmony of style: in effect, toward a perfected classicism. Michelangelo, more emotional than intellectual in nature, and more dependent on example and tradition, develops on his first attainment of maturity in ways that are, on the contrary, less conducive to a perfection of the classicism in his style. His growth in spiritual dimension, as in the *David*, is a development of an ideality; however, his simultaneous development of increased intensity of spiritual sensation does not promote a classicizing temper of harmony. An element of internal dissension appears in Michelangelo's style in the first years of the sixteenth century which is not propitious to his undivided pursuit of a goal that Leonardo had more purely intellectually defined. It is an oversimplification, but one which contains an essential truth, to say that Michelangelo did not instantly resolve this dissension, but for a brief but crucial moment made it explicit, dedicating himself essentially to the solution of formal problems of classical style that had been demonstrated by Leonardo. Toward 1504, the time most important for Michelangelo's activity in painting in this phase, his interest is dominantly in the problem of the aesthetics of classical structure, to the extent that spiritual values in his work assume a secondary place.

Leonardo's guidance of Michelangelo's formal research in this time is unquestionable; the Doni tondo of the *Holy Family* (Florence, Uffizi; c. 1504)[27] is the clearest demonstration of Michelangelo's obligation to Leonardo's example. The relation was, on Michelangelo's part, both one of dependence and of rivalry. He seems to have set himself, in the *Tondo*, the task of bettering, in its own terms, Leonardo's solution to the problem of classical structure. The structural basis of Leonardo's Florentine cartoon is also the basis of design of the Doni painting; and in particular the device of the inclusion of one main form, not only in the silhouette, but within the spatial embrace of the form behind, is reused here. It had already been adapted from Leonardo, but in more rudimentary fashion, for the design of the *Bruges Madonna*. As in Leonardo's model, Michelangelo imposes an uninterrupted continuity of contour on his group, but further reinforces its effect by the containing shape of the tondo frame. In a way that seems more consciously aggressive than in a work of actual sculpture, Michelangelo defines the plastic existence of the painted group and of its parts by intensest modelling and deep excavation; he then joins these parts in a connected sequence as if they were interdependent pieces of a single mass of stone. In this sculptural language he creates an absolutely compact unity, deeply differentiated, which is of a force of impact far beyond that of Leonardo's models. But as the basic idea for the containing unity of form had been Leonardo's so also is the basis for its mode of inner differentiation. The connected movements of the draperies and bodies in the *Tondo* is different in its temper from Leonardo, but not in its fundamental formal kind: the temper of these movements (and of the movement of the contour also) has more of a powerfully contained energy, somewhat blunt and strongly masculine, than it has of Leonardo's grace.

Even the difference in plastic articulateness of Michelangelo's group from Leonardo's models is one of degree and temperamental emphasis rather than of basic kind: one of the elements of style we can surely reconstruct for the cartoon of 1501 was the development in it, beyond the Milanese version, of the disposition of the forms in space, at once in a more solid and more expansive differentiation of their containing unity. Exploiting this precedent in the Leonardo with the force of his sculptor's sense, Michelangelo has developed Leonardo's manner of articulation into an assertive spatial contrapposto; it will reappear constantly in his succeeding works. The potential for such a differentiated movement of plastic substance within space was surely in Michelangelo's own earlier experience: its symptoms were in the *Centaurs* relief and, in part at least, in the *Bacchus*. The historical circumstance is this, however: that no work of Michelangelo's before the Doni tondo (and its complete digestion, in its process of invention, of Leonardo's ideas of the cartoon of 1501) is at the same time powerfully movemented and strongly developed in the spatial disposition of its forms; it required Leonardo's example to precipitate the emergence of this potential of Michelangelo's art.

The compositional structure of the Doni tondo reveals a development, on a basis afforded by Leonardo but exceeding it, of a principle of classical style: it is a significant progress in the exposition of controlled energy internally articulating a compact unity of form. The classicism of the picture is, however, almost confined to this character of structure; it was not created with a pervasive classicism of state of mind. The human expression of the subject matter, most unlike the Roman *Pietà* or the *Bruges Madonna*, verges on the conventional, almost recalling the habit of Michelangelo's first master, Ghirlandaio. Also recollective of that first training is the hard clarity of painting technique and the tendency to precise description of detail. The color, too, is based on Ghirlandaiesque precedent, but with such stresses of clarity and intensity — in places as assertive as the plastic form to which it is an adjunct

— as give it an essential, but not a classical, individuality. The profound ideal conception realized in the design of the picture is not matched, then, either by the spiritual content in the actors or by their specific forms. In no prior work of Michelangelo is there such a measure of disparity among levels of ideality as in the Doni tondo; an internal conflict of intentions, visible in the *David*, is still more apparent here. Yet, as in the *David*, the sheer force of the artist's primary intention absolutely dominates the work: here that primary concern is aesthetic, with the organization of the compositional structure. The content that emerges from it, a noble generalization of controlled vital power, is more meaningful than that of the persons in it.

The principles of classical composition which Michelangelo demonstrated in the Doni tondo are evolved beyond their model in Leonardo's work of 1501; however, by the time Michelangelo conceived the *Tondo*, Leonardo had already further evolved, and to a degree significantly higher than in Michelangelo, his own precedents of classical design. The occasion for Leonardo's development was offered by the commission for the *Battle of Anghiari* for the Great Hall of the Palazzo Vecchio late in 1503; the cartoon for this picture was ready for execution — never to be completed — by the end of [*] 1504. The subject given Leonardo for this painting allowed a wide latitude of interpretation: the Quattrocento tradition of battle painting, such as it was, permitted the consideration of a battle as a chivalric pageant, as in Uccello, as a chill confusion as in Piero, or merely as a narrative disorder, as in the *cassone* painters. It was Leonardo's classical development of mind that caused him to understand the subject in an altogether novel way, for which we know no precedent either in the Quattrocento or in Ancient art: he saw the idea of battle in terms of its typical and essential meaning, as a meeting, in its climactic moment, of opposing powers of physical force and spiritual will; and saw in this climactic moment, when the issue is at the point of decision but not decided yet, the contesting persons and their passions at their height of energy but, as much as in an act of love, fused and woven into one another. Leonardo's interpretation of the subject regards the actual historical data, but manipulates its presentation into the terms of an ideal. The historical Battle of Anghiari, as fifteenth-century sources have described it to us, was hardly so forceful or so noble an event as Leonardo's arbitrary presentation of it.

The evidence we have does not permit us to describe with any exactness the whole scheme of Leonardo's intended picture. It contained three main incidents: a subsidiary engagement on the left, with a decided resolution of its energies in the direction of the center; on the right, an onset of mounted troops, less violent than the scene that balanced it but unopposed in its progress toward the center; and in the center itself, the climactic *Battle of the*

Standard — the only section actually painted, and of which fair copies survive.[28-33] Though not in any sense literally symmetrical, the figure design of the whole work would seem to have been set within the general shape of a flattened triangle. The basic compositional idea, conforming to the intellectual conception of the event we have described, would have been of a confluence and discharge of energies upon the center, meeting and fusing in the passionate, tight knot of the Battle for the Standard.

The copies of this central group show a remarkable development of the principle of organization demonstrated in the St. Anne cartoons. Like Michelangelo's *Tondo*, this group is more strongly plastic in the definition of its parts; even more than in the *Tondo* these forms, as they express their necessarily more violent activity, move and turn into a depth of space. The whole group that includes these turning forms reflects the spatial development of its parts: the entire episode acquires a nearly spherical dimension, internally deeply excavated. All its parts in movement are continuously interwoven in warping patterns of which it is quite impossible to separate the spatial and the two-dimensional sense. The curves of pattern derive from and exploit every incident of shape and movement of the forms, particularly of the horses: and it is not necessarily the baroque accent of Rubens' famous copy [29] which causes us to sense, in this context of passion, a swelling and a straining of these curves as if of distending physical and aesthetic energies. This central group accepts into itself the contending energies of the whole battlefield around it and knots these together in one intensely charged, compacted rotation of forces and of forms. The conflict, in this moment of its highest power, is still equal and indissoluble. Differently from the Doni tondo, it is not this aesthetic structure only which is so contentually expressive. The postures of the soldiers are not mere fine formal inventions but demonstrations of the terrible inspiration with which they fight, and their faces, as we know them from the surviving preparatory studies,[30-3] are maximum expressions of Leonardo's power of typifying spiritual states.

Leonardo's accomplishment in the *Battle of Anghiari*, four years after the opening of the new century, is almost as significant as was his first invention of the High Renaissance style more than two decades before. The *Battle* contains the development of that invention to the degree which, in our later study, we shall recognize as almost a complete realization of the possibilities of a central idea of classical style: in this conception, Leonardo has articulated a completely cogent unity in terms of a maximum formal complexity, and at the highest level of contentual intensity. It is possible to regard the history of the High Renaissance style in the subsequent decade of its full fruition as a reconquest of the same position that Leonardo had already attained here. This achievement was generated out of Leonardo's relentless and dynamic development of the logic of his own classical idea, and at a time almost as historically premature as his invention of that idea had been.

Just as Leonardo was completing the *Anghiari* cartoon, Michelangelo, already in part seduced by Leonardesque example, was brought into a compelled and in a measure forcibly dependent relationship with him. Michelangelo's cartoon for the intended companion decoration to the *Anghiari*, the *Battle of Cascina,* was commissioned in August 1504. It is reasonable to assume that Michelangelo was asked to consider, in some way, the problem of accord between Leonardo's existing project and such a design as he would make, and there is evidence in Michelangelo's preparatory drawings of his study of Leonardo's cartoon. Certain motives in the design that Michelangelo evolved, in particular his idea for the subsidiary scene in his subject (the attack of mounted horsemen that decided the Battle of Cascina) could not have escaped the influence of Leonardo's model. More significant, however, was the impress made on Michelangelo by the whole character of style in the *Anghiari*: a profound impress, but yet not one of entire comprehension. Even Michelangelo was not prepared in 1504 — or not disposed — to grasp the entire meaning of Leonardo's contemporary art.

The distinction between the two *Battle* cartoons began in the very attitude with which the subject was considered. Michelangelo's decision to paint the episode of the surprise of the bathing soldiers at Cascina[36] would seem to be as arbitrary as was Leonardo's arrangement of the historical data of his given theme. For Michelangelo, however, the subject "battle" was not a datum of human experience of which the essential nature required to be summarized in terms of art; it was rather a pretext from which he could extract the main matter of real interest to him, the human anatomy in action: the sculptor takes the given problem on his own terms. The conception of the theme in this exclusively anthropocentric sense implies a kind of ideality, but one narrower and more exclusive than Leonardo's, and less synthetic; instead of a meeting, as in Leonardo's case, between artist and subject there is a constraint of the subject to the artist's interests and will.

The first impact made by Michelangelo's interpretation of his *Battle* — surely not wholly due to falsification in the copies — is not only of the arbitrary, but of artificiality in the theme as it has been interpreted and in its effect of content. We are confronted with a set of virtuoso demonstrations of a sculptor's supreme formal knowledge: the artist's pride is the most pervasive and convincing content of the picture. We sense the assertiveness of Michelangelo's genius that wills to compete with Leonardo and to demonstrate its drastic superiority over every possible analogy in the past, including those in Michelangelo's own art. The cartoon, while it survived, replaced the Brancacci Chapel as the academy of art and its matter, in effect, consists of what we call "academies." In them, Michelangelo's preoccupation, as in the immediately precedent Doni tondo, is primarily with problems of form. No force of gesticulation nor any urgency of physiognomic expression that the lost original may have held could have been more eloquent than the artifices of posture, or equalled them in interest. The alarm of the arriving enemy is more pretext than true motivation of the actions of the soldiery; they are moved by the artist, not by their situation. In spite of a development of classicizing structure in the figures, there is a disparity between bodily forms and their humanly expressive content which, by the Leonardesque paradigm, is not wholly classical. In this incompletely classical, unsynthetic, emphasis on formalism and virtuosity in the *Cascina* cartoon, Michelangelo anticipates the mentality of the postclassical generation which, indeed, the cartoon later helped to form.

The *Cascina* cartoon is partly a direct development of Michelangelo's thinking in the Doni tondo. But it is also inescapably influenced by Leonardo's still more advanced formal inventions in the companion battle piece. The development in the *Cascina* beyond the *Tondo* of the problem of plastic figures in turning movement is in the direction indicated by Leonardo in the *Anghiari*; again, in the process of adapting Leonardo's precedent, Michelangelo surpasses it. Michelangelo's figures, specifically sculptural, are precisely articulate in their complex actions and spatially evolved to a degree that Leonardo's painterly style does not attain. Each figure is, indeed, so superbly emphatic in its formal demonstration — so commanding and remarkable an artifice, so ingeniously differentiated from the rest — that it unclassically defies effective synthesis into the entire group. Unlike the forms within the simpler compass of the Doni tondo, and conspicuously unlike the corresponding central group of the *Anghiari*, these individual perfections remain a sum of parts. In this vast pictorial dimension Michelangelo's conception of organization reveals itself as still, in a measure, quattrocentesque. On the example of the *Anghiari* as well as of his own prior work he wills, but incompletely, to connect the figures by devices of rhythmical sequence into groups, and to relate the groups into a whole of sensible geometric shape. But the splendid figures are intractable; they are conjoined, but not synthesized into a larger order. The sculptor's mind is evident in the total compositional shape: it is a panel of relief, strongly differentiated in internal space: the *Battle of the Centaurs* in a later guise. More than the absence of Leonardesque devices by which formal unity might be attained, it is the absence of a developed classicism of original conception that accounts for the unsynthetic structure of the *Cascina*: there is, in its conception, no profound unity of content to compel an equal unity of form.

The *Cascina* project was interrupted, and, in the end, entirely suspended by Michelangelo's employment, in the spring of 1505, by Julius II for the design of the Pope's intended tomb.[35] In Michelangelo's personal artistic history his employment on the Tomb marks his reabsorption into the role of sculptor and with the sculptor's exclusive problems; it correspondingly marks his rejection of the influence of Leonardo's style and of those problems in it which were peculiarly pictorial. Michelangelo's rejection of a painter's ambitions was intendedly decisive; his flight from Rome in April 1506, when the project of the Tomb was abandoned in favor of the project for the painting of the Sistine Ceiling, was an indication of the intense conviction of the renunciation he had made.

In the first Tomb project he abandoned altogether the picture-maker's cast of mind that, in the *Cascina* cartoon, had caused him to think, however insufficiently, in terms of unifying groups of several forms. The Tomb design reverts in its conception to the basic unit of the classicizing sculptor's thought, the single figure: the affectation of pictorial unity in the cartoon dissolves, in the Tomb, into its — for Michelangelo — natural component parts. In the Tomb there is a very different concept of the mode of attaining a unity, quite unpictorial and, on the contrary, explicitly sculptural: it is more abstract in the terms both of form and content with which it works. Formally, this unity is achieved in the association of figure forms with forms of architecture: in this relationship the block of stone from which the figure grows is conceivable as a living outgrowth from the geometrical substance of the architecture, but conversely, and at the same time, the architecture is a consequence and geometrical reduction of the figured forms. In content, the unity is not illustrative, as in painting, but thematic, and this unity of theme is articulated not in concerted action but in diversified expressive human symbols. This sculptor's way of thinking toward a unity, which Michelangelo expresses here in monumental form, is immediately relevant to our argument for the history of painting, for it persists when, in the Sistine Ceiling, Michelangelo is again compelled to paint.

Also reassertive in the Tomb design of the sculptor's personality is what we can conclude — even from our very unsatisfactory knowledge of the first design — is Michelangelo's rejection in it of the spatial expansiveness of figure action which had been so pronounced in the *Cascina* cartoon; he now again accepts the limitation of spatial dimension which is implied within the sculptural block, and this limit now tends affirmatively to acquire, in a way that is quite distinct from the sculptural habit of the fifteenth century, the authority of an ideal geometrical value. This is a reinforcement of the classical character of form, in terms of the sculptor's basic figure unit; it is within the ideal including limits of the single sculptural form, rather than in a wider compositional totality, that Michelangelo expresses his will toward a more cogent unity. Again, this sculptor's definition of a factor of the classical style shapes Michelangelo's development as a painter when he begins the Sistine.

Even Michelangelo's vision of the *Laocoön*, Antique but quasi-baroque, on its discovery in Rome in January 1506, did not at first affect this affirmation of the ideal geometric limiting of sculptural form. The *St. Matthew* statue for the Cathedral of Florence (Florence, Academy; c. 1506)[34] was in all likelihood conceived in immediate succession to the first design for the Tomb and after the experience of the *Laocoön*, yet its movement is severely defined within the still visible boundaries of its block. Compared not only with the *Laocoön*, but with the figures of the *Cascina*, the actual physical activity of the *St. Matthew* is much less; it is in part by the very limits imposed upon the action of the figure that its power seems so much intensified. The *St. Matthew* is probably the first evidence in Michelangelo's art of what we may describe as the *Laocoön*-complex: for the next half-decade, all through the course of painting of the Sistine, Michelangelo would be in a state of intermittent war with this vaunted accomplishment of Antique art, trying with the terrible egotism of his genius to absorb and to surpass it. The dramatizing of sensation in the *St. Matthew* is without precedent in Michelangelo's art, conspicuously in the formalisms of the Doni tondo and in the *Cascina* cartoon, and this new access of expressiveness may well have been inspired by the *Laocoön*. If so, Michelangelo owes to the Antique example this reintegration of energy of content with energy of form, which had not been present in his work since the conception of the *David*.

In the intensification of energy that distinguishes the *St. Matthew* from the *David*, however, there is also the distinction from the character of its presumable inspiration in the *Laocoön*. While the violent responses of the *Laocoön* are a consequence of a physical and external cause, the *St. Matthew*, yet more than the *David*, reveals the generation of its energy from an internal spiritual source, a separately conceivable principle of intensest motive power. This spiritual energy is diffused through the body, yet far more strongly than in the *David*, has a resonance that projects around it like an aura; the greater tension of the spirit expands through the movements, not quite physically or compositionally resolved, of Matthew's heavy form. There is a higher generalization, of higher power, in this state of mind of the *St. Matthew*, and there is a corresponding magnifying of the power of generalization in his bodily form. It is not only the unfinished state of the *St. Matthew* that distinguishes it in degree of ideality from the *David*, or still more from the academies of the Cartoon; there is a perceptible distinction of intention. And it may be in the *St. Matthew* that Michelangelo first discovered, perhaps at first accidentally, the idealizing value of the *non-finito*.

In this sculptural organism, so strongly spiritually charged and physically movemented, but powerfully controlled in movement, Michelangelo approaches a level of development that Leonardo had attained in the *Anghiari.* In concentrated sculptural terms, the *St. Matthew* tends toward a similar final harmony, charged with the energies of motion and emotion of its component elements. The *St. Matthew* tends toward such a harmony, but does not reach it; and it is significant for Michelangelo's relation at this moment with the classical style that he did not intend it should. The body of the Matthew strains within its balances, and threatens imminently to break through the disciplines that control it, and the passion that is barely contained in the body strains yet more incontinently from the inspired head. Michelangelo has applied to the *St. Matthew* his experience in development of classical form acquired since the *David*, but now that he again instills an intense spiritual content within this mechanism of form, the spirit threatens to expand beyond it.

The nature of Michelangelo's ideal of harmony is not yet, as it already was for Leonardo, explicitly defined. As in the *St. Matthew*, a partial harmony is achieved only in the partial resolution of a conflict; and the struggle experienced in the process of the resolution is still felt. All the elements of the work of art with which Michelangelo chooses to concern himself are felt with a greater urgency than are those same elements in Leonardo: the matter that Michelangelo is attempting to resolve is less tractable than that with which the older artist deals. Michelangelo's very power of feeling, both for spirit and for substance, is an obstruction to their easy harmony.

For Michelangelo the portrait is an inconceivable vehicle, but for Leonardo, whose processes of thought were differently involved with the experience of nature, it was the form of one of his most remarkable creative acts. The given datum of the *Mona Lisa* (Paris, Louvre; c. 1503–06)[37-8] is an ineffaceable specific human actuality, but not, according to Leonardo's doctrine, an inalterable one. He has worked upon the form and content of the sitter with subtle pressures that reshape them, gently but ineluctably, toward his own artistic ends. The result is a rare miracle of synthesis between art and actuality: an image in which a breathing instant and a composure for all time are held in suspension. It is the very sharpness of the instant, however, which symptomizes a quality in Leonardo's mind that binds his art more than it does that of Michelangelo, and links it, in one vital respect, more closely to the tradition of the Quattrocento. The vibrant acuity of feeling — the core around which the *Mona Lisa's* harmony of spirit is composed — is an indication of the survival, in Leonardo, of the almost poignant sense of the identity of individual phenomena that comes from his education in the Quattrocento. This sense is evident not only in the personality but in certain of the descriptive details of *Mona Lisa*'s form, and above all in the exquisite finenesses of painting of the textures both of substance and of air. All these remain perfectly contained within the discipline of larger form, and their complementary play within it and against it is only further proof of the suspension in a harmony that Leonardo has achieved. Yet by the attachment to the special and even intimate identity of things as well as feelings, the level of generalization in this picture is constrained, and the ideal in it remains more nearly nature-bound.

This character is more likely to appear within a portrait, but something of it may have been in others of Leonardo's pictures of this phase as well. We must remember of Leonardo's works done in Florence, since the *Adoration* and up to this time, that not one of his paintings or cartoons physically survives: we know them imperfectly, through evidence that consists in effect of diagrams that reproduce their general, but not their specific appearance. In the case of the *Last Supper* in Milan, the process of ruin has created a like situation. The second of the two *St. Anne* cartoons or that for the *Anghiari* may have had something of the effect of surface that we see in the *Mona Lisa,* of a measure of equivocation between precision and generalization. The effect is part of the prodigious vibrancy of harmony in the picture's style, but it is also an indication of a historical limitation in this artist, who otherwise so wonderfully shaped the data of history, as he did of art, to his own will.

It is likely that the execution of Leonardo's third version of the *St. Anne, Virgin and Child,*[39] that now in the Louvre, was carried out mostly after the artist left Florence for Milan, intending to remain, in 1508. In part, the picture thus chronologically belongs to the next chapter in the history of classical style; more accurately, however, it belongs within the present period. It is the concluding episode in the development of a single image and a single idea, begun just before Leonardo came to Florence and certainly committed to its final design, as it is on the panel in the Louvre, before he left. With the Louvre *St. Anne* Leonardo fulfills, and also almost — except for one mysterious later work — exhausts the possibilities that he was temperamentally capable of developing from his own long previous invention of a classical style. As the *Anghiari* cartoon had already been before it, the Louvre *St. Anne* is a fulfillment of one of the possible ultimates in a development of classical painting style; and as such, at the moment of its invention, despite the continuing evolution to this time of younger artists, it still significantly exceeds the classical development of any of them.

As the two precedent *St. Anne* cartoons had represented a condensation and refinement of principles expressed in the large *Last Supper*, so the Louvre painting of the St. Anne theme stands similarly to the *Battle of Anghiari.* The developments of structure which we deduced in the *Anghiari* have been carried over into the *St. Anne* painting, with their powers of contentual expression transposed into an appropriately different key, but with their substantial mechanism unaltered. The breadth of forms and their variety of articulation into space is that which had been in the *Battle*; with none of the sculptural emphases of Michelangelo, the figures of this picture move yet more variously and roundly than do those of the Doni tondo, and with conspicuously greater grace. The quality of movement is unsurpassably melodious: a kind of visible *cantilena*, now full and sweeping-broad, now finely ornamental, of which all the lines are fugally interwoven. The attitudes that make the major rhythms of this movement are at once richly differentiated and inescapably interlocked, far beyond the standard of the first *St. Anne* cartoon. The containing shape in which these sequences work is as much an integer as that of the preceding versions, but its effect of geometry is not so obvious or so doctrinaire: this shape weaves the cursive oval of the first cartoon into the pyramidal design of the second. The balancing adjustment of whole structure, like the attitudes of persons by which it is attained, is more fluent and more subtle, and takes into account not only the counterpoise of masses but the counterplay of energies of rhythm. The effect of this stability is as sure as that in the earlier cartoons, but it is both more complex in artifice and deceptively more natural-seeming. The background is worked around the controlling composition of the figures in close dependence on it: its elements are arranged so as to make precise compensation for fine, slight, animating unbalances within the group. The background has a measure of independent illustrative virtue but, mostly, it is an obbligato to the music of the figured theme. The landscape space has no independent rationale, no measurable distances, and, above all, no identity of perspective shape. Its atmosphere of content, as well as its forms, is byplay to the figures.

In one respect, however, the landscape finds a particular accord within the figures. Its colors, most arbitrarily restrained and muted toward neutrality — a cool, silvered blue of distance and, in the foreground, a subtle vibration between dulled greens and browns — are made, just sufficiently more explicit, into the colors of the draperies; and the touches of a reddish tone, enlivening the earth, emerge into a paled rose on the blouse of the Madonna. The form of the landscape is obbligato to the figures, but the color of the figures depends, as if in a process of growth and differentiation, from that of the landscape. In this extent, larger than that of the *Mona Lisa*, the color — there as dense as the form; almost monochromatic — is also more extensive: as arbitrarily controlled, but less constrained than in the portrait. The figures and their setting make, in this reciprocity of color, an interwoven coloristic texture; and this texture of color is inextricable from the atmosphere in which it is suspended. The air is almost palpable, vibrant with the subtly nuanced energies of light. Color, and the forms that emanate it, are perceived through and as if within this living aether, and as we perceive them they are muted by it, but they grow out of it as well. The union of setting and its contents, and of the whole pictorial experience of vision, is determined in the *St. Anne* by this ultimate development in it of the Leonardesque *sfumato* — in the wholly finished passages within the painting, more sophisticated even than in the *Mona Lisa*. But where, in the *Mona Lisa*, the *sfumato* light had virtually consumed color, in the *St. Anne* color reemerges, renascent from the light, to claim a role again within the tissue that is woven, in Leonardo's art, into a harmony.

It is classical doctrine that the bodies, woven into this pulsing suavity of design, should express the same tenor of content as the heads, but these, here, still hold the highest essence of the picture's sense. There is, in the Louvre painting, a yet deeper research into the problem of suspension, in a vibrant compromise, of actuality and beauty: the hard-won experience of the *Mona Lisa* has been exploited further here. Few countenances in the whole history of painting show such a mobile harmony of form and are, at the same time, so compellingly inhabited as that of the St. Anne, the overwatching and chief person of this picture. In these heads Leonardo has achieved the seeming limit of a peculiar potentiality of the classical style: to make harmonious beauty, of feeling as of form, not merely plausible but poignantly believable.

There is a region of meaning in the *St. Anne* painting that transcends what it so wonderfully illustrates of a conception of humanity and even of a conception of art. In this tissue of a vital harmony Leonardo has projected what was, for him, part the consequence of his science, part the fruit of the intuition he had come to hold of the nature of the world. The *St. Anne* is, in Leonardo's own language, the finally effective act of "transmutation of the mind of the painter into the very mind of nature" and the "commentary in art of nature's demonstrations as they are determined by its laws" (*Trattato* I, 24v): less now, as he had often demonstrated before, in the study of separately perceptible aspects of persons and of things than as a symbol of his understanding of the entire process and mode of functioning of nature. This close-meshed, endlessly interwoven, vitally acting and reacting harmony is the visible pattern of Leonardo's comprehension of his world: not just of the earth that he inhabits, but of the universe whose laws the earth reflects in small. This image of persons and an earthly landscape is an image also of the mode of being and the mode of movement of the spheres: it is Leonardo's realization in art of his vision of the cosmos.

In one sense, the generalization that this symbol holds is vaster and higher than any that the subsequent history of classical art — or of all art — will attain. But in another, the matter upon which it has been made contains the limitation of Leonardo's possibilities of any different avenue of development of classical style than this one, in its own way ultimate, that he has achieved.

This is an ultimate of classical thought, but it is not the only one; if Leonardo's were the only possible conception of a classicism all other artists of the High Renaissance would have been condemned, from this time on, to uncreative recapitulation of his accomplishment. It is his very preoccupation with the world as an experience and interpretation of nature, an experience as much that of the scientist as of the humanist, that closed to Leonardo the further possible directions of development, more exclusively (in the literal sense) humanist, which the younger generations would explore. This naturalism, transformed long since beyond its origins in the Quattrocento, still relates Leonardo to the period out of which his art had come. He retains, within his prodigious capacity for inducing generalizations, the sense of the specific identity of each phenomenon of experience that we have seen at its most acute in the *Mona Lisa*, and of which the evidence is still ample in the last *St. Anne*, and this identity is too precious a datum for him to surrender wholly. The synthesis that his painting attempts, and in fact achieves, is almost of a defeating complexity: it has, so to speak, no limits either in the cosmic or in the infinitesimal sense.

It is not only physical data to which he responds thus; it is the data of human emotion also. For Leonardo, emotion is — in his own terms of intellectual redefinition — the apt response to specified situations: there are spheres of comprehension of peculiarly human idea and aspiration — of exalted, wholly internally generated, states of spirit and of mind — that he does not invade: Michelangelo's way of a transcendent thought about humanity is closed to him. So also, in this very private communion with experience that is Leonardo's way of making art, is he closed off from the realm of public rhetoric, with its burden of grand and surpassing emotions, that will be the basis for Raphael's highest acts of classical style. There is a touch still, within Leonardo's poetic transformation of the art of fifteenth-century Florence, of some of its familiar attitudes of mind; the style he invented would develop, still within his lifetime, into regions into which Leonardo, at last bound by generation and by place, could not move.

FRA BARTOLOMMEO AND ALBERTINELLI

For the first three, or perhaps four, years after the opening of the century, the third among the Florentines who had evolved a classical style, Fra Bartolommeo, retired to pursue another vocation in the Convent of S. Marco. Though removed from the practice of painting he continued certainly to draw, and he had a deputy in the person of his former partner, Mariotto Albertinelli. As we have seen already from what is still decipherable of his contribution to Bartolommeo's *Last Judgment* of S. M. Nuova,[21] a contribution made in 1500 and early 1501, Albertinelli did not then quite comprehend what was new in Bartolommeo's ideas of style. Yet, being a dependent personality by habit, Albertinelli was induced to imitate these, with singularly inconsistent results: for the first few years of the sixteenth century Albertinelli is artistically schizoid. On one hand he continued to work in a mode which is almost indistinguishably that of his latest Quattrocento pictures; on the other, he worked in a manner based on that of the Frate and which, in these cases, seemingly depends on and exploits the latter's drawings. The imitation of Bartolommeo is entirely deliberate, but so is Albertinelli's practice of a Quattrocento manner. The two manners at first touch each other only partly, if at all, and then toward 1503 begin to fuse. However, it is only after the Frate resumed painting in 1504, and thus provided Albertinelli with new full-scale models on which to form himself, that Albertinelli finally, with relative decisiveness, surrendered his quattrocentesque style.

Mariotto's small portable triptych (Milan, Museo Poldi-Pezzoli),[40] dated 1500, gives an excellent index of his habits of artistic style at the opening of the century. The inner portion of the triptych, with the Madonna, and two saints on the wings, is almost eclectically representative of the mean of good Florentine painting of the moment: it recalls all at once qualities that we associate with Credi, Perugino, Filippino, and Piero di Cosimo, and even echoes Piero's occasional affectation of the Flemish idiom. Its fundamental cast of style is readily identifiable: it belongs to the literal-minded and gently sentimentalizing *détente* of the nineties, that phase of style from which Fra Bartolommeo had, by 1500, emerged. The outer wings of the triptych, with a grisaille Annunciation, are quite different: they adequately reflect Bartolommeo's newer manner. The *Annunciation* is surely based on a design by Baccio, of which Albertinelli's transcription may even exaggerate, by simplifying, the smooth rotundities of figure and the proportioned regularity of space.

It is not possible to prove of Mariotto's *Visitation* [42] of 1503 that it is, like the *Annunciation* in Milan, in effect an "execution" of one of Fra Bartolommeo's designs. However, there are indications which may point to this, including the existence of a drawing by Fra Bartolommeo (Uffizi 465E; Berenson) which corresponds to one scene of the predella. The character of the figures is like that in the most advanced of Baccio's drawings for the *Last Judgment*: those for the heavily movemented forms in the lower portion of the fresco scene. In transcribing those drawings, two or three years before, Albertinelli had given the figures in them (more complex than those of the contemporary small *Annunciation*) a turgid awkwardness of articulation which changed their effect of style retrogressively, toward the Peruginesque. In the *Visitation*, his understanding of Bartolommeo's intention has become much more sure. The two figures have the gravity and breadth of the Frate's forms in the *Last Judgment*, and they move with the handsome slow deliberation which, earlier, Albertinelli had not grasped; the implication of monumentality in Bartolommeo's actors in the fresco has been not only comprehended but increased. The surface of the painting is still Peruginesque, as is, in most obvious fashion, the framing architecture of the background.

The picture most explicitly reveals its antecedents, and equally clearly demonstrates its adherence to the new mode in its displacement, by a monumental moving harmony, of a static one. How much of Fra Bartolommeo is in this positive achievement may be gathered by comparison of the *Visitation* with a wholly independent work by Mariotto, of equal scale, the fresco *Crucifixion* of the Certosa di Val d'Ema,[41] dated 1506. There much of the vocabulary of forms is borrowed from the Frate, and it is intended that the structure work like his; but no fluency within this borrowed, but still not yet assimilated, speech exists to fuse its parts into a harmony.

The *Visitation* is an accomplishment, by proxy, of a development that proceeds directly from Fra Bartolommeo's premises of style as he had laid them down in 1499. It is a simple development, on a basis that was itself the simplest of those invented for the new classical style, and its comparative place in the evolution of that style is not with the contemporary efforts in Florence of Leonardo and Michelangelo, but at best with their accomplishments of the later nineties. Yet, the *Visitation* is the most impressive and stylistically homogeneous work of its moment in Florence outside the production of the two great geniuses.

In 1504, when Bartolommeo again began to paint, his ambitions became more complex than those which Albertinelli had realized for him in the *Visitation.* It is not certain how much of the new impetus of Bartolommeo's art was self-generated, or how much was due to the experience of Leonardo's example of the intervening years; it is clear in any case that after he resumed his career in painting, Bartolommeo was touched by Leonardo's art as he had never been before. In the few works of the Frate's that have come to us from about 1505 there is an accenting of the shadowed softness which, in his figures of the *Last Judgment*, had been just visible: there is the sensation, not precise enough to be defined as imitative, of a Leonardesque *sfumato.* What had been still-Peruginesque reminiscences, in the postures of bodies and in the disposition of their draperies, diminish, and are replaced by fuller, softer, and more cursive patterns, more so than in Albertinelli's *Visitation.* Further, the increased fluidity in the design of figures is accompanied by a higher animacy of expression of face and gesture. For these changes, the influence of Leonardo's 1501 cartoon may be in part responsible, but this does not exclude Bartolommeo's now more understanding restudy of the ancient model of the *Adoration of the Kings.*

The new qualities in the Frate's style are associable with Leonardo's example, and certainly in part derived from it, but the comprehension and adapting of that example are the consequence of a personal development already conditioned, by Baccio's own creative past, to be in the same direction. On his much lesser level, Baccio's exploitation of Leonardo's inescapable precedent is a phenomenon like that we know in Michelangelo; not imitative but assimilative, and creative still; it is not like the relation of Albertinelli to Bartolommeo himself, by which the classical style accomplished another stage in its process of dissemination.

The alteration in Bartolommeo's style after 1504 is at once perceptible, but the direction that this alteration takes is not immediately consistent. His first commission after he resumed painting was of a nature to create an inconsistency: the *Vision of St. Bernard* (Florence, Academy; ordered late in 1504 but delivered only in 1507) [43] was intended for the Badia, where it would be in patent competition with Filippino Lippi's older version of the same theme.[44] The influence of Lippi's painting is manifest in spite of Bartolommeo's genuine, and on the whole successful, intention to create differently. Filippino's busy crowd of angels have intruded themselves into Baccio's picture, but more than their presence as a motive it is the admission, with them, of something of Filippino's uncoordinate variety that disturbs. A tendency to slimness of physical type also suggests the influence of Filippino: this makes a touch of preciosity which recollects an unclassical aspect of the recent past. In all else, however, Fra Bartolommeo's painting develops in a classicizing direction, and the contrast of the two *St. Bernard* pictures makes a sound demonstration of the different identities of the old style and the new. A contrast not less clear appears when Bartolommeo's work is juxtaposed with a term which, within Quattrocento style, is nearly opposite to Filippino's: Perugino's version of this same theme (Munich, Pinakothek).[16]

It is in Bartolommeo's work that there reappears — perhaps by invention rather than by imitation — a pre-Renaissance ideality of iconographic interpretation of the subject: the Virgin is no longer earthbound, but borne by angels in a clearly divine apparition, and St. Bernard kneels in formal adoration to receive her. In this divine circumstance the spirit that animates the actors is not more or less deeply felt than in Lippi's interpretation (though surely more than in Perugino's); but it is a different quality of sensation, resembling the radiance of emotion that we know in Leonardo. The mode of physical being of Bartolommeo's figures is more recognizably new: it seeks a monumental breadth of drapery like that in the *Last Judgment*, and more than in Albertinelli's *Visitation*, increases the cursive fullness of effect of folds and silhouette. Each major figure, even that of the air-borne Virgin, attains a classical gravity of ponderation. In the composition, the Frate clearly intends to put by the remaining restraints on his style of a *détente* symmetry and to create a balance more internally alive. He succeeds, in effect, in making a compositional harmony of relatively freely disposed forms, in which there is a resilient and equilibrated concord of movement and of rest. The arrangement is carefully, intellectually conceived and it is a novel one, based upon a principle of design not hitherto employed either by Leonardo or by Michelangelo. The principle is deduced from the nature of the subject: it is the bipartite balance of a meeting, in which two laterally disposed parts intersect upon, but do not fuse compactly in, the central axis of the picture.

The same principle had been used, less articulately, in the description of another meeting, in the Albertinelli *Visitation*, and it is repeated in the Frate's own picture of a physically similar event, the *Noli Me Tangere* (Paris, Louvre; c. 1506).[45] The application of this idea of design is in every way more developed than in the *Vision of St. Bernard*. The ambition is the same, to create an animate and responsive, yet balancing, conjunction between mass and movement. Here, however, the movement is at once stronger and more surely controlled, and more pervasively diffused within the mass. The intersection between the two main forms in the spiral sequence made of arms and hands is both highly formally effective and contentually eloquent. On both sides of this linking key there is a constant manipulation into balance of the only apparently informal asymmetry of the design. Both actors in the *Noli Me Tangere* are of more developed classicizing kind than those in the *St. Bernard*: they are of fuller form and have no vestige, now, of Peruginesque inhibition in their movement. The effect of a harmoniousness in the picture is increased by the fact that the quattrocentesque hardness of technique, still partly visible in the *St. Bernard*, has yielded to a gentle unifying softness of vibrating atmosphere that, certainly, is of Leonardesque origin.

Fra Bartolommeo's last major work of this phase, before his departure for a visit to Venice in the spring of 1508, was a large altar of the *Assumption* for the Compagnia de' Contemplanti (formerly Berlin, 1507–08).[46] It was left for Albertinelli to complete, especially in its upper parts, and the intentions of Fra Bartolommeo's design have been somewhat falsified in consequence. The picture is nevertheless important because it is the Frate's first essay in the field of the monumental altarpiece, in which he was to make his most significant contribution to the history of High Renaissance style. In an artist of no profoundly adventurous disposition such as Bartolommeo, the grand dimension of such a commission and the thought of the picture's public destination seem to have induced a leaning toward a conservative solution. The rather experimental character of design in the *Bernard* altar or the small *Noli Me Tangere* have been put aside for a renewed dependence on accepted compositional precedent, in Ghirlandaio and, in particular, in Perugino. Yet precedent has been translated into new classicizing language no less effectively than it had been in the painting for the Badia: like that picture, the *Assunta*, as the Frate conceives it, becomes an ideal event and not a translation of divinity into prose. In its design, the *Assunta* is projected in a symmetry, but of movemented and cursively connected shapes, and these are disposed in an elementary, yet carefully deliberated, counterpoise. The main patterns of the composition are generalized and instantly obvious circular shapes, each ornamentally elaborated into further curves; the two main circular shapes, one in the elevation of the upper portion of the picture, the other in the lower plan, adjoin and echo one another. They are not yet unified: in this scheme it becomes apparent that Fra Bartolommeo's conception of a harmony is far from developed to the stage apparent in the contemporary Leonardo or in Michelangelo. With the survival still of some of the additive mentality of a fifteenth-century classicism the Frate thinks in terms — as in his pictures of "meetings" — of a harmony of conjunction, but not quite yet of a cogent unity.

Altogether, Bartolommeo's position in the development of a classical style, at the end of this phase, remains substantially behind that of his two greater predecessors. A work like the *Assunta* still reflects the conservative nature of the Frate's own original act of formulation of a classical style, almost a decade before, and bespeaks his slower and lesser spiritual and intellectual genius. The place to which his evolution brings him, by 1508, is well advanced beyond his own classicizing beginnings, but not even yet equal to the level of development that Leonardo brought to Florence in 1501.

We must, in assessing Bartolommeo's position from the *Assunta,* discount the effects of Albertinelli's intervention. Where he touched the picture it takes on more of a quality of Peruginesque reminiscence than it was meant to have. Mariotto himself, in his independent work, had resolved the dilemma of competing styles by determining to follow Bartolommeo in his new manner, but his following was not again, within this phase, so comprehending as it had been in the *Visitation.* A painting wholly by Albertinelli of the same time as the joint *Assunta,* the *Annunciation with Sts. Sebastian and Lucy* (Munich, Pinakothek; c. 1508),[47] reveals a style still ambiguous, suspended between Fra Bartolommeo's balancing and cursive fullnesses of form and Perugino's somnolent, bland, stiffness. The happening is without aesthetic interest, but it is important as historical symptom. The suspension between two chronologically successive styles, with the character of a transition, that we encounter in the Munich altar as in other works by Albertinelli between 1503 and 1508, is not to be found in Bartolommeo's works of that or of an earlier time. The conception of transitional style seems, in the historical process with which we are dealing, to be applicable only to those artists who, like Mariotto, change style only by the imitation of an extant model — to artists whose new style is learned and not created. In the work of the authentic inventors of High Renaissance classicism — even in the Frate's most historically organic-seeming creating of this style — there is a clearly apprehensible moment at which the new style assumes its recognizable form. In its first moment this form is, of course, unfulfilled and still amply indicates its antecedents but it is, in a decisive act, a new gestalt.

RAPHAEL

Late in the year in which Fra Bartolommeo renewed the practice of his art the young Raphael, then aged twenty-one, arrived in Florence. He was already the possessor of a formulated High Renaissance classical style, of which the first evidence had been in his very earliest works. The genesis of classical style in Raphael resembled that in Fra Bartolommeo, at virtually the same date: both styles were, to begin with, regenerations and reformations of the classicism of the contemporary *détente*. Raphael was, more directly than the Frate, in the direct line of inheritance of the fifteenth-century classical tradition. His place of birth and early education was Urbino, a major center of Piero della Francesca's activity, where he had left not only pictorial models of his early classical style but had helped impose it on the architecture of the Palace and city. Perhaps more than any place where the Early Renaissance flourished the physical substance of Urbino, the cadre in which Raphael grew up, had assumed the shapes of reason. Piero's pupil, Perugino, had become the dominating model of artistic style in Urbino in the time of Raphael's youth, and Perugino's influence was reinforced by that of his temperamental and stylistic analogue, Francia. In the experience of environment, and in such teaching as Raphael had before he went himself to work with Perugino, the classical tradition of the fifteenth century was authoritative, in particular in its then current *détente* phase.

The calm and reasonable harmony of this late phase of Quattrocento classicism shaped the first artistic conceptions and ambitions of the young Raphael, and was the basis to which he in turn gave different historical shape. His first means of change, as with Fra Bartolommeo, was the infusion of a new animation into a vitiated classical style; and in its first evidences, this impulse in Raphael was of a gentleness temperamentally entirely like that in Perugino and his artistic kin. It was not for that reason any less instantly decisive of essential change. The first appearance of this animation, pervasive as it is gentle, does more than create an art differently ingratiating from that of the *détente*; it creates a basically different, and differently compelling, mode of order. In Raphael, differently from Leonardo or from Michelangelo, the invention of a classical style seems utterly unforced; it does not have the dramatic sense of a resolution of a dilemma of art or of cultural history, or the effect of a vast power of intellectual or spiritual decision. His making a High Renaissance classical style seems a working of sympathetic genius, formed by the heritage of early classicism, upon that heritage, but realizing in it that which was potential but not yet formed. Still more than with the Frate, Raphael's new creation seems a natural — almost an evolutionary — historical event, the consequence of an inherent logic by which classicism might move from an early phase into a maturity. The implication of an evolution is in one sense true, but it does not diminish the high significance of Raphael's discovery, alone in his milieu of art, of this "inherent" logic. The discovery of this logic was apparently, however, not intellectually made: it would seem to have been, almost purely, the product of a new gestalt, of which the psychic and aesthetic components are inextricable. For this, we cannot even tentatively adduce, as we can in the case of Bartolommeo, an external forming or precipitating agent; no outward occasion can account for the act by which Raphael infuses a transforming life into the shell of early classical *détente.*

Very differently from the passive harmony of feeling in late fifteenth-century classicism there is, in Raphael's earliest works, a dulcet radiance that is the analogue of that in Leonardo's baptismal angel of a quarter-century before. This gentle life inspires, in the bodies it inhabits, a slow ponderated grace; and, because its pulse is utterly pervasive, inhabiting all the actors of the image, it interweaves them in a single skein of action and reaction. Both spiritual and bodily existence and the shapes which, with their slow grace, express them are felt, as in the Peruginesque style, as a harmony of quiet; but this harmony is, now, of a single unity and not of separable parts. In the *détente* style a mentality that is not only additive but, even, divisive determines the relationships of parts: this mentality permits, among other things, irreconcilable ambitions of ideal order and realistic literalness to coexist. On the earliest Raphael this contemporary habit of mind has no effect. He adjusts the emphases in painting of details to their role within the definition of the whole so that — so unlike what we observe in Perugino's style — descriptive incidents articulate and define, but do not obtrude on, harmony. Answering to the intention that this harmony should gently move, the contours of figures as they are drawn, and their forms as they are modelled, smooth out irregular accidents of shape and round off angularities, to make images of an idealized nature, related in a cadenced continuity.

This first Cinquecento classicism in Raphael contains a special personal accent, again recollective of Leonardo's early angel, in that, in Raphael too, the figures wear the look of youthful automorphs. This quality attaches not only to the delicacy — the prettiness, even — of face and form but to the state of mind, so fresh and quietly bright, with which the whole pictured world has been conceived. The early Raphaels have the emanation of such a loveliness as was incipient in Leonardo's angel, but in them, more in the way of Leonardo's later accomplishment in the first *St. Anne* cartoon, this loveliness is attached to a fuller proportioned harmony of sensuous form: like Leonardo, Raphael recreates a simile for the Ancient classic sense of beauty.

Raphael's *Three Graces* (Chantilly, Musée Condé; c. 1504)[48] intuits more than he could have ever seen in his Antique model of Phidian and Praxitilean ideals.

The youthful gentleness in Raphael is the index of a remarkable modesty which existed in him side by side with his absolute creative gift. In the course *of his direct exposure to Perugino, in Perugia, between 1500 and 1504, he too readily accepted the older painter's great authority, with results that were in part unfortunate for the immediate development of the new idea of style he had come to earlier, and on his own. For a while, Perugino's stiffness and literalness intrude into young Raphael's manner and there appear, in certain of his paintings of this time, a character as of transitional style, come by in this case by a strangely opposite process to that in Bartolommeo's partner Albertinelli: by the inventor imitating the tradition.

Toward the end of these few years of apprenticeship and collaboration Raphael's own identity again emerged, if anything now more secure from the discipline of technique acquired in his Perugian experience. The *Marriage of the Virgin* (Milan, Brera; 1504),[49] the last work done by Raphael before his arrival in Florence, could not show its sources in Perugino's school more clearly, but these are once again transformed unequivocally into new terms. Its figures are in an enlivened and connective relation developed well beyond that of the earlier *Three Graces* or its obverse (*The Dream of the Knight;* London, National Gallery), and their composition is altogether infused with a new degree of energy and diversity of articulation. The movemented but yet centralizing arrangement of the figure group is supported, and its formal ambition symbolized, by the architecture of the background. In a way, this picture recalls the Perugino of the later seventies or earliest eighties, when his style still retained the vigor of a recent Florentine education and his order still held some of the sharpness of a Pieresque discipline. Raphael's revivifying and clarifying of Perugino's style recalls a prior moment in the history of Quattrocento classicism before its *détente*, but yet more points a fundamental difference: in that earlier moment animation and order were principles of contrast in their function and effect; in the *Marriage of the Virgin* they are coefficients of a new mode of harmony.

Raphael thus arrived in Florence with a Cinquecento classical style of which the basis had already been formed, and even in some measure internally developed. The degree of evolution of his style might be compared, in 1504, to the contemporary stage in Fra Bartolommeo, and the resemblance is reinforced by the strong dose of Perugino that existed also in the Frate's background. But more than the style of Fra Bartolommeo the style of Raphael in 1504, in spite of his superior genius, seems naïve: a young man's style, as it in fact was; and even more than personally so, it seems provincial — culturally naïve. By Florentine standards this art of Raphael's is too simple and its scope and its ambitions too constrained. If the contrast is sensible even against the monastic painter of S. Marco, it is crushing in the context of the contemporary accomplishment of Leonardo and Michelangelo. With his singular combination of intelligence and modesty Raphael proceeded quickly to rid himself of his naïveté and to lose his simplicity, but not his clarity, of mind. This clarity of intelligence and feeling had been, to begin with, a consequence of the very limitations and the simplicity of Raphael's background; but it became a positive force in his maturing personality. From this clarity, distilled out of his provincialism, would come the special contribution that Raphael would make in the next years to the Florentine evolution of the classical style.

Among his Florentine predecessors in the High Renaissance classical style Raphael chose, as was obvious, the example of Leonardo as the most illuminating. Despite Vasari's assertion of Raphael's sympathy for Fra Bartolommeo (IV, 326–27) — a sympathy understandable in the light of their liens of artistic situation — there is not more than one clear instance of Raphael's acceptance of the Frate's example: in the design for the fresco of S. Severo in Perugia, conceived during Raphael's first Florentine year. Raphael's sights were set higher than the Frate. He studied Michelangelo's *David*, the *Bruges Madonna* (sold only in 1506) and the Madonna tondi both in sculpture and in painting, and he drew from the *Cascina* cartoon. Above all, he studied Leonardo's work: Raphael's drawings as well as his paintings of these years indicate his knowledge of the *Anghiari*, the now lost *Leda*, the lost *Madonna of the Spindle*, and the *Gioconda*, and he must have known intimately the St. Anne theme in the cartoon of 1501 as well as, almost surely, the design Leonardo finally committed to painting in the version in the Louvre. Raphael's interest in Leonardo seems to have led him beyond the work that might have been publicly accessible; there is evidence of his study of certain of Leonardo's drawings. Leonardo was above all the chief educative force for Raphael in Florence, as he was in these years for Fra Bartolommeo and for the difficult, but not as yet intractable Michelangelo.

The *Madonna del Granduca* (Florence, Pitti; 1505) [50] is the earliest major step in the process of translation of Raphael's style into Florentine idiom, and it is already quite distinct from the Perugian tradition. It is not that the earlier basic vocabulary of form has been so much altered; the most immediate mark of difference from Raphael's style of the Perugian years is in the growth of the dimension of the human meaning of the picture. The content is as gentle as in Raphael's earliest pictures, but no longer so ingenuous; it is graver and more inwardly profound. The Virgin, the vessel of this feeling, is more mature, and her loveliness is more classically conceived, fuller and more sensuously handsome than before, but not less pure of form. Her new appearance, with its accompanying effect of expression (and that of the Child also), is only in part the result of a change in type; it is due also to a more important change, in Raphael's descriptive technique, from a near-quattrocentesque smoothness to a muted chiaroscuro, sensible both on surfaces and in the contours of the forms. The image acquires a higher unity in the melding, in this *sfumato* atmosphere, of its parts, and it acquires a greater breadth from the veiling and the generalizing, in the softer handling, of detail. The source of growth and change in the *Madonna del Granduca* is certainly in Leonardo: the likely model for the grander and profounder manner of feeling, and for the amplitude and unity of form, is in the earlier *St. Anne* cartoons. Raphael's alterations of form, of content, and of painterly technique are all in a Leonardesque sense; in his example, Raphael found a revelation, already accomplished, of the disposition of style that he already entertained.

Despite the authority that Raphael so quickly recognized in Leonardo, there was no question of surrender of his own integrity of personality — less, indeed, now that he was more personally mature, than there had been in his earlier relation with Perugino. Leonardo's authority was, in general, accepted by Raphael; but he did not accept with it the torturing complexities of Leonardo's artistic ambitions. There was not in Raphael, as there was in the older Leonardo, any symptom of the Quattrocento scientist's passion to know and describe all the possible subtleties of experience, and no consequent need that each achievement of a harmony should come from exquisite manipulations in the mind and the emotions. For Raphael, harmony was in the first air he had learned to breathe, and its components were — or had so far been — the simple personal and cultural data of his provincial youth. The *Madonna del Granduca*, within its cast of Leonardism, preserves a modesty and purity of feeling and a simple dignity of form that are almost a rebuke to the terrible wisdom of the mature Leonardo. Raphael's following of Leonardo assumes his simplification and reduction of Leonardo's style, but this process also is a clarifying of it.

In the next two years or so of Raphael's Florentine education, as his personal sophistication increased and his own art began to unfold its potential of classical resource, he learned to understand more of the richness and complexity of Leonardo, and he took Leonardo's advanced solutions in classicism as models for his own. However, what he took from Leonardo remained, through this time, the substance of the Leonardesque solution and not its tissue of involved overtones. Raphael's development in these years thus became a recapitulation of the evolution and a restatement of the principles of classical style in terms of greater clarity than those of Leonardo, and of more immediate intellectual and emotional accessibility. This Raphaelesque restatement, unlike the style of Leonardo and, in this degree unlike the style of Michelangelo, carries nothing over from the Quattrocento except its heritage of classicism; the style of Raphael is uncomplicated by an older generation's reminiscences. It assumes the historical significance not only of a redefinition, but of the first definition, of the High Renaissance classical style made in terms that are unequivocally of the Cinquecento. The succession of Raphael's great Madonna pictures of the next few years illustrates this evolution that translates Leonardo into clearer and unequivocally "modern" style.

The *Madonna del Prato* (Vienna, Kunsthistorisches Museum; dated 1505)[53] depends more than the *Madonna del Granduca* on Leonardo's St. Anne theme: perhaps not only on the cartoon of 1501 but on the version from Milan. More than one specific motive in the Raphael has been adapted to its different context from the Leonardesque source: these would seem to include the head of the Madonna — more specifically like Leonardo in accent of form and in expression than that of the *Granduca*; the long, pure curve of her sloping shoulder and arm; the posture with which she supports the Christ Child — like that in the cartoon of 1501; and perhaps, also, the arrangement of her upper drapery. Raphael's interpretation of his theme, with its deceptive and ingratiating informality, seems also to adapt the notion of a kind of content invented by Leonardo for the 1501 cartoon.

Raphael's composition is certainly derived from this same source, from its carefully defined triangle which precisely contains all the figure elements within its shape. Throughout his picture, however, Raphael has simplified — oversimplified, in this instance — the subtlety and variety of Leonardo's artifice. In spite of their Leonardesque modulation in chiaroscuro of modelling and outline, Raphael's forms seem, by comparison with Leonardo's, somewhat overgeneralized and hard, and the clarity of Raphael's shape of composition seems nearly stark. The differentiation into movement of design especially is less articulate: despite the sophisticated motive of the Virgin's contrapposto the structure of the design is touched, still, with a Peruginesque planarity. It is, in part, a residue of artistic innocence that accounts for the too-crystalline simplicity of the *Madonna del Prato.* But also, this crystallinity is due to Raphael's positive new enthusiasm for a doctrine of geometry in art which now, on Leonardo's example, has become for him a highly conscious aesthetic value rather than an unruminated inheritance from fifteenth-century classicism. Like Leonardo's geometry earlier in his own evolution, the geometry of the *Madonna del Prato* is touched with a quality of the doctrinaire.

The response of Raphael to Leonardo, of willing discipleship, but of comprehension impeded by innocence and restrained by an ambition significantly less complex, has no more cogent demonstration than in Raphael's portraits between 1505 and 1506, and most of all in the portrait that depends most explicitly on Leonardo, the *Maddalena Doni* (Florence, Pitti; c. 1506).[51] Raphael's drawing in the Louvre, freely after *La Gioconda*, already indicates an intention to simplify the model. The painted portrait is a still further reduction of Leonardo's form, and a drastic, almost pedestrian reduction of

Leonardesque feeling. The portrait of *Angelo Doni* (also Pitti; c. 1506),[52] pendant in design to that of his wife, is more flexible in its description of the countenance and its content; it is in the portrait of the man that Raphael more nearly — though still by no means closely — approximates the controlled and suspended intensity of expression Leonardo had captured in the *Gioconda*. Even with Leonardo's supreme essay in the field of portraiture to support him, Raphael at this date cannot resolve the issue, in the drastic terms in which the problem of the portrait poses it, between the specific human datum and the ideality. Yet the very reduction of the Leonardesque exemplar in the Doni portraits, so aesthetically unsatisfactory by contrast with the Leonardo, is the sole practical solution of the problem of a portraiture in classical style. It is only by making both sides of the equation simpler — both the actual and the ideal — that it became possible to paint portraits by a process which does not, as in the *Mona Lisa*, partake both of miracle and of an infinite expenditure of time and spiritual labor.

So seemingly like the *Madonna del Prato*, the *Madonna del Cardellino* (Florence, Uffizi; late 1505–06) [54] is a work of much higher sophistication. It reflects a development that is, at once, wholly internal to the artist, and external in the sense that it bespeaks a higher comprehension of Leonardo's — and in this case perhaps also of Michelangelo's — models of classical style. It may be less the Florentine cartoon for the *St. Anne* than the antecedent version that Raphael has studied for the *Cardellino*: the structure of Raphael's composition suggests the Milanese cartoon's primarily oval form. The posture and placing of the St. John, and something of his relation to the Christ Child, also suggest the influence of this same model. For the placing of the Child, however, Raphael may have thought of the example of Michelangelo's *Bruges Madonna* [25] — itself, as we have seen, with some likelihood influenced in turn by Leonardo.

It is not the adaptation of particular motives, but the profounder penetration of the whole sense of the classical models from which they derive, that is important in the *Madonna del Cardellino*. The figure of the Virgin, and the compositional shape that depends on it, now have the richer amplitude of dimension, both of contour and of plastic shape, that Leonardo had attained in his cartoons; and more according to Leonardesque example than in the *Madonna del Prato*, the generalization of shape includes enriching ornamental variations. The movement of the major forms within the unifying contour is more rigorous, and now includes a fuller differentiation of the forms in space. The body of the Virgin, in gentler contrapposto than that of the figures of the Milanese cartoon, reflects their slightly oblique placing. The old-fashioned element of planarity that had been in the structure of the *Madonna del Prato* is much less apparent here: the sequences of rhythm now tend to warp across the — still partly visible — planes of form and bind them, in a richer spatial being, in a unity. Also, more than in the *Madonna del Prato*, the landscape background here has been arranged so as to frame and support the unity of the figure group.

Almost of itself, the head of Raphael's Virgin could illustrate the deeper classical sense of the whole painting of the *Cardellino*. Its form depends less literally than that of the Prato *Virgin* on Leonardo's types, but it more compellingly approaches Leonardo's effect of warmth and softness of an ideal beauty. Feeling, too, is warmer and deeper than in the *Madonna del Prato* and, in Leonardo's way, seems at the same time more serene. The nature of the harmony of form and feeling is generically the same as Leonardo's, yet, with the generic likeness, Raphael's decisive difference remains: of a harmony achieved out of material far less complex but, in compensation, instantly accessible and clear. In this picture this clarity works, for the first time in Raphael's career, within and through a considerably developed classical mechanism of form and in the dimensions of a developed classical resonance of feeling; the *Madonna del Cardellino* marks Raphael's adequate integration into the advanced contemporary development.

Like Leonardo, it may be said of Raphael in his Florentine years that he was obsessed with the problem of the perfection of a single pictorial idea, to which he too gave three varying forms, each significantly developed beyond its predecessor. *La Belle Jardinière* (Paris, Louvre; dated 1507)[55] is a final stage in the evolution that had begun in the *Madonna del Prato* and a fulfillment of the promise of the *Cardellino*. Even as Raphael evolved this third version of his theme it would appear that he still sought Leonardo's guidance, and that this guidance may have come from Leonardo's own last version of *St. Anne*.[22] Certain characteristics of the *Belle Jardinière*, even within the new identity they assume in Raphael's handling of them, suggest an origin in the Louvre *St. Anne*. First among them is the less axial arrangement of the figure group than in the *Cardellino*, with the more pronounced displacement of the Virgin at an angle from the picture plane and toward one side; the Virgin's inclination also suggests Leonardo's model. A pattern of fluid movement, made of the postures of the children and by the drapery, has been woven across the Virgin's form, and its quick convolutions are like those in the Louvre *St. Anne*; in one movement of the drapery, of the fallen mantle toward the rear, there is a singularly close resemblance to the exactly corresponding motive in Leonardo's picture. It is also like the Leonardo that the axial displacement of the figures is in part compensated by a single tree form to one side. But more essentially the balance of the picture is secured within the figure group itself — as in the Louvre *St. Anne*, and not as in the *Cardellino* — not only by the adjustment of masses but also by that of energies of rhythm. The whole structure is not only more various and active than before but — and the distinction is that of Leonardo's picture against the earlier cartoons, as well as of the *Belle Jardinière* against its predecessors — its containing shape is of a far less obvious geometry. There is too much that is novel in the *Jardinière* precisely in the way of Leonardo's third *St. Anne* for Raphael's progress to have come without its example. In this picture Raphael has developed from an adequate mastery of the mechanisms of classical style into a comprehension of its most advanced contemporary form. He has himself made no new inventive contribution to the evolution of these mechanisms but, in two or three brief years, he has assimilated them completely, to the limit of their then development.

More precisely, he has understood the substance of Leonardo's classical accomplishment, perhaps more thoroughly and with less congenital temperamental obstruction than Michelangelo; at the same time he has adapted Leonardo's style to his own particular expressive purposes: the sophistication of form in the *Belle Jardinière* is still dedicated to the illustration of a limpid, un-Leonardesque harmony. The whole intensity of temper and the highly involved artifice of Leonardo's third *St. Anne* have been reduced in Raphael's picture. Forms which, in the *St. Anne*, are flexed in an almost difficult aesthetic tension are relaxed, and the ravelled unity of Leonardo's design has been a little dissolved and made more naturally casual. Leonardo's energy of moving forms has been transmuted in the *Belle Jardinière* into a lighter ornamental grace, more consonant with Raphael's notion of a harmony, which embellishes that harmony with a freshness and variety that are absent in the *Cardellino*. The same quality of grace, delicate but just in measure, and with no trace of a preciosity, is infused into the expressions of face and attitudes of body. Raphael's harmony, not less clear than before, is now more subtle both in content and in form, and more sensitively animated. What the *Belle Jardinière* has to say is now said with entire aesthetic sophistication; of Raphael's former innocence no more remains than its admirable core: his purity of thought and feeling.

The *Belle Jardinière* represents the extreme possible stage of Raphael's absorption of the principles of Leonardo's style without infringement upon his own identity. Raphael went beyond this point: sometime in 1507, after the conception of the *Jardinière*, Raphael began to follow Leonardo not only as a guide but with something of the fervor of discipleship. He seems to have recognized that, beyond that level of classical development he had reached in the *Jardinière*, there were, in Leonardo's art, resources of potential use to him that he had not mastered: of subtleties in expression of emotion, of complex finenesses of form, and, above all, of inexhaustible intensities of animation that were contained within the harmony of Leonardo's art. In Florence, in the presence of Leonardo's overwhelming example, it was not conceivable to search for these resources in any but Leonardo's terms, and in doing so Raphael for a moment compromised, but did not permanently surrender, his own temperamental integrity. A few works of Raphael of 1507 show not merely a generic Leonardesque dependence but an adaptation of the specific style — highly animated, shadowed and complex — of Leonardo's matured art. Such paintings as the *Bridgewater House Madonna* (Edinburgh, National Gallery) [56] and the *Holy Family of the Casa Canigiani* (Munich, Pinakothek),[58] and such a singular and beautiful drawing as that of a *Madonna and Child* in the Louvre [57] (Fischel 142; used later in the preparation of the *Baldacchino* altar) are the extremes of this nearly imitative conjunction with the style of Leonardo. There is no surviving shred of Raphael's purity in these pictures; no innocence could survive in the inmost atmosphere of Leonardo's art, corrosive to others and even, perhaps, to Leonardo himself. But because this intimate following of Leonardo was brief its consequences, in the end, were good: from it Raphael's style lost only the negative aspect of its purity, which was its simplicity; its positive character of clarity was not impaired, but only given richer and more various matter to work upon.

This episode was, then, more than an acquiescent yielding to authority. After it Raphael seems to take on a different and larger measure of personality, putting to one side his young ideal of gentleness and grace, and willing instead to explore a far wider range of expressiveness and master more complex ideas of form. His art is charged with new intensity: it becomes not merely more complex but genuinely more vital. The *Belle Jardinière* had demonstrated an effective maturity in Raphael's manipulation of classical form, but its kind of content was still, ultimately, that of the juvenile Umbrian: the works that succeed it aspire to a content that is more serious, more various, and more mature.

The *Entombment* for Atalanta Baglioni (Rome, Galleria Borghese; 1507) [59] is the most ambitious of Raphael's Florentine works, and the only picture of this time in larger scale that is a dramatic illustration rather than a pure image of devotion. The subject as commissioned did not itself demand dramatic interpretation; Raphael's first thoughts for the picture were in the quieter vein of a Pietà rather than an Entombment. It was the new dimension of his formal and expressive will that caused him to select this moment of the sacred history. To realize in what degree and direction Raphael had evolved since the beginning of his Florentine years, one has only to compare this response to his theme with the predella *Pietà* (Boston, Gardner Museum) from the Pala Colonna of 1504–1505.

In the Borghese altarpiece the problem is not only deliberately posed in complex, active terms; its solution was also profoundly deliberated: the process of the generation of the pictorial idea is as elaborate as in Leonardo, and is documented in a series of drawings more extensive than survives for any of the later frescoes. This problem, of powerful and diverse emotion conveyed through action of the human form, had been Leonardo's in the *Anghiari* in particular, but it also had been Michelangelo's in his Cartoon; and it is the *Cascina* rather than the *Anghiari* that is the model for Raphael's thinking in the Borghese *Entombment.* More explicitly than the *Anghiari,* the *Cascina* was an apprehensible demonstration — an Academy — of the classical mechanics of figures in action provoked by emotional stress. This was, for Raphael, a new field of endeavor in his style, and though he adapted Michelangelo's example adequately he also, in his adaptation, exaggerated its defects. The figures of the *Entombment* reflect the character of those in the Cartoon — which is, as we have observed of it, at the same time still imperfectly classical and anticipatory of postclassicism — in the actors of both works there is disparity of purpose between expression of the content of their action and the demonstration of its form. Raphael exaggerates this disparity beyond its evidence in Michelangelo: the figures of the *Entombment* tend to be congealed in crystalline, self-consciously handsome postures. Even Raphael's design in part reflects the influence, and the faults, of the *Cascina*: there is a like sense of excessive separateness of forms within the whole and a contrast, not sufficiently resolved, between centrifugal and centralizing force. Yet, within each group of figures in the *Entombment* there is, more than in the *Cascina,* an effort to apply Leonardo's lessons of deliberate interweaving of the movemented forms.

More even than its inspiration, the cartoon for the *Cascina,* the Borghese *Entombment* savors of the Academy. Its extreme deliberation and its striving are too apparent, still, in its realized form — a form rather, in another sense, not quite realized. That higher art which was Leonardo's, and which Raphael would learn soon enough, of marrying the most complex aesthetic artifice to the look of nature, is not yet mastered here. Despite the sincerity with which Raphael aspires to a new power and variety of style he is not yet enough mature in temper — not grown enough beyond his early grace and gentleness of nature — to be able to feel and work convincingly in a realm like that of Michelangelo; it is a while before Raphael's personality will be able to embrace a region of emotional experience never quite equal, but at least comparable, to Michelangelo's. However, the ambition of the *Entombment* is more important than its actual artistic result: in it a new perspective is opened up for Raphael, and an avenue of development which he will later wonderfully successfully explore.

In Raphael's more accustomed vein of a devotional art, the *Madonna del Baldacchino* (Florence, Pitti, 1507–08; left unfinished by Raphael on his departure from Florence, somewhat defectively completed by later hands) [60] is no less of great importance as a preliminary to his Roman future. In this altarpiece the accustomed mood of Raphael's actors has not basically changed; it is only in their Leonardesque accent of complexity of feeling that they are different from the persons in the earlier devotional images. The same Leonardesque variety appears, as well, in the physical description of their forms. This very intimacy of content and appearance is at variance, however, with the principal new ambition in this altar: to create, in the composition in which the figures are imbedded, a monumentality for which, in an easel picture, there is no precedent. In basic type the picture refers to a long previous tradition, practiced since the second half of the Quattrocento, and by Raphael himself, of the *Santa Conversazione* in an architectural frame. What Raphael has done with the tradition is to reshape its elements into classicizing Cinquecento terms, applying to it — as he had not yet thought to do in his earlier large altars — the idea of an embracing semicircular unity of structure both of figures and of architectural form. The elementary motive of form had been invented by Leonardo, improved by Fra Bartolommeo, and once before adapted from him by Raphael in his S. Severo fresco; but in no instance before this altar had the idea of design been used not only to dispose the figures but to make a resonance of architecture for them. In this altar, too, the scale of the architecture takes on, for the first time, its own grand magnitude, and its perspective system is manipulated so that the figures are relieved in a seeming rising, growing, power of silhouette against it. From the form of the design there emerges an expression not only of a perfected order but of an order higher in its dignity and grander in its dimensions than our own. There is in this design — and in enough degree to overcome the opposite, almost trifling humanity of the actors it contains — the incipient nobility of monumental form that will emerge entirely in the atmosphere of Rome. The *Baldacchino* is the last step in Raphael's Florentine education, and it is his own first important, and wonderfully pregnant, classical invention.

THE SECONDARY MASTERS

In this period when the proposition of a classical style was receiving so significant a first development, not only the development, but the proposition itself, remained almost entirely within the small circle of those artists who were its original inventors. The main exchange of classical ideas took place within the confines of this group and their style was, during most of this phase, virtually isolated from the general practice of painting in Florence. Until the last moments of the near-decade we have been describing, the classical style was the style of its creators only, without disciples. By its sheer impact of quality and ideal force the new style had very early acquired primacy of place in reputation in the art of Florence, but only relatively slowly did it come to take on really formative authority. When this happened even certain of the painters who belonged inextricably to the traditions of the Quattrocento made small efforts to reform their style; more importantly, the generation that was contemporary with all but Leonardo among the inventors, or younger still, began, though only imperfectly and late within this phase, to reshape their art in a classicizing sense.

Fundamentally, the older generation was of course intractable. It could not be expected that Leonardo's return to Florence in 1501 should make important new conversions among those artists who, for a decade or for twenty years, had worked in manners that showed small regard for his achievements of 1481. In the case of Botticelli, the little that we presume was painted by him after the turn of the new century seems no less aggravatedly anticlassical than it had been just before. Nor does the style of Botticelli's former pupil, Filippino, during his few years of survival after 1500, indicate any profound concession to the art of Leonardo. In fact, despite his earlier ingestion of elements of Leonardism, Filippino's style seems to have been one of the active influences that operated against the quick dissemination in Florence of a classicism. Raffaellino Carli, in turn a pupil of Filippino's, practiced in the first decade of the Cinquecento in a manner compounded of his master's, and of Perugino's popular conventionality. As his altar of 1505 in Sto. Spirito[61] adequately shows, his style was moderated toward that of the *détente*, but not toward a High Renaissance classicism.

The quantitative contribution of these artists to the painting of the first decade of the Cinquecento was relatively small; not so that of Lorenzo di Credi, whose shop continued to produce in significant amount, and furthermore continued as a center for the training of young artists. Credi's close connection with Leonardo in the past had conditioned his style only superficially; Leonardo's return to Florence, and the new development in general of classicism that succeeded it, again touched Credi, and again only superficially. It is impossible to date Credi's paintings of this period with any accuracy, but the essential immutability of his style is such that it is of little consequence to do so. Working from the evidence of those paintings by him which are generically datable toward 1510[62] it can be said that, by the end of this decade, his style tended toward a greater accommodation to the outward characteristics of a classicism, with heavier forms and more rounded drapery, and often with a deeper chiaroscuro than in his earlier, chronologically quattrocentesque works. However, this accommodation did not disturb the underlying literalism of his style; and the intent to imitate a grander manner than his own only made his figures and his compositions turgid. Credi's adaptation of classical example was a minimum and hardly comprehending concession, perhaps less to the classical style as such than to the mode it had by this time created in the Florentine market. His adjustment, like Carli's, carries more of a resemblance to the old style of the *détente* than to a Cinquecento classicism.

The pure practitioner of that late Quattrocento style, Perugino, was as much a force for tradition in Florence just after 1500 as he had been in the years before, and kept a busy shop there until 1506. The event which, according to tradition (Vasari III, 586), drove him finally to withdraw to Perugia, may be indicative of the recognition, slow to come in Florence, that his style was, even for conservative taste, too unchangingly old-fashioned. After completing, in 1505, Filippino's *Deposition* in the Annunziata, left unfinished at that painter's death, Perugino painted a companion piece for it, an *Assunta* still in that church. Only the mild Fra Bartolommeo seems to have paid it (in his own *Assunta* in Berlin) the tribute of respect by studying its formula of composition. The rest of the Florentine audience was moved by it only to contempt. With the new genius of his own pupil already publicly manifest in Florence, Perugino's long history of success there came finally to its uninteresting end.

PIERO DI COSIMO

Among the older generation the most nearly flexible response to the new style is in the personality from whom — granted his singularity and even eccentricity — we should least expect it, Piero di Cosimo. His style in his first pictures of the Cinquecento shows a slight but visible alteration in a sense that suggests, only very tentatively, some qualities of classicism. His *Innocenti Altar* (Florence, Ospedale degli Innocenti; toward 1503)[63] has a Flemicizing descriptive literalness not less than in his earlier works, and is as much devoted to the illustration of unbeautiful eccentricities of form. Nevertheless, there are respects in which the picture gives the idea that, however tardily and incompletely, Piero has taken cognizance of an experience he might have had twenty years before, in Leonardo's *Adoration.* Episodes of type, the heavy emphases of drapery and gesture, and the mode of composition evoke Leonardo's precedent, somewhat in travesty, and so does the dark colorism of the painting, shadowed in a kind of chiaroscuro. These qualities are by no means such as to give the altar a definable character of classicism, but they do impose on Piero's quattrocentesque speech at least an accent like that of the newer style.

Once thus begun, the alteration of Piero's style seems to accelerate, almost certainly in good part from Leonardo's inspiration. The eccentricities of type and proportion in Piero's hitherto exceptional humanity diminish quickly, and his stranger imaginations come to be confined among the flora, fauna and geology of his backgrounds. In the *Immaculate Conception* (Florence, Uffizi; c. 1505–06)[64] the actors are almost harmoniously proportioned; their garments are arranged in smooth and in mostly cursive patterns; and they pose in attitudes that suggest a cinquecentesque, slow and ponderated, grace. There is a resemblance in all this, almost as much as to a contemporary classicism, to the conclusions that Credi had some years before derived from Leonardo's youthful style; but more than Credi, Piero approaches the new classicism in the important respect of his whole pictorial design. In the *Immaculate Conception* the structure of the composition is measurably less additive than it had been in the Innocenti altar: in a more purposeful and ordered way this composition seeks a movemented unity — still symmetrically disposed, but bound together by a pervasive continuity of curves among its parts. In its animate balancing of entire structure the conception is comparable in basic kind to the contemporary design of Raphael in his Pala Colonna for Perugia (which it is more than doubtful that Piero could have known).

The development in Piero of a cinquecentesque sense of movemented unity of whole design is, so far, the most important symptom in him of rapprochement with the principles of classical style. It is this evidence of change, in the *Immaculate Conception,* of a major factor of aesthetic disposition that makes it possible, despite the insistent elements of Quattrocento taste, to bring it into a relation — as we cannot any other work of this time by a master of Piero's generation — with a contemporary work of the inventors of the classical style. The comparison with Raphael applies to no more than basic kind, but with Bartolommeo, the least advanced among the classical masters, it is partly valid even in degree. In its measure of development of a classicizing organism of design, the conception is not much different from Fra Bartolommeo's — admittedly partly recollective — *Vision of St. Bernard*:[43] both are elementary classical gestalts. This general comparison holds, and may be extended in part to particulars, to the attitudes and draperies of the figures. But beyond that the divergences become aggressive. Within his larger classicizing mold of structure Piero continues to apprehend the world much as he had before, describing a reality so luminous and precise that it becomes poetically poignant, and defining the inventions of his fantasy with such clarity that they become illusions. Even when, as here, specific eccentricities of form are diminished or relegated to the landscape, the essential way of seeing and imagining of this artist remains eccentric: not compromising imagination and reality, as do the classicists, but confounding them in an intense and sometimes hallucinatory image.

As the examples of the new classical style multiplied and its authority accrued Piero's rapprochement with it became significantly closer. Shortly after the middle of this decade the models of classicism began clearly to impose on him; there began to be a visible imitative adaptation by Piero of classical style, but more of its form only, more readily imitable. In the *Madonna with St. John* (Vienna, Liechtenstein Collection; c. 1505–08)[65] the Madonna herself, in anatomical shape, drapery, type, and even expression of her face, is modeled upon Raphaelesque, as well as on Leonardesque, experience. Piero's imitation of these classical models is deliberate and, certainly, sincere, but it is at the same time — whether or not it is purposely so intended — subtle and disturbing parody. Piero's enchantment with the beauties of classicizing form must still coexist with a more essential temperamental disposition quite opposite to that of classicism. His partial absorption of the new style has provided him, in this instance, with more matter for the delighted exploitation of antitheses; and such a point of view is in itself antithetic to that of a classicism. The Liechtenstein *Madonna* has a strong air of affinity with the incipient German Renaissance; perhaps, in consideration of the known interest Piero took in North European art it is there as a result of yet another act of imitation. More profoundly, the resemblance, deliberate or not, suggests that the processes of artistic history which enter into this moment of Piero's art and those of a seeming analogue in the North are not basically unlike. Further, at this stage in his evolution, the nature of the relation of Piero's style to that of classicism offers an anticipatory parallel — in the opposite direction of historical process — to the first manifestations, still a decade off, of Mannerism.

Piero's *Liberation of Andromeda* (Florence, Uffizi)[66] comes from a later moment in his rapprochement with contemporary classicism, probably around 1508. In it his adaptation of the vocabulary and the sense of classical example is considerably more faithful. He has by no means wholly given up that singular aesthetic and psychological identity by which we so far know him, but he has moderated it enough so that its cohabitation with a classicism is now possible. The authority of Leonardo has finally effected this near-conversion; the mark of his model is visible almost everywhere in Piero's picture: in the types, the modelling, the misted color, and in the softened landscape forms. Even the invented dragon recalls Leonardesque experiments, and his navigation is described in a way that suggests Leonardo's diagrams of hydraulics. A tradition at least as old as the later sixteenth century has recognized all this in an allegation of Leonardo's design of Piero's painting, yet to be entirely disproved.

The relation to Leonardo's style is not so specifically close, but it is adequate. The softened figures are posed with as deliberate a grace as Piero can achieve, and they are distributed in animated interwoven groups. These groups are disposed in curving counterbalance, in an illustrational as well as formal commentary, around the central episode of the painting. Figures and landscape are manipulated in an oval unity, both on the surface and within the space, in a way as carefully concordant, and almost as evolved, as in the compositions of the classical inventors of the period. There are many evidences still of quattrocentesque habit, but they are quite dominated by Piero's new intentions of description and of pictorial form. Equally important, Piero's former character of content, even in this fantastic narration, has changed. The accent of the bizarre — even granted the dragon — has diminished, and human responses are now not so intense or strange as they had been in Piero's earlier mythologies. Like the form, the mood of the telling of the story is also softer, and feeling is more nearly drawn into a compass which, conceivably, might be a harmony. With this work Piero enters, by no means into the core of the new classical development, but surely into its periphery. The place that his now tempered fantasy of forms and content takes within the prospect of this first development of classicism is again an anticipation of a phenomenon that will occur a decade later, when a reawakened fantasy will be evoked to relieve the serious and rhetoric tone of the last phase of the classical style.

GRANACCI

Born toward 1470, Francesco Granacci was of a generation between that of Piero di Cosimo and that of Michelangelo and Fra Bartolommeo. As with Piero, by the time the new century began, Granacci's style had been formed in a Quattrocento mold — far less individual, obviously, than Piero's. Granacci had accepted the disciplines of the Ghirlandaio shop with a willingness that would be possible only to a painter of the second rank or less; such individuality as he felt it necessary to express required not much more than modest changes in the Ghirlandaiesque pattern. Works of around 1500, such as Granacci's *Holy Family* in Washington (National Gallery, Kress Collection) [67] or his altarpiece of a *Madonna with Two Saints* (Berlin, Museums; formerly on loan in Halle) [68] show such changes in two respects. The first consists of a refinement of Ghirlandaiesque technique in greater delicacy, almost a preciosity of execution, both of drawing and of high-keyed light. The second change, more evident in the Berlin altar, is curiously opposite to the first: it is a tendency to inflate the figures in dimension in a way that may intend, but does not attain, a monumentality. The intention at least would seem to be in part like that of the contemporary Fra Bartolommeo, to achieve a grander and more ponderous impressiveness than is usual in the *détente* style, but in Granacci it is thoroughly *manqué.*

A half-decade later his *Holy Family with St. John* (Dublin, National Gallery; c. 1505–06) [69] still shows a similar Ghirlandaiesque basis, similarly modified, but the effect of monumentality has much more nearly been achieved. Instead of the lax and swollen bigness of the figures of the Berlin altar the Dublin Madonna has an articulated breadth, expressed in movement in her space and in a vigorous cursive definition of her form; her figure makes the effect of an expansion of its actual dimension through the movement it contains. There is no indication in Granacci's work till this, and none to be deduced from his development in the future, that would lead us to believe this new energy of form comes from his own creative resources. The Dublin picture has at times been attributed to Michelangelo — unwisely, surely, so far as its entire execution is concerned — but the attribution serves the purpose of pointing to Granacci's source for this partial reformation of his style. There is evidence which suggests that Michelangelo may have supplied some part of a design for this picture to Granacci; what is more certain is that Granacci has, now, turned his careful scrutiny upon the Doni *Tondo.* The *Tondo,* itself still Ghirlandaiesque in technique, is in this one respect attached to the common education that Granacci and Michelangelo long ago had shared; in Granacci's study of his old friend's revolutionary work, this technique was one obstacle the less to imitation. Granacci has borrowed from the *Tondo* the energy which he has infused into his tumescent forms, and he has adapted others of its ideas. The posture of Granacci's Virgin is not necessarily imitated from, but is similar to that of the Joseph of the *Tondo,* and the compactness of the Virgin's active silhouette and the inclusion in it of the lesser forms has been directly learned from Michelangelo. With some real comprehension and some measure of success the Dublin picture takes over, from the style of Michelangelo, at least its elementary characteristics of classicizing form. As with Piero di Cosimo at a corresponding date, a partial conversion to the new style has been effected of a formed Quattrocento painter.

This close dependence of Granacci on Michelangelo was, however, short-lived. Granacci was one of those invited to Rome in the spring of 1508 to assist Michelangelo in the execution of the Sistine and summarily dismissed, surely without touching brush to plaster. Probably just after his return to Florence Granacci succumbed, with the same imitative willingness with which he had given himself to Michelangelo, to the yet more authoritative mode of Leonardo — or rather to the more accessible partial transcription of it that was offered in the current style of Fra Bartolommeo. The *Madonna della Cintola* (Florence, Academy; 1508–09) [70] is related to Leonardo, in types and in *sfumato* modelling, much in the way of Piero in his *Perseus*; the scheme of composition and the postures of the kneeling saints, however, are like those of Bartolommeo's *Assunta* of 1507–08.[46] Granacci's altar has a still visible, but diminished persistence of the Quattrocento in its handling, and his comprehension of classical ideas of description and of form is evidently incomplete. Yet his result in this work bears comparison in basic character of style with the Frate's model, itself of a not yet fulfilled classicism. The character of a transition is less apparent in the *Madonna della Cintola* than is its resemblance to the newer style; and Granacci's conversion to what might be described as a minimal Cinquecento classicism may now be considered as confirmed.

BUGIARDINI

Giuliano Bugiardini was the precise contemporary of Michelangelo, and like Granacci had shared Michelangelo's first Ghirlandaiesque education. Bugiardini, however, was less than Granacci formed exclusively by this education: his earliest identifiable works already indicate a mentality more eclectic and more inquiring than Granacci's. Bugiardini is a worse painter than Granacci, but a more lively one. His *Madonna and Child with St. John* (New York, Metropolitan Museum; c. 1500)[71] is not specifically Ghirlandaiesque; it contains a strong element of Credi's style. Further, in its expression there is an aliveness that is not usual either to Ghirlandaio or Credi and which, instead, suggests Piero di Cosimo's paintings of the later nineties. The style of the picture is a compendium, but only of wholly quattrocentesque tendencies of this moment.

Bugiardini's response to more modern currents seems to have begun only toward 1505, as a result of an association with Albertinelli. The *Holy Family* (Turin, Galleria Sabauda; c. 1505–08) [72] shows a perceptible adjustment toward the manner of Albertinelli — variable as this might be — about the middle of the first decade. This is imitation, in the second power, of the appearances of classical style, and its result in Bugiardini is a still more accentuated effect than in Albertinelli of a character of transition. And here, confronted by Albertinelli's reflection, however incomplete, of the new ideas, a conflict emerges, never to be solved, between Bugiardini's personality and the classical principles of form. The concept of a harmony of form and of the kind of beauty that proceeds from it is simply inaccessible to Bugiardini. Lacking absolutely the sense of aesthetic relations, and impermeable to the meaning of proportion, Bugiardini constantly commits gaffes of scale and shape that, in a Quattrocento picture, might be thought diverting; but they are awkward contradictions in a context of intended classicizing form. His craftsmanship is wholly adequate; it is the gestalt of the new style which, by his nature, he cannot adequately learn. Yet his ambition to work according to the current authoritative mode is a force still more powerful than his aesthetic incompetence is an immovable object. By sheer application he was able to absorb the elementary and external elements of classical aesthetic system, and even certain of its more essential laws.

For Bugiardini, it was by a process of imitation almost like that of a copyist that the new style might most closely be approximated. Given an example on which he might exactly model his own work, his hand was capable of making an adaptation of some technical refinement, and even of reproducing much of the model's aesthetic sense. Just this has occurred * in Bugiardini's *Portrait of a Lady* (Urbino, Galleria Nazionale; c. 1508).[73] Often improperly ascribed to Raphael, the erroneous attribution illustrates the literalness with which Bugiardini transcribed Raphael's exemplar to the purpose of his own commission, and the transcription's relative success. In the Urbino portrait Bugiardini has temporarily detached himself from the following of his contemporary, Albertinelli, and sought a preceding but classically more advanced type in the younger Raphael. It is noteworthy that Bugiardini does not go behind Raphael's *Maddalena Doni* to its own Leonardesque model: it is precisely Raphael's reduction and clarification of the classical style, as he effects it in the Doni portrait, which make it accessible and imitable even to a Bugiardini.

RIDOLFO GHIRLANDAIO

The response to Raphael toward 1508 was not an isolated one in Bugiardini. He was accompanied in it by the two rising artists of the youngest generation then practicing independently in Florence, Raphael's own contemporaries: Ridolfo Ghirlandaio and Franciabigio. In both these younger painters, no less than in Bugiardini, their rapprochement with Raphael came only at the end of the period we are describing and follows on beginnings in a style unequivocally still quattrocentesque. Even among Raphael's exact contemporaries the new style is a learned one, not innate, and it is learned by them no more readily, and not necessarily more thoroughly, than by their elders. Both Ridolfo and Franciabigio are, by artistic rank and disposition, followers of given authority; and it is only as authority in Florence becomes wholly that of the great inventive classical masters that they change as well.

Ridolfo Ghirlandaio was possessed of a strong and stubborn artistic inheritance. His father's disposition was also very much his own, and it was reinforced by earliest training, not with Domenico — who died, like Raphael's father, when his son was eleven — but with his uncle. Upon this most conservative of Quattrocento bases there was then imposed the influence of Piero di Cosimo (as it had been also on the Ghirlandaiesque background of Giuliano Bugiardini). The earliest datable paintings of Ridolfo, the *Madonna with Sts. Francis and Mary Magdalen* (Florence, Academy; dated 1503)[74] and his *Coronation of the Virgin* (Paris, Louvre; dated 1504),[75] are in a style that tends more toward Piero's than toward the identifiably Ghirlandaiesque, but with an accent wholly of the Quattrocento which is no longer in Piero's own works of this same moment. By about 1506 this strict conservatism had been only slightly moderated. The *Road to Calvary* (London, National Gallery),[76] probably of that year, is less rigid in design than the preceding altarpieces: not only from considerations of the subject, for it is decidedly more flexible also than Benedetto Ghirlandaio's version of the theme, on which this one by Ridolfo still obviously depends. Ridolfo's design is developed in a more informal diversity in space, and with more richly differentiated chiaroscuro, so that it suggests at least an incipient appearance of Cinquecento style. Piero di Cosimo's developments seem to be in part reflected here, but a much higher authority has also been consulted, though hardly understood. The *Calvary* contains virtually direct quotations from the *Battle of Anghiari*,[28] but they are isolated in this stylistically backward context. The few modifications Ridolfo has brought to his style have been imposed upon the basis of the irreducible literalness of a born Ghirlandaio.

The *Calvary* is artistically effective only in those portions of it which are most precisely imitative of actuality, in the portraits it contains. In these there is a conviction which far exceeds that in the figures where Ridolfo has depended upon borrowings or on his unconvincing power of invention. These portraits are not merely a continuation of the Quattrocento's realist portrait style but a development, antithetic to the principle of classical idealism, upon the old techniques of the Ghirlandaio school; Ridolfo's portraits show an unsparing intimacy of description that exceeds his father's portrait mode. His effects of salience of detail and illusionism of surface are achieved by a new accenting of chiaroscuro, perhaps eventually suggested by a study of Leonardo, but more specifically related to and derived from Piero di Cosimo's Leonardism in his pictures of the first half-decade. In the form of a separate portrait, such as that of a man in the Art Institute, Chicago (c. 1505–06; perhaps an adaptation of an older Flemish image),[80] there is the strongest impact of a near-illusionistic actuality of presence.

This chief aim of absolute fidelity to nature could not be more different in the direction of art that it intends, if not yet in its accomplishment, from the course on which, in his portraiture, Raphael had just embarked. But it must also be remembered that, despite their incipient formal idealization, the Doni portraits — and equally Leonardo's *Gioconda* — no less than Ridolfo's portraiture intend and achieve a plausibility more complete than that of fifteenth-century images. Ridolfo's superior counterfeit of human presence, though evolved from an older mode, is in fact a Cinquecento quality of style. It is like an element of classical style in its intent, but its means and its degree are different and, most significantly, it does not as yet work within a context of other factors of a classicism.

This accomplishment was to remain the meaningful core of Ridolfo's painting, but as the classical style assumed authority for him, as well as for the other secondary masters, he moderated his degree of realism and surrounded it with imitated classical device. Again it is Raphael's example which, in its easier aesthetic and intellectual accessibility, commands the interest of the lesser artist; and in Ridolfo's case this influence was reinforced by friendship and exact community of generation. The first evidence of adaptation of a Raphaelism nevertheless does not occur until the last years of this phase, toward 1507–1508, in the *Marriage of St. Catherine* (near Florence, Istituto delle Quiete).[77] Even then Ridolfo's mentality is not so readily alterable; this adaptation is conspicuously incomplete. It is apparent in some measure in this picture's composition, in its management of draperies and postures and, more especially, in facial types; it is particularly evident in the displacement of a Pieresque chiaroscuro by Raphael's higher-keyed bland unity of tone.

Ridolfo's two *Altar Wings with Angels* (Florence, Academy; c. 1508)[78–9] are his most ingratiating exhibition of this newly but not wholly learned Raphaelism: gentle, almost graceful in their quality of attitude and in expression, soft in color, and lucent and subtle in technique. But most comprehensible of all in Raphael, and — as in Bugiardini's case — most imitable, was the compact and less complex demonstration of his style in portraiture: it was probably toward 1507 or 1508 that Ridolfo, like Bugiardini, transcribed the *Maddalena Doni.* Ridolfo's *Lady with a*

Rabbit (New Haven, Yale University Art Gallery)[81] is less literally dependent on the Raphael than is Bugiardini's portrait in Urbino, and its approximation of Raphael's vocabulary is at once more confident and close. The smoothed contours of Ridolfo's figure flow into an immediately sensible continuity as Bugiardini's more sharp-cut, compilative shapes do not. However, like Bugiardini, Ridolfo also follows only partly Raphael's intention to idealize features, and there is a reminiscent literalism in technique and handling of surface in this following of the Raphael style.

This degree of Raphaelesque approximation is nevertheless enough to justify Vasari's report (IV, 328) that it was Ridolfo who was chosen, after Raphael's departure for Rome, to complete the *Belle Jardinière.* It is not only the example of the Doni portrait but probably also that of the type of the *Jardinière* which shaped Ridolfo's image of the thoroughly Raphaelesque *Girl with the Unicorn* (Rome, Galleria Borghese; c. 1508–9);[82] Raphael's free version in drawing after Leonardo's *Gioconda* (to which a friend so close as Ridolfo would have had certain access) also served Ridolfo as his compositional model. The imitation of Raphael's manner is more deliberate than in the Yale portrait but, still more than there, there is the sense of contrast between the borrowed forms and their Ghirlandaiesque interpretation. Raphael's subtle modulation of the picture surface has become a ceramic brilliance, and his fine classical adjustment between generalization and detail has been replaced by a contrast between bland smoothness and a hard precision. Above all, Raphael's breathing harmony of presence, and his effect of confluence among all the elements of form, is stiffened into staring, disarticulate rigidity. For all his dedication, Ridolfo's picture remains at root unclassical; it is in a sense an unintentionally meretricious betrayal of the Raphael style, as finally uncomprehending as the Raphaelisms of the Nazarenes, which this portrait so curiously resembles.

FRANCIABIGIO

The traceable beginnings of the second of Raphael's nearly exact contemporaries in Florence, Franciabigio, are as close to the style of the Quattrocento as are Ridolfo Ghirlandaio's. Franciabigio's earliest surviving work, a tondo of a *Madonna and Child with St. John* (Florence, Uffizi 2178; c. 1503),[84] is firmer in command of form and more precise in execution than Ridolfo's painting of the same date, but the elements from which its style has been compounded are much the same: for Franciabigio's picture the formative sources also are the art of Piero di Cosimo and, secondly, the school of the older Ghirlandaios. Francesco's first symptoms of a reshaping of his style in Cinquecento sense do not seem to occur till toward 1505; and then, probably, in consequence of contact with Albertinelli — not, as Vasari says (V, 190), in the role of pupil but perhaps as an assistant. Albertinelli seems to have served Francesco, as he did the older Bugiardini, as a first imperfect model of classical style.

Franciabigio's *Temple of Hercules* (Florence, Palazzo Davanzati; c. 1505)[83] reflects an Albertinellian mode of softened, cursive handling of drapery and shows an ordering of form, intendedly within a deeper space, which is at least incipiently like that of the Cinquecento style. This picture is still most tentative in its response to Albertinelli's example and seems to exaggerate those qualities in it that, with still transitional effect, refer to Perugino; also, the accent of Piero's formerly dominant influence is still quite visible. A *Madonna* (Perugia, Collection Count Ranieri; c. 1505–06)[85] is a much more convincing adaptation of Albertinelli's style. In its landscape and in the posture of the Christ Child precise reference remains to an earlier model in Piero di Cosimo, but in more important matters the picture is as accomplished and as convinced a transcription of Albertinelli's manner of around 1503–1505 as it is possible to make. The products of Bugiardini's contemporary following of Albertinelli reveal, by contrast, both his lesser comprehension and his lesser flexibility. Not only has Francesco absorbed the manner of Albertinelli, but he has apparently referred to its eventual (but for Albertinelli, still not direct) source, Leonardo: the smoothed chiaroscuro form and part at least of the content of the Ranieri painting are identifiably Leonardesque.

With better preparation than either Bugiardini or Ridolfo, Francesco also turns, toward 1507, to the more accessible restatement of the new classical style that was offered Florence by the art of Raphael, and Francesco's response to Raphael is not in terms so literal as those of either of these other artists. In Francesco's *Holy Family* (Florence, Academy; formerly Uffizi 888; c. 1507)[86] a Leonardesque accent in the types persists, but with just such a modification as Raphael himself imposed on Leonardo's models. In the posture of Francesco's Madonna and in the fully plastic shaping of her form there is a free adaptation of developed Raphaelesque precedent, such as that of the *Madonna del Cardellino* of the year before. The approximation of a classical form is closest in the figure of the Madonna, precisely where Francesco depends most on Raphael; the other shapes and attitudes of figures in the picture still retain a trace of Piero's, or of Albertinelli's, awkwardness. Though all the figures are related, as in a Raphael, by a continuity of curving posture, Francesco's understanding does not extend to the idea that is in his Raphaelesque models, of a compact unity of structure. In his conception of relationship of forms Francesco is, and will remain, touched by a persistence of the Quattrocento's additive mentality, or rather of that mentality translated in more modern terms. These figures are strung upon their sequence of curves in a succession; they are not related as an intertwining unity of forms. The habit of mind is not unlike that of Raphael of an earlier time, before his own absorption of Leonardo's gospel of classical form. Further, Franciabigio is still temperamentally limited, and will continue to be so, in his assimilation of the contemporary Raphaelesque ideas of generalization, and of the concomitant Raphaelesque techniques which mute detail and make effects of atmospheric unity. More than in Albertinelli of this period, there are irreducible continuities in Francesco of quattrocentesque habits in these respects.

In the *Holy Family* (Vienna, Kunsthistorisches Museum 206; c. 1508).[88] Franciabigio has shifted altogether into Raphael's orbit. The picture is a freer and more confident work than any so far by Francesco, and its individual personality is much more pronounced, but the affirmation of identity is nonetheless accompanied by a closer dependence upon Raphael. The situation is not paradoxical; it repeats in small Raphael's own relation to Leonardo. Francesco has adopted altogether the blonder tone of Raphael (who at about this moment was inversely, in certain pictures, imitating the darker chiaroscuro of Leonardo). More than in the *Holy Family* of the Academy, Francesco takes over Raphael's typology and more nearly, but not entirely consistently, Raphael's mode of generalization. Francesco now better understands the notion — which Raphael himself had only recently come to appreciate — of a rich internal variety of form within this generalization. In the figure of his Madonna, but less successfully elsewhere, Francesco applies this conception not only to the figure's shapes but to the action of the body. In this development of cursive and contrapposto movement Francesco had evidently studied not only Raphael but, again, Leonardo: the posture of the Madonna strongly suggests that of the Virgin in the third version of the *St. Anne.*

He has successfully adapted the outward form of the developed classical idea of animation, but he does not wholly understand its mechanism or its meaning. Francesco's figures are deliberately posed according to an evolved classical formula, but they remain somewhat stiff and inorganically awkward: their postures seem imposed on them as if from without, for form's sake more than for the sake of meaning; posture does not, as in Leonardo or in Raphael, evidently take the shape of a state of mind.

In imitating such an advanced variety of animation Francesco comprehends one of its uses but not its whole; he sees its value to create a stimulating pattern of activity but does not see that, in his models, this activity is inseparable from a preexistent harmony. Francesco is imitating one advanced aspect of the classical style without having arrived at an entire understanding of its elementary kind. As much as before, his composition is a cursive succession of elements rather than a unity, and the introduction of the stronger emphasis of movement serves in the end to emphasize still more the divisive character of his design.

There is a stage still closer to an outward Raphaelism in this moment of Francesco's art. As with the instances of Bugiardini's and Ridolfo's works that most deliberately depend on Raphael, the *Madonna del Pozzo* of Francesco (Florence, Academy; c. 1508)[87] has also, in the past, been confused into the Raphael *oeuvre*. The imitative resemblance is in fact not less than in Bugiardini's *Lady in Urbino* or in Ridolfo's *Girl with a Unicorn*; equally, however, Francesco's imitation is more technical and morphological than essential. Because his picture is a more complicated structure than these two, portrait and portrait-like, by his Raphaelizing colleagues, it reveals its differences of style from Raphael more readily. The approximation of the Raphaelesque vocabulary is in the surface only of an organism of design such as Raphael himself could not at this time conceive: boldly, almost drastically movemented, with an urgent diagonal impulse of action for which the disquieting contrapposto of the Virgin is no effective counterweight. The inventive artifice of Raphael's recent style is equalled here, but there is small savor of its grace. Francesco transposes the animation of Raphaelesque images into something obvious and emphatic, intelligent in idea and in development of form, but almost impervious to the classical condition of a harmony. It is in this combination of aesthetic circumstances that Francesco defines the capacities and the limits of his mature personality. The accent and the surface character of his style would change considerably, and often, in his later works; but its substance will remain what it has become here.

By 1508 in Florence the classical style, which had attained its first clear formulation only a decade before, had undergone a considerable development. These years had been a time of experimental definition of the new style, but each experiment made by the masters who had invented the style had the value of an absolute artistic accomplishment. They were not content to rest on any one of their accomplishments; they continued to search out the possibilities of their invention in increasingly profound ways and in increasingly complex directions. Almost altogether this research had been confined to Leonardo and Michelangelo, and in much less degree to Fra Bartolommeo. In 1504, Raphael had joined this small, exalted, group: his career during the next four years was at once a recapitulation and a clarification of the evolution of the older masters. Among personalities in Florence who were less than these, the response to their example was relatively slow. The power of the creative acts accomplished in the classical style won it a quick authority; but it gained practicing converts only slowly and, even then, incompletely.

Leonardo had been the chief shaping force of this whole period, even among his great colleagues of first rank, but he was less effective in the process of dissemination beyond them of the new style. It was Raphael's clarified and more legible example that, only toward 1507, attracted secondary and younger painters into the orbit of the classical style. The attraction of his model was, still, greater than the understanding brought to it, but the responses to it suffice to show how, toward 1507 or 1508, the classical style had assumed the function, in Florentine artistic sociology, of reigning mode. A "school" of classicizing, if not essentially classical, painting had thus hardly been established in the city when its creators abandoned it: Leonardo to return to Milan, Fra Bartolommeo to go to Venice, and first Michelangelo and then Raphael to go to Rome. Only Fra Bartolommeo returned to continue work in Florence and become, after 1508, the *caposcuola* whose new authority would extinguish the brief ascendancy of Raphael. But from this time the level of accomplishment in Florence would yield place to that in Rome.

ROME

The antiquities of Rome had helped, before the beginning of the new century, to form the first classical style of the young Michelangelo. By early 1501, however, Michelangelo returned to Florence where he gave his first classicism its development, which we have described above. He left behind him three works of sculpture — the *Cupid* for Jacopo Galli, now lost, the *Bacchus*, and the *Pietà* — in an atmosphere of contemporary art in which they were yet more isolated than they would have been in Florence of the same moment. Bramante came to Rome in 1499 and he alone in the course of the immediately succeeding years represented the new classicism there. Bramante's art had been formed first in the atmosphere of Urbinate classicism of the fifteenth century, and subsequently shaped by contact with the architectural imaginings of Leonardo but, as with Michelangelo, Bramante's first formulation of a High Renaissance classical style was precipitated in and by Antique Rome.

Neither the example of the architect nor of Michelangelo as sculptor had the power to move, in their direction, the painters of this time in Rome. As in the fifteenth century, Rome of the first years of the sixteenth century was without a significant indigenous school. The artistic functioning of the city was through imports now as it had been earlier. The native painters were either mere decorative craftsmen or, as is the case of the aged Antoniazzo Romano and his immediate pupils and assistants, representatives at a mediocre level of an old-fashioned Umbrian tradition. The chief among the imported painters of the late years of the fifteenth century had been Pinturicchio, and it was his variety of an Umbrianism that continued, after 1500, to dominate in Rome. Pinturicchio himself twice returned during the first decade of the sixteenth century, renewing, at least on his first return, an authority that might otherwise have decreased with the passage of time. During 1505–1506, between bouts with his large undertaking in the Piccolomini Library in Siena, he worked under the orders of Julius II, presumably in the Vatican, but no trace survives of his activity there. In 1508–1509 he was again in Rome, this time engaged, with one or more assistants, in the decoration of the choir vault of Sta. Maria del Popolo.[89] Its style is distinguished from his earlier production only by its still greater lassitude of inspiration.

The other imported painters of the first years of the century seem to have been largely formed by Pinturicchiesque example, either by imitation or by actual collaboration with him in Rome, or by previous association with him probably during his activity in Siena. The accent of those works in Rome that are datable between 1500 and 1508 is dominantly Pinturicchiesque and Umbro-Sienese, whatever the actual (and mostly unidentifiable) place of origin of the artists may have been: so, for example, the anonymous *Sibyls* of the nave wall of S. Pietro in Montorio,[90] and the *Coronation of the Virgin* in a side chapel of the same church. The principal surviving decoration of the period, in the choir of Sant' Onofrio (c. 1504)[91] belongs generically to the same style. The paintings of its semidome (like the Montorio *Sibyls* which they much resemble) are anonymous, though their cast within Pinturicchiesque style has some rapport with that of two among the foreign artists, from Bologna, who were then in Rome, Jacopo Ripanda and Amico Aspertini. These frescoes have also been attributed to Pietro Volterrano and to his Sienese associate, Baldassare Peruzzi. In spite of recent critical tendency to deny all credence to Vasari's assertion (VI, 591) of Peruzzi's activity in Sant' Onofrio he may well be the executant of the central fresco of the semidome, the *Coronation of the Virgin*;[92] and he is more surely the author of the center fresco, a *Madonna with Saints*,[94] on the lower wall of the apse.

Peruzzi had come to Rome toward 1503, in company with Volterrano, and had attached himself briefly to the shop conducted by a painter described only as the father of Maturino. Peruzzi's beginnings in Sant' Onofrio seem unlikely when we contrast them with the style he was to practice after his exposure to the art of Raphael and Michelangelo, but they are wholly what should be expected of the artistic background which was Peruzzi's then, four years or so before Raphael's advent. The style of the altar fresco is more authentically Sienese than Pinturicchio's, with eccentricities of proportion that would be quite intolerable in any other artistic community than Siena around 1500. The attitudes of figures, and the effect of their proportions, contain an element of preciosity that we shall encounter in Peruzzi later, and the technique, where it is not obscured by overpainting, has his thin and luminous fineness. The archaic conception of pictorial form that we see here is wholly altered some years later, but numerous elements of type and conceits of incidental motive survive from Sant' Onofrio through this change.

Late in Peruzzi's career, when his style had passed through and beyond his phase of Roman classicism and into a Mannerism of provincial stamp, there is the most singular reassertion of the style of Sant' Onofrio: his decoration of the chapel at Belcaro,[93] thirty years ahead, reevokes the language of this early fresco. Its mannered and provincial late Quattrocento style, untouched as yet by classical example, is a premonition of the provincial and postclassical style of Peruzzi. This monument is the first Roman expression of a personality who was to occupy a place in the Roman High Renaissance close after that of its two great exponents, a place qualitatively far higher but quantitatively not unlike that which, in Florence, Franciabigio holds in respect to Fra Bartolommeo and Andrea del Sarto. In the case of Franciabigio, as of his contemporary Ridolfo Ghirlandaio, their styles circa 1504 were not more evolved out of their Florentine quattrocentesque education than Peruzzi's is here from his Quattrocento background in Siena.

Another work of Peruzzi's of this preclassical time, but of later date, is more securely documented than Sant' Onofrio but in unhappy compensation has been almost altogether lost: a decoration (executed in collaboration with another visitor, Cesare da Sesto) in the Castello at Ostia (c. 1505–08). Vasari's description (IV, 592) tells us that it was "in alcune stanze storie bellissime e particolarmente una battaglia da mano, in quella maniera che usavano i Romani . . ." with "molti instrumenti da guerra antichi, e . . . diverse sorti d'armi." We cannot reconstruct the figure style, but traces remain in these rooms of a grotesque ornament of which the manner is again a recollection of a Pinturicchio example, liberally used by him in his work both in Siena and in Rome. Like the grotesque ornament, the subject matter has an archaeological accent, which Vasari stresses strongly. Whatever the undeterminable influence on Peruzzi's figure style may have been of the Antique works he must have studied for the scene Vasari describes, his exposure to Rome had the clear effect of stimulating an archaeological interest, and in this peculiarly Roman concern Peruzzi is by no means unique.

Jacopo Ripanda, who had been in Rome at least as early as Peruzzi, since 1503, is known to have made drawings of the sculptures on the Column of Trajan before 1507. The fruit of this, and of other archaeological research, was embodied in a set of frescoes in the Palazzo dei Conservatori, illustrating the history of Ancient Rome.[95] The earliest of these may have predated 1504 when there is a record, but unfortunately no description, of work by Ripanda in the Palace. Frescoes do survive, in the *Stanza dei Fasti Consolari Antichi* and in the *Stanza delle Guerre Puniche* which are of later date, after 1507.

Their style is not changed in any significant particular from the tradition represented in Sant' Onofrio, but it is altogether overlaid with the Roman cast of archaeology. It is a serious and even proudly ostentatious archaeology, but Ripanda's study of Antique art has not awakened in him one glimmer of response to classical aesthetic.

The intellectual atmosphere of this new archaeology aspired less toward instruction in classicism of style than had the first researches of the Quattrocentists: its intent, certainly in Ripanda, and probably also at this time in Peruzzi, was literary and illustrative rather than aesthetic. The aesthetic imitation of the Antique by these artists was limited to the decorative divertissement of grotesque ornament, hardly related, as they saw it, to the essence of a classicism in style. It was, curiously, in this one field that Roman practice of this period had a minor influence on art in Florence. Morto da Feltre, who is credited with the first significant resurrection of Antique grotesque, presumably while he was an assistant of Pinturicchio in Rome in the early nineties, carried his mode from Rome to Florence, where he worked between 1504 and circa 1507 decorating rooms in the Palazzo Vecchio and in the Palazzo Doni; Andrea di Cosimo Feltrini, the Florentine master of grotesque decoration, was Morto's creature.

Painterly creation in Rome might have persisted longer in this vein, of late quattrocentesque Umbro-Sienese style tempered by a new accent of archaeology, if Julius II had not decreed otherwise. In his concern with art, painting seems to have come as an afterthought, behind ambitions that could be realized more reasonably and more enduringly in architecture and in sculpture. It was only after Julius had decided, in 1507, that he could not inhabit the apartment of his Borgia predecessor — "marranum, judaeum, circumcisum" — and transferred to other quarters on the upper story of the Vatican that he determined — emulating the sacred image of his uncle — to undertake a major campaign of pictorial decoration.

His powers of selection were initially not so distinguished as his uncle's, and his taste, at the beginning, showed no novelty. Two of the painters whom he summoned to work for him, Perugino and Signorelli, were old hands who had served with Sixtus IV; another, Pinturicchio, had been the favorite of Alexander Borgia. We have already assessed the nature of Pinturicchio's contribution of 1508–1509; what Perugino left, in his decoration of the same time in the vaults of the Stanza dell' Incendio, is also unchanged from his prior quattrocentesque mode. There is no trace of Signorelli's activity in the Vatican in 1508 but his dated altar of the same year in the Brera is an index of his immutability of *détente* style. The lesser and younger painters seem to have been chosen by Julius on grounds of opportunity rather than of discrimination, or even of reputation. Sodoma, when he contracted to begin work in the papal apartments on October 13, 1508, was apparently in Rome already, bound to the service of his Sienese patron Agostino Chigi. His talents were conceded to the Pope by Chigi, but only in that amount which should not exceed fifty ducats worth of painting. He began the Stanza della Segnatura, painting the ingenious illusionistic central motive of the ceiling,[96] fixing the system of painted partitioning of the vault, and designing and perhaps also executing eight small trapezoidal paintings within this painted enframement. What is unequivocally traceable to Sodoma's responsibility in the Stanza della Segnatura conforms essentially to a preclassicizing style and offers no ground for supposition that he may have done, or intended, anything too much unlike his immediately previous paintings at Monte Oliveto. The small trapezoidal pictures have a new accent, but only of the current mode of archaeology. Hired on the same day as Sodoma was a foreigner from the North, Giovanni Ruysch, miniaturist, cartographer, and perhaps also a specialist in such bizarre transalpine matters as fruits and flowers. Toward 1505, his presence had been recorded in Cologne. His contributions to work in the Vatican, if they have survived, are not identifiable.

On the fourth of December two further artists were engaged for work in the Vatican: Michele da Imola and Bramantino of Milan. Again nothing survives in the Vatican of either's painting, or is not recognizable, and this is the case as well with Lorenzo Lotto, who was hired to paint (in a room apparently adjoining the Stanza della Segnatura) as late as March of 1509. It is only certain, from what we can deduce of the style of these painters in the period preceding their work in Rome, that none brought a Cinquecento classicism with him. In the case of the younger artists of importance — Lotto, Bramantino, and Sodoma — they proved to be, in varying degrees, adaptable in the direction of the new classicism, but they were not capable of its independent generation. Of the older artists, none was even adaptable. The High Renaissance classical style did not have an independent birth in Rome, and neither the cultural climate of the city nor the temper of the Pope called forth such a classicism in those artists in whom it did not exist when they arrived.

The new classical style was brought to Rome, in a form already significantly developed, by Michelangelo and Raphael, and the role of Rome in the history of this style was limited first to the act of importation of their accomplished fact, and then to the inescapable recognition by Pope Julius — initially probably quite apart from any preference in respect to styles — of the genius of these artists. In May of 1508, before the painters of the older generation and the second rank were set to their historically futile labor in the Vatican, Michelangelo began the Sistine Ceiling, and early in the winter, Raphael started painting in the Stanza della Segnatura. With these events classicism was reborn in Rome and a new chapter begun in the history of High Renaissance classical style.

III

THE MATURITY OF THE CLASSICAL STYLE IN ROME

(c. 1508-c. 1514)

III

THE MATURITY OF THE CLASSICAL STYLE IN ROME (c. 1508-c. 1514)

ON his accession late in 1503 Pope Julius had set himself the mission of regeneration of the papacy in both its spiritual and temporal domain. His success was remarkable, and it continued all through his career with only one significant reverse, in 1511, and he had recovered even from that before the end of his reign, in February 1513. Not only did he repair the disastrous situation in which Alexander left the papacy but he built the papal power stronger than it had ever been. His accomplishment was an act of personal creative genius which was not dissimilar, in its force to reshape extant historical data, and in its exalted ambition, from the creative actions — in their very different sphere — of the artists of the new style. His accomplishment was sufficiently remarkable in fact: the papacy under Julius "had become the center of gravity of the peninsula and, indeed, of the whole political world" (Pastor V, 453), but it did not even then conform to the dimension of Julius' intentions. The Venetian ambassador Trevisani (Ranke I, 41n) reported that "Il papa vuol esser il dominus et maistro del jocho del mundo." Behind this aspiration lay a personality of profoundest force. Sanuto in his diaries spoke of it thus: "It is almost impossible to describe how strong and violent and difficult to manage he is. In body and soul he has the nature of a giant. Everything about him is on a magnificent scale, both his undertakings and his passions" (Pastor VI, 213).

The atmosphere of Julius' papacy was charged with the force of his personality and accomplishments and with the resonance of his ambition. In his intention for papal Rome there was a discernible Imperial analogy: to make his new Rome a fit capital of empire, imitative of ancient Rome in its pretense to rule in Italy and, by spiritual authority, beyond its borders. Rome was meant to assume again the role at least of focal point, if not of actual determinant, of Italian and of international affairs. Julius meant to regenerate truly the concept of a rule that addressed itself *urbi et orbi.* Under him the living Rome again took on some part of its ancient grand and general significance, and this generalization that Julius remade for Rome was charged with the expansive vitality of his spirit and his actions.

It was a proper consequence of such a policy that Julius wished to reshape the headquarters of the papacy into a tangible symbol of its restored greatness. Bramante was Julius' first agent in this effort, and in his own ambition to recreate the values of an Antique Roman architecture, Bramante offered the Pope the first appropriate artistic form for his aspirations. In sculpture, Michelangelo would have served a similar function in his first commission for the Julius Tomb. In painting, a program which might be described as one of cultural imperialism was begun in 1508 with the project for the redecoration of the Vatican, and the concentration for this end in Rome of painters imported from other cities. Yet, despite these beginnings, Rome did not at once become a teeming metropolis of art, even to that degree to which it had been briefly under Julius' uncle, Sixtus IV. The work of Bramante and his assistants during Julius' reign was for the most part limited to beginnings: Michelangelo's sculptural project was not realized; and after 1509 the program of painting was quickly and drastically restricted in the number of participating artists. The quantitative accomplishment of Julius' reign was not so vast, and what was accomplished was the work of a limited artistic circle. However, almost each accomplishment was of the highest possible qualitative import, and inspired with an ambition as splendidly pretentious as the Pope's: the atmosphere of these few great achievements was concordant with that which Julius had created in Rome.

Like Michelangelo's, Julius' own personality was not necessarily identifiably "classical," but by the same accident of birth into a cultural context Julius was disposed to feel and act according to the authority of a century's accumulation of classicizing aspiration. It has been argued that the temper of Julius' personality and actions, infused into the program of art he initiated, was a primary agency of the creation of a High Renaissance classical style in painting. He was already, before 1508, supporting a High Renaissance classical style in architecture and he had intended to give sanction to a similar classical style of Michelangelo in sculpture. Any speculation about Julius' primary influence in the making of a classical style must yield, however, to what we have so far demonstrated to be historical fact: that the High Renaissance classical style was formed in Florence well before Julius began his active career as a patron of the arts in Rome; the exertions of Julius in the first years of his reign had not reshaped the style of practitioners of painting then in the city or recently imported there. We have seen, further, that there is no proof of stylistic discrimination in Julius' first artistic importations, or even of any more precisely formulated grounds for his selection of Michelangelo and Raphael as his chief painters than those of recognition of vast reputation and of obvious genial skill. The classical style was not made in Rome, but came there as a precise consequence of the importation of these two great artists in whom the style was an accomplished fact. Yet, whatever the bases may have been for Julius' importation of Raphael and Michelangelo to work with him, there came to be a profound concordance of mood and mode between their art and the atmosphere that Julius made in Rome, and with the ambitions he conceived for his city — ambitions which were to be more lastingly fulfilled by his artists than by the Pope himself.

If Julius did not make the High Renaissance classical style in Rome he did eventually choose it, for whatever motives; and once chosen he certainly discerned its appropriateness to his own style as a historical agent. Julius provided the best matrix into which the ready accomplishment of Raphael and Michelangelo could be received, and created opportunities, and an environment, for their style that acted with powerful affirmative stimulation on its development. The style that Raphael and Michelangelo brought to Rome had already explored many of the possibilities of classicism, and surely the creative dynamism of these artists and their own maturing personality would have led them, in a Florentine environment also, toward new reaches of expression in their styles: it remains that the atmosphere of Julian Rome encouraged their development in a degree and to a level that they would not have attained in Florence.

In the Rome from which Julius spoke and acted *urbi et orbi* the meaning of the Ancient world, whose accent echoed in his speech, became fuller and clearer than it had been before to Raphael and Michelangelo. Michelangelo had already learned in Rome, and Raphael brought to it, a disposition that enabled them to comprehend the aesthetic of the monuments of Antiquity; but it was in the Julian environment that they learned to understand the collective emanation of grandeur and of power in these Ancient works. For them, and for the other agents of culture in Julius' court who were something like their patron in spiritual dimension, the physical survivals of Ancient Rome became, not the archaeological repository it had been for artists earlier in Julius' reign, but the fragment, at once grandiose and pathetic, of an ideal image, to be completed by creative acts of art and of imagination. With the stimulus of both the old Rome and the new, the art of Michelangelo and Raphael entered into another dimension of the mind and spirit for which they found new resources of form to fit.

The development of style in Michelangelo and Raphael in Rome was not much swifter than it had been in the antecedent phase in Florence, but in Rome, demonstrated as it was within the confines of great single decorative schemes, it is more assertively apparent. With the new maturity, of stage of style and of personal situation, of both masters their definition of their problems now seems more explicit, and their evolution of solutions more absolutely consequential; there is a new severity of logic of development in their Roman works as compared with their accomplishment in Florence. The stylistic point of departure for the Sistine Ceiling and for the Stanza della Segnatura is much the same, and the first stages of development in both — despite the sensible distinction of artistic personality and the difference of the decorative problem — are also similar. However, while Raphael is engaged in the development of the resources of the classical style in a wider and more peculiarly painterly dimension, Michelangelo concentrates on the development of the classical conception still in a mostly sculptural vein, concerned basically with its human core. In the later phases of the Sistine Ceiling he outstrips Raphael in the evolving of this essence of the classical proposition, testing it to, and even beyond, the limits that seem proper to it. It is in the decoration of the Sistine Ceiling that we are overwhelmed by the realization of the dynamism of development of the High Renaissance classical style, which Michelangelo demonstrates at its utmost. It is forced upon us that, in the very process of fulfillment of his classical style, Michelangelo — more only in degree than his creative rivals — was inspired by an unclassical restlessness; and we are reminded that the manner of this search after classical perfection is the possessed and frenetic inspiration of a personality shaped by Christian heritage. The passion of this search, and the extraordinary exaltation of its discoveries, though stimulated by Antiquity and willed upon its model, do not exist in the classicism of the past.

MICHELANGELO: THE SISTINE CEILING

The painting of the Sistine Ceiling [97-148] was forced upon Michelangelo in substitution for his first commission for the Julius Tomb, and he proceeded to make of it a compensation for that unfulfilled sculptural commission. The vocabulary of forms he projected on the ceiling was basically derived from his Tomb design (Justi), unfolded flat upon the ceiling space. Three of the major elements in both designs are the same: the great enthroned figures attended by putti; the Ignudi who are like the captives on the Tomb; and the architectural system of superimposed, interlocking shapes. Into this architecture, projected in paint on the ceiling (in a perspective internally "correct," but not illusionistic to the spectator) the Prophets, Sibyls, and Ignudi have been placed quite in the manner of single sculptured forms, as units of mass inserted in a niche or set up on an architectural base. The scenes from Genesis, in the central panels of the ceiling, are enclosed in the architectural frames as reliefs would be on the surface of an actual monument; and these scenes are in themselves more plastic than pictorial in style. In general they deny any strong sense either of spatial extrusion from, or of deep intrusion into, the plane of the ceiling. That they are conceived as parts of a closed monumental structure is affirmed by the arbitrary turning of these scenes out of perspective and into parallel with the ceiling plane.

The whole system of design of the ceiling is classically sculptural, densely built of solids and evading voids. Even the painter's coloring of this design remains dependent on the sculptural conception of its forms: the dominant tone is that of the fictive stone of its architecture and of the population of nude figures that inhabit it, whose flesh is muted toward the tones of ancient marble. Where the figures are clothed, as are the Seers, their colors — though they become, as painting proceeds, increasingly fluid and harmonious — seem often like the varied patinas of old bronze; the draperies evoke the memory of metal.

The whole scheme for the ceiling retains the sculptor's habit of thinking in terms of single figure units, and the concept of relations among them remains precisely that first formulated in the ideas for the Julius Tomb. Unity depends first on the formal interdependence of the mass of figures with the plastic mass of architecture, then on the progressive interlocking of units of architectural form, and finally — here more visibly than in what we can deduce of the first Tomb design — on balancing repetitive concordances among all the forms. With this sculptor's aesthetic Michelangelo achieves a unity as compelling as, and more vast than, any in his contemporary art. There is no wish to pursue, for the Sistine Ceiling, the idea of a unity of many figures in a single, naturally coherent space, which Michelangelo had explored in the *Cascina;* the shape of the ceiling was such as to exclude such a possibility for any artist of the time. The shape was still, however, not such as to dictate an arrangement so peculiarly sculpturesque as this.

In each of the longer transverse strata of his scheme Michelangelo builds an interlocking and balancing sequence of forms.[98] The small narrative panel in the center is framed by an architecture that builds outward in successive steps, first to the bases of the Ignudi, and then to the prophetic thrones. The Ignudi are disposed around the central panel in attitudes that are each in themselves contrapposto, and which are then set in concordant counterpoise to one another. Their figures move, with the architecture that supports them, more outward from the plane of the wall, shifting to a diagonal direction that serves as a transition to the mainly frontal plane of the enthroned Seers: these are the forms of greatest size and most massive formal impact in each long transverse bay. The progression of counterpoised and concordant forms builds outward and downward in balancing opposite directions, from relief-like planarity to architecturally and sculpturally substantial mass below.

Each major form in this system retains its sculpturesque identity, but it is bound to its companions in the order of concordances of placing and of postures. Each figure is distinct from the architecture, but it is also — in the way invented for the Tomb — at the same time a living function of the architecture, an elaboration or completion of its form; conversely, the architecture is the geometrical function of the figures, and the locking together of its energized masses completes this tissue of a plastic unity. In its formal order each long bay assumes a musicality, but it is unlike the yielding, cursive musicality that Leonardo had conceived. This concord is of brasses, sounding in massive chords across the ceiling.

The intervening shorter bays, given entirely to the narrative scenes in "relief," lie in the topmost stratum of the whole painted monument; they are for the most part simply planar and, architecturally, recessive. They are, by contrast with their neighbors, broader and simpler in form. The complex force of each long bay is resolved into this broader and simpler resonance of the large relief, and this in turn is succeeded by a structure richly chorded like the first. The sequence of expansion and contraction in these alternating bays is like the respiration of a vital being, deep, alternating and regular in measure. And, as the bays succeed each other, they build into a system of great balances of triads of which the emphasis and direction is inverted, as by the turning of an X, with each successive step. The progression of the ceiling, from entrance to altar, becomes a measured alternating sequence of great forms, interlocked and irreversible in direction. As Michelangelo himself develops in the course of painting on the ceiling the dimension of form and the temper of energy that inhabits it progressively increase: the logic of the structure, at the beginning irresistible, is expressed increasingly in crescendo. The ceiling, cover for a Christian chapel, articulates the Christian concept of the processional way, but it scans this progress with the most majestic classic dignity.

The actual scheme of the Sistine Ceiling is far more elaborate than the original intention Michelangelo had for it when he began to plan it in the spring of 1508. The first project we know, documented in a drawing in the British Museum (1859–6–25–567r),[99] was for twelve figured spandrels with Apostles in them; the rest of the ceiling treated only by abstract patterning of geometric fields. The motives that led Michelangelo to expand this simple scheme into its present complexity are not clear but we have his own account (letter to Fattucci, December 1523 [Milanesi, pp. 426–30]) of his remonstrance to the Pope about the poverty of the first project and his assertion that he was then given permission to "make what I wanted, whatever would please me." What pleased him, structurally, was the painted substitution of the Julius Tomb we have described. But we do not know surely to what degree the subject matter of the Ceiling, with its necessary effect upon the structure, was Michelangelo's own invention or the result of consultation with authorities available in person or in print.

As has long since been pointed out the theme of the Ceiling is, in general, a complement of the preexistent decoration of the walls below and illustrates the history of man *ante legem*, in prelude to the history *sub lege* and *sub gratia* that Sixtus' artists had depicted. The Ceiling dwarfs these two succeeding chapters, but its conception of subject is not, for this, less according to its character of prelude. It tells, in its middle range of panels, a summary history of Genesis: the creation of the world and man; man's first sin and fall and its echo in a second fall. The core of meaning of this story is in the central ones among these panels where man is made who then makes sin, and so requires redemption by the Christ. Around this history, in the prophetic thrones, are those who foretell man's redemption by the Son of Man, alternating Prophets of the Old Testament and Sibyls of classical Antiquity; the Sibyls appear in Christian context and are taken in the sense of their meaning for Christian dogma. Below these Seers are the Ancestors of Christ, in whose line is the long generation of his coming, and in the four pendentives there are Old Testament narratives which refer prophetically to Christ's mission of salvation and to his sacrifice of Crucifixion. The elements of subject matter in the Ceiling, with their intrinsic literary content of tragedy and prophecy, are deeply moving in their common theme, in which they cohere to make one general and unmistakable sense. With entirely adequate internal logic and with surpassing power of conviction, the Sistine Ceiling basically means what it instantly and evidently says.

Despite recent profound research it is not yet wholly certain how, in a more specific dogmatic or theological sense, all the various single elements of theme relate precisely to each other. It seems certain that the Prophets, and consequently the Sibyls as well, are connected by literary allusion with the scenes of Genesis they adjoin, and that so also are the subjects of the bronze-colored medallions which are hung between them. However, the explanations given for the specific motive of association of these elements are not always sure. It is not even possible, in every instance, to interpret the type or action of the single Seers in the sense of illustration of their writings, or of the personalities "officially" defined for them. The literary justifications that they may have seem to have been absorbed in, and in some cases obscured by, the transcendent expressive and aesthetic identity Michelangelo has invented for them; it is in this Michelangelesque personality of the Seers, singly and as a group, that they are meaningful, rather than for their precise literary connection with the surrounding scheme.

For the secondary figures who attend the Seers the available iconographic explanations are still less clearly specific or definitive. It is not likely that this vast population of nude forms — caryatid putti on the Prophets' thrones, bronze-colored men in the spaces between the thrones, and the great Ignudi above them — have no more than decorative meaning; Michelangelo could not have meant this by his assertion, which Vasari reports (VII, 226), that the artist need not use foliage as ornament because the human figure was so adequate for the purpose. It is true that any human form of Michelangelo's making — unlike those of Vasari — would create a content also: the question here is not of content but of its motivation in a subject matter.

There is no trace of evidence for the genesis of meaning, among these nudes, for the bronze-colored ones, and only little, and then not very helpful evidence of how the roles of the caryatid putti and the Ignudi were determined. In the first project for the ceiling (in the British Museum drawing cited before) the Apostles are accompanied by caryatid angels placed above their thrones. In a subsequent idea, preserved in a sketch in Detroit,[100] the angels remain but are no longer caryatids: they stand in a place above the thrones which corresponds exactly to that of the present Ignudi and serve as supporters for a medallion of which the content is not certainly defined. The angels of the first sketch, unwinged and descended from their perch, have become the caryatid putti of the actual design; the angels of the second sketch, in place and function, are the precise antecedents of the Ignudi. There is, in these angelic motives of both the drawings, no more precise meaning than that of an appropriate, and inspiring, heavenly company for the Apostles — it is doubtful that in the Detroit design they had yet become Prophets. The original angelic meaning cannot attach to either category of their descendants, in the caryatid putti or the Ignudi; both lack, or quite deny angelic appearance or attributes. The Ignudi, surely, are not any longer angels: their explicit sex, their sensuousness and the kinds of mood that they express are contradictions of angelic personality. It may be that the caryatid putti have been transformed from angelic beings into an Antique counterpart as Genii, and symbolize some inspirational force upon the Prophets they attend. But their appearance and their actions are little in accord with such a role; if there is such meaning in them it has been almost entirely submerged. They do not inspire, or even consistently react to the inspiration of, the Seers. Their conduct is that of children, uncomprehending innocents at play. The forms in general of two of the present categories of nude beings descend from their antecedents in the two designs for early versions of the decorative scheme, but their meanings do not. The precise present types of nudes and their meanings were conceived only when the basic subject matter of the Ceiling was changed, and instead of Christ's Apostles his Prophets became primary actors in the scheme.

The Ceiling, with its central theme of man's fall and the prophecy of his redemption, may be a summary, from the view of Christian hindsight, of the moral situation of the pre-Christian world. The bronze-colored nudes,[101-2] for whom we have no counterpart in the first designs, afford the clearest hint of what the whole constellation of nude forms may mean. They are the antitheses of the Prophets they adjoin: unillumined captives of ancient ignorance. Dark, and darkly imprisoned, they may represent the barbarian peoples of a pre-Christian time, inaccessible to the prophecy of Christ's coming; they have no sense of the history in which they are imbedded. The Ignudi suggest another place in the scale of awareness, between the absolute illumination of the Seers and the dark ignorance of the figures in the spandrels: they would be the creatures of the pagan, classical, pre-Christian world, who are half-conscient of the meaning of the history they attend and the prophecy they oversee. The bronze-colored nudes are almost animal in nature, moving in soulless contortions like those of caged beasts; oppositely, the attitudes and expressions of the Seers are precise and purposeful, dictated by an ultimate explicitness of state of spirit and of mind. Between the two, the Ignudi are possessed by moods and express themselves in posturings that are neither wholly rational and inspired nor merely physical and animal; they are beings in whom the mind and soul have not yet assumed, as in Christian habit of belief, a separable identity from the flesh. As for the caryatid putti: if we continue to assume that things basically mean, in the Ceiling, what they evidently say, it may be that they stand in fact for *Innocenti*: representing a state of man that precedes Knowledge; and they may allude as well, as Innocents, to the children whom Herod sacrificed, as later he would be the instrument of the sacrifice of Christ which the Ceiling entirely foretells.

The role we discern in the Ignudi would explain the conjunction in them of paganized beauty and Christianized disquiet of personality, and would justify the presence of these figures, so much more precisely recollective than the Sibyls of the Ancient classic world, in the Christian context. The history of pre-Christian man becomes, by their presence and that of the bronze-colored nudes, enriched by a symbolic and anonymous population of all of Antiquity. The nudes are not participants or spectators but concurrent presences in the Christian history, blind to its meaning or half-knowing of it; and at the same time its meaning resonates through and is differentiated in them. The conception — not only in the nudes but in the Seers — of a division of humanity into strata that are different in their proportion of spiritual and physical content, and in their articulation of a distinguishable and rational soul within the body, is the profoundest demonstration (and the first one intellectually formulated in terms of visible ideas) of the nature of man as classicism within Christianity conceived it.

The sources of this thinking are of course generally Neo-Platonic, but there is no definition we know in Neo-Platonic writing of a proposition quite like this. In the figures of the Ceiling it is demonstrated that the human physical being untouched by Grace is animal in nature and behavior; it is in proportion as the creature has knowledge — here fore-knowledge — of Christ that the soul is a distinguishable identity and no longer confounded with the tissues of the body. In beings like the Seers who know Christ, or in Adam who is made by God directly, the soul is inspired, and distinguishable from the mortal flesh; but that flesh is infused by the soul, directed by it, and expressive of its force and splendor. It is this last conception that the classical style within Christianity intends as its ideal. In the Ceiling this conception is exactly articulated for the first time, in the context of a history, and in the guise of a process that history reveals.

The general design and the subject matter settled, Michelangelo began the labor of execution of the Ceiling in January 1509 and in a campaign of work that lasted until September of that year painted the frescoes of the first three bays, the last in the order of the succession of the Bible narrative. His first effort was apparently the *Flood*,[103] the large panel of the second bay. Confronted with a large space to be painted and with a narrative episode that required the presence of many figures, Michelangelo inevitably recalled his own precedent in the *Cascina* cartoon. Here, however, the actors seem to be moved more genuinely than in the *Cascina* by the drama of their situation. In their expressions of countenance and sometimes in gesture Michelangelo has evoked, in powerful imaginative reconstruction, their sensation of primitive tragedy. The attitudes of body are, generally, less expressive: not so arbitrary nor so nearly athletic as in the *Battle* piece, these postures still carry something of its sense of inventions made first for form's sake and only secondly in consequence of the actors' state of mind. It is as if the development of expressive powers demonstrated in the unfinished *St. Matthew* [34] had not been; in this less accustomed role of painter Michelangelo is diverted by the painter's problems — not only of the many-figured narrative but of technique as well — from the concentration of purpose sculpture had permitted him.

More than in the *Battle of Cascina,* Michelangelo tries in the *Flood* to attain a structure of pictorial kind. There is more effort here to bind the single figures, still emphatically sculptural, into unities of groups but these are still related to each other conjunctively more than cohesively; each group remains a plastic episode in the design. The distribution of the groups into a depth of space intends to be pictorial, but his sculptor's sense is here — as in his design of the whole Ceiling — for solids rather than for voids. The space, a summary notation of environment, has neither a framework of traditional perspective nor of arbitrary geometric shape; it has no structure to support and unify the solids set within it. The *Flood* is inspired with pictorial intention but it remains in a limbo between a painter's and a sculptor's aesthetic.

The *Sacrifice of Noah* [104] was probably the second fresco to be designed and executed. In it, the less extensive narrative allowed a change in scale from the *Flood*, which must surely have accorded instantly with Michelangelo's disposition to work with monumental, and with solid, forms; the subject also permitted the reduction, to the same end, of the first fresco's extent of space. Nevertheless, Michelangelo's ambition in the *Sacrifice* is still pictorial: he is visibly concerned to "compose" the figures both in respect to their arrangement on the surface and in the limited space. He disposes them (unlike the *Flood* or the *Cascina*) in a sequence of carefully connected postures; these, linking one form to the next, make an oval unity of design around the altar in the center. In this binding of forms in a whole, clear, movemented geometry the *Sacrifice* develops, beyond its antecedents, a solution of classicizing kind to a pictorial problem. At the same time Michelangelo's ineradicable tendency to work sculpturally gives the composition, with its bulk of figures and restricted space, an effect of structure which tends toward that of classical relief. The formal problem of the *Sacrifice*, more than in the *Flood*, is the dominating one; the subject was not such as to inspire a compelling interpretation of the content.

In the third scene to be painted in this set, the *Drunkenness of Noah*,[105] Michelangelo seems to have overcome effectively the unclarities of purpose that had accompanied his first sculptor's attempts to work as a painter on large scale. The solution of his problem was already implied in the *Sacrifice*, in the tendency in it to fill the picture surface with large plastic forms in a reduced space, and thereby suggest an effect as of relief. In the *Drunkenness* Michelangelo is more confident in technique of painting, but he is no longer concerned with the making of a peculiarly pictorial structure. The fresco is composed quite frankly according to a classical sculptural aesthetic: it reduces the pictorial expression of space to a near-minimum, enlarges the scale of the figures within the frame, and distributes them along a narrow plane close to its forward limit. The figures are connected still more fluently, and with more energy than in the *Sacrifice*, but their arrangement is now not at all in space but in a lateral sequence. In the most forthright way the conception makes an analogue to that of a classical relief.

Now that Michelangelo has evolved, by this means, a solution in the language of his own aesthetic for the painter's problem and, simultaneously, gained facility in the painter's fresco technique, he is free to express himself with less impediment; he resumes, in the *Drunkenness*, his momentarily deviated development. The figures in this fresco are the first on the Ceiling to stand again at the level of expressive power that Michelangelo had sketched out in the *St. Matthew*. Here also, perhaps as the fruition of still more of an experience of Ancient art, the figures begin to assume a more developed classical appearance than in the first two frescoes. In their forms and movements they display, for the first time so clearly in Michelangelo's art, the wondrous consonance that he is able to establish between power and grace.

It was with this quota of experience behind him that Michelangelo began the first Ignudi and the first Seers of the Ceiling. In them there was not, even at the beginning, a conflict of pictorial and sculptural purpose: they were initially conceived in the sense of sculpture, as compact solids on a base of architecture. Probably the first one painted of the Seers, the *Delfica*,[106] retains (like the first narrative panel) Florentine reminiscences: of the gesture of the Madonna of the Doni tondo and the type, already sibylline, of the Madonna of the sculpture tondo in the Bargello. As in both those compositions the *Delfica* makes a rounded and compact unity of form, of which the breadth is greater and the articulation of the contrapposto fuller and clearer than in these antecedents. Her counterpoise between movement and static mass is contained within an implied sphere, and adjusted in a perfect balance upon both vertical and longitudinal axes: her structure is a consummation of the formal logic of the Florentine period. She is the end of a prior stage of research, which Michelangelo will now use as a threshold for the evolution of a harmony of massive forms continuously more energized and internally diverse.

The counterpart of *Delfica*, on the opposite side of the same bay, is *Joel*,[107] the Prophet of the vine on the fruit of which Noah has become drunk. He is of greater bulk, appropriately masculine, than the *Delfica* but not less constrained within a unitary plastic form. However, he is informed by an energy of spirit higher than hers: this contrast between male power and the lesser spiritual vigor of the Sibyls continues through the Ceiling. There is a profound force in the attention with which Joel reads and his body answers to it, shifting in the narrow space and turning slightly in diagonal torsion out of an attitude of rest. His movement implies a potential of energy far greater than is actually expressed, and this energy is at once intensified against and absolutely controlled by a discipline of counterpoise and by the whole containing shape. In the *Joel*, more than in his probable immediate predecessor *Zachary* [108] — and differently than in the *Delfica* — we are made aware that Michelangelo describes a dimension of humanity higher and more confident than he had conceived before. Joel has the intensity of the *St. Matthew*,[34] but not Matthew's irrationality: this personality is as clear and forceful in mind as he is powerful in feeling. His dimension of spiritual being is matched by the scale of his form, and by his controlled energy of physical response; we have the whole impression of a creature magnified far above the normal stature, of body and of spirit, of humanity.

Isaiah, who denounces the sacrifice that he attends, was the last of the Seers to be executed in this set. In him Michelangelo has described not only a higher humanity, but given a more complex interpretation of it. The *Isaiah* [110] has the same bodily dimension as the *Joel* and implies the same potential energy of feeling, but Michelangelo now wants to differentiate, more exactly than in the *Joel*, the resources of personality of this kind of ideal being. Isaiah shows a spiritual power not assertively expressed but in the process as of its unfolding: he is in a crepuscular state between melancholy meditation and the beginning of inspiration. To express this more complex situation Michelangelo displays a subtlety of articulation greater than in any previous image of the Ceiling; this subtlety is reflected even in a higher expertness of expressive drawing with the brush. Isaiah's body is made to echo, comment on and reinforce in its every part the state of mind that is revealed upon his face: the whole of his person communicates at once more precisely and more variously, and yet with a profounder power, the sensation of his slow-awakening might.

The Ignudi are even less bound than the Seers to illustrate a specific literary content and among them the development of expressive form is yet more free. From the evidence of the first set of Ignudi, around the *Drunkenness of Noah,*[111-13] it would seem that Michelangelo initially entertained a notion of their role that related them not only to the prophetic thrones which they surmount but to the central scene as well: the restraint of attitude of these first Ignudi and their veiled melancholy of glance suggests a function like that of a chorus, of commentary on the scene that they adjoin. A first pair of Nudes, above the *Joel,* are placed in quiet, literally corresponding poses in plane against the wall; the matching pair above the *Delfica* move only gently forward in their space. In the second set of Ignudi, around the *Sacrifice,*[114-16] their liberty of action and expression has already expanded to a point which the first, choral idea of their role cannot contain. Each pair of these Ignudi echoes the posture of his pair of predecessors on the same side of the earlier bay, but with a far greater energy. Their attitudes, though still carefully co-responsive, are more vigorous and more complex, particularly in their play of form in space. Their moods are much more individually assertive and more varied among themselves. What they express is not much less distinctly articulated than in the *Isaiah* or the *Erithrea*[109] of the same bay but obviously belongs to a different order of emotion and idea. It begins here to be clear how the feelings of the Ignudi are those of a lower category of humanity than that of the illumined Seers: they express melancholy or fear or joy that is tinged with the irrational; and their actions, for all their energy, are finally bound, slave-like, by the physical duty which they must perform of holding up the bronze medallions. It is, however, in these enslaved Ignudi of the third bay, executed before he went on to the *Isaiah* and *Erithrea* below, that Michelangelo seems first to have fully realized a new liberty of his own: that conceded by the painter's art which let him make, in the time of one true sculptured image, a dozen figures freer and more various than he had made so far in stone.

Probably in the autumn of 1509 the scaffolding was shifted and Michelangelo may have painted first, on the newly accessible area of the ceiling, the smaller central panel with the *Creation of Eve.*[117] He brought to this story the new dimension of power and the subtlety of articulation he had invented for the *Isaiah* of the third bay, applying it now to the service of the narrative. More than the last previous narration, the *Drunkenness of Noah,* the *Creation of Eve* is at the same time more painterly in technique and structurally even less pictorial: here there is an absolute organization of the picture in a mode of classical relief. The figures are expanded to the largest scale within the frame that the subject will permit: massively modelled, and set in lateral sequence on the foremost plane, they wholly prevail over any sense of space. The space, in turn, has been reduced to a notation still more summary than in the *Drunkenness.*

Like that composition this one recalls, more precisely, Michelangelo's early study of Jacopo della Quercia; and this reference recalls how Michelangelo's first formation of a classical style found authority not only in the idealism of Antiquity but in that of a still partly medieval, not yet realistic, Quattrocento art. The essentials of actors and accessories to which Michelangelo has confined his narrative are not different than in Jacopo's version of the scene; the force of Michelangelo's interpretation is, however, vastly greater. From Michelangelo's precisely expressive manipulation of his persons — impossible to Jacopo in this degree in his historical situation — the same idea acquires an altogether different virtue of communication: the spectator experiences Michelangelo's meanings almost empathically. Not only the crumpled posture of the Adam but the whole tissue of his body is infused with the expression of his sleep. The face of Eve communicates a dawning sentience, a still dazed, half-animal recognition which in this moment belongs to a lesser spiritual status than the sleeping Adam — and which is less also than that of the Ignudi. Her body demonstrates explicitly how she is in part lifted by the magic power of God's gesture and in part already stumblingly supports herself. Not so far had Michelangelo's art expressed ideas of a human situation that were at the same time so essential — so elemental — and so profound as these.

The Ignudi who accompany the *Creation of Eve* are of identical anatomical character with the figures in the panel, and as articulate of emotional states.[118-20] In posture these Ignudi are freer and more elaborate than the Ignudi near the *Sacrifice*; they are less bound by their nominal function as supporters, and less literal in their counterpoise of pairs. They assume, now, a more attention-demanding role not only for their freer and more various powers of expression but by their now quite noticeable larger size. There had been, not only in the Ignudi, a progressive magnification of the scale of figures from one bay to the next in order of their painting, at the beginning mainly for aesthetic reasons; but there is more now, clearly, than a formal motive to impel this process. This magnifying of the human form was an inevitable response to the growth in dimension of Michelangelo's ideas of its content. The figures do not merely grow in size, they grow in grandeur; their expansion results from the accretion in them of force and depth of meaning.

The most decisive change in figure scale occurs in the panel of *Temptation and Expulsion*:[121] it is in this scene that Michelangelo's actors in the narrative assume in splendor of physique, in power of movement, and in resonance of feeling, the character of the heroic. Not only the scale but the very conception of the body is changed to fit this higher role. Its forms of musculature become more complex and cursively energetic, and the shape of body becomes less heavy toward its extremities: the anatomy is grander but more lithe; its center of gravity has been raised (Wölfflin). These changes in the bodily structure make its power more finely and flexibly articulate; the figures are more resilient in action and in their expressions of response. And because their ideal regularity of proportion is now more touched with the quality of grace they seem yet more beautiful than before.

The figures of this panel act in a setting almost as drastically summary as that in the *Creation of Eve.* The environment in the part of the scene that describes the *Expulsion* is almost desolate, as abstract as that in the Masacciesque model to which it refers. However, the relation of figures to their background is not so purely relief-like as in the *Creation of Eve.* The openness behind and around the figures, though it is so sparsely defined, contains a painter's effect of spatial and atmospheric ambience; but this pictorial ambience is exploited to affirm, to a new degree, the force of plastic existence of the figures. Michelangelo sets them a little deeper in the space and rounds them, with a painterly chiaroscuro, into more wholly tactile substances. These figures look less like figures in relief than those of the *Creation of Eve,* or of the *Drunkenness of Noah,* and they assume, as much as the frankly sculpturesque Ignudi and the Seers, the character of presences in full round.

In this panel Michelangelo has come to the definitive solution of the problem the narrative panels of the Ceiling had posed, of conflict between the painter's and the sculptor's language. From the subordination, in the *Flood,* of sculptural figures to an intendedly pictorial scheme of composition and of space Michelangelo had proceeded to an evident compromise, the simulation in paint of sculptural relief. Finally, as he came increasingly to understand painterly values — but not necessarily the values of pictorial structure — and to control painterly techniques, he evolved the solution of the *Temptation and Expulsion,* in which sculpturally wholly plastic form, set within a summary pictorial ambience, is described with the fullest powers of a painter's hand.

The *Creation of Adam*[122-3] affirms this solution still more explicitly. Against an openness of sky and a strip of primordial earth are placed two great plastic masses, on one side the Adam and on the other God, enclosed with his angels in a cloud-like cloak. The composition is a simple formal and contentual equilibrium of these two masses, more direct even than the bipartite balance between the *Temptation and Expulsion* scenes. Almost altogether abandoned here is the close-joined sequence of forms, resembling that of the classical picture-designer, that appears in the compositions of the earlier panels in relief-like style. This composition is rather one of part and counterpart of sculpturally distinct units, such as had already been devised for the pairs of the Ignudi. This simple order is exactly proper to Michelangelo's conception of the content of the theme: the confrontation in a high bare world of the first man and his Maker.

For the moment of this fresco God and Michelangelo enjoy a confusion of role: God acts the classical sculptor. He has just shaped the first image of a man, giving him such beauty of physical being as should belong to the ideal ancestor from whom we imperfectly descend. He hovers above his creature, in the act of endowing it with its content of life and soul. The vital spark flows from the outstretched hand of God into the matter He has shaped, and in response this matter begins to live: to move physically and to feel. The body of the Adam shows precisely how and to what degree it is, at this moment, infused with vitality: each part of the anatomy articulates how much it contains of energy and how much is still inert flesh. The Adam illustrates the essence of the classical idea of interpenetration of the physical and spiritual being, but he also illustrates the nonclassical origin of this recreative synthesis: the flesh and spirit are conceived of as initially separate elements and it is the spirit, divine in source, which controls and moves the flesh. At the same time the splendor of the flesh and its worth of beauty are as much the work of God as its inner radiance of soul: the beauty of divine creation is in the archetypal substance of the first man as well as in his spirit. What Michelangelo thought God meant by the Idea of man and what, thus, humanity was meant to be was this Adam before the deformation of experience: by God's will and grace a hero, the mortal counterpart of God.

Not only the idea, but the forms also, of the *Creation of Adam* are sufficiently more grand than in the preceding scenes to justify an interval in time between them, occasioned by a brief absence of Michelangelo in Bologna, from which he had returned by February 1511: the *Creation* accords in scale with the last three central scenes. The other members of the decoration of these bays are, however, on a grander scale still; there is a marked acceleration in them of the process, until now relatively gradual, of expansion of external and internal dimension of the figures. The Ignudi, and still more the Seers, in the last bays grow remarkably in size, and still more remarkably in power of content; and in the last scenes of Genesis, even without further change in scale, there is also an expansion of the power of content. They contain a profundity and urgent motivation in idea that is suddenly beyond the level even of the *Creation of Adam.* As Michelangelo mounts backward in the history of Genesis to this phase where God creates omnipotent and alone, his own thought seems to enter into a vaster and more abstract realm and to be informed with the conception of the Creator's primordial and awful power.

On internal grounds of style it is likely that the large panel of the *Creation of the Sun and Moon* [124] was executed earliest in this last set. God is depicted here as creating with a terrible dynamic energy; He himself moves in the heavens like a celestial body. On the right of the panel, with a gesture of explosive force, He wills into being the spheres of sun and moon; on the left He hurtles like a meteor toward the new-formed earth. In the smaller panel which precedes this one, most often called the *Separation of the Earth and Waters,*[125] the temper of God's movement is altogether contrasting: in slow-gliding majesty He smooths into peace the forms and forces He has created. In both frescoes the shapes assumed by God in his three aspects are compact plastic units suspended, as in the *Creation of Adam* also, in an abstract space. In the *Separation,* however, God's image takes on a yet more concentrated shape which suggests, more than before, the merging of the human form of God with that of a celestial sphere. This whole form is extremely simplified, generalized without and within to a degree not so far shown in the Ceiling.

As Michelangelo dwells on the first episodes of Genesis his conception of God's nature and actions becomes higher and more remote: apart from incident, narration, and materiality. The *Separation* is concerned with God's presence and being, and hardly with the description of an action; it is for that reason that the fresco is not precisely nameable: the exceptional generalization in it of form and content is that of Michelangelo's idea. But the last panel of the Ceiling,[126] the first act of Genesis, is conceived by Michelangelo in an image still more remote, and at the same time intellectually and spiritually yet more profound. The beginning of creation is reduced to an essence which reaches as if above and through the first bald sentence of the Bible to a vision of a hardly apprehensible God, seemingly newly self-formed from the surrounding chaos. He turns in chaos — and again a cosmic simile suggests itself, unknown to Michelangelo, of a solar body in its process of formation — seeking to shape the dark reaches where there is as yet no form and no direction. The idea of this image, so exalted and so nearly abstract, is given us in a corresponding language, so general as to border on abstraction.

The Ignudi of the last two sets also seem, by comparison with their predecessors, to have been generated in a higher and more powerful range of Michelangelo's invention — applied still, however, to the thematic idea they are supposed to illustrate. Their various emotions are much more intense, but are of no less irrational, nature than before. The Ignudi still convey the sense of personality involved with and enslaved by bodily existence. Their bodies, proceeding from the conception of a physical splendor arrived at for the Adam, elaborate that conception and try, even, to surpass it. Around the *Separation*,[127-9] the Ignudi — not less physically remarkable than the Adam — move as he is not permitted to in his role. One of them, possessed by an incoherent fear, is wound into a posture at once uncomfortably strained and almost calligraphically ornamental. Another, satyr-like in countenance, moves on his seat as if seized by the impulse of a dance. A third is inspired with a furious energy which makes him turn quickly and violently, pulling toward him the swag of the medallion to which he is bound. His partner is as if locked into a pose of contrasting immobility, but not of rest; he is in an extreme torsion of contrapposto. In his rhythmic eloquence of posture and in the beauty of his head he exceeds the Adam as an ideal physical image of humanity.

The Ignudi of the last bay [130-32] are more profound in mood: melancholic, and bound in upon themselves. Nearest to the highest image of God, it seems as if their power of spirit has become more penetrating and more possessive, but still not liberated from their enslaved and now yet more massive bodily forms. These creatures, more but not yet wholly knowing, yearn and struggle still only half-sentiently within, and incipiently against, their flesh. Only one Nude here, as powerful as Hercules and beautiful as an Antinoös, sits in almost sullen meditation [128] as if he alone, a *summum* of the beauty of Antiquity, were reluctant to see his epoch vanish and the half-comprehended prophecy fulfilled.

Not only he but all these last Ignudi have bodies still more powerful than the Adam's, or both more powerful and fine: in these figures Michelangelo finally has won his long private war with the *Laocoön*, and surpassed the envied model of the *Torso Belvedere.* But we are struck, in the Antinoös-like creature in particular, as nowhere earlier so strongly in the Ceiling, with the sense that this figure is no longer a possible or credible being. The archetypal perfection of this physical beauty and, as well, the gigantic muscularity of the Nude opposite him share, in a way, the extreme ideality of the image of God above their heads: the proportion in them of ideal invention and of plausible description is decisively weighted toward the former. This shift of emphasis, by which the image is removed yet farther than before from natural appearance and toward an idea invented in the artist's mind, marks a change from what we may regard as a median of classical ideality attained in the preceding set of pictures of the Ceiling, as in the *Creation of Adam*: the images of the last bay already point away from the sphere of thinking that is in the *Adam* and toward that of the Medici Tombs.

More marked even than this change in the Ignudi is the contrast of the last group of Seers with their predecessors; in them new energies and depths of thought are released in awesome crescendo and finale. For all their massiveness and force the Prophets and Sibyls of the middle bay belong to a perceptibly lesser order than these last five Seers. The difference, as always in the Ceiling, is not only of scale but of dimension of personality. The ancient crone *Cumea,*[133] almost clumsy in her heavy-muscled compact shape, contrasts with the grave, suave, slow-unfolding power of the grander *Persica.*[134] The mood and movement of *Ezekiel*[135] are almost blunt by comparison with that of *Daniel,*[136] whose state of spiritual possession electrifies the swift and subtle action of his form. As in the Ignudi of the same bay, in the *Daniel* a higher energy and more complex emotion are articulated in a freer action of the body, here vastly more monumental than the nude forms just above.

The last three Seers are developed, in some ways, even beyond the level of the *Daniel* and *Persica.* They are touched with the character of a still higher ideality that appears in the other figures of their last bay and they each express this ideality in a seemingly deliberately differentiated way. The *Libica*[137] most of all resembles, in kind of ideal meaning, one of the aspects of the Ignudi who, in time of painting, just precede her: among the Seers she is the one who most intends an archetypal beauty of physical presence and of formal attitude. Her form, still more evidently than in the last Ignudi, has been invented for its ornamental value: it refines the conception of the last Nudes toward a poised quick elegance which becomes, in Michelangelo's necessary interpenetration of content and form, the coloration of her personality. She may be regarded as a development in a special sense of one of the ideas, that of formal beauty, which elsewhere in the Ceiling — except only in the Antinoös-like Ignudo of the same bay — had appeared only as one among the complex of elements that composed the synthetic whole of a mature classical image. It is as if, in the process of development of Michelangelo's thinking toward a higher ideality, this concept of formal beauty had assumed a degree of clear identity, as a separable idea, within the whole ideality of classical style. In the concern in the *Libica* for formal beauty as a specifiable primary ambition, and in her complex ornamental elegance, she takes on the role of art-historical as well as of religious prophetess, of the style of Mannerism. However, the intention in her of formal beauty is not, as in later Mannerism, a divorce of this element from a classical context but only a stress of this value within it. The thinking in the *Libica* remains a development — a special stress of one of its ideals — within classical style.

A similar development toward an ideal archetype of one aspect of the whole classical conception of the figure determines the character, very different, of Jonah. Here again the idea follows on the thinking of the last Ignudi — not from their beauty of form but from its power and diversity of expressive action. In the *Jonah* [138] this conception is enlarged by a tremendous increase, possible in him as a Prophet, of spiritual content. Where the Ignudi and most of the preceding Seers have emotion that is self-generated and self-contained, Jonah is inspired instead by an actual outward vision of his God. Symbol of Resurrection and ancestor of Peter, Jonah projects a bridge between the epochs of Genesis and Grace, looking up at the history that is past and gesturing passionately toward the world that is to come.

More terribly inspired and possessed than any other figure on the Ceiling, Jonah moves with a vehemence that strains the limits of a classical constraint. His energy of action, like his implication of content, expands beyond the bounds of his allotted place. As the *Libica* appears to prophesy a Mannerism, the *Jonah*, an ecstatic spirit in a dynamically active actuality of form, seems to prophesy a baroque style. But again, though his image explores a new reach of the classical ideal, it remains within it: the impulse of the figure is compensated externally by its accessories and internally by its absolute adherence to the principle of contrapposto, of equilibrium of energy and mass upon the body's core. Further, the emotion of the *Jonah* is not only passionate but clear and pure, exalted even beyond the emotions of the other Prophets; what moves him is an idea higher than that which had inspired his companion Seers.

Jeremiah, [139] Prophet of Lamentations, is a demonstration of a third archetype. In massive presence he is of a race as grandiose as Jonah's, but he is his antithesis in expression. The power of feeling in this Prophet, as great as the expansive passion of the *Jonah*, is oppositely turned in on itself: Jeremiah's great, compact, gathered form expresses the dimension of his thought and its concentration. Every other Seer had been given some pretext of action or of illustrative incident, but Jeremiah has no "motive" beyond that of his thought. This slow-breathing, meditating monolith embodies, more than any allegory, the concept of thought itself, in that dimension of it Michelangelo himself has now attained: Jeremiah is the image of Michelangelo's Idea.

In ways that are different in their form and in intent of content, these last three prophetic figures express aspects of the conception that dictates the image of God in the final bay. In that central image the idea is expressed in terms of generalization so high as to verge toward abstraction, and in the Seers the ideas are more substantially defined as well as specifically differentiated from each other. Yet like the God, all three Seers are not any longer idealized representations but, instead, representations of ideas; and Michelangelo's whole evolution in the Ceiling may be summarized in this inversion of a phrase. He has moved, in the process of this inversion, toward an ideality so high that it now stands at the limits of a classical expression.

In the pendentives that flank Jonah, the last works done before the first unveiling of the Ceiling in August 1511, Michelangelo in fact finally* trespassed beyond the limits permitted by a classical concept of style. What had occurred between the first and last bays of the Ceiling was all of it encompassable in a definition of classicism, but what has happened between the first pendentives and these last two shows not only a development but a cleavage between styles. The sculptor's mentality — more rather than less affirmative since the early portions of the Ceiling — is in part responsible for the character of the late pendentives. No longer concerned, as he had been in the *David and Goliath*[140] and in the *Judith and Holofernes*,[141] to make a pictorial unity of narrative, Michelangelo, in the late pendentives, thinks entirely in terms of figure-mass; in both the *Hanging of Haman*[142] and the *Brazen Serpent*[143] the ambience is not only summary and secondary, but drastically arbitrary. In the *Haman* four narrative episodes coexist with not even minimum logic of spatial relation; in the *Brazen Serpent* there is hardly any space but only a turmoil of great plastic forms. In the *Haman* the arbitrariness of Michelangelo's thinking of the narrative is such that it is told not in a discernible sequence but with a juxtaposition of concepts like that in the word order of a Latin sentence. The beginning and the tragic climax of the story, which in normal order would be most separate, inversely intersect in the most prominent central place, and initial cause and final consequence culminate in the figure, more anguished and desperate than *Laocoön*, of the crucified Haman.

In its violation of the rationale of space, in its blunt yet restless distribution of units of design, in its abstraction of narrative order and dark violence of mood this pendentive — despite its classicism of single forms — is no longer structurally or expressively classical. Michelangelo's urgency of spiritual sensation and his abstracting tendency of thought have carried him here beyond the limits of a classical discipline. Neither harmony nor unity, and little of classical constraint, temper the dismembered vehemence of this fresco.

The *Brazen Serpent* is more unified in order but not according to any classical system of design. Its form responds immediately to a terrible, and also pessimistic, vision of the subject, expressed in the serpentine twistings of the figures of the damned. Figures, as mighty in dimension as the Prophets, are inspired by terror and moved by agony; again Michelangelo returns to and exceeds the theme of the *Laocoön*. Not only the tormented action of anatomies but their eccentric foreshortenings deprive even the single figures of a character of classicism, which in some measure had persisted in the *Haman*. And where, as toward the background, there is no room for the whole body to express its anguish, single ghostly countenances, like the population of a nightmare, assume this function. By comparison with this pullulating melee of the damned the small group of the saved on the left are conventional and unconvincing presences.

Even more than the *Haman*, the *Brazen Serpent* depends on an interpretation of its subject in a willed unclassical sense. In violence of emotion, and in abstraction and illogic of form, it is yet farther from recognizable principles of classical style. In both pendentives, moved perhaps in part by the dramatic potential of their subjects, but more by a climactic and irresistible surge of his own expressive intensity, Michelangelo's force and ideality acquire, for the moment only, an apocalyptic nature. In this momentary breach of classical disciplines the pendentives assume, prematurely, the character of postclassical phenomena of style, Mannerizing in the *Haman*, and in the *Brazen Serpent* simultaneously Mannerizing and proto-Baroque.

*With the last pendentives the painting of the actual curved surface of the ceiling was complete. There remained to be done, to finish the extent of the commission Michelangelo had undertaken, the painting of the lunettes adjoining the curved surface. These lunettes [146-8] contain most of the representations of the Ancestors of Christ, of which some already had been executed, contemporaneously with their neighboring portions of the decoration, in the eight severies [144-5] between the prophetic thrones. The scaffolding for the lunettes seems to have been ready, after the interval of temporary unveiling of the ceiling, in October 1511. A year passed before their execution was complete and before the final unveiling of the whole decoration in October 1512. In this year it is evident that the impetus of creative energy which had expanded ceaselessly throughout the previous painting of the Ceiling, and which had exploded finally in the unclassical violence of the pendentives, had come to rest, and even receded. It may be that Michelangelo's conception of his present subject was in part responsible for this. The Ancestors already painted, those in the severies, seem to have called forth an interpretation different from that of all the other actors on the Ceiling. Michelangelo seems to have regarded them as more nearly actual human types and personalities, less susceptible of ideal interpretation than the Seers or the Ignudi and to be contrasted, in their lower level of ideality, with them. In countenance, dress, and posture they are simpler and more ordinary than their neighbors. None of the first series of Ancestors is inspired. Only two among them peer as if into a future which, however, unlike the Seers, it is not given them to see; the others sit as if waiting, mostly passively, some asleep, as if they were less actors than merely human accidents in the fulfillment of a destiny they do not know. Their station in the scale of prophetic knowledge is less than that of the idealized Ignudi but higher than that of the ignorant imprisoned beings just above them; as doctrine prescribes, the Ancestors are in a limbo.

This same conception persists in the Ancestors in the lunettes. Only one or two of them are conceived in a noble or possibly heroic vein of person or personality; in general in the lunettes it is also the common humanity of the

Ancestors that is stressed, even to the accenting in some of them of a Semitic character of features and, in others, of a caricatural ugliness of face. Expression and action tend to be ordinary: sometimes meditative, but more often merely domestic, even verging upon genre. The interpretation of specific persons almost surely depends initially on literary authority, but this is only a point of departure for Michelangelo's exercise of personal invention in the description of beings as unexceptional as it is possible for one of his habit of mind to conceive.

Some of these lunettes, according to Michelangelo's own later evidence, were designed in cartoon in the early winter of 1511, before he began his last campaign of work on the Ceiling proper. It has been assumed that the cartoons designed then were those for the lunettes from the entrance wall up to, but not beyond, the bay that contains the *Creation of Eve*; a perceptible change in style appears in the succeeding lunettes nearer to the altar. However, it is these latter lunettes that more nearly approach in character of scale, elaboration of posture, and variety of motive the figures of the ceiling bays executed in 1511: on this ground it seems likely that the cartoons on which Michelangelo worked in 1511 were for these adjacent lunettes. The Ancestors in the lunettes on the half of the wall toward the entrance correspond in style more nearly to the more restricted and, by comparison, more rigid forms of the ceiling panels above them, and it would seem reasonable to assume that their cartoons were roughly contemporary in invention with these nearby bays and with the Ancestors in the adjoining severies.

Despite the difference in time of their invention and the distinction that can be made in style between the two sets of lunettes, all share common characteristics which are a consequence of their common time of execution during the year that follows the autumn of 1511. The first of these characteristics relates to a development in the late bays of the Ceiling itself, the frequent tendency to describe form in terms of summary generalization: the Ancestors are mostly drawn with a very simple indication both of whole form and of interior shapes, sometimes so reduced as to seem a blunt shorthand. This generalization is not accompanied, however, by the effect of concentrated force that it has in the last scenes of Genesis. In almost all these figures there is an absence of energy in form that corresponds to their usual character of feeling: uncertain, reflective, weary, or asleep, while they wait through the centuries of their generations before Christ. Tending toward abstraction in form, yet not ideal in type and content, the Ancestors of the lunettes convey not only a spiritual but a formal lassitude that is a result of more than the interpretation of their subjects; it is the genuine accent of their creator's style in this moment: the Ancestors reflect a deflation of the vast creative force that Michelangelo had expended on the Ceiling proper.

Michelangelo himself, in the course of their painting, complains (in a letter of 24 July 1512 [Milanesi, p. 104]) "Io stento più che uomo che fussi mai, mal sano e chon grandissima faticha; e pure o pazienza per venire al fine desiderato." The sense of fatigue and distance in most of the Ancestors — the sometimes almost vacant simplifying of the form and the slackness of articulation — are confessional of Michelangelo's own exhaustion: they were painted not in inspiration, but wearily, with patience. They are, in reference to the whole evolution of the Sistine decoration, its *détente* of classical style: a phenomenon opposite in character and direction to that in the late pendentives, but just as permissible a sequel to the climax that had come before.

RAPHAEL, THE SEGNATURA PHASE

The Stanza della Segnatura.[149-74] The Sistine Ceiling is perhaps the highest and swiftest flight of spirit ever undertaken by an artist, and in the range of style it explores it may be the longest. In four-odd years of labor Michelangelo accomplished an evolution that embraced, in summary and essential terms, the possibilities of the classical style from a relatively elementary to an apparently final stage, and also tested its impossibilities. No development in any other artist is comparable to this one in succinctness in time and space. Yet the pattern of development is not unique, and though it was doubtless isolated in its process of generation within Michelangelo's mind, it was not historically isolated in contemporary Rome.

Essentially independently, owing only little to knowledge of Michelangelo's example, Raphael moved in a similar orbit through the development of a mature classical style: less high and swift, but in compensation investigating the regions through which it moved more broadly and more thoroughly. The distinction between Michelangelo's and Raphael's development depends not only on their different personality, and on their different quality and kind of genius but, as we have observed before, on the habit and aesthetic of their different métier: it is Raphael who explores the classical style in the more diffuse and more complicated range of the painter's problems.

At the beginning of their two great decorations the stage reached by Michelangelo and by Raphael in the development of a classical style is almost identical. In Michelangelo's first three panels of his Ceiling the description of nude forms is not different in degree of idealization, development of contrapposto movement, or even in sense of scale from the nudes in the rectangles of the ceiling of the Stanza della Segnatura. The time of execution must have been almost the same: Raphael had apparently begun to paint in the late *winter of 1508, and was engaged on his ceiling,[151-5] employing Sodoma as a collaborator, at least early into 1509. Even the Ignudi of the first bay of the Sistine do not develop in classicizing form or in articulation beyond the executioner of Raphael's *Judgment of Solomon*,[155] and it is only with the

Ignudi of the second bay that Michelangelo began to bypass Raphael in Michelangelo's own special competence, the description of the nude. The resemblance in the two ceilings between Raphael's personifications, in the large tondi, and the Seers of Michelangelo is obvious. Here, though Michelangelo's execution probably already slightly succeeds Raphael's completion of his ceiling, their figures are not different in stylistic kind, but Michelangelo's first Seers are more rigorous in degree of classicizing unity of form and in decisive integration of their movement.

There is even a resemblance of compositional character between the rectangles of Raphael's ceiling and the first two smaller panels of the Sistine, and this is a result of a momentary intersection, in the two artists, of sculptural and pictorial intent: in his rectangles, set for architectonic reasons on a mosaic-like gold background, Raphael's scenes assume a partial character as of relief. The system of painted architectural division of the ceiling of the Segnatura was not Raphael's invention but the preexisting work of Sodoma, but even this is not wholly without relation to Michelangelo's system of articulating the Sistine. Sodoma's scheme — in the conception of which it is not impossible that Bramante may have been involved — is based upon an interlocking of heavy additive elements, according to a mode that is still sensible as a substratum of Michelangelo's far more dynamic, unified design.

Beyond what he had inherited from Sodoma, the architectural preconditions of Raphael's decoration were as seemingly appropriate as possible to his own disposition of style, and perhaps even a factor in favoring its development. The Stanza della Segnatura was the antithesis in architectural form of the Sistine Chapel — which seems also, by good accident, to have been appropriate to Michelangelo. In its long and narrow form, the Sistine required an articulation into successive parts, and the resulting system could particularly be exploited to accommodate a population of sculpturesque forms; further, the dimension of his ceiling encouraged Michelangelo's expansion toward superhuman dimensions of form and content. Quite differently, the Stanza della Segnatura was a nearly cubical vaulted space, a compact central unit of stately but humanly comfortable scale; below the predetermined decoration on its ceiling it offered wide fields, set in balance opposite each other, of indivisible arched shape, each one inviting the projection of one large painting. Where, in the Sistine, the vast space between the spectator and the ceiling permitted its decoration, without sense of intrusion on the spectator, with a structure composed essentially of solids, the dimensions of the Segnatura encouraged an opposite, and for Raphael appropriately pictorial approach, of expansion of the architectural closure into space.

The given architectural substance of the Stanza was altogether such as to solicit, in the mind of a painter of mature classical disposition, a whole pictorial decoration that should conform to the internally balancing, centralized unity shaped by the walls themselves. The opportunity implicit in the architectural frame was not merely accepted but decisively exploited by Raphael; like Michelangelo in the Chapel, Raphael created a painted structure far more articulate than the actual Quattrocento space of its classical aesthetic potential. Each whole wall became, in Raphael's scheme, itself a centralized unit of scanned, controlled expansion into space: a unit that elaborates, extends, and concords with the given architectural form. Almost as much as the sculptural reference is pervasive in the Sistine Ceiling, so is the architectural reference of the pictorial form evident in the Segnatura. In Raphael's enrichment by fictitious architectonic spaces of the simple central structure of the actual room, its effect of form becomes profoundly like that of the contemporary conceptions (as for St. Peter's) of Bramante: the frescoed space becomes a domed quatrefoil, in which responsive curving movements are arranged into a central harmony.

The thematic material that was given Raphael for the decoration of the Segnatura was, even more than the fortunate accident of the given architecture, of a kind to stimulate a classicizing character of artistic thought. The identity of the author or authors of Raphael's iconography is not known; it is only sure that, unlike Michelangelo, Raphael did not command a culture sufficient to invent his themes or to conceive their symbolic associations. Raphael's problem, vast enough, was to translate a given program (perhaps already earlier invented for Sodoma) into its visible form. What he was called upon to translate was, in the style of its ideas, of one community with the principles of art that he had brought from Florence and which, in part from the stimulus of this program, he was to develop more fully in this place. Unlike the program of the Sistine, in which a classical cast of form and expression had been given to a profoundly Christian theme, the program of the Segnatura was, inversely, basically classicizing and only secondarily theological. Its content represents a culminating expression of the humanism of the Renaissance: the program for the Segnatura, produced in Julius' court, is as remarkable a landmark in the history of classicism within Christianity as is the form in which Raphael illustrated it.

The humanist inventors of the program considered, as their starting point, the functions of the room that was to be decorated. These seem, from old tradition, to have been two: this Stanza was apparently the meeting place of the papal tribunal of the *Segnatura*, usually presided over by the Pope in his role as chief officer of the canon and the civil law; and it seems also to have housed the personal library of the Pope, the visible evidence of his character as a Renaissance man of learning, and of his sympathy with humanist letters and Christian humanist philosophy. Both these functions, projections not only of a papal personality in general but of the particular personality of Pope Julius, were to be indicated in the Stanza, but the key to their union was sought by the humanists in the circumstance that was at once more personal to the Pope and most sympathetic to them: the role of the Stanza as Julius' library. The library was already a concrete expression of these functions, and to the Renaissance observer this was more immediately clear than now, from the habit of arranging libraries of the time according to "faculties," like those of the contemporary university. The Julian reference of the room led to the selection, as the thematic basis of the program, of those "faculties" which were pertinent to him, but these were in any case the ones of widest general significance: theology, law, philosophy (which included natural science), and arts (literary, not visual). These themes once selected, their specific origin, either in Pope Julius or his library, was mostly absorbed — characteristically for the High Renaissance mentality — in their possibilities for making of ideal generalization.

One wall was to be devoted to the description of each of these faculties, illustrated by a rich cast of historical characters brought together on an invented, but noble and meaningful pretext; the historical accent is more literal, but not more deeply felt, than in the Sistine. On the wall devoted to Theology [156] the invention is of an imaginary council of great defenders of the dogmas of the Roman Church, supervised by a heavenly senate of saints and prophets, and presided over by the Trinity. The subject of their disputation is the justification of the doctrine of transubstantiation: a theme at once vastly general in its central importance for Catholic theology, and also topical and personal in its reference to Julius' own veneration and defense of a then disputed article of belief. The wall opposite, which illustrates Philosophy,[163] is an ideal assembly of the great philosophers of the Ancient world, metaphysicians and scientists alike, led jointly by Plato and by Aristotle. In this juxtaposition of Christianity and pre-Christianity, one seeking revelation and the other possessed of it, there is an analogue, but in humanistic terms that are more respectful of the illumination of the Ancients, to the scheme of the whole Sistine Chapel. The wall to the right of the *School of Athens* illustrates the arts, chiefly literary, personified in a gathering of classical authors and of modern Italian humanists and poets.[159] Certainly, the inventors of this program must have been given the due compliment of a place in this Parnassian court, presided over by Apollo and his Muses. Finally, on the wall across the room the Law is represented.[170] On the lower portion of this wall, to either side of the separating window, are the historical foundations of civil and canon law, in the latter of which Julius acts the part of the giver of the Decretals, Gregory IX; and on the upper portion of the wall is the representation of the three virtues, Prudence, Temperance, and Fortitude, which complement the virtue of Justice.

These are the separate illustrations of the faculties, each one an ideal generalization of actors and of situations, but it is a much higher generalization at which the program aims. It intends to describe not only the dignity of each faculty, but their ideal community: their function in a unity which embraces the highest aspects of man's intellectual, spiritual, and social being. The order in which the scenes are placed upon the walls implies relations. Theology and Philosophy lie across from one another; contrasted, not as irreconcilable opposites but as the classicizing humanists saw them, as complementary avenues to truth: one by faith and spiritual revelation, the other by reason and observation. Poetry and the Arts, which men create by inspiration, contrast with but also complement the Law, which man administers by deliberation and by precedent. The different disciplines, and seemingly opposite ways in which men work within them, are matched and balanced to form together a unity of man's intellectual and spiritual endeavor. Reason and faith, discipline and inspiration, become four walls of one ideal temple of the human mind.

The ideal relation among the faculties on the walls is not only that of their complementary contrast, but of a still more positive association of ideas which is made between each faculty and its adjacent neighbor. Within each wall the actors are arranged in such fashion that those toward one half of the scene have a link in ideal character with those of the adjoining half of the next scene: so in the *School of Athens* [163] it is Plato and his disciples who stand toward the side of Parnassus, and Aristotle toward the Jurisprudence; on the wall of Justice it is the Civil Law that adjoins Philosophy, and the Canon Law that adjoins Theology; in the *Disputà* [156] St. Peter is on the side toward Law and the mystics and visionaries toward the side of Poetry; in the *Parnassus* [159] the Christian poets stand near Theology and the Ancient poets, for the most part, stand toward the *School of Athens.*

This association among the faculties is confirmed on the ceiling in an ideal demonstration which links them still more closely.[151] Between the four enthroned personifications of the faculties, and set at an angle equally between them, the four oblong paintings are so devised in subject as to refer to both faculties that they adjoin: their idea principally illustrates the faculty to the left, but also leads inescapably to that on the right. Between Theology and Justice the oblong painting shows the *Temptation of Adam*, which brought the Fall that made necessary the sacrifice of Christ commemorated in the Eucharist, the subject of the Disputation to the left below. Since this Fall brought a divine judgment upon man, it links the theme of Theology with that of Justice [153] on its right. Between Justice and Philosophy is the *Judgment of Solomon*,[155] the king who here acts in the roles both of philosopher and judge. Between Philosophy and Poetry [152] is an illustration of Astronomy, a branch of "natural" philosophy, in which there is implicit the Platonic doctrine of the harmony of the cosmos that is imitated in the harmonies of art, the "music of the spheres." Finally, completing the interlocking circle of ideas, the *Flaying of Marsyas*,[154] between Poetry and Theology, deals — at the most obvious level only of its meanings — with the double theme of art and the fatal consequence of a challenge of divine authority, implying the results of contest with the sacred dogma of the papal Church.

In the subjects on the walls there is the intellectual and spiritual sensation of ideas of grand dimension, set in complementary and elastic balance in respect to one another, and cohering into a synthetic whole. The analogue to the formal order Raphael creates upon the walls is obvious. In the ceiling scenes, as they take up one meaning and then, in continuity, project another, there is a yet more intimate relation to the way of working of the artist's forms. The scanned flow, as if in alternating current, of one theme into the next suggests the quality of a respiration, and its rhythm is like that of the measured cursive sequences that connect the painted forms; in the interlocking, literally in a circle, of ideas there is a unity no less compelling than in Raphael's groups and whole compositions. Such is the consonance of style of literary thought in the program of the Segnatura with Raphael's aesthetic that there must have come, from their reciprocal resonance, an effect which caused both to assume dimensions that either separately could not have had.

As with Michelangelo's Ceiling, the history of the Stanza della Segnatura is one of a continuous development in style which, in the whole extent of the High Renaissance, is less dynamic and internally consistent only than in the Sistine itself. As with Michelangelo's first contemporary efforts, Raphael's ceiling in the Segnatura refers back to his just prior experience in Florence, but at the same time initiates a new development. The designs of the larger panels in the ceiling are Raphael's own, except that Sodoma may have designed * (assuming an invention, before Raphael's coming, of the iconographic scheme), and more surely executed, the tondo that personifies Philosophy; Sodoma (or perhaps Peruzzi) may have helped only to execute the tondo of *Theology*. The tondi with *Poetry* and *Justice* are, however, entirely Raphael's own. The *Poetry*,[152] apparently the earlier of the two, is virtually interchangeable with the Florentine Madonnas of 1507 and early 1508: still Leonardesque in countenance, and not different in fluency of articulation of her posture from the *Madonna of the Baldacchino*.[60] The *Justice* [153] is already more advanced: not less graceful but more vigorous, unfolding her movement in a clearer geometry of cursive shapes, and in a more articulate movement in the space. Her technique of execution (and with it her modelling of form) is more sharp and clear, without the lingering *sfumato* imprecision that is in the *Poetry*. The *Justice*, in her new energy and decisiveness, has the incipient accent of Raphael's Roman style.

The oblong scenes diverge still more from Raphael's Florentine past. In three of them the dominant formal matter is the nude, evidently influenced by a study of Ancient sculpture for which there had been no stimulus and no occasion in Florence. In expertness of description of musculature and in freedom of movement the figures far exceed the only comparable forms of the Florentine period, those in the *Entombment.*[59] Among these scenes there is also a development in energy and fluidity of articulation: from the figures of the *Marsyas,*[154] too literal in their imitation of the stressed musculature of late Antiquity, and yet a little languid, to the smoother and less planar postures of the *Fall*, and finally to the swift, wholly unlabored spatial energy of the Executioner in the *Judgment of Solomon.*[155] In these anatomies, under the stimulus of his first close contact with Ancient art, Raphael completed an aspect of his education, only now — but so very quickly — learning the lesson of convincing expressive manipulation of the human body, not ordinarily required of him in the religious pictures he had done in Florence. Further, these scenes on the ceiling, even in their limited dimension, were Raphael's first attempts (except for the misfire of the Borghese altar and some still earlier predelle) at narrative communication.

The painting of the ceiling was a necessary prelude to the major decoration of the Stanza. Beyond the opportunity offered on the ceiling to acquire some mastery of the technique of fresco it was only on the ceiling that Raphael finally attained the capacity, so necessary to the works to come, to make the human form articulate an active human situation. Equally important, the time occupied on the ceiling was a necessary interval in which Rome, Ancient and Julian, aesthetic and literary, could make its decisive impress on the spirit of the artist who, until recently, had been a painter of pictures of Christian devotion for a cultured, but mostly mercantile, Florentine society. By the time Raphael began his paintings of the walls he was possessed by the exalting knowledge of Rome and by the disposition to think and feel — as Michelangelo, by longer Roman experience, as well as private temper, felt already — nobly and universally. What came to happen on the walls of the Stanza della Segnatura is more than a logical development from what we know of Raphael's art before; it is the result of a dramatic magnification, in his new environment, of his personality.

Raphael's first painting on the wall, begun probably fairly early in 1509, was the illustration of Theology.[156-8] This scene is conceived as if it were at once an ideal council of the Church, in which its divine and mortal members are gathered to argue and approve the doctrine of transubstantiation, and a symbolic celebration of the Mass; the Eucharist upon the altar is the central object of the energies of the council just as it is the central object of the Mass. It is fixed precisely on the middle axis of the picture and it is upon this object, so small in size but of such vast spiritual meaning, that all the rest of the design focuses. Above and to both sides of the Eucharist the mortal disputants and holy witnesses are disposed in simple, grandly sweeping semicircles which extend, into the depth of the picture, the shape of the arched wall. Higher in the picture is a third and smaller semicircle made of angels and of seraphim, close-packed in upward-rising tiers. The sequence of semicircles, each dense with figures, instantly suggests an effect as of an architecture, like the apsidal half-dome of a church. Exploiting the arched shape of the wall itself, Raphael has conceived an inspired intersection between form and meaning. From the figures who attend the symbolic Mass he has built an apse to house the Eucharist and the altar on which it stands, making a church more perfect in its substance than any architecture of stone, out of the divine Persons, the Prophets and Apostles, and the wisest of God's theologians.

The development of compositional form and the integration with it of meaning of idea is at a level that makes insignificant the obvious ancestry of the design in such an early monument of classical style as Bartolommeo's *Judgment*,[21] or in Raphael's own Perugian fresco of S. Severo. The living architecture of this fresco has a clarity, harmony and spaciousness, as well as a sense of scale, like that of an actual architecture; but this painted structure has the flexibility, unarchitectural, of the vital beings out of which it has been made. The great curves echo and reecho in a grandiose accord; but while, in one sense, they repeat each other, in another sense they are at the same time resiliently opposed. Throughout the composition each curve converges meaningfully toward the Eucharist, and every balance swings from it as from a pivot: upon the mute symbol of the Mystery are concentrated not only the spiritual energies of the actors but the formal energies of the design.

As in a real architecture, the solids of the composition here not only shape but give aesthetic personality to the space that they enclose. The unpopulated spaces of the picture have become an aesthetic agent on a scale, and with an emphasis, that, in Fra Bartolommeo's *Judgment*, had been no more than hinted at. The space has not only the accustomed effects of a perspective structure (here still traditional and conservative) but is informed with the animation of the solids that surround and define it. There is no longer, in this space, the quattrocentesque contrast between solids and a measured void but a unity in which space, itself inspired with personality, acts in flexible and complementary concert with the solid forms. This system, expressed for the first time on monumental scale in the *Disputà*, is the normative solution to the problem in classical pictorial style of relation between substances and spaces; it is a mature midstage in a historical evolution in which Leonardo's *Adoration* [3] and *Last Supper* [12] stand at one end and, as we shall see, Raphael's Tapestry Cartoons at another.

The figures who populate this structure have grown in scale beyond those of Raphael's style in Florence and beyond those, also, of the ceiling; they are as if magnified to accord with the grandeur of the formal and ideal scheme in which they act. Most of the figures tend toward slightly but perceptibly heavier proportion than before, which is supported by a more generous amplitude of drapery. The movement of the body is explicit in articulation in the precise way that Raphael had learned in course of painting of the ceiling, and the draperies are so manipulated as to increase the breadth and clarity of the body's action. The full form and movement of the persons of the *Disputà* conveys, as Raphael's actors rarely had before, a deliberation, a decorum, and even a stateliness that reflects, but even more ennobles, the ideal of behavior of the classicizing Roman court.

The dignity and Roman sense of decorum in these figure types is new, but the way in which Raphael works with them still depends, even specifically, on lessons learned from Leonardo. The *Disputà* is in a way a fulfillment of ideas first stated in the *Adoration of the Magi*, and several motives indicate that its model was still influential upon Raphael. The left figures of the fresco's lower range [157] particularly recall the by now ancient, but inexhaustible, precedent: there is the same preoccupation as in Leonardo with the differentiation of complementary ideal types, and with the diversifying of expression within a general ideal mood. What Leonardo demonstrates in the *Adoration* in a — by comparison — too tightly interwoven texture is here sorted out into a wonderful lucidity of the component parts.

This process of internal clarifying is in no sense achieved at the expense of the coherence of the whole; it is no more than a function of the whole new power of clarity in Raphael's gestalt. Each individual figure is welded into ineluctable association with its group; and in the group its single parts are bound into a formal and expressive chord of which the resonance is much more than the result of the addition of its parts. As with the figures that compose it each group is distinguished from, yet inescapably associated with the next to make, again, a finally inclusive chorded harmony of whole design.

Within each group Raphael's principle of assembly is, at once, an extension of the principle of counterpoise in harmony, which shapes the posture of the single figure, and a reflection of the synthesis of complementaries which, in ideas of content as well as form, controls the decoration in its entirety. Each posture is related in a rhythmic sequence to the next, and at the same time may be complementary in movement, mass, and place in space. Each group contains, in the meaning of bodily action, in types and in expression of face, a similar interwoven play of complementaries. The relation among groups extends the same conception, of connecting sequences and simultaneous complementary variation of the general idea of form and mood. In the ordering of groups still other considerations are taken into account: of relation not only to the adjacent group but to the countering, other, half of the balancing design and, almost a primary consideration, the expressive function of the group in the development of the picture's whole communicative sense. So in the *Disputà*, in its actively expressive lower range, among those figures who are (unlike the divinely knowledgeable Senate) the "disputants," there is a succession of diverse states of energy and gravity in the groups that move from left to right and inward toward the altar; on the right [158] there is a slower and more even-tempered progress, of figures almost in columnar sequence, which brings the movement of design to rest; here the articulation into groups is not so scanned or so precise.

It is in this manipulation of a multitude into a differentiated harmony of form and expression that Raphael does, in extent and in terms of quality, what neither he nor any of his predecessors in the painting of the classical style had done before. Conspicuously, the *Disputà* achieves that which Michelangelo, in his contemporary first stories of the Sistine Ceiling, had attempted unsuccessfully to do and then abandoned. Moreover, even in Michelangelo's own special domain of expressive working with the human form, there is no measurable difference at this stage (probably late in 1509) in the evolution of resources of a classical figure style. In the *Disputà* the compact, spatially developed figure of St. Augustine's scribe is a form at once as unified and as internally complex as is the *Delfica*; the "Bramante" in the foremost group at left is as handsomely counterpoised and as expressive as Michelangelo's *Isaiah*, and perhaps more expressive than the *Joel* whom, in features, he resembles; Raphael's *St. John Baptist* is almost as easy in his pose as the Ignudi of the Sistine's third bay; and the quiet-gesturing, erect figure at the middle left is as classically recollective in his posture, quite as monumental, and of not less grave a grace, than are the sons of Noah. In all but the magnitude of form and feeling that is Michelangelo's alone, Raphael's contemporary figures are as eloquent as his in the language of the classical style; and Raphael's development in this respect is as surely independent at this date of Michelangelo as is his remarkable development of composition, in which Michelangelo could offer no aid or example.

The compositional ingenuity that had conceived the idea of exploiting the shape of the wall in the *Disputà* to make of it the basis for a churchly apse is no less demonstrated in the second fresco of the Segnatura, the *Parnassus*,[159-62] executed probably in 1510. Here the misfortune of the irregular arched space into which the window juts from below is converted to positive advantage: on and around the intruding window Raphael built the hill of his Parnassus. In this poetic assembly the atmosphere is different from that of the theological gathering in the *Disputà*. Where the *Disputà* evokes a muted and solemn, appropriately celebrant, ardor the *Parnassus* is more lyrically warm, as if in recreation of the atmosphere of a poet's vision of Antiquity. In Raphael's longer residence in Rome, now, he has been exposed successfully to its climate of literary classicism, but it is more than the subject matter of this fresco that suggests the flavor of an Ancient classical world. The figures of the *Parnassus* have the accent of an archaeological experience, of Raphael's study in Antiquity of visible analogues of his own classical style. The Muses of the fresco [160] reflect this experience with something of the excess of enthusiasm of a novelty: they are reconstructions, in Raphael's most sophisticated current vocabulary, of the sensuous beauty of Ancient classical images, exaggerating (far beyond what is in this case the identifiable and rather insignificant precise Antique source) generic classicizing characteristics of almost arbitrary perfection of shape and musically cursive sequences of form.

Not only the Muses but all the inhabitants of Parnassus are more classically conceived than the actors of the *Disputà*, not merely in their imitative Antique cast of drapery and accessories but in the more essential fact of a yet fuller amplitude of form and graver dignity of posture and of movement. The *Sappho*,[161] who introduces us into this intended reconstruction of an Antique world, summarizes the grander classicism of figure style in the *Parnassus*. Her body is a more plastically ample, richly rounded presence, composed of suave sequences of rhythm. Her movement is a fullest development of contrapposto, slow and easy, yet instinct with latent strength — an impeccable meshing and balancing of muted energy with rich substance. She makes a spatial arabesque of such beauty as before — and only shortly before — only the figures of Leonardo's third *St. Anne* had achieved, and then not with the classical accent of sensuous splendor and Antique recall of this Raphaelesque form. Measured against the contemporary accomplishment of the Sistine, the Sappho seems a synthesis of Sibyl and Ignudo.

In the position of the Sappho Raphael exploits the awkward given shape of wall with quasi-illusionistic intention, more assertive than in the "Bramante" who plays a comparable role of introduction in the *Disputà*. As with the "Bramante," the movement of the Sappho is directly integrated into a group, here of poets whose measured dignity of stance complements and compensates the variety of her posture. As in the *Disputà*, this leftward and forward group is distinctly articulated from the group that next succeeds. The internal order of this second group is an inversion of the Sapphic group, beginning with the figure of the Ennias — so Ignudo-like — which echoes and varies, in reverse, the figure of the Sappho. The group of Apollo and his Muses is of singular melodiousness, visibly expressing in its form the suave music diffused through it from Apollo's viol. This melodic line rests in the figure of the last Muse at the right; it then turns gently to descend the slope, moving in accelerating cadence through the figures of this part of the company of poets. Altogether the movement of the composition has a measure of variety — a close-textured alternation of rich arabesque and yielding pause — that is in every way more developed than in the *Disputà.* Again as in the *Disputà,* but with more decisiveness, the figures at the rightward and forward side of the design act to connect their ideal realm and the spectator's space. The principal form here, that of the aged poet, is the complement of the Sappho in sex, age, in compact and forceful shape, and in the direction of his movement; he leads us back to our reality as Sappho led us beyond it.

The *School of Athens* [163-7] (executed probably from late 1510 through mid-1511) also reconstructs an Antique world, but in a mood unlike that of the *Parnassus,* not golden and sensuously warm but crystalline: an atmosphere of high clear thought pervaded by the energies of powerful intelligence. The architecture sets the temper of the scene; Bramantesque, but with a stricter accent than in his actual architecture of recollective classicism, it creates a stage for the figures that is of lucid order and extraordinary breadth. Its harmony and vastness is not only the frame for its inhabitants but the symbol of the intellectual structure they have built; this man-made architecture contrasts in form and in idea with the fictive heavenly architecture of the *Disputà.* Within this structure, upon the various levels of its deep foreground space, Raphael distributes its population of philosophers in a scheme that absorbs the experience both of the *Parnassus* and the *Disputà*: it has an internal variety still greater than that of one and the final grandiose stability of the other. By comparison with this fresco the design of the *Disputà* seems stilted; the basic harmony of structure, broader and deeper than that of the *Disputà,* has been immeasurably enriched from within.

The ordnance of the actors of the *School of Athens,* like that of the architecture which supports them, is according to a central scheme. Plato and Aristotle,[164] framed by the diminishing sequence of perspective arches, are the focus of this scheme: in them the axes of the composition intersect and on them the orthogonals of the architecture converge. On both sides of their slow-gesturing, majestic forms the other figures expand in counterpoised, but not symmetrical, waves of movement which accelerate in energy as they descend, in a curving and centralizing embrace, toward the front. Unlike the *Disputà,* where the apsidal design frames, but does not enclose space, this figure composition is developed in ground plan so as virtually to surround a central spatial core; this ground plan not only echoes, loosely, the visible system of the Bramantesque architecture to the rear but that of the central ordnance of the entire decoration of the room: it suggests a quatrefoil in shape. The space thus defined by the figures is not only more inclusively and more articulately shaped than in the *Disputà* but there is also here, in comparison with the *Disputà,* a freer and more vigorous intermingling between the figures and the space. Far more than in the *Disputà,* the space of the *School of Athens* is permeated by the higher and more various energies of the figures, and shows the more complex plasticity of their distribution and their individual design. As in the *Disputà,* this space that is shaped by the figures is accompanied by a traditional and conventional space of Quattrocento perspective and both spaces, that formed by the figures and that made by the setting in perspective, are much more effectively combined. The space of the architecture and that of the figures wholly interpenetrate, and reciprocally magnify each other.

Not only in the *School of Athens* but in the antecedent frescoes color serves, beyond its multiplicity of other purposes, to help define the unity of forms and space. Earlier, in Florence, Raphael's color had no particular aesthetic individuality: it had been the least meditated aspect of his art in those years of research toward acquisition of a classical form, and had indeed been thought of as a secondary, surface, property of form — much according to the Peruginesque tradition, and not much distinguished from it in palette. A new restraint in use of hues, and their moderation in a Leonardesque *sfumato* — but not according to consistent principle — had been the extent of Raphael's accommodation, in color, to a Cinquecento taste. In the course of painting of the Stanze, however, color assumes a role of a quite different power. It still is not — as in contemporary Venice — coeval in the artist's thought with form, but it is no longer only a descriptive, pattern-making adjunct, overlaid upon the plastic form; it becomes, from the moment of beginning painting — as distinguished from the preparatory drawing work — an indissoluble function of the process of thinking of design.

In the *Disputà* the most apparent hues are those of complementary blues and yellow-golds; secondary to these, and interwoven with them, are near-complementaries of muted reds and greens; and, as if deduced from these first two categories of hue, are extensions of them into softened violets, oranges and browns, rounding out almost the whole resource of the color circle. In the *Disputà* the blues and yellows are quite dominating; the secondary and tertiary colors make variety, but no equivalence in whole effect to them. In the *Parnassus,* however, red and violet hues, and greens (some of draperies, but mostly in the landscape), emerge to equal strength beside the blues and golds. There are no dominants, but a richly differentiated, warm accord, as fluent in passage from one hue to the next as are the rhythmic sequences of forms, and indissoluble from them.

In the *School of Athens* the basic hues are not more varied, but they are differentiated further, and with more sophistication. The resources of this fresco include admixtures of reflected color, strong *changeants,* and subtlest off-whites; the range that color has explored is much more extensive. Furthermore, the greens, which in the *Parnassus* had been — somewhat recessively — used mostly in the landscape, are now prominent among the draperies. The hues, of primaries and their subtler derivations, are interwoven in a single coloristic tissue, within which the amount used of each hue has been calculated, in intensity and in demand it makes upon the viewer's eye, to be equal to that of each other hue. There are no dominants, but also, in the weaving into one another of the hues, no conflicts; the result is an extensive and inclusive harmony, of richest internal variation, entirely a counterpart to the harmony of the substantial forms.

But the precise use of hues intends, in the *School of Athens,* even more than this: the color also has a major function in the definition of the picture space. It is this function that determines, in the — at first — seemingly aesthetically arbitrary distribution of the painting's hues, where the main loci of hue are to go (from which, then, their connections and differentiations have been woven). Raphael has evolved a system — certainly never thought out to this degree before — which is based upon the assertive or recessive "personality" of hues, and uses them according to this system to articulate his space; this is beyond the customary atmospheric diminution of intensities which, even in this compass of the *School of Athens*, helps to this same end. The blues, relating to the sky seen in the distance through the architecture, articulate sequences of recession among the figures into space; the yellow-golds establish contrary, forward, sequences of movement. The hues of red and darker violet (related to the color of the pattern on the floor) are deliberately inert, stable, spatial loci. Among these spatially articulating hues, the greens are threaded almost in the manner of a lace, not differentiating space but, conversely, making binding continuity within it.

These spatial functions of the distinct hues are analytically separable, but their working is entirely synthetic. No less in this respect than in others of the color pattern, the single hues are inextricably woven into one another: in the whole fresco, in the groups, and even, in one critically demonstrative place, within a single figure. The philosopher who stands in contrapposto in the left foreground fulfills, all at once, three spatial functions within what is, so to speak, also a contrapposto of color in his draperies: that of fixed locus in the red of his lower garment, of forward inclination in his golden-yellow shirt, and of impulse toward the rear in his blue skirt and mantle. And as each hue within this figure answers to its like in figures elsewhere in the space, and this same attraction between concords, or complementaries, is multiplied throughout the fresco's entire color scheme, the effect the plastic forms already make sufficiently, of charged intervals among them, is still more increased, and with it the sense of a whole vibrant integer of presence.

In the *School of Athens*, the inheritance of the quattrocentesque concept of perspective space, and Raphael's new concept, of a space made by the figures, work in reinforcing concord and in balance. What Raphael has here first realized so profoundly as a space of figures is, however, distinct in fundamental principle from a perspective system. The space made by perspective may be described as the Early Renaissance's rationalization of an experience of space still based on that of medieval art: perspective serves to rationalize a hitherto unmeasurable, or infinite, continuum. The apprehension of the measurement of space was accompanied by that of the measurement of solids; these were concurrent and consistent, but not synthesized apprehensions. The substances were inserted in the space as loci of the geometrically defined continuum: this projection of consonant but separate experiences, of void and solid, was suspended in an abstract harmony in the reticule of perspective. In this system, as Alberti had defined it, the construction of the stage preceded the setting on it of the players.

As, in the course of the Renaissance, a differently integral, vital sense of human substance was evolved, culminating in the first expressions of High Renaissance classical figure style, it became increasingly less possible to conceive space only as a preexistent geometric void. Figures of the new kind, as they developed in this mature phase of classical style, came to move in three dimensions into the air around them, charging it with the emanation of their energies. Space, not only in the intervals between such figures but in the immediate ambience even of a single one of them is no longer precedent to substance or distinct from it: the figure creates space around itself, and in groups and compositions, shapes it. Shaped and charged by the enclosing substances (and in itself observed, in the new style, as mobile textured atmosphere) the space becomes not measured void but a palpable phenomenon: a plastically responsive aether. It is an extension and accessory function of the solid forms, and in this sense, in the *School of Athens*, space and substance have become parts of an experiential unity.

The conception of substance and of its effect on immediately adjacent space is like that in the Ancient classic style, but no Antique work we know controls so wide and continuous an environment as is in the *School of Athens* with its sense of consistent and connected unity; to achieve this it is precisely the experience of Early Renaissance perspective command over void that must be presupposed. The spatial structure of the *School of Athens* is, like almost every other aspect of High Renaissance classicism, distinct from Antique analogue and synthesizes classical rediscovery with the consequence, however transformed, of an ultimately medieval, Christian apprehension of the world.

All this inner unity of space in Raphael's fresco has only limited relation, either by figural devices or perspective, with the space in which the spectator stands. As Leonardo had defined it first, this projection of an ideal world is distinct from ours; it is an accessible but discrete unity. What is in the *School of Athens* as a spatial structure is a synthetic equilibrium, of perspective inheritance and new classical invention of space shaped by substance; we have observed already that the new classical component was destined to increase its role. At the climax of Raphael's development of classicism it would not only eclipse the other; more than this, the sense and the authority of substance, as such, would virtually extinguish even the ancillary function, in design, of space. But now, in this fresco, Raphael has evolved a solution, in terms of purely pictorial aesthetic, of the working of space and substances that is as inaccessible to the sculptural mentality of Michelangelo as it had been to the mind of classical Antiquity.

The new component in the spatial mechanism of the *School of Athens* is, as we have suggested, a consequence of the matured High Renaissance classical conception of the human form. In this fresco, this conception has evolved still more; while part of its population is not different from the actors of the *Parnassus* its most prominent figures, those in the foreground, have once more been magnified in their dimension. These figures in particular,[165-6] but also almost all the others in the painting, are possessed by an energy which now by far exceeds that of the persons of the *Disputà*; they move in, and occupy, space with powerful assertiveness. Because each form is in itself so much developed plastically their gathering together into groups is now more elaborately articulated: to accommodate their spatial movement the enclosing group becomes at once more open within itself and more deep; more than in the *Parnassus* or the *Disputà* we are aware, in the groups of the *School of Athens*, of their expansion as if toward the imaginary fullness of a sphere. Like the organization of the whole compositional structure, that of its parts is more than before spatially inclusive and expansive.

As is necessary in the classical proposition, the growth of human form is not a growth of physical dimension only; it is equally a growing of the power of spiritual sensation. The size and breadth of action of the figures answers to their grander and more vital energies of mind. Furthermore, these states of mind, as the faces show them, are not only stronger than in the preceding frescoes but also more explicitly defined; and the body also, in its classical function of interpenetration with the spirit, is much more explicitly articulate than before of its content. What Raphael achieves in the figures of the *School of Athens* represents a measurably higher development of classical style. Where, however, in the two earlier frescoes it could be asserted that his development in figure style was, in all but force and magnitude, proceeding *pari passu* with that of Michelangelo, it is now evident that the contemporary accomplishment of Michelangelo in 1511 has explored possibilities of classical figure style that Raphael has not approached. This is despite the fact that in the *School of Athens* it becomes for the first time certain that Raphael has studied the Sistine Ceiling, perhaps at first in its half-completed state at the end of 1510.

There is nothing among the figures of the second plan of Raphael's fresco that is not wholly understandable as a consequence of his prior evolution, but the figures of the foreground, exactly those in which he shows himself the most advanced, demand knowledge of Michelangelesque precedent. The *Pythagoras* at the left — still, like the figures just behind him, reminiscent of the models of Leonardo — most strongly shows community with the Sistine Seers; in their developed musculature, complex postures, and extraordinary articulateness of body the youths around Euclid to the right are indebted to the Prophets and Ignudi both. It is the so-called *Heraclitus*,[167] the *Pensieroso* in the center foreground of the fresco (unforeseen in the original cartoon in the Ambrosiana),[168-9] who is most exactly dependent on the Ceiling. This figure, a compound of Michelangelo's *Isaiah* and *Jeremiah*, and so strangely like Michelangelo himself in features and in dress, was added only at the end of painting of the *School of Athens*, after it had been quite finished according to the cartoon. In freedom and immediacy of expressive technique it is advanced much beyond the other figures in its neighborhood. It surely succeeds, in time of conception and in execution, the first official unveiling of the Sistine Ceiling in August 1511.

This addition was provoked by more, however, than a wish to emulate Michelangelo's recent remarkable accomplishment in figure style; it is even more important for its meaning, purely Raphaelesque, within the composition. The *Heraclitus* literally rounds out, to fullness and near-spherical closure, the fresco's spatial scheme and serves in the composition as a final unifying key: it is, almost, a fulcrum for the several parts of the design. Before its meaning of relation to Michelangelo, this figure must be thought of in its significance of a correction to and further fulfillment of the classical character of Raphael's original design, a correction conceived by Raphael as the fruit of his own development in the interval between invention and completion of the fresco; in this sense it has nothing to do with Michelangelo. It is, however, in this figure that Raphael comes closest to — but yet does not achieve — the sense of scale and of expressive vibrance in the single human figure that is demonstrated by the Michelangelo of this time. The imitation must remain approximate, for it is not motivated, nor inhabited, by the inimitable power of Michelangelo's ideas.

Confined within a less exalted spiritual limit, Raphael's conception of individual humanity does not trespass, even with Michelangelo's guidance, beyond what may be described (in terms of Michelangelo's own development) as a median of idealization. The species of humanity to which Raphael's actors belong, here at his absolute attainment of artistic maturity in the *School of Athens*, is that which Michelangelo had created in the bays of his Ceiling which just precede, but do not quite include, the *Creation of Adam*. However, what may be lacking in concentrated force of each human image is compensated for in Raphael by his quantitative variety of images. Harmonized into a community by their ideal reformation — but a reformation based on their wide, actual, human diversity — the actors of the *School of Athens* represent a concept of mankind much less austere and exclusive than Michelangelo's, but far richer. Like Leonardo before him the mature Raphael continues to believe in the function of art as comment on the multiform experience of the world. Where Michelangelo's art is the expression of an isolated psyche, and his creatures in the Sistine images of man in an essential isolation, the *School of Athens* — and the frescoes of the Segnatura in general — are the expression less of man as an individuality than of the community of men: representations of the greatness that men attain and promote in social concourse.

In the close-woven texture that Raphael makes of this concourse of humanity he exploits a range and kind of orchestration, both of form and of expression, that is closed to Michelangelo. The sum of this pictorial texture is greater than that of its human parts: the single figures may not rise beyond, or even to the standard of Michelangelo's median in the Sistine, but the aesthetic and contentual measure of the whole is not less nobly ideal. More than Michelangelo's pictured world — superb in both senses of the word; too high, too private and too terrible to imply practical example — the world projected here by Raphael conveys an ethic as well as aesthetic sense; here the beautiful is identified with human good.

The *Virtues*[171] of the last wall of the Segnatura,[170] executed in the latter half of 1511, are as broadly and boldly painted as the *Heraclitus*, and as certainly as he conceived under the influence of the newly unveiled Sistine. The *Virtues* reflect, even more than the *Heraclitus*, Michelangelo's later canon of proportion — like that, for example, in the *Persica*: small-headed and mighty-limbed. In Raphael's figures, their effect of monumentality is increased by his consideration of relation of the figures to the spectator's point of view (a concern which Michelangelo's abstracting mentality is hardly willing even to entertain), setting their vast forms in slight *sotto in su*. The actions of the *Virtues* are as much developed in complexity of contrapposto as the later Seers but their movements, for all their fullness and variety, are in no sense of comparably intense energy. They are not conceived as single images, of isolated concentration, like the Seers; their action is not self-contained but passed beyond the limits of each single form into the complex of their composition. That composition, in the *Virtues*, is conditioned as nowhere before in Raphael by their Michelangelesque dimension; the design is grandiose beyond that of any of the groups of the *School of Athens*, with heavier, full-sweeping, turning cadences. However, the basic temper of design remains inalterably Raphaelesque; the reflection of Michelangelo's power serves to strengthen and deepen Raphael's suavity and meditated grace. Raphael is not tempted by Michelangelo's example into the dangerous and for him unreachable exaltations of the last phases of the Sistine. There does not emerge from the *Virtues*, any more than from the *School of Athens*, the sense of an expansion that, as in those last Sistine bays, strains beyond the evident meaning of the subject of the scene.

The difference in the flexibility of Raphael's artistic aspirations and those of the contemporary Michelangelo is demonstrated most of all in the two scenes that complete the decoration of the wall below the *Virtues of Justice*, the giving over of the Canon and of the Civil Law. In these scenes, presented in a traditional perspective of illusion and conceived as an assembly of portraits, there is a frank descent toward naturalism, impossible to Michelangelo in this degree. Both frescoes of the Law are intended to suggest an almost informal glimpse into a current actuality, as if we should look at happenings and persons truly present in a space extended from that of the room. The historical reference in these scenes is almost altogether submerged in their intention of actuality. Lighting as well as perspective, and the informality of compositional management support the effect of illusion, which is confirmed finally by the portraits.

The fresco of the *Canon Law*[172] is the more successful: later wear and restoration, and the hand of an assistant, probably Penni, have obscured Raphael's intention only in part, toward the right portion of the painting. The *Civil Law*[173] is not, in its present state, an altogether comprehensible document: what is now visible is not a finished work. Whether through initial incompletion or through subsequent loss, all that remains of this painting is its preparation in *buon fresco*; the modelling and the working of details *a secco*, usual in most of the figures of this Stanza, is lacking almost altogether. Contrary to a present current of critical opinion which identifies this preparation as being wholly by Guillaume Marcillat (here working as Raphael's assistant) the character of handling and drawing at least of some forms is not dissimilar, or different in quality, from what is visible of Raphael's first preparations on the wall in the *School of Athens*. The character of lighting in the *Civil Law*, intendedly illusionistic, also more than adequately transcribes — even in its present state — the intention of Raphael's brilliant sketch for it in Frankfort.

The portraits in the *Canon Law* are particularly striking in their frank primary interest in the picture; but they are not different in character from those which Raphael had inserted as occasional elements within the larger frescoes of the room. These portraits throughout the Stanza della Segnatura are collectively far more significant as evidence of Raphael's accomplishment in portraiture than the few isolated easel portraits of his preceding Florentine, or even of the present phase. Beginning not so much with those in the *Disputà* as with the portraits of contemporaries in *Parnassus*,[162] there is a sharpening of characterization and a decisiveness in rendering of form which makes the Doni portraits, for example, seem somewhat tentative.

In the portraits of the Stanza della Segnatura Raphael arrives at an effective, though not necessarily exclusive, solution of the problem of a classical portrait style, and the problem is no longer, as it had been in the Doni portraits, posed in Leonardesque terms: of compromise between the data of nature and an ideal preference of form. The portraits of the *Parnassus*, of the *School of Athens* and the *Decretals* are as effectively accurate as records of appearance as are the portraits by the realist painters of the later Quattrocento. Features are not reshaped ideally: the contrast, in the *Parnassus* in particular, between the represented and invented faces is in instances almost diametric. Raphael accepts the Quattrocento's proposition of an inalterable visual identity of the portrait subject. But what he does in the process of his representing this visible identity gives it a new function of artistic style. Raphael clarifies the geometry he finds implicit in the form of whole head and of features of the sitter, and in a measure summarizes their appearance from the actuality. He does this not with any Leonardo-like intention of beautifying the appearance, but to make it yet more cogent and impactful of its peculiar identity of form. The head is transcribed as a unit of emphatic, including, plastic form within which the features take their place as clear articulating parts. The aesthetic value that these images achieve, regardless of the beauty or the absence of it in the sitter, is not a consequence, as in the imagined faces, of any artificial harmony of parts but of the sense of forceful clarity in shaping of the form. This aesthetic value heightens and purifies, and adds its vitality, to the expression of the given human visage.

Into his portraits, furthermore, Raphael inserts a quality of content as clear and as precisely articulate as is his perception of the form. His persons are alive with keen communicative intelligence, yet decorously restrained in their relation with us: the emotions they express are those which are proper to intelligent, agreeable and well-bred social concourse; their sensations are of personalities in harmonious adjustment with their society and their selves. In the heads of the contemporaries in the Stanza della Segnatura (much more explicitly than among the imagined personalities) this adjustment is characterized as being a function of a wonderfully aware intelligence. In biographical terms, these portraits symbolize the way in which the high classical culture of Julian Rome is intellectually willed and intellectually achieved. It goes without saying that the state of mind and the character of behavior of these persons, as Raphael represents them, is in part a fiction: but it is a fiction contrived by the artist and by his contemporaries jointly and endorsed by them. It is in the guise of what they would be that Raphael's friends inhabit the frescoes of the Segnatura, as participants in an ideal world which projects their ambition for their own.

The main frescoes of the walls of the Stanza della Segnatura were completed before November 1511, but there then still remained to be done much if not all of the ornamentation of the lower walls, in grisaille and grotesquerie, which was necessary to complete the decoration of the room. The system of this secondary ornamentation, and much of its detail, depended on indications given by Raphael probably in 1511 but its precise preparation and its execution seem to have been left in charge of Penni; he is responsible for the definitive preparatory drawings (Oxford and Haarlem), as well as for the execution, of the two grisaille pictures of fair size beneath the fresco of *Parnassus*.[174] From the presence of the motto of Leo X among the ornaments in the embrasures of the windows it is certain that the execution of the accessory decoration of this Stanza continued into 1513, when Raphael himself was already well advanced in the painting of the next room.

As a system of decorative ornament Raphael's scheme is not new; there is no single element within it — in the grisaille paintings imitative of reliefs of marble or of bronze, or in the grotesquerie — which is separately an innovation. Precedents are numerous and immediate, particularly in the Roman decorations of Pinturicchio and his school. The effect of Raphael's ornamental scheme is nevertheless quite different from that of its predecessors. The single forms of which it is composed are in themselves, even in the execution of assistants, of mature classical character: their combinations into patterns, of false relief or of grotesque, is richly rounded and in deliberately cadenced rhythm. Like the Leonine motto they enclose these grotesques are *suave*, rather than thin, linear and astringent like their Pinturicchiesque antecedents. The temper and cadence of Pinturicchio's mode of ornament is altered by Raphael into an appropriate complement of his larger fresco style, and it is a complement not without importance. It is on this carefully ordered yet pervasive ornament that the final effect of decorative opulence of the room depends, and from it is completed the sense of measured luxury that so fitly frames the presence, within and before the frescoes, of the Julian court.

Works Contemporary with the Stanza della Segnatura. From the moment he undertook the painting of the Stanza della Segnatura Raphael was committed to a career as a decorator on large scale. Until the end of his life his major effort and his most significant expressions, with a few superb exceptions, were to be in this field. Quite opposite to his previous Florentine phase, the measure of Raphael's art in Rome cannot be taken from his easel pictures, of which his production, especially during the time of his largely unassisted painting of the Stanza della Segnatura, is understandably much diminished.

The earliest certain Roman one among his easel paintings, the *Madonna di Casa Alba* (Washington, National Gallery; almost surely contemporary with the *Disputà*)[175] is still, in technique and in finish, as precise as the easel paintings of the years in Florence. Its composition, furthermore, depends on Florentine experience: a combination of Leonardesque and Michelangelesque motives made by Giovanni Francesco Rustici for a tondo sculpture is, probably, the source of Raphael's idea for his design (Hauptmann). In every other way, however, the *Madonna di Casa Alba* asserts its Roman time of origin. The household mood of the Florentine Madonnas, intimate and charming, has been replaced by a profounder pathos; all three persons of this picture — the Infants included — are, as it were, emotionally more mature. The conception reaches toward a different dimension of meaning than that of the Florentine Madonnas. It is grave and strong in feeling and in action as they had not been. As in the finest figures of the *Disputà*, the posture of the Madonna Alba makes visible the controlled passion of her state of mind and bespeaks her power, as well as grace, of form.

Of the few other Madonna compositions invented by Raphael during the time of the Segnatura only one survives that is of unequivocal originality: the monumental *Madonna di Foligno* (Rome, Vatican Museum),[177] executed almost certainly in the course of 1511. Despite its monumental size the *Foligno* altar is not so nearly comparable as the *Madonna Alba* had been to the contemporary development in the frescoes of classical feeling and form. Like a fresco in the dimension of its figures, but not in sense of scale, this altar seems to incorporate only part of the advances made between the *Madonna del Baldacchino* [60] and the *School of Athens*. Its design returns, in a manner more literal than usual for Raphael, to precedents of the later Quattrocento, and carries over from them echoes of their planar and symmetrical construction. Color, too, has a somewhat reminiscent smooth brightness of effect, like a not altogether effective translation into present terms of the hard lucidities of Ghirlandaio or Perugino: particularly since its recent cleaning the surface of the picture suggests too much of the oleograph. In the figures themselves there is a degree of inconsistency in handling: while the Madonna and the Infant forms are in the more richly modelled, more massive manner of Raphael's developed style, the saints and donor are comparatively spare and timid, literal in drawing and handling of surface and conventional in expression to a degree that recalls the pre-Roman altar of the *Baldacchino*.

The mature virtues of the painting lie in the fluency of Raphael's ordering of its design, though that is, unlike the frescoes, so spatially restrained. The pose of the Madonna, gently inclined in a rotatory contrapposto, is framed within her aureole and by angels, just differentiated from the enclosing clouds. Both motives conform to the picture's upper curving shape; below, this rounding *leitmotif* is echoed in a catenary curve by the silhouette of the adorers. The composition is clearly harmonious and simply imposing, and its central group attains some measure of a classicizing full beauty; yet the altar as a whole suffers from its visible uncertainties of style. In its hesitant development of spatial structure and in its inconsistency in the conception of the figures, there is the evidence of conflict between lessons learned in fresco painting and the survival of a preceding easel style. Returning here to a task of easel painting, in monumental size, Raphael did not yet wholly presume to think and paint this picture with the resources of technique and form he had attained in fresco. For the moment, the easel form presents itself to Raphael with its impedimenta of pre-Roman conventions, and these are an obstruction to his painting altogether at the level of development which his contemporary frescoes show.

In one respect, however, the *Foligno* altar contains an advanced innovation. Its handling of landscape in a light-shot, feathery technique, atmospherically vibrant, is unaccustomed not only to him (though certainly by his own hand) but to Central Italian painting in general. The manner approximates that of the contemporary young Venetians, and it is not improbable that it was formed in part upon the work of Sebastiano del Piombo, at about this moment newly come to Rome. But perhaps coinciding with this probable influence of Venetian example is the possibility of Raphael's first acquaintance with instances of Ancient "impressionistic" style in landscape art. Should this be true, the background of the *Foligno* altar would be the first transcription of this kind of Ancient style and technique of landscape painting, and of its bucolic, near-romanticizing mood.

The latter moments of the painting of the Segnatura had been, as we observed, much involved with the impression made on Raphael by the Sistine Ceiling. Probably from the interval between the Segnatura and the Eliodoro room, the *Isaiah* fresco (Rome, S. Agostino; much restored)[178] is more explicit evidence of Raphael's concern with Michelangelo's accomplishment. More even than the *Heraclitus* of the *School of Athens* the *Isaiah* imitates the Seers, but the imitation, differently considered than in the moment of admiring excitement that produced the Heraclitus, is also a critique. The *Isaiah* reflects the concept of inspired and active monumental form that Michelangelo demonstrated in his Prophets; but less than an attempt to rival Michelangelo in grandeur of form and expansive power of expression this figure seems to "correct" Michelangelo in the direction of a more normative variety of classicism. The anatomy of the *Isaiah* tends less than that of the later Seers toward superhuman improbabilities; the action of his body is according to a stricter axial contrapposto and more self-contained. There is no sense, as in the later Prophets of the Sistine, of a tension between the form in movement and its frame of architecture.

In its continence of form and in its muting of expressive energies the *Isaiah* demonstrates the difference between Raphael's matured temper, which creates an image finite and complete within itself — aesthetically and contentually self-sufficient — and the Michelangelesque temper which seeks meaning that transcends the illustrative and apparent sense — the face value — of what he represents. After his initial wonderment at Michelangelo's achievement Raphael ponders it once more in the *Isaiah*, and what he accepts of it now is only that which coincides with what his own style would have been without the knowledge of the Sistine. Within its act of imitation, the *Isaiah* reaffirms the separate personality of its creator.

THE ARCHAEOLOGICAL SCHOOL

During the time of Raphael's work in the Stanza della Segnatura and of Michelangelo's in the Sistine, the school of painting that had existed in Rome before these great events continued to function, apparently without important change in its ideas of style. In its production, the archaeological accent of subject and of motives seems to have become, if possible, even more pronounced. The frescoes by Jacopo Ripanda in the Palazzo dei Conservatori (which we have characterized earlier) are probably, in execution, largely of a time about contemporary with the Segnatura, and it is obvious that there has been no contact between these two chronologically parallel, but aesthetically wholly distinct, works. This mentality of Ripanda's, archaizing in a double sense, can be documented in the drawing engraved for him around 1510 by Marcantonio, his Bolognese compatriot, then recently arrived in Rome. The so-called ***Triumph of Titus* (Paris, Louvre)[179] is in a vein indistinguishable from that of the Conservatori decorations and it has been supposed that it may represent a design for a wall, unexecuted or lost, in that same project.

A contemporary example of this style more interesting than the Conservatori frescoes exists in the exceptionally preserved complete exterior decoration in monochrome *sgraffito*, done probably about 1510, of a small palace in the Via Maschera d'Oro (No. 9).[181] This is the most elaborate surviving one of the external decorations of the period, far richer and more imaginatively conceived than the better-known, ineptly restored façade of the Casa Sander in the same neighborhood, dated 1508.[180] The Via Maschera house is wholly covered on its front and its one exposed side not only with bands of grotesque ornament (more inventive and luxurious than on the Casa Sander) but with narrative scenes between each window. The motives of the decoration are in part freely drawn after the reliefs on Trajan's Column — perhaps exploiting Ripanda's careful study of a few years before — and in part imitative of other Antique representations, of mythological and bucolic subjects. An archaeologically learned and richly discursive mentality is responsible for this scheme, which is not different in kind of subject matter and in ordnance from that which would become standard for High Renaissance and post-Renaissance façade decoration.

Neither the designer nor the executant of the Via Maschera façades is identifiable. The inventor of the type of decoration of which this is the prime extant example seems to have been Baldassare Peruzzi; but (despite a seventeenth-century reference which may describe this house as done by him) no sound evidence permits us to connect him with this work in particular. The genre that it represents, however, was of great importance in its time for the history of art in Rome. The Via Maschera façades are the earliest surviving instance, developed in scheme though not in style, of a series of neoclassic "public" decorations of High Renaissance Rome. These decorations, weighty with retrospective literary and visual allusion and handsomely elaborate in form, were to transform certain of the palaces of Rome and, along some streets, whole stretches of façades (as at one time was true of this same portion of the Via Maschera d'Oro) into opulent reconstructions of the imagined external splendors of old Rome. These painted façades, now almost altogether perished, were in their time the abundant counterparts of the great schemes of interior decoration.

PERUZZI, THE EARLIER DECORATION OF THE FARNESINA

Toward 1510 (or perhaps still within 1509) the artist whose invention seems to be reflected on the façades of the Via Maschera d'Oro completed work as architect-designer of the villa, in Trastevere, now known as the *Farnesina* and resumed, in this same new building, the character of painter in which we earlier encountered him. Peruzzi took the chief role in a program of decoration which, in its initial steps with which we are concerned here, was to enlist the services also of two other major artists: the transient Sodoma and the newly arrived Sebastiano Veneziano. The decoration was the most ambitious scheme in Rome of this time outside the Vatican, and the painters working on it represented a conjunction of the highest talent, except for Raphael and Michelangelo, which could be found in the city. The owner of the house, the Sienese banker Agostino Chigi, was the person of the most conspicuous private wealth in Rome, from whom the money often came, indeed, for Pope Julius' expenditures. Chigi's enterprise of building and decoration in the Farnesina was the projection of this scale of his means, as well as of his character of private taste and culture. Unlike the Vatican, the Villa Chigi was a private pleasure-dome and its decorative contents make not one reference to Christianity.

In this decoration of a house he had himself designed Peruzzi emerges decisively as the most important single artistic personality of the time in Rome next to Bramante in architecture, and in painting next to Raphael and Michelangelo. This place was to be challenged in the subsequent decade only by his colleague in the Farnesina decoration, Sebastiano. The style that here gives Peruzzi claim to such a place is most unlike his wholly provincial early work in Rome, in his contributions to the frescoed apse at Sant'Onofrio. The intervening years of Roman residence wrought a drastic change of which the course is difficult to document; his most important work since then, the decoration of the Ostia Castello, has in effect, as we recall, been lost. However, one fresco fragment does exist, of undetermined provenance, which makes a term of recognizable transition between Sant'Onofrio and the style of the Farnesina: the *Three Graces* (San Francisco, Collection Zellerbach, formerly in the Collection Chigi; c. 1508).[182] In it some of the Morellian idiosyncracies and some also of the habits of proportion of the paintings at Sant'Onofrio are still visible; but in general its style has passed into the orbit of Giovanni Sodoma. Sodoma had been in Rome at least for some time within 1508, but the occasion of Peruzzi's knowledge of his art did not need to wait till then. Furthermore, though Sodomesque in general, this painting comes nearer than Sodoma — and not in subject only — to the atmosphere and formal language of a classical style.

The frescoes of the Farnesina have proceeded measurably still farther in this sense. It is at once evident that Peruzzi has become the profoundest of all Roman students of Antique archaeology, but it is also evident that for him, unlike painters of the type of Jacopo Ripanda, this study has meant more than the exploration of a treasury of costume, trappings, and illustrative motives. Peruzzi's study of the Ancient world has generated at least a partial realization in him of the ideas of form that are in Roman sources. An attitude toward Ancient art unlike that of his archaeological colleagues may have been promoted, even in Peruzzi's painting, by contact with the personality and work of Bramante, from whom it is reasonable to suppose that Peruzzi's initial architectural discipline depends. This classicizing orientation must then have been confirmed, and in part specifically determined, by experience of the early work of Raphael in the Segnatura. This experience was certainly direct, and it includes the possibility (assumed by some critics) of Peruzzi's collaboration, along with his compatriot and fellow-employee of Chigi, Sodoma, in the execution of the Segnatura ceiling. Even, however, if this experience of Raphael should not have been initially direct the accent of classicism in Peruzzi's first paintings in the Farnesina could still be ultimately owing to him, by reflection of the impress left by Raphael on Sodoma.

Peruzzi's work of this phase in the Farnesina, mostly from 1510 (and perhaps early 1511) consists of three distinct parts. One was an external decoration in grisaille, now almost altogether disappeared, of which the extent and character are not determinable; all that remains of it are a few allegorical figures, nearly indecipherable, in the spandrels of the ground-floor windows of the palace toward the Tiber. In a room of modest dimension (behind the loggia later decorated by Raphael) there is a frieze which illustrates a series of mythologies, in small scale. The main work of this campaign, however, is the decoration of the ceiling of the grand salon which, from another subsequent intervention of Raphael's, is called the *Sala di Galatea.*[183-90]

The subject of this ceiling is the most extensive commemoration of a single individual in the High Renaissance, much more exactly and exclusively referring to its patron than do Raphael's decorations for the present and next Popes in the Vatican: it has been shown (Saxl) how Peruzzi's ceiling is an illustration, on grand scale and in the most precise possible terms, of the horoscope of Agostino Chigi. The stars are set out on the ceiling, in their guise of human figurations, as they stood in the heavens in the moment of Chigi's birth. To this description of the heavens there were appended, in the lunettes below Peruzzi's ceiling — as part of a continuing, stratified iconographic scheme — illustrations of the mythology of creatures of the upper air, these painted by Sebastiano just after his arrival in mid-1511; and on the walls below, adventures of the gods on earth and sea, begun with Sebastiano's *Polyphemus* and continued with Raphael's great *Galatea,* but not any further carried out. A later landscape completes simply the indication on the walls of a terrestrial sphere.

In the moment of invention of the decorative scheme it was conceived on the basis of concord between intellectual structure and physical illusion: of outlook beyond the limits of the roof and walls into populated regions of the heavens, of the air, and into vistas of the land and sea. Except in the novelty of the great scale of the room in which it is applied, the concept of illusion is not in itself remarkable for, as perspective illusion, it has more consistently executed precedents in the Quattrocento, including among others the then extant Mantegnesque works in the Vatican and in the Palazzo Venezia. The innovation here, indicative of a disposition more classical than realist, is in the primacy in the illusion not of its character of optical device but of intellectual conceit: it less illustrates a visual reality than a complex of figuratively embodied ideas.

Peruzzi's mode of compartmentation of his ceiling is still related to that of Pinturicchio's Piccolomini Library in Siena, a room approximately like this one in shape. The scheme of more precise geometric subdivision is also — not in detail but in general effect — like that of the pre-Raphaelesque ordnance of the ceiling of the Segnatura; as there, this system is composed of interlocking repetitions of geometrical shape and not of forms that decisively compel a sense of unity. In this, and in the angular and pointed look of pattern and astringent marking of the moldings — a startlingly successful fiction of perspective paint — the ceiling is by no means yet of wholly matured classicism in design. However, the ordnance of the whole is intellectually precise, and it has been projected with a great effect of clarity and discipline.

In the figures on the ceiling there is a more immediately legible indication of the situation of Peruzzi at this moment in relation to a development of classical style. In general character of form Peruzzi's figures approximate those of Raphael from the later stages of the painting of the Segnatura ceiling: if we may assume direct knowledge by Peruzzi of Raphael's work of the preceding year or two, it is on a model like the tondo *Justice* that Peruzzi would have based this classicizing reformation of his figure style. There is, however, an assertive accent in Peruzzi's figures that diminishes their classical effect. There coexists, with their neoclassic purity of features and plastic roundings of anatomy and dress, a concern — still quattrocentesque — for bright, precise description of contour and surface, and often for exact and complicated indication of detail. A light of exceptional variety illumines passages of alternating smoothed statuary modeling and sharp-edged drawing of drapery and detail; this lighting is of most unusual effect in fresco, and without sure precedent even in an easel style. In some places it glances in bright sparklings from the surfaces, and in others glows with quiet radiance on broader passages of form. However it works, it is like no

Raphaelesque conception of a lighting: its effect is faceting and diverse, and sometimes magically strange, not modulating and unifying according to classical prescription.

Still more distinct from Raphael's contemporary classicizing than this mode of execution are the attitudes of Peruzzi's figures. They show little of the suave contrapposti of the Segnatura style; in part they are simply less effectively articulate in structure; but more positively, their ideal of grace is, as yet, not wholly classical. The grace that Peruzzi's forms display is still allied to the pointed, precious elegance of some modes of the later Quattrocento; his figures tend to posture in a brittle and exquisite way as Raphael's not only now, but even in the beginning, did not do. And, as Peruzzi does not altogether comprehend the implication of the classical contrapposto, so also he does not understand the idea of its extension into the larger pictorial design. Like the ordnance of painted architecture that contains them, Peruzzi's figures relate in composition in a system of conjunction more than in a classicizing unity; in this his compositions transcend his Quattrocento education only to a limited degree.

The style of Peruzzi in this decoration should not be regarded in its sense only of historical event: of a convergence of traditions from the Sienese Quattrocento with the pre-Raphaelesque Roman archaeological mode and a first experience of Raphael's new classicism; its intrinsic aesthetic interest is more demanding still. Peruzzi's painting in the Chigi ceiling is the positive expression of a personality of the highest talent and extreme individuality, whose nature it is to interpret any aesthetic or intellectual data he may receive in terms of an astringent, complicating intelligence and wit. In a way, Peruzzi is an analogue in Rome to what Uccello had been in the style of the Florentine Quattrocento. Peruzzi's disposition has not much to do with his precise historical situation; he has powers of refinement and of fantasy which transform the archaeological style of the first decade in Rome — to which the Chigi ceiling in part still belongs — into something more pointedly articulate and of more personal immediacy than Raphael, in his pondered consideration of Antiquity, achieves. Peruzzi's temper can not, as yet, accept the prescriptions of decorum and rhetoric of the currently maturing classical style.

Peruzzi is concerned, however, with the acquisition of classical canons of form, as Raphael had begun to demonstrate them; Raphael's precedent revealed to Peruzzi, far more clearly than he had so far perceived it for himself, the nature of the Antique models that, archaeologically, he knew so well. His work on the Chigi ceiling is the beginning of an evolution in this Raphaelesque direction, and even within the ceiling it is possible to discern, among the figurations of the planets on the window wall, an increasing roundness and a more fluently articulated posing and grouping of the forms.

The small-scale frieze of the *Sala del Fregio* (late 1510 — early 1511)[191-3] shows the same tendency slightly, but visibly, more pronounced. The figures retain, though in less measure than before, Peruzzi's disposition toward slimness of proportion and precise, or even mannered, pose. Nevertheless the whole conception of the human form is more effectively associable with Raphael's vocabulary, though still in that stage of classical development which is on the Segnatura ceiling. There are, among the figures and motives of the frieze, intelligently transposed yet surely identifiable quotations from that ceiling, and equally identifiable quotations from Raphael's *Parnassus.*

Peruzzi's association with Raphael must by now have been amicable and close, but not in any sense of a discipleship. The figures of the Ovidian frieze are touched with Raphael's suavity, but are more inspired by a spirit that is not Raphaelesque. Their mood is not of composed harmony but of excitant sensation, sharply personal and high-pitched; it is tense, precise, and nervously articulate. There is some precedent for the mode of design and for some of the subject matter of this frieze in the figure panels of grotesquerie in Pinturicchio's Library, still present as a model in Peruzzi's mind, but Peruzzi's temper in the frieze much more recalls, though less directly, a finer and earlier quattrocentist, Pollaiuolo. In their energy of drawing and their tautness of anatomy and pose Peruzzi's creatures have an accent that evokes the memory of Pollaiuolo, but it is an accent which is wonderfully fused into what has now become a classically chastened form. There is another quattrocentesque echo in the frieze: of that brilliant recreation in the Antique myths of their poignant and immediate aliveness, which had been the special talent of the younger, but no longer of the contemporary, Piero di Cosimo.

Among the qualities of this painting is one for which there is, except in Peruzzi's antecedent ceiling only, no precedent or any contemporary comparison: its handling of light. Here the light is no longer, as it had been in the ceiling of the *Sala di Galatea,* of faceting effect, but more nearly classically modulated and consistent. The light retains, however, the power it had before, of intense differentiation: in the frieze, light is subtly graded from radiant reflection down to luminous and gentle shadow. This light seems to come not from a source within the fresco scenes but from some artifice, like a fire-light, as in a brazier, set below the figures and within the room. Behind the figures (rhythmically disposed in a succession on the foremost plane, but not classically grouped) is a low horizon, on which trees stand in half-light against a deep blue nighttime sky. In this light, against this background, the figures acquire a value of strong sculpturesque illusion, as if this might be a reconstruction of an actual Antique frieze; yet at the same time light reveals the subtlest resources of living color in the flesh and draperies, and the dark sky is not alone a foil, but a depth of sapphire space.

As in the ceiling, an illusion, here far more sophisticated, is not its own end but is transcended; in the frieze the factor of illusion is the agent also of a classical allusion which, at the same time, conveys an intense present life both of the poetry of narrative and of a poetry of vision. Like Raphael's, this art is conceived in the language of the humanists, but not in rhetoric; it is less purely Latinized and nearer to the native living tongue.

SODOMA

An admixture of elements, and a situation in respect to the development of classical style not unlike that in Peruzzi, but at a level conspicuously less, appears in the decoration by Giovanni Sodoma of Chigi's bedroom in the Farnesina. The date of this decoration, which may be *established with some certainty in 1512, is later than that of Peruzzi's work, but Sodoma's is not for that reason more classically advanced. Since shortly after his exposure to the style of the early Segnatura and his brief collaboration with Raphael in that room Sodoma had been in Siena, and in the few years until this return to Rome — again only temporary — his art had developed more of provincialism than classicism.

The source of the chief fresco of Sodoma's bedroom decoration, the *Marriage of Alexander and Roxane*,[194] is a Raphaelesque drawing (preserved in copies, as at Windsor), of only shortly prior date, which illustrates, in much more literal and decorous fashion, a description in Lucian of a work by the painter Action, a contemporary of Apelles. In Sodoma's free transcription of Raphael's model its classical character is not quite lost, but it is much vitiated. In place of Raphael's concentrated and spatially developed grouping of the figures, Sodoma distributes them loosely across the foreground of a perspective space which, in turn, seems almost altogether unrelated to the figures. Instead of Raphael's unity imposed on a diversity of incident, Sodoma's fresco is dissolved into episodes — of figures, architecture, and landscape — each separately (and, indeed, quite entertainingly) stressed. What remains as evidence of Sodoma's former relationship with Raphael is a mode of cursive rhythmical connection among the figures, resembling that used also by Peruzzi; and, more than in Peruzzi, a ponderated movement and proportion of the single forms. However, Sodoma's conception of the figures is by no means of a consistent classicism: beside the handsome easy contrapposti of the Alexander and Roxane there are other figures that show awkward misunderstandings of the classical norms and, in places, distortions, ornamentally intended, of an almost capricious, mannered kind. The most durable aspect of Sodoma's Raphaelesque experience is in his imitation of the classical ideal of loveliness of face; Sodoma's translation of this loveliness, sensuous and warm-shadowed, recalls its — and his own — eventual origin in Leonardo. The quality of color and of texture too is a translation, intending a more luxurious appeal, of the intellectually-planned sonorities of Raphael.

This painting, and Sodoma's companion illustrations from the life of Alexander on the other wall-spaces of the room (the larger part of one wall, to the left of the *Marriage* scene, was painted later) are planned, with the preoccupation that is pervasive in the Villa Farnesina, as an intendedly consistent illusionistic scheme. On three walls of the room a painted balustrade is drawn across the frescoes, as if the spectator were to look through and across it into Sodoma's discursive recreation of a (not altogether) classical past. On the fourth wall of the room the presence of a fireplace prevents the sensible use of the motive of the balustrade, and it is substituted by another appropriate illusionistic device: two cubicles are painted into the lower wall beside the fireplace from which on one side Vulcan, working at his anvil, and on the other *amorini* who are his assistants, astonishingly seem to emerge.[105] The illusionism of the room has been evolved more with fancy than discipline, and its mentality remains quite different from that in both of Peruzzi's antecedent schemes: Sodoma's idea of illusionism is still naively quattrocentesque, of simple making of connection of the spectator's with the picture's space.

Sodoma's style in the Chigi bedroom is both more and less classical, and both more and less persistently related to the Early Renaissance, than Peruzzi's prior paintings in the Villa. Sodoma's handsome languors are nearer to one mood of classicism than are Peruzzi's subtleties of intellect and wit. The *Alexander and Roxane* evokes a pleasurable atmosphere of sensuousness that is present in some kinds of Ancient art, but this evocation is without the recreative power and, in particular, without the consistency of an effective classical style; it is not only quattrocentesque still in certain of its mental habits but provincially quattrocentesque at that: untouched by discipline and episodic, and discursive both in manner of narration and in larger mode of form.

Sodoma's brief intrusion of this time into the Roman scene had no consequence for the history of painting in the city beyond the fact of his contribution to the decoration of the Farnesina. Sodoma was by now too far embarked upon a course provincially tangential to the classical development in Rome to make any influential impress on it. The direction of this tangent was shortly to become quite clear: the Sienese Beccafumi (who also was in Rome close to this time, circa 1511–12, though no Roman work by him can be identified) defined this direction earlier and more decisively than Sodoma. Out of the conjunction of an incomplete, and only incompletely sympathetic, experience of classical style with a dominantly quattrocentesque disposition — medievalizing beyond any other of the Renaissance styles of painting — the Sienese masters were to form, among the first (though not so precociously as has been asserted), a style that stands at the confines of Mannerism. Even in Peruzzi, despite his continued residence in Rome and his classically-derived discipline, the persistence of Sienese and quattrocentist elements would predispose him, more readily than other Roman masters, to a style that contains elements of Mannerism.

SEBASTIANO DEL PIOMBO

Another visitor made his Roman debut in the decoration of the Farnesina and remained, as Sodoma did not, to play a permanent and important role in Roman art. Sebastiano Veneziano arrived in Rome in mid-1511, already the possessor of a considerably developed High Renaissance classical style, a result of the independent evolution, Giorgionesque in origin, of the first decade of the century in his native city. The style that Sebastiano had formed by 1511 was, in the measurably different dialect of the Venetian classicism, comparable in its stage of evolution to Raphael's art toward 1510.

A close associate of both Giorgione and the young Titian, Sebastiano's development had been in part authentically creative and original, but it was still more the consequence of learning from these two greater colleagues.

Immediately on Sebastiano's arrival in Rome he was quick to seek the influence of new example; it was normal that first contact with the art of Rome demand a new orientation of the foreigner who came to practice there. His first work in the Farnesina, the fresco lunettes [196-7] beneath Peruzzi's ceiling in the *Sala Galatea*,[184, 187] were probably designed quite soon after his arrival, and executed still within the second half of 1511. When he came to Rome that profoundly important event for the history of Sebastiano, the Sistine Ceiling, may not yet have been a public fact but certainly it became known to him in the course of making his designs. His figure style in the lunettes is distinguished from that of his just preceding works in Venice by the willed accentuation in it of sculptural effect, by the careful articulation of anatomy, and by research into action and foreshortening; in other words by a visible attempt to master a Roman, and in part a specifically Michelangelesque repertory of form.

At the same time the manner of Sebastiano's painting, as he makes this effort, is also influenced by his vision of the frescoes just at hand: the sharpness and occasionally strained and pointed angularity of Sebastiano's figures here, so unlike both his previous and shortly succeeding figure style, show a momentary influence on him of Peruzzi's ceiling. Nevertheless, even with this Peruzzian accent Sebastiano's paintings are, from the sound base in them of his Venetian classical education, more nearly comparable in essential style to the current stage of Raphael's or Michelangelo's accomplishment than are those of the ceiling. Meanwhile, however, it would seem also from the stimulus of the example just revealed by Michelangelo, Peruzzi too had moved into a phase of style more like that of the two leading classical masters; probably before Sebastiano's taking over the lunettes, Peruzzi had given evidence of his new direction in one of them he had already painted, the *Giant Head*,[204] of markedly Michelangelesque cast.

A still more evident acceptance of a Michelangelism is clear in Sebastiano's *Polyphemus* fresco,[198] closely successive in date to the lunettes (at latest within 1512; in part overpainted). This figure was the beginning of a decoration on the lower wall that was interrupted after Sebastiano's painting of only this first fraction of an episode (the episode itself completed, in the next year, by Raphael). Still touched in slight degree by the stresses of drawing and anatomy that are in the figures of the lunettes, the *Polyphemus* much more closely imitates the precedents of Michelangelo, in particular of the Ignudi. The imitation is limited to the form: to the pose and to the idea, here altogether appropriate, of great physical dimension, but the spirit of this figure is not Michelangelesque. The *Polyphemus* is, relatively, relaxed and his pose is easy; there is still some reminiscence in him of a Giorgionesque (specifically, late Giorgionesque) temper. As in Giorgionesque example, his mood takes color from the landscape into which he has been set. With different effectiveness than in the lunettes, the *Polyphemus* is a trial synthesis of the Venetian variant of classical mentality, more sensuous and less exclusively anthropocentric than that of Rome, with the Roman vocabulary of plastic form.

Almost certainly before the *Polyphemus*, Sebastiano had painted his first easel work of Roman date, the *Adoration of the Shepherds* (Cambridge, Fitzwilliam Museum; late 1511-early 1512).[199] In it there is also much of Michelangelo, but not so imitatively or so exclusively as in the *Polyphemus*. There is, in the easel picture, a dimension of anatomy visibly grander than that of Sebastiano's last Venetian paintings, and a more pronounced heaviness of musculature (more evident than in the lunette frescoes, but not than in the illustrative gigantism of the *Polyphemus*); these are in general the result of study of the work of Michelangelo. Two specific motives also may be borrowings from Michelangelo: the pointing shepherd in the background of the *Adoration* may have come from the *Cascina* figure recently engraved by Marcantonio; the posture of the Infant Christ may adapt, not so much Michelangelo directly, as Michelangelo's own model for his early "Antique" sculpture of a sleeping Cupid.

These references do not, however, dominate the picture as the reference to the Ignudi dominates the *Polyphemus*; furthermore, Sebastiano's willingness to learn from Rome has, in this picture, not been directed only to the art of Michelangelo. He has also studied Raphael: the theme and motive of the *Madonna del Velo* (in its now lost Raphaelesque transcription, not that of Penni's later derivation in the Louvre) have been borrowed for Sebastiano's Virgin and Child, and the shepherd at the left hand of the group depends on the similar figure (itself eventually Michelangelesque) in the *Euclid* group within the *School of Athens*.[166] The figure behind him also may derive, rather than from the engraving after Michelangelo, from a figure to the upper rear of Raphael's fresco. The sense of making of a group more compact, more rhythmically connective, and spatially distinct within itself than in Sebastiano's easel works in Venice seems certainly to have developed from an influence of Raphael's example.

Already much infused with Roman precept, the *Adoration* is nevertheless still deeply involved with the recent precedents of Venice: there is still the echo in it of the memorable Allendale *Nativity*, and of the characteristic Venetian machinery, only a little moderated, of asymmetric composition; above all there is the scale and great affective role within the picture of the landscape. Evidently, Sebastiano was not only concerned to learn from Rome; he believed now, and continued to believe, that in this last marvelous respect at least, he had brought from Venice something that was worth conspicuous demonstration to the Roman public.

Probably after an intervening execution of the *Polyphemus* fresco, Sebastiano painted his second large easel work in Rome, the masterly *Death of Adonis* (Florence, Uffizi; c. 1512);[200] it is the culmination and solution of this critical episode in Sebastiano's career. When it was painted the memory of Venetian *Giorgionismo* was not diminished in Sebastiano's mind, while the virtues of the Roman style had come to be not only intellectually comprehended but profoundly felt. In this picture Venice appears specifically in the landscape, in a portrait of the *Piazzetta* seen from the lagoon, as veiled and tender as the image of an absent love. Its painting is wonderfully evocative of atmosphere, and by its handling of light conveys a vibrancy of sensuous emotion good enough for Titian or Giorgione; yet the tonality of landscape — muted, crepuscular and greyed — is already overcast by a graver Roman frame of mind. The optical character of painting in the landscape is extended to the figure of Adonis, part plastic, part consumed by the play upon his form of various and textured light, but in the major figures the Venetian accent of technique is much diminished. Their effect of texture is muted to something intermediate between flesh and statuary; and in color, Venetian luxury of carnation is altered into tones of paled bronze.

Even before coming to Rome Sebastiano had a tendency, partly native, and derived partly from the recent works of Titian and Giorgione, toward monumental increase of the weight and proportions of the human figure. In this picture, following the much more commanding example of the Sistine, Sebastiano still more magnifies the proportions of his figures toward an almost bulking massiveness, ponderous and sensuously splendid in effect. The nudes are truly grandiose, not with the transcendent implication of those of Michelangelo, but as monuments of sensuous existence. The monuments move, and with a rounding fullness in their movement and deliberation of its ornamental value generically like that in Michelangelo's or Raphael's contemporary forms, and more weightily impressive than in the latter. By their movement, Sebastiano's figures are knit into a rhythmically continuous and closewoven group; the evidence of Raphael's example is as certain in this as is Michelangelo's in the shaping of the single forms. Unlike Michelangelo, Sebastiano is ineluctably a painter, and his inclination is not toward sculptural isolation but toward association of his forms. The character of this group is unequivocally Roman, Michelangelesque in parts and more nearly Raphaelesque in its whole, but the larger composition of the picture is still based on a Venetian, Giorgionesque and Titianesque, device: rather than a counterpoise of figure masses, this composition, fixed upon its center in the Venus, balances a plastic group against a landscape space; and at the same time juxtaposes a right-triangle of figured light against an inverted triangle of receding atmospheric dark.

In its character of content the *Death of Adonis* is also a meeting of Sebastiano's two classical cultures. Much more than the *Polyphemus*, Venus and her court respond to their situation, here with a clear beginning of what will later be, in Sebastiano, a profound sense of drama. This part of the content of the picture works with the monumental pathos of form and ideas that belongs to the Roman classical style; but the content that does not come from the narrative is Venetian: a splendor of the visible and fleshly world, an experience not of ideas but of the senses. For the conjunction of these two to have the effect of conviction it makes in this picture it was necessary that both of its components, the remembered and the new, have the immediacy they had at this one moment only in Sebastiano's career. This power in synthesis between the two great schools of High Renaissance classicism, meeting in their common moment of first mature fruition, could not have shown itself before this and did not occur, on this scale, in Sebastiano's art again.

The subsequent direction that Sebastiano's art would take is indicated in his tondo *Madonna and Child* (London, Collection Philip Pouncey).[201] Not later than a year or two in date from the *Adonis*, it already shows a more marked generalization of the forms and what, in comparison with Sebastiano's works till now, seems an austerity of texture and of smoothed handling of paint. The design has assumed a geometrical severity simpler even than that then current in the Roman style; this is not only Roman but Sebastiano's own interpretation, more grave and chaste than that of the Romans themselves, of classical lucidity and dignity of style. The quality of content is the same in its effect, at once ponderous and pure. Even the sensuous resonance of light and the resource of landscape, the peculiarly Venetian properties of Sebastiano's style, have been chastened, to assume a personality less disparate from the Romanized vocabulary of the larger forms.

Shortly after his arrival in Rome, Sebastiano had introduced another compound of Venetian and Roman experience into the Roman school; one less ambitious but, because more imitable, more influential than that in such works as the *Death of Adonis*. This was a portrait style Venetian in origin, but modified in conception and technique by contact with the style of Rome. The *Portrait of a Girl*, improperly called *La Fornarina* (Florence, Uffizi; dated 1512),[202] is the first example of this creative compromise. In it, Sebastiano has made the image more plastically clear and monumental than in his Venetian portraits, and he has given an accent of almost rhetorical dignity to the pose. The features, too, have taken on a cast of Roman classicism. The underlying conception of the portrait is, however, unlike that entertained in Raphaelesque Rome and in Raphael's Florentine antecedents: it is based upon an ideal regularization of the face more summary and generalizing than in Raphael, and much less observant of the sitter's complex visible identity. A liberty so manifest as this to accommodate appearance to preference had not been taken in Rome before, but it was habit in the precedents of Giorgionesque style. Almost more than an actual portrait, the so-called *Fornarina* — though she is specifically without attribute — resembles those Venetian images (including among them some of Sebastiano's own) of ideal female beauty who wear the iconographical disguise of Salome or Magdalen or Flora; indeed, the purpose of this picture seems more allied to that Venetian conception of representations of the female for her beauty's sake than to the accustomed main Raphaelesque purpose in a portrait, of record of and commentary on a precise being. Even Sebastiano's shortly later *Dorothea* (so-called; Berlin, Museums; c. 1513),[203] where the individual identity of the sitter is more evident, shows this, as it were, supra-portrait character.

Sebastiano's demonstration of his willingness to make more arbitrary generalization of an actual face than the Roman mode allowed, creating thus a blandly ideal and less complex image, made a precedent that the Roman school on occasion found it opportune to follow. Apart from the influence exercised in Rome by Sebastiano's models of this kind, his own practice in portraiture became more extensive than that of any Roman contemporary except for Raphael. By the quantitative place Sebastiano's portraits would take up in the Roman scene they give an altered cast to the whole of the historical picture of this branch of High Renaissance Roman art.

In one respect, the contribution made by Sebastiano in the course of his amalgamation into the Roman school has been exaggerated. The optical and coloristic mode he brought from Venice made, beyond question, an impression on certain subsequent works of Roman art. Raphael was certainly touched by it, specifically in portraits which, in other ways as well, in instances reflect some influence of Sebastiano. There are also places in Peruzzi's art which suggest that the accent, though not the existent substance, of his interest in effects of light may have been changed by contact with Sebastiano. However, Sebastiano initiates no wide current of optically oriented style in Rome; on the contrary, as he goes on in Rome his own colorism and luminism persist only by virtue of Sebastiano's transmutation of them into elements that accompany, but do not prejudice, his increasing Romanism of a plastic style.

PERUZZI, c. 1511–1514

Sebastiano's full accommodation, about 1512, into the current mature development of classical style in Rome was a result not only of his powers of comprehension, but of the nature of the preparation he had received before in Venice. In Sebastiano's experience of Michelangelo and Raphael it was not necessary for him, as it was for Peruzzi — whose intelligence was as keen, and in many ways more sensitive — to deal with the residues of a quattrocentesque and initially provincial education. During his first campaign of working in the Farnesina, Peruzzi had known the accomplishment of Raphael in its immediately antecedent phase, at least through the *Parnassus*, and in the two rooms he had successively decorated he had made an effort to reflect some part of Raphaelesque style. After the further progress of Raphael's painting in the Segnatura, and of Michelangelo's in the Sistine Chapel, the authority of example of the matured classical style became altogether irresistible; and as much as it was possible to him Peruzzi surrendered himself, at least for a while, to it. Probably before (more logically so, but not so necessarily) Sebastiano had begun his work on the lunettes in the *Sala di Galatea*, Peruzzi painted one of them, an end space in the series, with a single gigantic head,[204] referred to earlier; it confesses the impress on Peruzzi of Michelangelo's art (perhaps experienced in the Sistine, as by Raphael, even before the date of the unveiling). The *Giant Head* reflects the models of the Sistine — the *Adam* surely, and perhaps also the *Jonah* and the Ignudo to the left of the *Libica*. It was left in place, as Sebastiano's decoration proceeded to completion, perhaps not only because it was too artistically fine to be removed but because it was then thought relevant to the content of the decoration.

No explanation seems to account for the presence of this image except one that makes sense of its context of iconography: the notion most often advanced (based more on modern than on Renaissance artistic psychology), that it is not more than a private and experimental fresco sketch, does not convince. In the habit of the time the *Giant Head* would rather have had some meaningful connection with the careful plan of illustration in the room. The direction of the gaze suggests relations: the creature contemplates the happenings in the lower "sky" of Sebastiano's lunettes to the side, as if he existed in their sphere. We might suppose that this great face, so round and very luminous, might be a personification of the Sun as we see him in his rising or setting. If such an explanation is acceptable there is reason for Peruzzi's magnifying, even beyond any suggestion in the Sistine, Michelangelo's ideas of scale. It is important that Peruzzi reflects, in this instance, not only the dimension, but something of the resonance of feeling that accompanies it in Michelangelo's example. But necessarily, Michelangelo's grandeur of spirit is transposed into a different, lesser key: Peruzzi's tone of feeling is lyric, not heroic, and of a yielding, almost romantic, pathos.

With some likelihood before the time of this sole lunette in the Farnesina, Peruzzi had become involved with the program of decoration in the Stanze.* There is record in mid-1511 that work was in progress in two *camere* of which it is reasonable to suppose that the second was the Stanza d'Eliodoro. Peruzzi has left evidence, never critically disputed, of his painting in the minor decoration of the ceiling of this room.[205] Only part of it may be certainly assigned to him, and what is his is in a style which much resembles that of the frieze in the Farnesina; its date may be of early 1511. Apparently, however, it may not have been at first intended that Peruzzi's employment in this Stanza be confined only to the ceiling. A drawing [206] exists, in the Louvre, which if not by Peruzzi himself is at least a copy from him, of a design for the decoration of the wall on which Raphael later painted the *Mass of Bolsena*.[214] The subject is the apocalyptic vision of the Seven Trumpets, and included among its figures is one that almost surely is identifiable as Julius II, as yet without the beard with which he returned from Bologna after June 1511. Not only the draughtsman's style, but the structure of design would seem un-Raphaelesque, and assignable with more likelihood to Peruzzi.

The opportunity to paint this wall was of course not ever given to Peruzzi, but Raphael does not seem to have intervened in the decoration of this room until after Peruzzi had been allowed to invent and execute, almost certainly within the second half of 1511, the whole painting of its ceiling. A drawing survives for one of the larger paintings on the ceiling in which recent research tends to confirm a long-asserted attribution to Peruzzi: it is for the figure of God in the *Moses and the Burning Bush* (Oxford, Ashmolean).[207] The cartoon for the *Moses* of this same scene (Naples, Galleria Nazionale, there attributed to Raphael),[208] though denatured in the drawing style by its large scale, shows the precise morphology of Peruzzi. The actual painting of the main parts of the ceiling [209-10] — despite the loss of *velature*, which causes it to recall, fortuitously, the look of the damaged (or unfinished) fresco of the *Pandects* in the Segnatura — is abundant with precise analogies to Peruzzi's execution in the Farnesina. There is a handling of light, high-keyed and of a singular translucence, for which only the Farnesina offers a precedent in contemporary Rome. In drapery style there are close likenesses to the paintings of the *Sala del Fregio* and, beyond this, some persistence from the frescoes of the Chigi ceiling of its kind of incised ornamental repetition in the folds. There are, further, numerous identities of type and detail, of a kind which could not come from the deformation of another personality's inventions, but only from Peruzzi's personal vocabulary of forms.

While it is not a valid argument in determining the attribution of the Eliodoro ceiling, the illusionistic scheme on which the four main central scenes depend suggests a character of thought of which only Peruzzi hitherto had given evidence in Rome. The paintings are conceived as if on *tende*, suspended on hooks from the fictitious painted ribs of the vault, and through the scalloped openings where the *tende* are stretched tight, we look through to glimpses of a sky. Like the systems in the Farnesina, the illusion rationally justifies the form we see, but is not in itself a realistic end; and more clearly than in the Farnesina ceiling, this device makes an intellectually acceptable solution of the conflict posed by ceiling painting between vertical and horizontal directions. The source of the device is in Antique art, and such an archaeological discovery, or rediscovery, is in line with Peruzzi's pronounced interests.

The problem of authorship of this ceiling has been confused by the attempt (Venturi) to assign its execution to Guillaume Marcillat. This confusion is more nearly forgivable than that of the current of opinion which believes that the design of its main scenes is not by the executant, but by Raphael. There is of course much influence of Raphael in design; when Peruzzi undertook his functions in the Stanza d'Eliodoro he was brought into such close contact with Raphael as he had not enjoyed before and into contact, further, with a Raphael of constantly more impressive accomplishment. Peruzzi's concern with Raphael's example, only partly evident in the Farnesina, now received new impetus. Also, as was the case with Raphael himself in this approximate moment, Peruzzi experienced the revelation — sufficiently imposing to Raphael, and still more to a personality of lesser stature — of the Sistine, and there is still more of Michelangelo's mark in the designs and motives of the Eliodoro ceiling than there is of Raphael's. Peruzzi's intense concern, in his conceptions for the Eliodoro ceiling, was for the reform in them of his style according to the advanced models of mature classicism. He succeeded considerably in this reformation, but the ways in which he did not so succeed are also an indication of his identity in these designs.

The motives of type and posture in Peruzzi's ceiling depend both on Raphael and Michelangelo — more, considerably, from the latter — but the figure style does not precisely follow either model. The character of drawing in particular is different: some forms are almost geometrically blocked out in somewhat angular silhouette, as if Peruzzi were here trying to transform the sharp style of the Chigi ceiling into a bolder Michelangelesque speech; other forms are almost elaborately cursive, as if enlarging the more fluid style of the Farnesina frieze into a Raphaelesque grace. In spite of these divergent responses to his models, it is the constant of Peruzzi's own personality that is still most visible in this figure style. The references to the Sistine and the Segnatura do not obscure the temperament, more high-keyed and less stable than that of the greater masters, which makes Peruzzi work on one hand more rigidly, and on the other with a febrility, that are both less than wholly classical.

The most apparent change in style is quantitative, in the anatomical dimension of the figures. Unlike the persons of both decorations in the Farnesina, where proportion still recalls the canons of the Quattrocento, the figures of this ceiling are much more ample, and approach a mature classical sense of scale in relation to their compositional space. The expansion of the figures is in terms of content, too; there is a magnitude of gesture, and in instances of entire pose, which is a not inadequate reflection of the mature classical language, which involves the grandeur of the body with its life of mind. The *Moses* is much less articulate than the contemporary dramatic figures of the two first masters, but he is not too differently imposing in his power of form and conviction of expressive attitude. The sleeping *Jacob*, more directly Michelangelesque in source, almost challenges the grandeur of the inventions from which he derives. In these scenes Peruzzi has been inspired by emulation and the power of proximity to a depth and scale of feeling different from the wit, the lyricism, or the learning his earlier decorations had called forth.

Despite their adequate approximation to a mature classical figure style, and their sure narrative effectiveness, these frescoes are resistant in one main respect to contemporary classical example. As in the Farnesina decorations, the compositions are still based on the conjunction of forms rather than on an initial conception of their necessary unity. More than in the Chigi ceiling, but not significantly more than in the Farnesina frieze, cursive motives of connection or responsive inclinations of direction are used to bring forms into relation with each other; but the relation remains one of succession, and each major form remains more distinct from than bound within the composition. The gestalt that is at work here can comprehend the classical conception in its parts, but can only incompletely grasp the idea of a finally determining totality.

The much disfigured fresco altarpiece of the *Adoration of the Child* * (Rome, S. Rocco; c. 1512)[211] may represent — as much as its condition lets us judge — the maximum concession in Peruzzi's art to classical example, in this case evidently Raphael's. The picture is softened in form and expression (and apparently in its mode of drawing also), and it is composed in a deliberately balancing, responsive, geometric scheme. Its Raphaelism is still not more than approximate, and the approximation is at most of a moment in the Raphaelesque style of a few years past. The accent of Siena is still evident, and it has perhaps been reinforced by renewed conversations with Il Sodoma who, as we have seen, was in 1512 again in Rome and working in the Farnesina. Peruzzi's extreme sensibility disposed him, as Raphael's did too, to respond to art as strongly as to nature; at this time, unsettled by the recent convergence on him of influences, Peruzzi is least himself. He was, however, too highly characterized a personality to continue in a state even of this relative submission to the style of others, of Raphael and Michelangelo, and less still to that of Sodoma.

Recovered from the overbearing proximity of Raphael and Michelangelo in the Vatican, Peruzzi again soon took on much of the coloration of his antecedent style, but with new effect: it is a differently compelling personality that we perceive in Peruzzi's *Holy Family in a Landscape* (London, Collection Philip Pouncey; c. 1513–14; an unpublished companion panel of the *Corona-*

tion of the Virgin in a private collection, Norway; Pouncey).[212] The content of this painting has the resonance that comes from an experience in the Vatican of the tone of the mature classical style, but with no effect of lessening of Peruzzi's former peculiar acuity of feeling or of his lyricism; and there is no trace in it of his earlier, still quattrocentist, tendency to preciosity. The drawing resumes the sharpness of the Farnesina phase but, classically chastened, has become less pointed. The figures now are heavy in proportion and plastically full, and suggest not only Raphael's and Michelangelo's example but, as well, that of Sebastiano del Piombo. The lighting intensifies the variety and brilliance that had been in the Farnesina fresco: not only the difference in medium but, again, Sebastiano's influence may have helped toward this (Pope-Hennessey); beyond its brilliance, peculiar to Peruzzi, the lighting has a richness like Sebastiano's, of Venetian accent. The role of landscape in the picture, not only consonant with the figures but as pronounced in emotive personality as they are, resembles what Sebastiano had demonstrated in his first works in Rome.

The counterinfluence of the Venetian painter on Peruzzi is an episode, as transient as Peruzzi's influence had been on him; the *Holy Family* shows a convergence in one moment of the common interests of the two most unlike personalities on the Roman scene. The tondo by Sebastiano in the Pouncey Collection, of close contemporary date, represents a continuing process of concession by the artist to the basic ideas of the Roman classical style; the Peruzzi *Holy Family* of the same collection represents the reassertion of an individuality who was not, even in his closest contacts with the style of Raphael and Michelangelo just before this, to be dominated by it.

RAPHAEL, THE ELIODORO PHASE

*The conception of a decoration of the walls of the Stanza d'Eliodoro[213] with Apocalyptic subjects, implied by the Peruzzesque drawing in the Louvre, may have been no more than an exploratory thought of Pope Julius or his literary deputies. The drawing was done, apparently, during Julius' absence on his Bolognese campaign; after his return in June of 1511 he seems to have conceived a different content for the decoration of the room. Just after that return Julius was in politically uncomfortable straits, perhaps the worst of his career so far. It may have been in a frame of mind that was prayerful, but also characteristically indomitable, that he caused Peruzzi to recollect on the ceiling, in the four large Old Testament scenes, the evidence of God's unfailing intervention for the salvation of His People. These subjects on the ceiling are not relatable to the abandoned Apocalyptic scheme, but they are relatable to the scenes actually painted on the walls, not by Peruzzi but by his successor, Raphael.

Raphael took over the actual work of decoration late in 1511 or at latest in early 1512, after he had finished the essentials in the Segnatura. It is possible that the subjects intended for him on the walls were invented concurrently with those dictated to Peruzzi for the ceiling, and that there is in fact the close iconographical connection between them that recent criticism

(Hartt) has tried to demonstrate. If this is true, then the references to events in Julius' reign that are in the frescoes on the walls must be sought in the years before mid-1511. These interpretations, while they are admissible, are, however, less convincing than interpretations that are based for the first fresco, the *Mass of Bolsena*, on the historical circumstances of the second half of 1511, and for the other frescoes on events of the year 1512.

The interpretations that require invention of the subjects of the walls at a date contemporary with those of the ceiling refer to past victories, which by the summer of 1511 had turned to frustrations and defeats. The scenes painted on the walls suggest nothing of this historical anticlimax; on the contrary, their temper is that of triumphant affirmation. This is the atmosphere of the events that succeeded Julius' return from Bologna, not of the time that just preceded it; the happenings the frescoes on the walls commemorate are much more likely those which, from the time of the papal proclamation of the Lateran Council in July 1511, marked Julius' final and greatest resurgence of policy and power. It should be assumed that the ceiling and the walls have not more in common than the general iconographic theme of debt to divine intervention for rescue from grave peril. Where a more intimate connection can be seen, it is probably the result of *a posteriori* rather than *a priori* provisions of programmatic thinking.

The subjects of the wall frescoes may, further, not have been invented at one time among themselves, but in consequence of historical events as they occurred; the best explanations of their historical references point to this conclusion. The *Mass of Bolsena*,[214] in a way a reprise of the theme of the *Disputà*, would seem to be, in its direct personal reference, a reassertion of Julius' faith not only in a central article of dogma, but in a relic that had helped bring past victories and would help bring them again; more generally, it is an assertion of the certainty of divine support to demonstrate authoritative truth against doubt and heresy. The *Bolsena* would be Julius' proudly absolute response to the challenge of divine, and his personal, authority by the convocation of the Council of Pisa in May 1511, and perhaps also indirectly a commemoration of his counterconvocation of the Lateran Council in July. The *Expulsion of Heliodorus*[217] would refer to a more developed stage of thinking about the Lateran Council, called for April of 1512 but opened actually in May: that of its good results in the Expulsion from the Temple, always with divine aid, of the despoilers of its treasure of authority and doctrine. During June of the same year, despite the prior unsuccessful issue of the Battle of Ravenna, the French invaders of Italy were compelled to relinquish all their Italian conquests: the *Repulse of Attila*[221] would celebrate this unexpected and surely divinely motivated event. In this fresco, conceived (as the copy of a lost Raphael drawing in the Louvre unequivocally shows) with Julius as the papal hero, Leo X was substituted after Julius' death.

The last fresco to be executed in the room, the *Liberation of Peter*,[222] is still explicitly Julian in historical reference and in personal meaning: a commemoration of the final liberation of the Roman Church from the constraints of temporal and theological troubles. In this fresco Peter, who is the person of the Church, alludes to Julius in a double sense, as his apostolic descendant and as the former Cardinal of San Pietro in Vincoli. In visual form the painting is the counterpart, and perhaps the symbolic record, of Julius' formal visit of thanksgiving for the "liberation of Peter" — the liberation, thus, of the Church of Rome — to San Pietro in Vincoli on July 23, 1512 (Pastor VI, 416).

The historical intention in the Stanza d'Eliodoro[213] made a task for its decorator very different from that which he confronted in the Segnatura. There he was required to paint not actions but situations, in themselves of ideal character, and in this intrinsically accommodated to the mentality and forms of an idealizing classical style. In the Eliodoro room the requirement was much more complex, and based upon material less obviously assimilable to the propositions of an idealizing style. The immediate historical reference — the actual and urgent motive of each scene — had to be expressed in terms of an older typology, from biblical or Church history. At the same time, the authority of tradition both permitted and required that the authors of the present event be represented (in three of the four frescoes) as witnesses, or as actors, in Raphael's description of the historical analogies from the distant past. Raphael's problem was not, as in the Segnatura, the harmonious embodiment of what was already a harmonious idea, but the reconciliation into harmony of disparate elements; of distant with current historical reference, and of imaginatively recreated with contemporary persons; it was necessary to endow the imagined representation with the vitality of the actual, and so to manipulate the reality that, while maintaining its distinction from the past, it could adequately coexist with it.

In each of the three cases where the imagined and actual are combined, their reconciliation takes the form of an exchange between them of their normally expected character: vital immediacy of action is given to the past, and the present actors assume the more passive role. At the same time the fact of difference between the imagined and the actual is preserved in the visible distinction of levels of reality of the two worlds. The actors of the recreated past are embodied, in general, in forms of idealizing correctness which derive from the vocabulary of the Segnatura; the contemporary persons are described in that mode, also initially developed in the Segnatura, which is Raphael's classical solution to the problem of portraiture. Where the persons of the past are emotionally or physically highly active, but removed in form, the personalities of the present are most restrained in temper but immediate in form; the mutual accommodation of the two worlds that is aesthetically necessary, and the distinction between them which is contentually necessary are thus both satisfied. For each fresco, finally, a pretext of narration and a device of form have been conceived which subsume both the historically remote and the actual factors in a dominating unity.

This embracing concept takes its character from the content Raphael understands within his subjects, and in each of them his understanding is of drama and assertive triumph. Already, within the states of being described in the Segnatura, there had been an increasing exposition of their vitality; here, the subjects are initially conceived as representing states of action: the thesis from which Raphael's thinking of them departs is that of their dramatic animation. This thesis is of course in part presented to the artist by the makers of the program, but it is at the same time a consequent next step in Raphael's own development, in the Segnatura, of vitality. The dramatic animation that pervades the Stanza d'Eliodoro is more than a consequence of subject; it is a meeting of potential in the subjects with Raphael's inclination and potential of development.

This dramatic life may also be an evidence of Raphael's response to the examples of dramatic pathos demonstrated in the Sistine Ceiling, expressed now not in Michelangelesque terms of single figure motives or even of small groups, but in terms, appropriate to Raphael's different genius, of whole pictorial structures. In his pictorial world in the Stanza d'Eliodoro, on the wide dimensions of a populated dramatic stage, Raphael creates his counterpart of Michelangelo's pathos, in circumstances of historical narrative rather than of lonely heroic fantasy.

The initial conception of the frescoes of the Stanza d'Eliodoro in states of activity develops from the Segnatura, but at the same time it requires an inversion of emphasis in primary components of the Segnatura style. In the Segnatura Raphael had infused animation into basically static structures; the vitality of form, and of content also, in those frescoes worked within a preexistent stable frame of reference. In the Eliodoro frescoes the mechanism of control — of regulation of the whole scheme into harmony — follows, instead, upon the first conception of activity. The will to final harmony is not on that account a fraction less; it is an embracing motive quite as absolute as it had been before. However, as the animation of the Eliodoro frescoes is more urgent, and in some ways more complex, than in the Segnatura so also is there a greater complexity of means by which harmony has been attained. The devices used to control and counterbalance action in the Eliodoro frescoes tend in themselves to be conceived of active elements, even in the architecture; in each of these scenes, harmony is achieved by the manipulation of substances and forces more highly charged than those in the Segnatura. The temper of harmony so made is, of necessity, not the same as that of the frescoes of the early Stanza. It is rich with energies and resiliencies that the Segnatura does not know: it is of a more complex, and also of a more distinct, articulateness, and it is instilled with higher power.

The Eliodoro frescoes explore a dimension of classical style different from that attained in the Segnatura and which, in intensification of expressive content and in elaboration of form, is a development beyond it. As in the Segnatura frescoes there is, among the frescoes of the Eliodoro, a progressively developing research of the basic idea of style which, at the beginning, Raphael had to find for them; but in this room the research is more boldly probing and dynamic, as if in consequence of the dynamic nature of the basic idea in itself. Each fresco is conceived with a different power and kind of dramatic urgency, and in each Raphael invents new devices of form which shall express this urgency and, at the same time, discipline it into harmony. By the time of his completion of the Stanza d'Eliodoro Raphael had searched out, to their apparent limits, the possibilities in monumental painting of the mature phase of classical style. The Stanza d'Eliodoro fulfilled the maturity initiated in the Segnatura; but this process of fulfillment also posed the problems which, in the subsequent moment of Raphael's career, would generate a crisis in his development of style.

In the Stanza d'Eliodoro the expressive urgency of each fresco is such that each wall seems to assert its own identity far more than — as in the Segnatura — its harmonious community with its companions. It is not only the dramatic concentration of each painting that is responsible for this: it is the result also of the episodic separateness of themes dictated for the illustration of the program. Nor do the Eliodoro frescoes show, in the design of each, the measure of relationship to one another that was worked out for the Segnatura; as with the subjects, the identity of structure in each fresco is more apparent than its relation in community. Nevertheless, a planned formal concordance does exist among the separate frescoes of the room.

Between the opposite frescoes on the short walls, the *Bolsena* and the *Liberation*, there is the responsive relation of the stair-motive in their architectural schemes, exploited in both for its value of illusionism, and a complementary relation between light of night and day. Between the *Expulsion* and the *Attila* there is the counterpoise of landscape with interior architecture that appeared in the two large paintings of the previous room, and a contrast, more developed than in them, of opened against closed foreground space. Within each fresco, there is a balance of an active against a passive part, and in the succession of one fresco to the next around the walls, passive parts and active parts adjoin each other in the separate frescoes (Wittkower). This adjacency of similars between two frescoes serves to make more firm their connection in sequence: the spectator completes his reading of one fresco in the same pace and temper as that with which he begins the next. More than these useful structural devices, however, what binds the frescoes of the Stanza d'Eliodoro in a community is their shared pervasive energy of forms, and in content, their common atmosphere of dramatic authority.

In spite of its different character of subject the first fresco of the new room, the *Mass of Bolsena* [214-16] (first half 1512), is strongly related still, in mode of feeling and in the accent of its final harmony, to the frescoes of the Segnatura. Its impulse of movement, though dramatically directed, retains the tempered suavity of the Segnatura and its general design depends, as much as in the Segnatura, on flexible but relatively literal balances of mass. The *Bolsena* is more compact in form and more immediate in effect of content than the *School of Athens*, but its tonality, of fluent and grave resonance, is still much the same. At the same time, the *Mass* decisively confronts the new problems that had not been presented by the Segnatura, and affords solutions that are the basis for the subsequent development within this room.

The equal division of the fresco into massive halves is a division between the two disparate spheres that Raphael is required to represent: on the left a dramatically expressive, idealized historical past, and on the right a physically and psychologically immediate present, of which the persons are cast in a more passive role, part actors in and part spectators of the historical event. In the Segnatura frescoes, their harmony was of an existence on one internally differentiated plane of ideality and of animation; here the elements which must be reconciled are separately distinct. Unity is not a consequence, as in the *School of Athens*, of the expansion and articulation of a central core, but of counterpoise achieved between initially contrasting things. The first step in the process of their reconciliation is that which we described before, of an exchange of properties of content and form between the actual and imagined actors so that, while they still retain their appropriate basic identity, they partake in the character of one another: the ideal figures infused with a vitality of the actual, and the actual touched with the form, and yet more with the personality, of the ideal. Though on distinguishable levels, they are made to inhabit a common sphere.

The necessary illustrative dramatic activity that inhabits one half of the fresco finds a relieving contrast in the opposite, more passive side, but at the same time it also finds an equal counterpoise of expression and of form. It is as if the principle of contrapposto had been applied to the composition not, as in the Segnatura, in an endlessly subtle unfolding of single form to group, and of group to whole, but in a far more bold and generalizing single act: as if the whole design were the decisive unit of the counterpoise. And in this new scale of Raphael's conception of contrapposto, it is significantly no longer the single figure or even the group that is conceived in contrapposto, but only the composition as a whole. Certainly, the figures preserve their rhythmical, deliberated grace; but it is now no longer possible, as in the *School of Athens*, to isolate almost any given figure, or any group, and find in it its own poised self-sufficiency. Among the historical actors their urgency of impulse projects its energy in action that exceeds the limits of the single form: the single figure is carried by its feeling with the surging of the crowd. As the figures are still tempered by a suavity of movement so also, in the crowd, is its sweeping action internally controlled and rhythmically scanned; but even the whole mass in action, discharging its passionate attention upon the miracle of the Host, is not self-contained and must depend upon the counterpoise of static figures to the right.

In turn, this counterpoise of active and passive is contained within a unity imposed by the architecture. Almost as grand as the architecture of the *School of Athens*, and comparable in massiveness and symmetry, this architecture is different in personality and in its relation to the figure composition it contains. The forms of architecture share in the higher energy that generally inspires the composition: it is an architecture which, within its necessarily geometric discipline, is more complex and movemented than in the *School of Athens*, and of which the movement is accented by an unaccustomed variousness of light. The nearest feature of the architecture, the great choir-screen, is more than a background or a frame: it obtrudes itself into the very body of the figure composition, binding its parts together with the curving energy of its embrace. On the left it is muted in effect, a diminished sounding board for the activity of the figures, but on the right it arches with accented force into the static portion of the composition, enlivening its stillness with an energy of architectural form.

The animating personality of light, as it is visible in the architecture, functions also throughout the fresco. Previously, Raphael's light had been diffused, not strongly differentiated; its character had been proper to the composed ideality of his previous frescoes. Here, in concord with the energies of form and mood of the historical figures of the *Mass of Bolsena,* the light too assumes an active role, much more vigorously and fully differentiated than before; it is manipulated with a decisiveness and with a force of contrast that are nowhere evident within the Segnatura. This activity of light does more than enrich the action of the figures, in the sense of their form; it adds as well to the dimension in them of dramatic expressiveness. Among the portrait figures to right of the *Bolsena* the light serves yet another purpose, somewhat different in means and in intent from its mode of working toward the left. The light toward the right becomes exceptionally strong and clear, searching out and emphasizing the actuality of portrayed persons: the light brilliantly relieves their presences and, even more than this, charges the air around them with its radiance. As the figures descend toward us, and assume more the role of spectators like ourselves, and less that of participants, the light on them acquires the power to create absolute illusion: as if, in their corner of the fresco nearest us, the Swiss Guards [216] were inhabitants not only of the fresco but of our present world.

In its power of contrast, the light carries a consequence for color, which depends on it for its intensities. With the stronger lights, the color, indissoluble from it, emerges — as in the reds to the right side of the *Bolsena* — with a strength and an identity more assertive than in the frescoes of the Segnatura. But the dominating novelty in the light is in its contrary variation into darks, and this more generally affects the tonality of color, giving it — as at the left of this fresco — a deeper, but also less saturated, richness than it had before. The tendency of color, incipiently in the *Bolsena,* but more pervasively in the later frescoes of this room, is to a darker, heavier power: less ornamentally beautiful than in the Segnatura and less finely variegated, but more appropriate to the new tonality in content, of more masculine dramatic force.

The activity of light and the development in it of a great range of descriptive and expressive power are explored in the *Bolsena* with virtuosity, and with the enthusiasm of a new interest. This interest, however, is not without its prior symptoms in Raphael's art: it had been adumbrated in the *School of Athens,* and in what may have been the latest fresco of the Segnatura room, the (ruined or perhaps unfinished) *Civil Law,* there had been a sudden onset of concern with active light. Such a development of light is, further, in entire accord with the development of other factors of style that the *Mass* attests. The influence of Sebastiano del Piombo which has been cited as a motive for this new interest is only dubious: at the time of the painting of the *Mass,* Sebastiano had given a limited demonstration only of the optical Venetian style, and was then more concerned to reform his Venetian character on

Roman models than to assert it. The origin of Raphael's new luminism should be sought less in an external source than in the logic of his own evolution in this time.

The harmony into which these many animating powers are resolved, finally, in the *Mass of Bolsena,* is as unshakable as that of the *School of Athens.* However, despite the role played in the making of this harmony in the *Bolsena* — as in the *School of Athens* — by elements of symmetry and stillness the *Mass* is charged — even throughout its static parts — by an animating power altogether more compelling than that in the *Athens.* The *Mass* vibrates within its harmony, in a synthesis created out of equal and interpenetrated forces of expansive energy and of authoritative control: the nature and the temper of this synthesis resembles that of Michelangelo's conceptions in the latter phases of the Sistine and, almost, rivals it. The *Mass* establishes, for the Stanza d'Eliodoro, the proposition of a classical style dramatically expressive and intensely charged, and it is Raphael's object to evolve this proposition farther in the other frescoes of this room.

The *Expulsion of Heliodorus* [217-19] conceived and executed most probably in the second half of 1512, responds certainly to a yet higher dramatic potential of its subject, but this has been exploited in the sense of Raphael's developmental will. There is a sharp distinction in levels of expressive urgency between the *Expulsion* and the *Mass*: in the *Expulsion* the impulse to power of dramatic illustration is so strong that, for the first time in Raphael's career, the effect of force seems surely dominant over that of grace. The suavity that, in the *Mass*, still linked not only its character of structure but even something of its expressive tone to the frescoes of the Segnatura, appears in the *Expulsion* in no more than secondary forms; in its entirety the *Expulsion* makes another gender of effect, and at once: of swiftly consummated, almost drastic, dramatic action.

Far more of the space of this scene is given over to the illustration of the drama. The passive contemporary portrait group plays a role not only quantitatively, but aesthetically and psychologically less, within the picture. More than the contemporary persons of the *Mass*, these are cast in the frank role of spectators, and of spectators who belong with us in our world rather than in the sphere of the painted history. The transition which they make between actuality and history is not deliberately smoothed as it was in the *Mass*; the pretext invented for their presence beside the history is adequate but Raphael is not concerned with its elaborate justification.

The required papal compliment literally put aside, the dramatic exposition begins with the female spectators in the second plane: [219] these figures are inspired by the appearance of the avenging angel with an intense astonishment, much less decorous than that of the spectators of the *Mass of*

Bolsena. Their force of look and gesture is directed toward the right, but at the same time an equal and opposite impulse of fear makes them recoil toward the left. On one hand they are possessed by an expansive power of movement and emotion, and on the other they contract, seeking mutual protection among themselves. Their urgency of feeling and energy of action are wound into an inclusive single form, of almost arbitrary spheroid shape and of opaque compactness. In this tight-knit shape the expressive value of the action is at once disciplined and, by restriction, also magnified. Like the whole structure of the *Mass of Bolsena*, this group reconciles equal and contrasting powers, but unlike in the *Mass* both these opposites are active and, also, at a level of urgency higher than that in the preceding fresco. Less than in the *Mass* is it now possible to extract a single self-sufficient component from the group: as the dramatic energies of forms increase, they become more dependent upon one another, as agents of expressive stimulus or as vehicles of response. Even the formally deliberated ornamental figure, of so eloquent a cursive style, that precedes this group is not isolatable; her energies so swiftly traverse and extend beyond her form.

Despite the fact that it contains its own machinery of counterpoise, this whole group is no more isolatable from the whole fresco than are its parts from it: the group in turn depends for its sense on the whole situation to which it responds. These women are like a chorus, commenting the action of the protagonists and directing our attention to it. However, with a sophistication in narrative technique that is without precedent in the history of painting, Raphael does not allow us to proceed directly from this introducing group to the concluding action. The tension of narration is increased by creating a suspense, and in this interval there is also a fuller exposition of the story. The eye is pulled by a perspective space deep into the open center of the picture to the priest Onias, whose prayer has been answered by the angels' intercession; only then are we impelled by an inverse energy of movement in the architecture to the climactic foreground group.

Like every other element of form the space has been made into an active agent, developing the conception in the *Mass of Bolsena* of an actively articulated architecture and introducing now, as well, the idea of a perspective of dynamic kind. The vacant foreground of the scene is marked out in a floor-pattern of movemented, perspectively-diminished shapes; the architecture to the rear is open not only in its center but at the sides, making a wider and more pervasive sense of the activity of space; in the center bay of the temple arches, cornices and moldings are multiplied, and insistently and quickly scan their diminution into distance. To this perspective activity of architectural shapes is added, in much more marked degree than in the *Mass of Bolsena*, the formal energy and dramatizing tone of active, richly differentiated light. Unobstructed to the front, and swiftly and irresistibly channeled to the rear, the space and its vehicle, the architecture, are of one temper of dramatic animation with the figures; more than their sounding board, the space becomes an actor in the drama with them.

The force of perspective recession is discharged upon the figure of Onias as if to be converted in his form into an energy of prayer; from him the eye is drawn outward, as irresistibly as it had just been drawn in, to the group [218] (inspired by the Antique, by a memory of Leonardo and by Michelangelo) which enacts the answer to the high priest's prayer. In size, in place, and in effect of direction this plastically assertive group is the precisely calculated counterweight of the whole structure of figures to the left; equally important, it is their counterpoise in energy of action. This group, in its function of climax and conclusion of the drama is, however, differently conceived in form and in character of expression from its counterpart at left. The left half of the composition is strung upon a rhythmic thread so swift in movement, precipitating toward this climax, that in it single forms are virtually obscured; but in this right group each element is oppositely explicit in the shape and in the force of impact of its action: the effect is of a hard, clear resonance, like that of a brassy chord. The cogency of action in this group is thus more positive, but by virtue of the explicitness with which the action is described it is more disciplined, too; the increase of expressive force has been accompanied by an equal higher power of control.

Even in the impetus of their hurtling charge the angels have been, as it were, stylized in action, not only tempering their meaning of dramatic violence but, more than that, distilling its effect into another, an aesthetic, sphere. Their urgencies of movement are suspended, no longer in ponderated contrapposto, but in a daring equilibrium between centrifugal energies and mass; the movement of each angel has been poised at that point where its maximum effect of force may coincide with an effect of calculated formal beauty. Moreover, each angel (and the Heliodorus too) is described in a vocabulary of shape of deliberately stressed geometricizing regularity: they convey a quality of structured beauty more evident and more emphasized than in any forms of this extent in Raphael's art before. The dramatic and formal energy which is the initial meaning of this group achieves another kind of equilibrium (beyond that of its powers of energy and mass): between its expressive immediacy and its eternal-seeming classical deliberation of aesthetic form. To these equilibriums the whole ordnance of the group adds yet another discipline: each distinct member in it is locked dependently upon the next, and all their poised powers are meshed within a form that itself assumes an inescapable, near-spherical perfection. But even this perfection is not, finally, an end; the group assumes the full dimension of its meaning only in the larger scheme, to the charged harmony of which its form and content are referred.

The *Repulse of Attila* [220-21] must already have been in course of execution at the time of Julius' death in January 1513. His successor, Leo X, figures in it in his initially intended role of Cardinal in the papal suite, and again, in consequence of his election to the papacy in March, in the place that had been intended for the former Pope. It is doubtful, however, that any major change was made in the design which Raphael had put into execution under Julius, and which may be, most imperfectly, documented in a copy now in Oxford (Ashmolean). This design, however, was already an alteration of an earlier conception, rather bolder, which it seems Raphael felt compelled to moderate; this scheme is recorded, again in a copy, in a drawing in the Louvre (3873). In the Louvre design the papal group is relegated to a place in the far distance at the left, barely evident participants in the event, and the whole foreground of the picture is given over to the single sweeping movement of descent and recoil of Attila's charge. This conception eliminated the problem — with which Raphael had already shown some impatience — of reconciliation of portraiture with drama; but this elimination was not a solution. It not only diminished the actuality of reference of the depicted scene but slurred over the role the Pope and his companions had played in it; in this conception the responsibility for the repulse of the invading Huns was assigned altogether to Sts. Peter and Paul, and no visible credit was given to the mortal actors. Furthermore, by its almost entire depiction of a scene of action this design did not accord with the preceding frescoes of the room, in both of which the principle had been laid down of a scene composed of balance between activity and stillness.

The revision made by Raphael in the Oxford design meets the requirement of concord in principle of structure with the other frescoes, and more properly than the Louvre scheme confronts the given matter of the subject in the sense in which the Pope intended its interpretation. In this scene, in which the contemporary persons were meant to be principals and not merely quasi-spectators in the drama, this requirement of the patron was harder to fulfill. In order to achieve, here, that sense of effective coexistence between past and present that was in the *Bolsena*, and still in the *Expulsion*, it would have required not only Raphael's genius of invention but also his execution; unfortunately, in the *Repulse of Attila* the tendency (already evident in parts of the *Expulsion*) to permit the intervention of assistants had drastically increased. Penni, apparently now finished with the secondary decoration of the Segnatura, was entrusted — with gravely diminishing results — with the painting of the major portion of the right half of the *Attila*.

It was in consideration not only of the subject but of the ordnance in a differentiated harmony of the entire room that Raphael determined his conception of the *Repulse of Attila*, inventing — as in the Segnatura — a scene of landscape wholly, without architectural support, to complement the wholly architectural *Expulsion*. The elimination of any architectural frame of reference (the walls of Rome or a monumental gate could appropriately have made a near background for the scene) disposed of a primary means of discipline of composition, but it was Raphael's intention despite this to increase, beyond the level of the *Expulsion*, the movemented urgency of drama in the new fresco. The whole theme of the *Attila* is in a way a magnification and variation of that of the right part only of the *Expulsion*: here there is the charge of a host rather than of a single horseman.

The movement of this host is the chief matter of design; the fresco is dominated by the description of excited action. The charge of the Hunnish cavalry comes toward us from the right, sweeping in a broad descending arc out of the depth of landscape; behind them in the distance a town burns against the darkening sky. The impetus of movement carries the riders across the middle of the picture field, into the territory defended by the papal group. This group is a figurative rampart for Rome, which lies in the landscape to their rear: they confront the rush of cavalry with an unshakable immobility, made of massive static shapes, columnar and pyramidal. The impact of movement breaks upon this barrier, but even before it does so the charge is already being turned back upon itself, in incipient recoil, by the aerial counter-offensive of the St. Peter and St. Paul. Responding to this countermovement, the Huns pull back upon the impetus of their charge, reining in their horses and shrinking or turning bodily toward the rear. Their movement, reacting to that of the Saints, contains its own restraining and diminishing force, so that it is only a residue of violence that is discharged against the papal group. The equilibrium that is made in the composition is not just of movement against stillness, but also of resilient response between action and counter-action. This formal equilibrium is, in turn, exactly expressive of a dramatic situation poised at its climactic point — not only at its moment of conclusion, as in the *Expulsion*, but in the very moment of decision within conflict.

There is some similarity between this theme and its manner of treatment with the only major antecedent in the High Renaissance style for a battle scene, Leonardo's *Anghiari*,[30-3] and it is not surprising to observe that in the *Attila* Raphael remembered certain motives from Leonardo's picture, which he had studied years before. Leonardo was to come to Rome in the autumn of 1513 (when this fresco was already finished, and a year or more after its design); and he must have been satisfied to observe that in some respects Raphael was still his disciple.

But Raphael has evolved, in the *Attila*, far beyond the ideas of the *Anghiari*, and in an important sense beyond his own style in the *Expulsion*. The composition of the *Attila* continues to employ the balancing devices of the previous works; it contains an approximately equal distribution of figure masses to both sides of a center of some stress, and its opening to space is balanced by a strong emphasis of forms distributed along the foreground plane. These devices — and also the more novel intersection in the composition of diagonal directions — are integral to the structure of the picture, and secure its inalterable final equilibrium. Nevertheless, in the context of pervasive movement of this fresco, these devices do not have the same character of measured, positive stability they had before; their role in securing the equilibrium of composition is shared with, and may be less than, that of the elastic adjustment in the design of forces and elements that are in themselves not only active, but asymmetrical. The impulse of activity in the *Attila* is so dominant that it can no longer be expressed within the prior system of symmetrical, containing and constraining compositional halves, but must trespass beyond these limits.

The initial thinking of design in the *Attila* is distinct from that in the *Expulsion*: in that fresco the idea of activity is still conveyed within the kind of classical scheme invented for the Segnatura, of symmetrical balances dependent on a central core; in the *Attila* its activity is conceived to begin with as a dynamically expansive, asymmetrical relationship of forces, on which a machinery of balances is only subsequently imposed. This is the first instance in Raphael's work where he has presumed to construct a whole composition which neither starts from, nor in the end primarily depends upon, an underlying centralized design.

The equilibrium which this design does attain is no longer sensibly related to a concept of classical contrapposto, by which the structure of the whole is, as it were, unfolded from that of the single human form. In consequence — extending a characteristic already evident in the *Expulsion* — there is less need in this fresco that the composition be built of elements so rhythmically connected and adjusted to one another as to seem parts in the growing of a single organism: its parts may be more separately and more contrastingly articulated. Still more, important elements of composition may now be virtually detached, with sharply dramatic effect, from the rest of the figurative design.

The *Repulse of Attila* explores problems and finds solutions that are in some ways significantly new and which, potentially, are avenues toward new directions of pictorial style. At the same time, however, the novelties of the *Attila* are fruitions of inventions that Raphael had made in each successive antecedent work: he does not intend here to trespass the limits of his classical style but to extend its boundaries. These novelties are part of Raphael's characteristic process of constant enrichment of the vocabulary of classicism, and in the end they serve, in the *Attila,* to promote the vital power of a harmony that is Raphael's continuing classical intention. It is only the internal mechanism of this harmony that is now yet more complex, and more important, more freely manipulable than before. The *Attila* does not, like

Michelangelo's *Brazen Serpent*[143] (a year earlier in conception), surrender to an impulse of expressive urgency so strong that it transcends not only symmetry but classical control. But, in historical hindsight, the *Attila* proves to be the limit of the probing possible to a classical style in this direction, of dramatic activity and of multiplicity of forms.

It was not a negative caution about further probing in this same direction, but a positive will to investigate an alternative, and in fact opposite, mode of dramatic expression that determined the very different structure of the last fresco in this room, the *Liberation of Peter* (late 1513–early 1514).[222-4] The given theme in itself has none of the complexity of the *Attila*, and little of its initial violence; however, as Raphael feels this theme it assumes an even higher power of dramatic content. Rather than seeking to elaborate the material of the narrative, Raphael accepts it in its simplicity, and magnifies that simplicity into an agency of dramatic force. In its contrast with the complex action of the *Attila*, the *Liberation* seems partly to return to the simpler ideas of the first fresco in the room, the *Bolsena*, which it confronts and which, in respect of the entire harmony of the decoration, it was in some degree obliged to match. Yet the character of the *Bolsena*, suavely clear, and that of the *Liberation*, assertively austere, are very much distinct, in form as in mood; the *Bolsena* precedes the powerful mounting of dramatic tension in the *Expulsion* and the *Attila*, while the *Liberation* is its consequence.

Where the conception of the *Attila* began with its idea of movement, the *Liberation* begins, oppositely, with decisive stasis; but both such beginnings are different from the initial equivalence of movement and stillness in the *Expulsion* and the *Bolsena*. In the *Liberation* the architecture assumes the role of principal agent of this stasis. Unlike the architecture of the previous frescoes, this shape has no internal activity of articulation; it is, with contentual appropriateness, heavy and unrelievedly severe. Its form and its austerity of expression do more than support and frame the composition; they dominate it. Contrary to the relief from symmetry that is sought in the *Attila*, this architecture reaffirms both centrality and symmetry with strongest emphasis. Even before the interjection of any figure, the composition is molded by the architecture into an inevitable central and symmetrical scheme. At the same time, however, the shape of architecture is also divisive, interposing its great piers between the center and the sides of the design. No effort is made in the placing of the figures to violate this division between the sides and center: each group is contained frankly within its architecturally established frame, with a minimum connection, or no connection, with its neighbor. The design of figures, like that of the architecture to which it is subservient, has its affirmative and dominating central core; but the composition is now not in the least conceived — much less than in the *Attila* — as a sequence rhythmically unfolded, in the manner of a bodily contrapposto, from this core. The figure composition is a projection of three separate units, which are also three units of narration, and these are bound together not in an organic community but by *force majeure*, by the irresistible primacy of the central theme and form.

Compared to the *Attila*, or even to the *Expulsion*, the movement of the figures within their static framework of design is much restricted. There is here, according to the system prescribed for all the frescoes of the room, a contrast between an active and a passive side within the picture: it is the soldiers, awakened and alarmed on the left, sleeping on the right, who fill this role. Except for the gesture of the awakening angel, the protagonists are of necessity quiet: in the prison Peter sleeps between the immobile figures of his armored guards; outside to the right Peter walks as if entranced, led by his rescuer:[224] "[he] wist not that it was true which was done by the angel; but thought he saw a vision" (Acts 12:9). In this context of stillness the liberating action of the angel, central and relieved in light, acquires a singular dramatic emphasis.[223]

The real agent of dramatic force is not movement, however, but the light: it is the activity of lighting in the *Liberation* that replaces, and creates the dramatic equivalent of, the physical and formal action of the preceding frescoes. And, as in those frescoes the force of action was not only controlled but emphasized by contrast with passivity, so here the force of light is magnified against the dark rigidity of the architecture. Like the inventions in the *Attila*, this new function of the light is both a fruition of earlier developments and a reaching into a dimension that, in the earlier frescoes, had not been foreseen.

It is not only this dramatic generalization of a light effect that Raphael seeks in the *Liberation*. The effulgence of the liberating angel — naturally interpreted but generated supernaturally — is the starting point for further and subtler explorations of new light effects, of moonlight and torchlight. Raphael's interest in these is neither only dramatic, nor, less still, is it only descriptive. He is concerned with the power, which resides in artificial light, to transform common incidents of nature into singular experiences, not only optically but emotionally affective: as in the light that makes the pattern of the prison bars vibrate, and the polished armor glow. The two guards who catch the full radiance of the liberating angel become lucent demonstrations of geometry, quite dehumanized, recollective of images of Piero della Francesca or Uccello.

This use of lighting in the *Liberation* is developed essentially out of Raphael's own resources, but it is not unlikely that some stimulation to it may have come from Venice, perhaps by verbal report more than by direct vision of a work of art. Sebastiano had not yet, as far as our knowledge goes, painted any work in Rome which could pretend to the distinction of serving Raphael as precedent for what he has done in the *Liberation*, but Sebastiano or others may have carried to Raphael reports of Giorgionesque experiments — now lost to us — with night painting: a description only may have kindled the remarkable illumination of this fresco. Whatever the role of light in this work, with its powers and variety, it must be remembered that it functions within the most austere discipline of form Raphael had so far invented. The severe, grave nobility and the concentrated impact of dramatic force depend eventually, in the *Liberation*, on its form.

In this form and in this mood the principal decoration of the walls of the Stanza d'Eliodoro was completed, and with it another stage in a development of style which, though not in fact more accelerated than in the Segnatura, was more various and searching. The nature of the given problems in the Eliodoro room permitted and encouraged the deepening of the expressive power of content of the mature classical style, and the concomitant elaboration of its repertory of form. In the *Bolsena* and the *Expulsion* this new research is comprehended, still, in terms that are extensions of those of the Segnatura; but in the *Attila* and the *Liberation* the development no longer refers to the Segnatura, but to the evolution just accomplished in the two preceding works. In the first two frescoes the classical synthesis, matured in the Segnatura, had been expressed in an equal participation of forces of activity and of stasis, each explicitly defined, and each mutually and equally intensified in respect to the other. In the *Attila* it is the potential of activity that receives special development and an incipient new form for its expression; in the *Liberation* it is the contrary expressive potential of a static system that is stressed. In both later frescoes, however, though the primary emphasis in character of form has been shifted, and into opposite directions, the shifts occur within a still absolutely authoritative ambition to final, classical, equilibrium.

It is not only the shift in these later frescoes from previous classical system that is significant but the fact that, in each fresco, inventions of form have been conceived which, with new means, manage to retain and, at the same time, enrich and diversify the ideal of classical equilibrium. The modes of both the *Attila* and the *Liberation* offer possibilities of yet further development, but in the very fact of the divergence of the avenues of exploration they offer there is the material of a creative conflict, and the possibility of a crisis. And, in the will to test these new-formed propositions toward a level of yet higher expressive power, there is the risk of violation of classical principle, so far secure. This risk, in the inevitable dynamism of Raphael's development, would be seen but nonetheless encountered. The time that follows the *Attila* and *Liberation* is occupied with test and striving, not always successful of a classical solution; what might be considered the natural development of the mature phase of classical style ends, in Raphael, with the Stanza d'Eliodoro.

The painting of the main frescoes of the Stanza d'Eliodoro was completed before July 1514, but it is likely that the incidental decoration of the room, its basamenti [226] and embrasures in grisaille,[225] was in process for a further time. These have been for the most part ruined and drastically repainted, but still show Raphael's intent. In the embrasures there are grotesque designs, basically like those which frame the windows of the Stanza della Segnatura, but developed beyond them in fullness and variety of form and in ingenuity of conceit. Their execution may in part be due to Raphael's prodigious boy-assistant, Giulio Romano, whose help had already been enlisted in parts of the larger frescoes. It is also Giulio who was responsible for the preparation in drawing (though not for the invention), and probably for the original execution, of the caryatid figures on the basamenti of this room. Raphael's idea in them is an ingenious coincidence of Antique reference, architectural pretext, and decorative effectiveness. The caryatids are painted with a restrained and limited illusion, into a plane of space pictorially excavated for them beneath the frescoes, of which they seemingly support the lower frame. In their monochrome color and their heavy dignity of pose they authentically recall the character of their Antique source of inspiration. Yet, given the liberty of paint, these caryatids gently move in space with a variety not allowed their prototypes, and in certain of them, their eyes are those of living beings, not of a sightless Antique statuary. Submissive to their function, they are still infused, within their monumental dignity, with a muted power of animate existence and discourse. In a sense that recalls the structure of music as well as architecture, the caryatids are a sustaining base to the richly orchestrated themes above.

The work which Raphael planned to be closest in spirit and in character of form to the frescoes of the Stanza d'Eliodoro was never executed. This was a *Resurrection* (c. 1512–13) — for what patron or what place we do not know — for which a series of elaborate preparatory studies survives (Windsor, Oxford, Chatsworth, London) [228–9] but of which the principal document is a design for the whole, apparently in an early stage of its development, in Bayonne.[227] This was Raphael's first essay in a religious subject of dramatic cast since the pre-Roman Baglioni *Deposition*, and all the sophistication of dramatic style he had acquired in the intervening years emerges in the contrast we may make between the two. The *Resurrection* is possessed by an energy as inspired as that of the *Expulsion* or the *Attila*, and in its motives of astonished soldiery recalls the guards of Peter in the *Liberation*. In the single studies for these soldiers, the forms of Michelangelesque anatomy and the sense of force of movement and of grand dimension is yet more compelling than in the figures of the frescoes. As in them, the urgency of action in the soldiers of the *Resurrection* is too strong to be constrained within the bounds of literal contrapposto, and they too are poised in movement (like the angels of the *Expulsion*) at the critical point where it is also ornament, various in form beyond the aspirations of the Segnatura style.

As a group their response to the miraculous event is too violent to be held in symmetry: Christ's rising from their midst has split them into tumbling, unequal parts. The energy that radiates from His ascent divides the soldiery and oppresses them, but their reaction to it is resilient, as of tightly coiled springs: they turn and, as if seeking to escape the force that presses on them, untwist upward and to the right; this diagonal direction of their action is reinforced by the line of the sarcophagus. On the tomb, the quick turning of the angel — a powerful isolated silhouette — intersects this impulse of direction and links it to the upper part of the design. Here, within a circular pattern as clear as that of the *Madonna di Foligno*,[177] but altogether differently charged, the Christ takes up the motion from the lower left and at the same time turns counter to it, supported by the rotation, in this countersense, of the flight of angels. The movement of Christ's arms and head does not seem quite to arrest but to suspend His rising: He is held, at the intersection of the forces He has generated, with a miraculous buoyancy in space. There is evidence to suggest that for this scheme, in which such energies of form are so dramatically poised, Raphael intended the further dramatic force of a lighting like that he used in the *Liberation*.

Even in its state of intention rather than of accomplished painted fact the *Resurrection* reveals, like the later Eliodoro frescoes, the expression of vast dramatic powers in the framework, still, of an unequivocal synthetic discipline of entire scheme. The meaning of this design in the history of Raphael's development of classical style will become yet more clear when, in the later *Transfiguration*, he would recall its motives, but with no possibility of recapture of this moment's character of style.

Other Frescoes of the Eliodoro Phase. The *Galatea*,[230] companion and complement to Sebastiano's *Polyphemus* fresco[198] in the Farnesina, is of 1513. In the *Galatea* Raphael returns, for the first time since his paintings in the Stanza della Segnatura, to a subject that is *ab initio* classical — for which classicism in style is not a consequence of imposition of the artist's will but of inevitable concord between will and subject. The harmony of form and content in the *Galatea* is, on this account, more apparent than that (very differently complex) of the Eliodoro frescoes, but it is also beyond that of the frescoes of the Segnatura. Into the harmony of the *Galatea* has gone that growth in power of communication of content, and the more splendid and various repertory of form, that are the products of the Eliodoro phase. Different from the only incipiently animate painting of ideal situations in the Segnatura, this fresco shades, in its thinking of the subject, toward an episode of action, taking up the cue of Sebastiano's watching Polyphemus in the adjoining bay. Yet, unlike the dramas of the Stanza d'Eliodoro, the *Galatea* is, like the *Parnassus*, also finally a description of existence more than of action: it is less a record of event than a celebration of a classical — an Antique classical — mode of being.

The physical perfections of Galatea and her court are, as Raphael tells us in the famous letter on this fresco, of altogether calculated invention, and they evoke such a sense of the splendors of substance of the Ancient world as only Michelangelo so far had known how to represent. Here, however, there is no trace, as there is in Michelangelo, of the shadow on this substance of a Christian conscience. In this picture where the content is, from its beginning, one of harmony, the concept of contrapposto resumes the character and authority it had held in the Segnatura. The pretext of the scene is taken from a contrapposto: the gliding progress of Galatea and her company across the sunlit sea and, in perfect counterbalance to it, her movement to look backward at the Polyphemus. From this equilibrium of the Galatea in her turning the rest of the design is generated: an unfolding of a resilient, ornamental spiral from her core, developing in a controlling planar motion on the surface but expanding at the same time — again in echo of Galatea's movement — into a spherical space.

The symptom of this idea of design had been in the upper portion of the scheme for the *Resurrection*, but devoted there to a very different purpose and effect. As quick and as buoyant as the movement of that part of the *Resurrection* is, so in the *Galatea* is the temper of design deliberate and suave. From the very substantiality of its figures its movement takes on richness and sonority, fuller and more deeply chorded than in any prior work. All this elaborate complex of forms and powers is poised in a supreme equilibrium, in which the sense of arrest is compounded, equally and almost miraculously, of the certainty of permanence of this instant of a golden time and of conviction of its actual vitality.

Except for the evidence in it of a grander mode of Latinized speech — the result of his thinking in the frescoes of the Eliodoro — the *Galatea* relates still to much in the Segnatura style. This is the case also with the *Sibyls* of the Chigi Chapel in S. M. della Pace, which are a reprise and a more eloquent restatement of a Segnatura theme. The Sibyls on the lower façade of the chapel [232-4] were designed, in all likelihood, in early 1514 and executed by Raphael close to this time. The execution of the accessory feature of this decoration, four Prophets in the lunette above,[231] may have been delayed; it was in any case confided to an assistant who (despite Vasari's assertion that it was Timoteo Viti, IV, 495) is not surely identifiable. The whole scheme of decoration was, however, invented at one time, in an iconographic (though not a formal) system that reflects the influence of Michelangelo. An architectural device once bound the two parts of the decoration in a unity: a common setting of perspective architecture contained the Sibyls and the Prophets both. This has been painted out behind the Sibyls, leaving the assistant's mismanagement of Raphael's idea for the Prophets in deserved unnoticed isolation.

The Sibyls are a reconsideration of the *Three Virtues* of the Segnatura,[171] and though they are not intended to be more imitatively Michelangelesque, they are depicted with an energy and spatial variety of movement which makes them in effect more like their counterparts in Michelangelo. By comparison with the charged grace, so richly articulated, of the Sibyls' forms, the *Virtues* seem a little bland, docile in temper and too generalized in shape. As in the *Virtues*, Raphael is again concerned not only with the value of the single figure but with figures as the matter of a composition: the Sibyls join their energies in concert, in a lateral sequence that is not less rhythmically continuous than in the *Virtues*, but which is more deliberately scanned; to this intent of stronger marking of the measure the lost architecture once contributed. This is a clearer, as well as a stronger speech, than that of its antecedent in the earlier room.

The composition contains its own equilibrium of mass and energy within each half of it, and — somewhat more in the manner of the Eliodoro schemes than those of the Segnatura — balances, not quite active against passive part, but a greater movement with a more muted one. What Raphael had taken, in the like theme of the *Virtues* of the Segnatura, in the temper of an ideal situation, only gently animate, he now conceives, in the *Sibyls* — as he had conceived the *Galatea* — as a more motivated and more active circumstance. He expresses an increased vitality in more complex, but also a more clearly articulated, ordering of forms. Its final end of harmony remains the same, but it is more internally vibrant and more powerful, and both the human and aesthetic dimensions of the painting have been increased.

The Easel Paintings of 1513–1514. Probably in 1513 (at latest in the early months of 1514) Raphael conceived and wholly executed his highest accomplishment so far of altar-painting, the *Sistine Madonna* (Dresden, Gallery).[235-7] The picture is the counterpart of style, in terms of a Christian subject matter, of the *Galatea*, which must shortly have preceded it. As in the *Galatea*, Raphael took precise account of the place for which this easel picture was intended: in this case a place like that of a fresco, high on the apse wall (beyond the high altar) of the Church of S. Sisto in Piacenza. With a sense for the drama of relation between the audience and the work of art that was not yet in the previous great altar, the *Madonna di Foligno*,[177] and which proceeds from the whole temper of his thought since then, Raphael has conceived a theme of plausible action in a context of illusion for the Sistine painting. He treats the area of the painting as if it were not a picture only but a window through the wall as well. The curtain which is so prominent a feature reads as if it were at once a simulacrum of the covering often hung before a painting and the curtain of a window. It has been drawn open to reveal the picture, and in the same moment to reveal a vision in the sky beyond the wall.

The curtain has been pulled open by the Saints, Barbara and Sixtus, and in this moment only; Barbara still holds the curtain wide. In answer to our prayer to them, the Saints, in their precise role as intercessors between us and the divine Persons, have besought the revelation of the Virgin and her Child to us. She has come before us in the guise of any mortal mother walking with her son, but hers is a marvelously stately promenade across the sky. She does not truly walk: this is a cloud-borne descent from some more distant reach of heaven higher to the right. Her garments still hold, like a restraining sail, the gentle wind of her oblique descent as she stands — in the attitude of the Ancient *epiphaneia* — in the instant of arresting of this timeless flight. She attests her moving and substantial presence, and yet is utterly immutable; in her person she resolves — more than does the *Galatea*, and far more than the resurrected Christ of the Bayonne design — the sense of a moment into that of an eternal poise: substance, gravity, and time seem to be suspended in a perfect equilibrium in her. Her human guise incorporates a classical conception of a cosmos, but the prime mover of this cosmos, as we perceive it in the Virgin's countenance and in the Child's, is the surpassing Christian reassurance of the love of God for man, for which, ultimately, all prayers ask — including the one to which this vision is the answer.

The figures and forms that accompany the Virgin are the foil and the complement for the — in all ways — central, and sufficient, meaning and appearance that are contained in her. By their placing, the Sixtus (with the face of Pope Julius, in whose honor, if not in whose lifetime, the picture was commissioned) and the Barbara complement the balance that is already adequately evident within the Virgin's form, and at the same time reciprocally make counterpart of form and action to one another. They also serve the purpose of differentiation of appearances and personality, both with each other and the Virgin; the *angelini* who lean on the simulated window-frame below are similarly a differentiation and a contrast for the solemnity of the Child. The attendant figures not only amplify the composition but serve to articulate the working in it of its space, both within the picture and beyond its frame, toward us. The situation of the two Saints implies the path, on a slight oblique plane, on which the Virgin is arrested in her movement; the Sixtus carries this more affirmatively in the direction of the spectator. The two angels (and the tiara, incidentally) at once mark the boundary of the picture's space and make transition through it. The effects of color support this spatial implication of the form: in rapport with the strong core of the traditional blue and red garments of the Virgin, the gold of Sixtus is assertive and the shadowed greens and blues of Barbara are recessive; the green of her mantle binds her, as it were, to the same color in the plane of the curtain she holds back. As if to confirm that these distinctions in the space, though clear, are meant to be discreet, the forms are bound together not only by their close adjacency and by continuities of rhythm but by echoing accents of color, and particularly a gold which, almost like a thread, weaves from one form to the next.

The disposition of the figures around the Virgin is such as to impel a slight sense of rotation, counterclockwise, of the design, which is simultaneously sensible as an effect upon the picture surface and in its space; in this latter respect it makes a complement to the gentle turning toward us of the Virgin. The composition is based on principles like those of the *Galatea*, but much moderated in kind and in effect: there is, appropriately, a different intention of content and affect of form in this religious subject matter. This does not intend, like the *Galatea*, the recreation of an Antique, terrestrial, paradise of lesser deities but a solemn vision into the Christian heaven, made imminent to us by the intercession of the Saints. Its persons have the same classical authority of presence and the same supreme beauty of substantial form as in Raphael's recreation of Antiquity, but they do not dwell in a simulacrum of an earthly space. This is a more abstract, literally an ethereal realm, vaporous and immeasurable, from which Raphael has drawn the curtain for us; behind the holy presences there is only light and the faint song of cherubim. Though the vision is granted us in the frame of an illusion, what we are given to perceive is clearly distinct from our mortal world. It is not truly like, but in its consummate seeming simplicity of forms and nearly planar ordering of them, and in its constraint of a great dignity, the *Sistine Madonna* — even in its profound humanity — makes an impress like that of the hieratic images of high Byzantine art.

The time of conception of the *Sistine Madonna* is close to that of the *Liberation of Peter*; the connection is assured by similarities of precise kind (that in particular of the angel at the right of the *Liberation* with the Virgin) and also by relationships between them of idea. The difference we have seen in the temper and intended character of form of the Sistine painting from the antecedent fresco of the *Galatea* is not dictated only by the different burden of their subject matter; it is the counterpart of such a change in Raphael's direction of exploration as occurred also, within the Stanza d'Eliodoro, from the *Attila* fresco to that of the *Liberation*. Expressed in the more moderated terms which, until the end of this phase, are usual to Raphael in his easel works, the *Sistine Madonna* is the analogue of the probing, in the *Liberation* fresco, toward a new severity and clarity of architectonically ordered form, and its hieratic dignity of meaning is the *simile*, for its subject, of the lucidity and force of drama in that fresco. As with the style of the *Liberation*, that of the *Sistine Madonna* is the basis from which Raphael would build, in 1515, his most austere construction of an ultimate of classical style.

Two major easel pictures of the time of the Stanza d'Eliodoro, the *Madonna of the Fish* (Madrid, Prado; c. 1513)[238] and the *Madonna dell' Impannata* (Florence, Pitti; 1514)[240] were left — for the first * time in Raphael's career — for entire execution by his principal assistants, Penni and the young Giulio Romano, who had also come to assume an increasing role in the painting of the Stanze. Raphael's delegation of the execution of these two works is an indication of the pressure of his business which, from these years on, began its irreversible expansion. For both pictures Raphael prepared compositional drawings which are preserved, respectively, in the Uffizi and at Windsor;[239] but it is not certain how far beyond this stage he may have gone in preparation of his assistants' work. Surely, he directed any alterations that they subsequently made from his surviving idea for design; and his close supervision of the process of painting in his studio is certain. Yet, despite such supervision, and despite the intention of the pupil to conform not only to Raphael's indication for design but to his precise vocabulary of forms, the Raphaelesque idea inevitably assumes, in the executant's interpretation, an altered and qualitatively diminished substance.

So, in the *Madonna of the Fish*, the execution, by Penni and by Giulio jointly, is generalized in contour and in surface and inarticulate in figure-stance as in no example of Raphael's own painting: the picture makes, on this account, a first impression of a ponderous vacancy. The time of its conception in design by Raphael surely antedates the *Sistine Madonna*; this effect of ponderousness awkwardly translates Raphael's ambitions of the time of the *Bolsena* or of the *Expulsion* fresco. The figures of the Prado picture compare in their dimension with the most substantial ones of the *Expulsion*, and in this respect contrast decisively against those of the last large altar of previous date to this, the *Madonna di Foligno*.[177] Further, these forms — arranged in a scheme that is distantly reminiscent of the simply monumental altars of Raphael's earliest, still Perugian style — are brought together into an assembly more compact and more imposing than in any earlier panel in the bulk they make within the frame. The heavy masses are approximately balanced, but within this balance Raphael works in a mentality like that of the *Bolsena*, willing to instill, even in the devotional image, a resilient energy of composition.

As in the design of the *Bolsena*, the left portion of this picture is a theme of rising movement, of which the physical and psychological direction is discharged upon a massive center; and on the right this movement is counterbalanced by a static form. To support, and by formal means to dramatize the movement, in which there is no intrinsic drama, Raphael has invented the grandiose device of the drawn curtain which sweeps, with the effect of a rhetorical gesture, in a rising curve across the upper part of the design. Oppositely, the architecture of the throne is so manipulated as to redress and stabilize this diagonal direction, so far unprecedented in an altarpiece. To the new degree of formal energy that is suggested in the movement of the design, the very heaviness of the moving forms, as well as of the static ones, serves as an effective counterpoise. As in the contemporary frescoes, the generation of a new and more expressive movement is accompanied by a compensating increase of those elements that affirm stability; and the contrasting powers mutually intensify, even as they balance, one another. Even in transcription by lesser hands the *Madonna of the Fish* reveals, in Raphael's conception in it, a potency and grandeur beyond those in the altar paintings of preceding years.

The design of the Prado altar certainly precedes, and that finally adopted for the *Madonna dell'Impannata* (not the same as the design first indicated in the Windsor drawing)[239] probably succeeds, Raphael's own creation of the *Sistine Madonna*. The *Impannata*, altogether of Giulio's execution, follows his helping in the Prado altar at sufficient distance to have allowed this prodigy, in the meantime, to affirm his expertness of hand and his incipient strong individuality of temper. Different from the perfect unity of surface and flowing relation between large forms and details in Raphael's preparatory drawing, Giulio's painting technique now tends not to overgeneralize (as in the Prado picture) but to harden and precise the description of the forms. Contours tend to a somewhat schematizing clarity, and details to a somewhat contrasting, but also sharp, identity within the figure; in Giulio's transcription, the sense of synthetic visual unity of Raphael's drawing threatens to, but does not quite yet, dissolve into its opposite component parts. Also indicative in this execution of Giulio's personality, as we shall come to know it, is another sharpening, of the acuity of psychological expression: the personalities of the *Impannata* are pitched in feeling at a higher key than, but in not so resonant a tone as, Raphael's own.

In the degree to which Giulio's personality is now evident in the execution, this picture is in its whole effect a document for Giulio as well as for Raphael: in the sense of personal artistic style, as with all of Giulio's subsequent executions of Raphael's designs, this is an interpretation rather than a literal fulfillment of Raphael's intent. But again, as much as the *Madonna of the Fish,* the *Impannata* owes its essential form to Raphael's conception; and this conception, probably just subsequent to the last frescoes of the Eliodoro room, is like them a culmination of the ambitions of this phase of Raphael's style.

In the *Impannata,* the intention to create an activity of form and situation is more emphatic than in the Prado altar. It is the quick turning of the Christ Child, recalling a motive invented for the *Alba Madonna,* but still more like an infant version of the *Galatea,* which sets the temper for, and is the core of movement in, the picture. Unlike the *Galatea,* His contrapposto does not generate movement, but rather serves, in contrary fashion, to lock contrasting movements into Him. The primary motive of design is the strong diagonal which, passing through the Christ Child, links the Elizabeth and Mary; in Raphael's first design in Windsor it is this motive, at once strongly active, yet formed into an opposite enframing balance upon the Christ, that is alone developed. The two remaining figure elements of the design, the female Saint and the young St. John, are so disposed as to complete and elaborate the compensation into balance of the picture.

As an X-ray examination of the picture has shown, these two figures were selected for inclusion in the composition not for iconographic but for aesthetic reasons: a Joseph who was at one stage in the design was canceled, and an importance of role altogether unlike that at one time planned for him was assigned to the St. John. In their present roles and places the two secondary figures make a balancing counterdiagonal to that of the Elizabeth and Mary and, equally important, they complete the design in a geometrically explicit and severely disciplined massive circular form, as evident as that in the antecedent *Galatea,* and more deliberately compact: the activity of structure, as complex and as vigorous (considering its different scale) as in the *Galatea,* is even more rigorously contained.

In its measure of complex deliberation such a composition risks, as neither the *Madonna of the Fish* nor the Sistine altar had, the effect of intellectual contrivance and of artificiality in form. Apparently aware of this, Raphael has adjusted the communication of content in the *Impannata* in such fashion as to compensate this risk of artificiality, and thus of unsympathetic distance from the spectator, with a more intimate and more assertive relation to him. The quality of expression in the faces bears Giulio's accent, but its aliveness is, generically, an extension of Raphael's own contemporary tendency. The figure of the St. John, who in his role is a compound of the John and of the young angel in the *Foligno* altar, is both physically and psychologically assertive in his relation to us, and in his summoning of our participation in the picture, as neither of his antecedents is. In the very types — though again the accent is Giulio's — there is a lessening of the sense of ideal removal. Finally, to convince the spectator that this scene, so carefully contrived by art, is in fact believable and near, Raphael permits, for the first time in his mature style, the partial specifying of a domestic environment.

In this adjustment between artifice and actuality in the *Impannata* there is a yet more complicated mechanism than in the contemporary frescoes. The picture remains effective classical synthesis, but even more than in the *Attila* [221] there is the sense that the classical equilibrium is made of matter imminently too complex and already, in this instance — with the disruptive tendencies contained in Giulio's execution — perhaps too fine. And in this work in fact, as in the *Attila* among the frescoes, it would seem, in hindsight, that Raphael has found the limit of enrichment of activity of form and content that it is possible to express within a wholly classical discipline of style.

As the *Liberation* fresco is the more austere, architectonically ordered, corrective of the tendencies of the *Attila*, and the *Sistine Madonna* of the *Galatea*, so is the *St. Cecilia Altar* (Bologna, Pinacoteca Nazionale; 1514),[241-3] contemporary with or just succeeding the *Madonna dell' Impannata*, a similar counterproposition in respect to it. Raphael, by 1514, was squarely faced by these alternatives of mode that he had himself deduced from his development of classical style and which, in their responsive confrontation are complementary but also are, potentially, antitheses. With each successive probing of the possibilities of either mode he affirmed its distinct nature more, and more strongly confronted each with the other. Shortly, they would in fact come to have the look of irreconcilables; and the search for the limits of the virtue of each mode would provoke a crisis in Raphael's development.

It is as if in response to the tight-movemented complexity of the *Impannata,* seemingly so far an extreme, that the *St. Cecilia* altar is contrastingly the most stilled and simplified design in Raphael's mature art: so rectilinear in its architecture as to recall to the beholder's mind something of Raphael's long-past Peruginesque education. The figures are arranged with an almost early-classical strictness of symmetry, and on a plan that only partially concedes the idea of a curve; the semicircular plan that had been usual for this kind of composition has been compromised toward a parallelogram. Only minimal movement is permitted in the design, and this too is indicated by clear straight lines more than by curves, in the diagonal that traverses the figures from lower right to upper left, with an opposite appendage at either end in the direction of the instruments below and in the inclination of Cecilia's head.

The figures themselves have assumed an immobility different from that in any earlier mature work: their stance and their articulation no longer certainly imply the continence by posture of a fluid energy. Paul, immensely monumental, stands flat-footed, completely inert; the Magdalen (a portrait of the Fornarina, appropriately cast), more movemented in her role of communication between us and the painting, has a brittle-seeming, statuary stiffness in her poise. Cecilia stands in an attitude of minimal, flattened contrapposto; her posture is no equilibrium of powers, but almost the least enlivening of a state of rest. Her situation recalls that of the earlier *St. Catherine* (London, National Gallery) but the very likeness shows how much, in contrast, Cecilia's contrapposto is discreet. Like the Magdalen, though not quite to her degree, the Cecilia seems less than the recreation of a vital form, and evokes a quality of statuary.

The extreme deliberation of the handling (all Raphael's own, except for the still-life of the instruments and some few details, of Giovanni da Udine's execution; the picture is not egregiously restored) reinforces this effect: not only the temper of design but that of vision and of execution is restrained. The processes of observation and of record both are slower and more cautious; the summarizing seeming swiftness of the painting in the Sistine altar, almost fresco-like, is quite put aside. The eye searches and the brush finds smoothed firmnesses of surface, on which folds of drapery and incidents of detail are brought out in precise relief; the light is given a greater strength of differentiation to assist this end. The surfaces seem lucent as in none of Raphael's panel pictures up to now, and of harder texture; there is a cast as of metallic substance in the draperies of the Cecilia and of stone, palely polychromed, in the Magdalen.

The vitally important difference of more accented contrast in Giulio's handling in the *Impannata* does not obscure the relation of his mode of painting there to Raphael's here, and the conclusion to be drawn is that the "Giulian" manner of the *Impannata* is his translation, subtly but effectively distorting, of Raphael's guiding indication: perhaps even in the model of this altar, not unlikely concurrent with the *Impannata* in its course of execution. In his figure of the Magdalen, indeed, Raphael creates an effect of style particularly sympathetic to Giulio's own inclinations, and more articulate of it than Giulio at that date possibly could be. The Magdalen comes from the same mold as that in which Raphael had shortly before cast, for Giulio's specific elaboration and execution, the caryatids of the Eliodoro basamenti; but it was on the later evolution of the pupil that Raphael's example in the Magdalen would have, not as motive, but in style, more significant effect. Precisely crystalline in form, compounding the sense of a most lucid presence with the aspect in her of another art, the Magdalen stands on a precarious divide between artifice and nature. For the first time in Raphael, it is her figure that makes an impress not of the recreation, classically shaped, of nature, but of the willed evocation of the Ancient sculptor's art. The role and the vitality of nature are deliberately less in this response of art to art directly, and we are in the presence of a first symptom, which only Giulio would then develop farther, of a neoclassicism. The Magdalen's cool, fine-chiselled statuary beauty is the progenitor of what, in Giulio's later art, becomes the matter of an explicit Mannerism.

The Magdalen assumes her place, however, in a context of responsive unity, even of these simply ordered forms, which Giulio never was disposed or able to achieve, and in a unity of light and atmosphere which, on this scale, he could not describe. Raphael's whole design and effect of execution evoke, in this pictorial architecture, a classical analogy we have not experienced in his art before, of the dense columnar substance of an Ancient temple, discrete from landscape but infused with the presence of the landscape's light and air. In this atmosphere the forms, like those of a Greek architecture, seem to respire, and their polychromy, of green and yellow-gold and pink, glows as if into the surrounding air. The stillness vibrates; it translates into terms of visual sensation the reverberation of the angelic music to which the Saints, their own instruments cast down, so raptly listen.

This fineness of record of effects of light and atmosphere in the *Cecilia* altar is an agent in it of harmony, but a concomitant effect of this sensibility of eye and hand, more precise than in previous works of Raphael, has the possibility in it, and some actuality, of different effect. A responsiveness of eye and hand so fine as this, and so careful to describe the qualities of surface and incidents of detail, works on a scale opposite to that of the monumental figures, and this extreme of sensibility contrasts also with the severity of intellectual order of the larger form. There has been a divergent development, each to a new degree, of these contrary purposes and their coexistence in the picture makes, in slight but still perceptible amount, a sense of strain. This again was matter for young Giulio to develop; Raphael, however, at once perceived the sacrifice that must be made, of the lesser end, in order to proceed to a new dimension of development of this direction of a grandly and severely architectonic style.

Two portraits only of the closing years of this phase survive as sure testimony of both Raphael's invention and his hand: that of Tommaso Inghirami ("Il Fedra"; Boston, Gardner Museum; c. 1513)[244] and that of the Fornarina (in the guise, originally, of St. Catherine, now with the symbols painted out) known as *La Donna Velata* (Florence, Pitti; c. 1514).[247] A third portrait, of *Giuliano de' Medici* (New York, Metropolitan Museum)[246] is the ruin of a Raphaelesque design, in which his own hand may once have been evident; its time of painting, to choose from the two brief and closely successive alternatives allowed by external evidence, was late 1514.

Inghirami, prefect of the Library of the Vatican, was one of the more singular among the appearances that Raphael, as a portraitist, was called upon to paint. Wall-eyed and almost grossly stout, it would seem that he must defy even Raphael's abilities to resolve a recalcitrant nature into a semblance of harmony. The wandering glance is not at all evaded in the portrait — it is too relevant a datum of this visual truth — but its abnormality is minimized by the sideward and upward inclination of the sitter's head. The plump body is taken as an almost welcome fact: the moment of design here is that of the *Madonna of the Fish*, and Raphael takes this bulk of person and manipulates it, as he does those of the ponderous invented actors of the altarpiece, in similar temper and toward like ends. The great rounded body — clad in a luminous brick-red such as only Raphael's palette can mix —

framed by the enclosing movement of the arms, is posed in an almost abstractly defined oval tight within the picture frame; the oval is turned on its axes, at once somewhat backward from the picture plane and diagonally upward to the right. The form of the head, not less geometrically clear than the body, and rounder still, repeats its shape and its direction.

The grossness of the body is as if annulled by its purity of color and its assimilation to a purity of geometric form — both stressed in clear relief against the opaque background; and its impressive bulk, immobile physically behind the desk, is made aesthetically to move in a lifting, rotatory pattern. With extraordinary efficacy for the expression and the stress of characteristic appearance in this sitter, the contrapuntal echo of this turning and ascending movement is in Inghirami's eyes.

The later repetition of this portrait in the Pitti (of 1516 ?, shortly before Inghirami's death; probably by Giulio but perhaps touched in the face and hands by Raphael himself) [245] does not merely reproduce the first version; it seems to have been brought up to date by reexamination of the living sitter, now a little changed and older, and not so geometrically plump. A more realistic accent, appropriate not only to the pupil but to Raphael's own tendency in 1516, pervades this new version of Fedra's portrait: the light is more searching and the color deeper and more intense, and more simulating of a texture. The slight changes in form which this more literal manner makes — not only in the face but, for example, in the sharper characterization of irregularities of outline in the right arm and in the hat — are, however, enough to vitiate the brilliant, almost humorous aesthetic point of the original design.

The chief difference in the style of the *Fedra* from the admirable portraits of the Segnatura phase (the so-called *Alidosi* and the *Julius II*) is in its concern with the animation of mass into movement — the preoccupation so much more elaborately expressed in the contemporary frescoes; by comparison with the Inghirami, the preceding portraits seem structurally rigid. The same concern still dictates the design of the portrait of *Giuliano de' Medici* [246] (a subject much more presentable than Inghirami): it also aspires to a counterpoise, between expanded physical dimension and movement impelled by aesthetic means into the mass.

The substance of Giuliano, unlike that which nature had afforded in the person of Tommaso Inghirami, is an invented one, made of breadth of pose and amplitude of clothing. The motive of movement is more forcefully expressed than in the *Inghirami*: only partly in the more evident turning of the body inward from the picture plane, and more by the marking of a diagonal of unprecedented emphasis in a portrait design. The stress in the placing in diagonal relation of parts of body and costume is supported by the drawn curtain, borrowed from the idea in the *Madonna of the Fish*; and the curtain is lifted to reveal, beyond Giuliano to the right rear, a deep perspective (also suggestive of the sense of movement) toward the castle of Sant' Angelo — the place and symbol both of Giuliano's office of Captain-General of the Church. The influence of Sebastiano del Piombo's portraiture may be evident in this detail, and Raphael's own ambition to a grander dimension in the portrait form may also, in the *Giuliano*, have been reinforced by experience of Sebastiano's example. No portrait of this or of earlier date by Sebastiano has, however, the energy of this design of Raphael's, nor a comparable acuity of psychological presence. Even the paled condition of the picture and weakness of what is evident of the original execution (by Penni, perhaps, for the most part) cannot obscure the cogency of Raphael's idea.

It is not possible to determine, in the close-grained texture of events of Raphael's art circa 1514, precisely where the *Donna Velata* [247] lies. If, as is almost certain, her countenance inspired the image of the *Sistine Madonna* and (as is altogether sure) the face of the Magdalen in the *Cecilia* altar, this portrait lies in style and in concept of the person in between these two. The variation in the record of the same face is considerable, but not surprising: their differences of context and, quite as much, of time and of specific intention of style in each work of art account for them enough. The *Donna Velata*, though explicitly a portrait in its form, is not a portrait only; it must not be forgotten that, in its original guise, it was also the image of a saint. Such an idea was related to a precedent, of the representation of single mythological persons in the form of portraiture, which was more accustomed in Venice than in Rome — to which, however, Sebastiano del Piombo had imported it. We have no idea of the purpose or the destination of this work of Raphael's: of whether it was a private picture for Raphael's or the Fornarina's use, and thus a portrait by first intention and a saintly figure only secondly; or whether, inversely and more likely, it was painted as the commissioned image of a saint, for which the Fornarina served as the convenient and irresistible model: this is the case in all her other appearances in works of Raphael's lifetime (the Czartoryski portrait of the Fornarina, often wrongly* dated in this time, is post-Raphaelesque and by Penni). There is, on many grounds, an excuse for the measure of idealization that the face of the Pitti portrait shows, so unlike the truth of record in every portrait work by Raphael but this.

However, the uncertainty that we may have about the category, of portraiture or of religious image, to which this painting may belong is an analytical abstraction: Raphael's motive in the making of it had no part whatever of uncertainty, and there is none in the realized work. What he intended was, precisely, not a category but an amalgam of categories: he wished, in the *Donna Velata*, to synthesize the measure of real presence that belongs to portraiture with the ideality of a religious picture. The tendency that is realized here is adumbrated in the motives of the *Sistine Madonna*, where ideality and the machinery of an illusion are made to coexist; and it is extended one step — a difficult, and as we have seen, a straining step — farther in the combination of grandly intellectual form and precise sensuous record of the *Cecilia* altar. As in other ways, the *Donna Velata* is their middle term.

In the picture, the face of the Fornarina is recast into a shape more rounded, of a richer, heavier harmony than the actuality (as we know it elsewhere). Her neck and shoulders describe a form, at once sensually lovely and almost geometrically pure, like that of a Phidian sculpture; her clothing rounds her body at once into fuller substance and into ornament. Her whole person is enclosed by her veil — a mantle, rather — as if within a shell, compounded of pyramid and curve, musical and monumental both. The form has the virtue of an almost doctrinaire idea: it is the clearest paradigm of classical harmony and purity of order. But this meaning of the whole form is in no way separable from its parts: meaning in this picture is not reducible to diagram. There is such a profound synthesis of general and particular, of intellect and vision, of aesthetic will and actuality, as makes it impossible to distinguish boundaries between these — for others — antonyms; and there is no way for us to know if this image happens on the canvas more by deductive or inductive process.

As much as its generalization is succinct and abstractly clear, so, in perfect compensation, is its particularity compelling. The garment, in its luxury of folds, makes a complex pattern of rhythmic life for which there is no counterpart, for richness and vitality, in Raphael before. This pattern grows on the sleeve as if out of the simple curve of the enclosing form, increasingly elaborating and differentiating its melodic temper; it then diminishes and grows subtler, to be resolved again on the forearm into the large curve of the mantle at the left; on the bodice the pattern pales into the smooth whiteness of the flesh.

The color — less color than a monochrome of greys and whites, touched for accent with yellow-gold — works similarly, making ceaseless vibrant difference within its arbitrary pure harmony. The color, and the brushwork that applies it, record the sense of texture in the garments and the respiration of the flesh more flexibly and more convincingly than in any portrait of Raphael's so far. And where the image most of all assumes the nature of a portrait is in its quality of gaze, so warmly alive and communicative as to convince us utterly of the reality of a precise psychological presence. The actuality, in all its aspects, is as cogent as the idea, and made one with it. In the next year, in the *Castiglione*, Raphael would achieve a yet higher demonstration of the same kind, and not then use the pretext in the subject matter of the *Donna Velata*, of compounding of the truth of portraiture with the liberty of a religious image.

The occurrence in this time of Raphael's development of the phenomenon we have characterized in the *Donna Velata* requires no suggestion from any art beside his own. Yet there is the virtual certainty that, while it is essentially personal and new, it also is a result of the recall to Raphael's mind of an old lesson, learned long before by rote but not then mastered. Late in 1513 Leonardo came to Rome, where he was to stay intermittently through 1516; his baggage certainly contained the *Mona Lisa*.[37] That magic picture, now a decade old, would have had the look of an archaism in the Roman climate of 1514, but no less of magic; and in it there was still apparent, with the force of its profoundly effortful first statement, the proposition of which the *Donna Velata* is the nearly final demonstration. The *Donna Velata* was painted with the renewed vision of the Leonardo clearly present to Raphael's mind: as well as being a culminating event of Raphael's mature classical style it is a reference, at once tribute and critique, to the formulation by Leonardo of its first principles.

Compared with its near context of Raphael's works of 1514 the *Madonna della Sedia* (Florence, Pitti)[248-9] is a picture of far higher power, at once of concentration and of generalization, than is attained in them; not only the easel paintings — the *Sistine Madonna*, even — but the great frescoes of the time of the Eliodoro have no like effect. The fact of concentration is assisted, but not determined, by a circumstance of size; the power of generalization is in despite of it. This power is the result, at first, of a different view of the transcription of reality from that Raphael had till now envisaged, and to which he came precisely from his experience in the making of the last previous altar paintings we discussed, the *Cecilia* and the *Impannata*, and in the *Donna Velata*.

In the two altar works — one of his own execution, the other deputized to Giulio — Raphael had intended to reinforce the sense of a visual reality in the same measure as he had reinforced, in one case the controlled complexity, and in the other the intellectual clarity, of larger form. We have seen how in both works — much more in that of Giulio's making — a potential conflict had revealed itself between these two intentions, opposite, as he had conceived them there, in sensuous and intellectual nature and in scale. In the *Donna Velata*, however, Raphael had attained a means of nearly perfect compensation between one intention and the other, in which visual actuality and formal abstraction seem to grow from one another, as if organically. Now, in the moment of the *Madonna della Sedia*, Raphael has determined that these intentions, though reconcilable in the manner of the *Donna Velata*, cannot be further simultaneously prosecuted, with the same technique: the search for detailed truth of sensuous existence is too much in conflict with the ambition to a higher ideality of design and, as in his own *Cecilia* altar, inhibits its effect.

The *Madonna della Sedia* makes deliberate sacrifice of the fineness of description that distinguished the *Cecilia*, and the *Donna Velata* also; Raphael is content here with a more summary report of the appearance of surfaces, and with fewer episodes of precise detail. In the *Sedia* these last are only in the scarf and headdress of the Madonna, and even these are not characterized as details had been just before. More than in the *Cecilia* or the *Donna Velata* these details seem softly luminous, seen as if through a denser atmosphere; more than hard affirmations of incidents of physical existence they seem revelations of incidents of light. These passages of red and gold *ricamo* communicate painterly sensation as details in Raphael rarely had before; they are not only a transcription of a part of visual reality, but a translation of the aesthetic sense of warmth of texture and of muted radiance of colored light.

This frame of detail around the head of the Madonna seems to grow, as in the *Donna Velata*, by rhythmical differentiation out of the passages of larger form, but more than there it is bound into the whole by the more pervasive and apparent working of a softer atmosphere. Elsewhere in this picture what is indicated of particulars of inner form is sparse but, in compensation, more strongly drawn and accented in the richer depth of air and light. In passages of flesh and areas of drapery conviction comes, not from draughtsman's indications of detail, but by painterly suggestion of a textural existence in the light. The sense of presence of the figures is not diminished by this more selective and more painterly manner of description; on the contrary, the persons of this picture make a quicker and more optically true effect upon the recognizing eye than do their antecedents, more hard and precious in their handling. They have, furthermore, so much more ample a physical dimension that they impose conviction on us by sheer sense of breadth and density of substance. By alteration of his descriptive mode from that he had employed in his most recent panel works toward one more nearly like, in the scale of thinking, that used so far in his frescoes — and in part in the large *Sistina* — Raphael has exchanged an intention of precise truth of detail for a more summary and more painterly translation of reality; and he makes, in the *Madonna della Sedia*, a higher cogency of sensuous existence than he had attained, by more labored means, before.

Part of the immediacy of impact of this sensuous presence comes, however, not from descriptive means but from what, in the *Cecilia* altar, had been their opposite: the registration on our eye of form in the *Madonna della Sedia* is, in a degree not evident in any antecedent work, not only of the conviction of appearance it describes but of its abstract value of a pattern, of instantly apprehensible synthetic force: a phenomenally legible compact gestalt. The higher generalization in description of detail serves the end of stricter resolution of the descriptive into the aesthetic meaning of the form;

there is, here, no incipient conflict but a shared virtue of generalization in the two. However, unlike the *Donna Velata* in which, earlier, large and small form had been so persuasively reconciled, there is no sense here of the reversibility, as if by organic process, from one to the other. There is no question now, in this conception, of the primacy of the idea of the whole design: the general structure dominates its content of lesser forms and determines their ordering absolutely, even arbitrarily. The aesthetic plan has an authority, as idea, unlike that in any easel work before, and of more concentrated efficacy than is evident even in the frescoes.

As the outward frame of his design Raphael has chosen a tondo shape — abstract and perfect symbol of the form and process of classical synthesis. Its appearance in this work is the consequence, almost in logic, of the aspirations of design in the *Galatea* and the *Impannata*; and it is the counterimage of the extreme rectilinear geometry of the *Cecilia* altar. In this tondo shape, the figures differentiate and realize its abstraction into vital human substance, of grandeur larger than the life. As much as plausibility allows, the forms of this humanity seem to seek approach to the harmony of their enclosing circle, and beyond that toward the fullness of a sphere. They are gathered into compact shape: a dense group, sensibly convex to the front (almost with the effect, still slightly distorting, of an image in a convex mirror), and implying rounding continuity to the rear. The group is articulated simultaneously as an order on the surface and in the space: the rhythmic sequence of deep curves, which binds the forms together, also warps across them to express their depth. Yet this depth implies no space beyond that made by the substance of the figures; and even this substance, of which the plastic mass is descriptively and formally implied, is not entirely defined. The group simulates, not sculpture, but pictorial relief; its spatial articulation depends from and is accessory to its order of design on the picture surface. This sense of the picture surface as a dominating plane of reference for the structure of the work — the idea that the picture, as a form, is first of all a projection on a field of two dimensions — is, for the first time in Raphael, so clearly indicated here. The special shape of the *Madonna della Sedia* peculiarly stresses this identity of the surface on which the picture is produced, and with respect to which its existence and design are then differentiated; this shape has the nature, and its image a way of optical functioning, like that of a mirror, not an Albertian window into space.

The forms of the design seem to grow out of the circle which defines the picture field: that of the Madonna unwinds like a tangent spiral from the circumference, and in deep curves, consonant with the tondo shape, her figure weaves across its vertical diameter; the form of the Child develops by inversion out of hers, and is locked inextricably with it in the picture's center; the St. John arches inward, as if at once from the circumference of the circle and the depth, to lend the impulse of his movement and psychological direction to this interweaving of the rhythmed substances. The arm of the Madonna's chair — a vertical assembling of lathe-turned shapes — is the descriptive and aesthetic term of reference to gravity, like a plumb line, of all this rounding form: its presence enables us to grasp more finely and more firmly the heavy equilibrium that is, of itself, already thoroughly established among the movemented shapes. Movement, in this image, is not imposed on monumental substance; it is, in ultimate demonstration of a classical idea, intrinsic to a concept of matter, in its inmost essence, as a vital stuff.

Here, a movement of such resonance and controlled power as even the frescoes rarely had attained, and a monumental shape and presence, are indissoluble, and in equilibrium, as power and presence. In the process of achieving this effect there has perhaps been some meditation on the Sistine Seers of Michelangelo, but there is no remnant in this picture of the personality or form of Michelangelesque experience: the affect of this image is of the suave and deep-toned harmony that is only Raphael's, and only of his middle years; and here it is in its culminating beauty of expression.

The form of the *Madonna della Sedia* not only describes a human situation but comments it aesthetically. Besides the illustrative meaning of a sensuous warmth in the rich texture and the atmosphere, and in the chastened radiance of color — paled red, light blue, green and yellow gold — the very amplitude of human shape emanates a quality of warmness. The full, warping movement of the rhythms of design conveys the affect of a plenitude and depth of feeling; the weaving together of the forms communicates not just the act but the sensation of embrace, and the gathering of energies and substances affirms its closeness and security. All this is given to us to understand, as well, in terms of simplest psychological communication, in the gaze toward us of the Madonna and her Child. In different, more real circumstances than in the apparition of the *Sistine Madonna* — not in the stately distance of an altarpiece but in the intimacy of a private image of devotion — an image is made of the Madonna in more earthly mood and guise, in which she shows, not so much her divine love for us as the human love between her and her Child — which we, as she reveals it so compellingly, must share. We observed that the shape of the frame of this picture, and the spatial ordering of form within it, carry in them something of the sense of a convex mirror. The interpretation of the theme that Raphael has given us, in this luminous, near, presence implies that it is, however splendidly transformed, a reflection, as in a mirror, of a human actuality.

In the *Madonna della Sedia* there is the consummate concentration of all Raphael's wisdom of art gained to date, and at the same time an affirmation of new clarity of purpose. In the making of this work Raphael has pondered the result of the difficult and diverging strivings of the year or two just past and selectively summarized them into a new synthesis of style. The act of creation of the *Sedia* refounds the ideas of the Eliodoro phase and prepares the climax of the Tapestry Cartoons. The painting is, in one moment, the culmination of this phase of Raphael's style and the point of entry to the next.

VISITORS

LEONARDO

In the autumn of 1513, when Raphael had arrived at the seeming fulfillment of a proposition of artistic style invented long before by Leonardo, the inventor himself appeared in Rome. The image of Leonardo's art had never left Raphael's mind wholly since the time in Florence, when he had learned so profoundly from it; even in the course of his vast and different progress since, Raphael had recalled this image on more than one occasion — and at varying levels of self-awareness. We have observed instances in the Segnatura frescoes of such recollection, and others more recently, in the time of the Stanza d'Eliodoro. There are motives in Raphael's easel pictures of these years that betray, directly, a debt to Leonardo; but there are also other matters, of more substantial import than the borrowing of motives which, less directly and more essentially, eventually depend on him.

This sympathy — and now, something like a sense of challenge — that Raphael felt in the presence of Leonardo's art emerged, as we have seen, on renewed acquaintance with it: we have observed the relation the *Donna Velata* bears to the precedent of the *Mona Lisa*, and there may be something of *La Gioconda*, too, in the Magdalen of the *Cecilia* altar. The *Madonna dell' Impannata* — beyond its single precise, but not new, Leonardesque motive of the St. John — may be a commentary and development on the older master's St. Anne compositions. Though now so obviously outmoded in specific ways — and none was more aware of this than Raphael — Leonardo's work still held for him a virtue like that of avuncular authority. The baggage of art that Leonardo carried, half incubus, half talisman, still held something of the fascination, for the mature Raphael, that it had for the young man, not so many years before.

Leonardo's own evolution had been as if arrested in the endless process of completion of the last *St. Anne* at a stage which, in its time, was in advance of Raphael's evolution then of a classical style: the *St. Anne* was a compact equivalent of the ideas which, in Raphael, were represented by the Segnatura; since then, Raphael had moved far beyond. Further, in these intervening years, Leonardo's art had been provincially isolated, not only from Florence, but more important, from the main Roman center of development.

He lacked altogether the *Romanità* — the air of absorption of and reference to Antiquity — which in the current accomplishment of Raphael and Michelangelo had become not just an element of imitation but a vital factor in their developed classicism of style. Leonardo's activity as a painter had also much declined in these years; we know from Vasari's unsympathetic account (IV, 46–47) something — mostly the eccentric side — of his occupations during his residence of three years, occasionally interrupted, in Rome. As a painter he produced only two small Madonna pictures, intended for the papal datary, Baldassare Turini, both of which are lost. Leonardo was on the Roman scene but — except for the effects, much masked, of his older art on Raphael — he was not effectively of it; he lived and worked in a private realm from which, unlike the solitude of Michelangelo, no reverberation came.

One work of Leonardo's of more recent date of invention than the Louvre *St. Anne* requires examination from the point of view not only of its relation to the art of Raphael but to the development of the classical style in general. The *St. John Baptist* (Paris, Louvre)[250] suggests a motive Raphael used twice, once before Leonardo's arrival and once afterwards, in the *Foligno* and the *Impannata* altars. There is no documentation of Leonardo's Louvre *Baptist* until 1517, and its time of origin, though certainly post-Florentine, cannot be established. As is the case with the Louvre version of the *St. Anne*, the *Baptist* is a work of which the present substance is a chronological composite rather than the creation of a given moment: in this case, of an idea of motive that seems considerably to antedate Leonardo's presence in Rome and of execution that may be partly of the Roman time, partly later still. Raphael seems to have known both this present version of Leonardo's painting and, by some indirect means, an earlier projection of a similar idea as well. Raphael's adaptation is, however, in both instances, of motive only. The Louvre *Baptist* is of so singular an expressive personality, so much an outgrowth of the private dilemma of Leonardo that, except in terms of simple motive it could have no resonance in the public climate of contemporary Roman art.

Yet the *Baptist* signifies more than a solitary event in the later art of Leonardo; it is also a document — almost as ambiguous in wider meaning as in private meaning — for the history of the development of classical style. In one sense the image is still retrospective, bound yet more than some of Leonardo's prior works to an idea of complex and oversubtle content, reminding us of the quotient that persists in Leonardo's personality of late Quattrocento preciousness. The equilibrium of expression in the *Baptist,* achieved in an androgyne conjunction that is in equal measure ideally and sensually motivated, is too imminently unstable: too fine and too pregnant with ambivalence. Expression of this kind is, in this picture, recollective, but it also remarkably foretells what certain Mannerist painters would develop as a mode of psychological communication. At the same time that its expression is so oversubtle the basic conception of the content of this work rests on a very generalized and — in its peculiar way — philosophically abstracting idea: the resolution into one synthetic, artificial image of the antithetic ideals of the male and female. In basic form, too, this image is highly generalized, of a reduced simplicity of structure for which there is no comparison in Leonardo's art, or in that of recent years of Raphael. There is no discernible influence from contemporary Roman art, or on it, in the style of the *Baptist* (as distinguished from its imitable motive); yet in its ambition of an extreme ideality of content, and in the reduction and extreme generalization of its form, it moves into a sphere of classical style that only Michelangelo had attained already, in the last portions of the Sistine, and which Raphael would come to only now.

The *Baptist* was the definition in the terms of a human image of Leonardo's late development of a classical style of thought. Still later, in a cultural isolation greater than that which he had imposed upon himself in Rome, Leonardo explored this same region of ideality at a higher level still, in images no longer of humanity but of nature. The drawings of catastrophes — of cosmic cloudbursts, earthquakes and deluges — preserved at Windsor,[251] are the exalted generalization, in the language of art, of Leonardo's highest reaches of thought as a scientist and of feeling as an artist. In these drawings the earth and heavens are not described in any literal sense; there is only the summary notation, in a plastically compelling shorthand, of ideas that Leonardo has abstracted from visual and intellectual experience of what was, for him, the cosmos, and from his emotions in the contemplation of it. The whole world is projected as a unity of substances and energies inextricably intertwined, and moved by terrible and splendid forces. Even in the moment of catastrophe these forces move in visibly beautiful, rhythmical patterns of a lawful order: the world as Leonardo sees it at its end — and he is moved to see it so as his own end nears — is infinitely harmonious even in its agony. In these drawings, majestic and universal in idea, and indestructible in harmony of form, Leonardo achieved an ultimate classical commentary on nature, comparable to Michelangelo's highest commentary on man. But these commentaries of Leonardo were not published to his time; as always had been true in some measure of his art, these last works were not communication but part of Leonardo's endless, restless dialogue with himself.

OTHERS

There were other lesser artistic visitors to Rome during this period in which the High Renaissance style matured. None of them has left an identifiable trace of his activity there, nor did all of them carry back to their native place any certainly recognizable influence of Rome. Among the visitors of central Italian origin, Signorelli had reappeared briefly, as was his more or less recurrent habit, in 1513, but he was not disposed to be changed from his archaic mode. In the same year Niccolo Soggi and Vincenzo Tamagni were in Rome, both too provincial and too inconsiderable to be affected by their experience in any historically significant way. Beccafumi, of very different dimension, spent the years 1510–1512 in Rome, almost certainly mostly in the close shadow of the Sienese colony. His first identifiable works, executed after his return to Siena, are remarkable for their refusal to admit such demonstrations as he saw of classical style.

The North Italians seemed to have been more receptive. It may have been toward 1514 that Correggio was at least briefly resident in Rome, with vitally important effects for his later art; a visit at this time, rather than at the later date that has more often been assumed, offers more convenient explanation of the Raphaelisms, as well as the Michelangelisms, which appear from then on in his works. Even Lotto, the least temperamentally suited of the North Italians to the atmosphere of classicism, had undergone a major change in style in his Roman years (c. 1508–12), though hardly an entire classical conversion. The most durable effect we can observe of exposure to the art of Rome within these years is in the case of a painter of only secondary stature, Garofolo of Ferrara (in Rome c. 1512–15), who became one of Raphael's earliest *epigoni.*

One distinguished visitor from Florence, Fra Bartolommeo, appeared in Rome in 1514 as the period of extraordinary accomplishment we have been discussing neared its end. The most advanced practitioner of classical style in Florence, Bartolommeo had been drawn to Rome by the fame of the work done there by the two great artists who, less than a decade earlier, had also been members of the Florentine School. Despite his own considerable artistic stature and his high development of classical style the impact of the art of Rome on this monastic — and by now, in a sense, provincial — personality was more than he could bear. He returned to Florence to deliberate there, at a less oppressive distance, on the achievements of the Roman School.

IV

THE MATURATION OF CLASSICAL STYLE IN FLORENCE (c. 1508-c. 1514)

I V

THE MATURATION OF CLASSICAL STYLE IN FLORENCE (c. 1508-c. 1514)

THE principal creators of the High Renaissance classical style had all abandoned Florence before 1509 to pursue their careers and evolution elsewhere: Michelangelo and Raphael in Rome and Leonardo in Milan; and Fra Bartolommeo had left his native city in 1508 to visit Venice. There is no way of calculating what the destiny in Florence of the classical style would have been if Bartolommeo had not chosen, after an only brief absence, to return. He was, at this time, the least close to maturity in development of style among all the four creative masters, but he shared their essential aesthetic disposition and in part shared their experience of evolution in the classical style. Though least evolved himself, he alone among the Florentines of this time was capable of comprehending and absorbing the examples of a classical development higher than his own, which had been left behind by, or could be remembered from, the other masters.

All three greater masters had achieved, before leaving Florence, what may be described, for Raphael and Michelangelo, as an effective personal maturity, and a stage in the development of art that was the immediate preliminary to the full maturity of style to which they would advance in Rome; and Leonardo had sketched out but, as was his habit, not wholly demonstrated, the program of the fully mature classical style. When they left Florence the three prime inventors had already adequately defined the example and intent of the new classicism, and established the conditions on which the least genial of their creative group, Fra Bartolommeo, could continue to build toward his own maturity. Bartolommeo was qualified by talent, disposition, and experience to consider the classical style as an integer and not merely — as we have seen already in the case of some Florentine masters of the second rank — as a matter of artistic mode. The direction of development that the classical style would take was in part determined by the nature of the style itself, but without the available instrumentality of the Frate it could not have been so soon or so fully demonstrated within Florence.

As an instrument and as a creator, however, Fra Bartolommeo was of a far lesser power than the artists who had now abandoned Florence. By comparison with Rome the accomplishment of this period in Florence, led and dominated by the Frate, suffers from the limitation of its leader's stature. But the less than Roman dimension of its chief painter's personality now became appropriate to Florence where, also in the sphere outside the world of art, there was no circumstance and no personality that could create an atmosphere of culture such as Julius II created at the time in Rome, or even equal opportunities of patronage. While the atmosphere of Rome expanded in this time — artistically, on genius expatriated from Florence — that of Florence seemed by contrast, not only with Rome but with its own Quattrocento, to contract. It is in this period that Florence, under the government of the Gonfaloniere Soderini, played perhaps more than at any time in its history a political role of bourgeois cast, in the pejorative sense of the word: a role of banker's caution, seeking neutrality among stronger forces in equivocation and half-measures. This policy succeeded only in provoking the forceful action of the enemies of Florence and the reimposition, late in 1512, of Medicean rule.

When, in the spring of 1513, Leo X became Pope, Florence became in effect a political dependency of the Roman Court, but a dependency which even then was not privileged to share Rome's splendors or its cultural abundance. The difference between Rome and Florence in the years when one had grown in pretension and magnificence and the other, relatively, had diminished, is expressed in the diary of Paris de Grassis, who, when he accompanied Pope Leo on his triumphal entry into Florence in 1515, noted his "modern" Roman and, surely excessively uncharitable opinion, of the town: "miserrima civitas . . . rerum omnium extrema penuria . . . miseria insupportabilis."

The judgment was surely an exaggeration, but the exaggeration was provoked by an evident force of contrast. Of this contrast the native practitioners of art in Florence were for the most part fortunately unaware, but they were its victims, just as the geniuses who had left Florence to go to Rome were its beneficiaries. In Florence, without genius to make a way for art, if need be in despite of history, art developed in this time in a sociological climate of mediocrity, which only Fra Bartolommeo, and in somewhat different fashion Andrea del Sarto, were able to transcend. The art of Andrea, who matured into this very period, was marked from its beginning by a character of spirit which, in all but its sensitivity, is "bourgeois"; and the religious experience of the Frate is always, in this time, unimpassioned and discreet. Yet both artists attain, never to Roman heroism or rhetoric splendor, but to a genuine nobility of style; not as a consequence of spiritual reaching above the level of their milieu, but through the character of classical form within their works: as if the formal proposition of the classical style, and its potential, as form, of expression had the power to elevate a lesser content to its own higher dignity.

FRA BARTOLOMMEO (1)

The situation of style in which Fra Bartolommeo found himself toward 1508 or 1509 is illustrated in his *Holy Family* (London, National Gallery; from the Mond Collection).[252] This picture reflects the manners of both Raphael and Leonardo, but the reflection is by no means merely imitative: the veiled, chaste gentleness of mood and the purity of softened form of this painting are not to be found in the works of the more difficult, ambitious masters who are Bartolommeo's models. Relatively, the London *Holy Family* is simple, both in form and content.

This simplicity is an expression not only of its author's tendency of personality, but of a stage in that personality's development of style. As in the art of Raphael (not in 1507–1508, but in Raphael's first stages of approach to Leonardo) Bartolommeo's picture represents a reduction of the propositions of Leonardo's style, but to terms yet more simplified. And, despite the elements of Raphaelesque analogy, it is much more from Leonardo directly that the manner of this painting has been deduced. More specifically than any earlier work of Bartolommeo's, this one depends in types on Leonardo; and its composition, with its gentle inclination within a triangular unity of shape, suggests the example of Leonardo's cartoon of 1501. Further, the lighting is more evidently Leonardesque: it is not only, as it had been before in Bartolommeo's paintings, atmospherically soft, but developed in variety of chiaroscuro. As with every other element of Leonardo's style, this one, too, is transcribed in reduction; yet Bartolommeo is able to suggest that quality of Leonardesque light which serves to enchant the feeling as well as the eye of the spectator, absorbing him into an intimate communion with the painted image.

In the degree of his conversion to Leonardo's mode of handling of light Fra Bartolommeo follows the course Raphael had initiated a year or two before, but which he had since abandoned in the atmosphere of Rome. The effect created by this light, of a private relation between the spectator and the picture, was precisely appropriate to devotional art, and to the private scale and ambition of the easel picture; and it was welcome to a patronage whose uses for art were more personally than publicly determined. In Rome, where the principal efforts of art had come to be dedicated to more generalizing, more intellectually ambitious, public, aims there was now small place for the intimacy which, in Leonardesque light, was one of its important functions. In the atmosphere of Florence Leonardo's lighting could and did persist. Its character was altered as Florentine art also came in time to acquire a more rhetorical intent. And not much later, the idea of private, as dominant over public, meaning in the work of art was to find, among Fra Bartolommeo's disciples, a potential of unclassical expression in Leonardesque lighting that was unintended by him or by the Frate.

Almost more than by any other single fact of form, it was by the persistence of Leonardo's light that Bartolommeo's style, and through his example, much of Florentine painting, acquired a cast distinct from that of contemporary Rome. And while the school of Rome proceeded to a more independent evolution, that of Florence continued to depend on the proposition of the classical style in the particular guise, and with much of the particular intonation, with which Leonardo had posed it. The style Leonardo had first formulated in Florence and then, on his return, affirmed there in a perfected form, had a genuine affinity with the personality of his city, where its accent, if not necessarily its whole speech, was comprehended as that of a native tongue. The final departure of Leonardo coincided with the acceptance of his style by the Frate, and this was an acceptance which, while not so responsive to the inner sense of Leonardo as Raphael's had been, was also neither literal nor only external, as was that of Leonardo's followers in Milan.

The London *Holy Family* bears its basic resemblance to the style of Leonardo, but there is also in it a less certainly definable character that suggests, but without the possibility of confirmation, the reflection of Bartolommeo's experience of Venice in 1508. It may be in the relative abundance of its landscape, or in the almost sensuous atmosphere of warmth with which both the landscape and the figures have been touched; but this picture, more than any other Florentine painting of the time, suggests some community with the art of the Venetians. It is not impossible that the vision of Giorgione, and still more of the old Bellini, may have been to some extent a precipitant for the Frate's interest in light, so as to cause him, on his return from Venice, to turn to a profounder study of the light of Leonardo.

What is probably the first major work executed by Bartolommeo after his return, the altar *God the Father with Sts. Mary Magdalen and Catherine of Siena* (Lucca, Pinacoteca; dated 1509),[253] was commissioned in Venice, and at first intended for a Venetian destination. Its kind of light is not identifiably Leonardesque but Venetian, and specifically suggestive of Bellini. As in the works that precede the Venetian trip the tonality of this one is also relatively high; the difference from the previous paintings lies in an extraordinary luminosity of surfaces and color. Bartolommeo has absorbed, as no other Florentine artist had either disposition or opportunity to do, the conception, and the technique to realize it, of the Bellinesque *existenzbild.* Such a luminous visual illusion represents the fulfillment of a quattrocentesque ambition rather than an intention specifically of classical style, but more than in Bellini the effects of light and texture here have been made subservient to their place in a bland, yet altogether explicit, tonal harmony: Bellini's light has been transcribed with a Raphaelesque modulation.

Still more important than the harmony imposed on the handling of light, and with it, on color, is the harmony of forms within which the lighting works: for the first time in Bartolommeo's art without any element of equivocation, the conception of single forms and of whole composition is in the gestalt of a mature classicism. Something like this in character and effect may already have been intended in the *Assunta* [46] of 1508, and been spoiled by Albertinelli's unintelligent interpretation; but what is imperfectly suggested there is here fully realized. The figures of the two saints are of the most deliberate smooth grace of form, and perfectly poised in their floating movement, like that of slow wind-borne vessels on a quiet sea. Above their matching postures God the Father is monumentally immobile, but enclosed in movement: that of the angels and of the grandly cursive, slow-sweeping pattern of His drapery. These large forms are not now, as they seem to be in the *Assunta,* merely juxtaposed; a gentle but compelling continuity of rhythm relates the saints to each other, and both of them to the angels and to God, in an entirely cohesive unity. To either side of the panel the architecture simply frames and contains this unity, and to the rear it is relieved against a spacious and untroubled sky.

Not only is this altar such a consistent classical conception as no previous picture of the Frate had been, but no other panel work of comparable scale before this date in Florence, except for Raphael's *Madonna of the Baldacchino,*[60] so clearly demonstrates the basic ideas of the classical style. The sense of monumental dignity is as great, in Fra Bartolommeo's altar, as in the Raphael, and the effect of harmony in form, and yet more in feeling, is more instantly accessible. Generically, both panels are substantial documents of an achieved classicism. However, where the Raphael demonstrates a harmony resolved from relative complexity, the harmony of the Frate's work is simple: it is precisely the basic proposition of a consistent classical style, but not more, that he at this point somewhat tardily achieves. We are reminded how, almost a century before, Fra Bartolommeo's Dominican ancestor, Angelico, had achieved his own conversion to the contemporary progressive style by a similar reduction of it to simplicity.

Reimmersed in the atmosphere of Florence, and confronted by the omnipresent residues of Leonardo's and Raphael's accomplishment, it was not possible for Fra Bartolommeo to persist in the simply lucid state of mind out of which this painting had been generated. The altarpiece with a *Madonna with Six Saints* (Florence, S. Marco; also dated 1509)[254] is once more involved with the stimulations and the complications of Florentine example. Leonardo's mode of lighting now asserts, with new force, its place in Bartolommeo's style, though he is not yet willing to forego the new-learned luminism of Bellini. The two modes are not wholly reconcilable: it was surely evident to the Frate how Venetian light functions through and reveals itself in color, while the light of Leonardo consumes color and neutralizes it. Nevertheless, Bartolommeo attempts their reconciliation in the S. Marco altar and almost achieves it, using Leonardesque chiaroscuro as a shadowing veil, as if in transparent glazes, over an underlying Bellinesque variety of colored light.

There is also an evident persistence of Venetian interests in the composition of this altar, but here too Florentine authority, in the form of Raphael's *Madonna of the Baldacchino*, reasserts itself. This design is more ambitiously complex than that of the Lucca altar, and its complexity is intended in the sense of Raphael's example: of greater variety of forms and deeper exploration of the space. To this variety of forms the activity of the chiaroscuro, and of the color it does not wholly overshadow, adds a dimension that is almost in excess. It may be from its somewhat uneasy compound of Bellini and the Florentines, in a complex of ambitions not satisfactorily resolved — particularly in Albertinelli's large share in the execution — that this picture, unlike the contemporary *God the Father*, makes a somewhat disarticulate and, in places, even a transitional effect of style.

A third work of the same year, the *Madonna with Sts. Stephen and John Baptist* (Lucca, Cathedral),[255] abandons all but a distant undertone of Venetian influence and surrenders frankly to the force of Florentine example. In this painting Venetian luminosities of surface are virtually suppressed. Textures are matt and color is discreetly muted, even tending toward harmony by neutralization. A lighting explicitly imitative of Leonardo's now controls color and holds it subservient: a light of soft radiances which emerge from and recede into shadow, and of which the play is carefully modulated within each form. Less subtly than in Leonardo, the figures are relieved in shining contrast of their dark shapes against the open background.

Bartolommeo does not achieve, nor does he intend, the exquisite, close-woven gradations of lighting that make the single visible texture of a Leonardo but, with a more generalized manipulation of the light, he makes it serve most of the functions it had served for Leonardo. Bartolommeo's light, in a manner simpler and more emphatic than in Leonardo, works as a prime agent to diversify and animate design. Among the figures — and in this respect the Frate's method departs from Leonardo's — light and dark are distributed in large responsive balances of pattern, articulating more separately than in Leonardo the distinction between substances and atmospheric void. This large pattern of chiaroscuro follows that of the figure composition, and adds to it its own major contribution at once of differentiation and of harmony. The "design" follows that of the substantial forms but is not accessory to it; the pattern of chiaroscuro is of equal significance with the pattern of the solids, and as much thought has been devoted to its manipulation into harmony. The equilibrium of form and the equilibrium of light in this altar are separately sensible, but equal, aesthetic factors. There is a remarkable sensation, never before so articulately communicated — and not again to be achieved by Bartolommeo — of a perfect poise within this picture between the ponderable and imponderable: between light and substance.

In the structure of this altar, Raphael's influence is evident as well as Leonardo's. Raphael's model in the *Baldacchino* has been understood far more surely than in the Frate's S. Marco altar, which is more ambitious only in a simple quantitative sense. The somewhat rigid scheme of that picture and the bland simplicity of the preceding Lucca altarpiece are both transcended here. The present work develops the direction that Raphael points out in the *Baldacchino*: it is at once more strictly disciplined in composition — more unified and compact — and internally more flexibly various than Bartolommeo's two altarpieces that had come before. There is no intention to approximate Raphael's *Baldacchino* in its impress of a monumental space; however, from the breadth of substance in the Frate's figures — more ponderous than in the Raphael — and from the coherence of their order, a comparable effect emerges of a monumental form. This altar is related, in its degree of classical development of style, to the *Baldacchino*, and its mode of thinking in design is more schematically clear. Some of the extreme lucidity that had served Bartolommeo in the creation of the first Lucchese altar persists here, and insists not only on the preservation, above all internal variety, of symmetry, but on an instantly perceptible geometry of entire form. Bartolommeo arrives at the formula of this geometry in the process of compacting the distinct motives that go into his design: it is as if he should have synthesized, into one condensed unity of shape, the upper and lower portions of the earlier Lucca altar, incorporating the balanced lateral symmetry of forms, a central triangle, and a circle, all in one; and it is the implied circle, the most arbitrary and harmonious of these shapes, which finally contains the others. This is an invention which, in a way, draws the ultimate conclusion from Leonardo's *Adoration of the Magi*.[3] On this compounding of geometrical perfections — at once more doctrinaire and more obvious than in the contemporary Raphael — here first evolved, the subsequent great altars of Fra Bartolommeo would be based.

ALBERTINELLI

The role that Albertinelli at this time resumed in Fra Bartolommeo's studio seems to have been, much as before their association had been interrupted, not only that of an executant but also of a relatively independent collaborator who could work, when the occasion offered, on his own designs. Though the Frate's measure of classical development had so significantly increased during this first year of their renewed partnership, Albertinelli was at first slow to respond to his example, even in his role of executant; we have already observed the retrogressive consequences of Albertinelli's intervention in Bartolommeo's S. Marco altar. Perhaps still in 1509, more probably in 1510, Albertinelli painted a *Madonna with Four Saints* (Florence, Academy)[256] imitative in part of the S. Marco altar and in part of the Frate's picture in the Cathedral of Lucca, but evidently of his own designing. Albertinelli has achieved a labored approximation of Bartolommeo's composition and of his types; what is missing is the classical substance of the Frate's style. The individual forms ape the largeness of those of Bartolommeo, but are clumsy in proportion and inarticulate in posture; they do not comprehend even the outward form of Bartolommeo's ponderous classicizing grace. So stiffly posed, these figures cannot be contained in a responsive and continuous design: their effect of composition remains additive. It does not help quite enough to overcome this character of structure that Albertinelli, neither unimaginatively nor uninventively, spreads a baldacchino wider than in Fra Bartolommeo's or even Raphael's models, attempting thus to embrace the elements of form beneath one unifying shape.

Bartolommeo's altar in the Lucca gallery is the basis for another design and execution of Albertinelli's, the gold-background *Trinity* (Florence, Academy),[257] painted almost certainly in 1510. By the time of this work Albertinelli had come to absorb, as effectively as he ever would, the new vocabulary of the Frate's style. He paraphrases the monumental silhouette of the Lucchese *God the Father*, but in a diminishing, more fussily ornamental pattern. He adds to this borrowed image, and also to his more personal invention in the Christ, a chiaroscuro adapted from the Frate's recent manner, and he adds as well an almost carnival assortment of rich hues. Left to his own devices, Albertinelli may still indulge, at this date, in a nearly naïve variety of color, a quattrocentesque inclination sometime since abandoned by Bartolommeo himself.

The picture seems a barely adequate and rather archaizing paraphrase of Bartolommeo's style, but there is evidence that Albertinelli at one time entertained an idea for it that was of different merit. A drawing exists in the Uffizi (556E)[258] in which the subject of the Trinity is conceived with some grandeur: four saints, amply draped, stand around the image of the

Crucified while God the Father looms dramatically above. The idea (which in distant fashion recollects the precedent of Masaccio) is articulated only clumsily in the drawing, but, as an idea, it undeniably conveys a monumentality, and even a certain power, that the executed picture wholly lacks. The question inevitably must occur of the responsibility for the conception the drawing records: where there is such a disparity between the quality of a concept and the quality of its notation it suggests that they belong to different persons.

Yet it cannot, from our evidence, be claimed that this unexecuted idea of a Trinity was Fra Bartolommeo's, rather than Albertinelli's own. To assume that it was Albertinelli's makes the most important of his independent pictures, the *Annunciation* (Florence, Academy; dated 1510),[259] a more nearly comprehensible event in his career. In this *Annunciation*, as in the *Trinity*, the mode of painting and the types are dependent on the Frate, and so also are the main motives of figure composition. The upper portion of the picture, with God the Father surrounded by angels, is transcribed from Bartolommeo's *Assunta* of 1508 (which Albertinelli had completed),[46] and to a less extent from the first monumental Lucca altar. The *Annunciation* itself is in general derived from the type of Annunciation with the standing Madonna, which Bartolommeo had long ago designed, and Mariotto executed, for Volterra.* Here, however, the Madonna has assumed a pose which is a simple reversal of that of the Virgin in the S. Marco altarpiece of the just previous year.

What is seemingly novel in this picture, and without identifiable local precedent — unless, as with the drawing for the *Trinity*, we choose again to look back to Masaccio — is the scheme of architecture, which contains and binds together the two otherwise disparate halves of the design, and which gives the whole scene, by its effect as form, an intonation so unexpectedly, and so impressively, dramatic. A consideration of placing of the altar no doubt entered into the planning in perspective of the painted architecture, and to have taken the function of illusion in such obvious account is a quality of Quattrocento, rather than of idealizing Cinquecento mind. The figures, furthermore, are not integrated with this spaciousness of architecture but are still, in the manner of perspective thinking of the fifteenth century, separately conceived. Yet, from its own perspective activity the architecture takes on an active function in the scene, dramatically supporting the actors with an effect precisely as of a stage. And by the scale of the architecture, and in the imposingness that scale achieves, the scene is elevated to the atmosphere of grandeur of the modern style.

Albertinelli had adopted Fra Bartolommeo's chiaroscuro with a somewhat arbitrary accent. In his hands, the Leonardesque mode of light was schematized a distinct degree yet more than it had been by the Frate himself. Little survived, in Albertinelli's transcription, of the two consonant and synthesized functions of Leonardesque light that Fra Bartolommeo had preserved, of animation and of modulating unity; what Albertinelli carried over were rather the effects of contrast: those effects which, by schematic juxtaposing of the light and dark create activity, but not harmony. In the *Annunciation* this manner of describing light is turned to purposeful account. Albertinelli uses the activity of contrasting light to add its effect of drama — somewhat incoherent but still forceful — to the drama present in the compositional form.

By a singular process, part willed and part accidental, Albertinelli achieved, in the *Annunciation*, the first expression of dramatic style in this post-Leonardesque and post-Michelangelesque phase of Florentine painting. The picture is only imperfectly classical in form, but it entertains an advanced ambition of the classical style, to make a dramatic monumentality; and it invents or adapts devices, of architectural setting and of light, to help to realize it. This ambition, even thus imperfectly achieved, is the first counterpart, in this phase of style in Florence, of the contemporary tendency in Rome to express a monumental pathos. In the specific inclination of this picture toward dramatic emphasis supported by activity of light, it anticipates a direction that Raphael will only subsequently undertake. Soon after the painting of this altarpiece Fra Bartolommeo altered the direction of his own art in the sense here indicated by Albertinelli. Even if some part of the essential idea of the *Annunciation* may prove to be traceable beyond Albertinelli to the Frate, the picture retains its priority as an accomplished artistic fact, and as such seems to have exercised a return of influence upon the greater master.

Vasari describes at some length (IV, 223) the effort Mariotto expended on this painting. Apparently, he never worked or thought so hard again, and the *Annunciation*, awkward yet effective, remains his sole and unexpectedly significant contribution to the history of creation within the Florentine classical style. The *Annunciation* had historical consequence for others, but not for Albertinelli himself. After 1510 he subsided into his more normal and less demanding role, that of adequate but undistinguished executant for the Frate. To this role he adhered, from this time on, with more literalness and even less assertion of individual personality than he had managed to display before. His own creativity exhausted, apparently, in the making of the *Annunciation*, he was content to depend upon the authority of Bartolommeo and be absorbed in him: to become altogether a nearly
* mechanical adjunct of the Frate's artistic personality. He retired from painting altogether toward the end of 1512, some two years before his death. This was not his first retirement from the profession; he had temporarily abandoned it before, when (according to Vasari, IV, 222) "prese in odio le sofisticherie e gli stillamenti di cervello della pittura . . . si risolvette darsi

a più bassa e meno faticosa e più allegra arte" and had turned to tavern-keeping instead.

FRA BARTOLOMMEO (2)

The direction of development that is implied in Albertinelli's *Annunciation* altar of 1510 emerges with far greater clarity and with a far superior aesthetic consistency in the Frate's own immediately succeeding works. There is more than a year's interval between the most developed of the altars of 1509, that in the Cathedral at Lucca, and the *Marriage of St. Catherine* (Paris, Louvre; dated 1511);[260] in that time Fra Bartolommeo evolved into a measurably different level of maturity of classical style. By comparison with the Lucca altar that in the Louvre is far more impressively monumental, more ambitious in internal structure and yet more decisive in its harmony of total form. The aspect of the actors in the picture has changed: they are less reminiscently Leonardesque, less intimately described in features and in bodily form, and instead more largely generalized. Their countenances are more broad and regular, and their postures and draperies more ponderous and grave; and in the expressions of the saints there is, compared with the second Lucca altar, an accent of a greater spiritual gravity. Compensating their more generalized effect as single forms, the figures are arranged in a relation to each other that is more complex, depending no longer on almost literal symmetries of shape and mass but on broad equivalents of counterpoise. More differentiated in their placing in the compositional scheme, they are bound together, as the figures in the works of 1509 had not been, in groups that are unified within themselves, and related indissolubly to each other, by an uninterrupted, irresistible, continuity of slow cursive rhythm.

Each of the larger elements of composition seems to have been molded toward a geometrical identity of shape: the Virgin and Child triangular, the saints to either side a semicircle; and these are fused, incorporating the geometry of the architecture, into a finally controlling and determining whole shape. This shape, more explicitly than in its first statement in the *Madonna and Saints* in Lucca, is a clear, including circle. But, unlike the Lucchese altar, the plastic substance of the single forms has here developed and extended into a depth of space. Finally recalling the concept out of which he had created his own first classical design in the *Last Judgment* for S. M. Nuova,[21] the Frate builds the figures of the saints into a perspective semicircle, which here not only curves behind the Madonna but tends incipiently to suggest a fully circular completion of its form toward the front. Above, the baldacchino is spread by the angels into a shape altogether circular in plan, poised like a halo over the Madonna. It is not merely a plane circle that is the determining whole motive of this design, but a circle that has been rotated in the space: the whole formal structure approximates and suggests the character of a sphere. The architecture at once supports, and helps to stabilize and monumentalize this form, but the architecture is not in any sense primary, or even indispensable, to its construction. In a most advanced classical sense this plastic form, so nearly of ideal clarity, is built of the idealized human substance that inhabits and animates it.

It was only two years since, in the S. Marco altar, that Fra Bartolommeo had first tried to approximate Raphael's *Madonna of the Baldacchino.* Now, in the Louvre altar, he has not only absorbed but clarified and transcended Raphael's own example. It cannot now be said that the Frate is following Raphael; he is rather proceeding along a parallel path of development of classical style with him. In this work of 1511 Bartolommeo has created a monumental unity of geometric space, constructed out of human forms, which is in small an equivalent of the *Disputà* — which owed some debt to Bartolommeo's own earlier example. An exact comparison is of course impossible, but in general the stage of development of classical style that Fra Bartolommeo has reached in the *Marriage of St. Catherine* is, in its essentials, like that of Raphael's Segnatura phase. Bartolommeo's picture is, in the nature of its commission, a project far less complicatedly ambitious than any major fraction of the Segnatura; it is also obvious, and more important than this external circumstance, that the Louvre altar is the product of a temper far less emotionally and aesthetically subtle, and less vitally complex, than Raphael's. Nothing like the diversity or power of formal and human energies of the Segnatura frescoes may be expected here. However, when the contemporary Raphael is reduced to working in the dimensions of a panel painting, even of monumental size, that is Bartolommeo's normal field of exercise in Florence, an adequate similarity of style emerges from their work.

The *Madonna di Foligno* [177] is close in time to the Frate's altar for Cardinal Carondolet, *The Virgin in Glory with Saints* [261] (Besançon, Cathedral; begun 1511, dated 1512; with Albertinelli), and certain more or less fortuitous circumstances assist in a resemblance: the presence of the donor as well as of the saints, and the relation of both compositions to the traditional iconographic type of the Virgin in Glory. In the original state of the Besançon altar the resemblance was less striking, for the Frate's work contained in its upper part, since severed, a crown piece with a *Coronation of the Virgin,* [262] this fragment (executed by Albertinelli) is preserved in Stuttgart. In both Raphael's and Bartolommeo's altarpieces the composition depends on a lateral and central balance, which has been interpenetrated with a strongly assertive, and in effect dominating, circular motive of design. To an equal degree in both works approximate symmetry is enlivened by adjustments of restrained counterpoise, either of attitude of figure or of gesture. The postures of the Virgins are especially alike, based in both cases on a contrapposto that takes up, rotates, and returns the direction of movement of the lower half of the design. The basic resemblance of elements of structure and of their mode of functioning is as pronounced as it could be short of actual influence of one work on the other, which must almost surely be excluded here.

In both works, further, the figure style is comparable in the general level of its idealization. Yet in the specific character of figures, and in the consequence this character exercises on the whole design, the marked difference of personality in the two artists comes out strongly. The actors in the Foligno altar are less elliptically described than those in Bartolommeo's work: the description that Raphael gives of the substance and the personality of his figures contains a much more complex energy. By comparison the persons of Bartolommeo's altar seem, in form as well as feeling, a little spiritless. Thus, though the quantity of forms in Raphael's picture is less than in Bartolommeo's, and though they are less movemented, the vibration that exists in each of Raphael's figures, and the resonance of relations among them, finally creates an equal or greater entire animating power.

Raphael may have thought of the *Foligno* altar as a contrast and relief from the rhetoric of his fresco works. He has shaded his style in it to accent, not a character of public impressiveness, but an accessible, devotional relation to the spectator. Fra Bartolommeo, however, had no outlet for his ambitions to a monumental style except in altar paintings, and the Besançon commission served him as a vehicle precisely toward this end. What is intended in this picture is not merely the impressiveness of an ideal, but almost passive situation, as in the Frate's Louvre altar, but an impressiveness of dramatic kind. Unlike the Madonna of Foligno the Frate's Virgin does not sit, a quietly self-sufficient vision in the clouds, but is borne in celebrant commotion by the angels. It is not her contemplatable perfection, but her drama and grandeur of appearance that are conveyed to us in the billowing of her drapery, in her looming place against the height of architecture and, as well, by the activity around her of the light. This painting inclines in the same direction of development — though with far less sophisticated means — that Raphael about the same time began to investigate in the Eliodoro frescoes. In this inclination, however, Bartolommeo is himself referring back to the precedent of the *Annunciation* painted by Albertinelli in the year before the Besançon altar was begun, and for which, we have speculated, Bartolommeo may have supplied a germinating idea. Bartolommeo's altar is a fulfillment and correction, a critique from a mature classical point of view, of Albertinelli's effort to achieve dramatic monumental style.

Far more than in Albertinelli's *Annunciation*, and differently from Raphael in his immediately succeeding phase of style, the Besançon altar realizes the potential of dramatic pathos that can be attained by manipulating monumental form. Unlike the Stanza d'Eliodoro, there is no given theme in this devotional picture that is in itself dramatic, or that stimulates dramatic interpretation; rather, the drama is imposed upon the subject in consequence of the expressive ambition that the author entertains for the form. More than by the psychological or narrative communication of the actors, it is by the impress of the elements of form that the spectator is moved to an experience of grand pathos; the population of the picture are almost less actors than acted upon by the aesthetic structure. In his specific response to the emotions of the humanity he represents Bartolommeo is less profound and far less vital than his colleagues in Rome, but in his capacity to understand and develop the aesthetic language of the classical style he achieves a grandeur of form, and through it a magniloquence of content, which is comparable to theirs.

The two last major works of Fra Bartolommeo in this phase are both monumental *conversazioni*, very similar in design, in which he takes up again the structural proposition made in 1511 in the Louvre *Marriage of St. Catherine.* The *St. Anne* altarpiece (Florence, Museo di S. Marco)[263] was commissioned by the Signoria in 1510, but apparently not designed or put into execution until 1512. The panel was carried only to the point of its complete underdrawing, and though the Frate returned occasionally to work at it until 1515, it never advanced to the point of being colored. The *Marriage of St. Catherine* (now Florence, Academy; formerly in the Pitti, and generally referred to as the *Pitti Pala*)[264] was also designed, and wholly executed — though with the excessive participation of assistants — in 1512. In both pictures the design of the Louvre altar has been expanded and developed in a grander scale, and a character of formal pathos has been given to it even beyond that in the Besançon painting. The geometrical logic of the Louvre design has been made yet more explicit: in the *St. Anne* altar the space within which the figures are disposed has been greatly deepened, and the circular basis of the figure plan is consequently more marked. Behind the central pyramid, the architecture, itself more spacious than before, supports this circularity, and to the front it is now completed by the kneeling forms of saints. Above, the plan is repeated in diminished scale by the flight of angels and, as in the Louvre altar, the circular scheme in space is fused with an equally emphatic circle on the surface. The sense of actually spherical completeness is less here, however, than in the *Pitti Pala.* There the solid forms of composition are more compactly gathered, and the design more nearly closed by the standing figures to the front, while the motive of the opened baldacchino, developed from the Louvre altar, at the same time shapes and virtually seals the structure in a full sphericity.

In both pictures, within the more dogmatically complete integer of whole design, the greater multiplicity of parts is articulated with more separate precision than in the Louvre altar; in accustomed classical sense, the development from the earlier work is not only toward a higher unity, but toward an internally more elaborated one. It is at this point, however, that the Frate's deficiency in the *humanitas* of classical doctrine obstructs his development of form. The actors in the *St. Anne* altar — where, in Bartolommeo's own execution, their expressions are legible exactly as he intended them — assume a more serious and feeling gravity than in the Louvre altar, concordant with the whole more impressive and pretentious tonality of their picture. But this profounder feeling is expressed almost altogether only in the heads; the painter — in this respect still monastic in his disposition — does not understand the resources of expression in the human body: he is thus denied not only the variety of communication that the movement of the body yields, but also the results of this variety in enrichment of the whole pictorial form.

This resource, of which the contemporary Raphael makes so much, was not available to Bartolommeo, but he had another device at his command with which, with almost comparable effectiveness, he could diversify and enrich the form and the expression of his pictures. We cannot speculate about Bartolommeo's intentions for the completion of the *Anne* altar, but in the former Pitti altarpiece its advance in complexity and force of style results from a development in handling of light. Bartolommeo's handling of lighting in the Pitti altar, more compellingly than its figure composition, assumes the function of diversifying the design, and instills it with variety and with intensities of contrast. The figures of this altar are not more moved or more inspired than their companions in the *St. Anne* altar, but in this atmosphere of active light, alternately veiling and sharply relieving form, they take on differently dramatic meaning. The activity of light and the exploitation of its affects is more than it had been in the Besançon altar; and in this development Bartolommeo has drawn the extreme conclusion of his own mode of illumination. A lighting which, to begin with, had been somewhat schematically deduced from Leonardo's example, has been differentiated in the *Pitti Pala* toward its extremes of contrast, to the seeming maximum that can be sought without trespass on the limits of a harmony. It must be remembered that in this *Pala* execution by assistants, whose tendency to schematize exceeds the Frate's own, exaggerates the disruptive implication of these contrasts; from this exaggeration the youngest generation of Florentine painters would derive an impulse that Bartolommeo did not here intend. This lighting of the *Pitti Pala*, which complements and actively supports the pathos of the complex monumental form, was meant to work as a device of matured classical aesthetic in the same way as Raphael, in the same year in Rome, intended his effects of dramatizing light. In Bartolommeo now, as in Raphael, this mode of dramatic light is an agency of forceful public declamation.

When Fra Bartolommeo undertook his trip to Rome in 1514 there may have been in his mind some element of recognition of what we know, from historical hindsight, of his work of this phase — as we know it for Raphael in the same time: that it had evolved, in such a painting as the *Pitti Pala,* to the limit of those potentials of development that his original conception of a classical style had contained — that it had, in sum, achieved its limit of maturity. No further development was now possible only in this same direction without risk either of violation of classical aesthetic or of mere self-repetition; the time had come for reassessment and for redirection. Bartolommeo's trip to Rome must surely have been meant to satisfy a need for new resource: to find, in the famed accomplishments of Raphael and Michelangelo, ideas which could help him meet the demand, self-imposed even by the apparently placid Frate, for continuous new exploration in his art. Rome served this purpose for the Frate, but it also acutely pointed up what, by Roman standards, was his comparative artistic insufficiency.

In Rome, Bartolommeo received a commission to paint two canvases, with figures of Sts. Peter and Paul, for S. Silvestro al Quirinale (Rome, Vatican Museum).[265-7] In them the lesser spiritual dimension and the lesser power of Bartolommeo's form became at once apparent: these pictures, conceived as if they were quotations from the former Pitti altarpiece, are weak by comparison with the contemporary Raphael, and vacant by contrast with the work of Michelangelo. Apparently discouraged by his recognition of this difference, Bartolommeo abandoned the *St. Peter* before it was completed, and then Rome altogether. Raphael himself, out of consideration for his good friend of an earlier time, finished the *Peter,* painting the head and hands and probably lightly reworking all the rest; assimilating it, in a way quickly distinguishable from the *St. Paul,* more nearly to contemporary Roman style. Bartolommeo's experience of Rome was brief, but he carried back from it what he seemingly had sought in coming — new ideas and resources, but not all of them would be advantageously assimilable to his disposition of classical style.

THE SECONDARY MASTERS

It is one of the characteristics of Florentine painting in this phase that, differently from Rome, there was room in it for independent practice by a larger group of secondary masters. The production of these masters is more in quantity, but less in quality, than that of their Roman counterparts, and it is generally of more conservative disposition. Where Roman art depended chiefly on a very limited and aristocratic patronage, of exigent standards, the older and better founded school of Florence had a wider public: a considerable class of cultured bourgeoisie, less cohesive, less selective, and more various in taste than the court of Rome. Painters of the quality who continued, in this phase, to flourish comfortably in Florence would, in Julian Rome, have been forced to practice in a craftsmanly anonymity, or else required to accept another form of anonymity as assistants in the corporate machinery of a shop.

Though Fra Bartolommeo assumed an unquestionably dominating role in this phase in Florence, his influence on lesser masters was neither immediately effective nor exclusive. The Frate established his own decisive personality of style only late in 1509, and the response of secondary painters to this style, though general, was in varying tempo and degree. At first, before it had become quite clear that Bartolommeo had taken over the place vacated, successively, by Leonardo and Raphael, their examples continued, briefly, to be influential; and in particular the mode of Raphaelism that had been established toward 1507–1508 still exercised some measure of attraction.

BUGIARDINI

Among the independent painters of Florence — those outside the Frate's actual shop — it was Giulano Bugiardini who became the most literal among his followers. Bugiardini had already been conditioned earlier, by his experience as an assistant of Albertinelli, to such an inclination toward Fra Bartolommeo. However, the earlier of Bugiardini's paintings that belong to this chronological phase still show his acquiescence in the Raphaelesque mode. A *Portrait of a Young Woman* (Paris, Musée Jacquemart-André; c. 1509–10) [270] is imitative of Raphael's models, though not to the degree of near-counterfeit, as the *Lady* in Urbino had been. In this field where there were no examples given by the Frate, Raphael's influence tended to persist. It is again visible in Bugiardini's so-called *La Monaca* (Florence, Pitti; c. 1512),[269] which not unintelligently combines virtues deduced from both the *Maddalena Doni* [51] and the *Donna Gravida.* The lighting on the smoothed Raphaelesque forms, however, is now imitative of Fra Bartolommeo. As Bugiardini had been able to grasp some part of the sense of classical form from Raphael's reduction, in his portraiture especially, of Leonardo, so is he now able to transcribe Bartolommeo's reduction of a Leonardesque light. With the aid of an architectural support — not uncommon in Quattrocento portraits but more recently fallen into general disuse — Bugiardini has contrived a stable and clear compositional pattern, of simply ordered alternations and balances of lights and darks. His obvious deliberation of effects of form reveals an elementary and entirely unsubtle understanding of the mechanism of the classical style, which, however, is no longer merely imitative, as it had been in the *Lady* in Urbino, but is now competent at least to recombine borrowed forms in an approximation of a classicizing whole. The internal qualities of this structure are still not classical, however; Bugiardini's effort of intellectual comprehension is not able to remake, as well, the innate awkwardness and pedestrian literalness with which he feels forms and with which his hand describes them.

Two Madonna pictures of circa 1508–1510 are, like the portraits just discussed, more involved with Raphaelesque example than with any other. One, a *Madonna Standing in a Landscape* (sold London, Christie's, 1946),[271] is a paraphrase of Raphaelesque forms and ideas, to which Bugiardini has given an attractive, but not a classicizing, immediacy of presence, as if in the manner of a portrait style. Another, a tondo *Madonna and Child with St. John* (last recorded in New York, Collection C. H. Holmes) [272] is based in part upon a borrowing from the *Belle Jardinière.*[55] Unlike the blond-toned standing Madonna, this one inclines toward Bartolommeo's, or Albertinelli's, mode of light.

It was only after Fra Bartolommeo's own defined mature style — or Albertinelli's variant of it — had publicly affirmed itself that Bugiardini came to reshape his manner with fidelity on that of the Frate. A *Madonna with the Infant St. John* (formerly London, Agnew; c. 1512) [273] adapts Bartolommeo's vocabulary at least as literally as Albertinelli, though far less aptly. Within Bugiardini's approximation of the Frate's types, however, there persists an ineradicable instinct to prosy, labored description; and what Bugiardini natively inclines to describe is often of an ugliness at entire variance with Bartolommesque precept. Then, in transcribing Bartolommeo's cursive generalizing of forms, Bugiardini commits ineptitudes of drawing and, worse than this, shows a fundamental inability to sense the harmony in Bartolommeo's moving rhythms: almost each single shape, and each sequence of shapes, becomes a wonderfully graceless warping of Bartolommeo's intent. Bugiardini is capable here (as in *La Monaca*) of an intelligent arrangement of static factors of design, but he cannot, in his essential gracelessness, create an efficient harmony of movement among them. The combination of serious classicizing pretense — and we know from Vasari the nature of Bugiardini's humorless ambition — and of naïve awkwardness makes, even at its best, a singular compound, of the academic and the primitive.

By 1512–1515 Bugiardini's absorption of the Bartolommesque style was as complete as was possible to his mentality and gifts. The *Madonna del Latte* (Florence, Uffizi) [274] approximates almost as closely as Albertinelli, and with something of Albertinelli's own accent, the model of the Madonnas in Bartolommeo's contemporary altars. Bugiardini's variant of Bartolommeo's form remains inevitably clumsy, and not much less emphatic than before of literal description: the conception of idealized appearance is still not accessible to Bugiardini despite a decade of repeated demonstration. At least the model of this Madonna (and the model's presence is acutely sensible) is not actually unbeautiful; she much resembles the sitter for *La Monaca*. Bugiardini quite convincingly approximates the breadth and dignity of form of Bartolommeo's Madonnas, and in this simply plastic composition makes that dignity imposing. In this dimension at least, Bugiardini has grasped the Frate's implication of the pathos of a monumental form and caught his seriousness of expression — but again with a less ideal and more actual accent. Neither the physiognomic expression nor the form is so carefully distanced from the spectator as in Bartolommeo's pictures: here the expression has an overtone of intensity that intends to reach us most directly, and the form — as in Albertinelli's *Annunciation* [259] of 1510 — translates Bartolommeo's model to the purpose of an illusion. The Madonna, in slight *sotto in su*, is presented to us in the light and in the situation of an actual presence. Even as he most nearly commands the vocabulary and the formal and expressive accent of Fra Bartolommeo's style, Bugiardini cannot believe that the painter's business may be to create a fiction.

A group of pictures from the period between 1510 and 1515 demonstrates in its acutest form the conflict in Bugiardini's art between imitative classicism and a persistent literalism of style. These are three reclining nudes of Antique pretext: the earliest, circa 1510, an *Ariadne* (or equally well a *Sleeping Venus*; Venice, Ca d'Oro),[275] and the two later ones nearly identical versions of the Leda theme (both Milan, Collection Treccani).[276] It may be an accident of survival, but it is more likely a usable index of taste in early Cinquecento Florence, that these nudes (except for Leonardo's unfinished and probably uncommissioned *Leda*) are the only large-scale nudes of this time that we know. For inspiration in his conception of these themes Bugiardini has returned to precedents expressly quattrocentesque. The *Ariadne* depends, even to its kind of setting, on the models of Piero di Cosimo toward 1500. The two *Ledas* more nearly approximate Fra Bartolommeo's painting style, but their more basic reliance is also still on Piero, as if Leonardo's exercise on this same theme had never been. The literalness of description in the nudes, the utter absence in them of recreative imagination, is shocking — not for its simple-minded sensual intent but for its ugliness. The literalness is like that of Piero, but Piero's delight in conscious exploitation of eccentric form, either for ornamental or psychological effect, is missing. What is clumsy, or even comical, in Bugiardini's figures is not there because the painter has intended that effect.

Yet despite the Pieresque motive and the relative archaism of technique these figures are not confusable with productions of a Quattrocento style. Their ponderosity of form is meant to accord with the Cinquecento's classicizing canon; if not the detail, then the contours of the figures are generalized, with that lumpy gracelessness which, at its worst, is Bugiardini's parody of Bartolommeo's manner of design; the strong patterning of light and dark and the heavy balance of figure against landscape are according to a current taste. It is unfair, but impossible to avoid comparison of these works, in their clumsy intention of a classicism, with the pure and perfect accomplishment of that intent in the shortly precedent Dresden *Venus* of Giorgione. But even in their awkwardness and internal contradictions Bugiardini's paintings, hammered together as it were in sheer stubbornness of misshapen artistic ambition, and with an artisan's patient will, have a strong personal identity. He does not, nor indeed could he become, like Albertinelli, a merely reflecting instrument for Bartolommeo's conception of the classical style.

RIDOLFO GHIRLANDAIO

The record of change in Ridolfo Ghirlandaio's style in this phase is very closely parallel to that which we have found in Bugiardini. The Raphaelism that had attained its climax in Ridolfo's imitative *Girl with the Unicorn*[82] persists in his work, though in diminished and less specifically dependent forms, at least to 1510. The absence of Raphael was taken by Ridolfo as a relaxation of classical authority and an encouragement to reassert his own insistently quattrocentesque personality: so a *Portrait of a Lady* (Florence, Pitti; dated 1509)[277] still follows the general formula of the *Maddalena Doni*,[51] but within it there has been a marked accentuation of descriptive realism. What is related to Raphael is now not more than the smoothed plastic clarity of the larger form. The concept of an idealized portrait image, which before had taken momentary hold on Ridolfo, has been given up.

Where he is dealing with invented matter rather than a portrait, and where his natural imitative appetite is thus less stimulated, Ridolfo still, as in the *Adoration of the Child* (destroyed, formerly Berlin, Museums; c. 1509)[278] retains a cast of ideality. In this picture the clarity of surface and of contour in the figures, and their full proportion, reflect, probably, Raphalesque example; the angels, and in particular the right one of the pair, are counterparts of the *Girl with the Unicorn* in the Borghese. For the most part, however, specific Raphaelisms have been almost altogether absorbed by the consequences of Ridolfo's reemerging sense of his identity as a Ghirlandaio. The blond lucidity of Raphaelesque surfaces has been transformed into an airless shining, and the postures of the figures have lost most even of their earlier small approximation of a Raphaelesque grace. Further, the Raphaelesque inclination in design that had been present in the altar at Le Quiete[77] has been abandoned to return, instead, to a scheme as stiff as those of the older Ghirlandaio shop.

A larger picture of similar theme, an *Adoration of the Shepherds* (Budapest, Museum; dated 1510)[279] seems yet more reactionary. The first impression that this *Adoration* makes is of an entire reattachment of Ridolfo's style to the tradition of his family's former school. Yet Ridolfo's contact with modern classicism has left its mark upon his art so that, for all his literalness of hand and eye, and despite his additive effects of composition, this picture cannot be confused with works of his more purely quattrocentesque beginnings. Differently from those early works, the figures here are of a more ponderous and regular proportion; their contours and the movement of their drapery have a generalized, slowly cursive continuity, which intrudes itself into and modifies the additive effects of the design; and the surfaces of flesh and garment tend toward clear, and even heavily emphatic, plasticity. Even the mood, as it is illustrated in the faces and in the character of gesture, has a slow pulse of harmonizing life: a diminished echo of a Raphaelesque variety of feeling. Ridolfo was, then, in spite of the reassertion of his sympathy for an archaic mode, confirmed in 1510 in many habits of style that were, at least at an elementary level, those of a Cinquecento classicism. When the void of classical example in Florence, caused by Raphael's departure, was filled by the maturing of Fra Bartolommeo's style, Ridolfo was disposed, and adequately prepared, to follow this new lead.

Ridolfo's conversion to the new reigning mode seems to have occurred not much later than Bugiardini's, in the neighborhood of 1512. Two small pictures, a triptych of the *Nativity with Six Saints* (New York, Metropolitan Museum; formerly Milan, Collection Crespi) [280] and an *Adoration of the Shepherds* (formerly London, Henry Harris; by an assistant),[281] neither more precisely datable than between 1512 and 1515, repeat the themes of the Berlin and Budapest paintings, but in a vocabulary altogether of the Bartolommesque school. These depend not only on Bartolommeo but on his reflection, even more accessible to Ridolfo's temperament, in Albertinelli. Even Ridolfo's portrait style was influenced by his preoccupation with the manner of Fra Bartolommeo, and for one exceptional moment, in the *Portrait of a Goldsmith* (Florence, Pitti; c. 1512–15)[283] Ridolfo seems to have caught a glimpse beyond the style of the Frate into its Leonardesque origins.

What Ridolfo imitates and adequately assimilates in this time is the surface of Fra Bartolommeo's vocabulary. He excavates no more deeply into the substance of the master's style than suits the only elementary character of his own classicism. Ridolfo does not follow the Frate in his exposition in these years of classical pictorial structure; his discipleship stops at the minimal level of Bartolommeo's mature classicism, and even this is altered by Ridolfo in a retrogressive sense. Ridolfo's most ambitious panel of this period, the *Madonna della Cintola* (Prato, Cathedral; 1514–15),[282] is patently a work in Bartolommeo's school, but its model of composition is not in Bartolommeo's spacious geometrical schemes of this same time but in his by now archaic Berlin *Assunta* of 1508; and such small independence as Ridolfo demonstrates in his design is in the recall of a tradition older still, of his father's shop. Despite his Bartolommesque vocabulary the essential measure of classicism in style of this picture is still not so much different from that in Ridolfo's *Adoration* of 1510, before his imitation of the Frate had begun.

It is a revelation of the nature of official taste in Florence at this time that the most important undertaking of public decoration, the *Cappella dei Priori* [284–5] in the Signoria, was entrusted, in 1514, to Ridolfo. It was not a style, but a sound craftsmanly competence within the reigning mode, which seems to have concerned this ruling, and more than only politically representative, gentry of the city. For the layout of the decoration and the execution of its nonfigurative parts Andrea di Cosimo Feltrini was called in, and he designed, for the ceiling, a system of partitioning not unlike that which, in 1508, Raphael had found existing on the vault of the Stanza della Segnatura. In this scheme, however, the thin and angular articulation of its parts gives a still more disjunctive and old-fashioned, Pinturicchiesque, effect. There was no Raphael to redeem this scheme; its frames were populated by Ridolfo with ponderous figures of the Evangelists of his own poor invention, with a Trinity adapted from Albertinelli, and with groups of putti inspired from Fra Bartolommeo but graceless in their form and action. There is a mild pretense to iconographic unity in the ceiling decoration — supported by written explanations borne by the putti — but no equivalent mechanism compels a unity in the design. The decoration is completed by grotesque basamenti by Feltrini, and by Ridolfo's *Annunciation* in the lunette of one wall, in which there is a representation of the angel in flight that rivals the worst of Bugiardini in ineptitude.

GRANACCI

Francesco Granacci had turned to Fra Bartolommeo for example earlier than either Bugiardini or Ridolfo. Except for Albertinelli, whose following the Frate was a result of their direct association, and among the independent painters, Granacci was the only one who had accepted Bartolommeo's leadership before it was generally confirmed. He had already drawn on the repertory of the Frate in his *Madonna della Cintola* [70] of 1508–09; and in a picture which dates probably from shortly after 1510, the *Madonna with Two Saints* (Villamagna near Florence, S. Donnino),[286] Bartolommeo's *Madonna of S. Marco* [254] provides the pose for the Virgin, while the drapery behind her throne is developed from the same example much in the way it had been by Albertinelli in his altar (in the Academy) of about 1510. In Granacci's painting the effect of suavity and unity of form is greater than in the altar by Albertinelli. Granacci has learned, more than in the *Madonna della Cintola*, how to describe his figures in generalizing terms, with cursive outline and broadly modelled surfaces, and how to relate them in a simply connected unity. He still paints with a hard lucidity, but the residue of Ghirlandaio that is in Granacci's technique has been much chastened, to that important point where the description of detail no longer has an independent value for him. He does not relinquish the strong clarities of Quattrocento color, but he deepens its tone and, as in the *Cintola*, glazes it over with Bartolommesque shadows. The effect of the Frate's example on Granacci, whose history of Ghirlandaiesque association is longer even than Ridolfo's, is to convert more than in Ridolfo of the substance of his style, but less of its surface, to the Bartolommesque standard.

Of close date to the Villamagna altar, and in much the same situation of evolution toward a classical style, is Granacci's second version of the *Madonna della Cintola* (Sarasota, Ringling Museum; c. 1510–12).[287] It is toward 1512 that Granacci comes to submit more wholly to the widening authority of example of Bartolommeo's style, and to accept some part also of Bartolommeo's classicizing conception of technique; in neither sense, however, does Granacci fall so grossly into imitation as do Bugiardini or Ridolfo. A painting of the *Trinity* (Berlin, Museums; c. 1512) [288] is based on the model of Albertinelli in the Academy, but as in the comparison of their two altars of circa 1510 it seems that Granacci's style is more simple and also in more close accord with the Frate's ideas of a classicizing harmony. Here Granacci's quattrocentesque mode of handling yields finally; he accepts at least in general the new prescription of a softer and more atmospherically shaded style.

In the *Pietà* (Quintole, S. Pietro),[289] of about the same time, Granacci entirely admits Bartolommeo's contemporary manner of painting surfaces and light. Unlike his first response to the Leonardesque and Bartolommesque mode of light, Granacci in this painting does not merely apply contrasting shadow to sharp-drawn metallic form but integrates chiaroscuro with form in a way that appreciates — as Ridolfo's more literal imitation never did — the resources of harmony in this device of style. The gentleness with which Granacci modulates this light reflects the mood in which he treats his subject: less imposingly than Fra Bartolommeo in his contemporary monumental altars, and rather with a temper that recalls the early Raphael.

It is this resemblance that suggests the situation of Granacci's style at this time when, around 1512, he seems finally to assimilate himself unequivocally to High Renaissance classicism. In expression, in figure style and in technique, and quite as evidently in compositional device, Granacci is creating in the manner of the earliest and least complex moment of the classical development. The substance of his style is not much developed here beyond — for example — Raphael's early predella *Pietà* from the Colonna altar. Granacci's design is in effect a revision of a Perugino scheme; and it should be recalled how, even when Granacci was, toward 1500, an adherent of the Ghirlandaio school, it was not — as with Ridolfo — only toward the realism of that school that Granacci tended, but toward its inheritance of early classicizing clarity and order. Granacci's acceptance of the outward form and of the elementary inner substance of the Cinquecento's classicism, though a slow development, is a congenial one for him.

The continuing relation of Granacci's Cinquecento classicism to his earlier classicism of the Quattrocento *détente* is most evident in his large *Madonna in Glory with Four Saints* (Florence, Academy; c. 1512–14),[290] where he still depends for his design on the durable but worn formula of the Ghirlandaio school for this theme: there is no evidence here that such an event as Fra Bartolommeo's Besançon altar had occurred. Granacci was not disposed to think, especially on this scale, in any terms as advanced as the Frate's. On a smaller scale, however, Granacci is, by now, more confident in his transcription of the Bartolommesque style: the little *Holy Family with St. John* (Florence, Pitti; c. 1512–14)[291] is an easy fusion of such a model by Bartolommeo as his *Holy Family* of circa 1510 (Firle Place, Viscount Gage; formerly Cowper Collection) and of Raphael's *Belle Jardinière*,[55] and of earlier ideas of Granacci's own. It approximates the combination that is in the classical models, of animation and compactness, but it is not so much deliberated or so intellectually "correct"; it has, in compensation, an engaging informality of action and communicative effect. Its vocabulary is only generally Bartolommesque: the new style learned, as much as he has learned it here, Granacci finds the means in it of personal expression, and idiosyncrasies of vision and drawing that for some time had been submerged now reemerge, in somewhat different guise. Color in particular resumes its previous unshadowed freshness. Bartolommeo's models, and those of Raphael, have supplied an avenue toward a new mode for Granacci, but he has not sought in them an imitative end.

In the large altar in the Academy there is a similar relation to the ideas, in figure style, of Fra Bartolommeo and, as well, of Raphael; the four Saints of this altarpiece are of fuller and more flexible form than those of the Quintole *Pietà*:[289] they are like those of the Frate or of Raphael's *Baldacchino* altar[60] in general effect, but not in any specific aspect of vocabulary. Among themselves they compose into a pair of broadly handsome, malleable, responsive shapes. However, at the same time that, within their larger context of a conservative design, they approximate a classical effect, there reappears in them an old and unclassical quality of Granacci's private style: a tendency to disproportion of the heads and bodies, and a pointed drawing in the features of the heads; and this now is accompanied by a slightly artificial grace of pose. Granacci's mastery, barely achieved, of the grace of the new style encourages his resurrection of a tendency to something more than grace: to preciosity. His figures take on an accent of personal mannerism, and the way in which this happens, by compounding quattrocentesque reassertion into classicizing form, suggests one aspect in the process of the imminent emergence of the historical style of Mannerism. But in Granacci this is not an anticipatory invention; it is a confirmation of his still reflective place within the contemporary artistic scheme of things.

PIERO DI COSIMO

Piero di Cosimo was older in generation and in experience of the Quattrocento than Granacci, and of a temper much more eccentric to classical conceptions of artistic style, yet his response to classical example had been much more sensitive than Granacci's. Despite his temperament, Piero had been led by his receptive spirit and fine intelligence to investigate the ideas of the newer style, in particular as they were made evident in the art of Leonardo. This process had required a chastening of Piero's personality, but not its entire sacrifice: the *Perseus*[66] of the Uffizi represented, circa 1508–1509, the accommodation between Piero and the Leonardesque style. In this succeeding phase, however, the authority of classical style assumed a different character than it had before; more than dominant, it had now become, in effect, exclusive. Moreover it was no longer Leonardo's style — so rich in overtones that it permitted a libertarian interpretation to Piero — that was the major model but Fra Bartolommeo's, whose aesthetic was so much more limited, and limiting. After about 1510 Piero seems to follow, with more docility than we should expect — a docility perhaps in part due to older age and lesser energy — in the Bartolommesque direction of the rest of the Florentine school. He completes the process of chastening of expression and of discipline of form that had begun in the Uffizi *Perseus*, and in this process all but surrenders the precious, unclassical, identity out of which his finest pictures had before been made.

From these years, the last in which it seems we can place a serious and certainly attributable artistic activity of Piero, only one altarpiece remains: a picture as full of verbal exposition as Ridolfo's Cappella dei Priori, the *Doctrine of the Immaculate Conception* (Fiesole, S. Francesco).[292] Its date can be established only loosely, as being after 1510; it depends rather literally, but also weakly, on the style of Fra Bartolommeo's works of 1508 and 1509. The approximation of the Frate is somewhat spiritless and empty, less in consequence of much inadequate execution by assistants than of Piero's own conception. This is a weary acquiescence in the elementary externals of Fra Bartolommeo's classicism, rather than a convinced conversion to it, that Piero demonstrates.

* In another effort of this period, two panels with the *Legend of Prometheus* (Strasbourg and Munich; c. 1512–15),[293-4] Piero is working in that narrative genre which, unlike the monumentalizing altar of Fiesole, is his own established specialty; yet Bartolommeo's vocabulary has penetrated equally into these pictures. An accent of the Quattrocento survives in Piero's rather pointed description of the forms, but this accent is imposed upon a substance of classicizing intent. The figure style, in proportions and in degree of generalization, is more nearly classical than in the Uffizi *Perseus*, and now has the cast of Bartolommeo's, and no longer of Leonardo's, models. In the landscape the fascinating, discursive, wealth of incident that persisted in the *Perseus* has been suppressed in favor of a new restraint and quiet; and this tonality of quiet is reflected in a modulated light, explicitly in the manner of Fra Bartolommeo. Even the composition has been constructed with a geometrical regularity that suggests the inspiration, not of Leonardo's convolutions but of the sparser and more cautious structures of the Frate. This classicizing deliberation of form is accompanied by a continence in mood: for the first time in his career Piero tells a story in tones that are more soberly discreet than they are fantastic. Yet, through all this atmosphere of constraint the peculiar flavor of Piero's poetic personality still emerges, in incidents of characterization — though these are among the subordinate figures — or more significantly, of vision: he preserves the power, even within the generalizing language borrowed from the Bartolommesque school, of communicating in each circumstance he describes, and in each form he sees, an overtone of its singularity.

One work survives, of an even later time, for which we cannot adduce even an approximate evidence of date. It is no more than a supposition when we assume that it succeeds, perhaps toward 1515, the stage of style that is represented by Piero's *Prometheus* panels. This is the *Adoration of the Child* (Rome, Galleria Borghese;[295] a spoiled variant, perhaps earlier in date, in Leningrad). It is evident in this work that Piero knows the vocabulary of the mature classical style in Florence. It presupposes, in the cursive drawing of drapery and anatomy, Piero's own experience of about 1508–1509 in the Uffizi *Perseus*, and its lighting requires a knowledge of Fra Bartolommeo's developed mode of handling light, of at least toward 1510–1511. The lighting in the landscape, distantly seen through the stable door, is particularly like that in Fra Bartolommeo's Besançon altar,[261] which suggests the possibility of an experience of Bartolommeo's works at a stage still more advanced, circa 1512.

A similar measure of experience of Bartolommesque style had been incorporated in the *Prometheus* panels, there in largely willing reflection of the classicism of the Frate's models. But in the Borghese *Adoration* the proportions of classical reflection and of Pieresque individuality have been reversed from what they were in the *Prometheus*: here it is the classical vocabulary that is overtone, and the remarkable singularity of form and expression that is the substance. The figures have been reshaped as if in recollection of the preclassical Quattrocento, as it were re-Gothicized: the suavity and cursiveness of drapery and anatomy have been remade to echo an archaic elegance, as of the younger Lippi or of Botticelli, but not Piero's own blunt and energetic early forms; the composition too has assumed an archaizing accent. The Bartolommesque light has been turned into an agent, not of harmony, but of unexpected contrasting relation: of luminous, almost ghostly paleness of flesh, which shines against matt, yet strong dark color in the drapery and against the darkness of the interior space. Elements of Bartolommesque style have been altered to express a value contradictory to that which they served in the classical model, so that they do not make generalization but convey experience in its aspects of individuality and uniqueness, of human appearance and sentiment, and of sheer visual response.

Piero returned from his exploration into the reigning classicism, even though with a style perceptibly altered by that exploration, to reaffirm what had been his primitive doctrine, of the power of the artist to make not public rhetoric, but private and even eccentric poetry out of his resources of sensation. As Piero does this in the Borghese *Adoration*, it is by a recall of the personality and forms of the preclassical world in which he had first practiced and matured. This archaism clothed his meaning about the role of art in a vocabulary that was, even with its elements of contemporary accent, not acceptable as a model to other artistic personalities of this time. But the meaning itself, in its essence, was not without an audience ready to understand it — not among the generation that had made classicism, or who now, in maturity, conformed to it, but among the younger generation still. And by this Piero made a living link, threading through the life of classical style, between what preceded and succeeded it.

ANDREA DEL SARTO (1)*

In 1508 two of the younger generation of painters set up common shop in the Piazza del Grano in Florence. Franciabigio, slightly the older of the two, already had a fairly wide experience as an independent painter but his associate, Andrea del Sarto, was only newly emerged from apprenticeship with Piero di Cosimo. The association of the two young painters was brief, but rich in mutual influences, of which the directions cannot always be certainly determined. Of a much superior genius, higher indeed than that of any other painter working in Florence in these years — except for another, yet younger pupil of Piero's, Jacopo Pontormo — Andrea soon radically outdistanced Franciabigio. Andrea absorbed, into the Pieresque basis of his education, the experience his older partner offered, and with it an equivalent position in the evolution of a classicizing style; then, like Franciabigio himself but more clear-mindedly, Andrea turned toward the dominating example of this time, Bartolommeo.

Unlike all painters of this phase whom we have so far discussed, Andrea, in his assimilation of Bartolommeo's style, also effected a personally creative contribution to that style. By 1514 Andrea had subsumed Bartolommeo's example within a related but explicitly distinguishable variant of fully mature, peculiarly Florentine, High Renaissance classicism. In consequence of this, Andrea's style then took on a shared preeminence with that of the Frate, though not as yet an equal authority with his. It would not be until well into the next phase of the history of the Florentine school, and only after Bartolommeo's death, that Andrea would inherit the primacy, but never the undisputed authority, that belonged to Bartolommeo's art.

What seems to be the earliest surviving example of Andrea's work is a predella with a *Pietà and Four Saints* (Rome, Galleria Borghese; c. 1508),[296] which may be from the earliest days of the *bottega* in the Piazza del Grano. This predella is strongly indicative of Andrea's recent apprenticeship. The composition of the *Pietà*, eventually derived from Perugino's altar of circa 1493, and in part directly studied from it, is much more explicitly modeled on the reworking by Piero di Cosimo of the Perugino, in the painting now in Perugia. The relation to Piero is deeper than of motives only; the pupil is disposed, like his master, to an uncommon individuality of feeling. This, in the pupil, is less masculine than in Piero: more intimate and tender, and almost sentimental. As with Piero, Andrea's individuality of response is not only psychological; it is also visual. No other eye than Piero's — except for Leonardo's own — had seen so finely, and recorded with such sensibility of hand as there is here, the vibration of light and air in landscape and on figure surfaces. It is Piero's most Leonardesque moment, that which he came to embody in the Uffizi *Perseus*, that shaped the education of the author of the Borghese panel.

However, it is not only from Piero that the Leonardesque inflection of style in this panel is derived but from a model imminently also to become Piero's own, and less involved than he with quattrocentesque impediment, Fra Bartolommeo. The Bartolommesque vocabulary in the *Pietà* is in general more immediately evident than are the affinities with Piero di Cosimo. The affinities with Piero — beyond the obvious region of similarity in motives — are in modes of sensation, not in the larger structure of forms. These reflect, in tendency if not yet in fully achieved fact, the breadth of silhouette and curving contour of Bartolommeo's style of around 1505–1508. Certain elements, such as the billowing loops of drapery in the Saints of the *Pietà*, are demonstrably after the Frate's example. The predella is a compound: of an aspect, not yet wholly absorbed, of the new, generalizing classicism with an inclination toward intimacy of vision and feeling that — in the Pieresque guise in which it is demonstrated here — seems almost archaic. This compound is unstable, made so by the very way in which sensation is expressed, in the context of the larger forms, with such febrility. In Andrea's earliest beginnings this is already a recognizable symptom for his history to come.

The Magdalen of the Borghese *Pietà* suggests that Andrea had been exposed, if with only tentative effect, to another agent of the new classicism. The image of Raphael's *Belle Jardinière* [55] seems to have obtruded itself into Andrea's idea for his Magdalen, altering her from the precedents either of Fra Bartolommeo or of Piero. A Raphaelesque inclination might be expected in any Florentine at this moment, but to a junior associate of Franciabigio's it would be inescapable. The small *Madonna* by Andrea (Rome, Galleria Nazionale; c. 1508–09)[297] is a partial and momentary result of Andrea's exposure to Franciabigio's Raphaelism, and in this picture the authority of the intermediary is more than that of Raphael's own example. Fairly certainly the Child in Andrea's picture reflects the type and motive in Raphael's large *Madonna Cowper* of 1508; nevertheless it is not to such a contemporary work but at best to the Raphaels of a significantly different moment, at the beginning of his period in Florence, that the style of Andrea's painting can be compared. The easy, too-smoothed simplicity of forms, bland as in Franciabigio's Raphaelesque pictures (but nothing like so hard), makes an effect of naïveté in shape and structure which exceeds that in Raphael's paintings of 1504–1505. The type of Andrea's composition, in which the Madonna stands beside the seated Child, less resembles any Raphael than it does a still Peruginesque Albertinelli, a *Holy Family* (once in a Roman private collection) of about 1503. Indeed, in his approach to the new classicism Andrea's accent is of one who has, as yet, only imperfectly made the distinction between the style of Perugino and that of Raphael.

At this date Andrea is farther from the contemporary mode of Raphael than his partner — and for the moment — guide. Andrea's conception of form is not so broad or so plastically full as Franciabigio's, nor has Andrea more than begun to comprehend the role that movement may play in composition, even when composition is of limited extent. In every obvious way Franciabigio's *Madonna del Pozzo* [87] reflects more aspects of a developed, contemporary, Raphaelesque classicism than does Andrea's *Madonna*. In Franciabigio, however, these aspects do not constitute a classical integer, while Andrea's work, for all its relative naïveté, contains an essential element of the Raphaelesque style: his picture demonstrates a warmth of response to sensations of vision and of feeling that are not unlike in kind, and not so far in quality, from the earlier Raphael. Because Andrea's sensibility is pervasive, and in turn itself pervaded by this gently vibrant life, the whole of Andrea's painting takes on a kind of harmony like that which had been a first factor in the making of Raphael's classical style.

It is, then, less in any specific resemblance to Raphael than in this affirmation in it of an elementary disposition like that of Raphaelesque classicism, that the *Madonna* of the Galleria Nazionale is important to the future of Andrea's style. The imitative Raphaelism in this picture is not only mostly indirect but less than its quotient of dependence on Bartolommesque and Albertinellian style. Andrea has, even at the beginning, an almost excessive attachment to the *campanile.* Of all that is accessible to him in the artistic world of Florence it is to that of which the accent is most identifiably Florentine that he inclines: in the view of this young Florentine, Raphael may well have seemed a foreigner.

There is no further evidence of Raphael's impress on the *Baptism of Christ* of the Chiostro dello Scalzo (1509–10),[298] the first of Andrea's long series of grisaille frescoes in this place. The vocabulary of form throughout the fresco extends that of the Borghese predella, absorbing of the intervening Raphaelism of the small *Madonna* only some part of its fuller and smoother rounding of the shapes. But this inclination toward suavity — here only incipient, and only awkwardly realized in the unaccustomed larger scale — could as well now be a further acceptance of local, Bartolommesque, authority. It is in the compositional type that local *manes* are most obviously propitiated: in the adaptation from Ghirlandaio's fresco in S. M. Novella, and in the evident reference to Ghirlandaio's own source in Verrocchio's famous altar. The style of the fresco, however, is in contrast to these compositional antecedents; it is identifiably in a sixteenth-century, High Renaissance mode, even if only rather hesitantly so. Otherwise than in his precedents, Andrea's figures tend to curving, and even to ponderous shape, and they are distributed in a tentatively cursive, slow, lateral sequence against their setting of landscape.

There is still an evident unclarity of purpose in Andrea's mind: he has not yet resolved the question of priority between rhythmic revision of form and its precise representation, or between the role of line and the role of chiaroscuro. On this account the accent of style remains old-fashioned, though its substance is no longer so. This quattrocentism in accent is less unexpected than the unselfconsciousness with which Andrea confesses his dependence in composition and motives on the Quattrocento. Andrea seems, less than his partner Franciabigio, and less even than his former master, Piero, to be concerned that a point of aesthetic principle may be involved in the difference between the "modern" style and that of the masters of the preceding century. Andrea's disposition and his generation predetermined that his allegiance should fall beyond question to the "modern" style, but in no other painter of his approximate age, of the first or even of the second rank, is there so strong a sense, as their careers begin, of continuity between the old tradition and the new domain of style.

Since 1500 no fresco painting had actually been executed by any major representative of the new style in Florence. It was therefore reasonable that when Andrea was assigned the first wall decoration of any consequence in the city (since the grand joint fiasco of Leonardo and Michelangelo), in the atrium of SS. Annunziata, his work should further attest, at least initially, a dependence on the older tradition. The earlier frescoes to be executed (not, as has been universally assumed, in the order of their narrative) of the five scenes of the *Life of S. Filippo Benizzi* in SS. Annunziata (1510)[299-303] at once imply a relation to the models of Domenico Ghirlandaio. The relation is precise only in the *Burial of St. Philip*,[300] which refers to Ghirlandaio's analogue in Sta. Trinita, while the other two of the first three frescoes, the *Healing of the Obsessed Girl*[299] and the dated *Healing by St. Philip's Relics*,[301] generally recall the S. M. Novella frescoes: as in them, there is an awkwardly movemented population disposed before an architecture that seems more naturalistically than aesthetically related to them.

The most Ghirlandaiesque, in this sense, of Andrea's scenes is the *Obsessed Girl*, in which the architecture is no more than a screen, intendedly monumental, erected behind the figures. In this structure, in addition, the perspective of the figure-stage seems ineptly, excessively abrupt. The figure composition, like the architecture, intends too much; it is quantitatively the most ambitious and at the same time the least well-articulated among all these scenes. The evidence that this is the most primitive of the Benizzi frescoes is supported by the style of the figures: clumsily proportioned, with an excess of drapery and substance toward their lower parts, but for all this gravitationally insecure; they are of marionette-like woodenness in action, and for the most part conventional in type and expression of face. These figures resemble closely the Christ and St. John of the Scalzo *Baptism*, but their insufficiencies are more brought to our attention by their increase in number. The two girls at the left of this fresco, on the other hand, suggest a happier comparison within the *Baptism*, with the more graceful forms of the attendant angels there.

It is likely that the *Burial of St. Philip* was the second to be executed of these frescoes. We have observed that it is the most literal in its dependence on a Ghirlandaio precedent, as if, by closer imitation, Andrea were determined to learn the lesson offered by his model more successfully than he had at first. The architecture here intends and achieves a more monumental role: it is denser and heavier, and effectively related to the figures. These, like the architecture, are more substantial and, now, better anchored to the ground. They are less mobile but, despite this, more anatomically articulate than their counterparts in the *Obsessed.* Conspicuously, they are more assured in drawing and in the command displayed in them of the new fresco technique. The *Burial* demonstrates Andrea's quick recognition of the defects in his conception and his execution of the *Obsessed*; in turn the dated *Healing by St. Philip's Relics* seems a critique of them both. The inadequacies that Andrea remarked himself in his first frescoes are less worth note than his swift redeeming of them. The Benizzi frescoes were, after all, a proving ground for painting by an artist, still quite immature, on monumental scale, and from whom, hitherto, no such range of resource had been asked. What is remarkable is Andrea's quick development of these resources, at a pace almost comparable to that with which Raphael, on his very different plateau of style, moved at this same time.

In the *Relics* the command of space is different from that either in the *Burial* or the *Obsessed*; the role of architecture is neither so merely incidental as in one nor so obtrusive as in the other: this is a freely habitable, and inhabited, space. As the figures are distributed in depth within this space their compositional order — basically similar to that in the first fresco — has been made far more distinct: it has been syllabified, as it were, so as to be much more precisely read. More than in either preceding fresco the figures are trenchantly described and convincingly articulated in proportions and in movement. Where the shapes and accents of their predecessors are, in one case awkward and in the other turgid, these are at least incipiently touched with both vitality and grace. And, instead of the insufficient differentiation of types and expressions in the first two frescoes, the faces here have a sharper individuality, to the point of portraiture in some instances, as Vasari assures us was in fact the case.

In part the difference of this fresco depends upon a more precise command of naturalism than in the former ones. In this descriptive sense the *Relics* reaffirms the relation of Andrea to Ghirlandaio and the Quattrocento. However, the acquiring of mastery over nature is, regardless of any Quattrocento reference, also a necessity for the artist in his course of maturation toward a classical style; and Andrea's mode of more specified description is now recognizably not Ghirlandaiesque. Atmospheric chiaroscuro — already present, but not in company with this degree of naturalism, in Andrea's initial style — tends, in Cinquecento fashion, to soften highly characterized details of form and unify them. This new-learned mode, by which optical facts are more articulately described, not disparately but as if within a governing unity, is the symptom of more than a change of ways of seeing and of habits of the hand; it is the visible revelation of a new state of artistic mind. Further, it is a concern distinctly to articulate a unity that dictates, beneath the record of appearance, the order in which appearances are arranged. This is the first instance in Andrea's art in which a whole composition is an order at once clear and complex: the figures in this scheme are distributed before and through their setting of architecture in a pattern that follows and affirms the chief loci of this architecture in plan and elevation. The result is a structure of design cinquecentesque and classical in basic form, essentially such despite the many evidences still in it of persistences of older tradition.

In one very important aspect of this fresco the tradition is particularly evident: its tonality of content. It is true that the mood in the telling of the story is recognizable as the gentle, harmonious liveness that is frequent in the earlier phases of development of the classical style. Yet, as Andrea presents it, this mood has in it sensibly less than is usual in the classical style, of his predecessors or of his contemporaries, of the quality of ideal distance. The harmony we perceive in this fresco is not the attribute of an ideally superior humanity but of an average-seeming, almost commonplace world: a natural disposition of the unrhetorical Florentine bourgeoisie.

When in the two remaining frescoes of the Benizzi series architectural backgrounds are replaced by landscape, Andrea composes in them by a different rationale, less instantly apparent as such but not less intellectually determined. His order in these frescoes concords with the nature he describes, working with its variety and asymmetry of landscape forms, and arbitrarily manipulating them to effect balance. The figure composition in these frescoes is an adjunct to the order evoked from these landscape forms: precisely deliberate, but also seemingly casual. This is no relaxation of Andrea's new intent of classicizing order, but the expression of an interest to find a mode of harmony of less stringent and less formal kind than that either of *détente* classicism or of the recipes of the newer classicism: a harmony of which the mobility and apparent naturalness should convey a more immediately plausible conviction as of life. The direction initiated in these two landscape frescoes leads, in remarkable swift fruition, to the easy harmony of asymmetrical design in the *Adoration of the Kings* of 1511.

The forms of landscape in the *Punishment of the Gamblers* [302] and in the *Clothing of the Leper* [303] are still much attached to the quattrocentesque example of Piero di Cosimo; the *Perseus* of the Uffizi is a suggestive point of reference. But these forms have separately been given a more decisive and more collective clarity of shape; and their combination is into a more instantly apparent order. In the *Leper* a single turning and rising movement, with some sense in it of a spiral, rounds the shapes and space of landscape in a unity; in the *Gamblers* an asymmetrical but balancing chiasma molds the superficial and the spatial extent of design. The thinking in design is, still more evidently than in the architecturally determined *Relics*, of its spatial substance: the manipulation into order is simultaneously in all of its dimensions. The figures move, within this space, in concord with and complement to its spatial order, and cohere into an integer of pattern. Despite the reminiscences in detail that still persist from the traditions of the Quattrocento, the relation between figures and environment is essentially not that of the older time: they have not been thought in separate episodes but as functions of a unity — obviously, as yet, imperfect.

In the course of these latter frescoes of the Benizzi series Andrea's conception of the figure itself acquired a further measure of classicizing character, in greater density of form and in its mode of movement. The figures begin, in these paintings, to act with the symptoms of that heavy grace, almost excessively deliberate, that will more explicitly appear in the works of the succeeding year. It is a conception of movement like that of this moment, close to or still within the time of the Benizzi frescoes, and a like conception of form, that appear in Andrea's *Noli Me Tangere* (Florence, Uffizi; c. 1510).[304] The figures here similarly tend toward full proportion; and in feeling, in their quality of motion, and in the temper of design in which they are contained there is a deliberateness greater than in any of the frescoes. Whether it is a result of chronological evolution or only of the more limited, manipulable problem of the easel painting, Andrea reveals, in the *Noli Me Tangere*, a newly distinct identification of a classical style. Andrea's picture is dependent in some measure on Fra Bartolommeo's painting of some four or five years before, in the Louvre,[45] in the motive of its composition and, more generally, in the admission in it of a richness of chiaroscuro which, in the frescoes, he obviously could not use. Comparison of the Frate's and Andrea's versions of the theme indicates Andrea's evolution to a stage of classical development that the Frate, in his earlier painting, had not then reached. In Andrea's picture the harmony in movement of the figures is more articulated: it is a grace of credible anatomies rather than the rhythmed posing, aesthetically but not humanly convincing, of the Frate's mannekins. Where, in the older composition, there is still the sense as of a confrontation between the two actors, in Andrea's design they are synthetically joined: the moving of the Magdalen is turned and stilled with eloquent slow suavity in the figure of the Christ. In Bartolommeo's work the landscape only stiffly balances the necessary asymmetry of composition; in Andrea's the setting altogether compensates, and is indivisible from, the figure design.

It must be remembered that this comparison is with a painting of Bartolommeo's of a half-decade before; at this present moment Bartolommeo's style is mature in its development of a classicism, and rich in its articulation of it, far beyond Andrea's accomplishment of about 1510. Andrea's reference in his *Noli Me Tangere* is to an earlier aspect of the Frate's work, but it is the symptom of a new regard in general for his example. The *Noli Me Tangere* initiates a brief but important phase in Andrea's early evolution in which he, no differently from the rest of the Florentine school, much more largely admits the authority of Bartolommeo's matured style, only recently affirmed; by contrast with this style, Andrea's accomplishment of classicism in the *Noli Me Tangere* is still relatively elementary.

FRANCIABIGIO (1)

It must be assumed that at the beginning of the association between Andrea and Franciabigio the latter was the giver, not only in the shaping of specific elements of Andrea's painterly vocabulary but as a guide to an experience of models of style in Florence of this time. The similarity between Andrea's and Francesco's manners during the two years or so they shared a shop, first in the Piazza del Grano and then in the Sapienza, is uncommon for artists of their rank and their decided personality. No instance now exists of any of their actual collaborations but their separate surviving works show the signs of constant practice in each other's presence. After the first moments of their association it is no longer possible to establish positively which of the two is the more determining of their like qualities of style; partly, the problem is resolved by their response not to each other but, mutually, to the outside example of the Frate.

A *Madonna and Child* (Rome, Galleria Nazionale; recently improperly reassigned from Franciabigio to Andrea)[305] is dated 1509; technically apparently authentic, the date nevertheless provokes a measure of distrust; it would make better sense in the history of Franciabigio's development if the "I" and the "X" were transposed. Whether or not the inscribed dating is correct this picture succeeds Andrea's smaller version of the same theme, based on the same motive of composition, in the same museum; where that work reflects Franciabigio's Raphaelism of the time of the *Madonna del Pozzo*,[87] this one seems already to have embarked upon another course, indicated by the model of the Frate. There survive, within this change (beside the Morellian peculiarities that sufficiently confirm Francesco's authorship), the evidences of the concern that earlier affirmed itself within a surface Raphaelism, and of which the mark is the desire to make an image more compellingly, but not necessarily harmoniously, movemented than in the available precedents of classical style. But this desire is chastened here, probably by the joint working on Francesco of the example of Bartolommeo's decorousness and of Andrea's quiet grace.

By 1510 Francesco had subsided — even too much — from that onset of vitality which had been in his works of circa 1508: his fresco *Adoration of the Shepherds* (from the former Villa Quaratesi-Baroncelli; Museo di S. Marco; dated 1510) [306] is almost passive. In it the vocabulary of form — the details discounted — is virtually interchangeable with that of Andrea's Benizzi frescoes of the same year, and it may be assumed, but not surely proved, that Andrea rather than Francesco is the giver of this style. The identifiable Raphaelisms of the paintings by Franciabigio that predated his partnership with Andrea have been displaced by this vocabulary, which is more evidently Florentine and much less novel-seeming than that of his Raphaelesque episode. More than Andrea's contemporary work, Francesco's fresco suggests comparison with the manner of Albertinelli, not quite of this moment but in a phase a little earlier. A local and personal allegiance has reclaimed Franciabigio; and the temper of the *Adoration* is as conservative, and of a formality only a little less guarded, than in the current paintings of Granacci, or even of Ridolfo Ghirlandaio.

The forms of the *Adoration* resemble those of Andrea of the moment; but they are less individualized both in content and in representation. Also, while Francesco's manner of design resembles Andrea's, it is less tense, and less probing of the resources of classicizing structure. There is small difference in the basic plan of figure composition of this fresco and, for example, the *Burial of St. Philip*, nor is Francesco's landscape setting less deliberately related to the order of the figures than that in Andrea's *Gamblers*. Franciabigio's composition is more smooth and easy, especially in its rhythmic sequences, than any of Andrea's; in this sense it seems more classicizing and also, in this ease, more personally mature. What is missing in the *Adoration* are those qualities that make Andrea's frescoes seem, in comparison, unquiet, searching and potential of development: an acuteness of description, a sharper articulation of forms and of intervals between them, and the animation that increases progressively in the Benizzi series as Francesco's animation in this fresco, oppositely, has nearly disappeared.

Franciabigio's other surviving monumental work of about this time, the *Last Supper* (Florence, S. M. dei Candeli; c. 1511, ruined by repainting),[307] is more than the *Adoration* an evidence of compromise between contemporary and older forms. The iconography of this subject had by now — Leonardo's Milanese excursus notwithstanding — been petrified, and Franciabigio has had the courage to modify it only in its parts, but not to that degree which might significantly affect the character of the whole. The figure types incline, as they had in the *Madonna* of 1509, toward Bartolommeo's mode, but an intended "modern" ease of posture and of gesture, and — if the repainted evidence may be trusted — a Bartolommesque light, do not give a meaningful dimension of new style to the structure, *à la Ghirlandaio*, of this *Last Supper*.

ANDREA DEL SARTO (2)

It is in this year, 1511, that the separation of Andrea and Francesco, already a fact as regards their residence and practice, became an assertive fact of style. In the very moment that marked a *détente* in Francesco's development toward classicism, Andrea, approaching his personal maturity, began to explore resources of this style that were new to Florence, even in the light of what Fra Bartolommeo had so far done. From this time on Andrea unequivocally takes preeminence over Franciabigio, not only in the quality of his art, but in its power for development. By contrast with the later frescoes of the Benizzi series Andrea's *Adoration of the Magi* of 1511,[308] in the same forecourt of the Annunziata, reveals a new measure of its painter's personality, large and boldly confident; and there is no more here than the slightest trace of persistence from the tradition of the Quattrocento. In the *Adoration* Andrea comes abreast of — and in some ways overtakes — the development of Bartolommeo, and attains a classicism comparable not only to that of the contemporary Frate but even, in essential characteristics, to that of Raphael in an only shortly antecedent time in Rome.

The potential for achievement of such a style was discernible in the Benizzi frescoes, but not to the degree where it might have been expected so quickly — indeed so dramatically — to mature. Some precipitate or some external model must have helped accelerate this maturation. It is conceivable that Andrea may have been exposed to some ideas of Roman style, in drawings brought to him by his close friend Jacopo Sansovino (who stands portrayed beside Andrea in the right corner of this fresco), returned from Rome in this same year. This is no more than supposition, and in any case such indirect experience would have been far less formative than the effect of the immediately accessible example in Florence of the art of Fra Bartolommeo. One of the major elements in the new aspect of Andrea's fresco is his grasp of the idea of massively ponderated human form: Andrea's conception of stance and attitude is — like his new sense for breadth of bodily proportion — derived from Bartolommeo, and given a still stronger emphasis. Also adapted from the Frate is Andrea's new mode of chiaroscuro, present in less pronounced form in his prior easel paintings but now for the first time made a major agency for harmonizing form and color in a fresco. Drapery style and, even, typology in the *Adoration* show the impress of the Florentine *caposcuola*. The very limitations of classicizing form that are apparent in the fresco — the only partial development of contrapposto and the residue of additive mentality in the building of the figures into groups — are the limitations of Fra Bartolommeo's art in 1511.

Andrea's figures are, now, conceived according to Fra Bartolommeo's most recent demonstration of classical canon. However, they possess qualities that had never been particularly apparent in the Frate, and which had diminished as he evolved toward fuller classicism in his style. Andrea's actors — even those who are most deliberately posed — are much more vital than Fra Bartolommeo's; they are more inhabited in body and in face by an energy like that of a real humanity. Within their classicizing cast they are observed and characterized with a cogency and variety far beyond what Andrea had shown in the Benizzi frescoes. It is not only the increased measure of classicizing form that distinguishes these figures but their new effect of actuality of appearance and of vital content; beside them the Frate's models of the moment look, more than ever, like studio conventions. From that aspect of Andrea's temperament that determined his affinity, in the Benizzi frescoes, to tradition, he has infused into Bartolommeo's figure style a quotient of vitality that — for reasons no less temperamental in the Frate — it lacked.

A similar effect, of form at once more classical and more vital, has been worked by Andrea on the *Adoration's* larger ordnance of form. There is a marked difference against the Benizzi frescoes in the manner of combining figures in this composition. It is a decisive step in mature classical direction that figures are no longer set out (as in the *Relics*) as sparse loci of a geometric pattern nor (as in the *Burial*) loosely accumulated into groups; instead they are assembled in broad masses, plastically full and patterned with connective rhythms. The sense of a slow-movemented largeness in the single forms is aggrandized by their resonance within a group. It is in Fra Bartolommeo's terms, not those of the earlier Florentine models of Leonardo or Michelangelo, that Andrea makes this alteration in his style.

However, the way in which Andrea arranges these groups into a composition is according to a system personal to him, different not only from Fra Bartolommeo, but from any scheme in Raphael to this date; it anticipates, in fact, an invention to which Raphael came toward 1513. Andrea's composition demonstrates, as much as do the single figures, an effect of heavy equilibrium. The figures are disposed, in respect to their design upon the surface, in a varied, gently undulating, and controlling pattern of near-isocephaly. Yet their division into groups is strongly asymmetrical, with a marked predominance of mass in the main, rightward group. An abnormality of iconography helps the artist justify this structure: strictly, this is not an *Adoration* but a *Procession of the Magi*, and Andrea's fresco is intended to be read, though hardly quite convincingly, as complement to the *Nativity* of Baldovinetti, in a bay to the left in the courtyard, beyond an intervening door. It is this pretext of direction that supplies, literally, the motive for Andrea's design. Its structural precedent, however, appeared before in Andrea where there was no such motive, in the *Gamblers* of the Benizzi series. In the *Adoration*, where the asymmetry is at once more powerful and more certainly controlled, the intention of its use is much the same: to endow the structure — now much more substantially classical — with the conviction of an apparently informal life, of a kind that Fra Bartolommeo's hieratic altar-schemes did not allow. The compensation of this asymmetry into equilibrium is most sophisticated in its means, but again is based on ideas first devised in the

Benizzi *Gamblers*. The forms of landscape, and of architecture also, are disposed so as to compensate, by their shape and impulse of direction, the mass and movement of the crowd; in doing so yet further, enlivening, asymmetries are made along with their effects of balance. Color is used in a comparable way, with a remarkable awareness of its effects of apparent weight or lightness and assertive or recessive hue. Then there is an adjustment, of more knowing kind than in any works in Florence since the cartoons of Leonardo and Michelangelo, between effects of mass and of implied directions of energy among the figures.

The whole procession has come toward us out of the distant countryside and approaches, front oblique to us, wedge-like across the center of the picture field. Within the procession there is both continuity and reversal of its evident direction, as most obviously in the two foremost Magi who, as they march deliberately toward the left, turn their attention, and their upper bodies, crosswise toward the right. The direction of the group is counterweighted to the right by the portrait-group of spectators: Andrea, Sansovino, and their musician friend, Ajolle; to the left the shape and movement of the cortège is countered, and its direction turned, by the broad, rotating form of the attendant in the nearest foreground. His movement is continued rearward in the space, arrested by the oblique mass of architecture, and unassertively returned toward the main group by the welcoming figures farther to the rear. Despite the very look of informality, which its asymmetry is meant to promote, there is hardly an element in the fresco that does not have a precisely-meditated role in its complex making of an equilibrium.

Beyond this sophistication in manipulating elements of classical design there is a development, yet more meaningful and profound, of Andrea's classical conception of the nature of pictorial structure. Far more than in its first evidences in the *Relics* or the *Gamblers* of the Benizzi frescoes, there is the sense in the *Adoration* that its whole form is an integer, and that its superficial order and its design in space are indissoluble and were, in Andrea's invention of design, coeval. Andrea thinks, now, of the whole contents of this illusive excavation of the wall as a malleable unity, to be wrought simultaneously in all directions and in all its elements at once — plane, mass, space, and colored light — to his pictorial purpose. And there is no remnant now of what, in the later Benizzi frescoes, had been sensible as a dualism of such purpose: a distinction between the function of the picture as a representation and its object of creation of aesthetic order. Both meanings now seem to grow from one another, as interpenetrated functions of a unity of vision and of form.

The structure in which Andrea presents this scene of a stately, yet mundane, processional is, in terms of the development of the older masters of the classical style, precocious. Andrea employs much the same motives of design, and many of the compositional devices, that Raphael evolved for his later *Repulse of Attila* [221] — not altogether unlike in the problem offered by its subject matter. It is as if Andrea, who had no more than newly grasped the discipline of the more conventional examples of mature classical style, should at once have invaded its advanced terrain. While we recall how much Andrea's accomplishment in the *Adoration* owes to Fra Bartolommeo, it is apparent how this picture is much more than a maturing of Andrea into conformity with the Frate's current pattern. The *Adoration* offers a variant definition of the classical painting style to Florence, more vital and complex than Fra Bartolommeo's, and potential of more searching and more various development.

Still, the *Adoration* lacks, in some respects, refinements which appear in Bartolommeo's more personally mature contemporary style. Andrea had not yet attained such polished suavity in drawing and in manipulation of cursive rhythm, nor quite such power of generalization, as the Frate demonstrated in his Louvre altar of this year. Bartolommeo remained an example of authority to Andrea for the next few years while the younger artist learned from him, and incorporated into his own basically richer art, the Frate's urbanity of classical manner. In his search for entire consistency in the new style Andrea accepted and adapted not only Bartolommeo's model of suavity of form, but much of its corresponding mood, and even exploited Bartolommeo's precedents of composition, manipulating them to his own ends. Andrea's *Annunciation* (Florence, Pitti; c. 1512),[309] once in the convent of S. Gallo, derives the motive of its figure composition not directly from Fra Bartolommeo, but from Albertinelli's altarpiece of 1510;[259] Andrea's alterations from this model are, however, a critique of Albertinelli's lapses from his master's style. First typologically, then in quality of expression, formal and psychological, and finally in smoothed grace of attitude and contour, Andrea's figures depend on the Frate's art in its most recent phase, as in the Louvre altar. But where Bartolommeo's example tends toward blandness, Andrea reinstills it with controlled and subtly vibrant animation: in the communicative power of a gaze, in the meaning of a gesture, gently tensed, and in the movemented variety of all his drawing. The composition itself, so seemingly dependent, has been given a unity quite absent from the model of Albertinelli, and more articulated than in the paintings of the Frate, by Andrea's feeling manipulation in it of responsive shapes and sequences of cursive rhythm. The design moves with a controlled and subtle scansion that is sophisticated beyond any previous effect in Andrea's own, or in any other work, in Florence of this phase.

Less obviously than in the *Adoration*, but with yet more disciplined coherence, the design of figures is inseparable from their space and setting. An architecture, more stable than in the *Adoration* but also asymmetrically disposed, enlivens and defines the space and amplifies the figures' monumentality, and the figures are explicitly dependent on it to complete a single texture of design. The rhythm of Gabriel's gesture is at once expressively suspended and transmitted by the architecture, and the face and body of the Virgin are given higher resonance in their frame of architectural forms. Andrea's calculation of relations of design like these is yet more self-conscious and more pervasive in the *Annunciation* than it had been in the *Adoration*, and it is the consequence of an awareness yet more developed of the role, as form, of each element of representation. It is in the *Annunciation* that we begin to sense the exceptional skill with which Andrea relates forms: it is the manifestation in him of a special quality of aesthetic intelligence almost comparable to that of Raphael.

A small group of panel pictures almost certainly of 1513, the principal one of which is the *Marriage of St. Catherine* (Dresden, Gallery; perhaps in part with Puligo's assistance)[310] is as much involved as the *Annunciation* in the example of Fra Bartolommeo's art. The Dresden altarpiece refers not only for general character of style but for composition directly to the Frate's painting of the same theme, of 1511. Compared with the *Annunciation*, the *Marriage* shows a still deeper assimilation of Bartolommeo's style, but this is no impediment to a more marked emergence at the same time of Andrea's own personality. More like the Frate — and immediately evidently so — is the different degree and force of generalization in Andrea's forms. The figures of the *Annunciation* were still touched with a traditional concern for small effects and for episodes of fine-wrought draughtsman's handling; in the *Marriage* the figures are described as broadly as Fra Bartolommeo's own. A sense of entire liberation from the past, and of more mature assurance, emerges from this new fact of style. The figures have a new, quickly graspable, rounded unitary shape; even more than in Bartolommeo's art we read them instantly in the whole and only in a second moment in interior detail. Only the proportions of the figures still seem immature, both in a personal sense and in the perspective of a classical development: their emphasis of rounded breadth, accentuated by their postures, takes less account than in Andrea's *Adoration* of the canon demonstrated by the Frate.

The whole picture is inhabited, in fact, by emphases which alter, with strong personal effect, the stylistic models of Fra Bartolommeo. The composition concentrates Bartolommeo's scheme into a more substantial, compressed mass, more contained and more expressly spheroid than any composition of the Frate's to this time. This substance is internally articulated with more richness, and with far more energy, than in the works of Bartolommeo. Despite its specifically painterly effects of color and chiaroscuro — these, too, more emphatic than in Bartolommeo's style — this structure has a character of sculpturally excavated mass. The idea may have been inspired initially by renewed contemplation of Michelangelo or Leonardo, but it is worked out here in a development of Bartolommeo's tectonics of explicitly pictorial space. This is not, as in the *Battle of Anghiari* [28] or in the Doni tondo, [27] an excavation around and toward a core of substance, but a building out of substances around a core of space.

What is least Bartolommesque and most personal to Andrea is the temper, both of form and content, in this picture. The gentle continence of the *Annunciation*, subtler than the Frate's but still like him, has been replaced by emphatically communicative action and emotion that only this massive formal substance is sufficient to contain. The almost tremulous emotion of Andrea's early *Pietà* [296] and the intimate affection of his earliest *Madonna* [297] — Andrea's initial, innate modes of feeling — have now reemerged with a new accent and with the assertiveness of a temperament approaching full maturity. More momentarily than in the processional *Adoration*, the *Marriage* seems to assert forms and mood in movement, and this movement is less physically than psychically inspired: an excitement close to rapture fills the actors in this picture. Their postures strain, not in conformity to the prescriptions of a contrapposto; even within the massive and symmetrical design that contains them the actions of the figures, like their emotions, seem imminently unstable. The category of emotion that is here expressed is not unlike that of Fra Bartolommeo in basic kind, but the degree of emotion is utterly unlike: it has been intensified, sharpened, and made subtle to that point where its difference in degree verges on translation into other kind. In consequence of Andrea's example his own best pupils tend actually to effect this translation, but only in the context of a mode of form either less classically developed than here, or evolved into a postclassicism. The analogy for Andrea's style in this altarpiece lies less among his Mannerizing pupils than in the North of Italy, with the roughly contemporary work of Correggio.

By contrast with the models that Fra Bartolommeo offers, Andrea's picture lies at an opposite pole within the range of content that a classical style permits. Where Bartolommeo's great altars of this time are emotionally bland, and make content mainly through the affects of their form, Andrea's *Marriage of St. Catherine* employs a less pure and more active method of communication. Bartolommeo's art accentuates a classical effect of ideal distance; Andrea's, on the contrary, intensifies the sense of physical and psychic presence. From this time onward Andrea's classicism carries in it, more than any other major variant of the style, the quality of accessibility, or even of intimacy, of his images. Andrea's idiom is in this sense the most peculiarly Florentine among the classical modes, and at its far lesser level it reflects, in this concern for the actuality of experience, some of the character and some of the limitations of the Florentine founder of the style, Leonardo.

Nowhere in Andrea's art is his attachment to the *campanile* so apparent as in his *Birth of the Virgin* in the courtyard of the SS. Annunziata (dated 1514).[311-13] The relation of this painting to Ghirlandaio's fresco of the theme has been so often characterized that it needs no iteration. Like the Ghirlandaio, Andrea's scene contains a strong element of *reportage*; and on Ghirlandaio's precedent the subject is taken as a pretext for a presentation that is mundane, opulent, and actual. Unlike the Ghirlandaio this, though rich, is less aristocratic. It is in the likeness of Andrea's fresco that we tend to form our image of society in the Florence of these years; it is a conspicuous example of the power present in works of art to mold, aesthetically, a concept of historical sociology. Descriptively, the fresco may well be a kind of journalism, a record shared with us of a visit of congratulation to a wealthy house to which an heiress has been born. The fact that this particular event is more than actuality, that it is miracle, is quite secondary; but it is at least referred to in the topmost reaches of the room where (perhaps adapting the iconographic idea of a print by Dürer) angels ecstatically celebrate the birth. This incident does not change the journalistic fact: no other picture since the founding of the Cinquecento style had so little in it of the classical tonality of ideal distance; conversely no other image on this scale had been so welcoming and accessible.

The effect of an actuality which invites, not only our approach but virtually our sharing, is achieved by means, and in a humor, different from those in the Dresden altar. We have remarked that the Dresden picture contains a reassertion in new, but only partially tempered, guise of emotions from the phase that preceded Andrea's discipline of classicism and that these emotions, in their emphasis and near-febrility, are only just amenable to control by classical devices of the form. This access of excitement in the works of 1513 is transitory and it yields, in the *Birth of the Virgin*, to a more maturely classical, more continent emotional mode. It is as if the energy of feeling in the Dresden painting had not so much subsided in the fresco as been diffused in it: as if the same quantity of emotion had been dissolved among more people and through a wider space, and as if, at the same time, intensity of feeling had been transformed instead into its subtlest articulation. The resulting content, a breathing liveness skillfully differentiated through the range of one harmonious, and pleasurable, mood is classical in the most obvious, but also in an entirely developed sense.

The conviction of actuality of these sensations of persons in Andrea's fresco is of course inseparable from what is, for the first time in Andrea's art, a conviction of the unexceptionable plausibility of their physical being. There is no problem now of skill in imitative drawing; nor is there any conflict between generalization and description of detail. One appears to grow in living process out of the other, and both have become functions of a single visual and substantial unity. Most important, there is no conflict between internal aesthetic predisposition, and its manifest habits of hand, and the data of appearance given by the object. The process by which these figures are described is neither imitative nor aesthetically arbitrary but, literally, reproductive. The seen image and the artist's mind, shaping as it sees, are in vitally responsive, synthetic adjustment to each other. We too, in our response to these figures, are encompassed in the orbit of this synthesis so that our easy act of credence in them is not, as in the Ghirlandaio, a willed act of belief but an involvement in the working of a vital process: this is, in its most convincing form, the *natura naturans* of classical style.

The canon of appearance and of attitude to which Andrea's personalities conform is more nearly than before like that in Fra Bartolommeo's mature mode, but it still retains, from Andrea's earlier predisposition, a tendency to broader forms. The tempered but rich energy these forms possess is expressed in their sonority of rhythmic structure: generous, slow-moving, and articulately suave beyond any aspiration of the Frate. These rhythms accompany the shape in space of bodily substances, and their smoothed plastic richness suggests a quality that is not only of the eye but tactile: a malleability as of real substances, shaped by a powerful yet gentle and responsive hand. Such structures of rhythm are of course entire artifice, but so coherent are they with the naturalness of appearance and feeling of the figures that they seem to grow out of them rather than to be imposed. The "design" of the actors seems the consequence of the kind of beings that they are in form and state of mind. Yet such effects are, inescapably, effects of art, and no matter how sensuously actual-seeming, or even how seeming-casual, these persons are, we recognize them as components of an aesthetically transmuted world.

The composition equally makes most careful pretense to be casual. Its figures and its setting are disposed as if by accident, without evidence of formal emphasis on axes or on symmetry. The idea is developed with much higher skill from that laid down in the adjacent fresco of the *Adoration*, already a markedly original invention. In the *Birth of the Virgin*, the compositional scheme fulfills the pervasive intention of Andrea for this work: to convey the sense that this picture's world is actual, alive in the manner of our own and, in effect, accessible to us. Nevertheless, the evidence of art in the whole design emerges yet more strongly than in its parts: the deliberation of each form is magnified in its relation with the others and in the context of the calculated whole. Within the clear cubical framework of the painted room the elements of setting are placed asymmetrically, just to the degree required to offset the asymmetry of figures; at the same time this interior architecture frames, or clearly points up, the actors. The figures themselves are arranged in a welling arabesque, of a shape which, as befits their fullness, is like a cornucopia. The rhythm of the composition unfolds, as it were, from that of the figures, and has not only its suave amplitude but its plasticity. From the door in the deepest space at rear left (where a porter bearing wood, now all but obliterated, is about to enter) an irresistible curve moves forward through the room, leaving a meaningful perspective hiatus for the Zachary; his movement, a kind of semicolon in this eloquent formal phrase, is taken up in the near-arrest of the monumental women nearest us — beings fit to occupy a pediment on the Parthenon, but masquerading in the prose of casual action and contemporary dress — and with deep slow grace is turned and diffused, again rearwards, toward Anna and her servitors around the bed. The design is, far more than had been adumbrated in the *Adoration*, a functioning of substances within the space, or rather — so strong is the sensation here of a pictorial integer — the design seems a differentiation of substances within a single whole texture of the work of art.

That this texture is a unity is affirmed, as never before in Florence except by Leonardo, and never at all in a Florentine work of fresco, by Andrea's handling of chiaroscuro and color. Light and dark are richly modulated as in the mature pictures of the Frate, but with a yet greater effect as of a respiration, like that we feel in the rhythm of Andrea's composition. The subtlety of chiaroscuro far exceeds anything in Bartolommeo; for such effects of sensibility, both of observation and of calculating manipulation, there is no precedent but Leonardo's. However, unlike Leonardo's, this sensibility to light is fused with an equal responsiveness to color.

Like the composition of the figures, the design in color seems to grow by differentiation from the texture of a whole lighted space. From a harmonizing and controlling darker tonality of atmosphere the colors emerge with gradual increasing brightness; as the forms to which color is attached grow more clear and substantial the color becomes equally more clear, but also, as if partly to compensate the greater mass of forms, less grave. The colors include all the familiar primaries that are found on the Quattrocento palette, but none is expressed with quattrocentesque simplicity: each hue is mixed and muted, responsive to the qualifying effects of chiaroscuro atmosphere. But accompanying this ultimate sophistication in description is the effect, hardly less evident than in the disposition of the forms, of deliberate design in color. Against the harmonizing background of darkish green the design in color emerges, with the pattern of figure composition to which it is attached, first as darkened lavender; this, becoming lighter and more assertive in a nearer form and more infused with red, is then differentiated into browned red-orange and into muted blue; at this point, in the seated handmaid at left center, a dusty golden-yellow is introduced as accent, but also as complementary contrast, to the violet. The foremost figures articulate the two tones of this figure, each separately and more palely. At the right, the color recedes again to blue — echoing the blue skirt of the nurse at the left — and to tones of warm or darkened violet. Through all the figures a weaving lace of color runs, threading them together: of white or, more subtly assertive, of the fundamental violet. Even Raphael's contemporary work shows a less nice calculation of color than Andrea's in this fresco; and the contemporaries in Venice at this exact date, though more assertive of their optical experience, are not so subtle in its description, and they are conspicuously less sensible of its possibilities of aesthetic manipulation. Andrea's colorism is more than any Florentine's like that of the Venetians, but his Florentine *disegno* is applied as articulately to color as it is to form.

The *Birth of the Virgin* is the evidence of Andrea's emergence to complete maturity, in personal style and in the classical idiom of painting. In this picture he has explicitly fulfilled the proposition of a classical mode, more vital than Fra Bartolommeo's, that he had laid down in the *Adoration*; and now the difference is not one only of vitality, but of subtlety and power of both human and aesthetic meaning. In his Pitti altarpiece of 1512 [264] Bartolommeo's own development had brought his style to a place where, quantitatively and generically, it was comparable to the paradigm of the current Raphael in Rome. Bartolommeo's style in that monumental panel, however, is the result of a continuous elaboration, in a straight line as it were, of the premises established in his work of 1509, at his first classical maturity. The *Pitti Pala* is the achievement of an end in a progression, and as we know from subsequent events, the Frate's style had no resource of truly effective development beyond this, at least in the same direction. Andrea's formulation of a fully mature classical style is intrinsically more like Raphael's accomplishment in his phase just closed. The possibility suggests itself that some part of this likeness in Andrea's fresco is owing to an experience of contemporary Roman art, in this case direct rather than merely through the agency of drawings or of prints such, as we suggested, may have served Andrea in the *Adoration*. The suavity of classical idiom that Andrea attains in the *Birth of the Virgin* has no counterpart in Florence of this time but is like that of Raphael's style in Rome; and it is also true that the change in style that this fresco shows, in comparison to Andrea's just preceding work, seems more than normal evolutionary expectation.

It may be that a trip to Rome — which, as Vasari says (V, 55) was too hurried — may have been the precipitant of this degree of change and of Andrea's ascent to entire classical maturity. If this is so, even the brevity of the stay that Vasari reports would not lessen its significance for the history of Andrea's style. But even if a Roman stay at this time was so brief it is surprising that no precise and certifiable effect of it appears in the *Birth of the Virgin*: one specific motive only, the attitude of Zachary, may uncertainly relate to the *Parnassus* or the *School of Athens*. Except for this there is no indication of what we know is a result in every other artist of exposure to the examples of contemporary Roman art: the reflection of its repertory of motives of appearances and actions. There is no provable acquaintance in the

Birth of the Virgin with this Roman treasury, nor is there any other certain index of such knowledge in succeeding works. The assumption of direct experience of Rome before Andrea's creation of his great fresco of 1514 is no more than arguable hypothesis; the date of the voyage that Vasari reports cannot provably be fixed here or, indeed, elsewhere. The general affinity in the *Birth of the Virgin* to Raphael's mature style may equally well be the result of Andrea's wholly independent process of development.

It is not only the supreme fluency of Andrea's style in the *Birth of the Virgin* that promotes this effect of an affinity with Raphael, but the comparable level of psychological and aesthetic sophistication, and beyond this, the vitality — different in temper but not in basic kind — which their art shares. Also, Andrea's style is like Raphael's in its creation of new possibilities of monumental form, less bound than those of the earlier maturity of classical style to receipts of symmetry. Andrea's variant of classicism is a summary and an affirmation of what had come before in Florence, but it is also now a new threshold for this style.

However, one of the very resources that made Andrea's style potential of a new development was at the same time a function of his own, and his style's, gravest limitation. Andrea's responsiveness to the aliveness of nature as a visual datum and to the aliveness of the beings who act in it was a source of energy, and of enrichment with variety, of his art. In this fact as in others Andrea's situation resembles that of the contemporary Venetians, who derive from closer contact with the life of nature an avenue of new development for classical style. But in Andrea the relationship to nature was not so vital as that of the Venetians; there is the tenderest subtlety and, often, depth, in his experience of the world, but no urgent passion. The naturalness of his actors is not only in their looks and in their environment but in their absence of any unaccustomed spiritual dimension. There is little in Andrea's achieved art of the hieratic, though often slightly vacant, grandeur of Fra Bartolommeo and less of the high drama of the mature Raphael, and he has no will whatever to strong conceptions of ethic or of intellect. Andrea does not have, thus, the motive — the aspiring tensions of the mind and spirit, as does Raphael; or even Fra Bartolommeo, though with less effect — powerfully to develop the resources of his own new flexible and energized variant in Florence of a classicism; he does not seek as much as they do higher dimensions of expression for the instrument of style he has made.

Vasari recognized this limitation of spiritual reach in Andrea, and characterized it gently but unsparingly. There is something in Andrea, temperamentally, of the quattrocentesque painter of the type of Ghirlandaio, whose work the *Birth of the Virgin*, in spite of all the differences, persistently resembles. Andrea's art is, of course, historically inseparable from its context, but it is an index of the inescapable authority of that context — as well as of Andrea's profound and malleable aesthetic sensibility — that a painter of this temperament should, in this context, have become a master of the classical style. It is not uncharacteristic for the history of this style in Florence that in Andrea, as in Fra Bartolommeo also, the forms of classicism, and their content as aesthetic forms, should weigh more solemnly than the specifically human content, and lend the illustrative meaning more of dignity and import than it actually contains.

Andrea was the latest born, and the latest to come to his maturity of the classical masters; and he would survive to be the last pure practitioner in Central Italy of the classical style. He attained his personal maturity in the moment when the classical style in general, in Rome as well as Florence, had reached its own apparent richest complexity of development, a complexity that Andrea's own style, in the *Birth of the Virgin*, shared. But even in this moment that, for Andrea, was a fulfillment, a fissure opened in the prospect of the classical development in Florence, and its most visible symptoms were evident just around him, in his very shop and in the painting of his own disciples.

FRANCIABIGIO (2)

Franciabigio's fresco of the *Marriage of the Virgin*,[314] beside Andrea's *Birth of the Virgin* [311] in the courtyard of the Annunziata, was contemporary in course of execution with it. Vasari (V, 192–93) tells how Franciabigio's painting was unveiled at the same time as Andrea's and how Francesco, enraged, supposedly, because the unveiling was premature, destroyed portions of his own work: the damages remain as he inflicted them. Actually no part of the fresco seems unfinished, or not ready for any other evident reason for presentation to the public. Franciabigio's rage must have been, not with the Brothers of the Annunziata for their haste, but with his picture — and himself — for the unhappy comparison it made with the work of Sarto. Four * years before, when the two young artists still maintained their common shop, their manners had been intimately related and not too disparate in quality. The difference already recognizable then was of superior potential in Andrea, which in the interval he had superbly realized. Francesco's development had followed a course less individually inventive than Andrea's and less quick, and of no comparable clarity of classical intent; the *Marriage of the Virgin* demonstrates that no matter what Francesco's capacity may have been to approximate an early stage in the development of classical style, its advanced mode was not entirely accessible to him. Insuperable temperamental limits, and with these, habits of eye and hand that persisted from the preclassical tradition, obstructed an evolution in Andrea's sense or in comparable degree.

The manner that Francesco and Andrea had shared at the time of the Benizzi frescoes, long since abandoned by Andrea, is still in part apparent in the *Marriage of the Virgin.* Almost as much as the earliest of the Benizzi frescoes the *Marriage* suggests the persistent influence of Ghirlandaio's older model in S. M. Novella. Inspired perhaps, in his present rivalry with Andrea, by an outmoded concept of how to demonstrate his skill, Francesco has regressed toward a literalness in painting of detail that is more than in the Benizzi style, or in his own contemporary *Adoration of the Shepherds,* and which preserves little of the Bartolommesque effects of the Candeli *Cena.* This literalness, particularly in the drawing of Francesco's draperies, almost submerges the effect of hints accepted from the classical mode, as in the greater massiveness of bodies or their deliberateness of movement.

The relative passivity that had characterized Francesco's just preceding works has been displaced by a new assertion of that vitality, somewhat awkward, which had first appeared in his translation of the Raphaelesque style. The figures are in part in active postures, sufficiently to generate a sense of energy, and this not only affects the appearance of design but at least intendedly creates a tone of drama. Despite the archaisms of handling, the fresco is conceived with the ambitions that are proper to the classical style of this contemporary moment; but there is a gap between intention and achievement. Francesco nevertheless suggests, with incomplete effectiveness, most of the ideas that belong to the present matured stage of classicism. There are, in the *Marriage of the Virgin,* not only a movemented composition and intended drama but a degree of monumentality in which both the actors and the architecture share. The figures are distributed in space with continuities of rhythm that bind them in linked pattern even across the differences in depth between them; and the setting is consciously, though hardly fluently, bound into the figural design. The machinery of form and the temper of content are conceived by an artist who is aware of, and aspires to something like, the current accomplishment of classical grand style.

In these basic factors the *Marriage of the Virgin* has advanced beyond the style that Francesco practiced around 1510, but not in such a way as to make a major transformation in the appearance of that style: the compositional pattern and the role of setting in the *Marriage of the Virgin* are still visibly like Andrea's fresco of four years before, the *Healing of the Obsessed Girl,* and the general resemblance is accented by the presence in the *Marriage* of a comparable handling of detail. There is no measurable effect in Francesco's fresco of the knowledge that he must have had of Andrea's *Adoration of the Magi* of 1511,[308] and no more than a minimal suggestion that he might have known Andrea's *Birth of the Virgin* while it was in process. Such measurable, but obscured, progress as Francesco has made toward approximation of the more advanced classical style would seem to be self-generated, out of the basis of ideas that he and Andrea had in common about 1510. However, certain evidence in the *Marriage of the Virgin* suggests otherwise.

No matter how incomplete Francesco's approximation of advanced classical style may be, the impetus toward it came probably from Raphael, and from a likely trip to Rome, undertaken in 1512 or 1513. In precisely opposite way to Andrea's *Birth of the Virgin*, the *Marriage of the Virgin* reveals the influence of Roman motives, of sufficient number to imply that the experience of Rome in this case may have been direct. Among these motives the most obvious is the rushing figure to the left of Francesco's fresco, of which the source seems surely to be in the *School of Athens*; also at the left, the group of spectators — no longer Ghirlandaiesque — recalls closely the group with Raphael's own portrait in the *Athens*; a third motive, of the mother who ascends the steps in the middle distance, may be an inversion of the figure to the center right of the same fresco by Raphael. Above the door in Francesco's architecture, a simulated relief of the Temptation and Expulsion seems to depend on inspiration of the Sistine Ceiling.

We know from Franciabigio's past history and from the future pattern of his work that he was not himself capable of classical invention, or of continuous development in an explicitly classical sense of propositions given him by others. The chief work that intervenes between his style of 1510 and the *Marriage of the Virgin*, the *Cena* of S. M. dei Candeli, is not an interpolable term in a classical development of style. The impulsion of Franciabigio toward a relatively high stage of classicizing style must be accounted for by an external influence, and our evidence suggests that this may have been of Raphael in Rome. As had been true of Francesco's earlier approach to the Florentine Raphael, this putative experience of Rome was also only partly understood. Francesco's relation to Raphael was such as to do both parties violence: his submission to the example of Raphael's mature classicism seems guided not by sympathy but by will, stubbornly compelling a not-quite-understanding temperament.

Franciabigio's intelligence discerns, adequately, the mechanics of form and the intentions of content which, literally apparently, make the classical image, but the quotient in him of preclassical, and inherently unclassical, disposition makes the essence of the style ungraspable. The whole of the *Marriage of the Virgin* is built upon relations that are still in part additive: classicizing contrivances of form make connections, but no absorbing synthesis, of the matter of design. In the basic unit of his art, the figure, the same effect is manifest in surface and in substance. Detail, as of drapery, is patterned in approximate classical convention around the figure mass, but that mass itself is without compelling shape, of no higher unity competent to contain detail. And despite experience of Raphael's example, no figure in the *Marriage of the Virgin*, in movement or at rest, effectively demonstrates the first proposition in the classical painter's repertory, of contrapposto.

This hybrid art evidently cannot have a classical personality, but it has, and strongly, a personality of its own. The somewhat graceless energy that Francesco urges on his forms, the emphatic sharp characterization of their physical existence, and the hard, even disruptive accents of design give a peculiar awkward forcefulness to the *Marriage of the Virgin.* In the context of Fra Bartolommeo's blandness and Andrea's suavity, this effortful art is not unwelcome in the Florentine scene.

To Franciabigio's presumable experience of Roman style there was added, in the moment of unveiling of the *Marriage of the Virgin*, the example of Andrea's fresco. Between them these experiences were decisive for Francesco's subsequent relation to the classical style. He had already grasped the classical ambition of a grand manner, if not its precise tonality of expression or its whole machinery of form. Now, confronting Andrea's new demonstration, Francesco recognized much more forcibly the gap between his own conception of a classicism and its latest standards of accomplishment. The *Last Supper* of the Convent of the Calza,[315-6] dated 1514, is conceived in an altered style that reveals the effects of Francesco's study of Andrea. Its differences are not only evident in comparison to the *Marriage of the Virgin*; they are still more striking when they are referred to Francesco's painting of around 1511, of the same theme. The figures have been given a new dimension, as broad as that of the largest figures in Andrea's fresco: each makes an effect of intendedly impressive mass, and asserts a character of shape strong enough so that we see it in its unity. This shape is generalizing and adapts, though roughly, the mature classical prescription for full, rounding forms. More awkwardly, the draperies are handled in a similarly generalizing, and assertively movemented, way. Constrained though they are in place, the figures move more convincingly, and because of their large bulk, more forcefully than in the *Marriage of the Virgin*; and their movements are in more deliberate, planned, continuous relation than in that fresco. These strong shapes, overlapped and rhythmically interlocked, make a frieze that, in all but its details of design, is of classical effect. Though here, as in the Candeli *Cena,* Francesco preserves a pre-Leonardesque iconography, it is evident that Leonardo's example, available in the not altogether enlightening engravings, had an influence on him almost as strong as — and, significantly, not deeply different in kind from — Andrea's recent fresco.

In the kind of pathos that the Calza *Cena* makes by its near-urgency of drama and the rough power of its forms, it suggests comparison, rare in Florence of this time, with the dramatic mode of contemporary Rome. The effect of drama is of course purposeful, and it is a positive manifestation of an element we shall come to recognize as special in Francesco's matured personality. However, it is also an unintended consequence of his limitations in respect to classical style that the force of this art lies partly in its — unclassical — roughness: in the bluntness of emotion and, still more, in the impactful awkward energy of form. The conflict between what has been classically achieved and what remains still stubbornly unclassical becomes, in effect, an agency of tension to generate still more energy. And the conflict is multiple, more than can be enumerated here: between literal description and generalization — more apparent than in the *Marriage of the Virgin*; between inertia of mass and modes of movement in the figures; between rhythmical continuity and stiffness in drawing of drapery; between color and chiaroscuro. Even in this work that seems so much of its moment Francesco's relation to classical style is a rapprochement, not an assimilation. But what Francesco cannot acquire of classical ideality or grace he compensates with emphases which, as he wills them, should match the effects of largeness, and exceed the effects of force, of contemporary classicism in Florence. His solution is, outside the close ranks of genius, the most significant of his generation in this phase of the Florentine development.

Franciabigio was to enjoy a role of some prominence as a portrait painter, quantitatively more important than Andrea's. While Andrea's few portraits were to be almost altogether private documents, records of his immediate family and of a few friends, Franciabigio — evidently less pressingly occupied than Sarto — accepted a good number of professional portrait commissions. His only serious competitor in this field was Ridolfo Ghirlandaio, whose practice had been much earlier established, and who had enjoyed a near-monopoly in Florence until Francesco chose to challenge it. It is not then unexpected that Francesco's first certain works of portraiture, which date only from 1514, should considerably resemble Ridolfo's current portrait style.

Like the Pitti *Goldsmith* of Ridolfo,[283] Francesco's two male portraits of this year, one in Florence (Uffizi 8381)[317] and the other in London (National Gallery),[318] have a cast that is distinctly Leonardesque. The basic formula, like that in Ridolfo, is of a dark silhouette of torso, hair, and hat relieved by landscape; within this silhouette are shadowed head and hands, more softly drawn and more yielding in chiaroscuro than in Ridolfo's style. The Uffizi portrait, seeking a model more interesting and authoritative than Ridolfo's, quite self-consciously returns to Raphael's *Angelo Doni*.[52] Francesco borrows, and somewhat accents, the spatial articulation of Doni's pose and, applying the results of study of more recent Florentine style, he makes a more nearly common texture, in lighting and in shapes, between the figure and its setting. The London portrait seems the product of experience acquired in the Uffizi picture: its formula is much the same but it is more confidently handled, and much more articulate. The modelling of the face is deep-shadowed, but plastically decisive, and the silhouette is no longer slack, but emphasized and differentiated in its movement. The body itself, turning within rest, and the expression also, have an energy that is incipiently intense.

In both portraits there is a marked difference from Francesco's exactly contemporary fresco work. The portraits bear no trace of the awkward dramatizing emphases that the frescoes use; they intend no rhetoric. Francesco's concern is with adequate representation of the person of his actual subject, and with the communicative interpretation of a personality. Both factors are seen through a convention that has been made up, eclectically, from the repertory of forms and feelings developed in Florence since the time of Leonardo. In the small compass of the portrait the classicizing character of this convention is not so dissipated or so much disrupted as are the elements of classicism in Francesco's ambitious frescoes. Still, there are perceptible impurities in the approximate classicism of these portraits, and in particular in that in London: in the expression, of moody, shadowed sentiment, almost romantical (like that to be found in passages of the frescoes), and in the too sharply characterized activity of shape. These less than classical qualities were to attract, to Francesco's portraits of this moment, the interest of the least classically minded painter of the rising generation and serve as a point of departure for a more evident deviation from the classical convention in portrait style.

THE YOUNGEST GENERATION

The personalities of the painters of the new generation, born in the early 1490's, begin to be discernible in pictures made by them toward the age of twenty, in the last years of this phase in the history of Florentine painting style. To understand the development of this generation it must be stressed how malleable still, and how much more impure than in contemporary Rome, the course of development to maturity was of Florentine classical style. These youngest men had not participated, as even Sarto had to some extent, in the time before 1508, of heroically impressive formulation, by the great masters, of the classical conception. The works of these inventors must have had, for the members of the youngest generation, something of the quality of things already a little distant, no longer quite immediate for many reasons: not only from the sense of different generation of their authors, but from the almost more than human measure of the works themselves, and from the quality — inherent in their classicism — of ideal withdrawal.

The achievements of the first phase of classicism thus did not exercise, upon this youngest group, the same immediate authority as on their elders. As had been true even with Andrea, though in him to a less degree, their tendency was to attach themselves to the equally available, and less intellectually and spiritually inaccessible, continuities of Florentine tradition.

Further, these young painters' vision of the classical accomplishment of the older generation was not psychologically direct; there intervened between them and the art of Leonardo, Michelangelo, and the early Raphael, and even of their less authoritative surrogate, Bartolommeo, the practice and personalities of their own teachers. These were themselves in varying degree of rapprochement to classical example and, except for the Frate himself, they were at best — like Andrea in this phase — still involved in the difficult evolution of a personal classical style. Even by Andrea that was achieved only in the last year of this phase. Like Andrea, but following his lead and tempo rather than the Frate's, the youngest artists also would, subsequently, arrive at a form of classicism, varying in duration and degree according to the individual. But in this moment, in their earliest emergence as artistic personalities, they were a remove significantly farther from it than their masters.

There is one quality that the members of this youngest group of painters seem to share, and it is discernible even — or indeed especially — in their beginnings, before their line of development tends to closer coincidence with the classical style. This is a tendency like that in the art of Andrea in his own beginning and again, conspicuously, in his Dresden altar of circa 1513,[310] toward emotional states that are non-normative, more private and individual than are acceptable in the mature classic code. These states may be touched with sentiment, or at times with rapture, or in some other way may be disquieting, singular, or strange. It is, as we have remarked, the intention of these young men to conform, in time, and in more or less degree, to the canons of the classical style, so this distinction in temperament in them cannot be explained merely in the obvious way, as the reaction of a generation against its teachers. Some part of an instinctive reaction of this kind may nevertheless be in it; and the familiar mystique of generations, loosely applied, would reinforce our observation of the seeming attachment of these youths to the Florentine tradition: in this case the sentimental, and often emotionally eccentric art of the latest Quattrocento, the decade of their birth. One major personality of this decade, Piero di Cosimo, continued to function in Florence through the current phase and was the influential master not only of Andrea, but of the young Pontormo. He, too, had the intention to conform to classical prescription, but could not or would not wholly alter his expressive habits to them. Something like Piero, the youngest painters may have confronted the firming conventions of classicism with a disposition to see otherwise, formed by an attachment to the temper of what had been Piero's time.

PULIGO

Domenico Puligo, born in 1492, was barely the senior of the three young artists, including Rosso and Pontormo, whose first identifiable works date within this phase. He was also the least gifted and by far the least creative individual among them, but the early stage of his career conforms, in general, to the pattern of development that is traceable in theirs. Domenico's first serious education had been with the most conservative of Cinquecento Florentines, Ridolfo Ghirlandaio, and what seems to be Domenico's earliest extant independent work, a *Madonna and Child with St. John* (Rome, Palazzo Venezia; c. 1512–13),[319] still much reflects Ridolfo's approximately contemporary painting style. The picture most inadequately transcribes Bartolommeo's manner, according to Ridolfo's example rather than from the original. More than in the contemporary Ridolfo and, indeed, still as in Ridolfo's habit toward 1510, Domenico displays a very nearly archaic insistence on line in this picture's execution. It refers, in this respect, almost to the most backward models of this date in Florence, those of the practitioners in Credi's still quattrocentesque style. The presence of a different kind of individuality than Ridolfo's is evident only in the quality of expression of this early work — not a consequence of youthful ineptitude, as is proved by its later deliberate repetition — of a stressed, intendedly communicative sentiment, or better, sentimentality.

Ridolfo's model was replaced for Puligo by a better one when, almost certainly in 1513, he was employed by Andrea del Sarto to assist him. In 1513 and also during the next year or two Domenico worked as if on a contract basis, less as a regular subordinate in Andrea's shop than as part or whole executant of a few specifiable works of Andrea's design. His help in execution of Andrea's Dresden altarpiece is frequently suggested, and he may be the main executant of the *Madonna with the Infant St. John* (Rome, Galleria Borghese 336),[320] which reuses, in the figure of the Madonna, part of the cartoon for Andrea's Dresden work. Puligo is also the executant of most of the *Tobias Altar* (Vienna, Kunsthistorisches Museum; 1513–14);[321] though here the portrait of the donor has been painted by Andrea from his own remarkable preparatory drawing (Paris, Lugt Collection). In these works Puligo's intervention is discernible not only in distinctions of technique or quality, or in expected alterations in the Morellian vocabulary of the designer. Puligo tends with his touch to smooth and slacken Sarto's form, to sweeten color almost to the look of candy, and dissolve Andrea's feelings into too-soft sentiment. The Vienna altar, where Puligo's execution dominates, shows this — if we may say so — best.

The earlier of these presumed collaborations comes at a moment in Andrea's career that we have described as demonstrating a recrudescence, in forceful mature guise, of his own initial, still late-quattrocentesque, emotional disposition. Andrea's content in these works is taken by his young collaborator as authority for his own sort of sentimental inclination. As we shall see, it is not only Puligo who extracts, from the emotional compound in Andrea's pictures of this year, support for unclassical tendencies of feeling. In an independent work, probably circa 1514, the *Madonna with St. John Approaching in a Landscape* (Rome, Galleria Borghese 358; a later free variant in Montpellier),[322] Puligo's mood is all too intimate, pressing its sweetness on us with more efficacy than in his earliest Madonna, in Rome. Partly this is because physiognomic expression is more lively, but even more it is because the whole image has been made active, with hardly any trace left of the Roman Madonna's archaizing stiffness and constraint. In general, Domenico's new vocabulary is Sartesque, but despite his intimate exposure to Andrea it is not exclusively so. The influence of Bartolommeo's style, already filtered through to Domenico in his earlier apprenticeship, persists. In this divided allegiance as in other respects, Domenico resembles his contemporaries. And there is, as well, an element of resemblance of more than merely generic kind to the earliest Madonna pictures of one of these contemporaries, Rosso, who had, even at this date, already affirmed in them his dissent from the classical style.

PONTORMO

Vasari tells us (VI, 246) that, for a brief moment after his arrival in Florence, the boy Pontormo was placed to study with the ageing Leonardo, but that his first serious apprenticeship was with Albertinelli. The duration of this apprenticeship is very uncertain, but it would appear to have begun before 1508, and may have endured only until approximately 1510; but it is certain in any case that Pontormo's stay with Albertinelli was longer than with any other master. This training was, at second hand, an education in Bartolommesque style, in the precise years when Fra Bartolommeo, and Albertinelli to a less degree, were evolving a first maturity of Florentine classicism. Vasari notes also that Pontormo studied for a time with Piero di Cosimo, presumably after his apprenticeship to Albertinelli. This phase of Pontormo's training would have coincided with the time of Piero's own conversion to the same Bartolommesque mode, and a stay with Piero would thus have strengthened an already established inclination toward the modern style of the Frate. On the other hand, the personality, and certain elements even of the "modernized" art, of Piero would have given the young Pontormo a sense of continuity from the Quattrocento. It is likely, too, that association with Piero could have reinforced in Pontormo, apparently already an uncommon temperament, a tendency to singular and highly personal expression.

Toward 1512, about his eighteenth year, Pontormo was competent enough to become — apparently on a basis more or less contractual, like Puligo — an assistant of Andrea del Sarto. Attempts to discern Pontormo's participation in works by Sarto have not been successful, and it is likely that the nature of their association did not in fact result in actual collaborations. Vasari (VI, 247) names one work specifically executed jointly by Pontormo and by Rosso, also an assistant at this time, for Andrea: a predella for the *Annunciation* of S. Gallo. This has been lost, apparently irretrievably; a recent effort to identify a predella by Pontormo in Dublin as this work of circa 1512 is, as we shall see, incorrect. A further painting by Pontormo, a fresco of *Faith* and *Charity* with the stemma of the Medici, on the outer façade of the Annunziata, is documented between late 1513 and June 1514 when, according to Vasari, Jacopo was still in some relation with Andrea; this fresco is no longer clearly legible. Vasari notes of it (VI, 249–50) that it was in a "maniera nuova," and "la più bell'opera" done in fresco to that time. It may be true, or only in the usual pattern of Vasarian anecdote, that it was so remarkable as to provoke Andrea's jealousy and cause the end of their professional connection.

When he came to Sarto, Pontormo had much in his education that should have disposed him sympathetically toward the maturer master. Both had been pupils of Piero di Cosimo, and both had — Pontormo from his beginnings —

in part been formed on the model of Bartolommeo. However, the elements of education that they shared were viewed by Pontormo and Andrea through very different temperaments and with differing results. Pontormo was, in time, profoundly influenced by Andrea and came, after a while, to entertain his classical ambitions and to wish to better them; but in this initial contact Jacopo's response to Sarto was equivocal and incomplete. Other than the nearly destroyed fresco on the façade of the Annunziata a further work in fresco survives that may date still within, or very close to the time of their connection. It is the green grisaille *Ospedale di S. Matteo* (Florence, Academy),[323] of scale not larger than a modest easel painting; on account of a resemblance in theme and, more particularly, in certain motives, to Andrea's *Birth of the Virgin* it is best dated into 1514. Despite Jacopo's experience by this time of Andrea's style the *Ospedale di S. Matteo* does not, beyond the similarities of motive, reflect his influence. The disposition we assume would have resulted from Pontormo's earlier training, toward Bartolommeo's vocabulary of form, has not been altered by Sartesque exposure.

In general, the drawing in the *Ospedale* is inflexible and rather angular, as in Bartolommeo's models rather than in Sarto's; in part, the pattern made in line and by rhythms of shape accents the tendency toward angularity that had emerged, in the Frate's work, in his *Pitti Pala* of 1512.[264] Also as in Fra Bartolommeo, the articulation of the forms is stiff, a little marionette-like, and it is by exaggeration of a property in Bartolommeo's work that Pontormo's figures seem so insubstantial; they lack the assertive chiaroscuro that gives the Frate's images the illusion, at least, of substance. Some single figures in Pontormo's fresco take postures like those in Bartolommeo's classical repertory, or Andrea's, but there is small sense in them of classicizing effects of contrapposto; and none of that quality, so conspicuous in Andrea's art by this time, of continuity of movement between forms.

Pontormo still sees disjunctively; his composition is not much less additively conceived than the design of the quattrocentesque arcade he copies to be the main feature of its setting. Equally unlike a mature classicism, and at once accepting and sharing in the character of the archaic architecture, the spatial system is divisive. The setting and its furniture, and hardly less the figures, are arranged as on a grid: in strata laid parallel, or juxtaposed at right angles to each other, in the space. It is the Bartolommesque vocabulary of this picture that relates it to the modern style, not its syntax; that has hardly accepted even the minimal classical conventions. Within this vocabulary and these conventions Jacopo is still working according to a preclassical aesthetic, and each alteration he effects on Bartolommeo's precedent devalues its character of classicism.

This picture is not yet an evidence of any purposeful process of unclassical stylistic change, and should not be so interpreted; it marks no beginning on a new road of style, but a backward place on the present one. In the context of the history of its contemporary art the *Ospedale* has not yet achieved a coherent style. Yet it has a personality — oblique in expression and somewhat slight, but still discernible, and none of the graspable qualities of this personality is classicizing. The picture has an atmosphere of unreality, as if it might be more the image of a dream than of a world of substance. Its inhabitants are not quite corporeal; their being and acting is unconvinced. Their faces are no more than faintly sketched, yet their expressions — vague and undefinable — are strangely arresting, as if they held some uncertain meaning more compelling than that given by their actions. And the wavering tonality of green that pervades the whole scene gives it the faint and disturbing accent of a subaqueous occurrence.

Within the same year, from a moment that certainly succeeds Jacopo's entire independence from Andrea, is the full-size fresco altarpiece of a *Madonna with Four Saints*, once in S. Ruffillo, now removed to the chapel of S. Luca in the Annunziata (and deprived, in the transfer, of its lunette).[324] It is a much more forceful, and altogether more articulate statement of the personality that is perceptible in the *Ospedale*. The difference between the two is not so much the result of an appreciable extent of time as of subject and, particularly, of scale. Where the *Ospedale* is tenuous and dispersed, the altar fresco has a power both in form and content that comes from concentration; its effect is of an opposite immediacy.

The vocabulary of the altar fresco is still closely related to Fra Bartolommeo: the Madonna is explicitly derived from him, by combination of a recent and a past example, one in the *Pitti Pala* and the other in the S. Marco altar of 1509; the facial types also markedly resemble those in the Pitti altarpiece. The tendency to angularities of shape and drapery, in body contours and in attitudes, persists, but much accentuated in complexity and activity; the surface of the painting makes a faceted, almost irritant visual excitement. In its larger design the composition is marked by strong effects of unclassical rigidity, with the sense in it still of a structure made of juxtapositions and not yet by synthesis. It remains basically, however, a reduction of Fra Bartolommeo's models. The process of reduction is also a process of compression, of substances now more nearly convincing than in the *Ospedale*, both in their superficial relation and, even more conspicuously, in their depth of space. These qualities are in part assertions of a disposition not yet classical but they are, without paradox, also indices of an experience of Sarto's recent development of propositions of the classical style. A measure of Andrea's style has now been compounded, in the S. Ruffillo fresco, into Jacopo's Bartolommesque foundations.

The operative model is Andrea's major work of 1513, the Dresden altar.[310] In lesser elements of style Andrea's example has conditioned the drawing and handling of Pontormo's fresco: where the folding of drapery and the chiaroscuro depart from Bartolommesque example it is by way of a starting point in Andrea. The proportions of Pontormo's figures, almost awkwardly irregular and compact, are willfully adapted after the models of the Dresden altar. But more importantly, this painting supplies the precedent to Jacopo of concentration, in design of surface and of space, of Bartolommeo's grand but vacuous paradigm of composition. In its concentration, Pontormo's structure follows Andrea one major step in the direction of a classicism more developed than the Frate's. Andrea's model also indicates to Jacopo, and he accepts it in part, that the elements within this concentration should be rhythmically interwoven. He does not admit, however, Andrea's demonstration of two corollaries of his proposition, which are essential to its character of classicism: first that the temper of the union among forms be harmonious, and secondly that forms be not only joined but at the same time separably articulated. Pontormo's rhythmical scheme intends connection, but while it in part connects, it also fragments and disrupts. Further, his figures are compelled together much too urgently, without interval in an almost uninhabitable plane of space. The concentrated substance of design makes only partly classical effect, for the whole contains and magnifies, by compression, the unclassical temper of the elements within.

The formal structure is the principal agency of expression in the S. Ruffillo altar, and this expression — on one hand of classicizing compact monumentality, on the other of unclassical excitement — is internally divisive. It is the ambition of the young Pontormo to attain the power and grandeur that reside in classical forms, but to inspire these forms with an intensity, and more significantly, with a kind of expression that is not consonant with their nature. The formal ambition is inescapable; it is the consequence of the massive authority of example of wholly matured, or imminently maturing, classical style in Florence of this time. In this respect Pontormo's case is not so different from what generally was true of his immediate Florentine predecessors: the authority of classical form prevailed, in both Bartolommeo and Andrea, over temperamental inconsistencies, or insufficiencies, in content.

A temperamental distinction from classicism is much more marked, however, in Pontormo, and this emerges in the S. Ruffillo altar, though in a quantitative subcurrent, in incidents of facial and bodily expression among his actors. Mostly, they behave acceptably conventionally. The contrapposto of the Madonna's body is perhaps too marked, suggestive of a torsion rather than of classicizing ease, and the Child seems more restless than His conversation with St. Zachary should, in reason, make Him. St. Lucy's gaze is fixed on us with a directness, and an effect of communication more insistent, than we are used to in her counterparts in Bartolommeo's altars, and a little disquieting. It is the kneeling Saint who alone urgently asserts a wholly unclassical disposition: consumed by violent and unbeautiful ecstasy, lost in private rapture, she is without concern for measure or decorum in her relation with her fellows or with us. There is no precedent, in any Cinquecento painting, that represents a spiritual sensation so personal and so intense as this.

This especially, but also the whole expression of Pontormo's painting, is different from the tender and compelling passion that infuses Sarto's Dresden altar. Jacopo's emotion, in its energy and in its susceptibility to rapture, may begin like Sarto's, but unlike his it has been expressed disruptively, in private fragments of sensation, in one place utterly extreme. We have observed that the emotion of the Dresden altar is a transmutation into classicizing discipline, both of form and content, of an earlier disposition in Andrea that was linked, still perceptibly, with the later Quattrocento. Pontormo approaches the model of the Dresden altar with a temper natively less classicizing than Andrea's, and as yet less evolved toward and comprehending of classical ambitions. The authority of Andrea's model is accepted save for the effective classical transmutation of its content: in the Dresden altar's — as it were — unprocessed emotional material Jacopo takes sanction for his own unclassical disposition of emotion. Pontormo's altarpiece may be described as a regressive interpretation, in preclassical sense, of Andrea's example.

In the light of Jacopo's own subsequent personal development the S. Ruffillo altar is certainly preclassical. However, because it is chronologically subsequent to the accomplished classicism of Andrea's Dresden picture, aware of it and dependent from it, the Ruffillo altar may also be described, in a broader and impersonal perspective of the history of style, as already postclassical. Though admissible, such a description too much stresses the potential, rather than the actual, in the historical and aesthetic character of this work. The potential was, certainly, soon to be realized, but in Pontormo's case only after it had been in part submerged within an intervening development of classical discipline.

The survival, not only in Pontormo, but in his contemporaries, of preclassical elements of style so late as this, when classical style in the older generation was at its climactic maturity, became one of the decisive factors in the future history of style. When, among the older masters, the problem of the ways of further evolution of their art succeeded their attainment of a full maturity of classicism, that which was preclassical or unclassical in the dispositions of the younger painters — an immediate and vital force of art in them — asserted itself in this moment of a crisis. Only then did these elements assume their power to redirect and positively change the destiny of classical style.

ROSSO

Giovanni Battista di Jacopo, Il Rosso, was of an individuality so pronounced as to make Pontormo seem, by contrast, almost conventional. Vasari, who came to know Rosso well, could identify no master for him. Though, as was the habit of this generation, Rosso studied Michelangelo's Cartoon (without perceptible effect on his earliest formation) "con pochi maestri volle stare all'arte, avendo egli una certa opinione contraria alle maniere di quegli . . ." (V, 156). Where Pontormo exercised himself to acquire the elements of the older masters' styles, and later also to submit to classicizing discipline, Rosso's "certa opinione contraria" — a contrast of temperament as well as of "opinion" — interposed itself effectively between him and the dominant artistic mode. Rosso very quickly came to show an eccentricity of form so marked, and an accompanying and partly consequent eccentricity of feeling, which exceeded even the results of the last resurgence, at about this time, of the individuality of the old Piero di Cosimo. If any personality was apt to be Rosso's master, at least on grounds of temperament, it was Piero; but he had been in fact not Rosso's master but Pontormo's.

Rosso's case in these first years is of a wholly conscious exposure to the style of classicism and, simultaneously, a willful and nearly perfectly successful evasion of it. By 1514–1515 the young painter's increasingly assertive style was no longer measurable in reference to classicism; his art by then became the demonstration of a personality to whom the classical style was, in effect, almost beside the point. This moment was a climax of unclassical assertion; like Pontormo — though with a pronounced difference of accent and degree — Rosso came, after 1515, to take renewed cognizance of the classical style in its climactic fulfillment, inevitably impressive, and to accept some of its conventions, though mostly as a cadre for his own unclassical exertions.

Our reconstruction of the few surviving pieces of Rosso's earliest *oeuvre* * depends on the identification (Longhi), as his work, of a *Holy Family* (Rome, Galleria Borghese 332; c. 1513–14),[327] and a *Madonna in a Landscape* (Florence, Uffizi Deposit 8309, on loan to the Gallery in Arezzo),[326] of slightly earlier date (c. 1513). To this pair there should almost certainly be added the small *Madonna and Child* at Finch College, New York (from the Kress Collection, no. 485),[325] there attributed to Albertinelli. Related intimately in drawing, handling, and in expression to the picture of the same theme in Arezzo, this reveals a still preceding stage, much less aggressively individual, in Rosso's first career, not later in date than 1512. The Kress *Madonna* gives us an insight, hitherto inaccessible, into Rosso's first beginnings. He may, as Vasari says, have acknowledged no single master but — as the present attribution of the painting testifies — he was, toward 1512, more involved with the example of Pontormo's first teacher than Pontormo was himself. Rosso's painting transcribes such an Albertinelli model as the *Madonna of Humility* (Venice, Seminario; c. 1506–09), and the transcription is less adapted than in the contemporary Pontormo toward a Bartolommesque language. The peculiarities of form and temper that Rosso would assert shortly are not more than an accent here; not only is his personality not yet developed but what there is of it is effectively constrained by a learned convention, of recognizable but unfulfilled classicizing style.

The Kress *Madonna* helps to account for the more accomplished classicizing substratum upon which, in the Arezzo *Madonna* of circa 1513, the emerging singularity of Rosso's temperament begins to work its will. A more personally mature experience of a classical style itself more mature underlies this painting; beyond the relatively crude Albertinellian formula of the Kress painting, Rosso has observed the refinements of chiaroscuro of Fra Bartolommeo, the rhythmical suavities and complexities of Sarto, and perhaps as well, from the inescapable example of the Dresden altar, the intimate yet complex energy of Andrea's emotional expression. It will be remembered that at this time Rosso would have shared with Pontormo (according to Vasari's testimony [VI, 247]; on evidence from Bronzino) an experience of assistantship to Sarto, in the execution of the predella for the S. Gallo *Annunciation.* The Arezzo picture has also — though it is vastly more subtle and accomplished — such a mixed resonance of Sarto's and Bartolommeo's matured classicism as is reflected in the contemporary work of another of Andrea's executants of this time, Puligo, in his Borghese *Madonna with the Infant St. John.*[320] Like Puligo's, but more articulately, Rosso's *Madonna* conveys the sense of muted, interwoven energies of form and feeling.

Rosso's first relation to the classical style is not, as it has usually been assumed to be, one of involuntary osmosis from his contemporary visual culture. Nevertheless, despite his evident awareness of a classicism, the whole cast of the Arezzo painting is in part imminently, in part overtly, at variance with its bases in models of the classical style. In an only apparent paradox, Rosso's approach to classicism coincides with the beginning of his divergence from it, caused by the emergence of a temperament possessed by values of expression irreconcilable with those of the classical style. It is not harmony or generalization that are the ambitions of this temperament but the special, singular experience, of feeling as of form: the unquiet poetry of an eccentric sensibility. This sensibility is not yet urgent in the Arezzo painting, and does not have the disruptive power that it will soon acquire. Nevertheless, it has embroidered the classicizing fabric of this work with a draughtsmanship that warps shapes into patterns that are ornamentally active, but disparate in character among themselves, and which tend, in their insistence, to make strange distortions of reality. Contours may be swift and sharp, or slack and veiled by *sfumato*; in either case they have no function of implying plastic form. The bodies, and the forms of landscape, are in fact not seen or felt as substances; their spatiality is an incident. They have no integrity of structure, and it is on this account that they yield, with such easy susceptibility, to distortion of their shapes. What the painter registers is an experience of the volatile factors of visual and aesthetic experience, not the substantial ones; it is an exquisite flux of sensation that he transcribes. The image is compounded of shifting perceptions of light and incidents of rhythmic energy: of febrility and evanescence.

The expression of the picture is more the consequence of these effects of form than of specific elements of illustration. The meanings, as illustration, of physiognomy and action are not unconventional, but the appearances they inhabit are; and they are in this way transformed toward strangeness. But for their accent the character of emotion is, as we have observed, not dissimilar to Andrea's in the Dresden altar; but with its unclassical overtones it tends more nearly to resemble the not-yet-classical sensation of Andrea's earliest *Pietà*. Rosso's feeling, however, is evidently of another psychological texture, neither so controlled in modulation nor so harmonious, and its cast of eccentric sophistication is unknown to the young Andrea. This is not a reassertion of an old, preclassical, emotional mode, but a consequence drawn from Andrea's latest demonstrations by a knowing personality, determined to express emotion yet more individual.

The Borghese *Holy Family* explicitly derives in theme and in its major motive from the *Madonna* in Arezzo, but it is significantly different in its style. The individuality which had made its presence evident in the previous painting here asserts itself entirely, leaving behind, almost as if they had never been, the former indications of approximation to classical style. The temper of the painter has expanded, and his expression has sharpened and grown more intense. Within the larger scale of forms — increased in its effect by simultaneous reference to architecture and contrast with open space — there is a new concentration, and at the same time a more complex aesthetic energy. These factors, interchangeable in terminology with manifestations of a higher classical style, here function with conspicuously unclassical effect. The concentration given to the principal forms is of a silhouette, less spatially articulate and substantial even than in the *Madonna* of Arezzo. This silhouette is of sharp-drawn, agitated contour; within, its surface is patterned by etched linear rhythms, close-hatched and brittle. Less than in the Arezzo picture does this irritant network suggest form; it rather fragments it. Reinforcing this effect is a new factor in Rosso's art: the perception of light not as chiaroscuro but, much more evidently than in his previous painting, as color; it is in this picture that one of Rosso's most significant devices of expression is revealed. Like the vision of form, the vision of color is improbable and singular, at once exquisite and eccentrically dissonant. The color in the Madonna — pale blue; thin mauve-pink, bleached in light and soured in dark; flat green — is faceted irregularly by the linear pattern. Color creates an iridescence that, within this shape, becomes a screen to substitute for form — floating, as it were, before it.

Rosso creates a new region of experience of color: its descriptive functions recede to secondary significance or less, and it is raised to a higher aesthetic power than the form, almost separable from it; transcending form and tending to consume it. The color becomes a primary factor of pictorial personality rather than, as in the classical mode, a concomitant one. It assumes a character of assertive, complex, visual and psychological excitant. This happening has no precedent within the classical style, yet the source beyond which this so independently proceeds is in an experience of classical accomplishment: Sarto's recent development of a variety and energy of color till then unknown in Florence.

Another important innovation appears, at least symptomatically, in the Borghese painting. This is the first self-conscious application to the handling of space of the willfulness with which Rosso treats (normally) substantial form. The architectural setting has no perspective measure, and in its middle distance the small figures of Joseph and St. John are in an ambivalent relation of scale with the foreground group. As in advanced works in the classical style, the distant figures are bound into the rhythmical sequence of the main group, in fact intersecting one another, but because there is no articulation of the interval of space a disturbing tension is created among the factors of scale, side-by-side relation, and relation in the depth of space. The landscape still farther to the rear is normally recessive, but in the context of the remaining structure it works to add another element of spatial tension to the scene.

The inventive individuality of this picture is made particularly evident by comparison with a painting of Granacci's done some few years later (c. 1518), which is not literally derivative from Rosso's but inspired by it, even to the eccentricities of drawing in Granacci's children. Granacci's *Madonna with St. John* (last recorded Munich, A. S. Drey)[610] would imitate the peculiar stimulant personality of Rosso's painting, but even this is modified; and Rosso's creative peculiarities, particularly of composition and of spatial structure, are almost conventionally recast.

More than the art to this date of Pontormo, Rosso's Borghese picture has the character in it of radical invention, and marks a personality who is, in despite of context and education, unclassical. In this invention lies the material, more early perceptible than in Pontormo, for development of an anticlassical style.

BERRUGUETE

The Spaniard Alonso Berruguete has been identified (Longhi) as another of the incipient dissidents from classicism at this time in Florence. A few works of his long period of Italian study, between 1504 and 1517, have been recovered, enough to establish an explicit painterly personality. His Italian residence began, apparently, in Rome where toward 1508 he made the acquaintance of Michelangelo. A letter of Michelangelo's, dated 2 July 1508 (Milanesi, 92), informs us that a young Spaniard (surely identifiable as Berruguete) was then about to leave for Florence where he intended to take up the study of painting; the letter recommends Berruguete warmly, and requests that he be given access to Michelangelo's Cartoon. Four years later another letter of Michelangelo's (Milanesi, 48) transmits an inquiry from a Spanish friend about Alonso's health; in this letter Berruguete is called "pittore" and is identified as being known to Granacci. The name of the older master does not necessarily imply a close connection; Michelangelo, thinking back to mutual friends in 1508, is recalling the time when Granacci and Berruguete were both — the former briefly — in Rome.

Vasari tells us nothing of the education in Florence of the Spaniard. There are the usual references to work before the Michelangelo Cartoon, one mention of a work in sculpture (a copy of the *Laocoön* in wax, surely done in Rome before 1508 rather than in Florence), and the indication of a partial execution of a single picture, the *Coronation of the Virgin* for the Church of S. Gerolamo in Florence (now Paris, Louvre),[331] left unfinished by Filippino Lippi at his death in 1504. The portions of this altar that are by Berruguete have been isolated (Longhi); they are the angels who surround the Coronation group in the upper half of the painting. With this work there has been properly associated a *Madonna and Elizabeth with the Two Holy Children* — a "Sacra Conversazione" — in the Galleria Borghese (there long attributed to Piero di Cosimo).[328] Some five further paintings have been certainly attributed to the Italian period of Berruguete, but only one among these, beyond the two just named, belong without doubt within the present phase of our discussion.

Berruguete's birth date is uncertain; born between 1486 and 1490, he was older than Puligo, Rosso, and Pontormo, and may rather have been Sarto's contemporary than theirs. However, he started his education as a painter relatively late, and the time in which we may best situate his apparently earliest surviving work is, as with the youngest generation, circa 1512. This dating, for the Borghese "Sacra Conversazione," is not secure; the "circa" in this case implies a flexibility greater than is usual for us. It would seem, however, that its degree of technical competence presupposes at least Berruguete's completed training as a painter, which had begun only late in 1508. Internally, the picture affords no explicit points of motive that permit precise comparison with surrounding dated works; its main references, to Leonardo's Louvre *Anna* and Raphael's *Canigiani Madonna*, antedate the time when Berruguete began to study painting. These references do not imply an early date, but a difference in attitude toward the great models of the classical style's first formative phase, appropriate to Berruguete's difference in age from the youngest painters and, perhaps, to his different reverence, as a foreigner, for them. Because of this dependence the painterly vocabulary is in a way old-fashioned, but in larger aspects of the picture's style there seem to be possible more recent allusions. As with every painter of this time in Florence, Berruguete suggests, in his forms, the influence of Fra Bartolommeo in their generalization, breadth, and magnitude of scale; and the young St. John suggests more direct comparison, with the infant type evolved by Bartolommeo only around 1511.

There is then, in this picture, evidence of Berruguete's willing subjection, over an appreciable length of time, to models of the classical style. The classicism of the "Sacra Conversazione," however, carries small conviction; his response to classical example has something in it of caricature. The forms of Raphael and Leonardo are recalled expressly, but curiously distorted in recall. Berruguete's contours slide too unctuously and surfaces are too smooth, and his figures seem pneumatic, of balloon-like vacancy; despite their breadth they are of ghostly lightness. Their insubstantiality is compounded by the absorption of their forms in a *sfumato,* and by barely modelled color. Two of the figures pretend elaborate contrapposto and two, not at all concordantly, are frankly flat. All are assembled in a group that is spatially inarticulate and which adheres, almost pressingly, to the front plane of the painting.

These qualities may be in part the result of Berruguete's genuine misapprehension of his classical models but they are at the same time an affirmative expression, imposed upon a borrowed repertory, of a personality as unamenable to classicism as Rosso, and with better reason. The fact that Alonso Berruguete was the second generation of his family to study art in Italy and practice there at some length did not give him an Italian, or a Renaissance, inheritance. He was attached, still, to a cultural context that partook far more than Quattrocento Florence of the Middle Ages. All his tourist's reverence for Italy and the accomplishments of its masters could not dispose him essentially to a classical style. He is, in this, the prototype of the foreign painters who, later in the sixteenth century, were to make the *studienreise* to Italy but who would find there then, in Mannerism, a more congenial artistic mode.

For Berruguete, in spite of classical experience, substance has no objective worth; all his world is malleable: as he would so drastically later demonstrate in Spain, a compound of ectoplasm and taffy. Here the forms are still, approximately, controlled by their classicizing reference, and expression —

insistently communicative, as we have seen is the general tendency of this moment — is specified in physiognomy. Yet the forms themselves insinuate a singular emotion, provoked in part by the tension between their reference to classical style and their simultaneous deviations from it. It is not unreasonable that this picture should have been so often attributed to Piero di Cosimo, for Berruguete's situation at this moment in respect to classicism is not unlike Piero's: of a personality disposed to accept classical example, but with strong roots still in a preclassical — in Berruguete's case, an extraclassical — culture, and with a will to strongly individual, and even eccentric, expressiveness.

A painting fairly close in date to the Borghese "Sacra Conversazione," but probably successive to it, a *Madonna* (Milan, Saibene Collection; c. 1512–13, much restored)[329] is clearer than its antecedent in its reference to the style of Bartolommeo, and in this reflects the general inclination of these years in Florentine painting. The picture also refers, however, to an early quattrocentesque antecedent, and one particularly sympathetic to a sculptor such as Berruguete, before and after his experience in Florence, was. The motive is that of a type of Donatellesque relief of which the most famous example is the *Madonna* of the Casa Pazzi, now in Berlin; in a way native to his own tendencies of style at this time, and proper to the character of this model, Berruguete's transcription of it is nearly in the mode of a relief. The accent of form and of expression is intensely serious, and at the same time touched, as is the Borghese picture, with unintended caricature. Berruguete's adaptation of the Quattrocento motive may not have been an original idea; the same Donatello model served a painting, attributed to Michelangelo but of uncertain authorship and of no less uncertain date, which once was in the Milanese Collection Crespi.[330] But in Berruguete's art this particular Donatellism was to have a significant continuing career: at least three subsequent pictures by him are based on it. As he evolves, in these paintings, toward a postclassical style, the basis of their motive in Donatello's work reminds us most tenaciously of the relation, in Alonso's art, between postclassical invention and the preclassical past.

By definition, Berruguete's contributions to Filippino Lippi's altarpiece for S. Gerolamo (c. 1513–14)[331] give only partial evidence of the development of the Spaniard's style. It seems, however, that his angels in the *Coronation* are yet more highly characterized images, in appearance and in expression, than the children of the Borghese "Conversazione" or the Christ of the Saibene painting. The angelic forms — part whole, part appropriately immersed in clouds — have small relation to Bartolommeo's classical typology, or to any other: they are rhythmically warped to the point of obvious unnatural distortion, with a different temper of design, but with the same liberty of procedure, as in the contemporary Rosso. Alonso's draperies in this picture are drawn in quick ornamental convolutions, complicated in pattern and small in scale, quite opposite the vacant suavity of drapery in the preceding pictures. As in the Borghese "Conversazione" there are elements in this work, in particular in the drawing of anatomies, that suggest Piero di Cosimo; in this case the contemporary Piero of his latest identifiable style, as in his panel, in the Borghese, of the *Nativity*.[295] Of itself the connection recalls, but in a more specific way, the relation to Piero we have adumbrated for the others in the group of younger dissidents. However, a further consideration enters in the case of Filippino's altar. There is some resemblance, though no provable one, between other portions of the present surface of this altarpiece and the late style of Piero. Is it possible that the other painters of whom Vasari speaks as having worked on it were from Piero's shop? If so, the implication may exist of some connection of Alonso with Piero's entourage; coupled with the confusion with Piero that long existed for the Borghese "Conversazione" the implication may extend to actual connection between these two painters, in a previous time, as master and pupil. Again, Piero would assume the character of a formative link with the younger generation from the preclassical style.

Even as fragments of a composition, Berruguete's angels sufficiently indicate his assertion of a new kind of independence from the precedents of classical style. Abandoning the equivocal attitude he had displayed toward classical example in the Borghese "Conversazione" and in the Saibene Madonna, he has begun here to develop a vocabulary more suited to his own innate unclassical disposition. That disposition, and the means for its expression, are akin to Rosso's, but not so explicit or assertive. After Rosso, but well after him, Berruguete's is the most evident unclassical pronouncement of this time, and it was a manner of pronouncement almost surely quite independently arrived at. In this moment of the history of Florentine painting style such an achievement was predictable, but not necessary, to the foreign and eccentric talents of this painter. It is more than doubtful if Alonso's portions of the Lippi altar, fragmentary as they were, would have impressed Rosso or Pontormo; it is equally unlikely that his peculiar manner should be touched by them. It is unrewarding to seek personal priorities in the history of genesis of the new style; we must be content with the more general historical fact: that these younger personalities, emerging in the surrounding context of a matured classical style, found comparably unclassical means to give a new direction to their art. They may be regarded as the first symptoms of the imminence of the historical style of Mannerism.

THE MASTER OF THE MANCHESTER MADONNA

One personality who seems, by our best estimate, to be a member of the Florentine school, is best considered in this place, in a postscript to the history we have so far described. This painter, known as the Master of the Manchester Madonna, is eccentric to this history as the younger painters we have just described are not. In a sense quite different from that in which we shall apply the word to Rosso, Berruguete, and Pontormo, he is a mannerist: in curious and exceptional disposition and in tricks of mind and hand, and also in the meaning that the word had for an older history of art — he is the first of Michelangelo's *epigoni*. No attempt to identify this painter by name has been successful; the least credible identification is that with an early phase in the career of Michelangelo himself. The names of various of Michelangelo's associates have been tentatively attached to him, among them Mini (Popp) and, more nearly believably, Jacopo L'Indaco (Zeri); a new possibility may be suggested here, not more convincing than those tried so far: Aristotile da San Gallo, early an unsuccessful painter but later an accomplished architect and scene designer. Certain properties of this unknown artist's style suggest that he may have been, by primary occupation, something other than a painter.

The problem of identification is complicated by the difficulty of fixing the artistic origins of this master. It is possible that a vocabulary like that we find in his early works may have been formed in Florence, in an exceptional and archaizing response to such teaching as might have been provided in Bertoldo's school. There is some accent of a sculptor's disposition, and one accustomed to the study of the heritage of Donatello, in these works. On these grounds the vocabulary, but never the artistic quality, of these pictures may indicate an affiliation, from the beginning of their author's career, with Michelangelo. Equally possibly, however, the earliest paintings we know of the Manchester Master — roughly dateable about 1500: a tondo *Madonna and Child with St. John* (Vienna, Academy) [332] and the *Virgin Reading with the Christ Child and St. John* (New York, Kress Collection) [333] — may call to mind, perhaps quite deceptively, an extra-Florentine style, like that of the late Quattrocento in Bologna or Ferrara. This impress has been described also (Zeri) as Umbro-Bolognese; from this it might be assumed that part at least of the early career of this artist may have had to do with Rome.

It is certain at least that a direct experience of Rome is required to account for his first precisely identifiable Michelangelesque transcription, of the *Pietà* in St. Peter's (Rome, Galleria Nazionale; c. 1500–05).[334] A *Madonna* (Baden bei Zürich, private collection),[335] perhaps of circa 1505, implies some likeness to the art of Pinturicchio and to that of Perugino who, however, in these years was more Umbro-Florentine than Umbro-Roman. Still more, however, this painting suggests connection with the Florentine following of Ghirlandaio: again we are in Michelangelo's orbit. The Baden *Madonna* is more archaic in its style and far less accomplished, but it compares to Granacci's episode of Michelangelism of the same time in his Dublin *Holy Family* (once, in fact, improperly included in the Master of the Manchester Madonna's *oeuvre*). The resemblance is enough to suggest that this painter may have been in some way close to Granacci among the community of Michelangelo's Florentine friends, and have been influenced by Francesco. In the Baden picture its author has been studying, again, an early work of Michelangelo, the Florentine *Madonna of the Steps*,[17] and may as well have had in mind an unassimilated vision of the *Bruges Madonna*.[25]

It is in his namepiece, the unfinished *Madonna with St. John and Four Angels* (London, National Gallery; c. 1510–12),[336] that the Manchester Master has emerged into a different competence and new appearance of modernity; and in this painting there is a dedication to Michelangelo's direct example more entire than by any other painter for two decades yet to come. The models of Michelangelo to which this work refers have been studied with a new, consuming interest, and are far more effectively understood than they had been in the Baden *Madonna*. There may be some reference in this picture to motives (the paired angels) of the Sistine Ceiling, but otherwise the exemplars remain those which Michelangelo had left in Florence before his transfer of residence to Rome. Conceivably, these may have included not only Michelangelo's published works but also some material in drawing. The *Bruges Madonna* is the painter's principal example, and he has certainly absorbed, less the lesson in structure than in technique, of the Doni tondo. More even than in that work of Michelangelo, the painted surfaces of the *Manchester Madonna* assume statuary quality, of patinaed metal rather than of marble. A relationship with Granacci still is evident: the lower posture of the Madonna and the figure of the Child are related to the painting, almost as Michelangelesque, in Dublin.

In consequence of devoted study of the art of Michelangelo the Manchester Master has attained, in this name-work, an approximation of a modern classicism, but the approximation is essentially by imitative means. The style of his painting remains aberrant, not only on account of its apparent technical deficiencies, nor from its few evident incorrectnesses of draughtsmanship. The very nature of this painter's submission to Michelangelo — later to become ordinary, but in this time unique in this degree — is of an uncommon psychological disposition, touched almost with a character of mania. The region of compromise in medium he wills to occupy, between paint and sculpture, is ambivalent, intellectually and in its visual effects. The colors, dominantly of earth tones, and all of metallic cast, remove the figures into a special atmosphere, strangely oblique in its reference to actuality, as the classical atmosphere is not. And the drawing is evocative of a temperament not yet disciplined to the habits of a classicism: thin and tremulous, it alternates between weak, almost feminine, sensibility and torment as it delineates these bronze-like forms. This hand projects a vision more dependent and, in a sense, more introspective than that usual to classical art; this mind does not make synthesis of artifice and nature, but functions in a closed sphere in which there is only art.

With this preparation, certainly not quite adequate, the Manchester Master proceeded, probably between 1512 and 1515, to what was the fulfillment of his curious painting career: a fulfillment achieved, appropriately for one of such obsessive dedication to Michelangelo, in an act of virtual surrender of himself. Unlike his previous works, the *Entombment* (London, National Gallery)[338] is not merely based on Michelangelo but is specifically of Michelangelo's conception, and in part of his execution;* this is not a quasi-independent effort of the Manchester Master but, in effect, an assumption by him of the role of deputy for Michelangelo, if not quite that of his assistant. The central figure elements had been laid out by Michelangelo on the panel and their painting done by him in part; the Christ and the lower portion especially of the St. John show his hand. The time of this happening intervened — by general consent of those critics who recognize Michelangelo's invention — between the Doni tondo and the beginning of the Sistine. When, after the Sistine, it became evident that Michelangelo did not intend to return to Florence to complete this waiting work it may have been turned over to this most faithful one among his followers. The Manchester Master's devotion could not sustain his own, insufficient, competence; apparently, what was left to do included not only the completion of painting on Michelangelo's figures but a need — only very doubtfully conceived by Michelangelo — to invent figures to surround the central group. One of these accessory actors, the Magdalen, the Manchester Master recognizably adapted from a drawing made by Michelangelo circa 1505 for some other purpose; his source for the Mary on the upper right was probably similar but is not identifiable, and we have no idea of his meaning for the figure to the lower right — at which point he seems to have resigned his task, acknowledging his inadequacy to it. But enough of him is in this painting to make it not only what Michelangelo had begun but a work of compound personality and internally contradictory style.

A *Madonna* (Florence, art market),[337] probably toward 1515, is the last evidence we possess of the Manchester Master's art. It indicates a draughtsmanship still unsure, but developed in clarity over that in his portions of the *Entombment*, and some liberty in his response to Michelangelo's ideas of form. This work, however, has no traceable succession; there is no subsequent career for us to follow for this master, and no quick consequence in Florence of the dedicated and literal Michelangelism of his style.

V

CLIMAX, CRISIS, AND DISSOLUTION OF THE CLASSICAL STYLE IN ROME

(c. 1514-c. 1520)

V

CLIMAX, CRISIS, AND DISSOLUTION OF THE CLASSICAL STYLE IN ROME (c. 1514 - c. 1520)

LEO X, symbol in his own person of the unity of culture between Rome and Florence, inherited, with the papacy, the sum of Julius' accomplishment. When he came to the throne, and for a brief while after, the papacy was at a climax, unparalleled for centuries, of its temporal and cultural authority; and this time was also that of climax in the classical accomplishment of art. In this beginning of the Medicean reign it could not be foreseen that its progress would be of a dissolving splendor, and that this new Age of Gold, like a smaller sun, would consume its own radiance.

Leo's election had been welcomed with almost universal enthusiasm. He was thought admirably suited to his new place and its duties — as they were conceived by the observers of that time. Alberto Pio of Carpi, Ambassador of the Empire, reported of him: "careful of his honor and good repute, he will patronize the learned, orators, poets and musicians; he will erect buildings and will not neglect either his religious duties or his care for the States of the Church" (Pastor VII, 28). To the Swiss envoy Falk, his temperament seemed a welcome contrast to that of Julius: "Giovanni de' Medici inclines to peace, and is as gentle and temperate as Julius II was violent and harsh. For a century the Church has had no Pope to be compared with this one" (Pastor VII, 26). Both estimates were substantially exact; it was in the spirit these ambassadors describe that Leo administered his state, and with just such an emphasis on the primacy of culture over politics as Alberto Pio had predicted. But in both statements there is the implication of the absence in Leo of the force, often violent but creative, that Julius had possessed, and this lack would decide the history of this regime.

Especially in Leo's first years the city of Rome continued visibly to flourish in prosperity and magnificence, in what seemed to be even an acceleration of the Julian development. Mark Antonio Altieri in his *Nuptiali* (c. 1514) writes with a mixture of pride and old-fashioned disapproval of Roman splendor: "Not only do we see fine and commodious houses springing up on all sides, but with them splendid palaces full of distinguished inhabitants, noted for the unwonted splendor of their appearance, and the number among them of young exquisites . . . women . . . are proudly adorned . . . and at home there is the revelry of dancing and music" (Pastor VIII, 128–29). Raphael has only pride in the city he had helped to adorn in the last papacy, and was to serve still more grandly in the present one; in a letter to his uncle Ciarli in July 1514 he asks, in an irrepressible parenthesis, "qual locho e più degno al mondo che Roma?" (Golzio, 31). Raphael's words refer to more than the splendor of the physical place; they are the echo of awareness of the historical conjunction between the Ancient grandeur of the city and the new greatness that Julius had labored so hard to effect — the sense of a present Rome that, in the semblance of the *Roma* of the past, had taken on again an imperial measure of authority.

Leo at first maintained this authority, not by a policy of action but by one of mediation. This policy was not adequate to meet the political challenges, basically more deeply threatening than in the previous reign, to papal power; and Leo had no resources — of personality, and later also of financial means — to deal with them. The papacy soon yielded place among the prime movers of politics to France and the Empire, both of them inspired with a decisive, historically new, political dynamic, and directed by men of contrasting but equal force of personality. Eventually more serious still, but slower of realization, was the challenge of the Lutheran heresy, confronted too little and too late by political or by spiritual action by the papacy, and unmet by moves for internal Church reform. The authority inherited from the Julian regime was dissipated beyond recovery by Julius' successor. It was Leo's nature to spend the inheritance that Julius had amassed for him in Rome, rather than to increase it — except in the sense that its resources could be transmuted into acts and artifacts of culture. But beneath this splendid stratum of a cultural alchemy the temporal and spiritual substance of Rome was in process of dissolution.

The culture of Leo's Rome, too, was in an important way more an inheritance than of Leo's making. It is in general in the nature of a time that succeeds the development of a cultural idea to its maturity that a phase of refinement should follow on an earlier creative force, and that elaboration should succeed invention. Under Leo's patronage there was no decline in cultural activity in Rome; the opulence of Leonine culture is greater than in the time of Julius. But this activity is, essentially, a dissolution, in acts of elaboration and refinement, of a cultural style: a spending of a cultural patrimony, on which the inheritance of money of Pope Leo was spent in turn. Art, for this reign, assumed another kind of necessity than it had for Julius: more than the externalization of an attitude and ambition of the spirit, it acquired the indispensability of an indulgence. For this time art was more than an ornament of civilization; it was its substance. It is conceivable that this pattern of culture could have been altered by the direction of a personality different from Giovanni de' Medici, but his personality was itself, so to speak, a late cultural form. He brought into the culture of Rome — already based in part on Florentine importations — a temperament that was a late development of an older Florentine society: as a phenomenon of cultural generation, Leo was to his father what the Magnifico had been to the Pater Patriae.

The arts of design shared the general situation of Leonine culture. A pattern of elaboration and dissolution of classical style, within an appearance of continued splendor, is visibly explicit in the art of painting. However, the chief personalities of fine art seem of a different magnitude than those who dictated the politics and church affairs of Leo's regime, or than the men of letters; none among them, even Bembo, seems to possess the creative dimension of a Raphael. Though Raphael is involved in the postclimactic consequences of the development of classical style he continues to exert himself in intense seekings and inventive redirections, and not only in elaborations, of classical style. The same dynamic of creation continues to operate in him, and not alone in him among the artists, as had operated earlier to create and mature this style. The pictorial world of classicism was, for Raphael, no easy inheritance but his own rich, hard-won domain, and his exploitation of it was irrepressibly vital. His continued exercise of creative power, searching and testing the possibilities and limits of his own classical invention, gives to the atmosphere of art in Leo's time a sense of energy and of higher spiritual accomplishment than that which belongs to its general cultural and historical context. The justification of Leo's reign for history lies in its identification with art in general, but in particular with this art.

The tendency of Leonine culture was toward the exhaustion in refinement of the classical cultural style, but not its substantial alteration and less still its extinction. However, such in fact was the inescapable consequence of the actions of this reign in the practical sphere. The classical style was, as we have repeatedly remarked, essentially an artificial structure, which depended for its existence on a historical environment not in itself discernibly "classical" but instinct with its own energy of political or economic creation, and sufficiently physically and psychologically secure to permit and encourage the realization of an ambition to classical cultural behavior. In Leo's reign these conditions of environment began as surely to be removed as, in Julius' time, they had been provided. Julius' Rome could not be unbuilt in a day, but under Leo the process began of undermining those historical foundations that made a classical superstructure of culture possible. This was a Golden Age literally, in its spending, of its treasury of cultural forms and, yet more prodigally, of its temporal historical substance: its gold was the plating of a dissolving core. The conditions of the next, disastrous, Medicean papacy were determined in Leo's Golden Age.

RAPHAEL

For Raphael, the beginning of the last half-decade of his life was marked by more even than the opening for him of a new phase of development of style. It was also the beginning of a new expansion in his professional career. From this time on his role as a decorator was vastly increased: his charges of decorative projects in the Vatican were multiplied to that point where it was necessary for a time, from 1515 through early 1517, to manage them concurrently. In addition Raphael assumed in 1517 and 1518 a decoration of large scale for Agostino Chigi, in the Farnesina, which may also have required to be executed concurrently with further labors in the Vatican. Commissions for easel paintings also multiplied so that it was impossible to fulfill accepted obligations. To Raphael's role as painter-decorator a whole new sphere of activity had been added in April 1514, when he was named architect of St. Peter's in succession to Bramante (the appointment confirmed by papal bull of August 1, 1514: "Cum praeter picture artem, qua in arte te excellere omnes homines intelligunt, is a Bramante Architecto etiam in construendis aedibus es habitus . . ." [Golzio, 33]). This post made considerable demands on Raphael's attention, surely especially in the earlier stages of his tenancy when he was reworking Bramante's plans; and to this principal architectural business other architectural work was added later.

In August 1515 yet another responsibility, originally consequent upon his function as architect of St. Peter's, was taken up by Raphael: that of a superintendency over Antiquities in Rome, with the duty of selection of Ancient marbles for reuse in the new construction, and also of preservation of Antique fragments from destruction. This prefecture, in combination with Raphael's new architectural concerns, seems to have been the occasion for a considerable research into the architectural archaeology of Rome. It was known to his contemporaries that Raphael was engaged in his later years on a "descrittione, et pittura di Roma antiqua" (Michiel, *Diaries*, 6–7 April 1520 [Golzio, 113]), in which he was in process of describing "gli edificii antiqui di Roma, mostrando si chiaramente le proportioni, forme et ornamenti loro, che averlo veduto haria iscusato ad ognuno haver veduta Roma antiqua: et già havea fornita la prima regione" (Michiel, letter to Antonio Marsilio, 11 April 1520 [Golzio, 113]). Michiel's diaries imply that the intention to create this reconstruction preceded, and was the pretext, of Raphael's prefecture over Antiquities.

Because the scope and character of Raphael's occupations changed during this last half-decade of his life, his relation to art, and in particular to his former exclusive occupation of painting, changed accordingly. Raphael was no longer, after 1514, a painter with important but nevertheless limited functions, but the great *régisseur* of arts in Rome: planner and designer of concurrent great decorative projects, architect of Rome's — and the world's — most ambitious building, archaeologist of Ancient architecture and protector of Antiquities. He was organizer of Rome's current life of art: a figure of public action, and of status in the Leonine court like that of Leo's ministerial officers. The antithesis of personality between Raphael and Michelangelo became, now, even more radically marked. After Michelangelo's departure from Rome in 1516 Raphael was without contest to his artistic domination there. Certainly, this role was of Raphael's seeking and willing acceptance. It is the expression of expansion to their full scale of factors present in Raphael's earlier personality, now matured into a force and clarity become public and overt, and altogether absolved of the only apparent softness of his youth. But this role itself, in the course of its acting, must have helped to shape, as well as to confirm, a change of character, and the difference that results is one of the motive forces toward the direction that Raphael's art in this time assumes.

The Eliodoro room and its attendant, only quantitatively lesser, works were the fulfillment of a seemingly continuous process of stylistic evolution. According to our observation, what happened in the time of the Stanza d'Eliodoro extended and completed, in a highly differentiated but uninterrupted pattern of development, the propositions of style made in the Stanza della Segnatura. Between the two rooms, and the works that may be grouped with each, there is a caesura in character of style that is sensible, but not emphatic. But between the works of 1514 and the Tapestry Cartoons of 1515 there is a distinction of style so strongly marked as to convince at once of the beginning of a new stylistic phase: the sense of change is almost as pronounced as that which, years before, had marked the first Roman efforts of Raphael's career.

We shall examine the motives and the specific character of this new change later; in general, the style of the Tapestries is distinguished by a concentration, a deliberation, and a monumental force of statement that are different from any prior mode of Raphael's expression. The character of classicism in the Tapestries is, by a long reach, seemingly more nearly absolute than in any works before. They represent an act of profoundly self-conscious and rigorously self-demanding creative will, by which Raphael has accomplished an ascent onto a new plateau of classical accomplishment. This plateau of classical style had been occupied previously only by the later images of Michelangelo on the Sistine Ceiling, and there only by single, quasi-sculptural images; nowhere before had whole pictorial schemes been so conceived. Michelangelo's example, and Raphael's awareness of the near-juxtaposition of his Tapestries in the Chapel with this example, may have been a specific precipitant for Raphael's decisive and, more than Michelangelo's, embracing change of style. In Raphael, the making of this higher classical style required a reformulation of the already wholly-matured style of the Eliodoro phase. The new style may be characterized systematically, in its relation to the antecedent phase of classical style, as an elevation and clarifying of its whole synthetic structure: a displacement toward a higher pole of ideality of the center of the synthesis; and at the same time an enlarging of its entire scope. The elements of which the classical synthesis is composed are not in themselves altered, but they acquire a different expressive tonality through the elevation of the whole.

It is ascertainable through historical inspection that such a classical style as is in the Tapestry Cartoons is the ultimate level of classicism in pictorial form attainable to the High Renaissance. Except by Michelangelo, the plateau this stage of style represents is not long inhabitable, and Raphael's tenancy of it is relatively brief. Since this high classicism is an apparent ultimate, it is not susceptible of further development in this same sense. Any measurable progressive sequel could be only toward a region of ideality so high as to verge upon abstractness, and thus upon another, and no longer substantially classical, style. At the same time no style, this ultimate still less than others, is self-repetitively imitable by an artist of Raphael's continuously searching temper. The very fact of his achievement of a seeming apogee of classicism posed, for Raphael, the critical problem of the subsequent direction, or redirection, of his style.

A redirection did occur, but it remained a redirection of, and within, a classicism. Self-imitation was precluded, but not the reuse of elements of the high classical style of the Cartoons in other contexts and with other intent, which occurs in fact throughout Raphael's later work. In most instances this continuation of high classical style is in incidents rather than in the integer of these works. In one major field of Raphael's late effort, however, much of the temper, and an important aspect of the character of form, of high classical style persists as a dominant; though in altered — as it were sublimated — guise, of which the relation to the style of the Cartoons is not instantly wholly evident. This is the field of Raphael's great decorative schemes of his latter years. In these, where the design is determined no longer by a painter's concept of the picture frame but by a system of architectural geometry that is in itself classical, and within which the figure schemes are incidents of this architectural classicism, the character of the whole remains comparable to that of the Tapestry Cartoons.

The high classical style of the Cartoons thus has a continuing vitality in Raphael's late art; inevitably, it is a consequence of the shop system of these years that its expression should be in some measure compromised — as, in general, it is not yet in the Cartoons — by the intervention of Raphael's assistants in execution. But even as a model for the independent efforts of Raphael's school, and of others, it was in the nature of the high classical style to invite its own betrayal. A style of this kind, from its — apparent — simplicity, and also in its recognizable completeness, tends to invite crystallization and codification by its imitators. This codification — a translation into learnable elements of style — implies the imminence of an academy, even without its accustomed later apparatus. In its extreme manifestations an academic practice, in which forms once authentically classical are transcribed as formulae, uninhabited by the vitality that inspired their original creation, becomes by its nature no longer classical but classicistic.

More than through any deformation by his pupils, the alteration of the high classical style in particular, and of the classical style in general in these years, is Raphael's own responsibility. We have observed that a character of style like that in the Tapestry Cartoons persisted in Raphael's architectural decoration; more rarely it was also the dominant in a devotional picture. The persistence of high classical character is in works that do not require either narrative or dramatic emphasis; and it is best preserved in a decoration like that in the Farnesina, where the subject matter is itself one of literary classicism, and where this subject is then contained within the serenities of classical architectural form. The classical attitude continues without marked alteration where the content is, relatively, humanly noncommital, or subordinate to a partly predetermined geometrical organization of form. This is unlike the Cartoons: in them there was a formidable equation of stringent discipline of form, entirely invented, and the utmost urgency of content. The works of unequivocal classical temper that succeed the Tapestries and resemble them in formal mode continue — to put it too schematically — only half of this equation. They are a grand, but only partly inhabited persistence of Raphael's highest classical style.

When, after the designing of the Tapestry Cartoons, Raphael was confronted by dramatic subjects of historical or biblical narrative — subjects which, unlike those of the classical decorations, required his strong emotional commitment — the high classical style was altered more positively, and in a different sense. The ambition of the high classical style to powerful and emphatic rhetoric remained; Raphael's subsequent dramatic pieces intend effects no less grand and impactful than in the Cartoons. As in the decorative works, the dramatic scenes also continue to be populated by the same massive, impressive humanity that was invented for the Cartoons. Much of the appearance and tonality of the high classical style persists, then, in the dramatic paintings; but what does not persist is the integer of high classical style. Differently, and much more visibly than in the decorative schemes, the later dramatic works rupture the cohesion of style that existed in the Tapestries. In these later dramatic pieces it is Raphael's intention to create an expressive force which, if it could not be higher than that in the Cartoons, should be still more explicit and demonstrative: this intention is the final stage of a continuous process of intensification of urgency in narrative that had begun in the Stanza d'Eliodoro. The chief means of this dramatic mode is a more assertively characterized and more movemented repertory of forms, both of single actors and of whole designs; in instances the effect of this new repertory is drastic. The nobly contained, purely classical rhetoric of the Cartoons becomes, in such works, a more obvious, almost gesticulative speech. In the sense that the devices for urgency of expression in these pictures obtrude themselves more strongly than the whole effect of pictorial discipline, the style of these works distorts the equation so rigorously maintained in the high classical style.

However, the will to discipline is not more relaxed than in that style; the intended standard is the same, but it is no longer applied with equal stringency to emotions and to form, but chiefly to the latter. Each device for accentuation of dramatic effect is accompanied by, or is itself expressed in, a geometrical ordering of form, at times so distinct as to seem schematic. Each motive of expression, and its concomitant form, is given massive emphasis, to that degree where each element of style seems no longer, in the high classical manner, to be a precise articulation of the whole but the object of an almost separate stress. Like the mode of expression itself, this too is an end development of a process that had begun in the Stanza d'Eliodoro, of more explicit, even contrasting, articulation of modes of emotion and of parts of form. But as they were not in the Eliodoro frescoes, nor in the Tapestry Cartoons, in the late works the urgencies of form and meaning are too many and too marked to be submissive to the whole; they resist assimilation into a synthetic pictorial unity. The stresses in the late dramatic style are to a discernible degree disruptive of pictorial synthesis; in a sense, they are analytic in tendency. From the force within it of marked, separating stresses, the principle of classical synthesis, despite its still sensible presence in the late dramatic works, is threatened and partly compromised.

It is as if the seams between components of the whole synthetic structure should become apparent, as they had not been before. The indispensable synthetic basis of the classical image begins, as it were, to fracture under the pressure of the late Raphael's expressive urgency. The classical synthesis is in a state of imminent, or incipient dissolution. Nevertheless, these works are not yet definitely unclassical; what exists in them is still attached to and dominated by the classical prehistory of their creation. What has happened in them may be described as a faulting of their classical style, by analogy with the cracking and shifting under pressure of a geological or architectural structure, by which its look may be much altered and its security impaired, but where the structure is not changed in basic character of function, or destroyed.

The faulting of the classical synthesis is the result of Raphael's own manipulation of the datum of his achieved high classical style. In the actual translation of his ideas into paint, in these years so very largely by assistants, they undergo a process that, as far as we can ascertain, was not in Raphael's intention. His separating stress, in his dramatic style, upon the parts that constitute the — for him — still classical image is exploited by his executants. Increasingly as they develop they tend to see Raphael's emphases not in their character of relation but in their separateness: the classical image, its seams made visible by fracture, is seen by the students yet more analytically. This tendency is pervasive; it is applied not only to Raphael's dramatic emphases of form and content but to all the elements of style that, in his high classical mode, had been synthetically fused. In the hands of his executants the integer of classicism begins actively to be decomposed, not only formally and technically but in significant respects of psychological character as well. Because, after the Tapestry Cartoons, the specific appearance of Raphael's art is for the most part given it by pupils, their incipient decomposition, and even fragmentation, of the classical image at the least makes an overcast upon — or, more often, is confounded with — the substance of Raphael's thought. This tendency among the pupils affects not only the late dramatic works, of which the intended character would seem most to provoke this course; it appears as well in the population of the decorative schemes where, as we observed, the intention is more unequivocally classical, and no less evidently in the devotional paintings of the late style.

Where, in the later works, Raphael's responsibility for design is most assured, it appears that his intention, in manipulating emphases, is to compromise as little as possible the classical system of relations; his stresses are reciprocally compensating in their distribution and degree. However, the intent of emphasis itself, in such degree, incurs the risk of loss of equilibrium. In practice, and especially in Raphael's late shop practice, emphases tend to be disproportionate and disparate. The students are particularly inclined to — in instances evidently willfully intent on — the creation of disparities. In their incipient decomposition of the classical image they may isolate one or more facets of its whole for special stress; they differentiate for development, within — or against — the synthetic whole, parts that, in Raphael's vision, existed in equilibrium within it. Such a differentiation of elements for specialized development necessarily results in a warping of the whole initially synthetic conception, and it results also in a shift of meaning between the specialized element and its remaining context. Such disparities are particularly disruptive of classical character of style; and a sharp shift of meaning of this kind, of form or content, may not merely warp but destroy the shape of classical synthesis.

Another related process of alteration of classical synthesis occurs in consequence of Raphael's own initial faulting of classical style. It tends, in the most aggressive personality among Raphael's pupils, to be concurrent with the process of decomposition and differentiation of the classical image that we have described. This further process does not work only upon separate elements of style but upon the whole basic fault in classicism, widening the fissures in the classical synthesis into confrontation, and turning the confrontations into oppositions, and so, eventually, inverting synthesis into antithesis. This is the imminent destiny of the Roman classical style in the hands of Giulio Romano, but no more than any other happening of entire and explicit unclassicism is it permitted to occur in Raphael's lifetime. All these processes we have described as successive to Raphael's faulting of classicism participate, however, in a generic dissolution of the synthesis of classical style, and they prepare, within the body of the last phase of this style, the groundwork of the classicistic Mannerism that would, after Raphael's death, so rapidly replace it.

The history of Raphael's late painterly activity is now no longer, as it had been through 1514, a history of the manifestations of one artistic personality. The increase in Raphael's responsibilities had required, even during the time of the Stanza d'Eliodoro, the cooperation in some measure of assistants. But from 1515 onward the execution of his projects depended perforce on a *bottega*; it became necessary for Raphael to multiply his hands to meet his enormously multiplied obligations. The master did not withdraw entirely from the actual work of painting in his shop, but except for his extensive participation in the execution of the Tapestry Cartoons the other major decorative projects were not touched by him. Easel works tended increasingly to be left partly or wholly to the handwork of his pupils. His authority over the shop did not decrease in any way, but gradually, as his assistants acquired experience and more explicit individuality, practice within the shop became more libertarian. The helpers were not only permitted to impress their personalities in the act of execution but were allowed the entire invention of lesser pictures. In works of larger scale there was also some relaxation in Raphael's precise supervision of invention and design. In most instances that succeed the Tapestries it appears he may have been content to dictate the design in general of a decorative scheme and allow its specific further definition to his helpers. This does not, however, imply Raphael's surrender either of authority or of responsibility. His guidance and correction were not only available, but certainly given when, in the process of elaboration or execution of a design, too-evident discrepancies from his intention may have appeared.

The resultant work of art must nevertheless in some measure show its compound procedure of creation. Even in those works where Raphael's first design was precise and his supervision rigorous, the risk obtained of intrusion, even before the act of execution, of the helper's personality. For large schemes especially the shop was organized to require the preparation in drawing by assistants of certain stages intermediate between Raphael's invention and the painting. In such instances the articulation of a pose, indications of drapery, and elements of setting and perspective structure might well contain the personal accent of a pupil. Even during his close supervision Raphael's intent might thus be altered — not even against his initial will, but with his welcoming assent — by the image offered him by his draughtsmen.

The shop system of this phase in Raphael's career was an evident mechanical necessity, and had the sanction behind it of familiar and accepted practice. This did not preserve it from critical stricture, even in the course of the sixteenth century. The cult of Michelangelo which Vasari entertained and the — not unrelated — romantic conception of the role of the artist held by the nineteenth century and by our own did not approve of Raphael's delegation, and the depersonalization, of the execution of the work of art. Vasari speaks of Raphael's shop practice as "dannoso e di biasimo" (V, 626–27), and quite correctly deplores its effect upon the level of quality of the master's late achievement. Vasari, nevertheless, who in the scale of his own operations approached the later Raphael, could no more than he avoid resort to this traditional system, nor indeed could Michelangelo himself when finally he was forced to come to terms with his most important sculptural commissions.

The practice Raphael sanctioned in these same years, of permitting his signature to be affixed to easel works not of his execution has also been condemned; yet this too was customary and traditional for other artists, including, conspicuously, the profoundly moral Fra Bartolommeo. None of those critics who pretend to a morality more stringent than the Frate's has troubled to observe that, without the help of Raphael's assistants, only a fraction of the remarkable ideas of his late career could have become artistic actualities. In this perspective the contributions made by Raphael's ancillary hands to the history of art far outweigh their faults, and overbalance any inappropriate question of creative morality.

It may be that there is a deeper justification for Raphael's late adoption of the shop system, beyond the warrant of custom and necessary artistic economy. Raphael's style in these years became intrinsically less intimately personal in character. His major efforts tended on one hand to forms of monumental rhetoric, and on the other to projections of elaborate decorative schemes, architecturally engendered. In both cases the intent of communication is not so fine, nor are its devices of form and expression so needful of exquisite adjustment, as in the artist's earlier phases of style. His late art is, in sum, more immediately referable to generalization. What Raphael has to say is always, certainly, of a superlatively different level of effectiveness when he says it, as in this time he rarely does, himself; in transcription by assistants there is an inevitable, but not a fatal, difference in quality and character of statement: the meaning of Raphael's late generalizations, as generalizations, is not lost in the process of transcription.

That Raphael's late style became to this extent one of approximately imitable generalizations gives to the collective functioning of his shop something of the character of an academy. It is preserved from the pejorative implication that, for us, resides in this word by the scale of personality of the master of the shop, by the aesthetic magnitude of his conceptions of these years, and by the dynamic inventiveness that possessed him and infects his pupils. There was, among Raphael's pupils, a hardly academic assertion of identity, and a fruition of personality more rapid and more evident than in any contemporary *bottega.* The school — and such in an almost real sense the Raphael shop became late in this phase — attracted young painters of great resource who, in the very course of Raphaelesque assimilation, developed, some of them with remarkable precocity, their own marked individuality of style.

What has come to us in Raphael's name from this period of his painterly activity is a phenomenon complex not only in its diversity of evolution of classical style but in its compound human, and thus aesthetic, personality; we are dealing in this phase with several kinds of artistic happening, which are not always securely identifiable in their kind. There are, first, the occurrences, from now on increasingly exceptional, of complete execution, as well as invention, by Raphael himself; and most nearly approaching these, the aesthetic amalgams made of Raphael's design and his partial execution in collaboration with assistants. A third case is of whole execution by one, or more than one, assistant of Raphael's design, with the possibility of its alteration not only in the course of painting but in the course of detailed preparation, by the pupils, precedent to painting. Raphael's design may itself vary in this case in its degree of specification, and the preparation and execution of the painting may vary greatly in the amount given it of Raphael's supervision. A last class of works appears only in the latest years of the shop and is confined to easel pictures, or to portions within large decorative schemes: of invention as well as entire execution by assistants, conceived more or less in Raphael's own vein but explicitly demonstrative of another personality.

The problem of the historian who seeks to assess so various a texture is, obviously, too complex for full solution in the compass of this study. To treat this matter properly it would be necessary to settle, first, the vexed philological problems in this field: to establish more securely than has so far been done the responsibilities for execution in the many, and mostly compound, categories of production we have described above. Still more critically difficult is the problem of characterization of the separable aesthetic personalities whom we find within these compounds, and the characterization of the relation of each to the history of this phase of evolution of the classical style. A major purpose in investigation must be the determination of personal responsibilities in the dynamic of the classical style, most of all, still, for Raphael.

Despite the diffusion of his personality into that of his shop — which resembles and is related to the process which occurs at the same time, of differentiation of the integer of classical style — Raphael remains the inventive genius and the prime mover of this phase of the history of Roman classicism. It is as important as before to characterize Raphael's own role, even though it is now mostly readable only in impure texts. But it must not be lost sight of that the pictorial actualities of this time are compound, much more than individual, expressions. The history of what actually happened in this time, as distinguished from the history of Raphael's, or his pupils', individual artistic thought, is determinable only by the characterization of the actual works precisely in their character as compounds. There is a dual, and almost unfulfillable responsibility: for the history of Raphael and his school, and the history of Raphael *as* his school — as, in these years, he is made manifest through them, and they achieve realization only through him.

THE TAPESTRIES OF THE SISTINE CHAPEL

The problem of the aesthetic compound does not exist in any significant degree in the Cartoons (London, Victoria and Albert Museum)[355-71] for the set of Tapestries of the Acts of the Apostles, woven for the Sistine Chapel (now Rome, Vatican Museum);[339-48] they are the last of Raphael's monumental works of which it is indisputable that their character, in sum, is overwhelmingly Raphael's responsibility alone. He is not only the inventor, almost or altogether exclusively, of these remarkable designs but the principal executant of five of the seven Cartoons that survive. Most of these, and presumably also the three Cartoons now lost (but of which the first reproductions in tapestry still exist in the Vatican) seem almost surely to have been executed in 1515, at least three and probably more of them in the first half of the year.

A first document of payment for the Cartoons is dated June 15, 1515 (Golzio, 38); in it three hundred ducats are assigned to Raphael as ". . . parte di pagam.to delli cartoni e disegni si mandarono in Fiandra per li pani razza si fanno per la capella. . . ." The Cartoons were paid for, we learn from Michiel (a note in his diary of December 27, 1519 [Golzio, 103]) at the rate of one hundred ducats each. A second document of payment for an odd sum, 134 ducats, is noted on December 20, 1516 ". . . delli Cartoni ha fatto p. la Capella" (Golzio, 151). One of the Cartoons, the *Blinding of Elymas*, had already been published in a print by A. Veneziano (B. 43) in 1516.

Further documents refer to the Tapestries themselves: the *Pasce Oves* was woven by July 30, 1517 (Golzio, 370); in July 1519 three finished Tapestries had arrived in Rome from Flanders (Sanuto, *Diaries* [Golzio, 101]); on December 26, 1519, St. Stephen's Day, Paris de Grassis recorded the exhibition in the Sistine of the Tapestries by then received, "de quibus tota cappella stupefacta est in aspectu illorum . . ." (Golzio 103); on the 27th Michiel's diary specifies which these were (Golzio, 103–04). Michiel names seven Tapestries, giving their titles in some instances wrongly but still without possibility of confusion for us; they are all of the main scenes of the set except the *Ananias* and the *Preaching of Paul.*

There is only sparse original evidence for Raphael's mode of procedure in his preparation of the Tapestries. Of the considerable number of drawings that are associated with the Tapestries, only two are with absolute certainty from Raphael's own hand (for the Christ of the *Pasce Oves*, Louvre;[350] for the Paul of *Paul at Lystra*, Chatsworth);[351] and two further drawings, both at Windsor[352] (one of them a counterproof from the Louvre drawing)[349] are probably properly attributed to Raphael himself. The other associated drawings include a few by Raphael's assistants, but by far the larger part are copies. A situation like this, of extreme scarcity of surviving drawings by Raphael himself for his monumental works, is more usual than otherwise in the late phase, nor is it new: it exists also in the case of the Stanza d'Eliodoro. Despite the incompleteness of the preparatory material, by using its various fragments as symptomatic indications we can surmise, with some degree of assurance, what the process of preparation of the designs must have been.

No trace now exists, nor any accurate reflection, of an initial invention by Raphael of a whole Tapestry design. It may only be assumed, but the assumption seems reasonable, that the first *invenzioni* were in the sense of the Tapestries; counterproofs of these, or tracings, would then have become the bases of detailed studies toward the Cartoons. The drawing in the Louvre for the Christ of the *Pasce Oves* [350] is a fragment from this first stage in Raphael's development of his studies for the Cartoons. Like the drawings that survive for the same stage in preparation of the cartoon for the *School of Athens*, this one is taken from the model, in casual contemporary costume. The counterproof from this drawing, in Windsor (worked over in large part, and perhaps altogether, by Raphael himself),[349] is taken from the Louvre drawing in its original extent. It indicates the continuing concern of the designer, while he prepared the Cartoons, for the effect his motives would have in their eventual reversed direction in the Tapestries. That the motives were still flexible is demonstrated by the changes that were made between the Windsor counterproof and the actual Cartoon.

The Chatsworth drawing for the *Paul at Lystra* [351] is, like the Louvre study for the *Pasce Oves*, in the direction of the Cartoon. With some likelihood it represents a stage in preparation subsequent to that in the drawing in the Louvre: this is no longer explicitly a model-study. The figure has been classically draped, and developed in poetic eloquence of pose in a way more artificial than direct observation of a model would permit; the image in the drawing is that which was directly transcribed into the Cartoon. Studies such as these two symptomatically indicate that Raphael himself specifically prepared the individual figures of his designs, probably in at least two stages, and elaborated their relation in groups; his mode of working, and his degree of personal responsibility, is not different from that in the Stanza della Segnatura. That the making of a final finished whole design, immediately preliminary to the Cartoon, was also by Raphael in some instances at least is indicated by the drawing, which we believe to be his own, for the whole *Blinding of Elymas* (Windsor 803); [352] no more than the detailed perspective setting has been laid in by an assistant (Popham).

In other instances it is possible, but not likely, that the reassembly of Raphael's elaborated partial studies into a final whole was left to an assistant, though surely only under Raphael's close supervision. Some evidence for this may exist in drawings such as that in the Louvre for the whole of the *Pasce Oves* (3863; [353] a squared variant,* also probably original rather than a copy, in the Uffizi, 1216E) or in the Uffizi for the *Paul Preaching at Athens* (1217E).[354] Unlike the drawings we have so far cited these are in pen and wash, and they are certainly to be ascribed to Penni; they belong without question (as do some other drawings of compositional kind, by the same hand) to the working material used in the preparation of the Cartoons. Rather than their being an assistant's summary of Raphael's prior stages in the preparation, however, it is more probable that these drawings were made as working copies of such a final design by Raphael as that which exists for the *Elymas*. These presumed working drawings would have served a double purpose: of preserving Raphael's original from defacement in the course of use, and of simplifying the original, especially in its pattern of chiaroscuro, for greater ease of transfer. They would have served the assistant who was their author in the process —

probably mostly left to Penni — of roughing out the actual Cartoon. Among the Cartoons that still exist, Penni was allowed to continue his execution in painting without significant intervention by Raphael in one scene only, the *Preaching of Paul* and, much less, in the *Blinding of Elymas*. Elsewhere throughout the Cartoons the painting of the major figures and most of the lesser ones as well was taken over by the master; the offices of Penni, and to a less degree of other assistants such as Giovanni da Udine, were solicited for settings, incidents of detail, and eventually for the painting of designs for borders.

The belabored problem of reversal between the Cartoons and Tapestries seems rather an invention than a problem of real historical or aesthetic significance. For every practical reason it must have been that Raphael's ultimate consideration in design was with the Tapestries, and not with the way-station toward their making in the Cartoons. If the Cartoons had been the objects of Raphael's final concern, and not the Tapestries, it is unreasonable that he should have executed them on a surface so ephemeral — that the larger part of them survives, and in legible condition, is a happy but hardly a certainly premeditated circumstance. It should be stressed that the Cartoons were, in the first place, working instruments, and not themselves intended for any public inspection competitive with the woven Tapestries. At the same time, it is obvious that these Cartoons are not so much merely incidents in an incompleted process as are ordinary cartoons. Given the medium into which these Cartoons would be transferred, and the distant place and foreign persons who had to be relied on to effect their transformation into final, public, form of tapestries, it was necessary that these Cartoons be in themselves exceptionally explicit statements — virtually complete works of art. Among the considerations to which the qualifying "virtually" applies is that of their finally intended reversal.

It is only when the Cartoons are reversed and set in their correct sequence that their individual designs make their completest, and not merely a partial sense, both in narrative and as units of an including, laterally connected, aesthetic structure. It is only when they are so seen that temporal relations of cause and effect, within each scene, succeed each other in their actual order. In some instances, however — and this is the source of vexation for those who have speculated on the effects of the reversal — it appears that the composition in the direction of the Tapestries is less dramatically effective than that in the sense of the Cartoons. The reversal matters least in the approximately axially balanced scenes, like the *Ananias* and the *Elymas*; obviously, the effects of reversal are more sensible in the more directional designs. It is, in general, true that when they are read in the direction of the Tapestries, the lateral compositions seem more fluid than in the Cartoons; they seem more easily continuous in their movement and less tensely dramatically charged. The second fact is certainly, in part, consequent upon the first, but this is not the only reason for the diminution of the effect of dramatic urgency in the Tapestry direction of the designs.

In the Cartoons, in the course of their preparation as well as execution, Raphael was working in what might be described as a countergestalt: a reverse image of his initial, and eventually final, compositional intent. We do not mean by this what is implied by that conception of directional gestalt which is at times applied to the reading of images in a classical style: that the "natural" tendency of the classical image is to read from the spectator's left to his right; and that a design which reads oppositely would be counter to classical gestalt. This is a cliché of characterization for classical compositions, but it is not, for all its frequent repetition, true. The intention of direction in designs in the Tapestries — as in general in developed works by Raphael and Michelangelo from their more mature phase onward — is as much from right to left as otherwise; the direction in which a composition reads, in the case of the Tapestries, is determined by considerations other than those of a supposed preference of gestalt. But it is true that, whatever the invented direction of a design, its gestalt is indissolubly identified with the original intention of direction. It is in this sense only that, in the reversed directions of the Cartoons, Raphael is working counter-gestalt. We suggest that the psychological consequence of this is to have introduced an element of opposition, and thus of tension, into the particular working out of form in the designs. Postures or gestures that might have a relative fluency in their original context of direction might, in their reversed sense, have assumed a quality of resistance or taken on an initially unintended degree of stress. Such tensions may have served to intensify, to a sensible degree, the temper of dramatic content in some of the Cartoons.

However, it is more important to the efficacy of dramatic effect of the Cartoons that it was in *their* direction that Raphael specifically and actually worked out his general meaning. His chief actual aesthetic and emotional involvement was, from after the first moment of invention, with the Cartoons; the precise articulation of an action or a feeling was in the figure as he prepared it for and executed it in them. Into this actual and tangible form in the Cartoons, and not into its eventual Tapestry reversal, Raphael injected his creative urgency.

It is not so surprising that, when the image in a Cartoon is reversed into the sense of its original gestalt, its details do not all work there with equal force; what is surprising is that they are, for the most part, only so little diminished by reversal. It was not intended for the Cartoons that they be final works of art, but because in some respects they exhibit, more precisely than their reversals, the vital processes of their creation they have taken on some measure of this final character for subsequent observers. It is proper that we should regard them not only as incidents in the making of the Tapestries but as separable, and far more profoundly personal, variants of the same artistic end.

When Michiel described the Tapestries on the occasion of their first exhibition in the Sistine Chapel he named them in an order which is that of the narrative of the Acts. Since, it will be recalled, he did not actually recognize all the pictured scenes for what they were, his sequence could not have been composed from any memory of the written text; Michiel's sequence must therefore indicate the order in which he saw the pieces hung. An obvious, but sometimes still disputed point is thus made clear: the principal Tapestries were displayed according to the narrative sequence of the text.

The exact disposition of the Tapestries in the Chapel [339] — a matter of great importance in our assessment of the way of working of the designs together, as well as in our understanding of each individual design — has a long history of inconclusive speculation. Only recently (White and Shearman) has a reconstruction been worked out that obviates the gross difficulties of previous suggestions, and conforms to the sense demanded by the Tapestries themselves. Recognizing the necessity in Renaissance aesthetic for conformity in direction of light within a picture with the actual, architectural source of light, and predicating a flexibility at this time still in assignment of Gospel and Epistle sides within a church — especially, as in this case, in a chapel of archaic orientation — this scheme reverses the hitherto accustomed suppositions for the placing of the Paul and of the Peter stories. The Tapestries of Peter, lighted from the spectator's left, and the Tapestries of Paul, lighted from the spectator's right, are assigned respectively to the north and south walls of the Chapel where (in the state of the building before Michelangelo's *Last Judgment*) each would have received its appropriate lighting from the windows then in the altar wall. Conforming to the order of narration in the frescoes on the walls above, each of the two sequences of Acts begins upon the altar wall: the first event of the history of Peter, the *Miraculous Draught of Fishes,*[342] rightward of the altar as we face it; the prologue of the history of Paul, the *Martyrdom of Stephen,*[340] in the space beside the altar to our left. Each story follows then in order on its lateral wall, proceeding away from the altar as the Quattrocento frescoes do, and as Michelangelo's Ceiling does as well. Besides the tapestries on the altar wall, all three subsequent scenes of the Peter series: the *Pasce Oves,*[343] the *Healing of the Lame,*[346] and the *Ananias,*[347] with their borders, fit into the space inside the chancel to the edge of the Cantoria. On the south side the *Conversion of Paul,*[341] the *Blinding of Elymas* [344] and the *Paul at Lystra,*[345] together with the narrow minor Tapestry of *Paul in Prison,* occupied the length of wall up to the former location of the Cancellata; opposite the Cantoria and, with good iconographic reason, outside the chancel as it then stood, in the space reserved for laity, would have been the place of the *Paul at Athens.*[348]

In this ordnance, evidence of planned and logical relation among the compositional forms of the Tapestries emerges as it did not from the systems of arrangement proposed before. The conscious order in distribution of types of composition that existed in the first two Stanze has been still more deliberately developed in the Chapel in a situation that, combining problems both of central balance and longitudinal sequence, is much more complicated than in the Stanze. A basic relation of balance is established in each series — excluding, in the Acts of Paul, the separable unit, beyond the chancel, of the *Preaching at Athens* — by the succession of two scenes in landscape with two scenes set in architecture; this balance in a lateral direction, adequate but unsymmetrical, is also a reflecting balance across the two sides of the room. The *Paul at Athens* outside the Cancellata is a massive architectural scheme, a pictorial counterpart for the Cantoria it confronts.

Each Tapestry is an uncompromised integer of design, but at the same time relations are made among them that articulate their situation in their sequence. The integrity of each design is altogether evident in the first scene of each series, an integrity supported by its distinct place on the end, altar, wall. As if, however, especially to ensure a continuity between this end Tapestry and the second member of each series on the side wall, the landscape is indicated to be — despite the break made by borders and by the corner — continuous between both (White). In the *Miraculous Draught* a strong impulse of direction affirms this continuity rightward, in the sense of the succeeding narrative. In the *Stephen* Tapestry, leftward of the altar, the impulse of direction is more internally diverse, but the rotatory movement of the executioners and their comprehending shape just as strongly make for continuity with the cavalry of Paul behind them in the next scene.

On the long walls the three subsequent scenes of both series are related in a scheme of balance among themselves and each composition, within its integrity, has been adjusted in consideration of its place within the three-part sequence. And, though there is no literal, and certainly no obvious, correspondence in form between scenes that confront each other across the Chapel, each confronting pair of compositions is concordant in basic indication of direction and in distribution of its emphases. In the *Pasce Oves* the movement of the composition in the sense of the narration is quite clear: the climax of the design and its place of emphasis are displaced affirmatively toward the right. At the same time, because this scene must sufficiently balance in relation to two succeeding stable schemes of architecture, its component figures are themselves arranged, against their landscape, with a stability of nearly architectural effect. The *Healing of the Lame,* the central element in the composition of this wall, contains a dense population of figures in a heavy architecture; essentially its design is central. Yet a continuity of lateral direction is, in minor key, indicated in this scene too, and its composition opens and relaxes toward the spectator's right. The final Tapestry on this wall, the *Death of Ananias*, has, as the terminal piece, the most decisive stability in structure — accomplished, rather as in the *Pasce Oves*, more through its figure composition than by architecture. Still more articulate of its central scheme than the *Healing*, at the same time the design expresses the function not only of arresting the sequence in direction but of countering it: its emphasis is displaced "backward," toward the left. In this diplacement it balances, on the whole wall, the opposite displacement of the *Pasce Oves* composition toward the right.

In the three Pauline Tapestries that hang opposite, the basic scheme in the composition of the whole wall, in its relation of balance and continuity, and in the placing of the major emphasis within each design, is a near mirror-image of the scheme we have described for the Petrine series. However, the precepts of developed classical style do not conceive of balances as mere literal inversions, but as differentiated and responsive counterparts. The side scenes of this Pauline triad are distinguished in the general character given their design against their opposites. Where, in the *Pasces Oves* and the *Ananias*, the compositions stress the stable and the architectonic, in the *Conversion of Paul* and the *Paul at Lystra*, which face them, the designs (despite the fact that their schematic loci are like those in the Petrine series) are assertively movemented. And in the central panel of the *Elymas*, for obvious reasons quite rigorous in its effect of stability, there is a conscious responsive differentiation against the *Healing* opposite: while the design of the *Healing* is, in primary effect, centripetal, that of the *Elymas* is — within an equally, or more severely contained whole structure — expansive toward its sides. Because of their overcast of movement the three Pauline Tapestries on this extent of wall cohere more fluently in a whole design than do their Petrine counterparts, in which the static, partly additive effect is stronger. Yet both groups of Tapestries remain counterparts; the sense of a unity that embraces both is magnified by this counterpoint of differentiation.

The composition of the *Preaching at Athens*, hung outside the chancel apart from the preceding Pauline scenes, is dictated by special circumstances of place and function of communication. Paul, in this Tapestry, addresses not only his pictured audience of Athenians but, by iconographic and structural implication, the actual audience of laity in the Chapel also (White). The scheme of the *Preaching* is that of a central composition altogether turned in profile; the audience of actual spectators is meant to complete to its full circumference the circle of Paul's listeners. The scene is, in composition, both an epilogue and an absolute term for the Pauline set. It backs up against the chancel, reinforcing its closure and abutment of the *Lystra* scene behind; the arcading in the *Preaching* extends and underlines the meaningful interruption in this whole wall's composition that the Cancellata made.

Raphael's planning of relations among the Tapestries is his highest development of classical decorative organization. The given situation was not only more complex in number of its elements than in the Stanze, but more intrinsically complex in its problems: beyond the problem of the Stanze, of complementary central relationships, the Tapestries required simultaneous consideration of lateral relation both of sequence and of balance, and of relation between side walls and the adjacent ends. The more complex application of classical principles in this organization is apparent not only in comparison with the Stanze but from the entire contrast this scheme, as we have described it, makes with the Quattrocento frescoes on the walls immediately above. Seven years earlier than Raphael, Michelangelo had faced a similar problem in the planning of the ceiling of the Chapel and had solved it in a way specifically very different, but also on the basis of the same essential classical principle of responsive concordances, both centrally and laterally related. Here as always differently from Michelangelo, Raphael's organization is of units of pictures and not of sculptural forms.

However, more than in the Ceiling and more also than in the Stanze each part that is assembled into the logic of the whole asserts, within that logic, its identity as a unit. The new level of classicism in the planning of the Tapestries is not only in the more complex coordination of the whole but in this more distinct articulation of each part. More than any other High Renaissance narrative-picture scheme, the Tapestries are telling in their demonstration of a principle of organization by which, within a whole including and immutable design, coordinate relations are established among picture units of which each is a distinct and separable, but not intendedly a separate, integer. The sense of unitary distinctness of each of the Tapestries within the series is to some degree affected, but not caused, by the external circumstance of the shapes required for them — simply and severely regular, unlike the arched areas in the Stanze. Rather, the distinct articulation within the series of each scene is the symptom, on its largest scale, of the new factor that pervades the style of the Tapestries, and which distinguishes Raphael's interpretation of classical style in them from the classicism of his antecedent phase. The clarity of each picture-unit is the consequence of the structure of the unit in itself: each scene is made with an intention to achieve a maximum articulate lucidity in definition of its forms and communication of its content. Each image of this series — much more visibly in the Cartoons than in their inadequate translations in the actual Tapestries — is in a style inherently more explicit, and more explicit in its character of classicism, than in Raphael's preceding works.

The style of the Cartoons demonstrates, in general, an economy more rigorously controlled, in some scenes markedly more severe, than in the Stanza d'Eliodoro or the Segnatura. The quantity and variety of elements that are contained in the design of each Cartoon may be no less in it than its smaller size, in comparison with the Stanze, might require. But regardless of its quantity of forms, each design seems, in its entirety, simpler. The whole shape in which the important elements of composition are arranged is more compact, and its outline and its character of shape are less complex, and certainly less ornamentally elaborated, than in most of the frescoes in the Stanze; the internal structure of this shape is also generally simpler. The geometrical basis of the whole order of design is more obvious, and more forcefully asserted than it had been in the frescoes of the Stanze: in the Cartoons each design is more quickly and more clearly apprehensible as a generalization.

This emphatic generalization of design is imposed upon a pictorial substance different in itself from that in the frescoes of the Stanze. These compositions are, literally, more substantial: in them space and spatial interval have been much diminished in their compositional role. The design of the Cartoons is built up of figures of which the relation in scale to the area of picture is larger than in the Stanze frescoes, and these relatively larger forms are assembled in a whole greater density of mass. The order given to this mass, in most of the designs, is primarily a shaping of the mass itself, as an integer of substance. The shape and sensation of space is no longer, as it had been in the Stanze, a virtually equal partner with substance in the structure of design; space is here an incident or a byproduct of the ordering of substance. There is no obvious violation of perspective and no significant dislocation in perspective scale, but this style no longer depends on perspective. Where perspective is used its rationale is yet more clear than in the Stanze — almost baldly obvious. What it is used for, however, is its value of geometry, far more than its value as an agent of effects of space. Space, as interval among solids, no longer has an identifiable aesthetic personality in the Cartoon designs: it is at best a representationally necessary but neutral aesthetic fact. And as extension — that expanse of setting which surrounds the density of forms — space is also an incident: a neutral descriptive field on which the figural substance of design is set.

This substance is itself arranged, in most of the Cartoons, in a way that minimizes meaning and effects of space. The figure masses are set out, for the most part in close community, in strata that are parallel to the surface of the picture and tend to fill it: in five of the Cartoons at least the shape and substance of the figure mass seems to fill the field, in a rough sense, foursquare. In some of these designs the rectangular whole shape of solid, or hardly excavated, forms seems (against its aesthetically-neutral spatial background) like a panel of deep relief. In some designs, indeed, the disposition of the figures suggests a principle of isocephaly. The kind of discipline in these compositions, and its means — of a rectangular density of figures in one clear plane, or subdivided into planar strata — are like that of a classical relief-style. This mode of discipline, with its Antique classical analogy, is a principal one among the devices that achieve the effects of clear generalization in these designs.

The whole clear integer of massive form in each of these schemes has, as a whole, an exceptional force of formal impact. This large effect of structure is then made precisely articulate by extending to its parts the principle of generalization that is evident in the whole. For reasons of content as of form, indissolubly from one another, elements are selected within the whole design and given a particular stress and clarity in shape and action. Each such significant part assumes a new force as an identity within the design, and in the same moment is related, by virtue of its generalization, more cogently to the whole.

As is necessary to a classical style, not less in this ultimate stage than in any other, the development of form is one with the development of the character of content. In this stage in fact, where meaning in every respect of style is more explicit, the sense of classical identity of form with content is more nearly absolute than ever before in Raphael's style. The concentrated substance of the Cartoon compositions consists, dominantly, of the humanity who are the actors of these scenes. The effect of scale that is given them, the impact of their force of shape, and their decisiveness of action, are determined not only formally but by Raphael's conception of the kind of content that is in them. The clarity of design and its instant legibility are at the same time cause and consequence of the artist's idea of the dramatic action. Emotions and their communication in dramatic incident are conceived with the same intense clarity and with the same power in generalization as the forms in which they are made visible. The major figures in the Cartoons wear expressions of countenance that are at once more strongly characterized than in their counterparts in the Stanze, but also of more typical significance; and their gestures are, by comparison, more emphatic and more lucid. Through condensation and generalization of their visible form, emotions that are specifically generated in the given dramatic situation are raised to the status, not merely of the typical, but the archetypal: there are instances in the Cartoons where such signs of states of spirit, without losing any of their force as particular signs, acquire, equally, the character of symbols.

This higher characterization is not indiscriminately imposed on all the actors in the Cartoons. Its use, and the degree in which it is applied, depend upon the kind and urgency of content of each figure, and the importance of the role he plays within the scene. Not only protagonists, but also the principal witnesses among the responsive audience of their actions, may be so emphatically described; among the lesser figures there may be a variety of types and personality similar, in its descriptive richness, to that in the frescoes of the Stanze. But even in this humanity that is incidental to the drama there is a difference from their earlier counterparts: they are sought out and described with a more intense and more sharply articulating vision. Their types embrace a wider human range, and each individuality among them is more flexibly, but also more succinctly characterized than in the Stanze; in this latter respect these figures, too, conform to a principle of generalization.[360-1] Even as new explorations of naturalism they embody a formal and spiritual force that their earlier analogues did not have. Their presence is a partial counterweight, and in a double sense a relief, for the high austerity of the protagonists. The new creative force in the Cartoons leads, then, not only into a higher and more abstracting reach of style but, in a secondary sense, into a broader one; the new reshaping of the classical synthesis not only heightens but extends its sphere.

In the way in which Raphael distributes his actors in his compositions in the Cartoons there is a coincidence, made much more explicit than in the Stanze, between the points of structural emphasis in the design and the strong points of dramatic content. The instantly apprehensible whole scene is articulated into major indications of action and reaction, which in their own emphasis are no less instantly apprehensible and explicit. In general in the Cartoons these indications are distributed within the evident direction of movement of each design according to their sequence of events in the depicted drama. However, there is no such sense here as in the Stanze of temporal interval between the moments of the action: a vastly higher condensation — an almost drastically concentrated unity — is imposed on the content of the drama in the same process that concentrates its visible form.

In the Cartoons it is easy to discern the relation of their different schemes of pictorial composition to precedents in the preceding Stanze. A scheme like that of the *Repulse of Attila* [221] — the most developed of Raphael's designs to that date in its curving, movemented asymmetry — relates most evidently to that of the *Conversion of Paul* in the Tapestries, and less obviously to the *Miraculous Draught* or the *Paul at Lystra.* The system of the *Liberation of Peter* — as we have seen, an opposite discipline into monumental stasis of design — is, in principle, like the *Ananias* or the *Elymas*; the *Preaching at Athens* is in some sense a combination of the two modes. These visible relations serve, however, to relieve only the more strongly the different way in which, in the Cartoons, these schemes have been employed. In the laterally moving, asymmetrical, designs it makes an evident difference that, in the Cartoons, the design consists so dominantly of substance, and that this substance is so precisely subdivided into its component forms: the temper of the new compositional movement is restrained, scanned, and made deliberately grave. The axial designs — the *Ananias* and the *Elymas* — are even more assertively deliberate in comparison with precedents in the Stanze: their higher symmetry of structure magnifies the effect of ordering of mass that is present in the components of design. In these axial schemes the idea of a rigorously controlled, essentially static order that was invented for the *Liberation* fresco is developed into an urgent and inexorable principle.

In all the Cartoon compositions alike, regardless of their particular cast of movement or stasis, it is the mentality developed from the *Liberation*, of strict discipline of composition, not the grandiose activity of the *Attila*, that is the consequent new element in Raphael's ordering of forms. Whatever particular intent of formal and expressive purpose may give one of the Cartoon designs its special shape, there is a high quotient in them all of this new degree of stringency of discipline. The specific tempers of design in the Cartoons embrace the extreme severity of the *Ananias* and the deliberated, large suavities of the *Draught of Fishes*, the columnar stillness of the *Pasce Oves* and the resilience of the *Paul at Lystra*. But in these compositions, and in the others also, a common denominator exists of that character which, among all the Cartoons, is most compellingly expressed in the austere *Ananias*. Far more than in the compositions of the Stanze, and much more even than in the *Liberation* fresco, it is a major motive in the aesthetic of the Cartoons to make deliberation manifest, and reason strongly and exactly sensible.

Unlike the Stanze the Cartoons are, in general, conceived in a mode of emphasis. The clarity and force of expression and of form that are intended in the Cartoons are not attainable except by selective stress. The suavities and graces that, in the Stanze, cohabit with — but also in a measure mask — their power are here largely dropped in favor of more bold and more compelling statement. Where motives of curving form persist, in composition or in postures, they are no longer gracile; they are made less suave and more simply and emphatically full in shape: subtlety of articulation is displaced by clarity and stress. But for the most part in the Cartoons there is a diminution of curvilinear elements of form and a marked increase of uncomplicated, straighter shapes; in this mode of emphasis it matters more that things be said forcefully than that they be said with grace. In many incidents in the Cartoons statements of human meaning and appearance are made in terms that are, literally, flat-footed — a directness unthinkable in the Stanze.

No dogmatic principle of severity is imposed without distinction on the figures of the Cartoons, any more than such a principle is imposed upon the whole designs; in respect of the figures, as of the compositions, each particular form is determined by a particular intent. But a new generic intent is evident in that large part of the population of the Cartoons that stands or moves in a way that seems, by contrast with the Stanze, almost artlessly direct: in the figures that are, in instances, gracelessly forthright, and in others that are rigidly severe. Their gestures and their mode of action may be absolutely simple or, where it lends visual and contentual force, abrupt. The effect of this new style of acting is to give, to the figures in the Cartoons that are conceived in this way, a hitherto unparalleled immediacy and force.

In the significant, and quantitatively dominant, population of the Cartoons that is so conceived it is apparent, for the first time in Raphael's art to this degree, that contrapposto is no longer a controlling and virtually indispensable principle of classical style. The grace of contrapposto movement is not reconcilable with the intention of severe emphasis in these actors of the Cartoons; a suave harmony would compromise their dramatic power. Further, the system of relations among figures that depends from contrapposto, of rhythmically woven continuities, implies a diminution of the clear identity of each figure; and the force of dramatic impact of the chief actors in the Cartoons relies in most instances on an unlike mode, of drastically clear relief, or even isolation, of the figure against the group. In the Stanza d'Eliodoro there had been symptoms — there hardly appreciable within their context — of a potential conflict between the intention of dramatic urgency and that of such a harmony, almost sensuous in its kind of beauty, as a contrapposto style suggests. In the Cartoons a decision has been made which, characteristically for Raphael, is not exclusive or inflexible, but by which contrapposto, as a principle of style, has been displaced.

This is a major alteration in the complexion of the classical style. However, it is in no sense an indication of a change from classicism in Raphael's art, but only of a change in the nature of his classicism. The Cartoons no longer seek so evidently for that which, in the Stanze, we have learned to describe as harmony: a system of finely articulated, contrapuntal compensations. In the Cartoons, minor figures may be merely stated, and with extreme simplicity, rather than ornamentally articulated; and they may seem almost passively conjunctive components of a figure mass. Against this mass, major actors may be set in bold relief, in a connection with their context that is almost blunt, and also in a sense conjunctive. Among the major elements of form the stress on clarity of each is such that they assume a degree, uncommon in the Stanze, of separateness; their manner of relation is not now one of suave continuity. The very clarity of purpose and its expression in design entails a process of analysis, of which the consequences are evident in the internal structure of the Cartoons: as the works of Raphael's maturity do not, these contain an element of additive mentality. But in the context of their whole design, this element has no meaning of incipient or even potential disruption of a synthesis, but only of a magnifying of its clarity of parts. For these parts are held together, with an aboluteness that Raphael had never before willed or attained, by *force majeure*, an inexorable logic of their compact designs.

Unlike the Stanze, the Cartoons do not ingratiate while they impress, nor do they act with richly ornamental, orchestrated harmonies upon the senses as much as on the mind. Nevertheless, the Cartoons have what we can also define as a harmony, but of an identifiably distinct kind: of a maximum clear unity which, in a literal sense, is more ideal. This harmony of the Cartoons is the consequence of the single force of each as an idea, and of the consistency of ideal value among the elements of form and content within each Cartoon. The sense of representational efficacy is not less in them than in the Stanze — in fact, as we have observed, the Cartoons include a wider natural descriptive range — but, since each major factor of style has been subjected to emphatic clarification and generalization, the value as a concept of each represented fact is higher than before. Each schema of design makes evident, in its very schematism, its ideal value of aesthetic shape; the posture of each major actor, explicit and deliberated, has a character of distillation of the artist's processes of thought.

This thought searches for the most cogent and most essential definition of a content and for its most explicit projection in a visual form; but wherever it can be done without compromising force it seeks also the highest value of a classicizing beauty in that form. There is, in many of the Cartoon figures, the utmost deliberation of aesthetic pattern, as if in them the armature of geometrical order that underlay the Stanze figures should have been made stronger and more apparent: within the Stanze the only partial precedent is in the remarkable group at the right of the *Expulsion of Heliodorus*.[217] What had been, in the figures of the Stanze, a vibrant suavity of shape becomes, in these figures in the Cartoons, crystalline and austere purity of pattern.[364] The beauty of posture of the figures of the Stanze seemed as if it might be transitory — the beauty of an organism held in complex equilibrium; the pattern of posture of the actors in the Cartoons has a differently enduring effect. More than we feel, in their postures, its function as an organism we feel its value of geometrical idea: each posture is conceived with a particular stress in it of a character of aesthetic concept. In this conceptual intent, and in the deliberation this conceptualizing entails, posture (and gesture evidently with it) seems, by comparison with the Stanze, more nearly stilled and almost immutable. The most dramatically specific content of a human actor is thus expressed in a vocabulary that conveys, by this stress in it of ideal value of its form as well as of its meaning, the sense that it consists of universals: an action acquires, and is identified with, the value of a concept.

The power of communication of these actors is of more, then, than their mimetic repertory. They convey high emotions in a style of acting that is gravely eloquent and deliberate, and from which there emerges, as nowhere in the Stanze, the sense of a nobility of drama. But this quality is exalted higher still by the value of concept that attaches both to the form and content in which it is made visible. The higher ideality of the Cartoons denotes a stratum of being not only aesthetically, but humanly, superior to any in Raphael's preceding art. As had been true also of the Stanze, an ethical value is associated with the classical aesthetic; the elevation to a higher sphere of one implies the raising of the other. The austere nobility of the protagonists in the Cartoons makes them, for the cultural mode of this time, ultimate ethical exemplars of a humanity inhabited by Christian powers of spirit, but classically supremely disciplined in their expression. There is a difference in this strain of beings, less beautiful in person but spiritually more noble, from the actors of the Stanze frescoes. If the actors of the frescoes are a projection of what Raphael's contemporaries would wish to be, the actors of the Cartoons are what these same men ought to be according to a higher ethic still.

The character of ethical exemplar that the Cartoons have, and the scanned, emphatic discipline of visual language in which this example is presented, give them a tonality very different from that in the frescoes of the Stanze. In comparison with the Cartoons — but only in this comparison — the histories of the Stanza d'Eliodoro seem diffuse, and their power of impact seems diminished by their care for suavity. If the histories of the Eliodoro are to be described as accomplishments of dramatic narration the Cartoons require a description that relieves their difference: yet more effective as narration, and different in their means, they may perhaps be defined as dramas of rhetoric character and intent. The higher ideality of the Cartoons does not imply a removal from the spectator of their immediacy of human meaning; on the contrary, they effect communication with an efficiency that the Stanze do not share. The means of this efficiency are those qualities which, in a verbal medium, we should recognize at once as distinctions of a high rhetorical style: emphatic and clear articulation of language, and force of ennobled statement deliberately controlled in form. From the beginnings of the classical style, narrative art had been subsumed and in part transformed into a dramatic mode; at the climax of the classical style a higher sublimation of narration has been achieved in the condensation of rhetoric with drama.

That a rhetoric ambition should appear in Raphael's later dramatic style was reasonable, and perhaps virtually inevitable. Since his first work in the Stanze Raphael's function had been not only decoration but the promulgation in visual form of doctrine: first, in the Segnatura, of a papal interpretation of classical humanism; then, in the Eliodoro, of Church policy and politics. Raphael's duty was, in a sense, as much as it was of the authors of papal documents and bulls, to find fit forms of public address. It was proper that, as his resources of artistic style increased, he should work also to increase the element in it of efficacy of communication. What is remarkable in the Cartoons is not the appearance in them of a rhetoric, but the effect in this rhetoric of absolute moral and artistic sincerity. In this, as in much else, Raphael transcends his cultural milieu, for the nature that this papacy was soon to manifest was precisely of disparity between grand form and diminished content: rhetorical in the pejorative sense in which the word is colloquially applied.

It was, of course, not the Cartoons themselves but their end products, the Tapestries, that were destined for a public audience. The fact that the Cartoons were not meant for public view, but only for the exploitation of the weavers, certainly to some extent conditioned their technique. So also, perhaps, did the relatively short time apparently permitted for their execution. As with other factors in the style of the Cartoons, these are conditions and not determinants: the technique in which the Cartoons are painted, at least where the execution is by Raphael himself, is the inevitable instrument of his ideas of larger style. The mode of handling that is most used in the figures of the Cartoons — forceful and general in modelling, and severely decisive in drawing with the brush — is to some extent surely more elliptical than it would have been in works intended for exhibition, and this reacts upon the character of figure style. But this is at most a minor qualification in our reading of Raphael's intent. In its character of generalization the technique of the Cartoons is coincident with the mode in which the whole work is conceived. The emphases and ellipses of this handling are necessary to a visual vocabulary of which the main purpose is no longer the description of sensuously recreated form, but the statement of ideas of form that underlie appearances.

The effect of Raphael's own handling in the Cartoons is of utmost efficiency and force; it is a vitalizing factor in the whole aesthetic texture of these works. In many passages there is an astonishing power of visual impact made by the handling,[356,363] not because of its effectiveness of illusion, but from its condensation of the described form and from the absolute control of succinct draughtsmanship and modelling: it is as a formal, and not a mimetic, experience that this handling tells. In other, rarer passages there is a contrasting gentleness and flexibility in execution, developed in subtlety even beyond the example of Raphael's preceding works. But on the whole the character of handling no longer has the inflection of an Italian, but of a Latin mode of speech. It is precisely the summary clarity of this inflection that is so much diminished when, among the figures, Penni imitates Raphael's execution; and it vanishes altogether when, as in the landscape backgrounds and in accessories, the matter treated by the brush is incidental and descriptive rather than ideal.

It was inevitable that Raphael's use of color in the Cartoons should conform, as a factor in their style, to the treatment of other — and for Raphael more primary — properties of form. There is in fact in the handling of color, even more obviously than in that of substantial forms, a distinction from Raphael's preceding works. In the Cartoons there is a reversal of the tendency, evident through the Stanze, to treat color more and more illusionistically, with an increasing richness of sensuous effect. The effect of color in the Cartoons is deliberately dry: the general sensation of color that comes from the assembled set is of a tonality like bleached bronze, seen in a bright and airless light. This tone results from the interaction of the grey or greyish green of settings in the paintings with the predominant hues in draperies of muted yellows and reds. Within each Cartoon there is of course some diversity of other hues, but they are, in contrast to the Stanze, most restricted and invariably in part neutralized. The choice falls mostly in the simple primaries; where climaxes of effect in color are desired they consist mostly of accents in the two dominant hues, of bleaching red or yellowed gold. The brushwork that applies color is broad, and in general textureless. Distribution of fields of color does not intend, as in the Stanze, to stimulate atmospheric interaction of tonalities but only to denote a local hue: color is a tint attached to, and circumscribed within, single elements of form. The color serves, inescapably, an ornamental purpose, but it seems more to intend a further differentiation, and thus clarifying, of the form. In the degree of identification of color with the separate forms, as well as in its primary simplicity, the color seems to heighten the presence that we have observed in the design of a trace of additive mentality; it is in the color system most of all that the Cartoons may suggest an element of likeness, in this ultimate classical style, with the modes of an earlier classicism of the late Quattrocento. However, color in the Cartoons is not applied only with its local field in mind; like the composition of substantial forms, colors also are related, though less evidently and less insistently, in connected schema. These color compositions, of sequence, contrast, or of repetition, are not only secondary in importance as design but — just as the local color is dependent on its form — are ancillary to the solid structure of the Cartoons' figure compositions. More than in any precedent in the Florentine tradition the proposition has been made explicit here that color is an adjunct of *disegno*, and like the design it must be, literally, ideated.

As with Raphael's mode of execution, it is possible, but here still less determining, that external circumstances contributed to his change of color style for the Cartoons. There may have been, but only very doubtfully, some intention to accommodate the color system of the models given to the weavers to their traditional resources. Certainly, there was some deliberate restriction on the brilliance and variety of colors in the Cartoons, so that their scheme might not conflict with the effect intended, in the actual weaving of the Tapestries, by the transcription of the highlights in gold thread. Seemingly there is some contradiction between the character of color in the Cartoons and that which, in their original state, must have existed in the Tapestries. The dry, bronzed, autumnal clarity of the Cartoons must have been much changed in its effect by the weaving into its color texture of the radiance of gold. A more persuasive harmony of tone, more atmospheric and, obviously, both visually and psychologically more opulent, must have been created by the gold. This change of visual and psychological tonality was not intended, however, to alter in any significant way the essential character of form and content established in the Cartoons. The sense of splendor — and, perhaps, even the idea of costliness that so much impressed contemporaries — was surely a not unimportant part of the impression Raphael wished the Tapestries to make: it is relevant to the aesthetic function of the Tapestries as decoration — specifically as ceremonial and papal decoration — and to the intention of public communication that their rhetorical character of style contains.

But this opulence is as far as it is possible to be from such naïve display as had once been made in Alexander Borgia's apartments. It is, first, the controlled opulence of the supremely civilized taste of Leo's time; and more important, its tone is dictated by the forms and meanings of which it is the epidermis: it is less opulence than a cast of splendor on an ultimate decorum. The paradox is present only in the words, but not in the Tapestries themselves as they once were, when they are felt as images of austere splendor. There is, further, more than a sensuous association with the radiance of gold in the woven scenes. This overtone of a precious and unnatural ambience is appropriate to the high ideality of what is seen and enacted in it; this is a fit atmosphere for archetypes. The use of gold to make both splendor and abstraction is a universal aesthetic device: in the Tapestries it recalls, however incidentally, its function in the paintings of the pre-Renaissance; at the same time it recalls, and in this case more relevantly, the mode and meaning of its use in Phidian Greece.

Whether in the Cartoons or the Tapestries the character of color is incident to the character of substantial form. Form, and content equally, have been made literally essential in these works. The whole design, the single form, the condensed technique, and the color all have in common the strong stress of their ideal value. The relation among them — among all important elements of style — is of a community of ideal values. This is different from the artistic construct devised by Raphael in the Stanze: there the work of art had been made by a process that we may describe as one of compromise between the sensuous and the ideal images of nature toward — roughly — a mean level between the two. The harmony of the Stanze frescoes — in more than the sense of that in their aesthetic structure — had been similarly made, of compromise between the actualities of human appearance and behavior and an ideal. In the Cartoons the actuality of nature has been yet more trenchantly observed than in the Stanze, but at the same time it has been more synthetically represented: the primary value of the image is its value of idea. The harmony in the Cartoons — again not only in the aesthetic sense but in the sphere and style of human being — depends much less than in the Stanze on adjustments made between nature and ideality, and more on relations among idealities as such. This harmony is one of coexistence among ideas, within a whole ordnance of form that is itself a manifest idea. The synthetic process in the Cartoons is one in which the separate elements of style, of themselves more ideal, are fused at a higher level of ideality than before.

If the style of the Stanze and their chronologically associated works are to represent for us the norm of classical style in High Renaissance painting then, evidently, the style which we have characterized in the Cartoons is no longer a normative classicism. Equally evidently, we are still dealing in the

Cartoons with a world of art that, in almost every fundamental way, belongs in one broad general community with the Stanze. What we observe in the Cartoons is a distinguishable, but not a separate phenomenon of style, which we have described as being, by inspection, a climactic development of High Renaissance classicism. In this ultimate classicism those propositions of style which are central and peculiar to the classicism of the High Renaissance are purified and magnified in aesthetic and spiritual force: in their demonstration of these propositions the Cartoons are clearer, more consistent and more nearly exclusive than any of Raphael's antecedent works. Not by imitation, but from this self-generated development of classical consistency, the style of the Cartoons suggests analogies, closer than it had been possible to make for Raphael's art before, with the classical style of Antiquity. One of the most important of these analogies is in the degree to which the style of the Cartoons has become, in a literal sense, humanistic: we have observed how, more evidently than in any earlier comparable works by Raphael, the formal substance of the Cartoons consists of, and is dominated by, the image of men, while space is no more than an adjunct to this humanity. This very mode of thought in which the Cartoons are conceived is like that of the Antique classical style in that it begins and, virtually, ends with the substantial image of ideal persons, whose setting in environment is aesthetically and contentually nearly neutral. The structure of these designs, made up of dense humanity, in some of the Cartoons displays an immutable geometrical logic, in others a crystalline discipline of cursive rhythm, which is like that of a Phidian relief style, as in the friezes of the Parthenon. And, though the actors of the Cartoons may be inspired with an intensity of feeling that is specifically Christian in its context, their expression of this feeling is distilled in a classical deliberation of its visible form: no matter how urgent their emotion, its form conveys the sense, as in Ancient classicism, of suspension or arrest. In these images appearances, emotions, and incidents are not merely transitory but partake, as in the older classicism, of the character of universals.

It remains true that this is not, nor is it historically possible that it could be, a classicism identical with that of any in Antiquity. What is impossible to this ultimate Raphaelesque classicism is the spiritual relaxation of the Ancient Golden Age. The emotion of the Cartoons is not merely Christian because their context of illustration is so, but because their mode of feeling is the consequence of a Christian history of experience of spiritual passion. It is a miracle not only of art but, in the larger sense, of cultural history, that this feeling should be expressed without compromise of its identity, and without loss in intensity, in formal distillates of such classical perfection. This feeling is a force in the Cartoons that shapes not only their contents but, in some instances, their character of form differently from an Antique classicism. When it is called into being in its full intensity by the subject matter, it may charge gesture with a severe explicitness of form, as well as of meaning, that is not usual to Ancient classical art, and may give to postures the sense of a particular power of impulsion or, contrariwise, of a tense rigidity. Even the general structure of design seems to partake, at least in the *Ananias* and *Elymas*, of this temper of intensity: by contrast with Ancient classical designs their clarity is almost too sharp. There is, so to speak, a strain of passion among the motives of this extreme intellectual precision.

While, then, on one hand qualities like those of an Antique classicism have emerged more strongly in the Cartoons than in Raphael's previous mature style, on the other hand there is also a growth in them of a particular element of Raphaelesque personality which, though it is expressed in classical forms — more exactly, in part sublimated into them — is not essentially classical. The specific intensity of spiritual sensation still links Raphael in his ultimate classical style — as it does also Michelangelo — to the Christian antecedents of his present culture. Because this intensity has magnified with the growth of personality, and because its expression is yet more explicit than before in the precise terms of this final classical vocabulary, the sense of relation to the tradition of a Christian art is now even more evident than in the period of the Stanze. There is, in the Cartoons, an element of resemblance — far less important than that to Antique classical style — to a much earlier, and unequivocally Christian, interpretation of classicism, in the art of Giotto. Some of the same figures in the Cartoons that, in their formal beauty, seem like those of classic Greece, seem also, in their archetypal simplicity and force of gesture, posture, and expression of countenance, Giottesque. And from what we have described as the strain of passion in Raphael's intellectualization of forms — in the intensity that, on occasion, forces an idea toward the character of dogma, or insists on the arbitrary clarity of schema — there is a likeness, in the most general sense, with Giottesque, protoclassical, abstraction. Thus the most elementary aspect of Raphael's clarity of composition in the Cartoons suggests an affinity with Giotto; so, even more evidently, does the handling of space, with its alternative modes of neutrality or of reduction to a geometrically condensed and simple stagelike scheme. The Giottesque analogy is incidental, but it is a point of some historical interest that there should come to be, in Raphael's most classically idealized images of Christian art, a kind of community with its first Italian, still abstracting, protoclassical antecedent.

In Raphael this reference to pre-Renaissance Christian art is not a result of any deliberate intent, and it is more than dubious that it should have had its cause either in any memory of the Giottesque style or in a renewed experience of Giotto's painting, as during Raphael's (only presumed) brief trip to Florence in the autumn of 1515. With the author of the other major High Renaissance decoration in the Sistine Chapel we have seen that the case is different: Michelangelo's reference to preclassical, or still primitively classical, modes of idealization was deliberate, and apparently an active factor in his own evolving of a mature classical ideal style. Within the classicism of Michelangelo's images in the Sistine, even more than in Raphael's Tapestries, the "modern" component that is the consequence of Christian personality is apparent. The emotional intensity that inhabits the later figures of the Sistine especially, and which permeates their entire substance of classically manipulated form, exceeds that in the actors of the Tapestries. What Michelangelo's creatures contain of passion is more urgent, and at the same time complex to a degree far higher than in Raphael; qualitatively speaking the distinction is still one between levels of the superlative. But it had occurred in Raphael's art before that, aside from any inherent developmental impulse, Michelangelo's example had precipitated in him the ambition to a higher spiritual power; that such inspiration had at least in part been Michelangelesque is specifically evident only in the instances, like the *Heraclitus* of the Segnatura,[167] that are recognizably imitative. Given the fact that the Tapestries were intended to complete the decoration of which Michelangelo's Ceiling was the crown — that Raphael's Tapestries were, so to speak, to be confronted, on each occasion of their exposition, with the Ceiling — it is more than likely that, in the course of creation of the Cartoons, the Sistine Ceiling became an even more particular object of study for Raphael than it had been before. The spiritual stature to which the content of the Tapestries has risen, in so far as it is distinct from that in the Stanze, may have taken some part of its initial impulse from Michelangelo's example.

No explicit imitation in the Tapestries documents this possibility. What is precisely Michelangelesque in them is not more than the incidents of anatomical emphasis, multiplied beyond the similar occurrences in the Stanza d'Eliodoro (but not much more evident than in other preceding works, such as the *Galatea*). Yet, in certain important respects other than that of spiritual stature, the Tapestries show analogies in their new characteristics of style to the style of the later Sistine; again the relation is of broadly general factors that yield no evidence to document a possible, or even likely point of departure in Michelangelo for Raphael's own formulation of them. The most tangible of these factors is what we have described, in the Cartoons, as their literally humanistic character of style, with their primary emphasis on human substance and their significant diminution of the role of space. No more aggressive instance of this interpretation of classical style exists than in Michelangelo's developed paintings on the Ceiling. Similarly, the dominating tendency in the Cartoons to compression of dense substance toward the forward plane, and to relief-like stratification and outline of the figure mass, recall the mode of Michelangelo in his central narrative bays. The color of the Cartoons too — and even that of the gold-heightened Tapestries — suggests the possibility of their intended harmony with the patinaed metallic tonality of the Ceiling. Certainly, in a much more basic matter, that of the stress of ideal values in all representational and aesthetic elements of the Cartoons, the precedent of the later bays of Michelangelo's Ceiling was inescapably exemplary and in some measure formative. We have indicated before that the Sistine Ceiling contains in its span the summary evolution of the classical style; Raphael's development, in the three years since the completion of Michelangelo's Ceiling, to the ultimate classical style of the Tapestries is, in an elementary sense, a recapitulation of Michelangelo's accomplishment.

Whether it was achieved independently or in possible partial derivation, it is to be expected that Raphael's evolution to a stage and kind of classicism comparable to that in the later Ceiling should exhibit the analogies with its style that we have discussed. The analogies, however, are general; they do not affect the vast repertory of particular ideas and forms that Raphael has evolved to demonstrate the general proposition of an ultimate classical style, nor do they diminish the power and novelty of his inventions. His particular accomplishment in the Tapestries is not less original because certain of its basic premises were anticipated by Michelangelo. In one respect, an area of distinction between Raphael and Michelangelo has narrowed in the style of the Tapestries, in that in them there is a lessening of Raphael's previous concern with specifically painterly and pictorial, in the sense of spatial, values; like the Ceiling — in fact reversing the tendency toward an increasing painterliness we observed there — the style of the Tapestries is, more than before in Raphael, draughtsmanly and plastic, "formal" in a way that in part suggests the character of sculpture. But what is ineradicably distinct in the higher classical style of the Tapestries from that of the Ceiling is the Raphaelesque personality, more than ever in this, his climactic development, intellectually lucid and intelligible. Since his beginnings it had been one of Raphael's historical functions to express the propositions of the classical style more clearly than his contemporaries — to resolve what were private meditations for Leonardo or Michelangelo into publicly accessible communication. It is this character that gives the Tapestries, within the history of High Renaissance classicism, canonical value, as of promulgated law, for the stage of higher classical style they represent; it is this clear and extended demonstration of its kind of meaning that is not shared by the work, similar in style, that Michelangelo left in his swift and lonely progress across the Sistine Ceiling.

THE STANZA DELL' INCENDIO

On July 1, 1514, Raphael wrote to his uncle Simone Ciarli to inform him of his appointment as architect of St. Peter's, and in the same letter told him "ho cominciato un altra stantia per S. Sta a dipignere" (Golzio, 32). This room was the Stanze della Torre Borgia. Flanking the Stanza della Segnatura on the side opposite to it from the Stanza d'Eliodoro, it would be known later, from the principal piece of Raphael's decoration in it, as the Stanza dell' Incendio.

There is only slight evidence to specify what Raphael meant by his bald statement of a beginning in this new room. On the basis of a preparatory drawing (Vienna, Albertina)[373] sent as a gift to Albrecht Dürer and inscribed by him with the date 1515, we may deduce that the probable first concern of Raphael in this Stanza was with the fresco of the *Battle of Ostia*.[374] Evidence of style, of the most general kind, supports this view. The composition of the *Ostia* looks back to, and in a sense develops out of, the probable penultimate fresco in the Stanza d'Eliodoro, the *Attila*,[221] and in the manner of its painting — heavy in chiaroscuro, with strong highlights, and darks often indistinct and weakly blurred — it relates to the *Attila* and the *Liberation* both, and to the parts especially in those frescoes that are, as this whole fresco is, the handwork of assistants. At the same time, a link exists to connect the composition of the *Ostia* and the earliest stage of planning of the Tapestry Cartoons. There is a drawing in the Albertina (S.R. 225),[372] by Penni, for an unused scheme for the presumable first among the Cartoons, the *Draught of Fishes*; in compositional system it most strongly resembles the fresco of the *Ostia*. This drawing could be regarded as an intermediate term between the compositional style of the *Ostia* and that of the Cartoons, and help (in combination with the observation on technique that we have made) to locate the design of the fresco either just prior to the first work on the Cartoons or roughly contemporary with it, in early 1515. That the development of design and the execution of the fresco are probably contemporary with the first Cartoons is further indicated by the presence, in the *Ostia* and the *Draught of Fishes*, of some common types and motives.

The evidence of subject matter for the dating of the *Ostia* is unclear, and not so decisive as the circumstances indicated above. The fresco describes a historical event of the fourth Leo's reign, a victory in naval battle with the Saracens off that port. The analogue to the current papal reign, necessary in these histories, has often been taken to be specific: to Leo X's escape from a pirate raid on Ostia in April 1516. Since, as Dürer's drawing indicates, the fresco was in preparation not later than 1515, it is more probable that the reference of the *Ostia* was more generally intended. From the beginning of his reign Leo X had been much occupied with the problem of military action against the Turks. Early in 1515 he had appealed to the Christian princes to help in a crusade, and had fitted out a papal fleet for this purpose at Ancona.

As Raphael had written to his uncle, he was burdened in the second half of 1514 with a double charge. In the first months that succeeded his appointment to St. Peter's it is likely that his chief concern was with that supremely important task, rather than with the active prosecution of yet another decorative scheme. When he did turn his attention to this scheme it was necessary for him, for the first time in his career — initiating a major precedent — to entrust not part alone of a large work, but all of its execution and certainly most of its preparation to a helper. The emergence into a phenomenal technical precocity of the young Giulio Romano, to whom the *Ostia* was given over, would have encouraged such acceptance of a surrogate. The receipt of the commission for the Tapestry Cartoons also intervened between Raphael and his obligation to the Stanza dell' Incendio. We have seen the nature of Raphael's involvement with the Cartoons, and the extent of his profound personal commitment to them. The Cartoons were, in every sense, much more interesting to the artist: much more honorific in the destination of their final products than this one more, and architecturally least agreeable, of the

Stanze; and the Tapestries were directly to be compared in their destined place with Michelangelo. It is not impossible, but unlikely that Raphael made any preparation of a design for a second fresco in the Stanza dell' Incendio while he was still heavily engaged with the Cartoons during 1515.

Of the subjects of the three remaining major frescoes in this room two, the *Coronation of Charlemagne*[380] and the *Oath of Leo*,[383] make specific iconographic reference to events that postdate the time of Raphael's work at least on the bulk of the Tapestry Cartoons. The *Coronation* explicitly refers to the happening of November 1515, when Leo X received the homage of King Francis I in Bologna; this subject could hardly have been assigned to Raphael before the Pope's return from this meeting in February 1516. The *Oath of Leo* is inscribed with the legend "God, and not man, is the Judge of Bishops"; the contemporary reference is to Leo X's repromulgation of the Bull *Unam Sanctam* at the eleventh session of the Lateran Council, December 19, 1516. The name fresco of the room, the *Fire in the Borgo*,[376] offers no such conveniently specific chronological reference. Usually, it is taken as analogy for Leo X's acts in connection with the termination of the Pisan schism in June 1513 — a metaphor for the extinction of doctrinal and political conflagration in the Church. No external reason makes it impossible that a design of some kind might have been prepared for the *Fire* concurrently, or just after, that for the *Ostia*, but even if this should have been the case, the style of the painting makes it clear that such a design would have been substantially remade, or altogether reinvented, at a measurably later date. The fresco depends so markedly on the style of the Cartoons that its precise ideation, as well as its execution, must be at earliest contemporary with the full definition of the mode of the Cartoons, and more probably succeeds them. Here, as in the *Ostia*, the development and execution of Raphael's invention was left to Giulio Romano. The level of his technical efficiency, and the development of his explicit personal style in the *Fire*, is advanced so far beyond the *Ostia* as to require, on this account as well, a later date.

While the *Fire* was in progress, probably in 1516, Penni (with incidental help) developed and executed Raphael's designs for the *Coronation* and then, in early 1517, for the *Oath*. The *Fire* finished, Giulio himself designed as well as executed the Royal Protectors of the Church in the Stanza's basamenti.[385] A date is inscribed in the embrasure of the window under the fresco of the *Oath*: "1517, anno Pontif IV" (March 19, 1517); before July 19, 1517 the Stanza dell' Incendio had been altogether finished. On that date Bembo wrote to Bibbiena that "le camere di N. S. che Raffaello ha dipinte" were "bellissime," and almost always well populated with Cardinals (Golzio, 57).

As had been the case in the Stanza d'Eliodoro, in the new room half at least of the subject matter was invented after, and in this case well after, the beginning of the decoration, and the times of invention of designs were spread out more than they had been in the preceding room. In the Eliodoro, vast care had been taken to accommodate each event of the whole decoration with the others; in the Incendio there is no such visible concern, and a most unlike effect. Each fresco is, in design, a highly characterized episode of its own separate moment of invention. The classical concept of relation among elements of one picture scheme, so highly perfected in the first two Stanze and in the Tapestries, and reused in all of Raphael's other late decorative works, is not operative here.

In the Stanza d'Eliodoro the partly occasional and successive subject matter was governed, in its incorporation in the room, by a general preconceived iconographic theme. The specific differences of subject matter were in part resolved and in part made dramatically meaningful for the basic theme by the unity of aesthetic structure in which the subjects were contained. In the Stanza dell' Incendio the same iconographic principle of relation to a pre-set basic theme controls the admission of successively found episodes but, unlike in the Eliodoro, the community of ideas is not reinforced by their relation in a community of form.

In general, the theme of the Incendio room is an extension of that in the frescoes of the Stanza d'Eliodoro. They treated, by historical analogy, of the intervention of divine power in behalf of the papal Church; the paintings in the new room refer to the powers that this Church, with its divine sanction, may exercise itself through the person of the Pope. Beyond the still uncertain specific reference of the *Ostia* is the idea of the exercise of the Pope's temporal power to defend his Church and state against the Infidel. In the *Incendio* the underlying theme is that of papal power to protect the Church, and its temporal seat in Rome, from doctrinal and civil disturbances. The *Coronation of Charlemagne* reminds civil princes of their subservience to the authority of the Pope, and the *Oath* reminds both civil and spiritual princes whence this supreme authority derives. Literally underlining the embracing theme, the Royal Protectors and servants of the papal power support it in the basamenti.

The whole message is apparent enough, but it is perhaps indicative of a growing concern that it be understood that the two later frescoes are more explicit as historical illustrations and as applicable analogues for current politics and problems of the Church. Under iconographic dictation from the patron the decoration of the Stanza dell' Incendio, as it proceeds, takes on the character less of a proclamation of the papal powers than of defensive assertion of them. By this pointed propaganda the room becomes less general in intent of meaning than it had set out to be, and descends to a level of ideality of content far below the high declaration of force and faith that had been made by Julius in the Stanza d'Eliodoro.

More than their tonality of content, it is the character of form in the frescoes of the Stanza dell' Incendio that has cost them, heavily, in critical reputation. They are distinctly less in quality than the preceding Stanze or than the Tapestry Cartoons, for the most part also precedent; and they are also different, and seemingly less, in their stylistic kind. In both respects, of quality wholly, and in part of kind, the reason for the difference lies with the execution of the frescoes in their entirety by assistants. This is the first vitally important instance in Raphael's career where we are dealing with a series of what we have described as aesthetic compounds. If, however arbitrarily, the differences of quality from preceding works can be set aside, the differences in style of these frescoes can be assessed in a historically meaningful way. Some of these differences are literally basic; they are in the essential structure of design of the painting, and in the general distribution of the forms to articulate the meaning of the subject. These, we believe, are Raphael's responsibility, in indications of varying exactness supplied for the design of each fresco. Other distinctions result from the visual epidermis the executant has given to this presumed Raphael design. In the case of Penni's scenes, such differences are not historically meaningful and are also of only negative qualitative effect. However, in the frescoes of Giulio's execution — and more particularly in the *Fire*, where his personality is matured and explicit — meaningful effects of style are not only in the surface, but in Giulio's own development of Raphael's first indications of design; to that degree where his execution and Raphael's controlling, but not inflexible, original idea have become an aesthetic amalgam.

It has often been the critical habit to read and assess the frescoes of the Incendio only in terms of their epidermis, and to consider that they are altogether the creation, from the initial design onward, of their executants. The evidence for Raphael's initial indications and for some measure of his continuing supervision is considerable, but it is not unequivocal. None of the assumed first inventions of design survives, and of the preparatory drawings that exist not one, the drawing presented to Dürer included, is by Raphael himself (though he well may have retouched this one); they are by Giulio or by Penni,[382,384] for their respectively executed frescoes. But such a situation in respect to the surviving drawings is not much different from that which exists for most of the later products of the Raphael shop. The literary evidence for Raphael's responsibility is more assuring. Raphael's own statement of July 1514: "ho cominciato un altra stantia per S. Sta a dipignere" (Golzio, 32) implies more than an involvement in the role of entrepreneur; Bembo's notice, four years later, spoke of the Incendio in an including phrase with the two preceding Stanze as "Le camere di N. S. che Raffaello ha dipinte." Much later, Vasari, in his life of Raphael (IV, 358–59), described the late shop procedure, and reported that the master followed "l'ordine che egli aveva cominciato delle camere del papa, e dalle sale, nelle quali del continuo teneva della gente che con i disegni suoi medesimi gli tiravano innanzi l'opera, ed egli continuamente ordinando ogni cosa."

It is Giulio who, among these assistants, is most often advanced as a claimant to independent invention in the Incendio, but in his life by Vasari — compiled, it will be remembered, on information personally given — no such claim is made. However, Vasari's language is not wholly decisive. He states (V, 524) that Giulio "Aiutò anco a Raffaello colorire molte cose nella camera di Torre Borgia, dove è l'incendio"; and without change from the locution "aiutò . . . colorire" continues "e particolarmente l'imbasamento." If any part of the invention of the Stanza dell' Incendio might be assigned with some confidence to Giulio, it is that of the basamenti. There is no doubt that, by 1517, the young Giulio was capable of independent entire invention of such figures as inhabit the basamenti, but it is more speculative that, a year or two before, he was already competent to create, without reference to Raphael, the complex systems of the *Ostia* and the *Fire*. Giulio's earliest wholly independent panel paintings show no such organizing powers. Penni was, as least chronologically, much more mature than Giulio, but at whatever age the Fattore lacked any significant power of independent invention. In all four of the Incendio designs their basic structure exceeds, in breadth and scale of effect, anything that is known of the surely independent exercises in design of Giulio during Raphael's lifetime, and of Penni through the whole extent of his career.

In the first three of the Incendio frescoes, the armature beneath the epidermis of design is in each case a significant inventive development of new possibilities of composition. They are not mere derivations from Raphael's prior or contemporary compositional style, nor only disfigurements of it by lesser personalities; they rather should be seen as experimental reachings, at once bold and calculating, in directions implied by, but as yet untested in the Stanza d'Eliodoro or the Tapestry Cartoons. The complex, multifigured and movemented style of the *Repulse of Attila* is charged, in the design of the *Ostia*, with a higher pressure of activity, both of narrative action and of form. In the *Fire*, the severe rhetorical style of the Tapestries is reformed for use with the scale and variety of the Stanza narratives. Whether from Raphael's intention or from Giulio's interpretation, this fresco explores, in its equal emphasis upon contesting powers of form and expression, a critical limit of the classical style. The *Coronation* — superficially the least attractive fresco in this room — is the most daring manipulation of a design in space since the beginning of the classical style; it is impossible that so unorthodox a novelty should have been generated in the mind of Penni. All three works — the *Ostia* just before or concurrently with the first Cartoons, and the *Fire* and the *Coronation* after them — are radical investigations of new directions in a style that intendedly extends the limits, so superlatively and finally defined in the Cartoons, of classicism. It is this temper of experiment, in part compromising of classical style, that dominates more than half of Raphael's production after the Cartoons of 1515. But, as we have also earlier observed, this temper was not exclusive, but concurrent with a continuing more nearly purely classical ambition. In the Stanza dell' Incendio itself the design of the last fresco, the *Oath of Leo* — or at least its original idea before it was dissolved and debased by Penni — represents this aspect of continuity, beyond the time of the Tapestry Cartoons, of an intent of style like that in them, of stilled architectonic discipline.

The structural inventions in these frescoes are, then, Raphael's responsibility and, to an extent impossible to determine, so also may be some part of the accent of surface style in these works. It is important for our history of Raphael's artistic personality to establish at least the basic factor of his responsibility; but in this case we can do no other than to read the Incendio frescoes not as they may have been ideated by him but as they exist, as aesthetic compounds. The element of personality in invention, whether it is accepted for Raphael or rejected, does not alter the meaning, for the larger and not merely personal history of classical style, of the facts of style as they are in these frescoes; for that history these facts remain the same.

The result, as Giulio has interpreted it, is very different, but a fundamental intention in the *Ostia* [374-5] was like that in the contemporary Cartoons: as in them, the intention was to magnify the force of expressive impact of the classical style beyond its level in the Stanza d'Eliodoro. As in the Cartoons, a heightened emphasis and clarity were employed as basic means to this expressive end. Each major figure in the *Ostia* is given a higher quotient of identity — a measure of distinctness as a separable form within the context of its group and of the whole design — which is like that we observe in the *Draught of Fishes*; and to emphasize further the force of impact of these forms, they are given (in comparison with the figures of the Eliodoro scenes) an increased sense of scale. In compositional arrangement the main group at least in the *Ostia* is defined with a schematic clarity that suggests the character of the Tapestry designs, and contrasts with the more interwoven groupings of the Eliodoro. There is an increased stress in the effect of clear arrangement on one plane of this main group also. As in the *Draught of Fishes,* the principal group in the *Ostia* is disposed on a plane behind which, and to one side, a secondary group is set. In both the *Ostia* and that first Cartoon, the basic elements of design consist of two interlocked arched shapes, disposed in parallel. The resemblance between the two designs is accentuated by the inclusion in both of similar motives, as particularly of the forward-striding figure in the center of each composition and the boatman to the farthest right.

A kinship of ambition to expressive impact, and of some means of design and motive, thus exists between the *Ostia* and the first Cartoons; however, the subject and the wall space of the *Ostia* — and of the Stanze in general — presented a different set of terms in which the primary intention had to be worked out. Where the Cartoons depend on strictest concentration of effects of form and content, the shape and subject matter of the Stanze scenes is more diffuse. In them incident and population are more varied, and their drama is of more complex historical narrative, more elaborate if only from the need to fill the given space. A sequence of incidents, not a rhetorically stringent near-simultaneity, is described in the *Ostia* and in the succeeding *Fire in the Borgo.* This greater internal variety of subject matter demands a corresponding variety in form; there is a continuing application of Alberti's old prescription for *copia* in histories. Where the Cartoons take their point of departure from the one experiment in formal simplification in the preceding Stanza, in the *Liberation*, the *Ostia* instead continues the mode of movemented complexity that had reached its apparent culmination in the *Attila*. The temper of activity in the *Attila* is here tested at a new level: the figures are, singly, more movemented, and because each figure is, as we have seen, more emphatically defined, its effect of action is more evident. The collective pattern of activity made by these emphatic movements in their sum is far more complicated than in the *Attila*. Other devices of the repertory of the *Attila* are extended here: the effect of asymmetrical composition is intensified, here almost with precarious result, and extension into space is more insistently explored.

These last devices in particular are unlike the contemporary intention of devices of form in the Cartoons, and they are by the same token not consistent with those elements within the fresco which resemble the Cartoons. The urgent spatiality is in conflict with the emphatic definition by the major figures of the forward plane; and the movemented asymmetry of composition is opposed by almost obvious devices that are meant to contain it in a final balance. These effects of contradiction are not confined to the larger elements of form; they are pervasively apparent. Almost every indication of activity in a figure, despite its stress of complex energetic pattern, seems organically inert: these are patterns of movement, but not communications of its vital force. Movement is as if crystallized by the too-specific emphasis with which it has been described. In part, these tensions would not seem wholly consciously intended, but there are places in the design where it is unmistakable that effects of opposition are deliberately meant. In the main figure group [375] there is an inescapable confrontation of opposing movements each, as it were, negating the other; and in the dense core of this group, utterly constrained within it, three further forms are literally locked in postures of extreme complexity. In the modelling of the figures in stressed light and accented dark — a technique schematized from the handling of the *Liberation* and *Attila* — there is a further provocation of effects of contrast. As much as the pattern made by the movement of the actors, the pattern of chiaroscuro that is attached to it creates the temper, complexly active and descriptive, of this scene.

It is self-evident that, whatever its elements of relation to the Tapestry Cartoons or to the preceding Stanza, the character of style in the *Ostia* resembles neither. The matter out of which the scene is made is, to begin with, the same as that from which, in the Cartoons and the Eliodoro, Raphael creates images in synthesis, but the *Ostia* does not achieve synthesis, even of its form alone. This result is not the merely negative consequence of ineptitude; we have seen that there are, in parts of this fresco, clear evidences of a different order of aesthetic intent. If we accept, as logically we must, the evidence that the contemporary Cartoons afford of the kinds of aesthetic intention that are possible at this time to Raphael, then we cannot accept, as part of his intent, the tensions and the stiffly articulate disharmonies of the *Ostia*. These are due to the working of Raphael's assistant, skilled in the vocabulary of classicism but in part impervious to its aesthetic essence, and in part actively dissympathetic to it; obviously, Raphael would have resolved the problem differently.

Yet, it is possible that the problem, even as Raphael had posed it, was not susceptible of an unequivocally classical solution. In the Cartoons, Raphael was able to accomplish a higher development of classical style through a process that was in important respects restrictive; the style of the Cartoons is deliberately less complex than that of the antecedent Stanze. In the *Ostia* the ambition to a higher urgency of expressive power is — or was, in its presumable original conception — as much as in the Cartoons, but there was not, in the fresco, a comparable limitation of the range of formal means. The *Ostia* was required to achieve its higher expressive end employing all, and not just part, of the apparatus customary to the Stanze scenes; and to achieve this intended higher contentual result the formal apparatus, too, had to be magnified. The magnification was achieved, as in the Cartoons, through stress — inevitably, as we have seen already in the Cartoons, to some degree analytic in its effect. The consequence of trying to say so much in a formal language so complex and — at least incipiently analytically — emphatic, could well have caused, even in Raphael's personal development of his idea, a visible strain within a structure of classical synthesis originally intended for this fresco. The fissure in classical style that occurs in the *Ostia* could thus be Raphael's responsibility.

That this may be so is indicated by the fact that in no succeeding narrative-dramatic work of approximately comparable complexity, even on much smaller scale, does Raphael again give his pupils a design that is resolved in unequivocally classical style, of that kind which we recognize from the manner of the first two Stanze. It is still explicit that, in the *Ostia*, its development and execution by Giulio is the final agent of disruption, but perhaps of a proposition given by Raphael that was of itself not wholly classically tenable.

Despite his vast precocious competence, the Giulio who was entrusted with the execution of the *Ostia* was not yet wholly technically formed, nor yet quite explicit in artistic personality. His effects in the *Ostia* are not consistently sufficiently premeditated; the image he creates is not altogether a controlled act of artistic will, either as a translation of Raphael's intent or as an expression of his own. The somewhat inchoate purpose of the *Ostia* makes it so in style as well; it is an important symptomatic work, but not a monument by which we may define a clear or decisive fact in the history of style. This is no longer true of Giulio's execution of the second of the Incendio frescoes, the *Fire in the Borgo.*[376-9] The time — less, almost surely, than a year — that had intervened since the beginning of the *Ostia*, as well as his experience in that fresco, sufficed to mature his hand and specify his personality. It is also likely that, the work on the Cartoons over or toward its end, Raphael's attention to the *Fire* could be more than he had given to the *Ostia*, not only in invention and development of the first design but in supervision and criticism of his executant. There is a change in Giulio's technique in the *Fire* that is also, by contrast with the *Ostia*, a remarkable improvement. The direction of this change is toward a close approximation of the manner Raphael had developed in the Cartoons; Giulio's fresco style no longer refers, as it did in the *Ostia*, to the chiaroscuro style of the preceding Stanza.

Almost the whole vocabulary of the *Fire*, not only its technique, depends on the Cartoons. The figure style is that invented in the Cartoons, with highly characterized and powerful anatomies, and so is the severe declamatory style of acting. The figures are, in the manner of the Cartoons, designed more for forcefulness of impact of their shape and action than for grace; here, too, contrapposto is matter for incidents, and not for the substance of design. The figures, and not only the main ones, are stressed in their identity, and the relation of their shapes to one another, into groups and in the whole design is, more than in the Cartoons, by an angular rather than a curvilinear geometry. In the content that has been established for its subject matter the *Fire* shares the rhetoric tonality of the Cartoons; it is less than the *Ostia* in a mode of narrative.

The incoherence, verging on disorder, of the *Ostia* gives way to a mentality of strict discipline: there are no unpremeditated effects in the *Fire*. The complex matter of the composition is not less than in the *Ostia*, but it has been, as it were, resymmetrized according to the most stringent canon of the Tapestry Cartoons. Within the composition, the active movement of the groups has been cast in patterns of severe geometric order, and the links of pattern from one group to the next are almost too apparently deliberated. The sharpness of intellectual and visual definition of each form, whether it is a category of design, like space or substance, or merely a detail, is not only modelled on the example of the Cartoons but intensified beyond it. But where the effects of definition in the Cartoons are of supreme lucidity, in the *Fire* they become even harshly insistent. This insistence of sharp statement is applied to factors of form and content which, by the very fact of their insistence, assume effects of contrast in relation to each other and to their entire context. The results of this emphasis of definition, applied throughout the extent of the fresco, are now explicitly, rather than, as in the Cartoons, only incipiently, analytic.

The increase of explicitness, of intention and of language, derived from the Cartoons promotes a higher force of content in this fresco than in the *Ostia*, but this force is also more disjunctively expressed. In the *Fire*, the official subject, the miraculous intervention of the Pope that halts the fire, has been inverted in order to attain a more vigorous affective purpose: in terms of a contemporary headline the subject would read "FIRE IN THE BORGO miraculously halted by the Pope." The action of the Pope has been displaced into the distant background, and what in a more literal report should be only by-play, the commotion of the anonymous crowd, becomes instead the major theme. These foreground figures [377] are, in general, represented in states of strong physical and emotional activity: their actions are described as moments of acute physical or psychic strain. The postures of action make movemented shapes, and these have been so drawn as to accentuate the effect of their activity, not so much as physical facts as in aesthetic impact on the viewer's eye. The figures have been arranged in a compositional pattern of which the effect of activity is more urgent, because more articulate, than in the *Ostia*.

The architecture also, in comparison to that of the Cartoons or even of the previous Stanza, has been made more energetically active. It has been spatially reexpanded from the types of setting that were in the Cartoons, to reacquire instead the full effect of perspective and substantial definition that was customary in the architecture of the Stanze. But this setting is no longer a symmetrical and stabilizing unity, only internally differentiated into movement; the background here becomes a set of multiple and fragmentary parts, which shuttle in alternating steps into the depth of the design. The parts of architecture are each sensible as an asserted, though fragmentary, identity, as much set one against the other as they are related in an including logic of design. The space itself — extending a device first used more tentatively in the *Expulsion of Heliodorus* — has been given a strong perspective thrust. Much more than in the *Ostia*, the urgent effect of perspective space is made in contrast to a strict definition by the major figures of the foreground.

The figures are not less subject to a process like that in the setting, of insistent, separating, formal and expressive emphases. Like the elements of architecture, the figures are so singly stressed that, to a degree not comparable in the *Ostia*, and unequivocally more even than in the Cartoons, they are distinguished by silhouette and spatial interval from one another. This analytic process is only just contained, as in the elements of setting, by marked and evident — and also emphatic — larger order of their groups and of the whole figure composition.

The analytic tendency so marked within the larger discipline of the *Fire*, and so much more explicitly articulate in it than in the *Ostia*, is a logical consequence — or better, a consequence that has been overreached — of a development that had begun in the preceding Stanza. We observed of the

Eliodoro frescoes that they were constructed by a process different from that in the frescoes of the Segnatura: not by a continuous differentiation of each whole but by broadly generalized division into complementary parts. There is, further, a tendency — first evident in the right half of the *Expulsion*, and still more clearly demonstrated in the *Liberation* — to articulate the elements, in one case of a group, in the other of the entire fresco, with more separate distinctness. This increasing clarity of articulation is the result of a purely classical motivation, and its culminating form, in the Tapestry Cartoons, is one of the components of the ultimate classicism of their style. As it is demonstrated there, this tendency is complementary to an increased power of synthesis, achieved partly by restrictive means, of those designs. However, in the *Ostia* incipiently, and precisely in the *Fire*, the process of distinction has been so far stressed, within their more complex contexts, that it is no longer complementary to synthesis but in contrast with it. Confirming and specifying the symptoms manifested in the *Ostia*, in the *Fire* the effects and intention of analysis are so pronounced that they create a conflict with the classical ambition, here still no less positively entertained, of synthesis.

In the *Fire* classical synthesis is compromised by separation in analysis of that which, in the previous history of the classical style, had existed in a fused and equal harmony: reason and emotion, ideal and real, order and accident, activity and stasis, and a host of other nominal antitheses. These factors are now used instead as if in effortful compensation of each other; but used in this way they do not produce the effect, so evident in the Eliodoro frescoes, of their resolution in synthetic equilibrium. It is at this point that a visible seam appears in the hitherto integral system of the classical style, and the structure of the style is, in our geological simile, as if faulted.

At most, effects of tension, at the least a sense of disparity, inhabits almost every element of style in the *Fire*. This disparity applies, too, to the relation in the fresco between form and content. Intrinsically, the subject does not ask so great a charge of drama as the artist means it to convey. Unlike the powerful vehicles of the Eliodoro scenes this subject is, in its bare essence, hardly a dramatic history. To make drama of it it has been necessary to invent richly, not only a repertory of human situations but a content of historical and archaeological reference. The inventions are appropriate to the occasion, but they exceed its intrinsic motive force of meaning: the dramatic repertory does not so much grow from the subject as it is imposed on it. The scene retains its air of an invention; the effects in this fine commotion are not wholly in proportion to their cause. This already sensible disparity is increased by a formal result of the application to the actors of the separating force of stress: because they articulate their content more separately from one another they are thus yet more detached from whatever dramatically unifying, but in this case already insufficient, motivation that the scene may have. In actors who are as removed as these from direct expression of a content it is their form of action that assumes the major value: the form acquires, by default of content, a disparate power of interest and impact.

There are specifiable symptoms in the *Fire* of a concern with forms as separable from a content of emotion; and such a separation is an index of the working of one among the processes we earlier described of dissolution of classical synthesis: the isolation of an element out of synthesis for particular development. In the group at the left in this scene, who descend from the wall with such visible effort (but with no clear indication of why it is necessary that they do so) it is evidently the form of their gymnastic actions that concerns the artist, far more than their meaning. In the figure of the nude, straining youth — gratuitously nude — there is an intention to emulate, more identifiably than in any incident in the Cartoons — the example of Michelangelo; a similar intention appears also in the group farther to the left in which reference is made to the legend of Aeneas and Anchises.[378] But in their excess of formal demonstration over motive these anatomical displays are precisely unlike the contemporary or recent Michelangelo. The precedent in him for such an exploitation of anatomy was long past and far away, in the *Cascina* cartoon. Oppositely, not masculine power of form but female grace is taken as a sufficient and separable theme: the famous *Canephore*[379] at the right of the fresco is the complement of the nude athlete. In the *Canephore*, narrative meaning is not more than a pretext for her calculated handsomeness of drapery and pose. And, like the Anchises reference to the left, she affords an opportunity for a classical quotation, carefully underlined as such quotations were not in their earlier use. Even in the central group of figures, whose actions are so dramatically developed, the meaning of posture and gesture on one hand, and on the other their formal handsomeness, call themselves to our attention separately. Their meaning is of response to a momentary situation, but the forms of their response are rigidly deliberate.

This disparity of form and content, in which the theme is not adequate to the charge of expression laid on it, and where the primacy of meaning tends to be assumed by form, requires the application of the pejorative sense of the word "rhetorical." It is a rhetoric *faussée* that characterizes the discourse of this fresco, and in this the *Fire* misfires precisely in the ambition, surely entertained for it, to emulate the expression of the Tapestry Cartoons. That the rhetoric of the *Fire* should go false is a necessary consequence of the faulted machinery of classical style used to achieve it.

The style we have characterized in the *Fire* is that of the actual image, the aesthetic compound. We have observed that, within this compound, the roles both of Raphael and of Giulio are more explicit than in the preceding fresco in this room: of Raphael in his presumed increased specific responsibility for design and supervision, and of Giulio in his more articulate development of hand and personality. The situation is thus more sharply defined than in the *Ostia*, but its basic components are still much the same: a given problem which, in the urgencies and complexities of its intent, was not wholly classically soluble; and a working-out in painting of this problem by an executant disposed to intensify, in the data given him, its aspects of unclassical potential. Whatever Giulio's positive imitative disposition may have been, he transposed Raphael's intention into, at best, an aesthetic synonym which, as is the habit of synonyms, does not quite mean the same thing.

Giulio's initial alterations were effective in matters particular to the role of an executant, more than in large factors of aesthetic structure. In Giulio's mode of drawing in the *Fire* he has exaggerated into hard incisiveness the clarity and force of Raphael's contemporary drawing style; of himself Raphael could not and did not so drastically or so quickly change the manner he had demonstrated in the Cartoons. Raphael's process of draughtsmanship remains synthetic; when he draws, he partially identifies himself with the shapes and vital energies of his object matter: he draws upon the forms as well as draws them. Giulio, however, regards the object as a separate datum upon which to impose a hard, dominating, and unsympathetic hand. His brush defines shapes with remarkable exactness, but with a line as uncompromising and as unresilient as that from an engraver's tool. Giulio's modelling is similarly inflexible, exaggerating Raphael's bold manner of the Cartoons just enough toward contrast and hardness so that it chills the forms and transforms them slightly, but suggestively, toward tinted statuary. Giulio's whole response to the human figure, as he demonstrates it so explicitly for the first time in the *Fire*, is neither to its whole content of vitality nor to its unity of form; he sees the human, as well as the inanimate, components of the picture in terms of analytic stress. His mode of seeing and projection in the *Fire* can in large part be thought of as the result of a willed imitation of the Cartoon style which, in the process of imitation, exaggerates and unclassically deforms that style. In Giulio's realization of Raphael's ideas he has made explicit what, in those ideas, is implicit of the reaching of a crisis in the ambitious development of the classical dramatic style, and he has made actual a potential of aesthetic conflict. The change that Giulio effects is not merely one of accent; it is a sufficient alteration of degree made at that critical point where it becomes a measurable change of kind.

This change of kind in the *Fire* is not, as has sometimes been asserted, into the first monument of Roman Mannerism. The basic character and intent of style in this fresco is that of a further testing of the possibilities of classical dramatic style, an extension from what had been successfully accomplished classically heretofore. Giulio has made it explicit that this was an overextension; he is the specific catalyst of an implicit crisis. In the *Fire* the incipient forces of analysis and the persistent intent of synthesis are still in suspension; and what is new in this fresco is still intimately related in its whole vocabulary to preexistent or contemporary classical forms. What has happened here, in this moment of faulting of the classical system, is the marking of a turning point, succeeding the climax of the Tapestries, from which potentially there could, and in fact did, proceed a dissolution of a major aspect of the classical style. Out of the disparities within a classical structure that Giulio has in part created, and in part only made manifest, in the *Fire* he would develop an unclassical, though still classicistic, style of antitheses; but this he does not attain while he is still under Raphael's control. This work is the first point in that process, by no means yet its accomplishment.

Giulio's role in the execution of the *Fire* gave that work a new dimension of interest beyond Raphael's intention for it. Penni's intervention in the *Coronation of Charlemagne*,[380-1] at least in part concurrent, has had an opposite effect. In the *Coronation* a difficult and radical invention of design has been almost altogether vitiated in its translation by Penni's hand and, probably, the hands of still less competent executants — and, as well, by restorers. The given problem for the *Coronation* was altogether unlike that in the *Fire.* The subject here is static and ceremonial, impervious to interpretation in terms of drama. Yet, in the temper of this moment of experiment with style, it was not possible to treat even this subject dispassionately. It had been necessary, in the *Fire*, to increase by invention the dramatic resources of a subject which, in that case, was at least potentially dramatic. Here no drama could be induced in the actors of the subject; the sole possible resource of any expressive energy lay in making an effect, hopefully equivalent to a dramatic value, by manipulation of the compositional form.

This effect was sought in a design, both of superficial pattern and of spatial form, of extreme unconventionality, more drastically asymmetrical in both respects than in any previous picture of the classical style. The picture field was, to begin with, of uneven shape: abnormally cut into by a high window at the left; and it was also disturbed by an assertive, not quite centered, door below. As in earlier instances in the Stanze, the architectural conditions are exploited in the process of design of this fresco and in the "natural" incidents that are invented for it, as it were to justify the accidents of architecture. The window at the left becomes the pretext of a raised choir loft, from which engrossed spectators look down at the ceremony in the church; the door below, by a more oblique but psychologically more adroit reference, marks the open landing of an unseen stair which ascends into the fresco, and up which porters come, illusionistically as if from our space, bearing trophies. Both these incidents serve to give abnormal — in the geometrical sense — direction and inclination to the design, but its major matter is more important in defining its asymmetry. Every element of composition save for the rearward architecture has been displaced on the surface and in space beyond the possibility of axial reference. It is as if a central composition — such as, indeed, this might have become in an earlier moment in the Stanza d'Eliodoro, or in the vein of the Tapestry Cartoons — should have been rotated rearward and rightward, and at the same time still more surprisingly tipped up forward in the space.

In the course of this manipulation this (fanciful) initial central structure has been strained, so that its sides are not now normal to each other, but disposed in a trapezoid. The whole scheme of design of the figures, and of the space that contains them, consists of irregular projections of diagonals. The assembly of actors has nevertheless been so arranged that, by their effects of mass and the patterning of light on them, they suggest, approximately, a sense of balance. But the final stabilizing of this eccentric scheme depends on outside aid; the architecture to the rear, aggressively marked with planar and rectilinear elements of form, and of ponderous proportion, opposes its inertia to the pattern of aesthetic, but not physical, movement of the design of figures. The architecture is distinct, too, in perspective from the figure space, and means to counterweight its abnormal inclination. This setting does not function, as did the settings of the Eliodoro, as a responsive complement to the figure composition but as its corrective. As in the *Fire* and the *Ostia*, but with yet more specified effect, large facts of pictorial structure — facts indicated by the designer, not by the executant — are conceived and stated disparately from each other, and each more emphatically, within an eventually still synthetic whole. Here these disparities are of figure composition and of setting, of forward and of rearward elements of space, and most important, of movemented asymmetry and of gross inertia in design.

Like the *Fire*, the *Coronation* conforms to a definition of a faulted classicism, of a system still intact but with visible seams among the elements of its structure; but the specific accent of its execution impairs its classical effect. None of Raphael's assistants has so manifest a talent as Penni for deflation of a Raphaelesque idea; his slack articulation in the *Coronation* is corruptive of all classical clarity of statement. There is one respect, however, in which the handling in this fresco is indicative of more than a deficiency of Penni's, and is a positive contributory fact of a new effect in larger style. Penni had tended before to relax Raphael's models, by his handling, into a more casual naturalism of appearance. Here there is not an unmeditated relaxation into naturalism but a willed increase of it: first in a merely quantitative sense, of specificity of detail, but more important in a much accentuated optical complexity of forms described by light. The intention of the handling to make an intendedly real record of visual experience is greater than any intention of ideally representing forms.

This is in a way appropriate to the domination in the subject of its contemporary over its historical reference, but — in this conception of the subject, as well as in the intended actuality of its forms — there is a distinction from the prior mode of presentation of such themes. It is as if one facet only had survived of the complementary distinction, made earlier in the frescoes of the Eliodoro, and before it in the Segnatura, between levels of naturalism in present record and in reconstruction of the past. The tendency to accent the actuality of presence resembles the strong element, in Giulio's handling in the *Fire*, of increased specificity of visual description; furthermore it finds precedent, in Raphael's own painting in the Cartoons, in his brilliant treatment of episodes of naturalism. In neither of these analogies, however, is the sense of optical reality so clear or dominant. In Giulio's manner the insistence on description is, as we have indicated, accompanied by an equal, and often contrasting, assertiveness in the characterization of the geometry of form; and in the Cartoons the values of visual experience and aesthetic order still eminently coexist in synthesis.

This new fact of naturalism in the epidermis of the fresco is an expression of Penni's peculiar tendency of hand, but it is not his invention. It is a revelation, through Penni's agency — deformed and exaggerated, certainly — of Raphael's intention for a subject matter, interpreted by him as a reportage and a gallery of portraits, that invited an experiment in descriptive naturalism. The same intention would shortly become manifest in other works partly or largely from Raphael's own hand that contain elements of an ambition to actuality and illusion like that in the *Coronation*.

That ambition lies deeper in the *Coronation* than the epidermis of the painting: it is present in its basic structure of design. No previous fresco in the Stanze marks so strongly, or so explicitly reports, the illumination of the scene as if from the room's actual main source of light. The handling of space also intends the suggestion of illusion: by the diagonal opening from the front of the figure composition, and by the device — at once physically relating and psychologically connective — of the group of trophy-bearers who mount, as if from our space, into the painted scene. The inclination of the floor means further to assert a continuity of space, as if by the spilling of the contents of the picture space into our own. All these devices that promote illusion are deviations not only from the canons of structure, but from the realm of ideas, of antecedent classical style. The concept of the picture world as a discrete space, a projection of a region credible to the spectator but only spiritually, not empathically, habitable by him, is no longer inviolable for Raphael. As in other uncanonical developments that have taken place within this room this new fact of style is the consequence of an experimental testing, in the course of Raphael's research for new directions, of an idea which was explicit, within a canonical synthesis, in a fresco of the Eliodoro room. The spatial energy of the *Expulsion* is, at a great remove of meaning and intention, the starting point for this. And subsequently, in his most important late design in a dramatic style, Raphael would reuse ideas of the *Coronation* composition, in the *Transfiguration.*

The new intent of illusion requires new means. New within this context, they are also resurrections, or recreations, of old means. The trophy-bearers recall the quattrocentesque devices of a Ghirlandaio, as in the Sassetti Chapel; but the orthogonal abnormality of space is, in one way, pre-Masaccesque. It is not based on a quattrocentesque perspective rationale but on a combination, as in pre-Renaissance or Northern art, of nonperspective extension with psychological suggestion. Again, a fact of antecedent development, of wholly classical intent, is prerequisite to this uncanonical innovation: the negation of perspective space in the Tapestries is the precondition to this revolutionary reuse of space in effect without perspective.

The *Oath of Leo* [383] has always been stigmatized as an assistant's poor plagiarism from the *Mass of Bolsena* [214] in the preceding room. The resemblance exists, but to read the fresco in this way is to miss entirely what has been left in it by Penni, his aides, time, and the restorers of what Raphael meant for the *Oath of Leo* in the context of this room in 1517. In the first place, the character of the *Oath* must have been determined partly by consideration for what had been already painted, or was still in course of execution, in this room. The research into new ways of formal and expressive animation in the preceding frescoes had already carried Raphael into difficult terrain, too commotionful, and potentially or actually aesthetically unsatisfactory. The most urgent impulse of experiment seems by now, also, to have been spent. It was reasonable that a different mode of design be attempted for the last fresco, one that should compensate the too-active structure of the other three; and it may have been in the nature of this time to seek extremes that the *Oath* should, in this respect, disparately overcompensate. The relation of the *Oath* to its companions is, but with this significant difference in degree, like that between the *Liberation of Peter* and the other Eliodoro frescoes.

The subject of the *Oath*, yet more actionless and ceremonial than the *Coronation*, was amenable to treatment in a static style, and the precedent for at least the form of such a treatment existed in the *Liberation*, and yet more in the Tapestry Cartoons. Activity in form having been renounced, and activity of content in the subject being nonexistent, the fresco was designed to recreate, in a language like that of the Cartoons, a similar effect of austere gravity, appropriate to its literally hieratic meaning. The structure depends on a symmetry more severe even than that of the Cartoons, to which it was possible to arrive only from their precedent; and this symmetry contrasts all the more with the eccentric design of the *Coronation*. In the *Oath*, setting and figures alike compose an architectonic order.

What Penni has made of this scheme, potentially as impressive as the *Elymas* or the *Ananias* of the Tapestries, is too obvious; the high classical exemplar of this compositional style has been made monotonous and disarticulate. This is, though negatively, an accomplishment of a stage worthy to be marked in the history of the classical style: the academicization, through devitalized translation of its forms, of Raphael's ultimate accomplishment of classicism. Penni had threatened, but not achieved as much before, where he participated in the painting of the Cartoons. Here, however, there is a purposeful difference, from Penni's execution in the Cartoons, in his handling of elements of form, and the difference is the same that we have observed already in the *Coronation*. It should be assumed here, as there, that the distinction is not of Penni's, but of Raphael's, motivation. As in the *Coronation*, the *Oath* is presented to us as reportage, with still less admixture of invented or historical reference. More than the *Coronation*, this is the description, with its actual participants, of a contemporary event. The descriptive naturalism of the *Oath* has here been one stage more developed in its intention of specific record, and that much of this intention lay with Raphael is again suggested by the portrait by him, begun later in this same year, in which three chief actors of this scene — Leo, Giulio de' Medici, and Cardinal Rossi — reappear. Devices of illusion, a logical accompaniment of this intent, are present in the gathering, more communicative than their counterparts in the *Bolsena*, of officers on the steps. A clear and measurable remove from the normative level of classical ideality was meant for the *Oath of Leo*, but not such a pedestrian accumulation of small facts as, in Penni's hands, it has become.

Giulio's grisaille basamenti (entirely repainted),[385] with their frieze of Royal Protectors of the Church, seated and partitioned off by caryatid herms, complete the scheme of decoration of this room. The muscular Kings are another admission of the influence of Michelangelo's models on Raphaelesque style of this time; in a general way, Giulio's figures are inspired by the Prophets of the Sistine. They function similarly in the relation of their forms to space and to the architecture, but in their context of nearness to the spectator they convey a different intonation of illusion. In some instances this intonation has been discreetly stressed, but the Kings make no spatial disturbance comparable with that of incidents in the frescoes; they are at least aesthetically recessive. They are the one element in the Stanza dell' Incendio which, on all four walls, proclaims a theme of unity, but this does not suffice to bind together the disparate matter of form and content in the scenes above them. Each large fresco, highly characterized by Raphael's intention and, for better or for worse, by its execution, manifests a different look and personality of style. More than any internal elements of style within one fresco, these four whole frescoes are disparate from one another; the very thread of community among them, of their temper of experiment, accentuates the character in each of difference. These four disparate aesthetic acts are distinct probings of new avenues of a single style in crisis: they are the visible symptom, in the compass of this room, of the end of the integrity of the classical style and of its first processes of dissolution.

THE LATER DECORATIONS

Concurrent with the Tapestry Cartoons and the Stanza dell' Incendio, and succeeding them, Raphael was engaged with other major decorative projects. His activity in the supply of easel pictures was also considerable in these years, but by no means so important as his work on monumental scale, and this situation continued to the end of his career. It was in the decorations that Raphael found the problematic challenge of ideas, of that scale and potential breadth of generalization that suits his temper of this time.

It was only partly of Raphael's determination that, of the decorative projects of these years other than the Cartoons and the Incendio frescoes, none had the subject matter of biblical or Church history that demanded didactic and dramatic treatment, on a pictorial stage of considerable scale. Among the other major late decorations, two of five are concerned with Christian themes, but with no intention for them of large-scale dramatic communication, and three are explicitly Antique and pagan in their subject matter. But whether the literary matter is classical or Christian, there is, in all these decorations, a strong overcast of the vocabulary of Antique classicism, in places assertively archaeological as it had not been in Raphael's art before; even the Christian subject matter is embedded in an Antique context. These subjects, both classical and Christian, are not necessarily emotionally neutral, but not one of them requires exposition with the urgency that had been found for the Tapestries or the frescoes of the Incendio: their character of subject is more readily resolved into their decorative context.

It is partly in the nature of these themes, but also in the nature of the spaces given Raphael to work with in these decorations, that the units of narrative, and the sizes of the picture field containing them, are, in general, smaller than in the Stanze or Cartoons. The units, of subject or of decorative motive, are smaller, and the scale and complexity of matter in each of them is less. Within the actual architecture that of course establishes the whole limit of design, a fictitious painted architecture may create frames for the invented, smaller, subdivisions of the scheme: each picture field tends to be defined within a shape of architectural geometry. In a double sense, both the form and the expression of content in these decorations are contained: a discreet content is presented to us in discrete units of pictorial form.

The clarity of parts this mode of geometric subdivision makes is not divisive: as much as each part is identified itself, it is also identified in its function of articulation of the whole design. This is, still more than its parts, eminently clear, and its large geometry of form depends from, and coincides with, the limits of the actual including architecture. This whole painted shape has authority not only as a commanding element of pictorial design; it also takes authority from the architecture with which it is identified. Its effect is of a geometrically rigorous, dominating unity, the clarity of which subsumes the clarity of its articulation into parts. The nature of the architecture evidently enters into the definition of the scheme that starts with it; in the projects of which we speak here, four out of five of the containing spaces are designs of the High Renaissance classical architectural style, at least one of them by Raphael himself.

The character of style of such schemes as these, where a whole including clear geometry is articulated with an architectonic — and in fact architectural — logic into clearly identified parts of ideal shape is very similar to that which we determined for the Tapestry Cartoons. Here, however, the wholly figurative matter that made this logic in the Cartoons has been translated into a vocabulary more actually geometrical, more made of forms of architecture and thus in essence more abstract; to a significant extent, the meaning of the later decorative schemes is dominated by their classical ordering of abstract forms, of real or fictive architecture. The human population that inhabits this geometry further articulates the abstract order of the architecture, and may diversify or markedly relieve its personality, of form and of mood. But in relation to the content that the form of architecture carries, that of the actors in it is not — especially by the standards of the actors of the Stanze or Cartoons — assertive. There is, in the abstract geometry, a discipline to which the human forms are ultimately subservient.

There is fundamental likeness in aesthetic with that of the Cartoons, but also a significant difference in the human content of this decorative style. The high classicism of the Cartoons continues with no apparent crisis in the late decorative works, but more as a principle of form than as that remarkable conjunction, in the Cartoons, of forms and human feelings. If we insist that the ultimate classical style of the Cartoons can retain its historical identity only in such an integer as it displays of form and content, then this separation, in the decorative schemes, of a principle of form into a dominating place belongs also — but in a way opposite to that of the Stanza dell' Incendio — to the process of dissolution of classical style.

It would seem plausible that this mode of decorative thought, and its means, are in some way a result of Raphael's concern, since 1514, with architectural problems. It might also be that a thinking about decoration from the viewpoint of a deeper intelligence of architecture could account for another character — often most pronounced — which these late schemes share: of elements of, or of a whole, illusionism. The relation of the decoration to the architecture in terms of formal order is secured by the extension of the forms of one into the other, but this extension is thought of not only in the terms of forms, but of the accustomed architectural functions of these forms. The decoration not only paints; it builds a further space of illusionistic architecture, which continues the reality. The functional, illusionistic extension of the containing room creates another relation beyond that of aesthetic concord: a psychological relation, empathic and representational. The abstract vocabulary of architectural order in decorative design is thus compensated with what is, in effect, a new device of naturalism.

The first adoption of a whole illusion in one of these decorative schemes predates, within this phase, the partial devices of illusion that are used in the Incendio fresco of the *Coronation.* Those devices belong, however, to the same tendency of style, and are part of the same general interest in experiment with heightened effects of naturalism. As in the *Coronation*, the decorative schemes revive some of the repertory of perspective illusion from the Quattrocento, but this is now employed within the context of a finally still-classical aesthetic. As it is not in the experimentally aberrant *Coronation*, in the decorative projects the sense of spatial continuity is controlled. A caesura is invariably made between the actuality of space and its fanciful extension; and its forms, both of architecture and figures, are for the most part disposed as if in reference to an implicit, but sensible, classicizing picture plane.

The first of the illusionistic decorations of this phase was designed by Raphael for his familiar patron, Agostino Chigi, for the mosaic cupola of his chapel in S. M. del Popolo,[386] of which the architecture also was Raphael's invention. Authentic studies by Raphael for figures in this scheme exist in Lille and Oxford,[387-8] as well as copies from his studies. The Lille and Oxford studies conform altogether in their style to that in Raphael's few certain drawings of 1515. This indication of the date of the design is supported by the date of 1516 inset in the mosaic, with his initials, by the executant, Luigi de Pace Veneziano. This date, incidentally, probably does not indicate the termination of the work which, from other evidence, may have continued until 1520. On May 31, 1520, a contract was drawn between Alvise de Pace and Madonna Francesca, Chigi's widow (Golzio, 126–27), for work in the fields between the windows of the drum and in the pendentive tondi, from designs still to be supplied by an unnamed artist; four years of the mosaicist's exclusive labor were foreseen for this new scheme. It was never executed; there was no obtrusive postscript in the same medium to Raphael's own design.

Agostino Chigi's tastes were strongly marked, and in specific traits unlike those in normal vogue within the Vatican. He was much more interested in the use of art for illustration of Antique legend than for Christian images; and he was obsessed with astrology, particularly in its application to himself. Also, whether it was an implicit quirk of his own taste or a recurrent accident, there is no patron for whom commissions were so constantly executed on illusionistic themes. The work of Peruzzi in the *Sala Galatea* and the *Sala del Fregio* in the Farnesina had strong illusionistic elements, as did Sodoma's *Alexander* room; and there was some intention of illusion, of a different kind, in the original conception of the Galatea-Polyphemus theme. Contemporary with Raphael's chapel in the Popolo, Peruzzi painted the Farnesina's well-named *Sala delle Prospettive*, and later Raphael designed for Chigi, in the *Sala di Psyche*, the most developed of his illusionistic schemes. The cupola of the Chigi Chapel would have been, without its illusionism, an exception in this catalogue of Chigi's commissions.

The astrological subject matter of the Chigi cupola invited treatment in illusionistic terms — almost inevitably, since Peruzzi had invented his brilliant conceit for Chigi's horoscope on the ceiling of the *Sala di Galatea*. As in that ceiling, the cupola here is thought of as a surface where a fictive architecture is projected, through openings in which (as from within a pergola) we may see the embodied planets in the heavens. The conceit is like Peruzzi's, but significantly differently developed; Raphael accepts the entire perspective consequence of the premise of illusion. There is a difference, too, in the interpretation of the astrological subject matter, probably inevitable in the circumstance of place and Christian context of this scheme. Here, in more orthodox view, the heavens are a clearly Christian province. Each planetary body is accompanied by an angel who guides his course, and each angel indicates by look or posture that his orders come in turn from higher up: in the center and summit of this heaven God the Father is the ruler of the planetary system. He looms majestically through an oculus of which the shape and radial enframement clearly refer to the image of the sun. Radii extend in alternating intervals beyond this symbolic sunburst to the circumference of the dome of heaven, and bring to mind the pattern of a horoscope, or of a wheel of destiny.

The structure of fictitious architecture that creates this pattern is severely, almost massively monumental, yet like a wheel implies rotation. Within its first meaning of perfect symmetry and order it contains a second sense, of slow majestic motion, as of the solar system that it represents. The movement of the figures within their heavy frames instigates this sense of a rotation. God the Father — an image remade in the mold of the most impressive actors of the Tapestry Cartoons from suggestions in the iconography of Michelangelo — incipiently turns as He hovers over us; as He does so He establishes an inclination leftward and counterclockwise across the diameter of the cupola. The planetary images take up this impulse in their own movements, mostly with measured gravity, but in places assertively; in each planetary "house" there is another pulse of counterclockwise rotation. Rarely if at all before, even in Raphael's own art, had there been so precise a coincidence established between the given form for decoration and its articulation in terms of the thematic idea. The Chigi cupola is an exposition more precise and far more impressive than any before of the iconographic content that is *associated with the dome.

This is Raphael's first unequivocal acceptance of the proposition of illusionism: in the use of an invented architecture to extend actual architectural space, and in the concordant perspective situation of the figures. The repertory of devices he employs necessarily recalls the Quattrocento, when, in the course of perspective experiment, nearly all of them had been discovered. The Melozzo apse once in SS. Apostoli must have been in some degree a precedent, and also, probably, some of the Roman work of Mantegna, now lost. But Raphael's use of these devices is in a context of style so unlike the Quattrocento that their meaning no longer is the same. Perhaps because the cupola is contemporary in invention with the Tapestry Cartoons, it is the most fully classical of the late decorative schemes in its effects both of form and content. The same temper that informs the design of the Cartoons has deduced, from the abstract perfection of the given architectural shape — given, here, by Raphael — a geometrically perfect ideal order: ultimately clear in its articulation, gravely monumental in its density of form, absolute in its coincidence of forms and meanings. Unlike the illusionistic paintings of the Quattrocento, the image projected in this cupola remains, despite its aspect of illusion, of an ideal, and ideally distinct, world — exactly a heaven, which we may contemplate but not enter. Equally, this scanned, deliberate, and separate region of existence has no relation to the style of the baroque. If Correggio ever saw the Chigi cupola, it might have given him some impetus of illusionist idea, but it precisely would not have given him the idea, so very unlike this, of an uninterrupted, energetically inhabited, extension of our world, which gives the first cupola of Correggio its baroque implication.

In the first half of 1516, while the Chigi cupola was in course of execution, and Giulio Romano and Penni were conducting experiments for Raphael, of very different character, in the Incendio room, a decorative scheme of yet another kind was invented by the master, and carried out for him by his assistants. Letters from Bembo to the Cardinal Bibbiena, between April and June of 1516, discuss the progress of work on two adjuncts to the Cardinal's apartment on the then topmost story of the Vatican, overlooking the present Cortiletto del Maresciallo. The items with which Raphael was concerned were a small loggia, the *Loggetta*,[389-91] of which it is possible that he designed or remodelled the architecture, and a bath, the *Stufetta*,[392-3] which adjoins it at one end. Bibbiena was away from Rome during the work of decoration and probably also during its first design; on April 19 Bembo writes to him to say that Raphael urges that the Cardinal send the remaining histories he wishes painted in the *Stufetta*, since the subjects sent already would be finished in a week; on May 6 Bembo informs Bibbiena, "La stufetta si va fornendo, . . . le camere nuove sono fornite e la loggia"; finally, on June 20, he reports to the Cardinal in Florence that "la loggia, la stufetta, le camere, i paramenti del cuio di V. S. sono forniti, et ogni cosa l'aspetta" (Golzio, 43–48).

What awaited the Cardinal on his return may have been a surprise as well as a delight. His setting of the subjects for Raphael to paint in the *Stufetta* may well have been all that he determined in this scheme. The scheme itself had no modern precedent; the two spaces are the first complete decoration *alla grottesca* since Antiquity. They are the first statement of the mode that was to be elaborated in the greater Logge, and by way of this more influential offspring, the ancestor of the whole tradition of grotesque decoration in the sixteenth century.

There had been, earlier, a considerable tradition of the use of Ancient grotesque motives by painters who worked in Rome. The history of the rediscovery of the grotesque style is told by Vasari, who connects it largely with the explorations of Morto da Feltre; Pinturicchio had also adopted a repertory of grotesquerie and demonstrated it not only in Rome but in his decorations in Siena, and Peruzzi may have taken his first models of grotesque ornament from this source. In all these uses by older artists of grotesquerie it is confined to a role of incident within a decoration; it is never the expansive basis for a whole decorative design. Its style as ornament is, furthermore, as much preclassical as is the more substantial figurative matter it adorns: linear, rigid and repetitive, and always additively combined.

Raphael had himself used grotesques as episodes of ornament since circa 1512 or 1513. The probable earliest occurrence is in the embrasures of the windows of the Stanza della Segnatura (of Penni's execution[?]), and then, circa 1514, in the corresponding spaces of the Stanza d'Eliodoro; these are still small and incidental picture fields. Their difference from earlier grotesquerie is in the fact that their intrinsic style as ornament is classical. They are made of a richer and more imaginatively varied repertory of shapes, flexibly and rhythmically combined; and they imply, as the Quattrocento grotesques rarely did, a content. Evidently they are inspired by a fuller understanding of the Antique models than the Quattrocento had, but they are much more inventive, in design and in motives, than they are archaeological.

What occurs in Bibbiena's decoration is an entire quantitative change from the previous limited use of the grotesque, and this is its most significant distinction. However, this change, by which the grotesque becomes the dominant, and not an incident, of a system of design, is accompanied by a change in relation of the motives to their Antique models. This scheme reinvents and freshly recombines its sources, but an archaeologically precise study of them, which did not exist in Raphael's earlier occasional grotesques, is now apparent. The multiform resources of such decoration in the Domus Aurea may have afforded Raphael his chief models: in the *Stufetta*[392] it is explicit that its vault imitates that of the *Volta Dorata* of the Golden House. The more exact dependence on the Ancient grotesque schemes is natural in this first essay at a similar extensive decoration, but the whole motive of this reference lies deeper: it is the most explicit index in Raphael's late career of the development in him of an archaeological interest in Antiquity.

This archaeological concern, stimulated further, but surely not begun by his role as prefect of Antiquities, does not imply a major change in Raphael's attitude toward Antique classicism; he is as much as before interested in its essential meaning of artistic style. Archaeology becomes another, parallel and added kind of interest for him in Antique art: a concern with it in another aspect than that of its aesthetic. This archaeological consideration of Ancient art seeks in it values that the literary humanist might stress, as distinguished from the purely visual artist. In Raphael, this attitude would understandably evolve from his longer experience of the literary court of Rome and his increasingly intimate association with its leading figures — the patron of this very commission and his delegate in it, Bembo, conspicuous among them. Indeed, the ambition of the new grotesque style of decoration is, in its learned refinement of imitative Latin style, like that of the *littérateurs*. Their wit, too, has its visual counterpart in the ingenious caprice of the grotesques. But so, also, has their ultimate decorum, for the larger pattern within which the grotesques play is as disciplined in order as in any of the figurative late decorative schemes, and — more than in its Antique prototypes — expressive of the rationale of its containing classical architecture. The result of Raphael's new invention fits the cultural personality of its patron as if it had been made deliberately to his measure.

The personality this mode accommodates, however, is a private rather than a public one. There is no intention of communicating, here, the kinds of content that are in the figurative schemes of decoration; this is, more literally, only decoration. It has no message and not even, specifically, a subject, and means only to ornament a private ambient with pleasant matter of a kind that is, in a way, the visual projection of a cultured humanist's small talk. Within a basic style not different from that in the figured decorative schemes, this deliberately explores a different mood, or mode. In it the content is yet more recessive in respect to form, and form — in no respect less rational in larger order, or less architectonically abstract — becomes, through its grotesque articulation, less severe. The system achieves a richly differentiated harmony, classical in substance, in appearance and in literary cast, but in a degree yet more explicit than in the figured schemes the active agent of this harmony is form.

Within the formal harmony its basic components are more disparate in scale and aesthetic character than in any antecedent system of the classical style: the rigorous large architectonic order and the fanciful small order of grotesques each represents an antithetic development of the possibilities of design. In this development of internal difference there is again the evidence of a process repeatedly observed in this late phase, of increased internal differentiation among elements of style. But in this mode no disruptive effect ensues from this disparity; the grotesques function both as relieving enrichment of the austerity, and as compensation for the scale, of the larger order. The two systems meld, in the diffused pattern of grotesques, into one another, but the more essential reason of their coexistence is in the near accord, in the two orders, of their measure of abstractness.

Each of the two spaces of this decoration is itself distinguished in a different variant of Antique decorative mode. The larger space, the *Loggetta*, is dominantly frescoed with grotesquerie in a light, open style, even a little sparse, which recalls the principal manner of the Domus Aurea. The small *Stufetta*, however, is modelled after types of the Roman third style, in which the grotesque elements are incidental. It is (properly for a bath) warm in color scheme, with remarkable approximations of Antique "Pompeian" reds and with rich blacks; and it is as close-textured as the *Loggetta* is oppositely sparse and light. The architectural space of the *Stufetta* is supremely lucid in the subdivision of its walls in paint: on the upper walls small inserts, of strict rectangular shape, contain mythologies in a consciously imitative Antique style. In a lower range of small pictures, with scenes of *amoretti*, the imitation of Antique models verges on counterfeit; the technique, and even the surface of these paintings (as far as it can now be judged in their considerably ruined condition), is like that of Roman "impressionist" encaustic work. The lunettes contain perspectives of spindly Antique architecture; the vault, as we have observed before, is closely derived from a Neronian example. The presiding deity of this rich archaeological order was to have been an Ancient marble Venus, a gift to Bibbiena from a friend. Unfortunately it did not fit the niche that had been provided for it. With Raphael's encouragement, Bembo asked that it be given him in turn (Golzio, 44–45).

Raphael's continuous supervision of this project is well attested by Bembo's correspondence. However, here, as always in this phase, his role in the execution of the work was nil; and given the nature of the motives of design it is likely that his role in their development was less than in the case of figure compositions. His particular agent to whom this scheme was entrusted must have been Giovanni da Udine, who was suited by his previous specialty within the shop to undertake this new development, of small motives, and who, furthermore, had the virtue at this moment of not being otherwise heavily engaged. Subsidiary assistance was given to Giovanni in order to complete the project in the relatively short time it took, but the specific matter of design and the substantial execution were by him. Giovanni would gain, in Bibbiena's apartment, the experience that would allow him to assume the same role, with a much greater scope, in the subsequent Logge.

Giovanni was a better instrument of Raphael's will than either of the two other principal assistants, Giulio or Penni; he was more malleable to Raphael's precise intent of style than, in their opposite ways, were either of those two. His work in this scheme may be taken — not in detail but in its whole effect — as an extension of Raphael's intelligence, and this intelligence is precisely what is revealed in the ordnance of the *Loggetta*. There, the openness and lightness of design accord with the architectural meaning of a loggia; the pattern in painting seems to make articulate the play within the loggia of the natural light. The division of the inner wall in picture fields responds to and continues the real forms of architecture: each arched bay of grotesque patterns is responsive to the opening opposite in the loggia; the rectangular bays, each with their painted niche and fictive statue, are responsive to the facing windowed piers. The loggia is reflected in a less substantial, crystalline, geometry on the painted wall.

This attenuated reflection of the actual architecture is not meant to tell as an illusory extension of it; for this the context affords no such compelling pretext as did the Chigi cupola. Yet, motives of illusionism run through this decoration in an obbligato: not assertive, but sensible in a subsidiary stratum of the meaning of the scheme. The machinery of the illusion is, consistently with the other matter of the decoration, in an Antique vocabulary. Its principal means are architectural perspectives imitated from the Ancient style, even to their falsity of projection, which make suggestive but not even intendedly convincing structures in the wall. More genuine in its intent of illusion, and Antique in motive but not in means, is the one large figurative incident, in each alternate bay, of a grisaille statue in a niche.[391] The idea of these painted statues was to extend, or rather preface, a real situation intended (but, as we recall, not realized) in the *Stufetta*, where a marble Venus was to occupy a similar niche. But even here the character of illusion is a conceit, rather than an assertive fact; its force has been deliberately diminished because no assertion, even of a fact primarily of form, could be permitted to intrude upon the urbane harmony of this scheme.

The next in time of Raphael's decorative projects seems to have been begun while the Stanza dell' Incendio was still not altogether finished and while Giulio Romano, at least, was still engaged with the basamenti there. A document of July 1, 1517 (Golzio, 56) records a payment of twenty ducats, not to Raphael himself but ". . . a li Gioveni di Raphaello di Urbino che hanno dipinta la stanza avanti la guardaroba," which is taken usually, and correctly, to refer to the *Sala dei Palafrenieri* (or *dei Chiaroscuri*).[394] The original decoration of this room was destroyed under Paul IV, but then remade, including some few surviving portions of the earlier scheme, by Taddeo Zuccaro and others in the early 1560's. Zuccaro's remaking was altogether in his contemporary taste; it recreated the essentials of Raphael's scheme and even some of its details, but in a vein of style radically different.

Our conception of Raphael's *Sala dei Palafrenieri* can take no more from the Zuccaro transcription than its general idea, but other evidence exists that helps us in some measure toward a reconstruction. Vasari knew the original decoration; he describes it in the *Life* of Raphael thus (IV, 361–62), ". . . fece una sala, dove di terretta erano alcune figure di Apostoli ed altri Santi in tabernacoli: e per Giovanni da Udine . . . fece . . . quegli animali che papa Leone aveva . . . ." In Giovanni's *Life* the description is a little amplified (VI, 555): "fece Raffaello in certi tabernacoli, alcuni Apostoli di chiaroscuro, grandi quanto il vivo . . . e Giovanni sopra le cornici di quell' opera ritrasse di natural molti pappagalli di diversi colori, i quali allora aveva Sua S$^{ta.}$, e così anco babuini, gattimamoni, zibetti ed altri bizzarri animali." Apparently, Giovanni's menagerie was at least as demanding of attention as the grisaille Apostles. These latter seem to have been prepared, and perhaps also executed, by Penni; two explicitly identifiable preparatory studies, for Saints Matthew and John Evangelist (Louvre 4261 and 28954; squared for transfer)[395-6] are from his hand. They resemble, but do not in fact correspond, to the two same Saints in the set of Apostles engraved by Marcantonio (B. 64–76), of which it is often, but by this token evidently unsurely, assumed that they closely reflect the lost originals. At Chatsworth a set of Raphaelesque copies exists of drawings for, or after, the Apostles, but there is no means of testing the value of their testimony for the appearance of the vanished paintings.

From this various evidence it appears that the lost decoration consisted of a fictitious interior architecture on four sides of the present room, with tabernacles framed by columns or pilasters; each tabernacle holding a life-size grisaille figure of an Apostle, with his attribute. That the colonnade by Zuccaro and others is not entirely their invention is assured by the one element which, by its archaizing look, they seem mostly to have carried over from the remains of the original decoration: the entablature with its frieze of putti and rinceaux. The present architecture is too massive, and too complicated in its perspective mode to stand for Raphael's original, but its system of structure and disposition is the same. Above each tabernacle was the population of Pope Leo's zoo, contrasting in its color — and certainly in its content — with the grisaille humanity below.

The whole scheme was, evidently, of pronounced illusionistic intention. The architecture was meant as if it were reality, and the birds and animals that perched on its perspective projections were, it would seem, also meant for real. The figures in the tabernacles, however, were identified by their grisaille — as in the *Loggetta* and in Giulio's *Kings* of the Incendio basamenti, in execution probably at just this time — as illusions not of living persons, but of statues. By contrast with the menagerie, the statuary Apostles must have maintained some dignity, even in these difficult circumstances. The two certain models we possess, in Penni's drawings in the Louvre, are exceedingly restrained in mood and movement. It is just this classicizing element of compensating marked difference — characteristic for this phase of Raphael's thought — that the Zuccaro translations of the Apostles, in their excess of action, miss. The principle was here, as in the *Loggetta* of the year before, of gravity of large form relieved by a deliberately different capriciousness of small forms, which here again — but more in our usual usage of the word — were grotesque. It is, however, difficult to imagine how, in such a scheme, a genuine and unclassical contrast in the content — almost as of the most surprising Mannerist conceit — could in fact have been avoided, between the animal grotesquerie and the religious whose peace they could not but disturb.

As in his preceding illusionisms, Raphael's reference to the repertory of the Quattrocento is obvious. There may be, here, some recollection of Castagno's frescoes from the Villa Pandolfini, and in the architectural system there is the likely inspiration of Mantegna, from such Roman works as were earlier in turn reflected in the Palazzo Venezia's *Sala del Mappamondo*. The influence also may be here of Peruzzi's very recent *Sala delle Prospettive* in the Farnesina, an illusionist invention remarkable enough to stimulate even Raphael's emulation. There was, in the structure and in much of the detail of Peruzzi's decoration, an unmistakable accent of the mature classicism, not only of vocabulary but of effects of form, of this distinguished architect; and it would seem proper to presume of Raphael's design also that here, as elsewhere, he controlled and transmuted the sense of his illusion in a classical formal cast.

This is the one Raphaelesque decoration of this phase of which the given subject is unequivocally and dominantly Christian. However, this does not prevent the artist from presenting it to us in the guise of an Antique analogy. This analogy results from the iconographic association of the particular architecture that Raphael has chosen to contain his Saints. This assembly of sacred statues in classic aediculae, framed by a Roman colonnade, has the look of a reconstruction — imaginative and only indirect — of the interior of an Ancient temple: the Apostles are presented to us as if they were the inhabitants of a pantheon.

On the 1st of January 1519 Leonardo Sellaio wrote, consolingly, to Michelangelo in Florence: "E schoperto la volta d'Agostino Ghisi,[397-409] chosa vituperosa a un gran maestro; pegio che l'ultima stanza di palazo, asai" (Golzio, 65; there dated as written, in Florentine style, 1518). Sellaio's sour judgment had the most uncharitable motives, but one of them was certainly the same as that which moved Vasari to say later (IV, 377–78) that these frescoes "mancano . . . grazia e dolcezza . . . cagione di averli fatti colorire ad altri col suo disegno." The situation is, in this respect, not, as Sellaio has it, of worse effect than in the "ultima stanza di palazo, asai"; the two principal executants are the same. A secondary role in the execution was given, further, to Giovanni da Udine, and a minor, but identifiable contribution made by another nameable assistant in the shop, Raffellino del Colle. Perhaps from late in* 1517, and through 1518, a considerable part of the efforts of this group was given to a translation into paint, not so inept as either Sellaio or Vasari would assert, of the grandest of Raphael's late schemes of architectural illusionism.

Raphael chose to convert the loggia of Chigi's villa (originally an open loggia) into something more than usually suggestive of its function of a link between the building and the outdoors space. As if the loggia were to be understood almost interchangeably as a compartment either of the villa or of its garden, he has transformed the loggia's vault into an arbor, open through its foliate architecture to the illusion of a sky. To shade the interior from an imaginary sun, he has stretched two *tende*, in the form of painted tapestries, across its roof; these tapestries contain the crowning episodes of the subject of the decoration: Psyche's reception in Olympus and her marriage. In the spandrels below, in a perspective so adjusted as to give the sense of near-verticality of their surface, are earlier episodes of the Psyche story — not all of them; only those which, in the text, take place in heaven. We see these scenes as if they were enacted in a heaven just beyond the limits of the arbor; each scene is framed in the foliate architecture, intersecting it or intruding a little toward us from beyond it.

In the *tende*[408-9] there is entire illusion in the device, but none in the situation of the figures in them. These are illusions, not of a figured extension of our space, but of tapestries so hung. The spandrel scenes, on the other hand, are wholly plausible illusions of a figural existence, but they achieve this illusion with only minimal concessions in perspective, and with far more emphasis on the separateness of being of their figures than on their spatial relation with us. The illusion defined in the spandrels is, further, of their figures only, with its immediately appertaining space; they substantially fill the area of each picture field, and the sky behind them is as if opaque, without optical indication of a deeper space. However, in the space between each spandrel (in the adjoining horizontal segment of the vault) the heavens genuinely open upwards: *amoretti*, birds, and mythic beasts fly, in a higher distance from us than the spandrels, in a sky defined by clouds, light, and effects of atmosphere, and by the drastic foreshortening of its inhabitants, as an intendedly believable reach above the loggia — a spatial and optical reality that extends our own.

In its first admirably appropriate pretext, in its whole system, and in each major part this scheme works, to intellectual and visual satisfaction, as illusion, and its apparatus has been controlled in such a way that no slightest rupture has been made by the illusion in classical aesthetic. There are literally three levels of illusion within the framework of fictitious architecture: the outermost completely assertive of extended space; the spandrels defining the existence, in an adjacent space, of figures but not of spatial extension; while, in the *tende*, spatial extension is entirely denied. The more present to the eye the picture field, by area or position, the more diminished is its assertion of illusion; the full power of spatial device is reserved to confirm the initial statement of illusionistic situation in the periphery only of the whole design, where the matter is not more than incidental to the subject. What the spandrels and the central ceiling more importantly present of narrative, in wider areas, is turned back, in two successive stages, towards a nonillusionistic norm. At the same time, however, the lessening of specific illusionistic effect in each stage is justified by a pretext that makes this diminution intellectually acceptable as consistent with the illusionistic functioning of the whole.

The scheme achieves the intellectual and visual sensation of illusion, and defines it, for both these motives, with entire plausibility. The higher credibility — the more affirmative sense of presence — that comes from an illusionism is established, but not in that degree (as in an illusionism more strictly perspectival) that the painted world is taken mainly in the sense of an extension of our own. Planar, not perspective structure, is dominant in this scheme, and the classical sense persists in it of an ideal limit interposed between us and the form, which, at the same time, tends to contain the content. What is projected here is still a discrete, ideal realm, appropriate to its Olympian nature. In more explicit way than in Raphael's earlier illusionistic schemes the effect of a planarity supports the sense of the integrity of the actual architecture, and with it, its value of consistent, unifying reference for the whole structure of design. This comes to what, in the cliché of much later criticism, is called "respect for the wall surface." The near-contemporaries of Raphael apparently also were impressed with Raphael's classicizing restraints upon illusion: Serlio (Regole Generali, 1537 [in Golzio, 285]), in his discussion "Degli ornamenti della pittura, fuori ed dentro de gli edifici," approves of Raphael's avoiding "le durezze di tanti scurci," and particularly applauds the invention of the *tende*.

Tende had been used before with quite similar effect, but in an altogether different context, by Serlio's master, Peruzzi, on the ceiling of the Stanza d'Eliodoro. Peruzzi's name intrudes itself recurrently into our consideration of Raphael's involvement with illusion in his later decorative style, and nowhere more strongly than in this building, of Peruzzi's architectural design. In the adjoining *Sala di Galatea* Peruzzi, in his role of decorator, had worked on a virtually identical space, with a theme which, like that of the *Psiche* ceiling, was celestial in its locale. Peruzzi's illusionist solution, and his ordering in painting of the given space is — not for consistency's sake, but for its evident appropriateness of solution — a clear starting point for Raphael's conception of his own design. What is different in Raphael's solution is its evidence of a near-decade of intervening classical experience. For all its careful moderation, Raphael's pretext and particular devices of illusion achieve a higher plausibility by far than in Peruzzi's ceiling, and a clearer and more consistent rationale; both these factors are functions of a higher classicism. Further, Raphael now articulates Peruzzi's own architecture in more wholly classical vein, with broader units of geometry that simply, responsively, relate to one another and cohere in a large unity of pattern.

This structure of form was to have been inhabited, in Raphael's intention, by a race of beings, and an atmosphere, much like those in his fresco of five years before on the wall of the *Sala di Galatea.* The tone of content means to recreate, here with more august and Olympian presences than in the *Galatea*, a like ideal splendor of sensuous existence. Unlike the *Galatea* this ceiling had, for obvious reasons, to make more in the way of narrative, and convey more, more specifically, than the *Galatea's* perfect distillation of a situation. In the ceiling the element of narrative and its consequent effects of content are still, however, not assertive; their meaning of narration is less, in most episodes, than the meaning of sensuous beauty of the actors' forms. There are more actors here than in any of the other of Raphael's illustrations of Antiquity, but by no means correspondingly more of dramatic action; despite its quantity and scale the classical literary content remains — as we have observed — unlike Christian narrative content, recessive to the form. Such is almost uniformly the character of content in the spandrels: the splendor of persons, not their urgencies of feeling, is the affective burden of — for example — the *Three Graces* [398] or the *Venus, Ceres, and Juno* [399]; and in the *Venus and Psyche* [401] it is not Venus's emotion but her nudity that, positively, claims attention. Where there is energy of action it proceeds — as in the three scenes of ascents or descent from Olympus — from formal causes, not from emotional circumstance. The case is yet more pronounced in the *Wedding Feast* [409] and the *Council of the Gods* [408] in the *tende*: each is taken as the pretext for assembling a tableau in which the figurants — not actors — are a nearly statuary gallery of gods and goddesses, in part made up of archaeologically minded restorations of known antiques.

Since the chief meaning of all this Olympian population is its beauty of physical presence it is understandable why, in this decoration still more than others, the ab-

sence of Raphael's own hand in execution should be felt so much, and invite such unfavorable comment in the older sources. In this project Raphael's autograph is preserved to us only in drawing, and perhaps in one only of the number of apparently preparatory studies that survive (Louvre, Windsor,[407] Haarlem, Dresden). A finished drawing for the *Venus and Psyche*[402] (Louvre 3875) has oscillated endlessly in the literature between Raphael and Giulio; a frequently favored compromise solution advances that it is by Giulio but retouched by Raphael. This drawing seems, however, to be a rare and authentic product of Raphael's own late draughtsman's style: it is from such examples that Giulio's draughtsmanship, and more important, his ideas of form about this time are imitated. Its aggrandized, but still wonderfully vital mass is what is translated by Giulio into a more inert style in the painting.

In his execution Giulio's figures may at worst assume a hard, stiff-jointed bulkiness, more wholly graceless even than the Roman statuary that may in part originally have inspired this mode. Giulio was the principal executant only of the spandrels: Vasari reports, too generously (V, 524), that Giulio ". . . lavorò anche la maggior parte delle storie . . . ." However, Penni's contribution of three spandrels (by common critical consent: *Venus before Jupiter*,[403] *Mercury Descending*,[404] *Mercury with Psyche*) and both scenes in the *tende* amounts, roughly, to as much. There is no possible disguise for the tendency to softness in Penni's execution, but here, working presumably on Giulio's cartoons and in the presence of his aggressive example, the lesser man reforms his manner toward that of Giulio. The result is still weak, but at least in Penni's spandrels it contains a happy, though unintended fact: Penni's slackening of Giulio's models restores to them a more human, less statuary quality of surface and, as well, a diminished variant of a Raphaelesque grace. This is not the case, however, with the figures of the *tende*, which most of all appear to justify Sellaio's harsh disgust; these have no affirmative merit, but only the diminishing effects of Penni's transcription of the Giulian figure style. One spandrel, the initial episode of the story, in which Venus points out Psyche to her son, seems to be the work of yet another hand, Raffaelino dal Colle[405] (Hartt), based equally on Giulio's mode, but more wholly soft than Penni in the adaptation of it. We have it from Vasari's most enthusiastic report (VI, 558), taken from the deposition of the artist himself, that Giovanni da Udine, specialist for the shop in still-life and grotesquerie, is the author of the foliate, floral and vegetal architecture, and of the foreshortened *amoretti* and animals in the outer spaces of the scheme. These last,[406] also Giulian in their general style, are nevertheless the most expert accomplishments of actual painting in the whole room, and their particular invention, like their brilliant execution, is most probably Giovanni's.

It has often been a matter of speculation whether this depiction on the ceiling of only Psyche's heavenly adventures is intendedly thus incomplete, and if the rest of the story, with its terrestrial scenes, was not meant to be later painted on the walls, or woven into tapestries to hang on them. The mere sense of the story would seem to ask for such completion, and certain motives of action and gesture in the existing scenes suggest they were intended to be complemented by further episodes below. There is an analogy, also, with the scheme intended for the *Sala di Galatea*, fully carried out only much later, of heavenly and earthly realms adjoining on the walls and ceiling. The hint that something should be done about the missing scenes was taken up by others: lost drawings, seemingly of the post-Raphaelesque Roman school, were the basis for a set of prints (B. 39–70 and B. 235–38) of the earthly history of Psyche, by the Maestro del Dado and A. Veneziano. Their design was erroneously given by Bartsch to Raphael, but they are in part inventions by a posthumous follower, and in part mere pastiches of the existing frescoes. There is no evidence that Raphael himself, or his own assistants in his lifetime, made any defined plan for the decoration of the *Psiche* walls.

A presumed intention to complete Chigi's *Sala di Psiche* may well have been interrupted by the need to turn the manpower of the shop, with reinforcements, to work on a papal commission for the decoration of the loggia,[410-12, 415-21] overlooking the Cortile di S. Damaso, on the principal story of the Vatican apartments. The construction of the set of superimposed loggie had been begun by Bramante around 1513, and responsibility for their continued construction had then come, with Bramante's more important inheritance, to Raphael. Building on the loggie may have continued into 1518. A document of March 1518 (Golzio, 68) cities payment to Raphael "per l'opera della Loggia," and it may refer either to completion of the work of architecture or, equally well, to work already undertaken on its decoration. By May 4, 1519 the decoration had been finished. Marcantonio Michiel writes from Rome on that date of a "loggia longissima" as if work on it were done (Golzio, 98), and this is confirmed by payment on June 11, 1519, not to Raphael but (as had been the case earlier with the *Sala dei Palafrenieri*) "A li garzoni hanno dipinte la logia" (Golzio, 99). Contemporary writings of near date (Castiglione to Isabella d'Este, June 16, 1519 [Golzio, 100]; and Michiel once more, in his diary, December 27 [Golzio, 104]) again refer to the completed decoration of the loggia.

Evidently this decoration depends from, but also profoundly develops, the remarkable invention of a grotesque decorative style in the *Loggetta* of the Cardinal Bibbiena, two years before. In this papal and public context, however, the matter of the decoration could less well be only archaeological and pagan; the grotesque scheme was used here not only on its own decorative account, but as the elaborate setting of a series of biblical illustrations. These small narrative scenes, set out by fours in each of the thirteen vaults of the loggia, are the so-called *Bibbia di Raffaello*. Archaeological classicism and Christian illustration were so intimately juxtaposed for the first time in the Logge; and the basis for their coexistence has been made, not by any mutual accommodation of their contents, but in terms of form. The harmony that is thus achieved recalls, in its effectiveness, but not in its means, the synthesis of classical and Christian matter in the Stanza della Segnatura. As in the other late decorative schemes, the harmony of form in this one depends much on the integer that has been made of architecture and of painted decoration; and, here too, devices of illusionism are employed to interlock the forms of architecture and of painting.

The development in the Logge from the grotesque mode of the *Loggetta* involves no change in its principle, but there has been an expansion and elaboration of its possibilities such that all the effects of larger style first attained, or even intimated, in the *Loggetta*, are realized at their utmost in the Logge. The grotesque system here is no longer so visibly imitative of its Antique sources; it is a freer development on the given Ancient theme. Individual elements of motive and pattern still considerably depend, in a spirit of intended archaeological reference, on the Antique; and so does the system of arrangement of these motives in the single decorative fields. The whole design, however, cannot be referred to a parallel in Ancient style, as had been the case in the *Loggetta*. The gestalt of pattern is that of High Renaissance, not of Ancient classicism: it is at once more precisely disciplined and more self-consciously subtle in the manipulation of design. In contrast to the *Loggetta* the scale of ornament is now smaller and its elements are much more closely woven.[411-12] The sense of geometrical definition of each element of grotesque is clearer, and the meaning of the relation of order among them is, in their close adjacency, more apparent. The effect of ornament is of a rich, close texture of geometrical design, at once surely disciplined and almost infinitely various. A major new means of attaining this effect is in the reinvention for use in the Logge by Giovanni da Udine, the chief executant of the ornament, of the Roman technique of stucco work. The patterns of relief in stucco make more than half of the ornamental scheme below the vaults. They extend the properties of the design literally into another dimension; and at the same time they are integral to the body of the architecture as the painting, except in its illusionistic episodes, is not.

This grotesque mode, enriched by the incorporation in it of the stucchi, conforms in the Logge to a preexistent architectural system of which the logic is more complex than in the *Loggetta;* this richer articulation of the actual structure has its response in the richer pattern of grotesque. This sympathy of ornament and architecture at the same time contains an element of difference between them — already, but less definitively, remarked in the grotesque system of the *Loggetta*: by its contrast in scale and variety of form, the grotesquerie make compensation and relief for the more rigorous geometry of architecture. However, in another sense, the grotesques but continue, with progressively more intimate and various differentiation, the process of articulation that begins in the logic of the architecture. Here, the close-textured ornament does not merely conform to the structure; it adheres to it. The decorated surface is like a living skin upon the body of the architecture: mobile and porous, giving respiration, as in true Greek statuary, to the pure, scanned substance of the underlying form.

For the invention of the details of this supreme formal unity Giovanni da Udine was certainly responsible, and where their execution was not his own it was directly supervised by him. But Giovanni never again, as an independent artist, achieved a result like this, either in quality or in the complete definition of a comparable idea. It must be assumed here, as in the *Loggetta*, and yet more positively, that the intention, and a plan sufficiently specified to realize it exactly, were given to Giovanni by Raphael: Giovanni's gifts, his research, and his industry are Raphael's instrument. Two minor offshoots of high merit come from the mode that is thus developed for the Logge grotesques: the added vertical borders of the Sistine Tapestries, of Giovanni's own design (c. 1519),[413] and the chiaroscuro embrasures painted at the same time into the Stanza dell' Incendio by a Logge assistant, Polidoro da Caravaggio.[414]

The scheme of decoration within the vaults of the Logge works, with different means, on basic principles like those in the entire grotesque design. This scheme also intends to extend the articulation of the actual architecture and, in so doing, be one with it; and, at the same, it means to give imaginative differentiation — relieving, enriching, and contrasting — to the architectural form. The vaulting scheme, however, is different in its scale and temper from the grotesquerie. Its motives are as affirmative as the grotesques are discreet. There is a different emphasis, in the painting of the vaults, on liberty and lightness, appropriate to the character of that part of the architecture; just as in the grotesques, on the supporting members, the emphasis is on restraint. The whole vault decoration is based on an exploitation, in different degrees, of a general illusionist conceit. In each vault fictitious frames are made, in the form of painted casements, for the biblical narrative scenes, and around these is projected a painted pseudo-architectural roof. Both the painted architecture and picture frames depend in each vault from a square *voussoir,* decorated with the stucco figure of an angel. Each of the first six vaults has an ingeniously different painted covering; the last six bays repeat in inverse order, but not literally, the types of roofing of the first six. The seventh, central, bay is a distinct composition, in stucco rather than in paint, and unique in its roofing scheme. In the first six bays there is an alternation of strictly architectural forms of cover with coverings that, for lack of a more exact word, may be said to resemble baldacchini. In the first bay the architectural form is essentially closed, to give a proper stable terminus, or beginning, to the set, but in the inner bays that are roofed with architecture their perspective opening is drastic, and makes contrast with the closed space of the alternate baldacchino roofs. This alternation of designs, however, is of elements almost all of which intend illusionistic effect.

The roofing of the first bay[415] is a fictive stonework lattice, with its members rendered conscientiously in perspective. Through each of its openings we see, as if into an adjacent heaven, a minuscule angel. This heavenly space is quite distinct from that of the casement frames within the lattice work, through which we look into the first scenes of biblical narrative. The lattice is in direct vertical perspective, and explicitly extends the actual architectural space; the pictures are in perspective as if hung against the surface of the vault (though they freely spatially penetrate it) at an angle meant to suit, more or less comfortably, the oblique vision of the spectator.

An ideal picture space is thus projected within a disparate context of illusion, which is applied even to the painting of the pictures' casement frames. This system of juxtaposition of ideal and illusive projections is maintained throughout the vaults. Their intended different reference is so clear that no evident conflict arises in the spectator's mind between them.

The second bay [416] is covered with a closed system, with no intention of illusion: the corners of the vault are painted with flat tone ornamented with discreet grotesque motives, and framed with bands of grotesquerie; the effect is, in rough analogy, like that of ornament in the Antique third style. The decoration of this vault refers back, as it were, to the lower architecture, and in contrast to the vaults before and after it, makes a caesura in the sequence of spatial and perspective play. It gives all the more relief to the sudden upsurge of extreme perspective illusion in the third bay.[417] A towering peristyle opens upward into the Roman sky, where birds soar at vast distance. This is the most surprising virtuoso conceit of illusion that survives to us within a classical scheme of painting: on this scale and in this context the artist permits himself a liberty of whole statement that would have been, by classical aesthetic, inappropriate on the ceiling of the Farnesina. This perspective insistence again recalls, as so often in these decorative schemes, the precedent of Peruzzi; and so indeed do some of the specific forms of the painted architecture. The suggestion has been made (Lanckoranska), not so far provable but not implausible, that Peruzzi may have had a part in the design of the Logge vaults.

The fourth vault [418] is painted with a more elaborate reprise, more richly figured, of the grotesque style of the second; the fifth vault [419] repeats the drastic motive of illusion of the third, with a severer architecture. The sixth bay [420] is roofed as if with a *tenda*, decorated with grotesques, stretched tight and tied down to the sides of the vault; at the edges of the *tenda* we can see bits of the blue of a supposed sky outside. The motive conforms to the sequence in the vaults of alternation of open and closed coverings, but it refers, even though with nonperspective means, to an illusion. The seventh vault [421] intends a stability and emphasis appropriate to its central place. A heavy central panel in the vault carries the framed papal arms; the stucco ornament below, in white and gold, which here replaces painting, is conceived in an ingenious reference to the inner peristyle of an Antique temple. Its major order helps enframe the painted illustrations, and a lower order has its own population of stucco Antique figurines.

In this sequence of the vaults richness and variety of form and of conceit, and a discreet luxury of ornament, function within a perfectly apparent rationale of whole order. Combined with the equal richness and yet more apparent order of the grotesque system on the lower architecture, the effect of the whole is without peer in its kind of classical expression.

The content of the decoration is of course in part that of its assigned matter of Christian illustration; in this context the Bible scenes have the character of paintings hung into a decor so remarkable that the meaning of these paintings, as a group, tends to blur into that of their surroundings. The subtly dominating tone of illustrative meaning is that which emerges from the smaller, diffused, yet pervasive incidents of classical subject matter. However, in a more important sense, the content of this decoration is less that of its subject matter than of its form: of the ideas and sensations that proceed from its aesthetic system. Here there is reason made evident in order, and the essential restraint of high classical decorum, enriched and relieved with wit, with fantasy, and learning. The atmosphere of the Logge bespeaks restrained opulence and suave delight; it is the product of a hardly surpassable sophistication. This character of content, an ultimate of its own kind, is that of a late stage in the evolution of a classical style. It is by no means yet a formalistic hedonism, such as that to which the next generation would arrive, but it is more nearly purely aesthetic in its matter and meaning than the earlier creations of High Renaissance classicism had been. The ethic import that inhabited classical pictures until the Tapestry Cartoons — defined supremely, but also finally, in them — has receded and given place, in the Logge, to a — still soundly classical —(in the colloquial sense) Epicureanism.

In the second half of 1519, apparently just after the completion of the principal loggia, Giovanni da Udine and his assistants were given the task of decorating the loggia *just below, on the ground floor of the Cortile. In this — in effect — public passageway [422] no such splendid company was served as by the loggia above, and there was no attempt to match its opulence. This was a job of decoration in the common sense, and harsh restoration has made it look today as if it belonged to a stage still lower in the aesthetic hierarchy, to house-painting. Michiel complained, in the note in his diary of December 27, 1519 (Golzio, 104), in which he says this Loggia is completed, that it was painted "assai volgarmente, et con poco spese, benche vistosamente." There is small doubt, from the way in which the matter is reported in Vasari (VI, 554), and from the look of the decoration itself, that Raphael gave it only minimum attention, if he gave it any. His role here seems to have in fact been that which some critics attribute to him throughout this late phase: in effect, of entrepreneur. The responsibility, apparently for invention as well as execution, was assumed by Giovanni da Udine, here working in quasi-independent status. This is the only instance among the decorative schemes where we are not dealing with an aesthetic compound, and in which the element, Raphael, is not definable; and the consequence brings out, into clearer relief, the same element in the invention and style of the Logge above.

Considerations of expense condition the mode and means of execution of the lower loggia but they did not dictate its system, or its quality, of aesthetic organization. The least effort was expended on the walls, where there are flat fields of color, containing sparse geometrical ornament *all'antica*, but no grotesques. The arch-faces are adorned with stucco panels, severe and monotonous in shape. The sole interest of decoration is in the vaults where, as in the Logge, the theme is of illusion. In a somewhat awkward dactyl sequence, a vault of closed architectural form is succeeded by two vaults both painted in the semblance of an open arbor; this order is repeated along the whole length of the loggia. In the closed vaults an effect of illusion, as of a vaster — obliquely, a Pantheon-like — space, is made by coffering arranged in diminishing perspective. The arbored bays are open to the sky, and (in Vasari's description [*ibid.*]) ". . . pieni di viti cariche d'uva, di vitalbe, di gelsomini, di rosai, e diverse sorti animali e uccelli." This latter conception turns into literal illusion the invention of the *Sala di Psiche*, there quite differently employed. Both devices for decoration of the vault depend eventually, though in free transcription, on models of the Ancient style.

The richness of texture and the great deliberation of variety of the Logge are understandably missing from this decoration, but not even its basic ordnance suggests a comparable harmony. Its intent of illusion does not, as in the Logge, finally respect the rationale of the existing architecture. This illusion does not imaginatively project an idea but literally represents a natural circumstance. In the arbored vaults at least, what is represented has novelty, in the Roman school, of meaning; it is the first intrusion here (though Mantegna and Leonardo had devised such things long before) of the *vigna* and the villa into the *palazzo*: a reference in the context of the court to the nostalgia — all the more felt in its atmosphere — for life *alla rustica.*

It is a support for our conception in the greater loggia of a classicism of style based chiefly on its decorative form that Raphael seems to have concerned himself very little with the pictorial illustrations in it of the Bible. With minor — and even then only dubious — exceptions the evidence indicates that he entrusted the invention and design of these to his assistants with, as Vasari tells us (IV, 362), Giulio in general charge. Almost none of the actual paintings (all damaged or painfully restored) explicitly reflects the master's style, and there is no verifiable reason to see his hand, or the projection of any identifiable state of mind of his, in the fair number of surviving original *preparatory drawings. Vasari identifies (IV, 362–63) the executants of some of the Bible paintings for us, and names other assistants who participated in the work, and he indicates that there were others still, unnamed. What seems to have occurred in the illustration of the Logge Bible was a relative liberation from Raphael's direct supervision of the younger artists in his shop. Giulio himself worked here essentially independently, and in his role as supervisor seems to have subcontracted his freedom at least to the most capable of the others among the assistants. The paintings that result are objects of some aesthetic interest, and, in some cases, historical importance. These latter include the first clear manifestations of the personalities of two new recruits to the corps of Raphael's assistants, who emerged shortly later than the time of the Logge to prominence rivaling that of Giulio and Penni among the painters of the post-Raphaelesque Roman school. The contributions of Perino del Vaga and Polidoro da Caravaggio to the Logge Bible came to have so pronounced an un-Raphaelesque individuality, and are so much more relevant to their personal future than to their present context of surrounding late Raphaelesque style, that they are better treated in a later, separate place.

THE PORTRAITS

The category within Raphael's late work in which his own identity is most clearly manifest is at the opposite extreme of his production from the great decorative schemes. The portraits of these years require Raphael's personal involvement to a degree not present in the larger works, including even their execution in the clear majority of cases by his hand. The portraits are, as an artistic problem, inherently unlike the other aspects of the master's practice, yet what is revealed in them of Raphael's thought is an index of his responsibility for analogous ideas that may appear in other, compound, works. In their relative simplicity of formal problem the portraits are unlike the more ambitious paintings, but for this very reason their design may show, in simpler guise, a symptom of Raphael's basic formal preoccupation of their moment. In one respect of content the portraits are a link between the works of decoration and the large religious works. In the portraits the human content is neither recessive to form, as in the decorations, nor dramatically urgent, as in the great religious pictures; the portraits record a human presence, of appearance and of psyche, in a normal situation. And because they are records, the portrait paintings pose with special stringency the problem of accord between reality and aesthetic order, which in this last phase becomes acute.

The subjects of the late portraits are identified save for a single sitter. One of the portraits only, that of Leo X with the Cardinals Giulio de' Medici and Rossi, is an official work. The sitters in the rest include some of the most distinguished representatives of literary culture at Pope Leo's court, who are, at the same time — as we know from the tone of contemporary letters — Raphael's close friends. They are the humanists into whose circle he was first introduced some years before, at the time of the invention of the program for the Segnatura. His first acquaintance with some among this group was evidenced by his painting of their faces into the *Parnassus*; two at least, and perhaps three of these men reappear as subjects of the portraits now. Except for the portrait done on papal command, none of these would seem to have been undertaken as normally — as it were commercially — commissioned works. Raphael could find no time to discharge all of his commissions for important princes and hardly touched his major ventures with his own hand. Yet he willingly assumed, and for the most part himself executed, these lesser but more personally compelling tasks that are the portraits of his friends.

Probably the earliest among the portraits of this phase is the *Baldassare Castiglione* (Paris, Louvre).[423] It is referred to in a letter from Bembo to Bibbiena on April 19, 1516 (Golzio, 43) as a past, but evidently not long past, work. Castiglione had been away from Rome from before April in 1514 and for much of 1515; however, he had been in Rome in the early autumn of that year (Golzio, 37). The portrait may date from this visit, but might also be from the beginning months of 1516. Of all the portraits, it is conceived most in the vein of the Tapestry Cartoons and like them it is, in its own field, Raphael's consummate accomplishment; it is a consequence of the same extraordinary, but unenduring, artistic state of grace. It is of an incomparable lucidity among the portraits, and this lucidity is occasioned in part, surely, by the degree to which the meeting of the artist and the sitter is a meeting of like minds: this is the exceptional instance where the maker and the matter of the portrait constitute, far more than is usual, an equation. In the artist, furthermore, there is that clarity of knowledge of his subject that comes from friendship.

No other one among Raphael's sitters shows so much in his gaze as does Castiglione of intelligence. His attitude is vitally alert, and at the same time of contained ease. His body is not, as is more usual in the other portraits, a nearly inert clothed geometric form, but seems to convey as if organically the powers that are in it, and in its inhabiting personality, of energies and disciplined restraints. The silhouette, defined in a bolder than the normal contrast of darks on light, has a force of ideal shape like that of the protagonists in the Cartoons and carries with it a like implication for the figure's content. Deliberately, however, this is nothing like so severe. Castiglione demonstrates decorum but not apostolic austerity; his image is not meant to be a fabrication of superior symbolic worth but an accessible, communicative human presence. His silhouette is tempered with descriptive incidents of varied shape, utterly premeditated but with the look of accidental nature. Their effect of pattern, alternately subtle and almost electrically charged, is a commentary in pure visual terms, woven out of the appearances of form, on the sitter's personality.

Far more than in any prior portrait, and unlike in the abstracting technique of the Tapestry Cartoons, the sense of presence in this portrait and its particular effect of personality are defined by the handling of light. In lesser incidents especially of the Cartoons an intenser sense of actuality had been achieved by draughtsmanly means alone; here a comparable result is gained by heightened truth of optical effect. This actuality of light is fused into the highest discipline of tectonic form so that, as is the case with the elements of sharper naturalism in the Cartoons, there is no compromise of classical synthesis but an extension of its including range. In the *Castiglione*, light is not so much intensified into effects of contrast as it is made more strongly and more richly internally diverse. The vigor of distinctions in the light between the figure and its background projects the bodily presence of the sitter into more actual relief; and at the same time fine distinctions in the light transcribe the sense of atmosphere to make a credible ambient of space for him — limited, but optically as if real.

The bolder differences of light adhere to and fuse with the substantial pattern and are the most persuasive factor in the definition of the whole design: this is the one instance in the art of Raphael where the process of the forming of design upon the canvas approximates a principle like that used by the Venetians. There is also an analogy with Venice in the way in which light gives actuality not only to the ambient but to the substance and its surfaces, in the guise of texture. But still more important than this working of light toward an illusion is the way in which it operates to qualify the substance of design: the vibration that is in the light casts an animating tissue on the whole tectonic form, enlivening it with oppositely subtle and intangible means. This diffused sparkling — a muted incandescence — is not only an effect of form; it is another emanation, made visible, of the personality of Castiglione. For all its complex inner differentiation this close-textured light is ultimately an agent of pictorial unity, and this role is emphasized by the near-absence in it of a content of color. There is opulent modulation, but of near-monochrome, of white, black and green-browned or reddish greys. As this harmony of tone is enlivened to the point of vibrancy, so also is the harmony — into which the working of the light is fused — of tectonic form; and the character of content which comes both from the human illustration and from form is one with these. In supreme degree among the portraits the *Castiglione* is the richest and most complex integer of form and content: the highest demonstration of the working on an actual humanity of the powers of classical synthesis.

It has been repeated often that what in the Castiglione portrait resembles the Venetian style is there in consequence of the influence on it (as on earlier episodes of more than normally "painterly" manner in Raphael) of Sebastiano del Piombo; the suggestion is supported by the fact that by this time unquestioned preeminence in the art of portraiture in Rome belonged to Sebastiano. But also by this time (as we shall see more precisely in a later place) Sebastiano's own art had become so much Romanized that it could offer no precept for such optical truth or luminous variety as is in the *Castiglione*; that hardly existed in this degree even in Sebastiano's first Roman pieces. If Venice must be called in account for the style of this portrait it can be only in the original, and not in Sebastiano's transmuted variant. There is no record to confirm it, but no reason to deny the possibility of Raphael's direct vision of an imported early Titian — brought to Rome, it might even be speculated, from Mantua by Castiglione himself.

Such an assumption, however, is not necessary to explain this picture, and would in any case explain no more than a part of the mode of handling even of the light. The *Castiglione* has its own antecedents within the art of Raphael, ultimately in the Guards of the *Bolsena*,[216] different in context and different of effect, but basically akin in their artistic means. More closely, the *Castiglione* depends on and superlatively develops the soft-lit, textured presence of the *Donna Velata* [247] of the year (or so) before. And like it, and still more closely, the *Castiglione* makes reference to a renewed experience of the *Mona Lisa*: [37] that precedent, more than any other, explains what is unique in kind and in degree in the style of the *Castiglione.* The *Castiglione* is, more than the *Donna Velata*, a transcription — into male gender — of Leonardo's model, and must have looked still more like it in its original, longer dimension (recorded for us in Rembrandt's drawing). More even than it resembles the

Venetians, the light of the *Castiglione* resembles that of the *Mona Lisa*: differentiated with subtle vibrancy within an including harmony, carefully defined, of tone; creating texture, but muting and absorbing color also into deliberated harmony. But the likeness extends beyond the lighting and the obvious close relationship of composition, into the manner and principle of manipulating almost every element of content as of form. Evidently, Raphael has "modernized" his exemplar, in a sense archaic, with a handling both of technique and ideas that is far more free but not less controlled; his effects of design and expression are bolder and more decisive, appropriately more masculine, and his naturalism is free of those constraints which, in the *Mona Lisa*, contain her still behind a veil of apparent artifice. Raphael's portrait is a reshaping, into the vocabulary and with the resources of the highest classical style, of the perfect statement of the portrait in the style's first phase; this is a meeting of ultimates, each of its context within the history of classical portraiture.

In the letter mentioned earlier, written by Bembo to Bibbiena on April 19, 1516 (Golzio, 43), he described the portrait of Castiglione as looking — as far as truth of resemblance went — like a pupil's work by comparison with the portrait Raphael had painted apparently recently, of Antonio Tebaldeo. Tebaldeo, another member of Raphael's circle of humanist friends, had been painted by him before among the company of moderns in the *Parnassus*.[424] This vaunted later portrait has been lost; a version, unpublished, which makes unconvincing pretense to originality is in Switzerland, and an old, apparently partial copy exists in the Uffizi.[425] There is no means of deducing from this evidence what must have been the artistic merit of the original. Since Bembo's praise for it was on the basis of its striking character of resemblance it would seem that, in style, it was distinguished from the *Castiglione* in much the same way as are the other portraits that postdate it: by a less exquisite balance between the interest of design and that of representation, and a more pronounced insistence on the latter.

An authentic portrait does survive of what must have been almost the same moment as the *Tebaldeo*, which demonstrates this more assertive naturalism. This is the double portrait (Rome, Galleria Doria)[426] of *Andrea Navagero and Agostino Beazzano*, two further members of Raphael's humanist circle — the latter of whom had, like Tebaldeo, also earlier appeared in the *Parnassus*. A famous letter of Bembo's, again to Bibbiena, of April 3, 1516 (Golzio, 42), tells of a trip intended on the morrow to see Tivoli, in company with Raphael, Castiglione, Navagero, and Beazzano; the journey would be undertaken "per dare piacere a M. Andrea" [Navagero] who at the end of April would depart for Venice. The *terminus ante* of the double portrait is thus fixed, and the particular pretext of its painting may have been just in this proposed departure: to memorialize the friendship of the two poets, whose names are coupled in Bembo's letter as their presences are coupled in the picture. There is no evidence for the suggestion (Fischel) that the two images may first have been conceived as separate portraits and then joined; the original sense of this picture is precisely in the association it depicts. It may explain the particular psychological character this portrait has that it was meant to document the association of the two men, not for each other but for a third person, Bembo, the friend of both. The picture was in Bembo's house in Padua, where it was seen by Michiel, and it was given by the Cardinal to one of the sitters, Beazzano, only in 1538 (Golzio, 162).

The problem of the double portrait was new in the Roman school. Precedents for the type existed, but less rarely in Venice than in Central Italy, and it is not likely that Venetian examples were known in Rome. One such Venetian precedent is attributable to Sebastiano before 1512: a portrait of the musician friends Verdelotti and Ubretto (last recorded in the deposit of the Berlin Museums; there assigned uncertainly to Titian); but there are no genuine instances of double portraits within Sebastiano's Roman phase. He did, however, paint the first Roman group portrait (excluding of course the numberless such representations in fresco) in this same year, 1516. As a problem of design this work (now in Washington) is expressly dissimilar from that which Raphael attempted in the *Navagero and Beazzano.*

Raphael's organization of this picture began, evidently, with the datum afforded by the norm he knew, the single portrait. Beazzano, on the right, is described as if he were indeed a separable portrait image, cast in a posture that, roughly, resembles the *Castiglione.* Navagero is confronted against this normative portrait form, and such compensations as are necessary to the sense of the design are imposed on him. His silhouette — especially indistinct in the rubbed condition of the picture, and imprecise in the pattern it makes of darks on dark — balances approximately, in reverse, the oblique pyramid of Beazzano's shape; the bases of the two pyramids are interlocked. Navagero's pose in space does not quite make a counterpart for that of Beazzano; the former's body is more nearly set into profile. His head turns rightward until its view and glance approximately match his partner's. The two figures make a responsive complementary design, but the few devices which assert their unity in pattern — for example, the diagonal connection from Navagero's hat to Beazzano's hand, the common base made by the arms for both triangles of the body forms — do not effectively achieve it. To some extent, the pattern's additive effect is relieved by the slight displacement of the figures to the left.

For all this deliberation in its formal structure, the portrait means firstly to achieve a stronger assertion — more than in the *Castiglione* — of the physical and psychological existence of its two persons. In no other portrait does the format in itself so much suggest the old Albertian precept of a window into space: improbable as the analogy may, on the faces of it, seem, the two poets are in a situation in respect to us like that of the putti in the *Sistine Madonna*. The frame works like a casement; it is as if we looked from the space outside a room — from a street or garden, or better, from within a loggia — at the two men sitting at a window. They have turned from their own converse to look at us; beyond them in the room's interior, at an indistinct distance, is the pattern (now almost obliterated) of tooled leather *paramenti* on the wall. This spatial situation is not forced; it is diminished in specificity to that point where it is more implied than stated as a precise descriptive fact, but its origin in actuality remains sensible.

The light, less tangible, is more actually explicit. A strong daylight reaches through the casement but is consumed in the darkness of the room; the light, unlike the warm diffusion of the lighting in the *Castiglione* is, in its very device and also — though with much moderation — in its effects, proto-tenebrist. By contrast with the *Castiglione* this fall of light searches form intensely, seeking its intimate accidents of shape and modelling them with accented chiaroscuro contrast. The light is unitary in direction, but not unifying in its effect on form: it tends to isolate the parts of form in contrast and to analyze detail. Yet, this lighting requires that of the *Castiglione* for its antecedent. A different order of presence is achieved here — and from Bembo's comment, in the *Tebaldeo*, too — than in the *Castiglione*: more immediate; partaking in its space, in lighting, and in the kind of description that this lighting makes, of the character of illusion. This illusionism is controlled, and the figures' continence of pose and their deliberation of design further hold this illusionistic reference within classicizing confines. But the sense that was in the *Castiglione* is diminished here: of an existence discrete from and superior to that of the spectator. A principle of classical portrait style — the synthetic self-containment of the portrait image — is incipiently compromised in the double portrait.

The pose of Navagero in the portrait is, at long distance and indirectly, Giorgionesque. Apparently in 1515, when Raphael chose to recollect Leonardo, Sebastiano del Piombo chose to remember his own earlier Venetian exemplars, and in his portrait of a *Young Violinist* (Paris, Collection G. de Rothschild; the inscribed date falsely extended to read as 1518)[456] he resurrected the posture of Titian's *Ariosto* which, in turn, depends on the Brunswick portrait of Giorgione. Sebastiano's picture may have served in part to inspire the posture of Navagero. Quite certainly, however, it was the direct source for the portrait, probably of Raphael's design but wholly of Giulio Romano's execution, of *Bindo Altoviti* (Washington, National Gallery, Kress Collection; c. 1516).[427] The *Altoviti* improves upon the design of Sebastiano's model in the sense of a classical correction: the posture of the sitter is more organically felt, and his movement is a proper contrapposto, in which the parts of bodily form mesh as they do not in Sebastiano's stiffer and more additive design. However, where Sebastiano's image quite preserves the earlier classical quality of an ideal distance, the *Altoviti*, like the *Navagero*, means to affirm a nearer and intenser presence. Yet more than in the *Navagero*, Altoviti's attitude implies movement; it is felt as a turning to communicate, and the glance — almost a stare — in which this turning culminates is insistent beyond that of either sitter of the double portrait.

What Raphael might have wished to stress of the sense of actuality has been put more pressingly by Giulio. He defines the hair in hard-drawn color of more tangible reality in effect than in a Dürer. The skin is painted with a close brushwork that is also hard, but which yet creates, by its response to light, a smooth-shining sensuous texture. The new force that Raphael had given light is exaggerated, so that here it no longer searches out and modulates the form but makes sharp contrast on it, of bright reflection and absorbent dark. As in his contemporary translation of Raphael in the *Fire in the Borgo*,[376] Giulio makes disparities of means which, in Raphael, still intend to be resolved in harmony. Almost most strikingly, Giulio's personality asserts itself in color. The hues are like those Raphael employs but their tonality is different, partly from their content of a stronger light: the darks are more smoked and glowing, the lighter hues more lustrous and intense. The color does not quite make, and precisely does not quite intend, harmony; its atmosphere of slight dissonance and its intonation of morbidity (in both the English and Italian senses of the word) are meant, and conform to Giulio's interpretation of his sitter's personality — more probably an imposition than an interpretation.

Altoviti's expression only superficially suggests the states of mind we are accustomed to in Raphael's preceding sitters. He has been handled in a way that approximates, but is not really like, Raphael's approach to a female portrait; but even in his images of the Fornarina Raphael was concerned more with intelligence, and less with sensuous beauty and sensuality of spirit, than Giulio in his painting of this young man. Each element of description and all the concomitant elements of form are so handled as to stress, now openly, now with veiled indirection, the content of sensuality that Giulio finds in Altoviti's beauty. The point is not that such a personality as Giulio creates for Altoviti was abnormal in its time, but that it is anormative from the point of view of this time's classical conception of personality. Not only is the insistence of Altoviti's communication unclassical, but so is the intimate and faintly morbid meaning he communicates. More distantly than in the case of the Castiglione portrait, Leonardo is again recalled to mind; there is an air here, in debased translation, of the late *St. John*,[250] which Leonardo probably had with him at this time in Rome.

The best version of the portrait of Cardinal Bernardo Bibbiena that survives to us (Florence, Pitti)[428] is not from Raphael's hand. It cannot be identified as the production of a nameable assistant, but it is in any case unlikely that among all his later portrait subjects Raphael should have entrusted this one, of his close friend and protector, and intended relative by marriage, to an aide. The Pitti picture is a copy, of close contemporary date and fair quality, of what was in all likelihood a lost original substantially by Raphael himself. From the accounts of Bibbiena's various diplomatic missions outside Rome the most probable date of painting of this portrait would have been 1517, and even in the copy the evidence of style confirms this date.

As does Giulio's *Altoviti*, the Bibbiena portrait grows out of the double portrait in the Doria. The motive of pose of Bibbiena develops, with particular stresses, that of Beazzano. The bulk of body in the *Bibbiena* is increased, and so also is the clarity with which that bulk conforms to a structure of geometry; the effect of large pyramidal design in the *Bibbiena* is emphatic almost to the point of seeming arbitrary. This massive presence is made to assert its occupancy of space much more positively than does Beazzano. The left arm of Bibbiena, strongly relieved in white, defines the front plane of the picture quite explicitly, but his torso is set obliquely to this plane; the right arm is no less suggestive of diagonal effect. The head also contains a duality of axes: the acquiline face is straight in line with the torso but the eyes incline sharply to the front. The whole form, more rigorously conforming than before to an apparent geometric order, at the same time indicates that this order is disposed in space: immobile in posture, the figure is instead made aesthetically active.

A near-tension is created between the severe and static pyramidal geometry of form and its sharp accents of spatial movement; and a like effect is present in the personality. The dark glance turns with almost gimlet sharpness out of the strongly modelled head, and its quality is relieved, but not quite relaxed, by Bibbiena's smile. The classical sense of an enduring image, vital in potential but, in the moment of its presentation to us, poised and at ease, has lessened in this portrait to give place to a sharper, more tensed actuality of psychological and physical moment. It does not restore an entire effect of a classicism that the oppositely permanent and abstracting character of formal order has been so much stressed. Such a counterweight restores a balance among the picture's elements, but does not recreate a synthesis; there is a disparity between the order of form and the character of content in the Bibbiena portrait that is sensible as such.

It is in the most important and ambitious of the late portraits, *Leo X with the Cardinals Giulio de' Medici and Luigi Rossi* (Florence, Pitti; second half 1517 or, less likely, 1518),[429] that the syndromes of unclassical tendency in the just preceding portraits emerge in overt and acute display. The actuality that is intended now, in the papal portrait, is in its degree and quantity no longer a malleable factor of artistic process, of such flexibility as incorporation into synthesis requires. We have observed of the Bibbiena portrait that it is possible to make, by formal order, aesthetic counterweight for what was, there, a lesser actuality, but not possible to remake synthesis with it; synthesis cannot be imposed on such hard facts of analytic truth. By his own account (Vasari V, 42) Giulio assisted Raphael in the execution of the triple portrait, and some of the effect it makes of realist insistence may be his. However, it is not possible to distinguish where his hand leaves off and Raphael's begins; the level of actuality is quite consistent through the entire portrait. The intention to make actuality of this kind is, here, Raphael's own, and Giulio in this case is no more than conforming to it.

It is possible that Sebastiano's group portrait of Cardinal Sauli and his secretaries of 1516 may have been some stimulus to the invention of the portrait of Leo with Giulio and Rossi, but there is closer antecedent in the group portraits in fresco of Raphael himself, as of that of Julius and his court in the *Decretals* of the Stanza della Segnatura.[172] But the recollection of this precedent is only of analogy in motive, and confronts us with the measure of Raphael's great change since then in style. The Pitti portrait brings to what seems an extreme conclusion the process of increasingly specific description of reality that had begun only so short a while before. Parts of clothing, the accessories, and — most marked — the heads are painted with an insistence of detail far exceeding that in the previous portraits. Leo's unbeautiful face is transcribed with the unsparing eye for record of the later Quattrocento, and with a nearly Flemish subtlety of hand. Giulio's countenance, handsome by contrast of nature rather than of art, is no less carefully described in its particulars of surface. Almost most of all, Rossi's portrait has the value of illusion. Each head is powerfully plastically structured with the same light, now more than ever forced, that seeks out its precise detail. The intention of analysis that is in this light is so marked that each portrait is a separate act of seeing; and this separateness is evident not only as a fact of the artist's visual, but of his psychological attention. The three persons have no psychological relation to each other; Rossi, however, is intensely in communication with the spectator.

The intention of this forced light is to find and reveal, almost as if with the power of a spotlight, but also with its inescapable effect of isolation, discrete parts of visual truth. Evidently, as the light breaks into contrast, the seen pattern breaks up with it, into relative discontinuity: it is disruptive of that kind of unity which had before existed in design, in the act of vision, and in content. But this light asserts — not in compensation for this loss of unity but in place of it — a more forceful and more active, and more vitally convincing, actuality. The image of nature is a less synthetic one (in both senses) than had been given us before, but its parts affirm themselves with hitherto unmatched power. In part only, a careful moderation of effects of color — of varied flat reds, with blacks and whites — tempers this effect of light.

Raphael's searching toward a more vital character of illusion is also evident in his handling of this portrait's spatial scheme. For the first time in a portrait — and in the only case except for the recent *Coronation* of the Stanza dell' Incendio — the space is projected in an a-normal perspective, oblique to the front plane and looked at as if slightly from above. With an effect more marked than in the *Coronation*, this space is opened to us and the physical contents of the picture, in their newly emphatic actuality, are made accessible to us. There is explicitly no intention of creating, in the portrait image, persons discrete from us in physical and psychic situation. These are revelations of real presences, as imperfect in appearance as ourselves and with no psychological disguise, existing in a space and light we share: its reality is commented finally — Flemish-wise — by the reflection of the source of light in the knob on the papal chair.

It is still Raphael's intention to present this actuality to us in terms of art: of an aesthetic ordnance deduced from classical principles, but accommodated in mode and means to what, in this structure of illusion, is necessarily new. More than in the *Bibbiena* there is stress on the elements of geometry in design, as if to compensate the stronger actuality by a stronger affirmation of aesthetic order. The composition is defined in triangular and diagonal forms, locked in intersection, and of hard decisiveness of shape. The lines and shapes that make energy of movement in the design are as sharp as those which, contrastingly, intend stability. There is an almost entire abolition of effects of rhythmic grace of drawing, even in incidents of drapery, and there is no evidence of contrapposto posture in the figures; their attitudes are no less severe than are their compositional shapes. Hard parallels, or still more, diagonals that intersect at strict right angles, make a reticulation on the surface and in the space of the design. This reticule does not resolve the movements of oblique direction; rather it checks them into counterbalance. Then, despite their distinct situations in the oblique space, the heads are aligned in something like an isocephaly; this, because it seems to refer to a unity in plane, works as if in opposition to the spatial movement, constraining it and closing it.

All this assertion and explicitness of geometric structure in design works with an effect of force and clarity like that in the light as it defines the portrait heads: in their definition, too, there is the same intention of a kind of statement which, in its ideal distinctness, should have classicizing value. But as the portrait heads, for all their clarity, are not only separate contents in the picture but disjunctive forms, so also are the elements of geometry that have been so carefully manipulated in the whole design. Classical devices and classical intent persist in the papal portrait, in some respects with even stronger stress than they had had before; but beside them, just as strong in stress, are those elements beyond the competence of classical synthesis to contain, which are in conflict with its means of discipline. We now have, unequivocally from Raphael's own mind and mostly from his hand, a clear case of a faulted classicism.

Raphael must have realized — without our critical assistance — to what extent the problem he had posed himself in the *Leo* X was a dilemma. No way could be found beyond the impasse made of its irresolvable equal and opposing ambitions except by breaking the tie, as it were, between them. The decision made was, understandably for Raphael's character, in favor of the potential of development in a new direction that the papal portrait, and the portraits that preceded it, contained. The resolution to pursue a portraiture yet more effective as illusion was boldly carried out; and, paradoxically, the very freedom of the new solution permitted that there be carried over into it elements of genuinely classical effect, not strained to doctrinaire extreme or denatured as they were in the *Leo.*

The vehicle of this new solution was the self-portrait with an unknown friend, called usually by the romantic title *Raphael and his Fencing Master* (Paris, Louvre; slightly enlarged all around, and drastically in need of cleaning).[430] The technique of its painting corresponds to those parts of the *Transfiguration* [438] that are of Raphael's execution and imply a contemporary date of 1518 or 1519. The motive of the main figure in the portrait — the turning posture of the swordsman with the outstretched hand — is also clearly the result of meditation on the Andrew of the *Transfiguration* (the figure in the foreground of the altarpiece that, by universal assent, is from Raphael's own hand). These two like figures share a strong intention of communication with the spectator, achieved in both instances by a movement of the whole visible physical form in projection toward the picture plane. In the swordsman the effect of projection is yet more positive than in the Saint, from the near isolation of his motive in the picture frame; explicitly, his pointing arm intends entry into our actual space. In both the Andrew and the figure of the portrait, too, the pose is a contrapposto of the body — not gracile, in the former manner of a contrapposto, but of high masculine power — in which the turning rearward of the head leads our attention to the further contents of the picture. In the altarpiece this communicative motive of illusion is an incident, and introduces us to a much vaster pictorial sphere; in the portrait the affirmation of illusion of existence in the foremost figure is primary in the picture's meaning, and is a coincidence between artistic means and end.

As in the preceding portraits, the business of this one is to recreate, as vital actuality, the sitters: in this instance not only the friend who introduces Raphael but Raphael himself. The informality of subject permits, as it did not with the august personalities of the papal portrait, the invention of a pretext of illusion of this great immediacy and ease. The swordsman's presence is instantly affirmed in his powerful, quick fluency of posture; and Raphael stands close behind him, at once recipient and cause of this diagonal movement into space: the two forms are apprehended in an unimpeded single oblique impetus. In the *Leo X*, the similar diagonal setting of the Pope and Rossi in the space had been scanned in separately successive steps. By the very boldness and vital force of his new motive Raphael has overridden the formal, separating stresses of the Pitti composition; he recreates a unity of structure, as well as of effect of presence, by the energy of movement and compactness of design.

Raphael has receded from the severe, even labored, insistence on elements of classicizing discipline with which he had tried to "correct" the unclassical innovations of the papal portrait. He has, at the same time, surrendered some of his insistence on what, in the papal portrait, had been elements of novelty. As if remembering the classical principle that synthesis cannot well be manufactured from extremes, he has much relaxed the searching characterization of detail he had given in the Pitti portrait. The descriptive drawing in the Louvre picture is as generalized at least as in the double portrait of the Doria, and but for its evidently later kind of stronger plasticity of form and greater force of light, would resemble that in the *Castiglione.* The lighting has the power of definition that is in the papal picture, but because it is not combined with an incisive drawing, it does not make distinctions which disrupt the forms. Again recalling something of the model of the *Castiglione*, the light is so modulated on the clothes and in the background as to suggest an optical effect of ambience, more boldly differentiated — as is the whole design — than in the *Castiglione.* In the slight measure to which the head of Raphael seems not to be absolutely resolved into this context of unity of light it reveals another element of his fidelity, in this picture, to optical data: while the head of his companion makes the impress of a form directly seen, Raphael's own head transcribes the effects of light (and also the quality of expression) given by a mirror-image, with its muted contrasts and its diminution of clarity and sense of substance of the form.

In some respects, Raphael has withdrawn from the position taken in the *Leo X*; but in another sense he has decisively developed its essential new idea: its effectiveness as illusion. This, in the Louvre portrait is the higher, from the far more powerful quotient in it of physical and psychological vitality; and this has been attained by the elimination, in this picture, of those disparities of elements of style — whether affirmative of classicism or disruptive of it — that, in the *Leo X*, were an inhibition of vitality. The Louvre portrait once more works as a unity of form and content, in which all the elements of style are subsumed into the dominating fact of liveness of illusion. The moderation of the former too-literal realism of detail "impressionistically" promotes illusion; and at the same time it promotes the visual and formal sense of unity. Within its vigor of illusion, this painting observes classical precept more effectively than the Pitti portrait did: in its unity, both of optical effect and of cohesive form, and in the equilibrium of substances and energies within its bold diagonal design.

What Raphael attains in the Louvre portrait is in effect a resynthesis of elements of style, restoring what had been strained to the point of a disruption in the *Leo*. This resynthesis is still in essence classical, but it attains a new liberty of form — still balanced — and a new actuality of presence and of personality — still controlled — that is different from what was in the former classicism, as of the *Castiglione*. It is as if the process that had occurred in the Tapestry Cartoons were here reversed in direction: a reformation, but not an essential alteration, of the classical synthesis has been achieved, now not toward a higher level of ideality, but toward a lower level of living actuality. This was not only a solution to the conflict of interest between classical and unclassical elements of style in the Pitti portrait; it was also a potential solution to the basic problem of how the classical style could evolve further, in a direction not yet tried. This solution has no further consequence in Raphael's own art; it stands in these latest years of Raphael's life as a terminal experiment. A solution in similar sense was known to some among Raphael's most gifted posthumous followers, but its currency was limited and its duration short; it was quickly compounded into, and its identity diffused within, the antithetic postclassical direction of Mannerism — of which this image of Raphael and his friend shows not the slightest evidence. The point of departure for the pupils was rather in the dilemma of classicism propounded in the *Leo* X than in its solution in the Louvre portrait.

No subject offers less ground for speculation than the possible character of Raphael's style had he lived on. But it might be remarked how the solution to the problem of a new, still classical, development in this portrait is in principle, though not in surface aspect, like that worked out in Venice in these same years from the datum of mature classicism, and with which, in that school, the High Renaissance style was endowed with a further generation's span at least of life.

A portrait exists from this late phase of Raphael's activity for which he saw fit explicitly to disclaim responsibility. The *Giovanna d'Aragona* (Paris, Louvre)[431] was commissioned by Bibbiena in 1518 when he was papal legate in France, it is assumed as a gift for Francis I. Vasari's report of the picture (V, 525) is more generous to it than it deserves; according to Vasari, Raphael did paint the head while Giulio Romano was responsible for all the rest. This is not borne out by the picture (which Vasari could not himself have seen);

its substantial executant is Giulio, and he is surely the author also of the design. Late in 1518 Alfonso of Ferrara solicited the cartoon for the portrait from Raphael. The correspondence which refers to this matter has survived (Golzio, 76–77). Its last item, on March 2, 1519, contains the report by Alfonso's agent, Costabile, of Raphael's disclaimer: "Ho parlato cum Raphael da Urbino . . . Lui dice non avere mandato quello ritrato a V. Exa. per cossa di sua mano; ma che havendo voluto Santa Maria in Portico el mandasse uno suo gargione a Neapoli per ritrare quella Sig. na, ha mandato a la Ex.a. V. quello proprio ritracto fece el suo gargione. . . ."

The style of the portrait precisely indicates its entire creation by another personality than Raphael's; Giulio would repeat its essential formula in independent productions that postdate Raphael's death. Its specifically Giulian character is not our concern in this place; what interests us is the evidence the documentation of this portrait offers for the attitude of Raphael toward the products of his shop. His libertarian attitude admitted the necessary intrusion of his executant's personality into his inventions; and as we shall see, he was tolerant also of whole invention by members of his shop. In the compound works, entire coincidence between the inventing mind and the hand of the executant was not expected; an alteration, or perhaps even some *détournement*, of style was expected and inevitable. Raphael's judgment of acceptability in the contributions of his collaborators was based on a standard of technical performance, and not on an impossible realization of his entire intent of style. The concept of style of a given work, in the sense in which we have used it here, was explicit in the actual performance, but not necessarily in the initial conception, of a work by Raphael; it is doubtful that, in the moment of invention of a design, he precisely thought through, in anticipation, how the idea of the design should be realized and articulated in its execution. Left to the assistant, then, this articulation would have been a distinct process, acceptable in its results unless it fell technically short, or less likely, blatantly betrayed the sense of the design as given. Thus the tolerance by Raphael of elements in the aesthetic compounds that, in historical hindsight, we may find inconsistent with his probable intent.

This libertarian view had its limits, however, and they are indicated by the repudiation of the *Giovanna d'Aragona*. Raphael's idea of what might adequately stand for him would permit alterations, and even grave strains, in the integrity of a classical style — and for some of these, as the evolution of the late portraits shows, he was himself responsible — but he would not accept the entire expression, even technically excellent, of another personality that was only classicistic, but essentially unclassical; that is already, in this work of 1518, the character of Giulio's independent style in the *Giovanna d'Aragona*.

THE LATE ALTARS AND DEVOTIONAL EASEL PICTURES

Except for the portraits, there is only one among the easel paintings after 1514 that may be attributed in its entirety to Raphael. Even this attribution, however, is made with a certain caution: it is not impossible that the formidable execution of the *Madonna della Tenda* (Munich, Pinakothek)[432] may be by Giulio Romano in an unusually assimilative state of mind and hand. We indicate this caution but do not observe it; for us (as for Fischel) the picture is, in surface as well as substance, a highly characteristic and informative production by Raphael himself, of 1516, or perhaps of 1517. It is his own critique, made in the light of his ambitions of this later time, of the mature classical perfection of the *Madonna della Sedia.*[248]

We recall that it is universally recognized that both compositions have their eventual origin of motive in sketches made about 1510, on the same sheet as the preparatory study for the *Alba Madonna*;[176] the including posture of the *Alba Madonna* gave rise to this early speculation on a more compact form of its compositional idea. Where the motive-sketches on the *Alba* sheet are rectangular in format, the *Madonna della Sedia* is, like the *Alba*, round; the *Tenda* picture is again rectangular, like the motive-sketches, but in internal arrangement it is developed much more differently than the *Sedia* from them. The changes in form from the *Madonna della Sedia* to the *Tenda* are not directed merely by the change in picture shape and the desire to accommodate the composition to it, but by the will to remake this picture-motive on ideas of style that did not exist in 1514–1515, much less in 1510.

Instead of the resolution of the forms and content into the ultimately contained stillness that is in the *Sedia*, the *Tenda* intends a physical and psychological situation of higher stress, in which the stresses are related in an equilibrium, but not resolved. The figures in the *Tenda* are not, as in the *Sedia*, in states that are essentially of rest, but in postures tense with the energy of unstable turning. The Madonna leans diagonally, and in leaning turns her compact form in heavy, energetically resilient, contrapposto. Her density of substance and the power of her movement are increased by the swelling of her form against the limits of the panel to the front, and by the spatial closure of the *tenda* to the rear. The Christ Child's posture is not knit into that of the Mother, as it was in the *Sedia*, but is an unwinding from it of its own full contrapposto, developed in an opposite diagonal stress; the edge of the *tenda* marks its axis. The impulse of the Christ Child, arching backward in the space, seeks union with the St. John, who meets His turning with a matching spatial movement from the rear; John's form and movement are not only contiguous with, but absolutely indissoluble from, those of the Virgin and the Christ Child. No other composition in the Raphael *oeuvre* has so much of the sense, recurrent in the art of Michelangelo, of an expanding energy, within an inviolable compact unity, of bodily forms.

The content of the *Tenda* is also, by contrast with the *Sedia*, more urgent and more complex, and at the same time it has been woven into a tighter tissue of psychological unity. It is as if the energies of movement in the bodies should culminate in the countenances, and be transmuted in them into a discharge of spiritual force: the faces project, as it were, psychic lines of force that extend the physical rhythms of design. The nature of emotion, lyric and impassioned, and its intensity of communication, are richer than in the *Sedia*; behind such a depth and differentiation of emotion lies the experience of the Tapestry Cartoons. Both the physical and emotional dimension of the figures in the *Tenda* have been magnified, but the effect of this is not, as it is in general in the Cartoons, of a spiritual and aesthetic distance but the opposite. The vibrant weaving of emotion in these figures seems, in its weaving, to ensnare our own; and the energetic, massive presences are as if compelled, within the close limits of their space, toward us. Light, and the technique of description of the surface, intensify the sensation of near presence. As in the portraits since 1516, the lighting is more powerfully differentiated, creating effects more assertive of substantial form. Here the light does not seek out — as it does appropriately in the portraits — the special properties of physiognomic form, but it does make a radiance of sensuous texture in the flesh and give a darker richness to the drapery. And in details — in the hair, at the neckline of the Virgin's dress, and in the gold embroidery of her dress and coif — the light finds out the subtlest incidents of optical and rhythmical effect, noted with a sensibility of eye and hand that is only Raphael's.

Like the contemporary portraits, the *Tenda* is a precious document for the late Raphael's personal intent. More appropriately than the portraits, its thematic matter justifies our seeking in it for indices of what his own meaning may have been in the great religious compositions he did not execute himself. Of these large late altarpieces, the earliest in order was the *Spasimo di Sicilia* (Madrid, Prado; so named from its original destination for S. M. dello Spasimo, *in Palermo),[433-4] designed probably still in 1516 but completed within 1517; an engraving of the composition by A. Veneziano is dated in that year. The picture bears the prominent signature of Raphael, but his role in its actual execution was very small. Raphael's own hand is visible in the painting of the head of Christ, and (as much as its condition allows judgment) in the head of Simon of Cyrene, whose lifting of the Cross from the fallen Jesus is the theme of action of the picture. All the rest of the execution is by Penni; to him, too, may be assigned the preparatory studies which survive in Florence and Vienna. As is usual, Penni's execution vitiates each element of Raphael's design, not just in detail but in his articulation of Raphael's basic meaning.

Penni has made the altar a *machine.* The force of Raphael's invention in it is, however, indestructible.

The *Spasimo* was conceived in the time of the later paintings of the Stanza dell' Incendio, and more than any altarpiece in Raphael's career so far this one is dramatic and complex in subject, as the frescoes are. It is understandable that its invention should pursue the vein opened in the Incendio frescoes. The expressive temper of the *Spasimo* is not what Raphael, or even Giulio, would have made for it, but its parade of rhetoric gesture and the intendedly strong characterization in it of physiognomic expression conform to the manner demonstrated in the *Fire,* and at one more remove, to the Tapestry Cartoons. Here, as in the *Fire,* there are some figures of an intended great force of posture, anatomically massive, with extremities extended into space. There are also figures — mostly these same ones — the meaning of whose action seems less pressing than its form. The foremost executioner, developed from the groom of the *Attila* fresco into a motive, here, almost of *maniera,* is the most evident of these; but part of the central meaning of the picture, the action of Simon of Cyrene, is also compromised by formalistic emphasis. By contrast, there is an almost stark dramatic literalness in the *Spasimo* itself, so moving because it is so seemingly — but only seemingly — unposed. There is a busy multiplicity, in Penni's poor articulation, of forms, of interest and incident.

These are marshalled, in Raphael's design, into a scheme that has no specific precedent but of which the general antecedents are clearly traceable, and equally its closely contemporary analogues. The straight-lined geometry in this composition was invented for the Tapestry Cartoons, but there applied in different orderings of whole design, and with a differently effective meaning of directness and severity. The strong diagonal impulsion the design makes here was first experimentally developed in the composition of the Incendio *Coronation,* in a very unlike context; it was there, too, that the idea was first conceived of a scheme of asymmetrical diagonals. It is in the very different guise of the *Madonna della Tenda* that the closest parallel exists, in its diagrammatic substructure of design, for the structure that is explicit in the *Spasimo*: a scheme made of the moving force of contrasting crossed diagonals, locked together at their place of crossing, but at the same time oppositely tending to expansion into space. It accords with the differently expansive nature of this theme that, here, the diagonal framework of design should indeed extend in space, and it is proper to its different intention of dramatic force that this framework has hardly any overcast of grace. Much more than in the *Tenda* the asymmetry of the crossed diagonals is stressed, with the evident intention of creating a more compellingly movemented effect of design.

With that extraordinary sense that is in Raphael of coincidence between form and content, the basic structure of the *Spasimo* fuses with the shape of the Cross that is the scene's thematic cause. The two strong thrusts of composition intersect in it, closely framing, in one quadrant, the head of Christ, and in the other, the helping Simon of Cyrene. The turning movements of both figures, opposite in their direction, serve to wind the coinciding energies of the diagonals together at their intersection but, still more, the Cross itself performs this function. Viewed as it were flatly, as implications of compositional direction, its arms are extended into the large diagonals of the design, but the perspective of the Cross — its actual spatial set — is in reverse to these directions. In the form of the Cross itself the movement of the diagonals is turned within itself, with the effect as of a knotting of the thrusts of the design in the place that is the center of its content. It is not only the framing in near-isolation of the Christ that gives His countenance its pathetic power but the sense as of acceleration of compositional energies as they coincide upon it, and their knotting together just behind His head; these aesthetic energies reinforce His piteous intensity of gaze.

The head of Christ,[434] as we have remarked, is Raphael's. It is painted with that fullness of modulation in light that is also in the head of the *Madonna della Tenda*, and with a similar soft glow of texture. It is smoother in surface and yet more fine in observation of detail, but it is not for these reasons alone that Christ's head suggests analogy with Northern art. The morbid details of tears and drops of blood, and the agonized expression, point surely to deliberate dependence on a Flemish model (not surprising in view of its Sicilian destination); and it is not impossible (in view of this same circumstance) that one of Antonello da Messina's transcriptions from the Flemish style may have served Raphael as a source. Even in Antonello's Italian renderings this iconographic type is explicitly unclassical; yet in Raphael's Christ there is an extraordinary assimilation of the image toward the classical vocabulary. Despite the tears, Raphael's Christ is not lachrymose: the head does not have sentiment, but a genuine pathos; and this ennobled vision of the theme is not the consequence only of Raphael's imposition on it of a classicizing canon of appearance, but of a state of mind that sees even this kind of experience as acceptable for classical interpretation.

Christ's head is an extreme paradigm for the process that is in general evident in this picture. The artist's will is, as it had been since the Tapestry Cartoons, to expression of an intenser dramatic urgency; here, from the nature of this Christian theme, this higher power of drama was to be combined with a more immediate and humanly compelling poignancy. Since the frescoes of the Incendio, the formal means of such effects were sought in more movemented schemes of composition, in which the force of movement is articulated with maximum directness. The design of the *Spasimo*, based upon two primary factors of diagonal thrust and of asymmetry, no longer conforms to the mature classical compositional system: of differentiation of a compact whole unity into responsive movemented parts. This design begins oppositely in its ideation, with forms that are intrinsically movemented, as if the parts of classical structure should have been developed in emphasis and energy to that point where they are now more important than any formerly containing, synthetic, core. The scheme of the *Spasimo* does not rely on any stable, central, compositional form: it is a pattern laid from a diminished center centrifugally across the surface and in space. As in a centrifuge, there is the sense in this design of opposing tensions between the expanding movement of diagonals and the, here, eccentric center. A unity of design and meaning is still emphatically willed, and it is achieved: in meaning, by the stringent direction of gesture and attention on the central forms; and in design, by the manipulation into balance, not of responsive movements, but of opposite and similar forms and forces. The tight knot made in the center of design between opposing movements needs all its power to hold their tensions in a unity. The — so to speak — centrifugal dissolution of the former mature classical mode of design is still accompanied by a persistence of classical intentions almost, but not quite, powerful enough to hold these dissolutive powers in check.

From before March of 1518 through late in May (Golzio, 66–68) Raphael's most pressing problem was the design and supervision of two large altar paintings for the most exalted possible destination. Commissioned by Lorenzo of Urbino and the Pope, jointly, the *St. Michael*[437] and the so-called *Holy Family of Francis I* (both signed and dated 1518)[436] were to be given, respectively, to the King and Queen of France; it was from this source that eventually the pictures came, with the royal collections, to the Louvre. For this market, much more exacting than the Palermitans who bought the *Spasimo*, Penni's ineptitudes would not do; the principal work of execution of both pictures was assigned to Giulio Romano. In the *St. Michael* it is possible that Raphael intervened in the execution of the head, but the rest of the * painting is unequivocally Giulio's, and his hand only is perceptible in the painting for the Queen. Preparatory drawings survive only for the latter picture (Uffizi, Louvre) as well as fragments of its cartoon (Bayonne, Collection Bonnat; Melbourne);[435] all are unequivocally by Giulio. According to Vasari (in his *Life* of Giulio [V, 524–25]) Giulio "lavorò sopra d'una Sta. Lizabetta, che fu fatta da Raffaello e mandato al Re Francesco"; for what Vasari's evidence on such points is worth, apparently Giulio made no claim to him for authorship of the design. The studies make it explicit in this case to what extent Giulio was entrusted with the exact development of Raphael's design; furthermore, his execution (as also in the *Michael*) is not only more highly technically skilled — to the point, indeed, of a remarkable standard of accomplishment — but more marked in personality than it had been before. We are dealing in these instances with aesthetic compounds of a different kind than in the *Spasimo*: not with Penni's negative vitiation of Raphael's intent, but with Raphael's intent compounded with a positive, and partly un-Raphaelesque, dimension.

However, it is not what Giulio has done in these two pictures that accounts for their difference in design and in temper of expression from the *Spasimo.* Each picture compared with the other, and both together with the *Spasimo* which preceeds them — and the *Transfiguration* which follows them — recalls attention to what by now should be a very apparent characteristic of Raphael's late style. Much more than had been the case in the previous mature phase of classical style, there is, within the broad generalization that may be established of a late style, a deliberate exploration of diverse possibilities of expression and development. The experimental temper that had first manifested itself in the Incendio frescoes does not diminish in these easel works — barely successive to them in time — though its effects are more carefully moderated. There is, in this searching out of diverse possibilities of formal and expressive directions, a tendency which — in the same language we have used to characterize the design of the *Spasimo* — is centrifugal in respect to the former integrity of classical synthesis of style. In the mature phase, all themes had been treated in recognizably common character, with less concern for their particular difference as theme. Now, in the late phase, freer from control by a single, synthetic ideal of style, there is a new motivating factor: that of differentiation of the general character of style into — in the musical meaning of the term — modes appropriate to particular thematic matter. In this sense the *Holy Family of Francis I* is not basically unlike in style, but explicitly distinguished in its modality from the *Spasimo*; and the exactly contemporary *St. Michael* has another modality than either. This phenomenon is, broadly, an aspect of what we have described much earlier as the process of diversification that occurs in the phase of classical development succeeding maturity.

The modality of the *Holy Family of Francis* has a counterpart — properly, for their basic similarity in theme — in the antecedent *Tenda.* Both intend lyric expression, not drama; and the immediately consequent difference from the *Spasimo* to the *Holy Family* is in the relaxation of the severity of design. The *Holy Family* reasserts the elements of structure which, in the *Tenda,* had formed its aesthetic sounding board for human meaning: the movemented curve, of lyric connotation, and (in this different context less assertive than in the *Tenda*) the convergence toward a unity of the persons and emotions of the theme. To charge this structure with intenser life, it contains, as in the *Tenda* — but much diminished from their urgency of contrast in the *Spasimo* — crossed diagonals. From the merely quantitative difference of its theme the *Holy Family* is of necessity more complex in form and in differentiation of its content than the *Tenda*, and that it seems perhaps more complex than the *Spasimo* is less the consequence of a year's development between the two than of the more precise and more effective articulation, by Giulio, of the picture's matter.

Giulio's surface grows so organically upon what has been given him that it is impossible, in the *Holy Family*, to distinguish Raphael's substance of design from the epidermis Giulio has given it. The pictures makes, as the *Spasimo* does not, a single texture of aesthetic fact; and even Giulio's visible un-Raphaelisms develop here, as if organically, by extension and by more extreme differentiation out of Raphael's own current ideas. The quantitative measure of movemented, complex, interwoven rhythm that is in the design we may assume is Raphael's, but its precious, almost brittle temper of articulation is the working on it of Giulio's mind and hand. He accelerates the sense of activity in design almost to the point of a sharp visual and expressive excitement. Also, the assertive chiaroscuro conforms to what we know explicitly are Raphael's intentions for it of about this time: strongly defining plastic form, complicating and enriching the design, and intensifying its life of content; again Giulio — as in the Altoviti portrait, and much like Raphael himself in the nearly contemporary *Leo X* — has raised Raphael's own pitch. The differentiation of the light is heightened into contrast, of lucent, smooth, sharp-outlined surfaces against absorbing darks — the tonality that provoked Sebastiano del Piombo's words about this painting and the *Michael*, in his letter to Michelangelo of July 2, 1518: ". . . che pareno figure che siano state al fumo, overo figure de ferro che lucino, tutte chiare et tutte nere . . ." (Golzio, 71). Still in classicizing manner, light adequately — even urgently — defines the substance and presence of any single form, but its multiple and active powers of contrast come near to dominating, and disrupting, the elements of structure that make a unity in the design. The color — hot, yet dulled, oranges and reds in the draperies, with flat greens and blues — does little to restore the unity of pattern; the color contains its own slightly sulphurous effect of visual unquiet, not quite in harmony.

More clearly here than in any earlier collaboration Giulio demonstrates his particular tendency to intensify one facet of an incipient process of disruption of visual form, already symptomatically evident in Raphael's own painting in the *Leo* portrait: this is the imbalance between effects achieved by linear description and those achieved by modelling. Giulio exaggerates Raphael's example in two distinct and opposite directions. In the foremost figures, those most strongly lit, an extreme generalization of modelled surface is confined by an incisive line, and its incidents of interior detail are hard-etched; in the less-lit forms line vanishes almost altogether and form is characterized entirely by *sfumato*.

There is a constant tendency in Giulio to seek out directions a degree, or more than that, still more divergent from the classical norm than Raphael had so far attempted. It is not only a variant, and less intrinsically classical, effect of form that is apparent in this picture but a variant human and expressive content: not forceful in dramatic tension as the *Spasimo* was meant to be, but implying subtler tensions; not quite explicit, but rather almost nervously excitant and suggestive. This image is hard, but it is also yielding; it is psychologically sharp and at the same time sentimental; it is febrile in its excitement and precious in its poise. It has, to a degree that is not in any other late work, a character of both formal and human artificiality. These persons have become, in Giulio's shaping of them, a gender subtly but surely distinct from those of the *Madonna della Tenda* — a distinct gender rather than a distinct kind. It is almost surely presuming too much calculation on both Raphael's and Giulio's part to believe that the personality of this picture is intentionally feminine, to suit the female royalty for whom it was intended. Yet such a conclusion is suggested when it is compared with the male power, almost even heroic, of the *St. Michael* painted for the King.

The *St. Michael* partakes of the character both of devotional and dramatic painting; in theme it is a middle term between the *Spasimo* and the *Holy Family* for the Queen. A mode has been conceived for it which, in effect, resolves the force of one into the lyric of the other, and which in dialectic consequence is a third and different thing. The *Michael* has been made into an image of superb masculine power, of virile grace in action and of high classical beauty in presence. He is a synthesis of such *virtù* and *grazia* as had before appeared together in the Paul of the *Paul at Lystra* in the Tapestries, or more distantly, and with less cogency of synthesis, in the avenging angels of the *Expulsion*. Here the vessel of these properties is grander in his isolation and in scale, and the meaning of these properties is more clear because they are an isolated content and not an episode in an extended text. Unlike these antecedents within larger pictures, in the *Michael* this content and its modality of form are the result of Raphael's concentrated and exclusive deliberation.

In its effectiveness of synthesis of high meaning and of perfected form the *Michael* not only recreates but reinforces, in its concentration of single subject, some of the essential character of the ultimate classical style of the Tapestry Cartoons. It is also like the Cartoons that, as with their primary actors, the *Michael* is — with obvious greater appropriateness — an archetype, whose beauty is contrasted with the Devil's archetype of evil. But, despite its synthetic effectiveness, it is unlike the style of the Cartoons that there is in this image a sense of contrivance, which emerges from both its form and content. It is not only from the different nature of their subjects that the protagonists of the Tapestries are a more cogent revelation of human and artistic truth.

The actors of the Tapestries have the force of concepts, while the Michael — for all his grandeur — is touched with the character of the different quality of artistic thought that abuts in the conceit. Less than in the companion *Holy Family*, but still evidently, the *Michael* has an atmosphere of artifice. In part, this character is due to Giulio's main share in the execution. He has given this figure a metallic high gloss of surface like that in the *Holy Family*, though in this outdoor setting it is not so forced by light; and he has used, in many passages, a similar incisive draughtsmanship to define detail. The effect of his touch is to diminish the vitality of the *Michael*: to chill his energy of movement and give his form a faint overcast of preciosity.

The elaboration and extreme deliberation of design beneath this overcast, however, is not necessarily Giulio's except in slight degree. The given structure of the design intends, with its power of movement, the most finely calculated equilibrium and the most precise articulation of its ornamental grace. The design is invented as a theme of movement, more bold than in any previous large easel work, and also more complex both in its motives that make action and those which effect its control. The scene is as much symbol as it is narration, but it refers to and arrests the climactic moment of Michael's pursuit of the Devil through the heavens to the earth. The demon has fallen heavily, in abrupt perspective torsion; Michael has descended on him in oblique flight and with opposite outflung motion turns, threatening the prostrate figure with his spear. Michael's posture makes a contrapposto both of form and energy, but one that is powerfully centrifugal from an axis thrust diagonally into space. His form only initially suggests the familiar late motive of crossed diagonals; from this elementary schematic, and controlling, shape multiple extensions, as of spokes, have been developed, of diagonal directions in the space. This diagonal rotatory posture is linked below into the more drastic perspective twisting of the Devil. For all its diverse energy this activity is not thought of as a discrete physical or aesthetic force, but as inseparable in very concept from the effects it also makes of equilibrium: these are not ideas in antithesis, but differentiations more extreme — on one hand bolder, and on the other more subtle — of the synthesis of powers of movement within, and of gravity without, the major figure. The complex movement of the massive form is suspended, but not fixed, in an exquisite equilibrium, so finely calculated that it cannot avoid the air of artifice; and the powerful exploration of the figure's space is so managed, by mutings and forcings of light — of somewhat theatrical effect — that it seems subject to a classical domination by the picture plane. The temper of refinement that is in the equilibrium is achieved by, and extended into, almost every visible detail. The least rhythmic movement: of a contour of anatomy, or of a wing, or a curve of drapery, suspends movement in a crystalline deliberation of its formal beauty, its value as of ornament. But this ornamental fineness is —

or would be except that it is too preciously described by Giulio — not separate from the boldness of the larger forms; again the boldness and the fineness are the widely differentiated limits of a whole image synthetically conceived.

The *Michael* provides its own commentary on the destiny, in this late phase of the classical development, of the High Classical style. With ambitions more complicated than in the Tapestry Cartoons and a formal machinery more sophisticated still, Raphael has recreated in this picture all that was in the Cartoons, and in some ways more, of High Classical style, except for its profound genuineness of artistic and human meaning. This recreative act does not have the power of the climactic act of creation in the Cartoons. It is an act of elaboration, on a substance of form that is of increased richness, but on a substance of content that is not so profoundly felt. For all the grandeur that is still in this work, the rhetoric drama of the Cartoons is diminished here to something more identifiably theatrical, more concerned by a definable shade with its effects rather than with the matter that is making them. It is understandable how this picture could be read by the painters of the Baroque Age, with an inevitable distortion, as a sympathetic model.

The *Transfiguration* (Rome, Vatican Museum)[438-45] had been an earlier commission than both the *St. Michael* and the *Holy Family of Francis I.* Like them, it was originally destined to go to France; it had been ordered, probably in late 1516 or in January 1517, by Cardinal Giulio de' Medici as a presentation to the Cathedral of Narbonne. At the same time the Cardinal commissioned a *Resurrection of Lazarus* from Sebastiano Veneziano for the same church. It was clearly understood in the art world of Rome, and by the two painters themselves, that they were thereby set in competition. Despite his known habits of delay Sebastiano was more prompt to set to work than Raphael. Letters from Michelangelo's correspondents tells us something of the progress of this "competition"; where Sebastiano was well begun by September 1517 (Golzio, 59) Raphael had not yet started painting by July 1518 (Golzio, 70). It is not to be excluded, however, that preparation of some kind for the picture had been made in 1517. Apparently once put forward on account of other business, the substantial portion of this large undertaking had to wait again on the completion of the more pressing gifts for the Royalties of France. Even then Raphael was slow in progress on the *Transfiguration.* It was still undelivered in his studio at his death, when it was exposed at the head of the artist's bier — perhaps then not quite altogether finished. Payments for it were solicited by Castiglione on behalf of Raphael's heir, Giulio, in 1522 (Golzio, 146) and made finally, with not uncommon slowness, only in 1526 (Golzio 156–57).

Raphael's responsibility for the design of this difficult and important picture has never been questioned, but there is less agreement on his role in execution. The head of the foremost seated Apostle toward the left, Andrew, is assigned by general consent to Raphael himself; and there is sound support in the quality of two further heads, those of the old and young Apostles most in view in the middle of the lower group, for the opinion (Fischel) that they too are by Raphael. The distinction between these and the head just above them, and also that of the pointing Apostle to the left, is not such as to exclude the possibility of their execution by Raphael. In most of the rest of the lower portion of the painting the executant is Giulio; in the upper figures, and probably also in the landscape, the hand is mostly Penni's. Raphael does not seem to have intervened in the upper section, even where it would seem he would most appropriately have done so, in the head of Christ. The only documentary reference to an executant is to one whose hand cannot be identified, Battista Dosso. It was he who was supposed (according to report by the Ferrarrese Ambassador of Raphael's statement [Golzio, 106]) to finish the painting finally, before Lent of 1520. The work of preparation, like that of execution, also was partitioned out: the studies which survive are variously distributed between Penni and Giulio Romano.[445] However, two of these drawings (seemingly auxiliary cartoons) are almost certainly by Raphael himself: with good claim, a study for the two heads in the center of the picture that are also fairly surely of his execution (Oxford, Ashmolean),[444] and with still better claim, a drawing for the head of Andrew (British Museum).[443]

Quite properly, considering its size, this altarpiece is the most compound in execution of the late works, but the sense in it of differences that cannot be quite reconciled is not due so much to the execution; the fault lies, oppositely, at the beginning of its process of creation. It is not known to what extent this peculiar iconography of the *Transfiguration* was dictated to Raphael. The subject of the whole picture, as it is painted here, has no precedent. It consists, in its upper part, of the Transfiguration enacted by the persons indicated in the Bible text (Mark 9:2–13; Matthew 17:2–13), but accompanied by two incidental spectators, the martyrs Felicissimus and Agapitus, whose feast day, the 6th of August, is also that of the Transfiguration. The scene is represented as it had never been before, not only in its dramatic energy of supernatural event but in the stress of allusion of this event to the future Resurrection. The scene below is that which follows the Transfiguration in the text, but which there has no relation with it (Mark 9:14 ff.; Matthew 17:14 ff.), of the Healing of the Possessed Youth.

What the sense is of the pictorial conjunction of the two events has yet to be satisfactorily explained. Theological pretexts can be found, and were certainly invented, for this union; but none accessible to us seems to justify it adequately. The two scenes are irremediably disconnected, and in character of subject each contrasts with the other: on the hill, a symbolic visionary happening, enacted by a few beings of superhuman station; below, a crowded human tumult, of lesser beings helpless to perform the action that is sought of them. The handling of the theme deliberately expands the inherent contrast in content of the two parts of subject matter.

Given the control of the patron over subject matter that is normal to this time, the speculation that we wish to make is dangerous, but perhaps correct. Knowing of the virtuoso richness of Sebastiano's competing picture, earlier begun, it is possible that Raphael may himself have sought expansion of his given theme, feeling of it that it was too limited, by textual requirement, in quantity and kind of its expressive possibility; and that he received consent for this expansion: the added episode was sought in order to give opportunity for complex dramatic demonstration and for strong incidents of emotion, action, and appearance such as were denied him in the central scene alone. That the two themes were of contrasting nature would have been a stimulant, rather than a discouragement to their combined treatment; this would have given Raphael his first opportunity to examine the proposition of strong differentiation within content on a massive scale. That the risk was implicit of disparity in expression of the two parts of subject would not, in his temper of these late years, have been an impediment. It sufficed the view of religious narrative he had taken since the Incendio, or even since the Tapestry Cartoons, that both themes have the common ground of powerful, even though different, dramatic implication. The chief will in this work is a development one step more removed than in the *Spasimo* from the canons of mature classical synthetic style; still seeking synthesis, it seeks yet more urgently for strong effects.

Whatever the iconographic pretext for the combination of the two scenes may have been, Raphael worked it out in the terms of illustration of a narrative, to which he has given the dramatic energy and sense of true presences as of the theatre. The biblical text itself may be so read as to imply, but it nowhere directly states, the situation Raphael has represented in his picture: that the two events, told successively in the Gospel, were actually simultaneous in occurrence. It is as if Raphael had inserted a "while" between the thirteenth and fourteenth verses of the text: *while* the Transfiguration was taking place, the Apostles on the plain below were presented with the possessed boy they could not cure. The two scenes are treated as happenings diverse in matter and in place, but of a single moment in time. As in the text, each event is unknown to the participants in the other. The Transfiguration takes place in a high and separate world, distinct from the other and of closed form. The gestures of the group below refer to it, but without knowledge that the event occurs; no gaze is directed to the miracle. The gestures point out to the father of the possessed child that he must wait for aid for the return of Christ who is absent on the hill. They call our attention, but no other actors', to the Transfiguration.

As removed as is the miracle from us, so is the earthly scene made near. The Andrew embodies the most powerful device of illusion yet conceived by Raphael: his whole great form, an almost Michelangelesque compact of mass and energy, projects toward us; he compels our attention and discharges it, with his own, inward on the scene. In the right foreground a female figure, back to us in intense light — perhaps the mother of the possessed boy — stares left at the Apostles, but her gesture whips rightward and inward toward her son. Between the two foremost figures the space is opened to us in a deep oblique cleft between the confronted groups of the Apostles and the supplicants. All that inhabits this near and accessible space makes strong assertion of its actuality. A light more vigorous in contrast than in any previous dramatic work gives high stress to the modelling of form. Illumined surfaces of draperies and bodies stand out smoothed and full, in lucent relief against the darks. Especially in the heads, and in the few incidents of anatomy, this light searches out and strongly characterizes detail. Even among those heads that are attributable to Raphael there are episodes of imitative realism more literal-seeming than in his late portraits. To heighten the conviction of reality the heads display a marked diversity of type — not, however, altogether sacrificing their typology — stressed in at least one instance to the point of caricature. An affirmation of a variety of presences is also in the strong gesticulation of almost every actor; these persons are not only plastically but intensely energetically present. Their gesturings and postures are forthright, with minimal or no pretense to grace.

Relieved in light, the heads, the outflung pointing gestures, and portions of the bodies make a pattern of quick, positive activity, most complex in its variety of directions on the surface and in space. This pattern is controlled with great deliberation by an angular geometry, made of repetitions and of right-angular intersections laid obliquely in the space. The calculation in this asymmetrical order is decidedly apparent; it disciplines the urgency and complexity of pattern, but does not diminish it. Despite this variety of motives and appearances that make up the design its tempo of activity is so swift, and its tone of statement so emphatic, that its comprehension as a whole is almost instant: it has, in its diversity, a unity of impact which, like that sometimes seen in the Tapestries, seems of a *force majeure*. The excitement of dramatic happening that this scene has derives at once from its actuality of illustration and from this shaping of its form.

This scene is distinct as narrative from the scene above, but not as a content or a form; the relation of simultaneity that exists between them is expressed not just by physical conjunction in the single frame but by movement — of the nature of time itself — which connects the two parts. The almost drastic energy that is generated in the lower scene is a prelude to the Transfiguration and is discharged into it. Not only the pointing gestures specifically, but the whole sharp diagonal inclination of the lower group, inward and upward in direction, lead toward the upper scene. There the closed spheroid form of composition, substantially symmetrical — the Christ aligned on the central axis between the almost heraldically disposed Prophets — seems self-contained and, by contrast, calm; and there is a clear shining of the transfiguring light. But this seeming calm is more truly a suspension, in their moment of equilibrium, of great forces, as if in the bright eye of a tornado. While the three Apostles are splayed upon the ground by the impact on them of the vision, the Prophets are blown in an upper wind, counterclockwise around the Christ; the Christ too rotates, but as if more heavily and slowly, His head and body turned slightly to the wind. There is no mere natural logic in the scale assigned the figures in this vision; they are seen in an arbitrary space of miracle, somewhere intermediate between the hill and plain, and in such relationship of size as they would have had not for any human eye but for the eye of the motivating God. All this activity has been "caught" when its elements are in one plane, parallel to the picture surface. Its forms and forces hang in the transfigured moment's stillness. But this moment is charged not only with its own implicit energies; it receives the thrust of the powerful diagonal motion from below, discharged against the right side of the upper group with an aesthetic force that seems more compelling than that of the supernatural wind. This force, rather than the descriptive indication of the blown draperies, induces the sense of rotation of the upper sphere and inspires a tensing energy within the seeming calm of its suspension.

The passages of Raphael's own handling in this painting are of a greater richness in internal contrast than in any other of his personal works, but each such passage still conveys the sense of a visual entity. This is not so in the pupils' execution. We are already familiar with the nature and effects of Giulio's and Penni's intervention, and they are apparent here, with the usual attendant sense of difference from Raphael's example not merely doubled, but multiplied by their dual, and in places, interwoven contributions. The unity of effect the picture makes is achieved despite these diversities in handling. It is remarkable that, beneath the merely painterly epidermis of the *Transfiguration*, so high a measure of unity of sense and form has been created between its two substantially unlike main parts. Their unlikeness remains evident, and it is deliberately meant. The two scenes are set in contrast both of temper of expression and of character of form, and of this contrast artistic capital is intentionally made; each is foil to, and intensifies the character of, the other. It is as if Raphael had willfully attempted to remake one whole new construct in this picture from the two possibilities of dramatic style open to him since the Tapestry Cartoons: the one, the exalted and supremely disciplined style of the Cartoons themselves, the other, the more movemented and irregular expression of the frescoes of the Incendio.

But these modes are too disparate to permit their synthesis, and in this picture Raphael has, if anything, made the distinct character of each yet more apparent by their confrontation. What he has achieved in the *Transfiguration* is no longer a genuinely synthetic image but one in which disparates have been forced to coexist, effectively, in unity, created in this case from an overriding utmost power of dramatic idea, supported by brilliantly contrived devices of aesthetic form.

The conception of the subject indicates quite clearly that the initial invention of the whole work was based on an idea of contrast, then to be resolved in unity: this is a reverse of the normative classical principle of differentiation, even into extreme contrast, of an initial unity. Yet, in the working out of the final sense and structure of the picture unity has been achieved; the power of contrast is nearly, but not quite equal to, the including whole and for all its force internal to it. No work demonstrates more clearly than the *Transfiguration* not only the retention but the still effective assertion, in Raphael's late style, of basic classical principle, and, at the same time, the strain and alteration of such principle by new and not quite classical intentions. The *Transfiguration* shows, with almost schematic explicitness, the fault that has opened in the structure of classical style. In one sense the *Transfiguration* may be taken as the extreme manifestation of the crisis of Raphael's late classicism, but in another sense it belongs beyond the point of crisis; the fault in classical structure has been riven so wide that it seems beyond repair, and the style is in effect entered, from the impetus of Raphael's own research, on its process of dissolution.

We can only unprofitably speculate how Raphael would himself have resolved the problem of the next step beyond the style of the *Transfiguration.* The decision was not made by him but by his heirs, and Raphael's personal decision need not necessarily have been the same as theirs. Historically, our last evidence for Raphael's dramatic style is the style of the *Transfiguration.* What occurs in it is no necessary index of the destiny of style of all the aspects of Raphael's wide artistic practice. As we have seen, an unfaulted classicism coexists, in the contemporary late decorations, with this dramatic faulted one; and in the portraits there is, for obvious reasons inherent in the genre, no such grave stress laid on classical system as there has been here. The late style has not only its diverse possibilities of mode, but its diversity of genres, in each of which a distinguishable variant of classical expression may appear. However, in the late phase it is only in the dramatic style, as of the *Transfiguration,* that Raphael confronts, not a part only, but the whole range of problems with which his art could be involved, of urgency and variety of human expressiveness and of complexity of form. As the nondramatic works are not, this is the whole test of what the classical style had come to be in Raphael; it is the significant representative symptom of his latest art.

It is only speculation to assume that the next step — which Raphael did not live to take — in dramatic style beyond the *Transfiguration* might have been toward the example of one of the other genres. The only evidence we think we have for Raphael's personal intention and realization which, by our reckoning, postdates the *Transfiguration* is in portraiture, in the *Self Portrait with a Fencing Master* in the Louvre,[430] and the conclusions we have drawn from it are by no means surely transferable to the more complex dramatic style. We have seen how this work resolved the disparities of style in the *Leo X,* which in diminished form resemble those in the altarpiece, probably of contemporary invention. The solution indicated in the Louvre portrait implied an alteration in the character of classical style, but its style is still classical, and no longer faulted. We noticed the analogy of this solution with that which, found in Venice at about the same time, permitted a continued life to classical style. The likeness of the *Transfiguration* to Titian's contemporary *Assumption* has often been remarked, but it is not observed that while the *Transfiguration* propounds a dilemma of the classical style, the *Assunta* proposes its solution. The dilemma could be otherwise resolved, and in Rome the artistic circumstances — including among them the *Transfiguration* — in which Raphael's pupils worked, and their personalities, which he could only form in part, made it — as much as historical event could be — inevitable that the resolution should be in terms of Mannerism. With shifts that need be only small to be decisive, Mannerism can be generated out of the style of the *Transfiguration.* In parts within the picture the pupils' hands have already effected such a transformation, but it is not in Raphael's determining whole of vision and idea. The *Transfiguration* is pregnant with postclassical style, but it remains itself the last and extremest statement of Raphael's classical ambition.

In rare and minor instances before 1518 it had happened that one of Raphael's assistants had been allowed a virtual complete freedom in the execution of an easel picture. From 1518 onward, however, the production of all easel pictures commissioned to Raphael, other than those of the first importance (which we have discussed), was in effect given over to the pupils. From this time on the lesser easel works not only show no intervention of the hand of Raphael, but give no sign of his inventing mind. Whatever notions of design and interpretation Raphael may have given his assistants for these works — and it is entirely possible he may have given few, or even none at all — they were too slight decisively to shape their evolution, or offer much impediment to the assistant's expression of his own personality. These pictures are "aesthetic compounds" in an only tenuous sense, in that (whether they begin or not with Raphael's indication of design) they are generated in his closest ambient and out of his late art, so that he is, so to speak, behind these works if he is not in them. Some of them are inscribed with his name: no misrepresentation, but an index of his acceptance of ultimate responsibility for them as *capomaestro* of the shop; Raphael's signature now is more like a warrant of inspection than a guarantee of personality. We have observed that the standards held for pupils' work were those of technical performance and, in terms of style, an adequate but not impossibly specific conformity to the master's models. There was no point, now, in interference with the pupils' manufacture of the less important products of the shop; the chief ones, Giulio and Penni — each with his particular competence and inescapable limitations — knew both these aspects of his job. Furthermore, with increasing maturity, both assistants were more set in personality — Giulio, indeed, had affirmed the elements of creative individuality; they were less easily amenable to exact control. The freedom that Raphael allowed them in the lesser easel pictures was partly an economy of his own time and partly a matter of creative common sense. This liberty permitted the more individual assertion of the pupils' manners with different effect, in these contexts largely of their own consistent making, from that which their hands make in a work invented and controlled by Raphael.

In this moment of the history of Raphael's style its classical identity is preserved only by the force and intelligence of Raphael's personal intent. With his control held in abeyance from the pupils' work their derivation of Raphael's current style cannot achieve his difficult equilibrium in classicism: both Penni's and Giulio's late creations accelerate, in different ways, the process of dissolution of Raphaelesque classical style; and Giulio's last works from the shop complete it. Raphael could not prevent this consequence of the liberty he conceded to his pupils except by exertions that would have defeated the first purpose of his concession, the economy of production of the shop. But his acceptance of these consequences is more than a matter of economy; it may be indicative of his attitude toward what we think of as the problem of artistic style. His noninterference in the pupils' late work is, by implication, also a noninterference in their unclassicizing alterations of his style. He seems not to have considered that, even within the closed precinct of his shop, style could be promulgated and imposed like dogma; his style could not, in the last resort, have superpersonal validity. Raphael's classicism was, ultimately, an essential expression of his artistic personality. Other similar classicisms might exist, but they too were functions of a personality. It might be hoped for, but not expected — and certainly could not be required — that different molds of personality should adopt this ultimately personal expression. Style consisted in both the appearance and essence of the aesthetic construct, and while one was imitable the other was not. The approximation by the different personalities of Raphael's pupils of the outward form of his late classical style was, of necessity, sufficient.

The extent to which Giulio's art, even in its quasi-independent exercise, could still depend on Raphael in 1518 is demonstrated in a small Holy Family (called the *Madonna Piccola Gonzaga*, Paris Louvre; probably of that year).[446] The painting combines (into what may be a distant evocation of the early *Cardellino*) [54] a motive (the Elizabeth and John) from the *Holy Family of Francis I* [436] with an adaptation of the posture of the *Madonna della Tenda*;[432] both of these have been arranged according to what is still evidently, even in this different form, the compositional scheme of the lower part of the *Transfiguration*. The pose of the Virgin here develops the leaning, turning posture of the *Madonna della Tenda* diagonally toward the depth of space; as in the design of the *Transfiguration* this diagonal is extended to an opened landscape, and redressed toward balance by a hillock toward the left. Other elements as well control diagonal imbalance: the Madonna contains her own leaning pose by a compensating torsion much more pronounced than in the model for her movement in the *Tenda*; and, most explicitly opposing the movement toward the space, the other figures are disposed in near-planarity — actually on a slight contrary diagonal — across the Madonna's form. The design tests asymmetrizing movement, and controls it, with a force that may have been in a suggestion of design by Raphael, but which he had so far reserved for use in his large dramatic works. These contrasting movements have been resolved by Giulio toward a unity, though one highly tensile, of whole structure; and the expressive content of the picture has been similarly treated in the psychological exchange of gesture and charged gaze among the actors. In its quality of expression and in handling the picture has a fineness and sharp sensibility which (with due allowance for their different scale) recall Giulio's execution in the *Holy Family of Francis I.*

Entirely unlike the *Madonna Piccola Gonzaga* in scale and in subject, and also different in relation of its style to Raphael, the *St. Margaret* (Paris, Louvre; much damaged and repainted)[447] was done, according to Vasari (V, 525) ". . . quasi interamente da Giulio col disegno di Raffaello." It was sent to France, in view of its subject matter presumably to Marguerite de Valois, Francis' sister, and it was evidently in the nature of a female companion piece and afterthought (1518–19) to the *Michael* for the King. As much as it resembles the *St. Michael* superficially, the *Margaret* is in every deeper sense unlike it; not merely by distinction of its mode, expected in this late phase, but in effect of style. The Raphael *disegno* to which, on Vasari's eidence, Giulio admitted has been engulfed in Giulio's working over of it; no parallel for the effect this picture makes is evident elsewhere in Raphael's identifiably personal late style.

It is the conception of the figure which, evidently, is first responsible for this sense of difference. It is made in a proportion, heavy-limbed and rather broad, which adequately resembles that used sometimes by the later Raphael, as in the upper figures especially of the *Transfiguration*; it is rather the manner of articulation of the figure that has no analogue in Raphael. The limbs and torso here do not convey even that measure of conviction of organic connection that is still in Giulio's figures painted into Raphael's more strictly supervised designs; the *Margaret* does not seem at all to be inhabited by a human energy. Less than moving of herself, she *is* moved, as a lay form is manipulated. The concept of the human image is, as never within Raphael — and as it conspicuously is not in the *Michael* — of a physical existence only, without a necessary content of vitality. Yet even this physical presence is not entire: despite its heaviness of shape the figure hardly exists, or moves, in space. What is felt in it is not coherent substance but an assembly of smoothed surfaces, projecting or receding in a pattern of contrasting light. It had already been Giulio's symptomatic tendency in the collaborative works, which he now makes explicit, that his sense of the figure is not of its entity of physical, no more than of its vital, presence; it consists for him only of the surfaces the eye perceives, as they are described by an aesthetically predetermined light. The light is virtually frontal, and what it lights up — in a manner learned from the execution of the *Michael*, but schematically exaggerated in effect — is aligned with the picture frame. Movement is aesthetically made by contrast of projection and recession in the light, more than by the action of the represented form. The figure, in the frontal light, is also almost altogether frontally disposed, in a pose that is not a contrapposto but a lateral adjustment, not quite in balance, of the body forms. The displacing of the forms makes a pattern of movement, but no effect of action; the figure is as if suspended, at once stiffly and preciously, in uncertain equilibrium, in a limbo between activity and stillness. Confirming the resemblance her articulation suggests to a lay figure, the *Margaret* seems to hang within the picture puppet-like, as if from strings.

The adjustment of compositional pattern in the background helps to compensate her balance, but cannot rectify the un-human quality of Margaret's posture. Her figure is in fact not only no longer effectively related to the supporting pattern of design, but, more important, it has no discernible relation to the containing frame. Not just the figure, but the whole pictorial image, no longer seems a necessary integer. In the *Michael*, as well as in Raphael's more populated late altarpieces, the frame contains its human substance closely, and its limits are felt as those of the design; the sense of shape of the picture field is inseparable from its inner structure. Differently, the *Margaret* hovers in an unclear space, and on a wider, looser surface of which the whole shape has no clear connection with her own. What fills the area in part is the monstrous arabesque made of the conquered dragon: an oversize grotesque, a fantasy painted in Giulio's most literal technique, meant to convince, alarm, and amuse the spectator all at once. The attribute is almost more the real interest of subject in the picture than the Saint. The dragon makes a stronger content than the stilted preciosity of the heroine, but neither has to do with the varieties of feeling or idea that Raphael had investigated so far. Both the Meissen-like *minauderie* of the Beauty and the whimsical horror of the Beast are special, and specializedly personal, expressions of sensation, eccentric to Raphael's classical repertory of content. Only the fact that the manner of execution in this picture is still so clearly based on Raphael's — that its outward forms are still so recognizably like his — holds it tenuously in allegiance to Raphaelesque classicism. The symptoms are all here, but yet indecisively expressed, of what in substance, as distinguished from appearance, makes an unclassical style.

The further and more decisive step in the unmaking of classical synthesis is in Giulio's *Madonna della Perla* (Madrid, Prado; 1519–20).[448] Like the* small Louvre picture in its theme (except that the aged female here is Anna rather than Elizabeth) and resembling it somewhat in composition, it too recalls the *Holy Family of Francis I.* There is, evidently, a close connection in the style of all these three pictures. What has happened in the *Perla*, however, is such an alteration in degree in treatment of certain elements of style as results, finally, in an identifiable alteration of whole stylistic kind. Taken separately, the distinction among the elements of style in the *Perla* and the large *Holy Family,* or even the *Madonna Gonzaga,* is not so much, and measured against some facets of Giulio's execution in the *Transfiguration,* it is still less. But here these separate facts of style appear, with their small, but yet pervasive measure of intensification, in a discrete whole of Giulio's personal invention; the same forms, under higher pressure in a separate frame become a new gestalt: a distinguishable new order of artistic style.

It is almost characteristically perverse of the maturing Giulio that he should refer so strongly in this work, in which he hastens the classical style to its end, to the beginning of the style in Leonardo's cartoon of the same theme, of twenty years before; this Giulio may well have seen during Leonardo's recent time in Rome. The figures of the *Perla* are compacted and interwoven almost as they are in the Academy cartoon, but not in order to effect a dominating unity. The concentration that is given to the group is not the statement of a synthesis but of one term in an antithesis: its apparent unity exists as a term of contrast for the multiple disruptive forces, still more potently effective, in the picture. The outer contour of the group is almost schematically severe, sharp-faceted like an irregularly hewn rock. Within, it is richly articulated: a spiral movement rises from the young St. John on the left and traverses the main incidents of form, finally intersecting on itself in the crossing of the Virgin's arm upon the Child. But growing from this spiral and twisting back on it, the Virgin's body exercises a still stronger tension, opposing the including action of the spiral like a restraining spring, and opening what it attempts to close. Neither movement is, however, actually confined in its effects within the limit of the group: the posture of the Virgin lies on a diagonal, from lower right to upper left, that passes from the rightmost foreground of the picture into a virtual tunnel in the architectural setting to the rear (where Joseph lurks inside a Roman ruin); an opposite diagonal, of equal power, crosses this and penetrates, across the shoulder of St. Anne, into the depth of landscape. The group is riven structurally by these contrasting lines of force, and its identity, both of formal structure and of human separateness, is compromised by these insistent connections with the landscape.

This scheme of statics and dynamics is inseparable in its operation from the functioning of light, which in the *Perla* assumes a particularly active role. Vasari (IV, 351) speaks of this picture as "una natività . . . con un'aurora molto lodata . . . ." This is not a Nativity, and thus not a *Notte*, but neither is it a *Giorno*; the condition of light selected is exceptional. Certainly, part of the reason for its selection is its effect upon the picture's content; again the precedent of Leonardo is suggested. But more than for this reason, it would seem that the time of day is pretext for a kind of light that will have certain willed effects upon the picture's form. By this pretext, the lighting in the *Perla* has been forced a strong stage beyond its differentiation in the *Holy Family of Francis I*, and to the degree of urgent contrast that exists in the dramatic, half-miraculously illuminated lower scene in the *Transfiguration*. In the *Perla,* however, there is no dramatic content to inspire this dramatization of the form: the effect of activity and force of contrast of the lighting is sought initially as an effect of form itself. From the veiling or obscuring dark, polished high-lit surfaces of flesh and drapery emerge, more subtly shaded than in the *Transfiguration*, but not less in their range of contrast. These surfaces, incisively defined by Giulio's line, are smaller and more sharp-faceted than in the earlier paintings, and thus more variously active. A complex visual excitement is in this activity, which at once defines, elaborates, and breaks up the larger pattern of design. Color has no primary effect within this scheme; it is entirely subservient to light. Its hues, initially not unconventional, bleach at high value or become glittering *changeants*, and are recessively muted, sombre and smoky, in the dark.

No whole forms are sensible in this illumination, but only fragments: there are only parts or planes of persons. More evidently than in the *Margaret*, these work inorganically, not frozen in the midst of movement, but more from the beginning without the power of it. The actors have no vitality in them, not only to continue or complete their action, but not even initially to start it; the bodies are no longer inhabited by *pneuma*. They are less recreations of the life, as well as look, of a humanity than they are projections of aesthetic artifice, something between statuary and persons. The expression of a human spirit is confined, in unclassical fashion, to the countenance alone; and what is there is psychological sensation of a peculiarly sharp, or else an oppositely shaded kind, precious and veiled but not profound. In certain fragments, both psychological and physical, the actors are almost too intensely real, and in others as intensely artificial.

There is no norm, either of reality or of artifice, to which this scene refers; what has happened here is an unclassical *verlust der mitte*. In this whole shifting, arbitrary context even the apparent affirmations of reality assume a singular, sur-real, effect, and this is true not only for the parts of persons but for the setting. There is, in passages within the figures, and even more evidently in the landscape, a development of complex optical response, and of precision in its record, that exceed any precedent in Raphael's own art. The landscape is like those of Venice in the measure in it of visual sensibility (and the influence here may be in part Sebastiano's), but its graphic mode of definition is quite native to the Roman school. However, this extreme development of illusionistic power of the eye and hand is not used to recreate a normal ambient: this setting is part fantasy, part learned archaeology; it is singular in the substance it contains, and it has been made more singular by the exceptional, transforming light.

The whole image is a demonstration of extraordinary artistic powers, by a personality who has all of Raphael's sophistication, but not his basic point of view. The brilliant complexity of this picture is distinct in its effect and in its process of achievement from Raphael's late demonstrations of his classical style. What had been, in Raphael, a severe testing of the limits of classical expression here has become, finally, a working primarily with those limits only. What had been in Raphael still classically synthetic, though faulted by experimental strain, becomes, in Giulio's hands, the knowing exploitation of antithesis as the chief constructive principle of the work of art. That the outward guise of form is still deliberately like Raphael's is not so important as the fact that its content is no longer merely symptomatic, but explicitly expressive, of a style distinct from that of the master. The *Perla* is the first definition, still within the latest moments of Raphael's own shop, of an art, still faithfully classicistic in surface, which has become unclassical in substance: this is the first quite explicit event of Roman Mannerist style.

Giulio's personally creative transformation of the Raphaelesque style could not of course be expected from Francesco Penni. Yet even in his latest easel works within the shop an operation is performed on Raphalesque classicism that is of historical significance: negatively rather than constructively, appropriately to the way in which Penni's change in style was made. His most important effort was the *Visitation* (Madrid, Prado; c. 1519; signed for Raphael, and inscribed also with the name of the patron's family, Branconio dell'Aquila).[449] The picture is a large one, and though simple in theme and composition its main lines of design were surely indicated to Penni by Raphael, with more care than in the case of Giulio's *Margaret*. The design recalls an obvious Florentine iconography (in Albertinelli, perhaps reseen by Raphael on his possible reported brief visit to Florence), but it is not based (as has been suggested; Fischel) on any early Raphael invention. The intention of style, perceptible even through Penni's deformation, is entirely that of the latest years: it is meant to be in the grandly monumental vein of the *St. Michael*; and it is further intended to be not only grander, but more impressively simple, than the precedents in the Tapestry Cartoons from which this mode derives. The upper figures of the *Transfiguration* are, but more successfully, of similar intent. What Penni has developed in this design, less supervised than his execution in the *Transfiguration*, extends, to the virtual point of caricature, the effects of his participation there. It is no novelty to find a Raphaelesque invention weakened and deflated in Penni's transcription of it: it is rather that this accustomed effect is now so much increased, in the context of the scale and the isolation of the figures of the *Visitation*. The grander the physical and moral dimension is of Raphael's invention, the vaster the discrepancy is between it and Penni's petty blandness of technique.

But the result of this disparity between idea and realization is no longer, in this instance, only technical, or only of a devaluation; on this scale and with this consistency it makes a decisive, although negative, alteration in the basis of classical style Raphael had given for the picture. It is for the first time so explicit that the classical form is made vacuous: not only diminished altogether in its human content but deprived even of its life as form. Unlike Giulio, Penni invents no new vital factors that transform the old; this is obedient and empty observance of classical prescription. In the *Visitation*, classical style has turned into academic formula.

It is conceivable that this negative solution to the destiny of classical style might have had a longer life in the history of Roman art, but fortunately Penni did not shape the character of style in the shop. The responsible personality was Giulio, and increasingly in these very latest years of the shop's functioning he began to operate as Raphael's deputy, and in a more important sense, as the actual model for the manner of painting to be practiced by the shop's other members. It should not be forgotten that, in these years, Raphael had almost altogether ceased to paint; he conceived and directed, but did not realize, the projects that occupied his shop. What the other pupils saw most often, as the most frequent as well as most skilled level of production in the *bottega* was — with the rarest, fragmentary exceptions — from the hand of Giulio, not from that of Raphael. It is Giulio's actual manner that thus tends to influence the others; and his quasi-independent designs, too, acquire the value of imitable source. Penni falls already into the dependent and ancillary relation to Giulio that was to characterize the years that followed Raphael's death. Penni's *Madonna del Divino Amore* (Naples, Galleria Nazionale; c. 1520 and perhaps later than the death of Raphael) [450] does not derive from any design by Raphael but, like Giulio's contemporary *Perla*, is independently conceived; independently, that is, except for its visible inspiration from *La Perla*. This is a partial, but not entire, surrender; despite the many references to Giulio's model, Penni still insists on working, for the most part, not in Giulio's sharply shadowed style but in an only slightly altered version of his own bland technique, as it were recalling the better days when he had learned from Raphael himself how to paint, however badly. His composition in this picture, too, attempts to moderate, while yet imitating, the spatial and directional complexities of the new style of design.

Giulio's authority in the shop was apparently more, however, than that of *primus inter pares*. It would seem that on occasion his responsibility was extended to the preparation, perhaps quite without initial indication by Raphael, of a design for execution by another pupil, and to control over the subsequent execution. Such would seem to have been the case with the *St. John Baptist* (Florence, Academy, ex-Uffizi; c. 1519–20),[451] which conforms wholly in conception of the figure and in composition to Giulio's late manner in the shop, of the moment demonstrated in the *Margaret*; but where the hand is, by general assent, Penni's. Over another of the late assistants in the shop, Raffaellino del Colle, Giulio exerted an entire domination. In Raphael's studio probably since 1517, Raffaellino is, with unintended accuracy, described by Vasari (V, 556) as Giulio's pupil, not as Raphael's. The *Madonna della Rosa* (Madrid, Prado; c. 1519–20; the rose from which the picture takes its title added) [452] is, in all likelihood, of Raffaellino's execution on what, essentially, is Giulio's design. The relation, established in these terms in Raphael's lifetime, continued afterwards. The *Madonna of the Oak* (Madrid, Prado),[453] a virtual companion piece to Giulio's *Perla*, is signed for Raphael and may in fact have been commissioned to the master before April 1520. There is nothing decipherable of him in it; the style of the picture has no counterpart either in the late Raphael or in Giulio's exercises still within the master's shop. However, it precisely reflects Giulio's manner as it had come to be in the autumn after Raphael's death, when the new young *capomaestro* was painting the first Popes of the Sala Constantino. The design of the *Oak* is his, conceived about this time, and part also of its excution; Raffaellino is the discernible executant of the rest. Assuming a commission during Raphael's lifetime — as there must have been to justify the signature remotely — the inscription is a venial misrepresentation, not out of character with the prior workings of the shop, and not unexpected from the men who claimed, when the commission for the Sala Costantino was in doubt, to hold designs by Raphael for it. Later still, when Giulio had opportunity to revise, more maturely, two of his own inventions made in his late master's shop, he also turned to Raffaellino for their execution: these are the redesigned variants of the *St. Margaret* in Vienna [454] and of the *St. John* in the Louvre.

In the last year or two of Raphael's lifetime Giulio was, in anticipation, assuming his inheritance. The decision for the future that, from our knowledge, Raphael might not have made, was made by Giulio even in the master's life, and the future in this sense already belonged to him.

SEBASTIANO DEL PIOMBO

Raphael and his shop enjoyed a virtual, but not an exclusive, monopoly in Rome. By 1515 Sebastiano Veneziano had gained a sound position in this market where competition was so difficult, establishing himself in the few years since his arrival firstly as a portraitist. We have observed already how his practice in this field was influential even upon Raphael. Sebastiano's art had, almost immediately from the beginning of his residence in Rome, begun to assume a local coloration, but by no means with the effect of quick displacement of the style he had brought from Venice. His loyalty to Giorgionesque tradition is still evident in portraits painted by him around 1515. The portrait of a *Man in Armor* (Hartford, Athenaeum, formerly London, Sir Giles Sebright; which probably just antedates that year)[455] still depends upon the precedent of the Brunswick Giorgione. The figure turns in heavy contrapposto, still much in the manner of the Giorgione, and leans upon a strip (possibly cut down from an original larger size) of familiar Venetian parapet. The tousled head strikes a romanticizing note that would be foreign to a purely Roman portrait, and the expression is still touched with what, by Roman standards, is Venetian *schwarmerei.* Yet this is moderated by comparison with Venetian example, and so also is the handling of light: it is a clearer and less various luminosity than in the Venetian style. With this clearer definition of the light there is a corresponding greater clarity of form; not only the shapes of armor — which invite geometrical transcription — but the whole contour and setting of the figure are, for Sebastiano, newly explicit in their definition.

The portrait of a *Young Violinist* (Paris, Baron G. de Rothschild; c. 1515, the date falsely extended to read 1518)[456] is again Venetian in its composition; we have observed before how this recalls the early Titians that Sebastiano could have known before leaving Venice. The depth of chiaroscuro and its dark warmth are also still suggestive of Venetian origin. But what seems less

Venetian is the sense, much increased beyond that in the Hartford portrait, of clarity in definition of the figure's parts of shape and the insistence on an evident order in them of relation. The spatial effect of the sitter's contrapposto, still marked in the Hartford portrait, is much diminished: the light is either muted in its use for modelling or (as in the face) tends to more decisive contrast; the result is a seeming greater adherence of the form to the picture's surface. This discipline within planarity is much strengthened by the effect, still more sensible, of rectilinear arrangement of the pattern made upon the surface; no previous work of Sebastiano's is so deliberately geometrically ordered. In this degree, Sebastiano's clarity of shape and almost schematic discipline of composition quite exceed any precedent in the portraiture of Raphael, where a more flexible adjustment than this is made between a rationale of form and the complex actuality of the model. The resemblance of Sebastiano's portrait style, in this instance, is rather to the most doctrinaire, and exactly contemporary, aspect of Raphael's art, as it appears in the architectonic logic, but in parts only of the internal form, of the Tapestry Cartoons.

Sebastiano's tendency before had been to generalize form in excess of normal Roman practice. Not by first training or by disposition a draughtsman, he had not wished to characterize those incidents of actuality which, in Raphael's work in general, or in Michelangelo's, relieve purity of shape and vitalize it. And at the same time diminishingly Venetian, he had less and less given to his generalizations that differentiating life of light, texture, and color that belonged to his earlier tradition. Now, generalization of form, still more apparent than before, is combined with equal generalization of pictorial structure, and Sebastiano has become in a way more Roman than the Romans. By contrast with the *Violinist*, the contemporary *Castiglione*[423] is not only less aesthetically doctrinaire but more suggestive of Venetian analogy in optical conception and even in its character of brushwork.

But aside from the vitalizing effect of more complex diversity within Raphael's mode of generalization, there is another significant distinction between his formal logic and the Romanized formalism of Sebastiano. Sebastiano's discipline of form is evidently idealizing, but it does not achieve the meaning that it has in Raphael, not only of an idea, but of an ideal force. The shapes in Sebastiano's *Violinist* cohere adequately, but they are not, as in Raphael, compellingly related; Sebastiano does not exercise — he does not have it to exercise — Raphael's power of synthesizing energy in design. There is, in Sebastiano's manipulation of his whole artistic matter — the interpretation of the personality in this case as well — a touch of blandness, a willingness to settle, in his relation both to forms and contents, for something less than passion. This is not merely personal and temperamental; it is perhaps, beneath the Roman look and interests of Sebastiano's present art, a survival of the abstracting temper of form and the introverted feeling that are in *Giorgionismo.* Expressed with much less of the compensating Venetian luxury of sensuous effect, and in the intellectual vocabulary of Romanizing style, this temper can seem vacuous.

This certainly is the effect made by the *Portrait of a Young Man*, sometimes incorrectly called of Raphael (Budapest, Museum; c. 1515–16),[457] where the schematic character of Sebastiano's *Violinist* has been exaggerated almost into diagram; like a diagram, the image seems virtually uninhabited. The extreme purity and simplicity of shapes has become banal, and the geometry of whole design too obvious. It is as if the idea of the design had been set down and left almost in its ideal form only, insufficiently articulated and not even enough representationally realized. The interpretation of personality in the too-handsome face is not enough to reinstill this portrait with vitality; and even the expansive incident of landscape seems, by contrast with Sebastiano's normal habit, somewhat arid. Nothing in Raphael, not only in his portrait style, but even in the extremest passages of the Cartoons, is so doctrinaire a demonstration of geometry as this, or of so lofty a monotonousness. This is the datum of high classical Roman style interpreted in the spirit of the Giorgionesque *sogno,* and thereby made relaxed, distant, and unvital. These, however, are the qualities that emerge when the portrait is measured in a Raphaelesque context; taken more charitably, for itself alone, it has its due effect of impressive amplitude and serene clarity, and of stilled warmth of atmosphere and texture. The face is curiously Leonardesque, and the possibility exists that Sebastiano, like Raphael, had been impressed with what, for him, would have been his first vision of *La Gioconda.* It is a further positive distinction of Sebastiano's picture that it is the first instance in Rome of a portrait in this expanded format, in effect of three-quarter length. It is not Sebastiano's independent invention but another recollection of Venetian experience, as of Titian's *Schiavona* of circa 1510.

The portrait of *Cardinal Antonio Ciocchi del Monte Sansovino* (Dublin, Gallery; c. 1517)[458] indicates clearly that Sebastiano's insistence on the geometry of the forms he paints has become an ineradicable fact of his interpretation of the Roman style. The shapes that compose the Dublin portrait are even more decisively defined than earlier; and now preciseness of effect in definition is secured not only by contrasts of light and dark but — for the first time so explicitly in Sebastiano — by Roman draughtsmanly means, of line-sharp contour. These shapes are, however, in themselves not so arbitrarily simple as in the Budapest portrait, nor are they combined in quite so abstract a geometry. The Dublin portrait recedes from that somewhat vacant purity of ideal form and makes, in compensation, a more nearly energetic pattern. The extreme simplicity of light in the earlier picture has also yielded, and has been replaced by a reasserted fuller chiaroscuro, more warm in tone, in general more richly differentiating of effects of texture, modelling, and place of forms in space. This chiaroscuro is not merely a resurrected element of Sebastiano's Venetian style: it functions differently from his light as it had been before 1515 or so. In parts, as in the drapery, the light seeks almost no detail; it minimizes the descriptive meaning of the area that it defines, and conversely increases its impress as a whole shape upon the eye, intensifying thereby its value of abstraction. In the face, however, the lighting works with an opposite variety, and with a descriptive efficiency like that in the exactly contemporary portraits of Raphael, searching out the actuality of form.

These are two new differentiating extremes for Sebastiano in the use of light; and they are relieved in this portrait against a context of a normally complex, still identifiably Venetian, chiaroscuro of the architectural and landscape background. The whole range of differentiation in chiaroscuro is not different from what had been before in Sebastiano, but its uses are: on the one hand, a new increase of a value of abstraction, and on the other, an achievement of a newly specific descriptive force. These do not make unclassical polarities, for (unlike the similar phenomenon in the painting of young Giulio) both extremes are generated out of a still present and containing norm; and it is yet more important that these differentiations made by light are contained within the highly characterized geometrical system of design. It is this insistent and exceedingly apparent formal structure that, in the end as in the beginning, is the dominating matter of the picture.

It is only in Sebastiano's portraits of this time that the particular human identity is so much treated as a vehicle on which to impose a system of aesthetic form, which, in the measure of its emphasis as form, assumes a value separable from the represented human content. There is not, in Sebastiano's images, the responsive coordination, inevitable in Raphael's portraiture, between the expressive effects of the design and the quality of the sitter's personality. The countenance of the *Cardinal Ciocchi* has a bright immediacy of expression — quite new for a portrait by Sebastiano — which in temper is not like the still abstraction of the forms that frame it. Ciocchi's face is, as it were, set into the design, and also into the rest of the representation from which its degree of realism differs; the person and the picture do not make, as in Raphael, a single, though differentiated, visual and expressive texture. However, it is the expression and the relative realism of Ciocchi's head that first suggest that there is a more than casual connection between this portrait by Sebastiano and Raphael's *Bibbiena.* Because this conception of a sharply animate psychological reality has antecedents within Raphael, but no precedent in Sebastiano, it is likely that it is Sebastiano's picture that is the dependent work; Ciocchi's pose as well would then derive from the *Bibbiena.* By this time the two artists were entirely *brouillé,* but Raphael's painting, once published, would surely have been accessible to Bastiano. The relation affirms the community of interests between the two, and of stage of development in general within classical style, but even more serves to stress again their differences of personality.

Raphael in turn may have been indebted to Sebastiano for at least a motive, but a motive only, when he composed his *Leo X with Rossi and Giulio de' Medici.*[429] Sebastiano's group portrait of Cardinal Bandinello Sauli, his secretary, and two friends (Washington, National Gallery, Kress Collection; formerly the Earl of Harewood)[460] is dated 1516, from the year preceding the *Ciocchi,* and preceding also Raphael's invention of the *Leo X.* Sebastiano's group portrait, the most quantitatively ambitious venture in easel portrait painting so far undertaken in the Roman school, depends in part on Sebastiano's own previous Venetian experience, but in a double portrait only: of the musicians Verdelotti and Ubretto (destroyed, formerly Berlin).[459] The compositional problem of the present more complex case is partly solved for two of its figures by almost exact memory of what had been done in the portrait of the two musicians; the dependence is so close that, aside from Morellian resemblances of detail, it confirms our attribution to Sebastiano of the Berlin work. The two "new" figures, of the Cardinal and his secretary, have been more imaginatively represented, in a relation of pose interesting enough to have been, possibly, suggestive to Raphael when he began the *Leo X.* But the whole arrangement of the figures is quite uninspired: it is an additive conjunction of forms, so much separately conceived that they are not quite reconciled in scale.

Sebastiano's thinking here is still, mostly, in the vein of his Budapest picture: insistent on a maximum clarity of single shape, and on an obvious rationale of larger order, in this case meant to be achieved by the repetitive rectilinear disposition, in near-planarity and near-isocephaly, of all the figures. The intended — and in such a composition, necessary — accents of variety in the placing of the forms are not enough to make the effect either of vitality in the design or vitality of presence. To achieve the sense of presence, Sebastiano has labored instead with another means, of smoother realism of descriptive surface and of incidents of detail: this is a variety of Roman practice he would henceforth use at will and frequently, but by no means to the necessary exclusion of Venetian techniques from his work. Except in its details — or, indeed, in the masterly execution of each portion of this unsynthetic whole — the picture does not work; it is defeated by its problem. A single human actuality could be subjugated and transformed by Bastiano into an image of abstracting art; but these four models all at once, and the problems of relation among them, are more of literal reality than the painter can control.

We tend too often to remember Sebastiano in the character Vasari unsympathetically created for him, a portrait sketched from Sebastiano's later years when he was, admittedly, a relatively unproductive and perhaps even lazy painter. However, in the half-decade between 1515 and 1520 Sebastiano's accomplishment was as much as could be expected from any artist who, unlike Raphael, was not a compound personality. Furthermore, the importance of Sebastiano's accomplishment was second only to that of Raphael himself, not only in portraiture but in the field of major works of religious painting. Sebastiano's challenge to Raphael was a strong one, in productivity, and in the aesthetic interest and spiritual dimension of what he produced.

According to Vasari (V, 568), Michelangelo had chosen Sebastiano to lead the Michelangelesque party in Rome in their by now long-standing feud with Raphael. This role as deputy for Michelangelo was assigned to Sebastiano apparently in 1515, before Michelangelo's departure from the city, and it became still more important afterward. Vasari's statement of the situation is that Michelangelo meant to use Sebastiano as a kind of straw man, who would present Michelangelo's ideas to the public in painted form; without risk to the latter, but with credit to both and, in the expected comparison, with discredit to Raphael. Already Michelangelesque in artistic orientation since soon after his arrival in Rome, and always disposed to think in large terms of human forms and sentiments, Sebastiano was the best available instrument for such a purpose of Michelangelo's, if — as Vasari alleges — it in fact existed. What Sebastiano may have lacked to fit him to compete with Raphael, Michelangelo would, in Vasari's presumption of the case, have supplied.

What was envisaged at the first in this relation may in fact have been what Vasari, in his description of its beginnings, implies: that Sebastiano was meant to undertake the function of a quasi-independent executant for Michelangelo's ideas, not altogether different from what Giulio Romano, in this time too, began to be for Raphael. But any such intention was quickly undermined by Michelangelo's return to Florence in the autumn of 1516; even a *quasi-bottega* could not be run successfully by correspondence. In any case the relationship between Sebastiano and Michelangelo could not have been, in its way of working or its results, like that within a shop. Sebastiano was not and had not been Michelangelo's pupil or assistant; he was, when this relation began, a differently, and independently, formed mature personality.

Beyond Vasari's allegations of Sebastiano's dependence on Michelangelo we have, within this period, only one documented instance of solicitation by Sebastiano from Michelangelo of a design; this case coincides with the surviving visual evidence. In no other case is the older artist's intervention provable; nevertheless, it existed. However, such suggestions as Michelangelo may have made in the form of a notation, in drawing, of motive or of composition have been subsumed entirely, in Sebastiano's pictures, in his own subsequent personal artistic process — except in one work only, from the very beginning of the phase we now discuss, which is in addition to the unique documented case. In general, what Michelangelo seems to have supplied to Sebastiano was taken by him not as Raphael's assistants took the *disegno* of their master, but as a basis for Sebastiano's own distinct, and wholly personal, meditation. A Michelangelo *disegno*, where it may be presumed, assumes the value not of an invention made *ad hoc* but of an experience external and previous to the particular picture by Sebastiano, as of a previously extant work of art. The dependence in this time of Sebastiano on Michelangelo is not so much more than earlier on specifiable artistic facts, but rather on Michelangelo's general example of a dimension, and an expressive tonality, to which the human image could be formed. This does not make Sebastiano's style, in his pictures of this phase that Michelangelo's designs may be supposed to underly, an approximation, even in rough sense, for a hypothetical style that Michelangelo might have exercised in painting in these years. The whole aesthetic personality of Sebastiano's works, and even their expressive temper, more formed on Michelangelo's, are distinct from what is at any point in the style of Michelangelo. The comparison of Sebastiano's allegedly derived works with the art of the Florentine only finally confirms how little, still, the latter thinks as a painter. The identity of Sebastiano's art is not only in his personality, but in the problems and solutions of a painter that he shares, not with Michelangelo but with their mutual opponent, Raphael.

We remarked that one picture, from the beginning of the Michelangelesque association, seems surely to support, from internal evidence, Vasari's contention (V, 568) that its "invenzione . . . ed il cartone fu di Michelagnolo"; this is the great *Pietà* (Viterbo, Museum).[461] Its dating had vacillated much in past years, but in more modern criticism tended to a place between 1517 and 1520 or shortly thereafter. Recently it has been established that the year 1517 must be a *terminus ante quem* for the *Pietà*, because its figures are paraphrased with some literalness in a picture dated in that year by the insignificant Viterbese, Costantino Zelli (Viterbo, Museo Civico 29). Considering the normal circumstances of production and publication of a picture like Sebastiano's, and the time required for its elaborated imitation by Zelli within 1517, it is reasonable to place the beginning of Sebastiano's *Pietà* at least in the year before. If its inception is assumed in 1516, however, it requires that we admit a community of style between the *Pietà* and the painting of the same theme in Leningrad by Sebastiano, dated 1516; this community does not exist. The Leningrad *Pietà* demonstrates the first distinct appearance in Sebastiano's art of a linear squaring of forms, especially of drapery: a tendency which, once manifest, persists uninterrupted through the succeeding years. The manner of drawing in the Viterbo *Pietà*, and also the quality of rich-textured surface, rather suggest a measure of relation, still, to Sebastiano's large easel pictures of the preceding phase, the Fitzwilliam *Adoration* [199] and the *Death of Adonis*.[200] Other factors, too, suggest that the Viterbo picture antedates the *Pietà* of Leningrad: the handling of light is still richly modulated, and the response to optical experience, as of details of form, is not yet so generalized or stylized so selectively as in the pictures after 1515. The figures are conceived more vitally, and are not so much posed aesthetic constructs as they become from the Leningrad altar onward. Despite the domination of the figure style and figure composition by the Roman mode, this work is still — and it is the last work of Sebastiano's so to be — profoundly Giorgionesque, though it is a *Giorgionismo* made, far beyond any Venetian example, physically immediate and heroic in its scale of form and idea.

The chronological place of this expression within Sebastiano's style is not after 1515, and it is not to be excluded altogether that the *Pietà* of Viterbo may have been invented in the year before. Vasari describes this painting first in sequence among the major commissions of this phase, which in fact fall in the order of his narrative; his evidence of sequence coincides with the date we have deduced from the evidence within the work itself. It is also of this picture that Vasari states explicitly that its invention and cartoon were by Michelangelo, the first product of their intended association. Vasari's statement is not to be dismissed, as it has too easily been in recent criticism. He does not attribute the invention of the setting to Michelangelo, nor does he give him any role of supervision over the picture's particular interpretation and execution, and these factors finally determine its substantially Sebastianesque personality. The *invenzione* is of not more than the basic compositional idea and the attitudes only of the figures; and this can with more plausibility be credited to Michelangelo than to Sebastiano.

We have remarked that, before and after the Viterbo *Pietà*, Sebastiano thinks as much as Raphael in painter's terms of pictorial organization, of populated compositions arranged in space: the *Pietà* in Leningrad is Sebastiano's own conception, pictorial in essential kind, of what this theme should be. This iconography in the Viterbo altar is a sculptor's, not a painter's notion of the *Pietà*. Its figure composition is entirely the projection of a sculptor's thought, without concession to pictorial effects. Each figure is separately sculptural, closed in contour and resistant to intrusion of the space, and their compound makes a massive isolated formal unit. Despite Sebastiano's painterly touch, his sense for optical effect cannot conceal the haptic origin and essence of these figures. They were not conceived to inhabit a landscape but to be set, like sculpture, into an aesthetically neutral space. What is here is not imitation by Sebastiano of Michelangelo, or such quotation as appears in larger contexts elsewhere, but the transcription of the idea of another kind of mind, an idea so powerful and of so highly characterized an identity that it is, even in translation, fundamentally inalterable.

Aside from Vasari's statement that this idea is Michelangelo's, the motives in themselves bespeak him: not so much retrospectively, though the Virgin is generally related to the Seers of the Sistine, and the Christ to the conception of the male form that is in the *Dying Slave* of nearer date. The figures are less derived from precedents than they are precedents themselves: the Christ for the type and anatomy that Michelangelo would use in the sculpture of S. M. sopra Minerva, and the Virgin for the much later Rachel of the final version of the Julius Tomb. Michelangelo was not in the habit of quoting others, but he properly had no scruple about self-quotation; the first appearance of these motives, later used by Michelangelo, in the Viterbo altar is further indication of his invention of them. More generally, it should be observed of the whole design in this picture that it makes reference both backward and forward in Michelangelo's own work. In its severity, it is an intermediate term between the early *Pietà* of St. Peter's and the late *Pietà* for Vittoria Colonna. The *invenzione* then, but of the figures only, must be assigned to Michelangelo, as Vasari properly asserts, but it is more doubtful that, as he asserts also, it was ever put down for Sebastiano's exact guidance in a cartoon. The rear of the Viterbo panel contains some sketches, of which one group only, for the head of a Madonna, are clearly relevant to the picture on the front. These sketches are quite tentative; if a cartoon by Michelangelo existed such preparatory probing of the motive would hardly have been necessary. Beyond Michelangelo's notation of the first idea, then, the picture is Sebastiano's own. That idea, however, no matter how slight the form may have been in which it was conveyed to Sebastiano, was indomitably Michelangelo's.

We are thus dealing in the Viterbo *Pietà* with a compound work of art, which in the problem it presents resembles those which at this same time began to assume importance in the shop of Raphael. The elements in the compound are, in this case, easier of solution. Michelangelo's figural *invenzione*, in its status of idea, is, as it were, one clear and separable element in this picture. What Sebastiano has done with this idea: in setting, in handling, in interpretation of its content and particular appearance, and in the remarkable conjunction of Michelangelo's purpose to his own, is another, and to a decisive degree, effectively a Sebastianesque matter. In a sense, the *invenzione* is Michelangelo's critique of his own early *Pietà*, made in the light of a different stage in the evolution of classical style. This idea is in every sense larger and more generalized: more ample, broad, and distinct in geometry of form, and more expansive in its character of content. The conception is in the strain of the late images of the Sistine, including a suggestion of resemblance, in the figure of the Virgin, to the style of the lunettes. Still more than there, this image is presented to us with a stressed simplicity, both of content and of form. An idea of high tragic power is expressed with absolute explicitness, in a structure of severest geometric rigor. The style of this group, in the generalization we discern beneath Sebastiano's hand, is a variant of the high classicism Michelangelo had sometime since achieved, but it is a variant which, in its extreme directness of idea and austerity of structure, suggests close analogy with Raphael's exactly contemporary ultimate classical style, in the Tapestry Cartoons.

The outward guise that Sebastiano has given Michelangelo's idea, and the inflection he has given to its meaning, do not quite belong on this same exalted plane of classical conception. Sebastiano still thinks, Venice-like, of a need of painting to recreate a palpable, textured substance. One of the things he has learned from the Roman school (as had been incipiently visible in the Pouncey *Madonna*)[201] is its tendency to smoother and more precisely modelled surfaces, in which draughtsman's handling reinforces the effects of brushwork. This is the lesson less of Roman fresco style than of the manner used particularly in the easel pictures, appropriately imitated here. This Roman precision of technique, combined with Venetian sense of surface, results, in parts of the Viterbo altar, and in the Christ particularly, in an illusionistic literalness that, in this, exceeds the Roman norm as well as what is in Sebastiano's own preceding works. In the figure of the Christ there is, to reinforce this intention of illusionism, surely a wish to approximate the sense of plastic actuality that belongs to sculpture: another indication of the presence of Michelangelo close to this work.

This particular power of illusion is articulated in a light which — though it too is manipulated with new precision, no longer in Venetian shorthand — is still Venetian in its basic character and use. The lighting here competes with form, and effectively takes equal place with it as an agent of expression in the picture. In 1514, Raphael had himself come to one exceptional such conception of a role for light, in the *Liberation of Peter*,[222] and we have observed how light increasingly became a formal and expressive factor in his later works. But this lighting in the *Pietà* is different: its content of dramatic power is, as not in Raphael, at the same time a lyric content. Further, Sebastiano's light is not forced as if by artifice; it is a single optical consistency, rich with the depth and vibration of an experienced visual truth. It is this which moderates the austerity of pose and structure of the figures, and suffuses their statuary essence with a warmth like that of life. The light makes the high ideality of the image more nearly accessibly human, and even poignant to us in its sense of presence.

It is an indication of Sebastiano's personal power of invention, and of the power of the principle with which he works, that he is able to overcome, at least in part, the statuary isolation of Michelangelo's intention for the figures; by the functioning of the light they are made, in some degree, to partake of their setting. It is in the landscape, the most imaginative and poetic of Sebastiano's such inventions, that the pretext in reality for the mode of light is found: a full moon darkly illumines the rolling hills of the Campagna. A shimmering light sketches out the forms of earth, trees, and half-ruined rustic towns within the gloom, of which the dark depth seems infinite. Color is absorbed or muted in this moonlight; its original intensities, as of the blues of the garment of the Virgin, are dimmed or chilled to make a dully glowing radiance within the dark; the whites, in the coif of the Virgin and around the grey-bronzed body of the Christ, are luminescent. Save for the working of the light on them and around them, the isolation of the two figures would be absolute, formally and in meaning; but by the degree to which they are incorporated in their setting, the loneliness of the Virgin and her Son are made less abstract: more humanly poignant because of their context that other beings might share, but do not. It is by Sebastiano's extension of the mood of the landscape, almost romantic, to the Virgin that her emotion, too, becomes less entirely ideal and risks the perilous distinction between nobility and bathos. But the setting that contains her form also serves to magnify the sense of grandeur in her. She becomes a looming and heroic presence, immovable in her solitary grief, the least impermanent feature in the landscape. It is again Sebastiano's doing that this grandiose appearance is larger in its effect of form than in its intensity of meaning; there is always in him this slight but sensible discrepancy between the magnitude of physical presence and, not its scale, but its vitality of content of idea. The whole image remains, nevertheless, one of the most impressive in this phase of Roman painting, in which Michelangelo and Sebastiano — as they meant to do — effectively challenge, in similar terms of style, the highest accomplishment of the contemporary Raphael in the Cartoons.

Unlike the Viterbo picture, the *Pietà* of Leningrad (Hermitage; signed and dated 1516)[462] contains no element of Michelangelo beyond its one evident quotation from the *Sacrifice of Noah* [104] (in the figure to the upper right) and repetitions of quotations already incorporated into Sebastiano's repertory. The invention is Sebastiano's altogether and, as we have remarked, it is, in contrast to the Viterbo *Pietà*, a painter's iconography and development of the theme. To give the theme a higher possible complexity, both formal and dramatic, it has been interpreted as a compound between two events, the Lamentation and the imminent Entombment. The intention of enrichment by thematic synthesis is here, with better pretext, what Raphael would much more forcefully evolve for the *Transfiguration*. The richness of conception is the antithesis of the Viterbo picture, and again an analogue with Raphael is brought to mind. Sebastiano is not responsible for the character of design of the earlier term in this sequence; but the sequence, of a rigorous architectonic stability followed by an elaborated and dramatically highly movemented work, resembles what, in the same two years, we have seen in the art of Raphael.

In general, indeed, the Leningrad *Pietà* seems to share ambitions of style that are apparent in the exactly contemporary art of Raphael, in its dramatic aspect. More decisively than in the *Battle of Ostia*,[374] and more radically even than in the *Coronation*,[380] the *Pietà* is designed asymmetrically, its main forms arranged on a diagonal that thrusts leftward in a shallow depth of space. The line of thrust is forthright and severe; less than in the Viterbo *Pietà*, and less than in Raphael's *Spasimo* [433] of this same year, is there equivocation between the claims of urgency in expression and of ornament. Like the impulse of design that contains them, the figures move forthrightly, with a squared yet not unhandsome bluntness in their shapes of action. As in Raphael's diagonally asymmetrized designs, the strong oblique movement here is compensated, in this case partly by a crossing axis (in the Virgin and St. John), and partly by a motive, now familiar in Sebastiano, of counterthrusting gesture in the Nicodemus. His motion, pointing to the figures at the tomb, more distant in the space, finds in them the substance and energies of posture that finally effect a balance of the urgently moved masses in the picture.

The idea of working with asymmetrical design was more easy to Sebastiano than to Raphael; this was part of his original experience in Venice of that more flexible and movemented version of the classical style. His two great early Roman easel works had been composed asymmetrically, but neither one had ventured so aggressively as this. This composition is of a drastic novelty, as daring in its temper of experiment as the current Raphaelesque researches, and substantially like them in its devices and in its intent. There is no specifiable precise relation between this work and the *Spasimo*, but they are evidently, beneath the gross difference of personality, of a close community in style. It is barely possible that Sebastiano should have seen the *Spasimo* still within 1516 and in time to paint this considerable work subsequently, but still within the same year. He could have seen it, however, only after its completion and public exhibition, for by this time the rival shop and all that went on in it certainly was closed to him. So also would the *Coronation of Charlemagne*, which also has some resemblance in design to the *Pietà*, have been in all likelihood still invisible to Sebastiano in 1516. He almost surely did not see the Tapestry Cartoons, yet these too show common characteristics with Sebastiano's painting, not in respect of design but of other circumstances almost equal in importance. It is in this *Pietà* that, for the first time so explicitly and so pervasively (there are symptoms on lesser scale in the contemporary portraits), the difference in conception of form appears that we remarked briefly in distinguishing, in comparison, the manner of the Viterbo altar.

As in Raphael's Cartoons, form in the Leningrad *Pietà* is described succinctly, almost summarily, with a generalizing and abbreviating stress of geometric values. In Sebastiano, this tendency goes farther than in Raphael, nearly to the point of schematizing shapes. Rhythmical refinements of modelling of surface or of ornamental curve of contour are largely sacrificed to make patterns, almost blunt, of angular or squared geometry. More explicitly than in the Viterbo *Pietà*, these shapes are defined by draughtsman's outline and reinforced by a chiaroscuro as generalizing as that in the Tapestry Cartoons, and only slightly less decisive in its force. Unlike Sebastiano's preceeding works, the lighting here suggests less of sensuous experience than its conversion to aesthetically arbitrary use. As in the Cartoons, form assumes a very highly characterized ideal identity.

In Sebastiano's picture, this ideality of shape is not the product of a condensation of the form so powerfully aware as Raphael's, nor is it aesthetically so vitally inhabited. As Sebastiano proceeds onto a higher plane of Roman intellectuality there is reasserted in him a way of regarding form like that in his earliest Venetian experience, and in the monumental works of Giorgione himself: form is felt — as we have remarked already of the portraits — in the distant and abstracting state of mind of the Giorgionesque *sogno.* What, in the style of the Cartoons, is a supreme ideal force of form becomes in Sebastiano, with means artistically similar except for their energy, in effect formally abstracting. The shapes that are created from the figures seem, in places, as if they might be separable from their substance; despite the figures' monumental amplitude they are a little vacant. The counterweight for this patterning abstraction is in the contrasting efficacy of individual descriptive incidents, and in the sense of habitable actuality, in space and light, of landscape setting; these restore the whole effect of the image to a classical domain of plausibility and power of impress. Perhaps still more, the abstractness of the form has been redeemed by the power of expressive pathos in the faces and the gestures of the figures. These are as deeply serious as in the Tapestry Cartoons, and they are expressed as much as it is possible to Sebastiano with the same directness. These emotions, furthermore, are touched with the particular slow gravity which, from now onward, will be recognizably Sebastiano's: his emotion is more decorous than in Raphael, as profound but not so intensely charged.

At the end of the year 1516 the rivalry of Sebastiano with Raphael was put to explicit comparative test when Cardinal Giulio de' Medici commissioned both artists to paint intendedly companion pictures for Narbonne: the *Transfiguration* by Raphael, and by Sebastiano, the *Resurrection of Lazarus* (London, National Gallery).[463-5] If we are to believe the reports from Sebastiano's camp the competition was not to Raphael's liking: on the 19th of January 1517, Leonardo Sellaio wrote to Michelangelo, then in Carrara, that ". . . Bastiano aveva tolto a fare quella tavola . . . Ora mi pare che Raffaello metta sotosopra il mondo, perche lui nonlla faca [sic] per non venire a paraghoni." (Golzio, 53.) The history of Sebastiano's progress on his picture, and the careful concealment of the work of each artist from the other, is more than usually well-documented. Begun before Raphael actually set to work on his *Transfiguration*, Sebastiano's *Resurrection of Lazarus* was completed first; on May 1st, 1519, Sellaio informed Michelangelo in Florence that Sebastiano had finished (Golzio, 98).

According to Vasari, Michelangelo's partisanship of Sebastiano once more extended to the point of direct help with the creation of the *Lazarus.* Vasari asserts (V, 570) that it was done ". . . sotto ordini e disegno in alcune parti di Michelagnolo." This phrase may be interpreted in several ways, but its literal meaning is that Michelangelo supplied ideas, not for the entire composition but for some motives in it. The evidence of the work itself, as well as the literary evidence of correspondence between the persons most involved, indicates that Michelangelo indeed had no part in the design of the whole; but the contention that Vasari does make, in our reading, may contain the kernel of a truth. The motive of the Lazarus alone — hardly, by any estimate, "alcune parti" — is with great probability based upon a suggestion in drawing made *ad hoc* by Michelangelo at Sebastiano's plea; the figure as painted is not at all literally derived but worked up, and worked away, from Michelangelo's original suggestion. The three drawings by Sebastiano for the *Lazarus* (Bayonne, Musée Bonnat, and two in the British Museum) show, in the course of the evolution of the motive toward the form in which it finally was used, a decreasing literalness of Michelangelesque style in draughtsmanship — which, however, in the initial drawing (Bayonne) is dependent to the point of possible confusion: Sebastiano is nowhere else so deliberately Michelangelesque except in instances where, provably, he is working after Michelangelo's example. But in the end the alteration made of Michelangelo's presumed suggestion is so much that the motive, as Sebastiano has transformed it, has become his own and no longer Michelangelo's invention. The *Lazarus,* indeed, less literally evokes Michelangelo than do certain of the fragmentary quotations in this picture from the repertory of the Sistine Ceiling — such, for example, as the citations, in the arms of Christ, of both the *Separation of Earth and Water* [125] and the *Creation of Adam,*[122] and in the attitude of Martha, of the Adam of Michelangelo's *Expulsion.*[121] Even such reminiscences are few; as much as the Leningrad altar that precedes it, this painting is Sebastiano's essentially personal creation.

Following so closely as the *Lazarus* does on the Leningrad *Pietà* it is inevitable that the two works should be markedly similar in most respects of style. The *Lazarus,* from its nature as a competition picture, is more extensive and more complicated in its apparatus of form, and it seems also to be — perhaps for the same reason — not only more careful in its execution but more flexibly and precisely calculating of effects of handling. The resemblance of one work to the other confirms a mutual resemblance to the contemporary art of Raphael; the *Lazarus,* furthermore, is almost literally like the *Spasimo* in the basic structure of its composition. As in that picture, in the *Lazarus* the armature on which the design is projected consists of asymmetrically crossed but counterbalancing diagonals, laid back into a depth of space; in Sebastiano's structure the exploration of the space is deeper, and the integration with the landscape setting is — as also in the Leningrad altar — more effective. In this case there is the explicit possibility of Sebastiano's knowledge of Raphael's design for the *Spasimo,* but this is still no assurance that the scheme of the Lazarus was not entirely independently invented. For a similarity exists which, though less exact in the design alone, is yet more convincing in whole character of style, between the *Lazarus* and Raphael's *Transfiguration* [438] with which it was in competition; and we recall that the *Transfiguration* was started later than the *Lazarus,* and that Sebastiano did not see it until after the *Lazarus* was finished.

Part of this similarity proceeds from the like ambitions that were generated by the competition of the two great paintings. In the terms of this moment in the development of style in Rome, and of the taste of Roman patronage educated by this development, it was understandable that both artists should seek to impress by virtuoso demonstration of grandiosity and complexity, of form and content. Each of these works inevitably would seek powerful effects of drama, and equally, their most complex articulation. Sebastiano was more initially fortunate than Raphael at least in one sense, in his subject matter. His theme was a dramatic unity, susceptible of rich differentiation, in the beginning; it was not necessary for Sebastiano to contrive a unity as Raphael did, out of themes disparate in dramatic temper and disconnected in narration. At the same time, Sebastiano's simpler problem did not generate the challenge that Raphael so remarkably and finally so excitingly surpassed. There is no motive in Sebastiano's theme for such an ascent into sublimity as Raphael makes in the heavenly episode of his *Transfiguration*; though miracle, Sebastiano's subject is an earthly happening. It is richly dramatic in interpretation, but it is also not like Raphael's earthly episode, a passionate commotion. Sebastiano's dominating temper in his reading of the drama is of majestic gravities and deep, slow-unfolding powers: there is a bass resonance of content in his scene, by comparison with which Raphael's episode of the *Obsessed Boy* [440-1] seems strident and less decorously classical.

The tone of Sebastiano's scene is set by the monumental shape and posture of the Christ,[464] ponderated like a Polyclitan image, but with the potency of wide-flung, simple, and rhetoric gesture that (though its motives here are specifically derived from Michelangelo) had been for the first time used in Rome with this effect in Raphael's Tapestry Cartoons. The *Transfiguration* repeatedly employs this same style of gesture, more intensely charged, and without the profound, slow deliberation that is in Sebastiano's Christ. Also as in the *Transfiguration,* such gesture is used by Sebastiano as a major and explicit determinant of formal and contentual directions. In both works, not only this mode of gesture but the disposition in general of the actors conforms to a clear pattern of straight-lined diagonal design, equally insistent but in each case differently severe in its effect. In the Raphael *Obsessed*, the stress of thrust is repeated and inflexible; in the *Lazarus* it is equally explicit but less harsh. In both cases the schema of design is differentiated with a multiplicity of incident, more various than the matter strictly calls for. These intend, obviously, to diversify and complicate the central content as they do the basically forthright form. As much as in Raphael's picture, Sebastiano seeks in his to make maximum variety of types of persons and of psychological response; the effort in both works is as self-consciously programmatic as it had once been, long before, at the beginning of the classical style, in Leonardo's *Adoration*. In both works, too, this diversity of characterization is in part accomplished by a newly insistent fragmentary realism of the heads, less forced by Sebastiano than by Raphael. In the denser population of the *Lazarus*, however, the quick succession of varied physiognomies and gestures create a more complicating effect; Sebastiano's differentiation of his theme is more elaborate than Raphael's, but not so articulately sharp. But despite such distinctions, the two altarpieces are less unlike, and more in fact companion works, than the artists could ever have intended. They share a common formal and expressive character to a higher degree than do any other independent works of major personalities of the Roman High Renaissance style. This measure of coincidence, independently achieved, might not have been possible at a moment earlier than this, before the resources and ambitions of Roman classical style had been so clearly indicated. Both the *Lazarus* and the *Transfiguration* are most precisely characteristic products of the last vital phase of this style in its mode of grandiose and complex declamatory drama.

It is the level of complexity which, more nearly accustomed in the art of Raphael, is new to Sebastiano in the *Lazarus*. This particular aspect of Roman style was the one least readily accessible to Sebastiano: it demanded the continuous and unrelenting exercise, in extension and in depth, of the calculating mind. The Giorgionesque temper that lay deep within Sebastiano, beneath the assimilated Romanism, was not natively disposed to this extended, intense and precise intellectual exercise. Only in the *Lazarus*, where Raphael's challenge stimulated it, does Sebastiano finally achieve this measure of complex intellectuality; and though from now on its possibility is open to him he never wholly reattains it. It has, in the *Lazarus*, effects upon his style that are best appreciated by comparison with the Leningrad *Pietà*. In that picture the manner of describing form had been intellectual, in the sense that form was generalized toward an evident geometric value. But this generalization had been too elliptical; its effect was of schematizing abstractness of form. In the *Lazarus* Sebastiano manifests the same new tendency to generalize toward a rectangular geometry, but this geometry is not now so oversimplified and vacantly abstracting. His analysis of form — quasi-cubistic, if we may use the term only suggestively — is more complex and connectively articulated. He continues to induce a geometry from the parts of body and of drapery, but this now reflects the richer and more vital order that is in their actuality. It is, further, not so exclusively and uniformly a rectilinear mode of order as he made in the Leningrad *Pietà*: relieving varieties of shape and connective episodes of pattern are expressed with sharp-drawn curving rhythms.

Light, too, had been almost schematically generalized in the Leningrad picture. As it now inescapably accompanies, in the *Lazarus*, the definition of its more complex forms, it too becomes more vital and complex. The light retains Sebastiano's particular reminiscence of Venetian depth and richness in its modulation, but this now seems less romantical — differently precise and powerful, and more vigorous — in this context of its more sharply articulate behavior. The accent of Venetian sensuousness that remains in it does not prevent the light in the *Lazarus* from functioning in a dramatically active role, like the light in the *Transfiguration*.

The content of color in the light has become, like the form, decidedly arbitrary but its richness is again a symptom of a once-Venetian education. The figure of the Christ is coloristically isolated by a pure bleached pink in the dress, with a mantle of ice-blue; the subsidiary figures are a wonderfully differentiated unity of complementary greens and oranges. The flesh tones of the male and female forms are so distinct as to suggest a convention almost Egyptian in its stringency: the men (except for Christ alone) browned and dark, the women pale to the point of greenness. Bands of sharp white and lighter tones weave a rhythmic thread of continuity through the color composition. More than it has ever been evident before, it is now clear that Sebastiano's color no longer means to convey, in accustomed Venetian manner, an intensified sensuous experience. The colors are initially fantastic — inventions made on the palette, singular, surprising, and visually exciting, not hues encountered even in the most opulent actuality, and surely not in these sequences and combinations. They retain a deep, Venice-like luminosity that makes them sensuously pleasurable and enchanting to the eye; yet they do not transcribe, but rather profoundly transmute, a sensuous experience.

In the distant background the color is autumnal, and in it light does not warm, but bleaches color where it strikes, or is reflected from the coldly bright cerulean sky. The landscape [465] seems a sear and urban transformation of a dimmed memory in Sebastiano of Giorgione's *Tempest*. It is a setting which, immediately on its publication, would assume authority as model even in Raphael's own school, for Giulio in particular. The figure composition more deeply penetrates the landscape than in any earlier Sebastiano, yet the sense is in this picture — supported partly, but not entirely created by distinctions in color and tonality — that the figures and the landscape are more separable elements than in Sebastiano's works before. Even more than in the *Pietà* of Viterbo, where the figure scheme was not Sebastiano's doing, landscape here — adroitly connected with the figure composition as it is — seems not to be integral in conception with it, but the product of a discrete, less important thought, as in the making of a backdrop. Sebastiano's cast of mind has so much altered from that of Venice that he has begun to think, as Raphael has especially since the Tapestries, in terms of absolute predominance of figures over setting, and not any longer of their reciprocity.

In the *Lazarus* Sebastiano in effect completes the process of his Romanization. Dislocated by his translation in milieu, it is only when this process is achieved that Sebastiano, at this late date, attains his entire and explicit artistic identity — a tardy maturity — which subsequent experience or even strong influence, as from Michelangelo, will alter but not substantially disarrange. The character of this style, and its place in the development of Roman classicism, are distinct from that of his preceding works: as they are not, this is an elaborate expression of late classical rhetoric, supremely articulate of Sebastiano's special sense of grandeur and decorum. The human and the formal language in it stand, in the classical evolution, in a reach between Raphael's Tapestry Cartoons and his *Transfiguration*: lacking the sublimity and force of either, it has the magnitude of thought and ideality of one, and the intent of formal and expressive complexity that is in the other. Unlike the *Transfiguration*, the classical style of the *Lazarus* shows no apparent fault; unlike Raphael, Sebastiano is not possessed by so urgent a creatively experimental impulse that it strains the sense and structure of the style that, in its fullest moment of accomplishment, he finally had wholly mastered.

The *Holy Family with St. John Baptist and Donor* (P. F. Borgherini [?]; London, National Gallery; c. 1519)[466] is like the *Lazarus* to that degree where its conception and most of its execution must have followed immediately on it. This picture is almost certainly that referred to in the correspondence with Michelangelo, once in a letter from Sellaio and the second time, much later, in a letter from Sebastiano himself. The Sellaio letter, of March 1, 1517 (Frey, *Br.* LV), tells Michelangelo that Pier Francesco Borgherini (the Florentine art-patron and friend of Michelangelo, who late in 1516 had commissioned the decoration of a chapel in S. Pietro in Montorio to Sebastiano) was "disperato" with a picture being painted for him by one Andrea, presumably del Sarto. Sellaio reports that Bastiano would like to have a cartoon from Michelangelo from which he, instead, could paint Borgherini's picture; if Michelangelo is willing, Sebastiano will send the dimensions and "uno aposta" — a sketch idea, perhaps — for it. There is no indication of any favorable reply from Michelangelo to this request. On April 22, 1525 Sebastiano still had what was apparently this picture in his studio; he had already begun to suffer the partial paralysis of will which was to blight the later years of his career. He tells Michelangelo then (Milanesi, *Corr.*, p. 32) that Borgherini's *quadro* will be ready in two days, in this context: "a me mi par più faticha a far una mano over un semplice panuzzo ne la nostra arte che far tutte le scelle del mondo."

Despite the unconscionable delay, the picture had been substantially painted — as its style unequivocally indicates — probably in 1519. Typology and handling are virtually interchangeable with those in the *Lazarus*; only a somewhat drier and more chill, and thus more abstract-seeming, quality of surface indicates a possible slight distinction in the date. The composition of the *Holy Family*, for all its very different format and contents, is also related to that of the *Lazarus*: it equally contains a framework of intersecting diagonals, of uneven emphasis, which works spatially — though here in much limited degree — as well as on the surface. In the *Holy Family*, this framework has been synthesized with an including broad horizontal curve of the posture of the Madonna so that, unlike in the *Lazarus,* the temper of the design is not dominantly severe and slow, but swifter in its movement and more resilient: the Madonna is the nexus of expansive arching impulses that are opposite in direction but of finally compensating power, and of almost arbitrary rigor in their geometric pattern. The intensity of movement in design is precisely channelled and controlled, and its energies surcharge the monumental breadth of forms through which they pass, which equally counterweight and control them. The composition is a synthesis of energies and disciplines both stated at their maximum of power, in a structure of most strongly ideated order.

The design is an extraordinary invention for the subject matter, which in the Raphael school was generally differently taken, in a more intimate and conventional expressive vein, and with more lyric than dramatic intention in effects of form. The conception here is strong-willed and masculine as it is not in the late Raphael Madonnas, and grandly monumental; it wears the air, despite the presence of the private donor, of publicly impressive statement. It is touched, too, in the Virgin, with the nearest approach that is in Sebastiano to Michelangelo's heroic — or in this case Sibylline — conception of the scale and behavior of the human personality. We observed that there is no trace of Michelangelo's reply to Sebastiano's request for a cartoon for this picture, and its whole nature of design so much bespeaks what might be expected of Sebastiano's own character and powers in this moment that it is certain there was no such cartoon. The starting point of Sebastiano's personal process of invention still may have been, however, a note by Michelangelo for the posture of the Virgin. As in the case of the Viterbo *Pietà*, this image does not literally relate to any contemporary or previous work by Michelangelo, but suggests a later development by him of the thought he may have generated for this picture: the conception of the *Medici Madonna* may grow out of this idea for the *Madonna* of Pier Francesco Borgherini. But it is one of the indices of Sebastiano's responsibility for the whole design that altogether in contemporary Roman language as it is, it still refers to Venetian precedent of format and of motive for Madonna compositions with a donor.

The works of this brief moment, the *Lazarus* and the Borgherini *Holy Family*, are the climactic expression of Sebastiano's full development of artistic powers; and this climax is not the consequence just of a private fulfillment of personality, but of the coincidence with it of the climactic development in Sebastiano's Roman atmosphere — in Raphael, and in the example, present in Rome and communicated from Florence, of Michelangelo — of the possibilities of the classical style. When the moment of this coincidence dissolves, as it does shortly, the stature of Sebastiano's accomplishment grows less, as it had been before it.

The commission for the *Lazarus* had interrupted Sebastiano's work on a more involved project of religious decoration, which he undertook in late summer, 1516: the painting in S. Pietro in Montorio of a chapel [467-73] for the same Florentine patron for whom, later, he was — also as a result of Michelangelo's intercession — to paint the *Holy Family* in London. Our first notice of this decorative project is in Leonardo Sellaio's correspondence with Michelangelo, when on August 9, 1516 he recalls to Michelangelo that he is to send a drawing (which we are able to identify as the design for the *Flagellation*, the principal painting in the chapel); this was received on August 16 (Frey, *Br.* XXIII and XXV). A cartoon was begun by Sebastiano in late September, and a clay model prepared for the figure of the Christ in the *Flagellation* (Frey, *Br.* XXIX and XXXI). Sebastiano did not begin the actual painting with this scene, however, but with the frescoed figures of two Prophets on the outer arch-face of the chapel; these were done within November of this year (Frey, *Br.* XXXV and XLI). It was shortly after this that work was interrupted. Nothing came of the "grande animo" with which, as Sellaio reported on March 1, 1517 (Frey, *Br.* LV), Sebastiano intended to begin work in the chapel on the morrow (presumably within the chapel, as distinguished from the outer faces). His attention was taken up altogether with the *Lazarus*, and it was only after that picture had been done that, on May 1, 1519 (Frey, *Br.* CXXX), he indicated his intention of returning to work in S. Pietro in Montorio.

However, there were further interruptions. A letter of September 6, 1521, from Sebastiano to Michelangelo (Milanesi, *Corr.*, pp. 30, 32), implies that he had already painted the upper portion of the chapel (that part which, in the semidome, contains Sebastiano's fresco version of the *Transfiguration*); the letter further indicates that he was working in oil on the lower wall, on what is in effect the chapel's mural altarpiece, the *Flagellation*, and hoped soon to have the whole project finished. It was nevertheless not until March 24, 1524 (Frey, *Br.* CCIX) that the chapel could be opened, though it contains, beyond what has been mentioned so far, only two frescoed figures on the side walls of the patron's name saints.

Sebastiano's first effort in S. Pietro, the Prophets on the outer spandrels of the chapel,[468] are very closely related to the *Pietà* of Leiningrad, dated in the same year. Types and bodily proportions are virtually interchangeable between the two works; these figures have not yet acquired the saving touch of attenuation that, in the *Lazarus*, relieves the squaring of proportions. Drapery style in the Prophets is also much like that of the *Pietà*; but it already indicates the tendency toward more complex notation of abstracting shapes, which becomes more explicit in the *Lazarus*. The supposition, implied by their known date, that the Prophets succeed the Leningrad *Pietà* in time, is supported by this slight shift in character of style.

Given the nature of the problem, it was almost inescapable that Sebastiano's Prophets should recall the recent example of Raphael's Sibyls for S. M. della Pace.[232] The dependence of Sebastiano on Raphael is obvious, yet he would not necessarily himself have regarded this as conceding much to Raphael's authority. What Sebastiano may have seen in the Pace Sibyls was, rather than Raphael himself, Raphael's own reference to the precedent of Michelangelo. More than Sebastiano looks here to Raphael, he looks through Raphael, to a mutual model in the Prophets of the Sistine. Sebastiano's Prophets try to recreate a sense like that in the Sistine Seers of overpowering scale and shape, and of great — at least physical — vitality. But in this first reuse in three years of a fresco medium — with which he never wholly felt at ease — the effects of draughtsmanship are fussy and the color wan, and what was intended to be grand monumentality in the two forms, over life-size, of the Prophets, becomes instead pretentious, but unimpressive bulk.

Though the *Flagellation*[469] had to wait for its execution until 1521 and later, and its technique — in oil on the wall, more sympathetic to Sebastiano than fresco — reflects a later moment in the evolution of his painting style, its cartoon was prepared by Sebastiano (as is indicated almost certainly in the correspondence; Frey, *Br.* XXXI) at the same time as that for the Prophets, late in 1516. The situation of the *Flagellation* between Sebastiano and Michelangelo is like that of the Viterbo *Pietà*: an aesthetic compound in suspension between the two personalities. It is now clear (Popham) that, contrary to the general contention in the recent literature, Michelangelo did supply an *ad hoc* drawing for the composition of the *Flagellation*. The drawing mentioned in the correspondence, which Vasari cites (V, 569) as Michelangelo's "piccolo disegno," is preserved, not in the original but in a well authenticated copy (Windsor 451).[471] As *invenzione* and as design it was literally followed in the figures of Sebastiano's painting. It was from this *modello* of Michelangelo's that Sebastiano made the "fighurina di tera per Christo" to which Sellaio refers in his letter of October 11, 1516 (Frey, *Br.* XXXI) and elaborated the large study of the figure of the Christ alone (British Museum 1895–9–15–813)[470] that is one of Sebastiano's most admirable drawings. His intention to reproduce Michelangelo's model literally was uncertain at one moment only, when he experimented in a drawing (British Museum 1895–9–15–500)[472] with another posture for the Christ, and made variations in the attendant figures, but most of all attempted — as he had done for the Viterbo *Pietà* — to give the figure group a larger ambience of his own conceiving. This more individual solution might, at least in supposition, have been the better one.

What Sebastiano, after five years' delay, began to paint upon the wall — at a moment past that of his own highest inspiration, and in a labored and unsuitable technique — was an essentially faithful but also a vitiated transcription of Michelangelo's conceit. The painting gives evidence for Sebastiano's manner, but of his manner after 1520; but in style it represents more of Michelangelo than of Sebastiano. As has been correctly observed (though with an incorrect deduction; Tolnay), Michelangelo's invention is related to his ideas for the Julius Tomb of 1513. The *modello* for the *Flagellation* is, however, not a cast-off from among these thoughts but a separately intended further outgrowth of the same set of creative processes. In relation to the Michelangelesque idea, even as it is perceived in the Windsor copy, Sebastiano's realization stands — almost — as Penni's realization does to an idea of Raphael's. The energies of Michelangelo's *modello*, and their charged differentiation, have been much diminished in Sebastiano's version. The forms have decreased in content as they are enlarged in scale: what is most apparent in them is not their inventor's monumental power, but their executant's effect of artifice. The grandeur of the *Flagellation* is a little hollow; Sebastiano here has academicized Michelangelo's originally inspired classical conception.

In a very different frame of mind, not submissive but aggressively competitive, Sebastiano painted, late in 1520 or early in 1521, his fresco *Transfiguration* [473] in the semidome of the Borgherini Chapel (in the space above that where, at that time, the painting of the *Flagellation* was still to be begun). Sebastiano's *Transfiguration* was his rebuttal to the Raphael, and his critique of it; it rounded out the argument of the recent competition. Later, in 1523, the comparison of Sebastiano's fresco and Raphael's altarpiece could be immediately made, when the Raphael was placed on the high altar of the same church.

Almost literal as a critique, Sebastiano's painting begins with the very data supplied by Raphael: the posture of the Christ, the attitudes of the Prophets and Apostles, and even something of the composition are based on, and intendedly bettered from, the rival master's work. In the leftmost figure of his scene Sebastiano paraphrases further, from the Andrew in the lower episode of Raphael's *Transfiguration*. Almost immediately Sebastiano scores one strong point: his execution, unlike that in the earlier Prophets, and still more unlike the later, gelatinous, *Flagellation*, is dry and brilliant, far surpassing the pupils' dominating share in Raphael's *Transfiguration* — which, for the unsympathetic observer, suffices to belittle the extraordinary concept. Sebastiano replaces Penni's actors in the upper portion of the Raphael, too polished and precious to support their burden of intended meaning, with a very differently virile cast. These types are more suggestive of a Michelangelesque canon, and of Michelangelesque amplitude and powers, than the figures of the *Lazarus*, yet are so without any literal dependence on Michelangelo's example.

These powerfully movemented shapes, relieved against a sky radiant with *changeant* hues, converge dramatically upon the hieratic figure of the Christ, who is fixed, unlike Raphael's Christ, upon the earth, but spiritually transfixed. Exploiting the perspective situation of the half-dome, Sebastiano has made three appropriate gradations of physical and spiritual presence in this scene's painted space: the darkest and illusionistically foremost in the three Apostles, the lighter and farther in the Prophets, and the most removed in Christ, suffused in supernatural brightness lighter than the tone of sky. Seen in a perspective which suggests that the miracle occurs in the spectator's presence, Christ's figure seems to rise upward and away from us, His majesty of presence spiritualized and made imponderable by His Transfiguration. The concept is no less intellectually remarkable than Raphael's, and its urgency and effectiveness of dramatic articulation are not less compelling; furthermore, in this case the visual language of the execution coincides with its author's — and executant's — precise meaning.

This is an effective critique of Raphael's *Transfiguration*, yet does not surpass it despite the faults — or what Sebastiano felt were such — that it corrects. In more limited compass than the *Lazarus*, this is on the highest plane of classical ideality accessible to Sebastiano's thought. It is exactly in the differently exalted level of ideality that Raphael attains that his *Transfiguration*, despite its shortcomings in particular, is finally impervious to criticism. Sebastiano has given a more cogent actuality than Raphael to his handling of this theme; his conception of its content and his devices of form may even make his version the more powerful communication of its human and dramatic meaning. But what Raphael has found is a form of intransigent purity, inhabited by irresistible yet exactly ordered powers; and this Idea of form — for it deserves the capitalization — is one with the supreme conception of the event, more divine than human, that it describes. It is this reach of the mind and spirit that is closed to Sebastiano.

Sebastiano's *Visitation* (Paris, Louvre),[474] painted for the Queen of France, was signed and dated by him in 1521 but it had already been exhibited, and had received the kind of comment usually given only to a finished picture, in July 1519. The actual year of its painting coincided, therefore, with that of Raphael's *Visitation*, and there is no way of determining which work had precedence. Unlike the case of the two *Transfigurations*, a comparison may never have been consciously intended between the *Visitations*, but in the presence of the similar accomplished facts it now is unavoidable. The comparison is once more between a Raphaelesque compound and a work of entirely consistent texture by Sebastiano, and in this respect the result cannot be in Raphael's — or Penni's — favor. However, beneath Penni's academicizing epidermis there is a basic likeness in Raphael's mode of thinking in design of the theme and that of Sebastiano. For both, the central matter of the picture is the effect of monumental dignity, almost stilled and gravely simple, that is in the principal confronted forms. In the Raphael this effect is more intellectually clear — as Penni has transcribed the idea for us, almost stark. The sense of largeness and of dignity is as much in Sebastiano's picture as in Raphael's, but it is less exclusively architectonic in its means. Raphael's figures are an intellectually removed structure of stringently ideal form; Sebastiano, applying to the religious image a format previously used only in portraiture (and eventually Venetian in invention) confronts us more closely with the persons of his image, projecting his structure as if toward us by the effect of the three-quarter length, making its power of shape and of imposing scale more immediate. There is a nearer presence in Sebastiano's actors and a closer impress on us of their meanings and emotions. These are different from the conventional physiognomy and gestures that Penni, in the place of Raphael, has given us. Sebastiano's actors are not inflexible in their decorum: their slow gestures hold a powerful constrained eloquence, and in their faces a warmth of emotion infuses the overcast upon them, still evident, of the Giorgionesque dream.

More perceptibly even than in the preceding *Lazarus*, in his *Visitation* Sebastiano thinks in terms of what we called, in the Tapestries of Raphael, a "humanistic" style — one in which the figures absolutely dominate the image. Yet, what remains of setting in Sebastiano's picture is not, as in Penni's development of Raphael's *Visitation*, merely appended to the figure composition. The mood and lighting of the setting actively support the figures, and give their depth of mood a greater resonance. The sense of the setting is integrated not only with the form, but equally with the narrative, of the figure composition: the background gives the sequence of what has preceded and what is to follow on this only momentary arrest of the chief actors. The curve of the country road, along which the Virgin and her handmaids have just come, projects its slow turning impulse into the movement of the

Virgin; the same slow pressure of rotation passes from her to the Elizabeth. This curve then moves, more abruptly, into the commotion of welcoming figures — strongly Michelangelesque — on the staircase at the right toward which, the climactic moment of their greeting over, Elizabeth will turn to lead her guest.

As we have already seen, in anticipation, in Sebastiano's version of the *Transfiguration*, his intellectual deliberation of the relation between form and content is not the same in nature or in ultimate purpose as Raphael's exercise of intellect; it does not subject either form or content to so pure and powerful a force of idealization. But there does appear, in Sebastiano's *Visitation*, further evidence of the growth in him of his particular tendency, manifest since the Leningrad *Pietà*, toward abstraction: not so much of the whole formal order of the picture — though that tendency, too, is more sensible here than earlier — but of its parts of form. In the *Visitation* the geometrically analyzed elements of shape are not more arbitrarily defined than in the *Lazarus*, but their content of texture and color is now rather different. The muted warmth that is still present in the handling of light seems, less than in the *Lazarus*, to suggest, even by indirection, the sensation of depths of color or of textures. The surfaces of the *Visitation* are powdery-dry, matt and virtually opaque. The color on them is applied, much more evidently than in the *Lazarus*, by aesthetically arbitrary decision: bright-hued and flat, and bleaching broadly in the lights, the mode of color seems no longer to equivocate between Central Italian and Venetian tradition. For the first time in Sebastiano, color seems dominantly to be arbitrary local tone, with only the barest persistence in it of Venetian optical experience. This abstractness in the look of surfaces and color coincides now with the arbitrary shapes of parts of form; one adds its character of statement to the other. Much of the whole surface of the picture thus assumes, more evidently than before, abstracting character, and we see the monumental logic of the larger form, almost ponderously classical, through a stronger overcast upon it of abstraction.

In this approach to a nearer conformity between abstracting effects of surface and of underlying form there is a danger to the classicism of Sebastiano's style. Without the force of statement that is in either Raphael's or Michelangelo's higher ideality of form, Sebastiano's abstracter forms depend for their vitality on their cast of surface — on the effects, however transmuted, that result from Sebastiano's responsiveness of eye and hand to actuality. A coincidence between surfaces that are abstracting and forms that work, not only toward abstraction but — as Sebastiano's tendency has seemed to be — a perceptible bit toward vacancy, would denature classicism. This coincidence eventually in fact occurs in Sebastiano's art, and his style then becomes no longer classical but classicistic only. The *Visitation* is the critical document of the beginning of such a process of evolution into classicistic style — a style, however, which as Sebastiano practices it often achieves effects of art not less impressive than those of his authentic classicism. But this process is not quickly accomplished, nor is it rectilinear in its progress.

One of the delaying factors in it is the persistence in Sebastiano of his particular classical temper of response to human content — of his profoundly felt and grand pathetic eloquence. It is nowhere more evident than in his *Martyrdom of St. Agatha* (Florence, Pitti; signed and dated 1520),[475] where, stimulated by the dramatic poignance of the subject, he has given an interpretation of it that is profoundly moving, and utterly authentic in this context that carries so great an expressive risk. In a format once more reminiscent of Venetian tradition Sebastiano has projected figures which, as in the *Visitation*, are of three-quarter length; they give, as there, the sense of looming closeness to us of the scene. The cutting-off of figures by the frame promotes the sense of nearness: the effect of isolable entity of more normal classical format is decreased, and we see this event, both physically and psychologically, as if in an extension of our space. Such an intention is precisely emphasized by Sebastiano in the *Martyrdom*. To the right and left of the composition he introduces elements which, more frankly than in any recent work of Raphael's, or his own, indicate illusionistic projection toward and continuity with our space. Immediately, however, these devices lead to a structure, dominantly planar, of artificially arranged forms: illusion serves only to intensify a monumental, deliberately ordered, classical compositional presence.

The composition reflects — as in the nature of the subject would be natural — Sebastiano's preoccupation with Michelangelo's scheme for the *Flagellation;* but there is a different, more felt energy in this design, where Sebastiano is not transcribing, but inventing. In the frequent usage of this time, crossed diagonals form a partial energizing framework of the composition; these are more than before deeply flattened in projection into the space so that they tell almost more as an effect of ground plan rather than of design on the surface. As in the *Holy Family* for Borgherini, the diagonal impulses are fused into an arching horizontal curve, which includes the foremost figures of the picture in a compact unity. The temper of movement with which Sebastiano articulates this armature of composition is different from any previous use by him of like structural means. The movement is tensely charged but slow; it warps toward and closes on the Agatha inevitably but as if reluctantly.

The figure of the Agatha, ponderously beautiful, is an index of how wholly personally Sebastiano could remake a motive given him initially from Michelangelo. For her figure Sebastiano uses, in reverse, the pose of the Christ in Michelangelo's *modello* for the *Flagellation*, but nothing survives of Michelangelo in the identity that Sebastiano has remade for Agatha. Her slow, yearning pathos is only in Sebastiano's vocabulary of emotion; and there is the memory of Venice, still, in the idea — now transmuted altogether into idea, and without sensuous devices or effects — of sensuality that her almost statuary handsomeness contains. A superb drawing in the Louvre for the Agatha (10816; Pouncey),[476] full-length, shows the more impassioned, but also lyric, nature of Sebastiano's thought about her before the distillation in the painting took place.

In the Agatha, but also in all the other figures in the picture, there is a charged specificity of emotion — implicit also in the specificity of the moment of narration in itself — which is somewhat different in its accent from the more diffuse character of feeling that prevails, in general, in Sebastiano's preceding pictures. Feeling here is more sharply differentiated, and more immediately compelling in its effects upon the spectator; like the element of illusion that is in the form, this quality in narration and emotion brings the image nearer. This is the climax of a tendency that had been evident in Sebastiano in proportion as he had assimilated the principles of Roman style; but the degree of specificity of feeling here is less likely an internally motivated development than externally inspired. The exemplar is probably in Raphael, and the source of Sebastiano's lesson may well have been in the former's *Transfiguration.*

That the influence of Raphael, as the ultimate representative of current Romanism, is in the *Martyrdom of Agatha* is evident in Sebastiano's abandoning in it, finally, almost every reminiscence of Venetian handling: the surfaces of this picture are as much smoothed and polished as in any painting of unadulterated Roman descent. Color is still arbitrary, and its hues are the familiar ones on Sebastiano's palette; however, as it did not even in the *Visitation,* color now adheres with entire fidelity to its plastic form. But, in Sebastiano's abstracting tendency, this same plastic form is denied authentic sense of substance by a handling so smoothed as it is here. The amplitude of figures no longer reads as plausible monumental existence, but as hollow grandeur. In this formal sense, and in the contentual affect of this happening in form, Sebastiano has proceeded another step in the evolution that will carry him beyond the bounds of classicism.

Sebastiano's process of evolution beyond a recognizable classical style was relatively slow. Later than Raphael to achieve this style wholly, he was the last painter of the Roman school to abandon it. In generation — in the time of formation of his personality in Venice, and in his maturity in Rome — Sebastiano belonged with Raphael, not with the younger radicals. Something of the form and content of the classical style remained in Sebastiano's art longer than in any other painter of the Roman school; and even after that, the formulae, and the outward resemblance to the temper, of a classicism persisted in him. There were, as we have observed, tendencies personal to Sebastiano which, allowed positive development, would of themselves have dissolved the substance of classicism in his style. In the context of art in which he lived after the death of Raphael it was inevitable that this development should occur; as great an artist as he was, Sebastiano had never in his career decreed the artistic shape of his environment. Slowly, in the course of the 1520's, his art experienced the transformation, less of semblance than of essence, that would make it Mannerism.

PERUZZI

Baldassare Peruzzi's role within the development of classical painting style in Rome had long since been defined as assimilative rather than inventive. He had absorbed much of the look and a great deal of the meaning of the style of Raphael, and to a less degree of that of Michelangelo and Sebastiano, but he had not penetrated its deeper working principles. The inaccessibility to Peruzzi of an entire and pervasive classicism could not have been from a lack in him of the power to comprehend it; there are few artistic intelligences in this time that are comparable to his. It was rather that he was enough differently temperamentally disposed to make his entire subjection to a classical idiom unwilling, and finally impossible. There was a level in Peruzzi's personality that was ultimately impervious to the contemporary conception of classicism. In his native reaction to the content of human experience, and to the visual experience, that first make the material of the painter there was too much wit, too febrile a sensibility and too strong an impulse to poetic fantasy to be contained within the disciplines of classicism. Least of all could these qualities find place in the machinery, so often ponderous, of the high classicism to which, in these years, the reigning style had grown. Of the three great masters of the Raphael generation, Peruzzi was the least suited temperamentally to the tone of Roman classical style in its last phase.

Nevertheless this tonality of current style was not altogether escapable, even by Peruzzi; his response to it, however, remained more superficial than essential. Peruzzi's personal classicism had been marked since the beginning by a more explicit cast of archaeological reminiscence than in his chief contemporaries. His reaction to the example of a higher classicism was less in his apparatus of formal structure or in character of content than in a still stronger accent in his style of archaeology: his former tendency was confirmed and encouraged by the emergence, in this phase of classical development, of an interest which, in this respect, was like his own. He responded more evidently, too, to the current canon of proportion in high classical example. His figures had already lost, before 1515, the archaizing quattrocentesque elegance that earlier distinguished them; they now became, in general, blunter and more broad, according to the latest Roman mode. But even in these reactions —

to matters of mode rather than of style — there is no necessary consistency in Peruzzi's pictures of this phase. Because he was not involved with classicism by aesthetic conviction and spiritual compulsion, as his great contemporaries were, he was, relatively speaking, a freer agent: he might use the data of classicism, or not, as they suited his particular and momentary purpose. His practice and his development were more flexible than those of his contemporaries, and his works need not show that consistency in its successive events that is in Raphael or even in Sebastiano. Also, in those respects precisely in which Peruzzi chose not to function classically, he conformed to what might be called the obverse of the picture of classical development in this phase, to the aspect of dissolution that now incipiently appeared within it. Some of the facets of Peruzzi's style that a short while before had seemed only *retardataire* now assumed, in this new context, the look as if of progressive innovation, and some of these innovations may have had exemplary effect.

It is difficult for us to remember, in the state of survival of Peruzzi's *oeuvre*, to what extent his influence and reputation in contemporary Rome depended on his activity as a decorator. Part of what he did in this field, where he was Raphael's only worthwhile competitor, was ephemeral, consisting — as did virtually the whole major effort of the younger Polidoro later — of painted façades and of scene designs that have disappeared with time. Only scant reflection still exists of Peruzzi's mature activity in this field. There is one extant façade by a pupil, Virgilio Romano (Vasari IV, 607): a faded *sgraffito* decoration on the Vicolo del Campanile in the Borgo.[477] It uses, fairly literally, figure motives and compositions of Peruzzi's original invention (identifiable in the Siena sketchbook), but there is no indication that its whole design stems from him. What Vasari ascribes precisely to Peruzzi of this kind had, from the descriptions, a very differently ambitious character. In a sequence in Vasari's narration that suggests a date toward 1515 he speaks of a house façade (on the present Via Giubbonari), which in his time belonged to Jacopo Strozzi "passato Campo di Fiore per andare a Piazza Giudea, una facciata bellissima con prospettive mirabili" (IV, 594); shortly later in Vasari's sequence (IV, 596) there is a more detailed description of a façade, apparently yet more elaborate, for Messer Francesco Buzio near the Piazza degli Altieri: this included at its topmost level figures of the Twelve Emperors ". . . i quali posano sopra certe mensole e scortano le vedute al di sotto in su." In 1515 there had been another major decoration — condemned from the beginning to be ephemeral — a scene design for a performance to accompany the ceremonies of election of Giuliano de' Medici to Captain-Generalship of the Roman Church: in this ". . . fece stupire ognuno . . . la prospettiva o vero scena d'una commedia . . . perciò che la varietà e bella maniera di casamenti, le diverse loggie, le bizzarrie delle porte e finestre, e l'altre cose che vi si videro d'architettura, furono tanto bene intese e di cosi straordinaria invenzione, che non si può dirne la millesima parte" (Vasari V, 595–96). In another context, describing Peruzzi's stage sets for Bibbiena's comedy *Calandra* (first performed in 1513) Vasari credits him with the invention of the entire genre: his designs ". . . apersero la via a coloro che ne hanno poi fatto a' tempi nostri" (IV, 600). A reflection of this kind of work by Peruzzi is in the drawing for a comic stageset in the Uffizi, almost certainly correctly attributed to him. Such a catalogue of major, but vanished, accomplishments by Peruzzi as a decorator could be extended farther still.

In this field, quite like Raphael in these same years, Peruzzi was working much in a realm intermediate between that of architect and painter; and even more than Raphael Peruzzi painted far more architecture than he built. From what remains of Peruzzi's decorative works within this phase, and from the literary evidence about them, it would seem that there was no substantial distinction in the temper with which Peruzzi painted architecture from that with which he painted persons. The same cast of mind that disposed him to a less than classical relation to reality disposed him to delight in manipulation of architecture's abstract forms — particularly when they did not require to be built — and to the attendant games of mathematical perspective. The wit and inventive liberty with which he could project a painted architecture was like that with which he could make figure compositions; both could be chiefly exercises of his power of creative fantasy. Also, both painted architecture and figure compositions could invite the demonstration of his interest in archaeology. However, just as he was able to achieve a more substantial classical intention in his figure paintings when he wished, so also, when occasion or his own will directed it, could he make manifest — much more explicitly than in his figure compositions — the classicizing consequence of a logic of mathematical thinking in his painted architecture.

There could hardly have been a more important one among Peruzzi's lost decorative projects of this time than that single one which still survives, the *Sala delle Prospettive* (or *delle Colonne*) on the *piano nobile* of the Farnesina, in the building of which he had been the actual architect and, circa 1510–1511, the first decorator.[478-85] There is no external evidence from which we can assign a precise date to this newer decoration. From the difference in style between the figures painted in the frieze and on parts of the wall below it, but more from the absence of logically planned connection between the sections of this frieze and the articulation of the painted architecture, it would seem that these two parts of the decoration were not necessarily conceived together. The figured frieze, which runs around the whole upper portion of the room, may have been painted before the idea was evolved for an illusionistic architecture to decorate the walls (Carroll). Both parts of the decoration are, however, from, or in the closest vicinity of, 1515. The frieze may have been begun the year before (a quotation in it from Raphael's *Galatea* makes any earlier date, on external grounds, unlikely), and it is possible that the painting of the architecture may have run on into 1516. Here, as he must also have done elsewhere in others of his lost large-scale projects, Peruzzi employed assistants, though not so extensively in the figure compositions as the scale of the work would lead one to expect. Unlike the members of the Raphael shop, none of these assistants is identifiable.

Fifteen scenes freely illustrated from the Ovidian *Metamorphoses* form the subject matter of the *Sala Prospettive* frieze,[481-3] making the richest repertory of Antique literary illustration that survives to us from the High Renaissance; we can compare to it only Peruzzi's own earlier virtual mythological dictionary in the frieze of the smaller salon on the ground floor of this same building. Not only the fullness of literary reference of that earlier frieze but its wealth of archaeological citation is at least equalled here, and with the same entire absence of any character of pedantry. The poetic authenticity of this frieze comes in the first place, as it had also in the earlier one, from the sense of actuality with which Peruzzi feels the subject matter. There is a difference in degree from the earlier frieze, however, in precisely this respect. In the first frieze the immediacy of feeling and action in the figures was touched with a qualifying Raphaelesque ideality: their forms and their patterned rhythms of behavior recalled a classical perfection. What was spontaneous and naïve in feeling in them seemed, in this context, like a removed, more than ordinary, purity of spirit. In the second frieze feeling is much more sharp and differentiated, and less remotely pure, and the ideality of form is less; despite their continuing stressed classicizing guise the persons and events of the Ovidian text exist for Peruzzi here as if without the aura and reserve of classical distance. Little convention, and no rhetoric at all intervene between the artist and his sense for the aliveness of his subject matter. Psychological characterization is brilliantly various, in some places filled with humor and in other places verging on the bizarre; and in the description of physiognomy there is a frequent element of caricature. In the personality with which these actors have been endowed there is a kinship with the mentality of a grotesque style, in state of mind, though not in particular vocabulary, like that which Raphael only shortly after would evolve.

The canon of anatomy is also much more flexible: there is no such concern as in the first frieze for gracile harmonies. A less deliberated energy defines the contour and modelling of these forms, and these do not, except in incidents, seek a recognizable classical proportion. The shapes of body and of drapery are set down with a more impatient hand, which accentuates, beyond classical correctness, movemented irregularities of pattern and of structure. With a bolder range of rhythmical vocabulary, now almost blunt, now propulsively curvilinear, Peruzzi evokes a wonderfully active, and in places eccentric, patterning of varied human forms. The temper of this pattern is yet further accented by the handling of light, which — unlike the fine descriptive differentiation in the first frieze — here is also sharper and more elliptical, almost faceting the surfaces of form.

The whole absence of rhetoric in these paintings extends to their designs. There is almost no recognizable convention in their compositions; within each episode the design seems informal almost to the point of casualness. The contents of each scene are in fact disposed so as to make an adequate pictorial balance, but this is an altogether secondary matter. Much more consciously and explicitly than in the earlier mythology, design is primarily determined by the shape and, still more, by the purpose of successive narrative that is in the frieze. Within each episode the forms are strung upon a cursive armature that literally unwinds the narrative from left to right. The temper and complexity of this armature are differentiated in each scene; and it suggests but does not actually make a rhythmical continuity between one scene and the next. Between the scenes, caryatid herms mark off these different shapes and tempers of curving impulse, but do not interrupt the undulating progress around the whole extent of the room. It is again in the nature of a frieze that this long arabesque, as it unfolds, and the figures that give it narrative and formal substance, should adhere mainly to the plane of the wall. Yet it also makes some diverting excursions into space, and more than in the earlier frieze the design of figures partly inhabits, and partly is projected against, a landscape. The landscape, again night-lit, is as informally described — as ungeometrically projected — as the figures are upon the surface. Neither space nor figure composition has the classical value in these scenes of ordered substance; what mainly defines existence and specifies its meaning are the intangible aesthetic agencies of line and light.

This frieze is almost the antithesis — and by some might be regarded as the antidote — of the exactly contemporary tendency of classical style among the Roman masters. What is asserted in it is not a protest against the elevation of art into the Grand Manner, but only the liberty of the artist to think and paint otherwise: to make personal and informal poetic communion with the Ancients, rather than public Ciceronian rhetoric. The need was felt as much by Raphael and by Raphael's most literate patrons — among whom was Chigi, patron of this frieze — as by Peruzzi; Raphael's invention of the grotesque mode was his compensation for the mental and spiritual exertions required by the highest reaches of the current Roman classicism. It was easier for Peruzzi than for Raphael to make fantastic *poesie*; he had never wholly ceased to do so. In this given subject matter and particular architectural space Peruzzi's idiosyncracies, still persistent in part from his pre-Roman and preclassical inheritance, emerge more strongly than they had since Raphael had intervened between him and his origins.

It is not unreasonable (though an incorrect conclusion has been drawn; Brizio) to see in these frescoes some analogue with the art, barely classically contaminated by his brief, earlier, experience in Rome, of Peruzzi's compatriot, Beccafumi. The strain in Peruzzi of preclassical disposition facilitates the dissolution of the classicism that he had acquired, and this process is accelerated in him as the Roman classical style in general came to be compromised in its authority. Peruzzi's eventual Mannerism is not so much a conversion as a substantial shift of emphasis among the classical and unclassical components already coexisting in his art. However, that shift has not yet occurred within the frieze of the *Sala Prospettive*. The relation to Beccafumi is, at this point, stronger in its meaning of contrasts than of comparison.

It is more immediately historically relevant that the informal mode of composition and the figure style of this frieze resemble somewhat, and anticipate, what happens in the fresco style of Raphael's assistants in the small narrative scenes of the Logge of 1518–1519; it is not impossible that this small-scale fresco manner of the younger men owes something to Peruzzi's precedent in the *Sala Prospettive*. One idea, of motive rather than of style, still later found particular favor with the decorators of the younger generation: the use of herms as scene-dividers (not as caryatids only, as they had been used by Raphael and Giulio in the basamenti of the Stanza d'Eliodoro). Peruzzi's notion soon became so widely spread that his invention of it — itself an elaboration of an isolated thought in the frieze of 1511 — has become obscured.

The completed decoration of the *Sala delle Prospettive*,[478-9] with its painted architecture on the walls (though, as we observed, the unity may not have been initially so conceived), makes a still more important historical anticipation, perhaps specifically influential but, more likely, significant only for its presentation in general of an idea. The conception of a monumental painted architecture, inhabited partly by painted figures, which makes an illusionistic entity of perspective structure in one room, is a reevocation by Peruzzi of a quattrocentesque theme rather than an innovation of his; we have seen how it anticipates, and in part may have inspired, the generation of Raphael's idea for his *Sala dei Palafrenieri*. Peruzzi is the first in Rome within this century to recreate this genre of architectural decorative style and, equally important, rework it in the contemporary classical vocabulary. The genuinely innovative character in the decoration of the *Sala Prospettive* is more oblique in possible influence and in the nature of relation that exists between it and the art of Raphael: this is the first association in a single decorative space between a monumental classical style of painted architecture, imposing in form and inflexible in logic, with a figure decoration of contrasting fantasy — akin in variety of form and quality of content, as we have remarked, to the grotesquerie. This association in the *Sala delle Prospettive* anticipates the conception Raphael only began to investigate in the first grotesque decoration of 1516.

As an architecture, the painted structure of the *Sala Prospettive* is more austerely classicizing in vocabulary and more monumental in effect of scale than any realized building up to this time in High Renaissance Rome; as with Michelangelo's painted sculpture, Peruzzi's painted architecture had the advantage of possible quick succession of idea and execution. Its design shows the most precisely calculated balance of effects between fictive mass and equally fictitious opening, and between severities of larger shape and the animating smaller system of articulation. Within this order's perfectly apparent rationale there is, in the handling of proportions — as expecially of the shapes of columns and the spaces of intercolumniation — a touch of lightness and of elegance, the symptom of the same fine, sometimes pointed sensibility which appears in Peruzzi's figure style. The effect is one of opulence as well; Peruzzi counterfeits with paint the richness and variety of color of a purplish marble. The structure is imposing, of a handsome *Romanità* a little flavored with a Tuscan salt; but it is also, in a way different from any quattrocento antecedent, a conceit and a witticism.

As in Peruzzi's own earlier conception for the *Sala Galatea* (for the whole of which, as a conception, he must have been initially responsible, given its unity of iconographic program), and as in the conceit of the *Sala di Psiche,* in which Raphael followed Peruzzi later, the object of illusion in this room is to penetrate the wall into the outer space. These conceptions in general, and in particular that in the *Sala delle Prospettive,* derive in part from the role as villa of this house. Its decoration is devised so that the presence of an outer air, or of a landscape, shall be pervasive in it, but in almost excessively civilized fashion: not with the ordinary character of reality but as a world contrived to order. In the *Sala Prospettive* the view through the windows into the actual world is ancillary to the fictitious world that is projected through the walls; the windows serve primarily to light the artifice, and we take our stand back to them on the principal station point to grasp the fiction's machinery of perspective.

It is made to appear that we are in an isolated hall, something like the interior of a temple on a lofty hill. The wall is opened largely to the right and left, but also on the other longer sides, by apertures framed by piers and articulated in perspective depth by further piers or columns; through these lucidly divided spaces we look out and down, across a balustraded porch, upon a seeming surrounding landscape. Inverting the reality, what is left of the appearance of solid wall consists of the closed doors, which in actuality give egress from this room. The painted landscapes are full of the luminosity and variety of a real nature: on the side wall, which in fact looks in the direction of the countryside, we see a rustic landscape; and on the other that looks toward Rome, as it then was, is an urban landscape.[480] Motives appear that exist in actuality — some of them adequately identifiable in the city 'scape — but this painted environment is not meant to reconstruct the view the real walls interrupt; it is a projection, suggestively tangential to reality, of the artist's fantasy. Even now, in much repaired condition, it is a remarkably vivid evocation of the look and quality of seen places, but no reproduction of them. The freshness and visual sensibility of the landscape painting is the obverse of the intellectuality and discipline with which Peruzzi has conceived its architectural frame.

The painted walls have an illusionistic figured population of their own, aside from that of the frieze which surmounts them. In the one visible embrasure of each apparent side porch of this structure, there is the convincing perspective simulacrum, in grisaille, of an Ancient statue in a niche, recalling somewhat the motives in the architecture of the *School of Athens*. On the wall plane of the painted architecture, in the "solid" spaces that, pier-like, include the doors, there are life-size figures,[484-5] in color, that are meant to give the illusion of living presences, inhabiting the architecture and communicating — though with some classicizing reserve — with the spectator. On the plinths painted on to the entablatures of the doors stand paired *amorini*, who bear garlands that enframe an actual small niche; these *amorini* are supporters of a horizontal rectangular space, excavated by perspective in the wall, in each of which sits or reclines a figure of the classic pantheon, with less offense to probability than might be imagined. Only two of these figures, and their attendant putti, are of Peruzzi's own execution; these are the *Venus* and *Apollo* on the side wall opposite the main entrance to the room. The others are by assistants or, as it seems from their present condition of surface, even of later invention (as, almost certainly, is the decoration with the *Forge of Vulcan* on the *camino*). On the wall that is actually by Peruzzi, his figures do convey a keen sense of their existence. Their mode of painting is a development on that used earlier in the ceiling of the *Sala di Galatea*, but even more than there these figures are described in high-keyed light, which searches out and reflects back from a sharp-etched, polished surface, to make an effect in them like that of brilliantly illumined statuary. But they are not psychologically characterized as statuary; their attitudes are reserved, but not the sharp vivacity of glance that Venus and Apollo fix on the spectator.

Unlike the small-scale figures in the frieze above, these large forms evidently seek much more of an accustomed classical appearance and proportion. This "building," which in its form suggests a pagan temple, is meant to be inhabited by classical divinities who suggest, at once, the character of statuary and of living beings; and the frieze above them is a classical equivalent for what, in a Christian altar, would be their narrative predella.

Within this single scheme there is the evidence of very varying degrees of fidelity to current classical conventions. The walls, and what is in them of a figured population, are much more conformist than the style of the frieze. Especially when he was moved by archaeological impulse Peruzzi could impose, on the only adequately classical substructure of his style, the most distinct look in contemporary Rome of a reminiscent classicism. Such is the case in two designs of this moment, which survive as prints. The attribution of one of them is not certain, but Peruzzi is the best candidate for the design of Marcantonio's *Quos Ego* (B. 352) of 1515,[486] the most archaeologically ambitious, as well as archaeologically literal, print published in Rome up to this date, and certainly strongly influential afterwards in promoting the increasing taste for Antique imitation. The chiaroscuro print by Ugo da Carpi, *Hercules Expelling Envy from the Temple of the Muses* (B. 12),[487] is after Peruzzi's design, in date from 1516 or shortly after (the *terminus post* suggested by a possible quotation from the Raphael Cartoons); its matter, as the title might suggest, is also an archaeological compendium, of carefully worked correctness in each imitative classicizing form. One small painting is an index of Peruzzi's temper when he functions in this vein, the *Apollo and the Muses* (Florence, Pitti; c. 1516; the correct attribution due to Pouncey).[488] Precisely antiquarian in costume and appearance — and labelled, furthermore, in Greek — the Muses dance, supposedly, a round, but in a pattern so much flattened as to make what is in fact a frieze. This frieze is disposed across a wholly neutral background, in this case of gold, but imitative nonetheless of those backgrounds in Antique painting that cancel all environmental space and setting. The figures are precisely in the current mode of interpretation, broader and more squared than earlier, of the classical figure canon. Even the handling in this panel has an imitative air: the rough, small-faceted stroking looks like that of an Ancient painterly technique. The kind and the degree of archaeological reminiscence is almost that which appears in the near-quotations of Antiquity by Giovanni da Udine (especially in the figured inserts *all'antica*) in his initial work, the Bibbiena decoration of 1516, in the grotesque style. There is no way to determine precedence between Peruzzi and Raphael's Giovanni in this culmination of archaeologizing process in the Roman school.

Despite their common imitative purpose, Peruzzi's picture contains, much more than Giovanni's paintings, the accent of creative personality. Peruzzi is concerned, as he is often, with the look of the Ancient apparatus more than with its underlying character of form. He draws the Muses with a brittle energy: with a sharp thin filament of line, which moves too quickly to be merely academically or imitatively correct. The energy of line makes forms of anatomy swell and undulate, or points them precisely. Surfaces and contours flex and facet as if etched in metal; the color, also metallic, in cool off-hues — greens, pinks and ice-blue — reinforces this effect. The whole pattern of rhythmic sequences, woven through the frieze, is dry and febrile at the same time. Peruzzi's peculiar, somewhat mannered sensibility has found a new mutation, still more complex and more sophisticatedly artificial within the outwardly wholly archaeological guise. Even this apparent most dependent reference to Antiquity in Peruzzi is marked sharply with his individuality.

The content of individuality that is in this archaeological image found — probably in close consequence of the thinking that went into it — a freer and more natural outlet in the use of its motive (and of some of its particular passages of pose and drapery as well) in a scene of contemporary life. A wash drawing (Florence, Uffizi 638E, in three parts, in shape suggesting a design for a considerable length of frieze)[489] describes a festival in the Campagna. Figures on foot and horseback come to the celebration through the landscape from the right. Their destination is a country dance in which, before a rustic audience, country cousins of Muses perform a round in company with their swains. The air of the event is quite opposite that in the panel of the Muses. Here a sense of slow measure, as of the dance itself, hardly constrains the effect of informality in the scene, which in its temper is like a bucolic theme of Sannazzaro's. Because this drawing is in the vulgar, rather than the learned and sophisticated Ancient idiom of the Pitti *Muses*, it is not more or less, but only differently, personally poetic.

The flexibility of Peruzzi's practice in this time is evident within the single context of his fresco decoration of the Ponzetti Chapel in S. M. della Pace (dated 1516).[490-2] The decoration consists of a fresco altarpiece with the Madonna, Sts. Brigid and Catherine of Alexandria, and the donor, and of a semidome divided into nine rectangular compartments. These contain, in the broadest central band, a *Nativity*, an *Adoration of the Kings* and a *Flight into Egypt*, and in the lesser bands above and below, small scenes of prophetic reference from the Old Testament.[490] For each of the three different scales in which the parts of the decoration are conceived Peruzzi uses a slightly but perceptibly different manner. In the smallest panels from the Old Testament — free transcriptions from the comparable scenes on the Sistine Ceiling, and from Peruzzi's own ceiling in the Stanza d'Eliodoro — he employs a very quick and cursive mode, of composition as well as of handling, suggestive of the manner of the *Prospettive* frieze. The larger panels are much more formal, and there is a distinction made within them (between the *Adoration* and the two flanking scenes), of a relatively conventional manner, and one appropriate to what Peruzzi chooses to interpret, in the *Adoration*,[491] as partly Antique and archaeological. In this, a sharply linear drawing and metallic modelling of the Romanized — Roman provincial, at least — figures of the Kings recall the panel of the *Muses*,[488] but in this theme there is no comparable rhythmic inspiration; the figures are deliberately and correctly defined by an insistent line, reinforced in its effect by strong differentiation of the light. The *Nativity* and the *Flight into Egypt*, to either side of the *Adoration*, have no classicistic pretext, and are set down in the simplest and most conservative formula for type and composition available to a practitioner within the Roman classical style. They seem, in 1516, almost archaic, but they refer in fact to a phase through which Peruzzi had passed, as in the *Adoration* of S. Rocco, only a few years before.

In the altar fresco[492] the style conforms essentially to that Peruzzi used in the wall figures of the *Sala Prospettive*, but without the accent which results there from their classicistic guise. Thus stripped — except for the Antique-matronly figure of St. Catherine — of the outward cast of reminiscent classicism that, in the paradox of this moment, makes the *Prospettive* frieze "modern," it becomes evident how little in the most advanced contemporary vein these figures of the altar are. Raphael's *Sibyls* of the Cappella Chigi, two years earlier, lie just across the nave of S. M. della Pace, but Peruzzi's conception of a humanity is far from being so classically fulfilled as they are. The breadth of form of Peruzzi's figures in the altar responds to a high classical canon, but their outward shape is inhabited by a spirit like that of an earlier time in the development of classicism. Peruzzi is not sympathetic to high classical rhetoric, or even to the gravity of its modes of expression; the suave temper of his actors, and the kind of posture and psychological communication that it motivates, is still virtually interchangeable with Raphael's earliest Segnatura style. The whole of this decoration is qualified by one act after another of retrospection, but the least expected of them is that which, in the altarpiece itself, particularly accents its partial disassociation from current Roman style: a Sienese reminiscence, not from the time of Peruzzi's first origins, but of the types and the personality in expression of his compatriot, Il Sodoma.

The dense and rhythmically interwoven group of figures in the altarpiece is placed, almost too tightly, into a perspective space made in the semblance of a colonnaded room — the one evidence in this decoration of Peruzzi's architectural specialty. This setting reflects an idea of perspective situation that existed, in the original state, in Raphael's fresco opposite. Peruzzi's figures do not occupy their excavated space, even less than Raphael's in his composition that is intentionally frieze-like, but are set against the surface, in the foremost plane. Their assertion of large human presence is in the manner of high classical style, but as Peruzzi uses this device it rather serves to bring to mind an aspect of his art in which he never functioned wholly classically. Despite their breadth of form, these figures are not completely plastically convincing; the sense of an authentic substance is not in them.

This is a persistent symptom, even in this late moment, of a quality constantly apparent in all Peruzzi's varieties of style: in the polished and metallic figures of the *Adoration* here or in the Pitti *Muses*; in the Venus and Apollo of the *Sala Prospettive* and in the figures of its frieze; and still more visibly in the preceding works. Peruzzi apprehends the world he means to reproduce more optically than haptically: for him actuality is in the look of things that light reveals, more than in their massive presences — which a classical conception grasps not only by visual but by intellectual and empathic means. Peruzzi's transcription of his world in paint was, in effect, like his transcription of the classical style, more of its look than of its substantial matter. And though Peruzzi was an architect, and the foremost manipulator of perspective in the Roman school, his conception of space, too, was never wholly classical: he felt it less as extension than as a datum of appearance, existent primarily by virtue of the light that revealed it and its occupying forms. Space could be defined at will and projected by perspective; but Peruzzi never came to the conviction, present to the more profoundly classical mentalities from Alberti on, that extension could possess its own plastically malleable aesthetic personality.

There is one incident in the Ponzetti altar so rare in Peruzzi's art that it deserves brief comment: a sample, in the donor, of Peruzzi's portraiture. More than any other element in the picture this suggests to what extent ties with the Quattrocento still survive in Peruzzi; but for its modern boldness of handling this portrait might find place, for its surpasssing literalness, in a fresco by Ghirlandaio. Only one portrait in oil by Peruzzi is known, of a *Carmelite* (Rome, art market; c. 1514–15; assigned in the literature to Sebastiano del Piombo, the correct attribution due to Pouncey).[493] This portrait is based in composition, evidently, on Raphael's *Inghirami*,[244] but though Peruzzi has taken over Raphael's motive of the rounding bulk of form he does not approximate Raphael's idealizing handling of it, neither in this linear description of the drapery nor in the seemingly literally realistic face. The former attribution to Sebastiano is not incomprehensible, for despite the sharpness of Peruzzi's handling of parts, the whole large, simple shape, a little hollow, resembles what is in Sebastiano's exactly contemporary portraiture.

Peruzzi contributed to the changes that were being worked in this time in the Roman school, but he came himself to be at least as much affected by the more important alterations made by Raphael. The last important work of painting by Peruzzi from this phase, the half life-size fresco of the *Presentation of the Virgin*,[494] also in S. M. della Pace, is in part the result of a renewed consideration of the art of Raphael, in particular of the recently published *Fire in the Borgo*.[376] On evidence of style, and in Vasari's sequence, the *Presentation* succeeds the painting of the Cappella Ponzetti. Its earliest *terminus* is in 1517 and its latest 1520, and on the interval between these years certain historical questions of precedence depend. A confident precise dating is not possible, but the likelihood is that the fresco is rather of 1517 or perhaps 1518 in time of invention than later; it is still closely related in motives and in manner of painting to the Cappella Ponzetti. It may also be an indication of the fresco's date that no identifiable motives by other Roman painters of a later time than 1516, the date of Raphael's *Fire in the Borgo*, appear in it, and that picture in particular seems to be a source of influence.

It is in its setting and in staging of the subject that the *Presentation* first of all suggests a likeness with the *Fire in the Borgo*. There is, in both, a complex architecture, partly modern and partly archaeological, projected in a perspective depth unusual before this time. The fact of the resemblance in setting may, however, ultimately be more Peruzzi's responsibility than Raphael's: the first appearance in Rome of painted architecture of this kind had been in Peruzzi's stage designs, which may have influenced Raphael in his invention of a setting for the *Fire*. A reference of setting to Raphael in the *Presentation* would thus also be a reference to Peruzzi's own still prior precedent. Such scenic apparatus in Peruzzi had, however, not before been given a painted population of actors, and it is for his stage management in particular that Peruzzi seems to refer to Raphael. On a stairway in the right middle ground — like that in the *Fire* — Peruzzi has placed the nominal main subject matter of his picture. He has, not quite as drastically as Raphael, displaced the nominal subject to a rearward plane, while the foreground space and largest area of the fresco is reserved for secondary actors.

In Raphael's *Fire* one among such secondary figures, the *Canephore* (but more than one in the other frescoes of the Incendio room) is placed so as to make an illusion of connection between the painted space and that of the spectator. In Peruzzi's *Presentation* — as might be expected of his stronger preoccupation with illusion — a number of the secondary figures are so devised as to project toward, or even through, the picture plane; his entire figure composition has been more assertively brought forward. As an added conceit of illusion — a Peruzzian witticism — the whole fresco has been surrounded by a stucco frame, to give it the appearance not of a fresco but of a *quadro riportato*: an important early use of this conceit. It is like the Raphael *Fire* also that in this fresco the foreground opens to a contrasting extreme depth of space, scanned by figures set in diminishing perspective. None of the resemblance to the *Fire* is in terms of literal quotation — only the woman on the left of the *Presentation*, seen back-to, seems to paraphrase the *Canephore*; the quotations are rather from the earlier style and, perhaps, from certain of the Tapestry Cartoons. The resemblance to the *Fire* is in more important general ideas, of pictorial construction and handling of the given theme.

The relation to the Raphael is apparent, but it seems also and inevitably to confirm the difference of Peruzzi's personality. What is most obviously not in the *Presentation* is Raphael's precise pictorial economy: Peruzzi has adapted the kind and the complexity of Raphael's construction, but does not approximate its discipline. By comparison with the *Fire* the *Presentation* seems not only busy — as the Raphael is, too — but inchoate. The ambitious scenic space is imperfectly clear; despite its seeming great extent it has no distinguishable personality, as the space does in the *Fire*. Only the limits of the scene, defined by the architecture, are given adequately; the content of space that these architectural forms enclose is almost indecipherable, and without effect, as spatiality, on the structure of the picture. In fact, each main point of the perspective system that falls within this "stage" is masked, concealing or disguising spatial sense. We have remarked the abstractness of Peruzzi's apprehension of space: it is apparent here that perspective theory is not understood by him to have the possibility, within a picture, of making space a sensible aesthetic agent.

In his mode of ordering his actors on the stage Peruzzi shows none of Raphael's geometric stringency. The main figures are set out in paramilitary sequence, disposed side by side across the front plane in a way that distantly suggests the columnar figure order of certain of the Tapestry Cartoons; but no comparable logic of geometry contains them. A curious and novel conceit, of near-alternation of poses taken from the front and from the back, makes variety in this lateral parade of forms, as does even more the stressed gracility of almost every posture. The figures are related by the passing from one to another of them of their curving rhythms of attitude and drapery, and as in the altar of the Ponzetti Chapel this mode of connecting forms suggests that used in an earlier phase of classical style. But the temper of pattern in this warping rhythm is not like that in the Ponzetti altarpiece, nor does it now recall the temper that had been in Raphael's Segnatura style. This is not a suave and mellow *cantilena* but a pattern of tensing and contracted rhythms; tight, dry, and in passages acutely precious. This pattern resembles those evolved in the *Prospettive* frieze but it is made, in this larger and plastically more explicit scene, more deliberate and pointedly self-conscious of its effects. As in that frieze — but for the first time in Rome in a painting of this scale — this arabesque is in effect a composition in its own right and not, as in normative classical style, an equal agency within design with an underlying geometric scheme.

The temper of this arabesque is large part consists of, and is determined by, the temper of design of the figures. In the most prominent of them their postures are developed from the classical conception of a contrapposto, but with a tendency to exaggerate the figure's turning, in degree or in complexity of rhythm and direction, to that point which makes tension rather than a harmony: rhythmic impulse is pulled tight and fine-drawn upon the figures' substance. These attitudes are too precious, or else too extreme, to seem naturally plausible. Their effect is of manner and of aestheticizing artifice. And only aesthetic considerations prompt this behavior in the figures: there is no expressive pretext for the action of these persons who are only bystanders, not even an attentive audience, of the Presentation. Each of them, almost separately, is an invented motive, preeminently of form, and there is none but the most casual thread of connection in meaning among them. Their mannered attitudes are more pronounced than in any work in Rome of presumable contemporary date, and more nearly the result of purely formalistic invention. The preciosities in Giulio's interpretations of Raphael's devotional pictures, or in his own, come later by our reckoning, and are not so assertive then as they are here. Shortly later than the *Presentation*, another painter of the youngest generation, Perino del Vaga, Tuscan by origin like Peruzzi, would evolve a like mannered mode of behavior for the human form. In Peruzzi this mannered posturing is not an innovation except in its degree — though the accentuation of degree is what, precisely, is historically important: it is the reassertion, much more highly stressed and characterized, of a tendency in his first classicizing works, as in the elegant inhabitants of the *Galatea* ceiling. There, this tendency had been evidence of a preclassical persistence in the style and mentality of Peruzzi; here it has the value of postclassical anticipation.

If our dating of the *Presentation* is correct, it is the earliest prognostica-* tion, clear to this degree, of the shape of things to come in the evolution of painting style in Rome. It contains, in more nearly explicit definition than in any picture of its moment, elements that may appear in Mannerism: a complex and devalued space; a rhythmically involved and geometrically unstructured composition, of complicated ornamental temper; a mannered articulation of figures, which have only formal and not expressive motivation; a strong cast of archaeology. The personality in the Roman scene who is least involved with the creative history of classical style, and in whom the disposition of the late Quattrocento still persists, is the earliest to reform the classical style so nearly positively toward Mannerism.

Yet, despite its quotient of elements that are in Mannerism, the *Presentation* is not yet a Mannerist picture. First, these elements are not individually so strongly characterized as to assume the personality we recognize in unequivocal works of Mannerist style. Further, these elements are not consistently characterized within the sphere to which each applies: for example, in the figure style, figures of quite conventional classicizing cast exist among the mannered ones. Finally, no whole will works to shape the style of this picture in a new consistency, in which each mannerizing element functions in an accord, conscious in the artist, with the meaning of the others. A new meaning of parts is adumbrated in the *Presentation,* but no whole new meaning for the work of art. It is just this meaning that the members of the younger generation positively find — perhaps partly in consequence of what they saw indicated, but not wholly stated, in the *Presentation.* Peruzzi's picture is not yet a work of the new style, but still of the old style in its process of dissolution — not of dissolution only, but of creative alteration toward a new end. When the new invention of style clearly came, Peruzzi, despite his role as a progenitor, became a follower rather than a creative leader within Mannerism, and relatively conservative in his interpretation of it.

Peruzzi tended, indeed, toward 1520, to assume a relationship to the school of Raphael that was more evidently dependent than, as it had been in the few years before, suggestive to that school of new ideas. A small decorated room in the apartment of the Cardinal-Vicar of Rome in the Palazzo della Cancelleria, recently rediscovered (correctly attributed by Pouncey; published in part with an improper attribution to Perino, Griseri; c. 1520),[495-8] reveals Peruzzi's response to the promulgation by Raphael and his school of the Logge style. The vaulted ceiling of this room is painted with a system of figured geometrical inserts of varied subject and shape, densely and elaborately framed by grotesquerie. The style of the grotesques is partly like that newly evolved by Raphael's assistants, and partly reminiscent of Peruzzi's own earlier, still Pinturicchiesque, grotesquerie; the figured scenes are also partly personally reminiscent and in part derived from the repertory of the Logge. The ceiling contains, like the Logge, selected Old Testament themes, but still more than there they are accompanied and surrounded here by a context of Antique citations. The lunettes below the vault illustrate, on larger scale, further episodes from the Old Testament, among them some that are the same as those in the Logge, with discernable quotations from them.

Not all the lunettes have been executed by Peruzzi but the designs all seem certainly to be his. Where his hand is surely visible it gives his expected brilliant accent to the matter of design, and the design itself inventively transforms even the borrowed elements in it of mode or motive. Peruzzi's manner in the vault is deliberately various, just as it had been in the similar scale of the semidome of the Ponzetti Chapel; it ranges here from a mode like that in the *Adoration* of that decoration to an archaeologizing manner more explicit, but also drier, than that of the Pitti *Muses*. The lunettes call forth on one hand, as in the *Joseph Put into the Well,*[497] a design more fluid and an execution yet more lucent than that of the *Sala delle Prospettive* frieze, and on the other hand, as in the *Meeting of Sheba and Solomon,*[498] a scheme of staging more strict and a handling more neoclassically pure than in the *Presentation of the Virgin.* These two manners make even more apparent than before the divergent directions of exploration within Peruzzi's art, and indicate how each, one unclassical in tendency and the other classicistic, promote the dissolution of classicism. But what they adumbrate for the future of the classical style the disciples of Raphael had already, in the Logge, achieved.

THE SCHOOL IN THE LOGGE

The Emergence of New Personalities. The painting of Raphael's Bible into the Logge of the Vatican [499-526] must have been done under considerable pressure of time. We have little more than a single year of documented activity, from March 1518 to early May 1519, of Raphael's shop within this loggia. In this time, in addition to the grotesquerie and architectural ornamenting of the vaults — which had to be done first, presumably, since the frames for the narrative inserts depend on them — it was necessary to provide designs for and execute fifty-four narrative panels, of varying complexity. Quick work, and a division of labor, were obviously required. The supervision of this job and the initial burden of its execution fell to Giulio Romano, assisted in a rather special capacity by Penni and, in addition, by at least three identifiable further painters new to Raphael's establishment: Pellegrino da Modena, Perino del Vaga, and Polidoro da Caravaggio (the last taken on from the group of craftsmen recruited for Giovanni da Udine's program of grotesquerie). Giulio's general charge over these narrative paintings apparently was exercised with little or no interference from Raphael, and as the decoration proceeded and the new recruits became visibly proficient, Giulio deputized his own creative liberty to them. This narrative program was Giulio's job, not Raphael's, and the assistants equally were not Raphael's, but his; they worked in what seems to have been a virtually separate shop from Raphael's own, a subsidiary enterprise constituted for this project and intended for no more than its duration. This was an "outside" crew, distinct from Raphael's personal helpers in his private shop.

The nature of what was to be done and the time permitted for its doing encouraged freedom in the designers and executants. These small scenes were meant first of all to tell their story, and it was not expected that they be formal structures of the profound deliberation required for the larger efforts, and for those of more complex content, elsewhere in the Raphaelesque style. Intellectual considerations of order were quite secondary to ease, and where it could be attained, efficacy of narration. Originality of thought was not required: if an effective precedent for the given theme existed, it was sufficient to adapt it; but conversely, where there was no precedent there was no obstacle, of conformity to classical structural convention, to the free expression of a new idea. As the painting of the narrative scenes got under way the recognition of this liberty became increasingly apparent; compositions became less formally deliberate and more casual: quick, facile, and sometimes strikingly elliptical in their temper of narration.

Already granted a large quotient of creative independence in his role within the "inside" shop, Giulio was quick to exploit the freedom of this fully delegated responsibility, and to take the stimulus to inventive liberty that was in the nature of the task. He is the author, in the scenes of his invention in the Logge, of some designs that are dull and some that are merely imitative, but he is also responsible for many more highly interesting and even radical innovations of design. In his panels in general, however, even in the more radical of them, there is a perceptible quotient of allegiance to Raphael's style. The consequences, in Giulio's contributions, of his close relation to the master are quite evident in comparison to what occurs in the work, as it matures within the Logge, of Giulio's assistants. These were men who had not been exposed before to Raphael's direct authority, and who were not now; nor did they even necessarily experience, in the "outside" shop, Raphael's increasingly rare personal demonstrations of actual painting. Their direct example was, instead, that of Giulio himself, in his relatively libertarian role; this liberty, deputized in turn to Giulio's assistants, permitted the emergence of artistic individuality that was not constrained even by his measure of Raphaelesque allegiance. The two significant creative personalities among Giulio's helpers were, furthermore, younger even than he was himself, yet more removed in the time of beginning of their education from the epoch of a seemingly unfissurable classicism. Perino, born in 1500 or 1501, and Polidoro, born toward 1505, emerged in the Logge to identifiable artistic personality — as precociously as Giulio had himself, and still more than he in a climate of dissolution of classical authority and beginning redirection of the classical style.

Quite the dominant designer and executant at the beginning of the painting of the narrative panels, Giulio yielded place as the decoration proceeded to the still younger men, and to Perino in particular. The assignment of authorship among these panels is made exceptionally insecure by their condition, almost entirely repainted or, in some cases, now nearly obliterated. With this conspicuous reserve, it would appear that the narratives of the first four vaults were in large part of Giulio's execution.[500–02] Possibly in the fifth vault, and certainly within the sixth,[504] Perino made his first appearance as executant; he is also the principal painter within the seventh. While the eighth [505] and ninth vaults [507–08] were again mostly of Giulio's doing, from the tenth vault through the last it is Perino's personal style, here much more explicitly emerged, that dominates.[509–13, 517–20] Polidoro's contributions are sparser: he first appeared, with most likelihood, in the panel of *Jacob and Rachel* [503] in the sixth vault. He is the likely author of *Moses Striking Water from the Rocks* in the eighth vault,[506] and the two latter scenes of the Legend of Solomon in vault twelve [515–16] are his, in his most developed personal style within the Logge. The personal style of a third painter may also be identified among the narrative scenes, in those which are the least apt of the whole series: perhaps first in the *Dream of Pharaoh* in vault seven, in the *Anointing of Saul* in vault eleven, and in the *Consecration of Solomon* and his *Judgment* [514] in vault twelve. On the basis of comparison with what survives of his independent work, slightly later, in the Cappella di S. Giacomo in S. M. degli Spagnuoli, this painter is probably Pellegrino da Modena. His efforts in the Logge are of the least aesthetic, and of no historical, consequence.

Penni, it will be observed, is missing from the catalogue of executants so far. He almost certainly participated in the earliest work of painting in this series: the very first panel to be painted, the *Separation of Light and Darkness*,[499] and some of the *angioletti* of the first vault were almost surely once by his hand. Some of our tentative ascriptions to Giulio Romano in the early bays might also, were their original condition visible, rather require to be assigned to the Fattore. However, his importance for the Logge scenes is not as painter, but as draughtsman. He is, in our opinion, the certain author of the several authentic preparatory drawings that survive for panels in vaults one through nine (British Museum, Windsor, Uffizi, Louvre, etc.),[521–4] a conclusion to which we come not by elimination but by close Morellian comparison with drawings by Penni for other late Raphalesque enterprises: the *Sala Palafrenieri*, the *Oath of Leo*, the Tapestry Cartoons. Penni's authorship of such working drawings, however, no more indicates his necessary responsibility for design than it did in these other cases. Some of the designs — the earliest in the series, which include the feeblest and most imitative-minded, may in fact be wholly his. But his more considerable role in the Logge, as we recall it was in the process of preparation of the Tapestry Cartoons, must have been in the handling of the intermediate stages of preparation, in drawing, between the first invention and the final painting * of the compositions. The dominant inventor in the first nine bays — despite Vasari's assertion of Raphael's responsibility — was Giulio. The designs are either too imitative (and by Penni), or of too unconventional an inventiveness (and by Giulio), to have been conceived by Raphael himself. Penni's execution of the working drawings accounts also, evidently, for the reflection of his draughtsmanly style that is in the best copies after them, such as the group in the Cabinet of the Albertina.

Three original preparatory studies survive (Windsor,[525] British Museum) for scenes in the last vaults that were executed in painting by Perino del Vaga. The author of these drawings is not Penni, but — also unequivocally — Perino. Here, too, it is conceivable that ideas in rough form of Giulio's may underly Perino's specific preparations in drawing of these designs; certainly their style in general could not have come to be without the precedent of Giulio. But in the drawings (as in the corresponding paintings) the vocabulary of form is of such marked individuality, and so consistent within itself — the mentality of whole composition and of particular shapes is identifiably the same — that the stronger likelihood is that each entire drawing is, from initial conception to final development, of one creative piece. We know no Logge drawings by Polidoro, but since his paintings, too, in these last vaults are so strongly individual in style it is reasonable to assume that, like Perino, he was here the author of his own designs. Within the earlier vaults, however, neither Perino nor Polidoro had been conceded such a liberty. Among the Albertina copies of lost Penni drawings are instances of designs for the earlier vaults executed in painting, in our opinion, by each of the younger men; and the style in the painting of these indicates in every case derivative, not yet individually creative character.

Within the scenes of Giulio's personal initial invention there must originally have been a considerable compounding of personalities — of Giulio's idea recast by Penni, and retranslated into Giulio's own painterly idiom, or into the idiom, still flexible, of Perino or Polidoro. Repainting has not only added another element to this compound, but confused it nearly to deformity. Only the most general deductions of style are permissible from the present evidence these paintings give. In some cases, the designs have the air of a careless adaptation of a classical precedent or of a classical convention; those are the worst of them, and are no more than classical formula unthought-out, dissolved and boneless. But more often the designs are not made merely by so negative a process; an incipiently conscious principle determines, more or less consistently and effectively, their nature. We have remarked that the primary intention of this series was narrative efficiency rather than the making, in the accustomed classical way, of intellectualized formal constructs. The more interesting designs are set out in an order and according to a logic that is not determined by a structural geometry, but by their sense as narrative. By comparison with large-scale classical compositions the contents of these scenes are almost casually disposed, with minimal concern for classical conventions of arrangement. They retain — where condition has not wholly inhibited this effect — something of the quick impulse of the first narrative notation in a drawing: the elements simply and directly given, quick in temper of their action, and related in a rapid cursive sequence that conveys the rhythm of the designer's hand and his state of mind in the telling of the story. This is not, as in normative classical style, a cursive system incorporated into underlying geometric form; this cursive system is the controlling essence of design, resembling, and having an intention like that of, a literary script.

There is quite enough of residue of classical disposition in these designs to impose moderation on this cursive impulse of narration; the majority of scenes shows informality of order, but not drastically unconventional arrangement. In a few, however, there are surprising and inventive asymmetries, in particular in those instances where the rhythmical direction of design is extended to project in space. More than any other factor of design, it is the persistence of a classical sense of identity and substance of the human figure that makes counterweight to, and disciplines, this rhythmical activity of composition. The cursive movement traverses the figures, and in part shapes their form and manner of behavior to its *glissando* pattern, but the form itself is heavily emphatic in plasticity: the figures are in general in Giulio's small-scale version, yet more squat and dense, of the current late classical canon.

What Giulio has invented here is new to him, and to the school of Raphael, but not altogether to the Roman school. Peruzzi had conceived a cursive narrative mode a few years before, in the frieze of the *Sala delle Prospettive*, and there had permitted its less inhibited expression. Less involved with classical style than Giulio, Peruzzi operated with no comparable restraints — of the sense of substantiality of figures, or of spaces — upon his energy and variety of rhythmic impulse. Giulio's innovations in the Logge designs are, by comparison, still classically tempered. Only seemingly paradoxically, it is for this reason that they are more significant for the future course of style in Rome where, yet more than in Florence, a historically meaningful Mannerist style would develop only from the fullest prior realization of a classicism.

PERINO DEL VAGA

The accent of Perino's paintings in the Logge is from the beginning — even in those paintings where, presumably, he still works after Giulio's design — more mannered than those of Giulio. There is, on this account, a suggestion of likeness to Peruzzi's most recent demonstration in the *Presentation* of the *Pace*, and much more than their common Tuscan origin is required to account for it. The style this very young Florentine had brought to Rome on his arrival, toward 1517, and first practiced there (after liberation from his assistantship to the provincial painter from whom he took his name) is of a personality already interesting, but still unformed. Probably before Perino's invitation into the Logge corps is his first large-scale Roman work — perhaps his first large independent work altogether — the now nearly ruined fresco altar of the *Pietà* in Sto. Stefano del Cacco (c. 1517).[527] Awkward and immature* in painting, this fresco is much more reminiscent of Florence than it is, as yet, touched by Rome. Its types, drapery, and composition still much reflect the Florentine climate of Fra Bartolommeo, and its space and landscape, and its color in particular, are closely based on Sarto's early fresco style. Any evidence of Roman influence is superficial: perhaps from Peruzzi in the type and in the drawing of drapery of Joseph, and even less certainly in the St. John; and, almost unavoidably, from Michelangelo's early *Pietà.* There is no evidence of awareness of the contemporary Raphael; yet Raphael is in this picture as a Florentine, rather than a Roman, might know his art, in its pre-Roman guise. A drawing in the Louvre (3858, there attributed to the* school of Raphael),[526] which served Marcantonio as the model for his engraving (B. 35), is unmistakably related to the central figures of the Sto. Stefano *Pietà* not only in theme but in types, technique, and in expression; it is not specifically a preparatory study but rather a tangential product of the same process and moment of inventive thought. This drawing relates in turn, however, to Raphael's earliest inventions of 1507 for the Baglioni *Entombment,*[59] which somehow, in Florence or in the course of his wanderings with Vaga, young Perino must have come to know and study. This, so far, is the Raphael style that Perino had experienced effectively and understood.

A panel of Perino's early Roman time, the *Adoration of the Child* (Rome, Borghese 464; 1518),[528] is more evidently Raphaelesque but still is not explicitly related to the models of the master. Perino's painting derives instead from a drawing by Penni, or from the painted version of it, in tondo form (Museum, Cava de' Tirreni, near Naples); but Perino's derivation is farther than its source from comprehending of a "modern" Raphaelism. It compounds the retrospective character of Penni's picture with an accent like that of the conservatives of Florence, recalling the way an earlier Raphael had been interpreted by them. Perino's substantial early education had been close to, and actually in, Ridolfo Ghirlandaio's school, and this work in oil still has the mark of such an education on it. Its vision of Raphael's newer Roman art is still, in part, through archaizing eyes.

Perino never, in fact, came to be exposed to the direct influence of the "modern" Raphael. His recruitment into the Logge corps made him a disciple of Raphael's pupils rather than of Raphael, and his view of the mature and the contemporary classical style of Raphael was only indirect, filtered through the pupils' intervening personalities. Perino's education bypassed, as it were, the experience of Raphaelesque classicism. Perino's possible first appearances in the narratives of the Logge, in the *Isaac and Jacob* and the *Isaac and Esau* of the fifth bay, are, like the Borghese panel, dependent in their cast of style from Penni; but his first certain executions (in bays six[504] and seven) are, as we have suggested, not only based, most probably, on Giulio's compositional ideas but are imitative of his specific formal vocabulary; these panels more follow Giulio's own models in the preceding paintings of the series than they do the style of the working drawings made by Penni, we assume also at this stage for Perino's use. Giulio's repertory of types and attitudes, and — evidently — his mode of composition are skillfully transcribed by the new disciple, obliterating the traces of his former Tuscan style and the cast he carried, in his first works in Rome, of awkwardness and of provincialism. Perino is, with remarkable swiftness, technically mature, and Romanized not only in a general way but in the exact terms of the context in which he works as of this moment.

But even in the moment of this imitative assimilation the symptoms emerge of an individuality distinct from Giulio's, which extends and makes more evident the implications of unclassical kind that are in Giulio's models. The difference in Perino is in his change of the relation within Giulio's style between substance and rhythmical activity: in Perino there is no such classicizing sense as in Giulio of resistance offered by plastic forms to impulses of movement, and the movement itself assumes a proportionately freer and more dominating role. Its temper becomes distinct: more elaborately differentiated and ornamentally fine, more pervasively involving the matter of the picture in its activity. Not the principal impetus of composition only, but the whole design, becomes a complex rhythmic texture. The Giulian anatomy is worked by this mobile patterning into more artificial, and more mannered, gracile shapes, and the particular quality of attitude a figure takes may be determined more by its articulation of such ornamental pattern than by the function that the subject calls on it to represent. Bodies may assume the ornamental torsions, tensed and precious-seeming, that we have seen them take in Peruzzi's *Presentation* in the *Pace*: motivated by an aesthetic, more than by an apparent physical, energy. But these postures in Perino do not emerge from their context as singular episodes, as they do in the *Presentation*; instead they are the climactic points of articulation of a rhythmically consistent texture of design. Perino's images make what Peruzzi's *Presentation* still does not: a unity of stylistic purpose and effects. Even within these early Logge scenes Perino has imposed on Giulio's precedent of style and idea a seemingly slight, but sufficiently decisive alteration, which makes of them an explicit demonstration of postclassical style. Roman Mannerism emerges in the work of his disciple from the matrix Giulio had formed for it, by means and with a meaning different from those Giulio would shortly use to the same generic end.

The style that is thus defined in Perino's earlier Logge frescoes is affirmed and specified in his paintings in the later vaults.[509-13, 517-20] Part of this process is the simple result of Perino's phenomenal rapidity of maturation; now, inventing for himself, he conceives of ideas of far greater formal complexity, or of more novel force, than those which Giulio had supplied to him, and he develops these with a much more sharply conscious sense of the new identity of style he has discovered. There is now, in Perino, a self-knowledge yet more precocious than there had been in Giulio; and there is not Giulio's conflict of interest, still active, between personal impulse and Raphael's authority. It is not a paradox that Perino is now prepared to learn, better than he had before, some things that could be found in the models of the classical style. These do not compromise his new identity; he uses them to his own ends, to strengthen it.

In these later scenes Perino adapts more of the general outward look of Raphaelesque late classical style than was in Giulio's variant of it, in this place only. His interest extends to archaeology of accessories and costumes, or the absence of them; his anatomies become more — distantly — Michelangelesque and more vigorously muscled, in the accustomed current Roman mode. His definition of figure substance and of space becomes, at will, more plastically sure, and his meaning of design becomes clearer and more decisively articulate. The strongest evidence of these latter qualities especially is in the frescoes of New Testament illustration in the latest bay.[517-20] In these scenes the forms are — by comparison with what comes before — almost sparsely distributed, in a clear, including rhythmic sequence of whole composition. A higher clarity of articulation is in the drawing of the figures, too (where it still can be discerned, as in the *Adoration of the Shepherds*): the line is thin, quick-moving, and sharply differentiating. Beyond this, the surfaces of form are faceted by light. There are incidents in this last bay of a kind of use of light that is frequent in the Mannerists: in which an acute sensibility to optical experience selects actual, but singular, effects of light that finally promote the sense of fantasy within the picture. Giulio more or less contemporaneously, in the *Perla*, used light in this way; but differently from Giulio, Perino's light — like every other element of form in these paintings — finally subserves his cursive ornamental patterning.

Not only in the New Testament scenes, but in those of the preceding bays, which contain the Joshua and David stories, there is a similar decisiveness of main cursive compositional pattern, but not such relative simplicity in the mesh of ornament that grows from it. Where the subject in the least affords a pretext for a multiplicity of forms, Perino takes it; in these scenes he invents patterns of complex-woven interlace, or — even more original — sequences of forms in repetition, which make precedent for the coming Roman school. These patterns depend, nevertheless, from an explicit, broadly indicated cursive armature of whole design.

Like what had come before, of Giulio's invention, Perino's scenes are adequate as narrative and illustration, but they are no longer primarily these things; primarily they are projections of ornamental form, of complex, quick, and gracile temper. Subject does not dictate the shapes or the affect of form but lends itself to an aesthetically predetermined character. The human content of the subject — Joshua's and David's battles, David's contemplation of Bathsheba, the Nativity or Baptism — almost regardless of any possible emotional actuality, is conceived of, and transposed into, the affective key of the design. Content and form are one, but the meaningful content is that of the form.

There is, evidently, some reason in the semantics of the historical appellation "Mannerism." The style that Perino has evolved in the Logge is so explicitly identifiable as Mannerist — more readily so than the style of Giulio's *Perla,* or even of his first post-Raphaelesque fresco works — because it is, simply, so evidently mannered. It conforms not only to the basic conditions that we observe, from 1520 onward, in other manifestations of post-classical style but, in addition, demonstrates the temper that we most associate with developed Mannerism. There is just hesitation as to the correctness of the application of the term "Mannerist" to some of the happenings of Roman art that succeed the time of Raphael, but hesitation is not justified in the case of this demonstration, in 1519, by Perino. To point out its particular resemblances of style to what, subsequently, will become a major, if not the dominant, vein of postclassical painting — not only in Rome but more widely in Italy — is in part at least a historical tautology, since it is Perino's own production that becomes one among the major models for the subsequent *maniera.* Its model is more imitable, more nearly possible to "far di pratica" than that of other varieties of postclassical style. It is desirable to imitate because it is so pleasing: aesthetically engaging, intellectually facile, and contentually unproblematical; and it is easy to imitate because it can be done adequately by the hand alone, and done well if the hand is supplemented by no more than sensibility and wit.

Even the mantle of Raphaelesque authority that fell to Giulio Romano could not make his style finally so widely influential. Unlike the Mannerism of Perino, Giulio's personal Mannerism did not have an easy birth. Giulio faced, and grappled with, every possible problem that the complex triangular relationship of classical, unclassical, and classicistic aesthetic could contain; his art is full of difficulty, and its new identity of style was achieved with profound effort. Its making was at the same time subtle as a treachery and forceful as an act of violence; the uniform and the professed loyalties of his new style remained much the same, but not its principles. Rather than Giulio's powerful inversion of meaning of the classical style, Perino's art seems an easy transmutation of it, not facing the problems of its crisis but dismissing them; taking the decorative capital only of classicism, elaborating it, and converting its humanity into ornament.

POLIDORO DA CARAVAGGIO

Once made, the basic form and personality of Perino's invention was indestructible, but it was not inflexible. In the climate of acute change and experiment that followed 1520 Perino's own searching curiosity — he was as intelligent as he was precocious — and the influence of his peers and contemporaries led him in a variety of directions, not all of them consistent with the character of style first demonstrated in the Logge. An important one among Perino's post-Raphaelesque impulses of research resembles, and may initially have been stimulated by, the most strikingly individual characteristic of the two late scenes in the Logge (in vault twelve) by the youngest of the executants, Polidoro. In some respects Polidoro is here, in the panels of his own design — as he had been also in his earlier executions after Giulio — a more faithful disciple of his foreman than Perino. His types and anatomies conform more literally to Giulio's example; an occasional fox-like profile and a more elaborated musculature are personal, but not essential, distinctions. More even than Giulio — and quite opposite to Perino — Polidoro lays stress on plasticity of bodies, and he is also more assertive in his definition of effects of space: not so much as depth as in its own, as it were, substantial role, of interval among solids. The sense of substances and intervals is so strong that it seems to resist the gathering of figures into groups. Nevertheless, on Giulio's and Perino's inescapable example, Polidoro's compositions are arranged on asymmetrical armatures of cursive rhythm. But unlike those examples, they are still more fundamentally conceived as orderings of solid form within a space. In this aspect of Polidoro's scenes there is a kinship with classical style that seems more genuine than in Giulio's manner of this moment, but the temper that inhabits Polidoro's form gives it other than a classical effect.

In total contrast to Perino's mode of making figures act by imposed aesthetic motivation, and with the same preciosity that is in the character of his design, Polidoro's figures are self-propelled, by impulses that seem almost violent. The cursive pattern laid upon their movements is not convinced enough to give them grace, nor even to constrain their urgency. Their actions are wide-flung, almost drastic: Sheba throws herself at Solomon with unqueenly impetuosity;[515] and the builders of his Temple work as if possessed.[516] The painter's sense of the existence of his actors is sharper than prescribed by the conventions of the classical style, and his sense of their energy is unconventional altogether. The precedent for such force is in Raphael's late dramatic works, and in Michelangelo before that, but not as here unaccompanied by their counterweight of classical controls. Polidoro's impulse of energy, unclassical in its intemperate expression, is more than classical structure — here in part still present — can contain.

A quality of mind like that of a baroque style is in ferment in these panels, in a context that surrounds them, in Giulio's scenes, of a classical style already attenuated, and in Perino's of a classicism already transformed. Not only Perino but Giulio as well would experiment in the succeeding years in a direction that the young Polidoro here was the first so urgently to explore. But more than his tendency would work on them, theirs would work on Polidoro. The accent in his Logge scenes that only superficially is like Perino's, but more genuinely is like Giulio's, would grow, before the history of art in Rome was interrupted by the Sack, into the common basic language of the younger generation, that of the Mannerist style.

VI

CLIMAX AND CRISIS IN FLORENCE AND THE GENERATION OF FLORENTINE MANNERISM (c. 1514-1520)

VI

CLIMAX AND CRISIS IN FLORENCE AND THE GENERATION OF FLORENTINE MANNERISM (c. 1514-1520)

THE highest pomp that Florence could put on in 1515, for the triumphal entry of Pope Leo X, could not disguise the contrast her situation made with Rome: provincial in comparison, old-fashioned and relatively poor — "miserrima civitas," as we recall, by Paris de Grassis' harsh reckoning. The real responsibility for any betterment that might be made lay with Paris de Grassis' master, who was ultimately the master of Florence in this time. Leo, however, had small concern for Florence as such; his concern with the city was as an accessory of his papal policy in Rome, and still more as an appanage of family, as if it were a fief that had been restored to him.

He had entrusted the government of the city to Lorenzino de' Medici, who in 1515 took the title of Captain-General of the Florentines. From this time onward Lorenzino abandoned the pretense, more or less maintained since the restoration late in 1512, that the Medicean rule was of *primus inter pares*. The republican institutions of Florence had already been effectively vitiated, mostly by manipulation but partly by force, and Lorenzino's personal conduct became that of a prince. As always, there was a substantial Medici partisanship in Florence, but even most of those who disagreed with Medicean rule were willing to take profits from it when occasion offered. Regardless of political conviction, the merchants and craftsmen of Florence were concerned with the pursuit of business as usual; but this pursuit did not necessarily interfere with their holding their political convictions. Side by side with the partisan Palleschi, and with those who were merely acquiescent in the Medici regime, there was a considerable opposition, overriding considerations of caste and class — not only republican, but specifically of old-fashioned Piagnoni — to Lorenzino's government. It was exasperated by what, in Rome, would have been taken for granted, Lorenzino's assumption of aristocratic manners, perhaps even more than by his inefficiency.

Fractious and divisive by old tradition, the citizens of Florence lived, in these years, in a conspicuously imperfect internal peace; and that they were the most politically articulate population of any Italian city-state made their unrest not only a matter of economy and domestic instinct but of ideas. It is not an accident of culture that the principal literati of Rome in this time were poets and rhetoricians, and those of Florence historians and philosophers of politics. As in the late fourteenth and early fifteenth centuries, the most active form of humanism in Florence was not merely literary in its ends, but an applied speculation on government and history. The death of Lorenzino in May 1519 and his replacement by the Cardinal Giulio, more temperate in his rule, appeased unrest in Florence, but only briefly. When, after the death of Leo in 1521, the Medici power seemed less unassailable, and it became evident that Giulio's temperateness was also a temporizing of political reform, the most ardent group of humanist intellectuals in Florence, the members of the Orti Oricellari, turned from theory to political action; a conspiracy by them to restore Soderini's republic was frustrated.

Florence shared the burdens of Medicean Rome in these years, but little of its benefits. The atmosphere of cultural opulence that Leo made in Rome had little or no reflection in Lorenzino's, or in Giulio's, city. Its culture remained for the most part resistantly individualistic and bourgeois; Lorenzino's aristocracy and his autocracy were equally not tolerable in Florence. Also, Florence no more shared the responsibilities of Medicean government than it did its benefits: political action that concerned the world outside the city was determined in Rome, where it was equally determined that the Florentines should pay for it, as with the costly and unpopular war of despoliation by Lorenzino against Urbino. Florentines were without the power of decision or of meaningful action in the larger world; their political restlessness and their intellectual ferment of it were introverted and intramural.

What occurred in Florence in the development of the arts in these years was not the consequence of this political and social climate but was, obviously, conditioned by it. There was variety in style of art as in political opinion; it was not required of the members of a predominantly bourgeois Florentine society that, as patrons, they conform, in a social and cultural context as complex as theirs, to one fashion only. For the artists, there was more freedom of individual practice in Florence than in Rome: personalities of the second rank who, in Rome, would be conscripted to the discipline of an atelier were, in Florence, relatively independent painters, at most — and then sometimes only uncertainly — describable as members of a school. A relative conservatism of artistic style was quantitatively dominant in this phase in Florence, but it had more different shades of personality than can be found in contemporary Rome. However, the Florentine climate of individualism and of faction could encourage, also, the emergence of radical opinion in the arts, of a kind and a profundity of dissent that was unthinkable in autocratic Rome. The habits of personality of young Pontormo and Rosso, and their manner of assertion of a revolutionary style in this phase, may well have to do with more than the artistic aspects only of their Florentine environment.

The dissent of these young protestants from the dominating order of Florentine painting achieved its first maturity within this phase, and the quality and significance of their accomplishment was in itself enough to give a new complexion to the image of art in Florence in this time. They altered the historical gestalt, but by the mere fact of their working in it rather than by their action, as yet, on others. What surrounded their dissenting art, and prevailed in Florence in these years was still — in the looser and more internally differentiated way of Florence rather than of Rome — a classical style. The example of Fra Bartolommeo was still predominant, though not nearly so exclusively as in the preceding phase; Andrea del Sarto's art now came in part to supplant its authority as model. Neither of these styles, however, was any longer quite that which we knew in the phase before. The ambitions of Fra Bartolommeo had been changed by his experience of Rome, and his achievement of his few last years until his death in 1517 pretended to, but did not quite achieve, a character like that of art in Rome. Andrea, in this time, fulfilled his highest potential of accomplishment in a style as profoundly, but not so strongly, personal as that of the young dissidents. His expression resembled theirs in individuality, but his individuality did not, like theirs, require the trespass of the limits of a classicism. This phase is significant for more than the dissidents' important innovation; as in Rome also, it is the time of ultimate accomplishment, within the limits and the special disposition of the Florentines, of their classical style.

Among artists of the second rank, loyalties did not yet shift significantly. Their art continued, where it was susceptible of development, to evolve according to the way laid down by Bartolommeo and, increasingly, by Andrea. But there is in general, even among the secondary painters, a higher differentiation of artistic individuality in this phase of Florentine painting than in the last, and a richer diversity of directions of development. And as Pontormo and Rosso acquired greater prominence upon the scene the whole tempo of changing style appears to assume a pace, and to operate with a freedom, much in excess not only of that in the preceding years in Florence, but in Rome of the same time. In Rome the first expressions of postclassical style within this phase seem only incidental to the late development of classicism and to the process — almost heroic — of its own dissolution; but in Florence it is the unclassical invention that takes on meaning much beyond that of its quantitative place. In Florence the invention of new style and the climactic expressions of the old seem, in historical perspective, events of equal scale.

FRA BARTOLOMMEO

Fra Bartolommeo had learned more, and more quickly, in Rome than the two pictures that he painted there — or rather did not quite finish painting — indicate. The almost inert image of *St. Paul* in the Vatican gives no hint of the vigor of the idea that preceded it. A study, probably the first *invenzione*, for the *St. Paul* exists in the Uffizi (1270E):[268] in it a massive silhouette, expansively powerful in rough-chalked pattern of drapery and contour, is projected slightly *sotto in su*; the monumental form emanates an energy that proceeds not just from its draughtsmanship but from the power of the image as idea. In spiritual stature and in physical impressiveness the figure of the drawing is not much less than the contemporary images of Raphael; and more than in Raphael of 1514 something is in it of the dimension of the Seers of Michelangelo. Nothing of this is translated into the painting: it is as if the enormity of this new Roman conception should have frightened its own author, or as if the monastic painter should have yielded to a now long discipline and considered that in art, as in life, the first impulse of expression should be chastened. On other occasions after this there would be a similar disparity between the power of a drawn idea and its tame reduction into painting, even when the transcribing hand is the Frate's own.

By Vasari's account, Rome was apparently as much inhibition as it was inspiration for Fra Bartolommeo. But, just after his return, he was more courageous than he had been in the *St. Paul* about allowing some measure of expression to the vital impulse of art he had acquired in Rome. Again in Florence, his first essay after his return must have been a private image of devotion, a fresco of the *Virgin and Child*, in half-length (Florence, Convent of S. Marco; documented July 15, 1514).[529] In this place, far removed from the possibility of Roman criticism, and removed even from the general public view, Bartolommeo made the first tentative application of his Roman lessons. Here, instead of the rather vacant inwardness of his earlier Madonnas, he has made this one intense in her relation with her Child. The two figures are rhythmically wound in an embrace that is physically convincing and emotionally meaningful; the full and sweeping movement of design conveys, in terms of form, the ardor and the richness of the figures' feeling. There is, in this small fresco, a gathered energy of form and an animate power of pathos that are too rare in the Frate's pre-Roman works.

A suggestion of resemblance, but not provable analogy, exists between this image and the Madonna and Child of Raphael's *Sedia*.[248] A possible inspiration of Raphael's design, or of some drawing preparatory to it, cannot be excluded. What is more important than any hypothetical resemblance in motive is the fair approximation by Fra Bartolommeo of the contemporary Raphael's resonant and movemented form, and the likeness in the power — though not in the specific temper — of the feeling. However, rather than any dependence on a precise current model by Raphael, the Frate, back in Florence, seemed rather to prefer to reconsider and, as it were, to modernize — almost as Raphael might now do himself — an accessible example of the earlier, Florentine, Raphael. Bartolommeo's fresco is the *Madonna of the Casa Tempi* remade in the contemporary vocabulary of classical style, as he understood it since his trip to Rome. This fresco served as an approximate model for at least three shortly subsequent frescoed Madonna compositions: one of them now in the same cell in S. Marco and two, in tondo form, in the Academy. In all of these the design is still more compact and richly movemented, and more active though not so genuine in spiritual pathos as in this one of the series that is nearest the experience of Rome.

A much more obvious response to Rome is in the gigantic *St. Mark Evangelist* (Florence, Pitti, from S. Marco; second half 1514).[530] Twice life-size, of the dimension of a fresco but in oils, it imitates the Seers of Michelangelo even in its scale. In 1514 the Sistine Ceiling was still a very new and utterly prodigious event of art; Bartolommeo's partial transcription of it in the *St. Mark* is the first attempted revelation of the prodigy to Florence. As much as it is possible to him the Frate makes a figure of Michelangelesque density and breadth, and inspires its mass with physical and psychic energy. He tries to recreate the force and the diversity of Michelangelesque contrapposto, and Michelangelo's resilient rhythmic differentiation. What is imitable of Michelangelo by intellectual comprehension has been imitated in the *St. Mark*, but what in Michelangelo depends on his spiritual and aesthetic quality is not there. If Michelangelo had a Francesco Penni in his studio to execute his Seers, they might have come to look like this; Bartolommeo has performed just such a dubious service for his chosen model. The *St. Mark* makes us realize, now, the justice of Michelangelo's dismissal, even when the Ceiling had only been begun, of his intended Florentine assistants.

It was inevitable that the Frate, with his acute limitations of anatomical science, should not possess the means to inspire this bodily structure with conviction, either of its movement or its mass. The drapery surfaces, more actively articulated than they were in Bartolommeo's style before, still seem vacant of a vital body. Even the enframing architecture seems inert; no tension exists, as in Michelangelo, between the body and its confining space. Somewhat paradoxically, a notion taken over from the style of Rome serves further to diminish the vitality of form: where, until toward 1514, an increasing activity of light had served to dramatize Bartolommeo's work, in the *St. Mark* — on Michelangelo's and also on Raphael's then current example — he much restrains the role of light, clarifying and diffusing it and using bland colors, fresco-like, of a higher key. The effect in the *St. Mark* of this abandonment of Leonardesque light in favor of a Roman mode is deadening; unlike the Roman models this work has no compensating depth or resonance of color. This higher-keyed and smoother-surfaced manner will persist in the Frate's works that follow.

The comparison that is disastrous to the Frate is of his own suggestion; if it were possible — as historically it is not — to consider the *St. Mark* for its own positive merits, and in the prospect only of the Frate's own career, it would assume a different value. It has the merit of its understanding of the basic problems of Michelangelo's developed Sistine style, even though Bartolommeo's powers of spirit and of hand could not give them similar solution. In this sense of comprehending Michelangelo's developed, though not his most radical, artistic thought Fra Bartolommeo is not less advanced than the contemporary Raphael; this comparison is again, unfortunately for the Frate, only quantitative.

The Frate's perception, in 1514, of the properties of Roman style that made it so seemingly superior to his own had been accurate. His art before his visit possessed the equivalent in formal grandeur, and in pathetic power of form, of that in the contemporary style of Rome, but almost nothing of Roman energies or passions; Roman painting had a variety of resources of pictorial structure and a dimension of dramatic content that no Florentine so far had explored. Much of this was, as we have seen in the *St. Mark*, learnable as principle. The Frate's willingness to learn was not an index of mere pliability, but of recognition of higher possibilities and purpose than his own. He accepted direction now as he had, not so long before, in the time of first maturing of his style, and from the same men.

Fra Bartolommeo's most ambitious essay in *Romanità* followed relatively shortly after his Roman visit: it is the monumental altar of the *Madonna della Misericordia* (Lucca, Pinacoteca; dated 1515).[532] Unlike the *St. Mark*, Bartolommeo is not here translating a Roman model into Florentine but, oppositely, adapting a Florentine precedent into Roman. There is no radical alteration, in this painting, of the Frate's customary structure for an altarpiece but rather an imposition on it of new energy of emotion and of form. It is not only the requirement of subject that has caused the Frate to populate the scene so densely, and with so conscious a variety of attitudes, sentiments, and types. The Florentine altar is compelled — as the altarpiece in Rome is not yet, at this date — to reshape itself on the model of the Roman dramatic fresco. The remembered source of inspiration is Raphael's Stanza d'Eliodoro; not anywhere literally imitated, though the groups of gesticulating spectators recollect both the *Bolsena* and *Expulsion.* It is rather the general temper of excitement of the frescoes and, at least in intention, their impulse of crowded, dramatizing movement that have been transposed here. In the outflung, turning, declamatory posture of the Virgin — so unlike her gentle antecedents in Bartolommeo's other altars — there is inspiration from Raphael's most energetic protagonists in the Eliodoro. The complexity and activity of the whole design is increased by its crowding and by its stressed rhythmical differentiation: there is an intended urgency of directed movement in the figures that is unprecedented in Fra Bartolommeo.

In all this energizing of the form, the clarity of basic structure, still like that of the precedent great *pale*, is by comparison not so instantly apparent. What is more clear, however, is the plastic definition of the elements within the scene; as in the *St. Mark*, the lighting and the handling have been altered toward the Roman manner. There is relatively little of the veiling chiaroscuro of Bartolommeo's earlier technique. The major figures are hard in surface and sharp-drawn, and color is untextural and matt. But rather than Roman in effect, this handling seems archaizingly Florentine. Comprehending the ideas, but unresponsive to the sensuous epidermis of the models of the Roman school, the Frate's surfaces in their new guise take on the look not of Raphael but of Ridolfo Ghirlandaio. This is not the only evidence of local accent: the tenor of emotion is not Roman, less indeed than had been the somewhat vacant majesty of the actors in Bartolommeo's prior works. Where new power of emotion is attempted, as in the expression of the Madonna, her pleading pathos is not grand or deep enough. Bartolommeo's higher stress of feeling is not of generalizing states of mind but — not inappropriately to this subject — of a common humanity's sentiments and sensations. In places, among the heads in the background, emotion touches on that region of unhandsome private ecstasy that we have seen in the young Pontormo's recent S. Ruffillo altar;[324] more often, Bartolommeo is content with a vivacity which, inadequately, resembles that in the contemporary paintings of Andrea. That he has observed Andrea's latest efforts is evident in the adaptation, in the mother and child at the lower right of the altarpiece, of the former's figures in the Annunziata fresco of the year before.

The *Madonna della Misericordia* does not quite fulfill the ambition of a style not only monumental, but dramatic, that the Frate had conceived for it. We have observed once before, in the case of the *St. Paul* of 1514, the disparity between initial conception in drawing and the painted work; the gap here is less but still measurable. The fragmentary preparatory study for the *Misericordia* (Uffize 475E)[531] has a power of movement of full forms and an immediacy of expressive pathos that are absent from the painting; the gathered force of the idea in the drawing has been dissipated in the finished work. The Frate deliberates too much, and in deliberating chastens, changes, and in part nullifies the dramatic value of his first idea. The alterations he makes in his pre-Roman style are not enough to accommodate it to the new end; Bartolommeo cannot sufficiently liberate himself from the conventions of mind and habits of hand that he had himself established for painting in the Florentine school. What he effects in the *Misericordia* altar is not a dialectic between the styles of Rome and Florence but a compromise, and there is unresolved conflict in it between the ideals of his preceding style and the notions he formulated of a new one: between restrained monumental gravity and dramatic activity of form; between containedness of content and immediate communication; between generalizing ideal distance and realizing nearness; and, in technical conception, between a chiaroscuro style and one based on plastic form. Bartolommeo's first thought, in the invention of the draughtsman, had a promise of the powers and virtues of the full maturity of Roman style; the second thought, as painter, inhibited and dulled them, and made confusions of stylistic purpose. On Bartolommeo's personality as a painter, that in which we see the final realization of the Roman experience, dramatic classicism was not a natural growth, as it had been for Raphael, but a graft.

Differently from Raphael in the nature of the process, but with a like result, the *Misericordia* altar evokes some of the internal disparities that at the same time occurred in Raphael's art in the course of his searching for new dimensions of expression for the mature classical style; this work also is a manifestation of crisis in the development of Fra Bartolommeo's classicism. Its disarticulate personality is the result not only of its disparities but of the uncertainty that is in it between past and present — and, by implication, future — of stylistic direction. In Florence, however, the significance of such a personal crisis of classical style is not what it is in the art of Rome. Fra Bartolommeo's art, though primary in influence in Florence was not, like Raphael's in Rome, almost autocratically exemplary. Further, the problem of intensification and change of expressive values in art was differently posed in Florence. The intimation of a solution had been made already, by the time of the *Misericordia* altar, in the work of the younger men, who proceeded less in the channel indicated by the Frate than by tangential routes, not so much confronting as skirting the problem of a new development for classicism. What happened in this altarpiece was in part the effect of the working, on the painter's concerns of this moment, of its scale and subject. No challenge — or provocation — quite like this was offered to the Frate again in his lifetime, yet the awareness of the problem that the *Misericordia* does not solve is in each major effort of the remaining years of his career.

The fresco *Annunciation* in the Convent of the Maddalena (Le Caldine; documented finished October 1515; heavily restored) [533] is conceived in the same mentality that determines the novelty of the *Misericordia* altar, but with none of the complex and partly contradictory ambitions its scale and subject matter stimulate. Here Fra Bartolommeo demonstrates the extent to which his ideas had grown, since before the Roman journey, in energy of form and communication: a dutifully traditional iconography and an accustomed formula of composition assume new force — or intend it; there is the inevitable constriction of the power of idea by the action of the painter's hand. Again the full meaning of the Frate's thought has not been carried over from the drawing (Uffizi 462 and 463E),[534] where the figures have a richly articulated density of form, and the sense of movement in its very process; and where the action and countenance of the Virgin wonderfully suggest — so unlike the painting — the strength, yet also the intimacy, of her feeling.

In another dated work of 1515, however, there are tendencies that at once confirm and contradict the major new impulses of Bartolommeo's post-Roman style. The small *Annunciation* (Paris, Louvre) [535] is exceptional to begin with in its singular iconographic form, combining narrative and altarpiece. The arrangement of the scene is wholly in the manner of an altarpiece, with a supporting architecture like that in the earlier grand *pale*, but in this case open to a landscape at the sides. The figures are traditionally symmetrically disposed, but not immobile; they are aware of and are psychologically, and to less degree physically, responsive to the narrative event: not as to an actual appearance but to its symbolic evocation. There is a muted quality of drama in the Virgin only; in the attendant saints there are rather varied kinds and depths of contemplative or devotional emotion, all genuine but not impulsive. Yet the figures seem to move; the movement is less in their own action than in the rhythmic thread that has been spun among their forms: not heavy and forced, as in the *Misericordia*, but quick and almost exquisitely light.

The figures are almost insubstantial, quite opposite those of the *Misericordia*. The plastic assertiveness of form in that altar has been abandoned for the moment, and in its place Bartolommeo has recalled his older chiaroscuro mode, but not as he had ever handled it before. This is not merely a chiaroscuro, in part constructive and in part dramatic in its purposes, like that in the great machines of 1512, but almost literally a *sfumato*. A flickering, soft, atmospheric light, filtered in from the adjacent landscape, pervades the picture; it plays through a thin and broken brushwork on figures and on the architecture, breaking up their surfaces and veiling substance. The drawing is quick, delicate, and pointed, accenting the seeming fragility of forms. So nearly evanescent, the figures are more easily caught up in the swift thread of whole compositional rhythm. The temper of the form is precisely that of the emotion of its human actors: gentle and withdrawn as the Frate's earlier actors had been, but unlike them in that these are articulate almost to febrility of their emotion.

This picture is in important respects the antithesis of the *Misericordia* altar. Where the *Misericordia* is declamatory, this is introverted in emotion and intimate; where the larger altar is aggressive in plasticity and in formal tone, this is exquisite and insubstantial. Yet, as much as the *Misericordia*, the *Annunciation* is distinct from the pre-Roman works of Fra Bartolommeo, and what is new in it depends also on the lesson first impressed on Bartolommeo in Rome, of a style more active in form and more complex and communicative in content. The means used in the two works toward this end are only in part the same — as in the rhythmical sequence, which animates both compositions; but there is less in the *Annunciation* of Roman import and more that exploits, and applies in a new way, ideas that belong to the Florentine tradition and to Bartolommeo's own previous history in it.

The lessening — in comparison with Fra Bartolommeo's own pre-Roman works — of architectonic rigidity in the *Annunciation* is in itself a concession to the general Florentine habit of interpreting classical modes of composition; the Frate's stringency of design had been exceptional in Florence rather than the rule. More faithfully here than in Bartolommeo's preceding pictures, the character of light evokes the unceasingly influential Florentine ideal of Leonardo: in contrast to the *Pitti Pala* [264] this reconstitutes a former unity of light, but in new fashion makes of it an agent that not only animates the form but subtly corrodes it. This near-fragility of form — its verging on a dissolution of attenuated shapes in light — is conspicuously un-Roman, and the degree to which this tendency has been developed here suggests analogy, surely unintended by Fra Bartolommeo and unimitative, with occurrences in the painting of the young incipient Mannerists. The intimacy of emotion is also a concession, from Bartolommeo's own prior standards, to Florentine personality. Like the incidents of it that are in the *Misericordia* altar, but here in the *Annunciation* pervasively, this temper of feeling, private and intense, at once goes back to an older time and resembles a most recent manifestation, in Andrea, in Pontormo, and in Rosso. The same generic impulse that inspired the change in style in the *Misericordia* altar, here exercised through alternate means, present in the Florentine repertory rather than derived from Rome, results in — almost literally — a dissolution of the classical image, and in a direction of style that accords with the first explorations toward Mannerism.

As the scale of the *Misericordia* has something to do with its conception, so also does the small size of the *Annunciation* altar, of the dimension of a modest easel picture, have something to do with its style. Its size cannot command a tendency that is not in the painter, but it can invite an intimacy of mood and delicacy of handling (entirely autograph in this work, as it is not in the large altars). Without the factor of its size it is doubtful that the Frate would ever have been inspired to investigate such a possibility of style as he has here. Some of its effects appear again, in ancillary ways, in subsequent and larger works, but he does not again pursue this line wholly, perhaps for the only fortuitous reason that he does not again have occasion to paint, with his own hand, a picture of similar internal scale. The model of style that he offers in the Louvre *Annunciation,* however, would seem particularly to have impressed young Domenico Puligo, but again only in pictures by him of small scale.

The *Annunciation* is our first encounter with a phenomenon of some interest in the history of the Florentine school of this phase: the increasingly evident emergence in certain artists of a manner in painting pictures of small scale that is different from their accustomed mode in larger works, not merely for understandable reasons of technique but for more compelling causes. The painter may regard the small-scale picture as a relief from the kinds of classicizing discipline he exercises in his large compositions — as an opportunity to paint in a more intimate and spontaneous way; it would seem that he may even seek a measure of contrast in his small works with his formal larger style. These excursions into a more libertarian and subjective manner in small scale reflect a tendency that also appears in this phase, though less frequently, in Roman art, there earliest and most evidently in the painting of Peruzzi. In Florence, where there is no significant practice of grotesque style, the distinguishable small-scale manner seems an equivalent outlet, on the periphery of classical style, for the painters' less classically restrained expression. In instances, as is true of Bartolommeo's *Annunciation,* the difference in the character of the small-scale work implies more than a distinction within personal manner; it implies a different tendency — but does not actually achieve a different kind — of historical style.

The paintings on small scale may preserve, much more nearly than the larger works, the qualities of form and personality that their author expresses in his drawings, but for a multiplicity of reasons they need not and, usually, do not reflect them wholly. Bartolommeo's *Annunciation* contains the *sfumature* of his later drawing style but not its more essential nature; that is of a freedom and inventive force that is not in any instance transcribed in the paintings. In this year after his return from Rome and in the next the Frate developed, in his drawings, a style possessed by movement: the intensity of energy in form is more than any in the art of Raphael, and is comparable only to the Michelangelesque; inspired in its temper by Michelangelo it is still, in Bartolommeo, not imitative. His technique in these latest drawings is impassioned: urgent, fluent, and richly differentiated in activity of line; and his former gentleness of chiaroscuro becomes a coruscating, roughly faceted vibration of the light. In some drawings figures may have an extraordinary density of substance, more plastically compact even than in Michelangelo; in others plasticity of form is fractured and consumed by light. Each form, regardless of its posture or its function, is a vehicle of action, in instances powerfully self-motivated, in others only caught up in the draughtsman's impulse of dynamic flux. In his inmost nature, confided only to these drawings, and among them wholly only in his uninhibited and unreformed first statements of *invenzioni,* the Frate not only understands the direction of style of contemporary Rome but gives it a dimension of expression for which there is no equivalent in Rome itself, save for some exceptional ideas of Michelangelo's. The gravely impressive formal pathos that Fra Bartolommeo had achieved before becomes, in such drawings, an inspired pathos of movemented form, so urgent that it strains against — but does not trespass — the limits of a classical constraint.

Had the late paintings been executed in the vein of these drawings the result would have been the creation of a style in Florentine painting like that which Raphael's *Transfiguration* in part intended but, within its own unresolved disparity of ambitions, did not achieve; or more like that which Titian did achieve in the Frari *Assunta* of this same time, implying the possibility of a baroque, but not willing it: a classicism so vitally resynthesized as to give the style another generation's life. But this was a consequence the Frate was not ready to express in painting; in the paintings the passion of his late inventions was tempered, diminished, and finally vitiated to the standard of his own prior published example. The vigor and originality of the drawings grow, but that of the paintings actually lessens in Bartolommeo's last two years. As the first impact of Rome recedes from him Bartolommeo recedes also from his most courageous demonstration of its effects, in the *Misericordia* altar of 1515.

There is, indeed, an apparently willed suppression in the painted works of 1516 of the energies that had been permitted some expression in the *Misericordia,* and that were increasingly manifested in the drawings. There are no drawings in the Frate's *oeuvre* more dynamically charged than those among the *invenzioni* (Uffizi, British Museum) for the *Salvator Mundi* (Florence, Pitti; dated 1516),[536] and no painting by him that is more consciously classically disciplined. The lesser complexity of subject than in the *Misericordia* had not influenced the drawings for the *Salvator* toward a lesser variety of form or power of dramatic action, but in the painting the restriction of the subject matter has deliberately been made evident, asserted in its simplicity. The design admits only the essential forms; there is no dispensable elment except, perhaps, for the angel-putti who alone retain, but in much diminished key, some trace of the energy of pose that had been intended in Bartolommeo's first thoughts for the Evangelists.[537-8] These latter stand, compact in shape and ponderous, like columns on a square ground-plan around the pedestal of Christ. His posture resembles that of the *Mater Misericordiae,* but so adjusted by discreet changes in the head and hands that it is self-contained, and no longer outflung and declamatory. The accent of the Eliodoro style that had been in the *Mater Misericordiae* is replaced in Christ by a suspended gravity which, in fact, is more like that of Fra Bartolommeo's ultimate model for this pose, in Raphael's *Sistina*.[235]

His chastened movement, here properly that of an *epiphaneia*, is framed and contained by the architecture. His divine apparition is distinguished ideally by larger scale than that of the Evangelists, and he is exempt from the operation of perspective law that fixes them, on this stage-like platform, in slight *sotto in su* — appropriate to the point of view from which, intendedly, we see the picture. The architecture is of an unusual severity even for Fra Bartolommeo; it does not emphasize the curve of space, as in the earlier altars, but its planarity and its decisiveness of limits. Except in the form of Christ, and there in moderation, Bartolommeo's customary cursive and chiaroscuro modulation of design is almost thoroughly suppressed. The composition is conceived in elevation and in plan as if on a grid, with an almost doctrinaire rectilinearity. It is of an utmost willed simplicity, nearly graceless and as explicit in its clarity as the Frate's deliberation can achieve: the painting is the antithesis of the near-baroque conception of the drawings.

Such a happening is not merely a concession, in Bartolommeo's public form of art, to customary taste, to habit or to the authority of his own classical precedent, though there is something in it of all of these. More positively, this stilling of the first dynamic invention into rigorous classical form is a purposeful expression, in which the classicism of the picture's style is preferred because it is the higher aesthetic, and also ethic, value. There is an analogy in the *Salvator* altar to the occurrence, just previous to this but not known to Fra Bartolommeo, of the ultimate classical style of Raphael in the Tapestry Cartoons. In Raphael, too, an intensification of expressive urgency, a stage beyond that of the Eliodoro style — from which the Frate had departed in the energizing of his art — encouraged experiment, as in the *Ostia*, with more active and unconventional formal means. At the same time this urgency could be turned to the account of a yet higher exaltation of classical values, in clearer discipline of stronger contents, and in a system of controlling form as much more rigorous as its contents were intense. There is a similar transmutation in the *Salvator* altar of higher passion into disciplines, and a similar achievement in its basic facts of form and content, but not in quality, to Raphael's highest classical style. In Bartolommeo the power of the first conception does not sufficiently survive the process of its transmutation, and the final image, for all its austere impressiveness, has his too frequent mark of blandness and of a grandeur that is slightly vacant. We have said that the Frate is his own *Fattore*; the analogy of the *Salvator* altar to the style of the Tapestry Cartoons may be made yet more precise: it is to those vitiations of Raphael's idea accomplished by Penni in the Cartoons given him for execution.

As in the style of the Tapestry Cartoons, the assertion in the *Salvator* altar of geometric clarity of parts of structure gives its composition something of an additive effect; and more than with this similar circumstance in Raphael, in Bartolommeo it is recollective of an older mode. The reason for this is the rectilinear and grid-like basis of the composition, suggestive of the early classical tradition of Piero della Francesca and of Perugino in which, in his beginnings, the style of the Frate had been formed. A smaller altar of contemporary date, the *Presentation in the Temple* (Vienna, Kunsthistorisches Museum; dated 1516; entirely by Bartolommeo's hand),[539] still more suggests the character of structure of a Perugino, almost as if with conscious archaizing intent. However, its order is not truly additive; this distinctness in the setting out of stilled, columnar forms is an opposite process to that in Perugino: as also in the Tapestry Cartoons this effect results from the separation into clear identity of parts within a unified design; the eye feels, within this deceptive simplicity of pattern, the quiet and considered pressures which, as it were, hold the forms apart. The place in space of each form, as well as in the dominating planar composition, is defined with an extreme consciousness, not only of identity of shapes but of their whole relation. This picture is no archaism, but a demonstration, more obvious and also more extreme than in the Tapestry Cartoons, of a problem peculiar to the apogee of classical style. It is the product of an ultimate deliberation even in its air of great simplicity. Nor is the human content, despite its apparent conventionality, any less carefully meditated.

It is again parallel to the contemporary case of Raphael — always, in the Frate's much diminished key — that this most chastened classicism that is manifested in the *Salvator* and in the *Presentation* is one aspect only of his late development. Like Raphael, though much more tentatively, Bartolommeo also explores — perhaps in part concurrently with this rigorous classical expression, but mostly just afterwards — a more active mode, in which something is allowed to penetrate into the paintings, though palely, of the energy of his first conceptions in drawing. Also in 1516, but later than the *Salvator* altar, Bartolommeo painted two panels, of the Prophets *Isaiah* and *Job* (Florence, Academy),[540-41] similar in scale to the figures in the altar, which were placed as flanking pieces for it in its chapel in SS. Annunziata. In these he takes up his own obvious precedent of the *St. Mark*, but with a lessened force than in it of the memory of Michelangelo. The two Prophets act in much the same way as the *Mark*, but less vigorously; their conception as plastic images of movement has not been quite extinguished, but softened and chastened much in the temper of the figure in the altar of the Christ. They are appendages to the composition of the altarpiece and are intelligently related with it; read with the altar their movement carries over rhythmically to the form of Christ. They are not, however, integral to its separate, and basically different, static conception of design.

Close to the time of his painting of the Annunziata *Prophets* Bartolommeo invented designs in drawing (Munich 2158–2159)[543] for an *Assunta* for S. M. in Castello, Prato (Naples, Galleria Nazionale).[542] He did not himself make the subsequent preparatory drawings but assigned the task of development — and inevitable chastening — of his inspired first idea to his principal assistant, Fra Paolino (Berenson). The execution of the picture was also left largely if not wholly to him. The conception in the drawings is perhaps the most daring in Bartolommeo's career; it is possessed by energies, freely and brilliantly expressed, that verge far more toward a baroque than in Titian's contemporary altarpiece; the idea and the form given it remarkably anticipate the most advanced Correggio. Whatever brake Bartolommeo intended should be placed on this power of activity in the final work, it was not in the form of such a stiffened and insipid caricature as Paolino made. The picture is of interest only historically, in that it documents what is not merely the readmission by the Frate of a movemented style like that in his works of 1515, but a new admission into the actual paintings of some at least of the now still more advanced ideas of movement of design that he explores in drawing.

Something of this more impulsive temper is allowed to manifest itself, though with discretion, even in the late Madonna paintings that emerge in 1516 from the Frate's shop which, like that of Raphael in Rome, was a favorite manufactory of superior devotional images. Two of these Madonna compositions — varieties, actually, of Holy Families — are signed and dated 1516: one in the Galleria Nazionale, Rome,[544] and another formerly in the Cook Collection (now London, Kenwood, Iveagh Bequest).[545] Both are painted from the same cartoon, reversed, and with the substitution in the latter picture of Elizabeth for Joseph. This cartoon served again with other variations, once in the Pitti with both an Elizabeth and a Joseph, and again in the National Gallery in London with neither. The invention once made, small effort was expended on its subsequent revision; the making of such smaller devotional pictures seems to have been considered by the Frate at this time more in the light of industry than of art. Among these pictures that in Rome is probably the first of the series. It is distinguished from earlier compositions of like theme by the activity of its design: by the energy of movement of the Holy Infants and the tensile posture of the Virgin. These impulses of movement are arranged according to a pattern familiar to us in the exactly current work of Raphael in Rome, in an asymmetrical balance of intersecting diagonals. Their energies are controlled by gathering of the picture's forms into a triangular pattern of almost doctrinaire insistence in its clarity of shape. Bartolommeo's mode of management of form and movement is once more, in these Madonna pictures, analogous to a mode in the contemporary Raphael; this picture is in fact a "modernization," with means of which Raphael himself might have approved, of elements from Raphael's early altar of the Casa Canigiani.

There is no failing of inventive power in the latest years of Bartolommeo's career, but there is an increasing lassitude of hand, occasioned almost certainly by the illness that overtook him and contributed to his early death, at forty-two years of age, in October 1517. Of the larger paintings begun probably in 1516 the *Pietà* (Florence, Pitti)[546] could only be sketched by him on the panel; left unfinished at his death, the entire execution was given over to Bugiardini. Bugiardini's surfaces are wooden to a degree that would have been intolerable to Bartolommeo; his drawing weakens and deforms the master's sketch, and his rendering of expression is at once forced and empty. Yet the power of invention is apparent even through this surface. The mode of composition is, with appropriate differences, like that of the Madonna series of 1516; and as in them there is, in this design, an element of Raphaelesque reminiscence, of the early predella composition now in the Gardner Museum. The resemblance must once have been stronger, for in its initial conception the *Pietà* was accompanied by flanking standing figures of Saints Paul and Peter, perhaps (as is the case with the Prophets of the *Salvator Mundi*) in separate frames. More than in the contemporary Madonna pictures, the design in the *Pietà* is constrained: overlaid with grave, full, curves, which are held within an asymmetrical triangular shape. The figures of Mary, the Christ, and John are interwoven in a rhythm which, in its temper, comments their emotion: a pathos that is deep and tender, yet measured like a tragic music. The Magdalen, however, is almost isolated in her different, literally prostrate grief. Her power of meaning is not only in her poignant act but in the visual impact of her separate, humbled shape; and the Frate exercises a beautiful discretion in the way in which he lets these sufficient factors work, and half-hides the figure's stricken face.

Bartolommeo's last work, the fresco *Noli me Tangere* (dated 1517; partly ruined),[547] in a garden chapel of the Convent of the Maddalena at Le Caldine (to which he had retired in his illness), is of his own execution but by a hand now visibly grown unsure: in places labored, and in others careless of its draughtsmanship. But there is in it, more freely than in any preceding painted work, an admission of the idea that a picture might be permitted to consist dominantly of movement: here — encouraged partly by the pretext in the subject matter — of impulsive postures, and of a composition unimpeded in its diagonal and turning sweep. This fresco was the weakest in its execution and the boldest in idea of Fra Bartolommeo's late paintings. It had no sequel.

FRA PAOLINO

No member of the shop of S. Marco in these later years was competent to carry on the directions of development initiated by its master. Indeed, Bartolommeo's admission of his own inventions into his painted work had been too cautious to encourage any tendency to new ideas among his helpers. Bartolommeo had been, in a sense, his own agent in the academicizing of his classical style; his entourage not only academicized but petrified it. The chief among them, Fra Paolino da Pistoia, hardly can lay claim to the stature of creative artist. He was so acquiescent an assistant during his long term of labor with the Frate and Albertinelli that, for years after Bartolommeo's death, he was incapable of personal invention or even of individuality of hand. In addition to the deformations by Paolino, as executant, of Bartolommeo's designs (as in the *Assunta* for S. M. in Castello),[542] he was permitted even during the master's lifetime to practice independently; but this opportunity never seems to have stimulated Paolino's inertia of mind.

Three works by Paolino within this phase may serve as indications of his practice, relevant to our historical view in that it represents — and by no means at its lowest level — a fairly widespread phenomenon in the Florentine school, of devaluation of Bartolommeo's style into a popular banal religious art: a respectable *bondieuserie.* Paolino's fresco *Crucifixion* (Siena, Sto. Spirito; dated 1516)[548] frankly derives in composition, not from Bartolommeo, but from Albertinelli's fresco of 1505 in the Florentine Certosa. This old-fashioned model has been revised toward Bartolommeo's more modern example: its scale of forms has been increased, and its design made smoother, more rhythmically coherent, and more dense; and the specific vocabulary of form has been, woodenly, translated into the Bartolommesque. A *Holy Family with St. John and Angels* (Rome, Galleria Doria),[549] from the same year or shortly later, is not more inventive than the *Crucifixion.* Its sources are, again, in an older Albertinelli (the angels, from the *Annunciation* of 1510),[259] and perhaps as well in more recent examples of the Frate's (the Holy Family series of 1516); but mostly, Paolino has relied upon an old design of the Florentine Raphael (which was also worked up into painting at about this time, by Penni probably; Vienna, Kunsthistorisches Museum). All these sources have been calcified by Paolino; yet his picture has, perversely, the charm of awkwardness — though this is the last climate in which one would expect to find the value of the primitive in art.

Paolino is more at home, and more nearly conventionally successful, when he follows his master literally, and this, with the store of Bartolommeo's drawings preserved in the shop in S. Marco, he was able to do even after the master's death. The *Pietà* (Museo di S. Marco; documented 1519; formerly in the Academy and once at Le Caldine)[550] is after a design by the Frate preserved among the Weimar sketchbooks. Related to the Pitti version of the theme, this design is, however, more conventional and thus better accommodated to Paolino's temperamental needs. His execution is still weak, but since Bartolommeo's death it has become in slight degree more identifiably personal: as schematic in drawing and as hard in surface as before, but more rhythmically fragmented. As Paolino continues in independent practice both his hardness and his fussiness increase, but the substantial matter of his style — a stock of Bartolommesque types and compositions, and a timid simile of Bartolommeo's content — remains unchanged. In Paolino's art the ghost of Fra Bartolommeo haunts Florence, but more especially the provincial towns of Tuscany, for a decade after his decease.

ANDREA DEL SARTO

With the frescoes of the atrium of the Annunziata, in which Andrea del Sarto had already taken so conspicuous a part, the small courtyard of the Confraternity of the Scalzo was to be the principal decorative project of the time of dominance of the classical style in Florence. This project, illustrating the life of St. John Baptist (now much damaged), was essentially Andrea's own. He seems to have been the planner of its ordnance in general and was designer and, entirely personally, the executant of all but two of its sixteen grisaille frescoes; assistants helped him only in the painting of the frames and ornament. The two exceptions among the major frescoes are by Franciabigio, done by him in 1518 during Andrea's residence in France, at a time when it appeared to Andrea's patrons that his stay might be indefinite, and that the completion of the project should be confided to another man. Andrea's first fresco in the Scalzo courtyard, the *Baptism of Christ,*[298] had been painted in 1510; he returned to paint there intermittently until the decoration was complete in 1526.

Andrea's first intervention in the Scalzo since his early *Baptism* was in 1515, after he had done the *Birth of the Virgin* in the Annunziata. In this year he painted three further frescoes on the same wall as the *Baptism* (opposite the entrance to the courtyard), completing this wall: one of the same dimension as the *Baptism of Christ,* the *Preaching of St. John Baptist* (paid for November 1, 1515)[552] and two of narrower format, a *Justice* (paid for on the same day)[553] and a *Charity.*[554] On October 30, 1516 the decorative framing of the frescoes on this wall was paid for. The general plan of decoration may have been evolved at the time of Andrea's first fresco, but it need not have been fixed and certainly was not specified in its architectural or ornamental detail until 1515. In subject matter, the plan was simply to illustrate the life of the Baptist in counterclockwise order around the court, with the beginning and end of the sequence at the entrance door. In addition, the entrance and the exit doors, facing each other across the court on its shorter sides, were to be framed each by two Virtues: at the entrance *Faith* and *Hope,* and at the exit *Justice* and *Charity.*

All the frescoes, roughly two-thirds life in scale, are projected in a painted architecture,[551] the flat surfaces of which are ornamented with simulated carving in grisaille, mostly of grotesque design. The system of architecture painted on the walls is a counterimage of the actual architecture of the *cortile.* In the lunette-spaces on the wall the painted entablature is surmounted by a fictive balustrade, heavily "carved" with swags and heads of cherubim. Mortuary symbols — urns and death's-heads — surmount the balustrade, across the top of which we see into a painted open sky. Other death's-heads are set out, illusionistically, along the shelf formed by the top of the entablature.

The grotesque decoration of the frieze is similarly serious: it consists of a repeated motive of the Veronica Veil surmounted by a Cross, framed by angelic and cherubic forms whose wings or bodies are transmuted into ornament. Below the frescoes a painted wainscot, with a design of strap-work, provides a continuous basis, like a stage platform, for the depicted scenes.

Andrea's scheme of architectural framing is not different from that used for fresco decorations in the later Quattrocento, in particular in the school of Ghirlandaio to which Andrea makes, in other respects also, such frequent reference; nor is it a new idea that he constructs a believable fictitious architecture, which extends and elaborates the existing one. Such a notion had been frequent in the Quattrocento, and one Florentine example in particular was of relatively recent memory, Filippino Lippi's Strozzi Chapel in S. M. Novella, finished only in 1502. Nevertheless, the effect of Andrea's scheme of painted architecture is unequivocally distinct from its precedents. These do not have so continent a harmony among the painted architectural forms, or so natural-seeming a concordance with the actual architecture. More than in any Quattrocento type, Andrea's painted structure seems more functionally and illusionistically believable — more natural — and higher in the unity of effect it makes between its fiction and the actuality. In part from its internal character of harmony, but also from this seeming naturalness, Andrea's structure does not, like most Quattrocento systems of illusion, insistently assert its illusion to the eye: more natural, it brings unforced acceptance; as illusion it is at once realistically more true and aesthetically more discreet. It creates an ambience which, more convincingly than in any past Florentine or contemporary Roman example, is like that of a continuous stage on which the episodes of drama are to be enacted.

An internally consistent perspective is used, within the scenes, to extend the space implied by the painted proscenium-like enframements, and in instances the result is remarkably that of a projection as if through a nonexistent wall. However, here, too, there is deliberate restraint on the assertion of illusion. As is Raphael's custom also, the perspective is calculated in nice compromise between effects of plausibility on the spectator and the internal spatial order of the scene itself, so that what is seen is believable, but no counterfeit in viewpoint of the actuality of a stage. Finally, the grisaille technique seems, like a veil, to moderate illusion; it is constantly — and like the tonality itself, unobtrusively — present in our mind that what we see evokes, but does not wholly physically relive, the drama of St. John.

The reasons for adoption of a grisaille technique are not now clear but they are unlikely to have been economic; the sums received by Andrea for his paintings in this place are in proportion, considering their size, to those received by him for fresco works in color. It is more probable that the grounds for this exceptional decision lay in the penitential nature of the Confraternity of the Scalzo and in their concept — or perhaps Andrea's — of an appropriate, even funereal, decorum in tonality of decoration; and it may also have been prompted by consideration of the small scale of the place, in which color might have made, at once, too much commotion and too pressing an effect of illusion. In any case, the decoration required the renunciation by Andrea of his resources, unique to him in Florence at this time, of color, and his dependence instead, surely not reluctantly, on his still more remarkable and more peculiarly Florentine talents as a draughtsman. The decoration was to become, in much more than the limited meaning of the word, the monument of Florentine *disegno.* It would also be the one complete work of decoration in Florence in the classical style that could be offered for comparison to the multiple, rich, and diverse decorative schemes of High Renaissance Rome.

In the course of Andrea's long execution of the frescoes of the Scalzo, no distinction in style would again be so marked as that between his first venture, the *Baptism of Christ,* and his three works of 1515; for these contain the experience of the intervening years that had led him to personal maturity and to maturity in his classical style. Like the early *Baptism,* but like the recent *Birth of the Virgin* also, the largest fresco of the three of 1515, the *Preaching of St. John,* is at the same time a reference to, and a critique of, a model of the Quattrocento style. Again the reference is to the inescapable precedent of Ghirlandaio; Andrea seems to have regarded the decorations of S. M. Novella as a treasury of ideas and motives on which he could freely draw. The composition follows Ghirlandaio's fairly literally in its components, but condenses it — not only for reasons of a different format — into an immediately apparent unity and order; an additive dispersion of forms and content in the Ghirlandaio becomes, in Andrea, a synthetic concentration. But beyond this, Andrea here makes evident to what degree the mature classical style depends not only on coherence in design but also on an optical and psychological unity in the painter's method of perception: on his differentiation of form within the image out of an including texture of its light and space — in this case, by means of a still Leonardesque chiaroscuro. There is in fact some resemblance in Andrea's fresco to the first demonstration of a classical image in Leonardo's *Adoration of the Magi,*[3] in compositional scheme and in certain motives, as well as in the light; and the resemblance may not be fortuitous. Doctrinaire expositions are not in Andrea's vein, but his *Preaching* seems almost like a demonstration of the new style's contrast with the old.

In his explicitness of classical intention in the *Preaching* Andrea seems to have returned, more rigorously than in the *Birth of the Virgin,* to classical first principles. The deliberated symmetry of this design is, on one hand, more apparently conservative than the freer structure of the Annunziata fresco, but at the same time this intention of a reasserted clarity of order is not unlike the impulse which, in Raphael, in the year or two before, had first prompted his investigation (as in the *Liberation of Peter*) of the possibilities of strict designs, and then, in the moment contemporary with the *Preaching*, had culminated in the austere style of the Tapestry Cartoons. Andrea has the sense of order, but not the severity of temper of the contemporary Raphael; there is no Raphaelesque urgency of discipline in Andrea's fresco. On the contrary, its mood is gentle, yielding, and sympathetic; there is no need of exhortation by the Baptist to this audience. As in the *Birth of the Virgin*,[311] we are in the presence of beings who are only in slight degree a bettered version of ourselves. These persons are plausible inhabitants with us of an unexalted world; intimately moved in their emotion but not impassioned. Into their number, further evidencing an interest that had begun in the *Birth of the Virgin*, Andrea has introduced three motives adapted, for their illustrative interest but not for any interest of style, from prints by Dürer.

In the smaller niche-like space to the right of the *Preaching*, the single figure of the Virtue of *Justice* evokes, despite grave damage, the most impressive of the personages of the *Birth of the Virgin*. The *Justice* displays an amplitude and gravity, and a measured contrapposto, like that of the central figure in that fresco. The resemblance in posture between these figures is such as to suggest that both not only derive from a common principle of style but relate to a common model, which is more identifiably reflected in the *Justice*. It has long been known that her pose depends on the statue of the same Virtue by Andrea Sansovino, on the tomb of Ascanio Sforza (1504) in S. M. del Popolo in Rome; with this Andrea was acquainted, if not directly, then most probably by means of a *modello*, which his good friend Jacopo Sansovino might have owned. The inspiration of the statue in the painting is apparent not only in its motive of pose and in passages of drapery but in the accent in the painting which suggests, but does not quite achieve, an Antique classicism. The changes worked on Sansovino's model are quantitatively rather slight, but of great qualitative meaning; they serve to underline strongly the distance, chronologically relatively brief but stylistically vast, that intervenes between the two works. An accident of iconography provokes comparison, still more useful to us, between the painting of the *Justice* and Bartolommeo's *St. Paul*,[266] done in Rome in the preceding year. Andrea's figure is, in general, indistinguishable in the kind and measure of its classicism from that of the Frate; but, beyond the generality, there is in Andrea's painting the quality that is not in Bartolommeo's, but which was in Bartolommeo's drawing (Uffizi): the evidence of energies of form and state of mind that charge the repose of the massive presence.

From the *Caritas*, much better in its state of preservation than the *Justice*, it is more clearly legible that the figures of the Virtues were conceived with a different intention of illusion than the narrative scenes. These grisaille figures, larger in scale than those in the narratives, and contained within a constricted niche-like space, are meant as simulacra of statuary. In the *Caritas* there is still visible, precisely, an effect of smoothed and whitened surface meant to suggest the nature of a statue. There are frequent analogues, both in contemporary Rome and in Florence before this time, for this idea. One of them contains, as well, the particular theme of the *Caritas,* in a guise sufficiently related to Andrea's version to have been relevant to its invention: this is in the decoration, already noted among the antecedents of the Scalzo, by Filippino in S. M. Novella. The relation is only of motive and arrangement; there is no common ground here, as there is for the *Justice* and its precedent, which might permit comparison of style.

Like the *Justice,* to which the *Caritas* is counterpart in place and pose, this figure is interchangeable with the women of the *Birth of the Virgin;* she is like a translation of one of them into classicizing *déshabille.* As rounded and as suavely full in form as they, the *Caritas* conveys — despite the implication that she is a statue — a yet more intimate and sensuous loveliness in her *déshabille,* and in the quality of expression that her role calls forth. Her infants are the same lively, restless creatures who, in the *Birth of the Virgin,* make improbable statuary ornaments for the fireplace; they are affixed to the *Caritas* like limpets and communicate their weights and action to her form. Answering their pressures, her ponderation becomes flexible, a resilient adjustment of her body into gently arching, incipiently turning movement. Into the slower pattern of her pose the infants weave a secondary, more energetic, rhythmic line, expressive of their own quicker, lighter, childish impulse. The group, as close-textured in substance and in rhythmic organization as any image of the contemporary Roman school, condenses in one equilibrium, and concentrates in their effect, the powers that are diffused through the larger compass of the *Birth of the Virgin.* In this concentration, the energies that possess the form emerge yet more evidently, and the intensity of psychological life becomes more pointed still.

For what must have been a relatively short but frantic while in the early autumn of 1515, the services of almost every competent painter in Florence were enlisted in the preparation of a festival decoration for the ceremonial entry into the city of Pope Leo X, on November 30. Vasari speaks in several places (V, 24–25, etc.) of this unfortunately ephemeral decoration; had more evidence of its appearance survived it would have given precious testimony to the collective situation of art in Florence at this moment. Andrea's part in this effort was the painting "in diverse storie di chiaroscuro" (Vasari, *ibid.*) of a wooden false façade erected on the Duomo by Jacopo Sansovino. Of all the paintings done for this event, the only sure surviving pieces are three of the chiaroscuri by Andrea from this false façade, and a fourth companion painting of which the author is Jacopo Pontormo (all Florence, Uffizi; held in the Gabinetto dei Disegni).[555-7] Of long and narrow format, each of Andrea's canvases depicts an unidentifiable classical subject: in the largest of them two female nudes recline in company with two putti, who hold pieces of armor; in a second a warrior in Ancient costume and a nude man are disposed before more trophies; in the third are three nude faun-like musicians. The symbolism seems indefinite and rather casual, and only one detail may be construed to indicate that this work celebrates, precisely, a Medicean occasion: the crowns of laurel that the figures wear, in reference to the leaves of the Medici *Broncone.*

As an even approximate exercise of classical allegory these paintings would not satisfy the most relaxed Roman standard; only their nudity and their summary accessories testify that they are meant to represent an Ancient world. The conception of an archaeological recreation of Antiquity, by now so thoroughly developed in the Roman school, had no currency at all in Florence, even at this date in the history of the classical style. Andrea's view of Antiquity seems as little, or less, controlled by reference to the grammar of a visual humanism than was Piero di Cosimo's, and — to judge by these insufficient yet unique examples in the whole of Andrea's art — are not even so precisely illustrative of an Antique matter in a literary sense. For Andrea — as it had been sometimes for the artists of the later Quattrocento — the Antique subject is an invitation to express a playful and engaging mood. These panels have a quick and lively, but also virile, informality of drawing and a sketch-like roughness in their setting down of forms. A swift-accented energy of arabesque-like sequence, almost careless of any meditated order, makes their compositions. As in the *Caritas* there is a diverse and pungent life of psychological expression; it is as if the temper of the *Caritas* and her infants had been lightened and made altogether unserious, and diffused in charm into these canvases.

The so-called *Holy Family with St. Catherine* (Leningrad, Hermitage; 1515 or early 1516; a replica by Puligo in London, a copy from Andrea's school in Windsor)[558] is intimately related to the Scalzo works of 1515. The head of the Madonna almost duplicates that of the second woman from the left in St. John's audience in the *Preaching*, and the children are close kin to those in the *Caritas.* As an invention of design this picture, like the *Preaching*, has an air of conservatism, but the first appearance of simplicity is specious. What seems to be an almost archaizing lateral, nearly isocephalic, order of the three adult figures is actually a subtle disposition of them, in a shallow arc of which the chord is laid diagonally in space. This spatial order concords exactly with the motive of design on the surface: a counterclockwise arc, which binds, irresistibly, the outer contours of the figure group, and of which the diagonal chord ascends from left to right. The scheme is not — as its description might suggest — a coincidence of separately conceived ideas of surface and of spatial order; no motive of organization on the surface is meant to work separately from its function in the ordering of space. The pattern made upon the surface and that made of substance are not only interlocked and concordant; they are, in their essential conception, one. In profoundly classical way, design is thought of from the beginning as a simultaneous manipulation of form in all dimensions, in a single process and with one effect.

In Andrea, as is not usual among the Florentines, this process of manipulation includes a role for color as an inherent property of form, not as an afterthought. In this picture color (assessed here from the accessible copy in Windsor) serves not only to articulate the spatial factor in design but to compensate the asymmetry of form in space back toward a coherent unity of surface — as if to reestablish the aesthetic, but not the representational, illusion of a classicizing integrity of the picture plane. As the figures are set deeper in the space color in them becomes more luminous (as in the different depths of violet in the garments of Mary and Elizabeth, or in the flesh tones of the Christ and John), or an assertive color is introduced, as in the vermilion and yellow-gold of Catherine. In terms of color Catherine's shape is projected toward the foremost plane; it becomes equivalent in aesthetic effect of near place in space and, thus, in the picture's surface pattern, to the mantle of Elizabeth. By a principle present within the *Birth of the Virgin*, but not so important in its diffused form, Andrea here achieves what is more than a color harmony; it is a use of color that promotes, beyond harmony, an integrity of the design.

Beneath its novel handling of structure — and more obvious than it — is the evident relation of this composition to ideas remembered still from Leonardo, and to Fra Bartolommeo's notions of a spheroid system of design. But there may also be a newer and a less expected relation of Andrea's composition to a foreign source: it may owe part of its particular form to a work of Raphael apparently recently arrived in Florence, the *Madonna dell' Impannata* of 1514,[240] painted for Bindo Altoviti, which, says Vasari (IV, 351) "egli mandò a Fiorenza." The similarity in the two designs of a whole enclosing rounded shape traversed by a diagonal suggests a starting point for Andrea in Raphael's invention, and there are possible communities in type in the Elizabeth, and in the roles taken by the Christ Child and the young St. John. The example of the *Impannata* probably supplied a compositional type that was by no means literally transcribed by Andrea, but still was new to his experience, and to that of Florence generally. Also in Raphael's painting Andrea might have found confirmation for a tendency he had often manifested in his work, of intensifying its activity of form and content. The kind of animation within a classically integrated structure that Andrea makes in the Leningrad *Holy Family* is only seemingly less than in the *Impannata* because it is more subtly given us. What Raphael asserts more evidently of an animating will by energies of bodily action and of plastic form, Andrea communicates instead by less forceful, but ultimately not less complex or intense, means of line, light, and color.

There is an almost febrile energy of drawing in Andrea's picture; broken, various, and intimate in its description of the rhythmical activity of forms, but even this excitement of draughtsmanship is not a primary factor in the picture's style. The character of drawing is dependent on and determined by the character of light, so subtly complicated and so alive as in no Florentine painting since Leonardo. The light is more shaded and crepuscular and, at the same time, more vibrantly differentiated than in Leonardo; it is more responsive to an actual — though singular — effect of nature, and less intellectually controlled. There is a muted excitement, or even excitability, at once sharp and exquisite, in this recreation of an optical experience.

This physical atmosphere of the picture is also its atmosphere of emotion, in which Andrea transcribes — with a sensibility that again recalls Leonardo, but which is more dispersed, and varied in accent — feelings that range from the shaded, subtlest tenderness of the Madonna to the inspiration, by no means a childish joy, of the Christ Child. All these states of mind are intimately felt and characterized, as they were in Leonardo, but there is then no subsequent imposition on them, as in Leonardo, of a measure of reserve. These sensations are meant to be shared by us immediately and entirely, with the effect more nearly of our identification with the actors than of our contemplation of them. The tone of the emotion is, basically, like the gently vibrant harmony of feeling that is common to devotional pictures in the classical style, but the acuity and range of psychological effects are unaccustomed, as is also the specific character of feeling — an ecstatic possession — in the children. The intimacy of sensation is such that it abolishes almost all the customary classicizing sense of distance. This picture brings into narrower focus the temper of emotion that had been diffused within the *Birth of the Virgin,* and at the same time refines it more precisely; and in particular it refines that quality of pathetic excitement which had been in the *Caritas* or the Dresden altar, among others, but of which the promise was explicit even in Andrea's first surviving work, the small *Pietà* of the Borghese.

The same theme of the *Pietà* seems to have served Andrea again as a major vehicle, in 1515–1516, of this mature development of a pathetic sensibility. The picture, commissioned by the Florentine merchant G. B. Puccini for export to France, has been lost, but its design survives in an engraving by A. Veneziano (dated 1516),[559] so little successful that (according to Vasari, V, 23) Andrea wished never again to have a picture of his engraved. Andrea's composition seems itself to have been inspired in part by prints: both the central motive of the Christ and the play made in the design by angels' wings derive from Dürer's woodcut *Trinity* of 1511; and the attitude of Christ is also, but less clearly, dependent on the *Deposition* from the *Small Passion* (1507). The exploitation of Durer's example is, for the first and only time, of more than an incident or motive, but there is still no valid influence on Andrea of the Dürer style.

The composition of the *Pietà,* as it is recorded (in the direction of the original) in Agostino's unsatisfactory print, is very like that of the Leningrad *Holy Family.* The figures of the *Pietà* — a symbolic rather than a historical image, in which three angels mourn the Christ before the Hill of Golgotha — are gathered in compact unity by an including curve which, more evidently than in the *Holy Family,* inclines on a diagonal axis rightward and rearward into space. This axis is strongly marked by the posture of the Christ, who lies back as if into an oblique apsidal concavity framed in by the angels. As in the Leningrad design, the including motive of the curve is incomplete in front, so that an opposite diagonal inclination rises leftward and to the rear away from the lower foreground plane. More developed than the Leningrad design and in the same sense, this suggests still more the character of an asymmetrically disposed spiral form. It can still be read, in the engraving, how Andrea wished to compensate this asymmetry in space by manipulating the poses of the angels in such wise that the farthest to the rear of them are turned most strongly toward the picture plane. The devices of color which, as in the *Holy Family,* must have supported this effort are unhappily irrecoverable; there is no known old copy of this work.

The theme was one to stimulate (as it had done in the Borghese predella long before) Andrea's intense pathetic sensibility. The descriptive postures of the actors convey, even in Agostino's transcription, how they are moved in grief ("con atti mesti e pietosi" [Vasari, *ibid.*]). The rhythmical involvement of the pattern communicates a temper of constrained excitement, and the structure of design itself assumes, as it had not in the analogous scheme of the Leningrad painting, a more differentiated and exciting energy. All that survives to us of Andrea's specific intention of expression for this painting is in a drawing (Uffizi 639E)[560] for the head of the angel on the left, of an almost romantic loveliness: the tenderest possible image of a shadowed mourning.

The same veiled and ultimately subtle sensibility, yet more compellingly expressed, is in the small bust of the *Redeemer* (c. 1516),[561] still on the altar of Michelozzo's tabernacle in the Annunziata for which it was designed. Evidently a generic recollection of a Northern iconographic type, this work intends — as does that type — the sense of an immediate physical and psychological being. Andrea's resources of style, as they have now developed, enable him to make that sense entirely convincing. In his painting the softly luminous flesh of head and hands, and the glowing red of Christ's garment, seem to grow out of their *sfumato* almost as actual substances might do within the obscure lighting of the tabernacle, with the effect of veiled yet tangible presence. The intensity of light within the form indicates, however, something more than optical revelation of an actuality; this has a power as of emanation. So also, the Being that the light reveals to us is distinguished from our mortality in quality of features and in spirit. The expression is ineffable: it is the subtlest resolution into gentle harmony of the feelings both of love and suffering, and a condensation of the sense of both an actual and a remembered presence. Like its Northern antecedents, this image skirts the edge of sentiment, but does not trespass into it; its effect is of an utterly convincing sincerity, and of quasi-hypnotic power. As in the beings of Leonardo's creation — whose means and ideas Andrea still evidently here employs — an utmost complexity of psychological and visual sensation, and of actuality and idea, are suspended in equilibrium in the Annunziata *Redentore*; but the level of suspension is, more than in Leonardo, on a nearer and more accessible plane to us.

The sensibility of these last three works we have discussed, so fine and tender in feeling and concordantly refined in form, could hardly be developed farther in this same sense without risk to the classical identity of Andrea's style. More subtlety of psychological responsiveness like this — already a shade feminine in its gentle and receptive temper — could verge too near the sentimental, and a further softening of form to match this content could result in form's incipient dissolution. What Andrea has done, in this moment of extreme sensibility, has the potential in it of morbidity, in both the English and Italian meanings of the word. In these pictures Andrea has reconsidered, not imitatively but with the inclination and accent of his private personality, the central conception of the art of Leonardo, and explored it to a like dead end.

A withdrawal from this extreme position and a shift in the direction of Andrea's style is apparent in his so-called *Holy Family* (Paris, Louvre no. 1515; 1516),[562] a reconsideration of the theme of the Leningrad painting. In the making of that picture Raphael's *Impannata* had been partly influential; in the Louvre painting its influence is more profound and quite precise. The redirection of Andrea's style in 1516 seems to be at least in part a result of his study of this physically present model of the nearly contemporary Roman school. In the Louvre *Holy Family*, the *morbidezza* of the Leningrad picture has given way to a more decisive, emphatically more plastic, handling of form, far less *sfumato* and much more like the *Impannata* in its vigor of contrasts in the light. The drawing is no longer febrile, but firm in contour and sharp in accents that it makes within the forms. The composition, now very like that of the *Impannata,* is at once more compact than in the Leningrad painting and more energetic in articulation of its parts. The resemblance in composition between the Louvre picture and the *Impannata* is such that it would almost seem as if Andrea had filled the same diagram of composition with another arrangement of dramatis personae — some of whom are, however, also intimately related to the Raphael, as is the Elizabeth or, almost altogether literally, the Christ Child.

Not only form, but the quality of emotion has changed in the direction of Raphael's example. Emotion is not — and in Andrea's devotional pictures will not for some years be again — wholly free of the extreme of sensibility that was in the works just past; but in this picture feeling is less exquisitely, and also less profoundly, characterized than it had been in them. Here there is a trace at least of constraint of emotion, which restores something to this image of the classical values of discretion and discreteness of its personality. Even Andrea's ecstatic angel, paraphrasing Raphael's Christ, has assumed, in expression of face and in quality of deliberated gesture, almost an air of moderation. After this partial emotional repression, the psychological depth and the variety of feeling in Andrea's actors remains at a level not less than in the *Impannata*; however, Andrea's emotion is nowhere so sharp as in Giulio's definition, in that picture, of his master's expressive ideas.

It does not follow that an adaptation or even an imitation should produce equivalent substantial results of style, and it is an index of the similarity in evolution of Andrea and Raphael within a classicism that Andrea's exploitation of the *Impannata* should create effects of style so genuinely alike. In Andrea's picture, as in Raphael's, a dense and compact unity of geometric shape is articulated into distinct plastic forms, the principal ones of which are so arranged, like offset parentheses, as to create an impulse of rotatory, yet matching movement. Also as in the *Impannata*, countering diagonal directions intersect across the whole containing form, and swift connective threads of cursive rhythm run all through it, warping simultaneously across its surface and into its plastic depth. The effect of a synthetic image at once most forceful of whole discipline and highly internally complex gives evidence of as high a development of classical structure in the Louvre painting as is in the *Impannata*, and of an application of classical aesthetic more stringent than in Andrea's art before. The Louvre *Holy Family*, absorbing for the first time a nearly contemporary Roman discipline of classical style, makes another threshold, in its way almost as important as that made in the *Birth of the Virgin*, for Andrea's subsequent development. The supreme works of the few years that immediately follow take their point of departure in the reformation and consolidation of Andrea's style in this painting.

Much less meaningful to the development of Andrea's art than his encounter with Raphael's *Impannata* is his brief succeeding episode of Michelangelism. The grisaille fresco, the *Baptism of the Multitude* (late 1516–early

1517; paid for March 15, 1517),[563] continuing the series in the Scalzo, is obsessed with Michelangelesque recollection. Surprisingly enough there is no earlier evidence of any interest of Andrea in the art of Michelangelo. Perhaps this tardy response was stimulated by Michelangelo's return to Florence in 1516, and by such personal interchange as must have occurred on the occasion of the transfer from Michelangelo to Andrea of a commission for Pier Francesco Borgherini sometime after August 1516 (Frey, *Br.*, XXIII, XXVI, LV). Evidently, in this time of redirection of his art Andrea was particularly welcoming of ideas from the acknowledged great men of the Roman style. All that was available to him of Michelangelo, however, seems to have been the master's work of his early years in Florence. Andrea's awakened interest leads him, for his models for the figures of the *Baptism,* to the early *David*, to the *Cascina* cartoon, and probably also to the *abozzo* for the *Matthew*; but there is only one uncertain indication (the Ignudo-like straddling putto at the right) of possible knowledge — not necessarily at first hand — of any work of Michelangelo in Rome. The *Cascina* cartoon – more precisely by this date, its fragments — was evidently the most influential model, for it demonstrated not only the anatomical style that Andrea imitates in the chief figures of his fresco but also an appropriate mode of draughtsmanship.

As much as his very different innate temper would allow, Andrea approximates the forceful and sharply differentiated accent of contour in Michelangelo's early style, and transcribes his faceted modelling of musculature. Andrea extends this character of drawing and modelling beyond the nudes — they are, more modestly than in Michelangelo, only near-nudes — also to the handling of draperies. The tendency to sharper articulation of both line and light is the same as that in the Louvre *Holy Family*, and so also is the whole more decisive and energetic temper in which forms are made; but under Michelangelo's more drastic stimulation these tendencies are given — for Andrea — unprecedented stress. The stimulus of Raphael's example to more plastic form had left its impress on the Louvre picture; now the example of Michelangelo's statuary style encouraged Andrea to more marked efforts in the same sense.

These stimuli, in this dosage, were not wholly successfully digestible by Andrea. His simulation of the *Cascina's* powers and activities of form is not, obviously, in Michelangelo's dimension. Andrea's anatomies are too broken in descriptive accent, and the movement of his line is too — almost agitatedly — various; his effect of energy in drawing is discoordinate. Further, Andrea's intention of plasticity is not sufficiently adjusted, in this atmospheric scene, to his recent immersion in chiaroscuro, from which he has not emerged. Intending a new force of plastic values, he is at the same time reluctant to diminish, even so much as he had in the Louvre *Holy Family*, his enriched chiaroscuro mode. He does make an alteration in its temper, imparting to it the same energy of sharply varied accent that is in his line, so that modelling of form equally seems agitated. In spite of the assertion of plasticity of parts, the sense of coherent substance in any whole form is, actually, less in the *Baptism* than in the works that had preceded Andrea's recent extreme development of a *sfumato* style. There is an evident conflict in this fresco between the demands of a tectonic and a highly developed optical mode, and this, in places, is disruptive of the unity of form. Fra Bartolommeo, in his first access of Michelangelism in the *St. Mark*, had confronted, but also not successfully resolved, a similar dilemma. It is least of all consonant with the sense in general of classicism, but not altogether unlike the character in particular of the early cartoon of Michelangelo, that the expressive content of Andrea's figures is not enough concordant, in spiritual inspiration or in meaning of their action, with their outward forms; still more than in Michelangelo's old model, Andrea's nudes have the effect of academies. It is a difficult and not altogether useful lesson that Andrea has tried to learn from his study of the early Michelangelo, unsuited not only to Andrea's temperamental purposes but to his kind and present stage of development of classical style. The Cartoon was more properly and effectively exploited by the Mannerist generation, and what the study of it has provoked in Andrea is, in its negative effects on his existing classicism, suggestive of the contemporary — but in them positively intended — impulses of Andrea's pupils.

In the *Capture of St. John* (paid for July 19, 1517)[564] Andrea has retreated almost altogether from the untenable Michelangelesque position he had taken in the *Baptism*. Here, the figure of St. John is still, but less literally, reflective of Michelangelo's anatomical style; and it is also possible (A. Venturi) that the motive of the whole group at the left of the composition depends on Andrea's having seen, late in the previous year, the drawing sent by Michelangelo to Rome for Sebastiano, for the *Flagellation* of the Borgherini Chapel. More generally, but perhaps more significantly than in any probable relationship of type or motive, there may be the stimulation of Michelangelo's expressive power in the force of dramatic effect, exceptional in Andrea, which this scene intends. The possibility admitted, such a stimulus is so oblique and so wholly personally transmuted that its result cannot be assessed as a Michelangelism.

In contrast to the disruptive energies of design in the *Baptism*, the description of form in the *Capture* is once more definite and clear — as it had been in the *Caritas*[554] or the *Birth of the Virgin*,[311] before Andrea's extreme *tenebrismo*, and as it had begun to be again in the *Holy Family* of the Louvre. The look of clarity of form is like that in the penultimate group of works, and though there is no essential difference in the means by which this clarity is now achieved there is an important difference in the role these means play within the work of art. What has happened here is the result of a finally effective dialectic between a plastic and a chiaroscuro mode, each of which had been developed, since the time of the *Birth of the Virgin,* to a new degree of competing interest. It is not only that the busy chiaroscuro of the *Baptism* has receded here, but that the lighting is applied — with no less energy but with far greater clarity — explicitly to the modelling of whole plastic forms, not to disruptively asserted parts. Further, the clarifying light has been applied not only to the forms but in the space that intervenes between them: there is no longer the sensation, as in the *Baptism,* of entanglement of substance with its surrounding space. The idea of a finally containing unity of chiaroscuro is by no means abandoned, but it is precisely adjusted to the plastic content of the lighted — or darkened — space. The force and clarity of light diminish in careful and almost measurable gradation as the space recedes, as if the lighting were an inseparable function of the structural perspective; and in the background, the muted light becomes a unifying substratum into which form is absorbed and out of which, inversely, it proceeds.

This system is not basically different from that to which Andrea had come in the *Birth of the Virgin,* where it was less positively articulated, and in color more evidently than in light. Its distinction in the *Capture* is in the degree of explicitness, even of stringency, with which the concept has been stated and described, and — equally important — in the higher power of both its tactile and its optical components, in the parts of form as well as in the whole. Forcefully effected, this synthesis of plastic and chiaroscuro style assumes a new measure of meaning — almost, indeed, a dominating value — in the formal system of this fresco; and it is a major factor in the paintings of the imminent climactic moment of Andrea's career.

The purposeful clarity that is in Andrea's handling of this crucial problem of perception and projection of form underlies the whole disposition in which the *Capture* is created. This is not the first time in his career that Andrea has encountered a narrative subject with some force of drama, but it is the first place in which he has chosen to exploit it. This is as sparse a rendering of the theme as the allotted space permits, without extraneous incident, and with minimal accessories. The figures act their roles simply and decisively, with precise economy of attitudes and movement, and in a setting that is descriptively exactly adequate. The impact of the event is instant and explicit. Its cogency of narrative effect is intensified by Andrea's first full realization, in this fresco, of an action projected as if on a stage. Its content of actors and of setting has been ordered with the utmost clarity, with a nearly rectilinear stringency of pattern both in surface scheme of composition and in space. There is the strongest contrast between this severity of geometric logic and the straining complexity, verging on disunity, of structure in the *Baptism.*

The *Capture* is strong and explicit in its means and in effect; but it is not conceived in either the spiritual or aesthetic dimension of dramatic painting of the contemporary Roman style, nor even in the temper of the later works of Fra Bartolommeo. In this fresco the scale of form and feeling is less than monumental, and there is more of illustration than of rhetoric in the interpretation of the drama, and in the measure that is in its actors of descriptive naturalism. The persons of the drama forcefully represent the human event, but they do not magnify it. Nevertheless, the *Capture* makes a parallel with a recent occurrence of Roman style, and it is directed by as much as is temperamentally possible to Andrea of a similar intention. Emerging, like Raphael in 1515, from a moment of style of apparently insuperable and potentially disruptive complexity, Andrea reacts, as Raphael did in the Tapestry Cartoons, toward a discipline more rigorous than in any earlier episode of his career. Like Raphael, Andrea imposes an austerity of deportment on his figures, devises a laconic clarity of narrative, and enforces a stringent geometric order in his composition. At the same time, also like Raphael, he finds it necessary to resynthesize divergent and potentially conflicting possibilities that had developed in his art. Andrea's accomplishment of these like ends is at a level very different from Raphael's: by comparison with the Tapestry Cartoons his means and his solutions are dry and poor, but the generic resemblance of purpose and achievement within the course of evolution of the classical style remains. Andrea's ultimate classicism is of no such height as Raphael's, but its principle and the manner of its ocurrence are alike.

The similarity to Raphael's Tapestry style extends, in the *Capture*, to a suggestion even of particular resemblance to one among the Cartoons, the *Blinding of Elymas*; the enthroned Herod and the figure who, at the left, is a counterpart of Raphael's St. Paul, especially recall the *Elymas*, and there are other more hypothetical similarities as well. There is no provable connection, however, and it is likely that these resemblances are fortuitous and not the result of an acquaintance, either *in situ* or indirect, with the Tapestry Cartoons. The Paul-like figure seen from the rear can properly be considered a recurrence and development of a motive that appears repeatedly, from Andrea's early paintings onward (for example, in the *Funeral of S. Filippo Benizzi*; in the Scalzo *Preaching*). The enthroned Herod and his priests recall, more than they do Raphael's Sergius and his Lictors, the figure motives and the composition of a local precedent, in Fra Bartolommeo's *Salvator Mundi;* Andrea's group compounds the Frate's central panel and the flanking Prophets of this altar. This work of Bartolommeo's is obviously an accessible source for motives in the *Capture* that Andrea seems to have derived. Equally evidently, the *Salvator* altar makes a far more precise analogue of style for the *Capture* than do Raphael's Cartoons. In Andrea, the invention of a severe classical style arose in circumstances like those in which a similar phenomenon occurred in the art of Raphael; but these circumstances also resemble those in which, in Florence, Fra Bartolommeo had evolved a parallel discipline of style, in the year before it happened in Andrea. It is inescapable that this important happening in Andrea's art was, to begin with, stimulated by Fra Bartolommeo's just prior example. However, Andrea went on to make of this Florentine variant of the ultimate classical style a more consequential and far more sophisticated vehicle than it is in the Bartolommesque precedent.

There has never been the least doubt of the general dependence in composition on the *Salvator* altar of Andrea's *Madonna of the Harpies* (Florence, Uffizi; dated 1517).[565] The basic arrangement of motives is much alike, and Andrea's composition indicates — as it had not before except in the *Capture*, similarly influenced — an insistence like that in Fra Bartolommeo's altar on rectilinear elements of order. Andrea's composition, compared with Bartolommeo's, seems still more absolutely clear, but at the same time not so rigid or so baldly doctrinaire. It is more surely unified than the Frate's, and also much more internally complex. Andrea has condensed the elements of his composition in a more compact relation, of surface organization and of space; as clearly marked as the discrete rectilinear place in composition of each major form may be, other forces, equally assertive, operate to bind them in community more cogently than in the *Salvator* altar. A sensible vestige still remains of the whole including oval shape of design that had been in Andrea's earlier altars (as in the *Holy Family* in the Louvre);[562] within this, manipulations of drapery and of flexible anatomy — in which Fra Bartolommeo could never think effectively — work to make a unity of pattern and a connected sequence of behavior among the figures.

Andrea's Madonna is far more contained in posture than the rhetorical Salvator Mundi, but a deeper reservoir of energy is held within her quiet contrapposto than is expressed overtly in His movement. Her poised broad form suspends in equilibrium (the fulcrum marked by the pressure on her hip of the Christ Child's foot) a complex of ponderative forces as articulate, but *con sordino*, as in a figure of Michelangelo's. The structure of anatomy, hardly visible in itself, only adumbrates this effect of form; it is communicated rather by the eloquent differentiation of the pattern of drapery and by variations of the modelling in light. The form and the energy of movement of the Christ Child are incorporated into, and controlled by, the Virgin's form; below, the *angelini* ornamentally elaborate, but also organically extend, the impulses of movement that are contained in her. From the left, the Madonna receives the slow but compelling pressure of the movement of St. Francis as he turns from us toward her: his glance is toward us, but veiled, because his more profound awareness is not of the audience, but of the Virgin; his body shows a slow yet poignant torsion toward her presence. Toward the right, the St. John oppositely frames the Virgin's statuary form; also poised in movement, he echoes and seemingly supports the Virgin's weighing convexity of shape, and at the same time precisely complements the posture of St. Francis. John (apparently a portrait of Sansovino, who provided a *modello* for this figure [Vasari VII, 488]) confronts the spectator in a measure that is the counterpart, in gaze as well as attitude, of Francis' contrary inward turning.

With yet clearer demonstration of that sense (already more developed in Andrea than in Fra Bartolommeo) of design as an indissoluble integer of silhouette and substance, each relation in this composition is plastically conceived. Movements are spatially developed to create an almost spiralling continuity from one form to the next. The manipulation into a responsive equilibrium of the figures' substances and play in space, and of their order of design on the surface, is in one indivisible process. Yet, as this still more explicit role of substance and substantial energies within design is confirmed it is also controlled with a new stringency: not only by the extreme clarity of superficial pattern but by the positive reference, within each attitude, of it to the picture plane; and more evidently by the careful restriction of the depth of space, limited by a planar architecture toward the rear.

As we have seen Andrea do before, he again uses color in such a way as to compensate the differentiations made of forms in space with an approximate equilibrium of visual attraction made among them on the picture plane, achieved by manipulating areas and intensities of color. In this picture, the most forward form in plan, the Francis, is the most restrained in color, a greyed tan; the *standbein* of the Virgin is covered by a drapery of matt, but assertive blue; the lower garment of the John is a high-keyed, pale red-orange, which brings him, who is actually slightly deeper in the plan than Francis, apparently as forward as he and into more demanding confrontation with the spectator. This compensatory purpose of the color is evidently not its only one: there is a sequence of development and differentiation of hue and intensity yet more carefully negotiated than in any of Andrea's earlier works. At the same time, color in the *Harpies* does not make the impression to which it tends in other paintings since Andrea's maturity, of a factor of major aesthetic interest, assertive of its own particular seduction for the eye. It is, here, relatively matt, without brilliance, and uncharacterizing of effects of texture; color has been qualified by the whole atmosphere of more intellectual deliberation that is in the making of this work. With greater clarity than before it subserves the definition of the tectonic form, in its compositional entirety and in each plastic part. And, in a way closely like that in the grisaille *Capture*, chiaroscuro works toward the strong modelling of whole plastic shape, and at the same time still defines the integrity of visual texture out of which form is differentiated.

Because the effect not only of color but of light is seemingly less sensuous than in previous pictures of Andrea's, the look of surface of this painting, as well as its compositional mode, confirms the generic resemblance, but only that, of Andrea's ideas of this moment to Fra Bartolommeo's in the *Salvator* altar. However, Andrea's far greater sophistication of aesthetic resource and, inextricable from it, his utterly articulate sensibility to the look and life of nature make this a specifically very different document, with no trace in it of the noble vacancy of the *Salvator.* There is no more in the *Harpies* than Andrea had shown before of his special power of perception of variety of visual experience, but this is — like the entire form — remarkably more precisely controlled. For the first time in a painted work Andrea's draughtsmanship exhibits a consistently exact refinement: the definition of rhythmic shape, in parts of body and of drapery, is uniformly fine and subtle. Both large and small forms lose the somewhat heavy and coarsely proportioned look they often had in his preceding works. There is nothing exquisite in this new manner of description of the form, but rather a more sensitive precision; and no elegance but rather a finer evocation of the quality of *grazia.*

Each element of observed nature thus transcribed — the patterning of a passage in the drapery, a contour of body, the drawing of a hand — seems in this picture to grow as if by an inevitable and organic differentiation out of, or upon, its larger and containing form; and these are just as ineluctably, and seemingly organically, related to each other in the entire pictorial unity. In no other image of the classical style since Leonardo does the synthetic equilibrium of large and small form consist of so subtly nuanced and so continuously shaded a gradation; and more even than in Leonardo this conveys the sense that what is here suspended in equilibrium is the flux of visible nature. What has been arrested in this harmony is not an exaltation of existence but a controlled, preselected actuality: as many values in this picture are induced from actuality as are imposed on it by acts of ordering artistic will. There is no trace of conflict of these tendencies; they are not envisaged by Andrea as even possibly antithetic but as reciprocal functions of one another. But for the first time in Andrea's art to this degree, a superlatively intellectual order is as strong a function in the work of art as the subtlety of actual perception.

The character of form and that of the illustrative human content are basically in accord. This too is an unexalted, but controlled and measured spiritual disposition: grave, gentle, and contained, and evidently utterly sincerely felt, and intimately characterized as living psychological expression. The range of feeling is as much differentiated into responsive nuances as is the form, from the inward adoration of the Francis through the exquisite humor of the Christ Child. Yet neither the depth nor the intensity of feeling is much more than conventional, nor is there, in Raphaelesque or Michelangelesque sense, a transfiguring power in any countenance of a content of sheer thought. The texture of emotion is rich, but it is not profound, and — as in Fra Bartolommeo's art as well — it takes its resonance from the larger affects of the picture's form. This image of an *epiphaneia*, much more than the *epiphaneia* of the *Salvator Mundi*, is earth-bound — quite unlike the Raphael *Sistina* from which, by indirection through the *Salvator* altar, it in a way eventually derives. But the reference to the *Sistina* is already, at the distance of these few years, only thematically relevant, and no longer wholly relevant for comparison of style. As we have indicated, this work of Andrea's, like Bartolommeo's *Salvator*, belongs to a succeeding stage in evolution of a classical idea. The *Madonna of the Harpies* is Andrea's exposition of his classical style at its point of climax. Compared with the *Salvator Mundi* or with Raphael's Tapestry Cartoons, it is at once the distinction of personal style of this picture and its special resource, and its limitation also, that it transcends nature less than they.

The depth of the impress made on Andrea in this time by Fra Bartolommeo's example in the *Salvator Mundi* is confirmed in Andrea's *Disputation on the Trinity* (Florence, Pitti; late 1517–first half 1518).[566] In this composition the order of the four main figures, and even part of their repertory of gesture, is inspired by the *Salvator* altar. Beyond this, Andrea refers also, in the two kneeling Saints at the front of his design, to a repeated precedent of the Frate in his other monumental works (as in the unfinished *pala* in S. Marco or the more recent altar of the *Misericordia*). There is also a generic, but almost certainly fortuitous resemblance of Andrea's composition to that of Raphael's *St. Cecilia* altar; but no influence beyond that of the Frate is required to account for the structure of Andrea's picture.

Like the *Madonna of the Harpies*, the *Disputà* effects important alterations on its Bartolommesque precedent, all of them in substantially the same sense as there. Andrea's order is more concentrated, in all three dimensions, than that in the *Salvator*, and it is more geometrically strict either than in that picture or in the *Harpies*: this latter circumstance is much promoted by the subject matter, more than normally untractable, but is not determined by it. The affect of this schema of design — severe, austere, and of intended architectonic impressiveness — accords with the only content adequate to a theme like this, as if it should communicate the — indisputable — logical and spiritual certainty of the dogma it proclaims. The four great Saints (Augustine, Lawrence, Peter Martyr, and Francis) stand clear and firm, almost without contrapposto grace, each with his sure but different conviction of the common truth for which they altogether vouch; in the foreground a gentle Sebastian and an adoring Magdalen contribute their rapt assent to the proceedings. The design implies, but does not more than minimally develop, a Bartolommesque circularity in plan. More than in the composition of the *Harpies*, this scheme stresses its component of rectilinearity, to the degree where this effect dominates the cursive elements of form, in spatial as well as in superficial structure. This is a virtually columnar setting-out of shapes, which despite its somewhat greater differentiation into depth than in the structure of the *Harpies* is as much bound into relation with the picture plane: or even more insistently, by the isocephaly of heads, by the horizontal continuity of gesture, and by the virtual suppression of all spatial contrapposto. The rectilinear basis of design itself serves to refer the plastic contents of the painting constantly to its frame.

There is no architectural support, as in the *Harpies*, for the condensation of the space, but the background, a *sfumato* texture of olive-green and brown, has a not dissimilar effect. This texture optically implies a space but does not construct one; it is a neutral and indeterminate aether, and not extension. As in the *Harpies*, it is the unifying matrix from which plastic substance grows and into which it is bound. The figures stand before this intangible yet sensible limit in a narrow depth; there is no independent dimension of space, but only that which exists in consequence of the existence of the figures. The analogy to the phenomenon in Raphael's Cartoons, as we have analysed it there, is obvious; this is equally characterizable as an instance of the exclusive — in our special sense of the word — "humanism" of the climactic stage of evolution of classical style. The figures are projected as if they might be elements of statuary: it is not without good reason that it has been observed (Wölfflin) that the composition recollects, probably not altogether casually, the early fifteenth-century *Quattro Santi Coronati* of the Orsanmichele.

The structure is not, in any literal sense, a planar one, but the imminence of its substances to the picture plane imparts to that plane a different importance than it had before in the designer's mind. Since spatial meaning is diminished, the superficial order becomes proportionately more significant; there is the heightened sense in the *Disputà*, as there was equally in the *Harpies*, of design felt as a projection on the picture plane. The ordering of substance within the lesser depth is not less purposeful; rather, it is integrated in a new strictness of relation with the dominating order on the surface and this, in turn, is more responsive to the logic of geometry that seems immanent in the whole shape of the picture field. This is not yet to proclaim a separable aesthetic identity for the picture plane; this remains for Mannerism to deduce from Andrea's — and, in somewhat different measure, from Raphael's — ultimately classical conclusions. What is meant by this new principle of structure in Andrea's art is clear in the contrast of the *Disputà* or the *Harpies* with his larger works of about 1514, such as the Dresden altar [310] or the *Birth of the Virgin*; just as it is evident in Raphael in the contrast of structure between his Cartoons and the frescoes of the first two Stanze.

Unlike in Raphael, the sense of strigency that is in the application of this compositional principle does not invade the more specifically painterly concerns of Andrea's style. His draughtsmanship in the *Disputà* is as precise, and in this subject even more intimately descriptive of the look of nature than it had been in the *Harpies*; there is an almost portrait-like immediacy in Andrea's presentation, only barely idealized, of his types. The temper of drawing is, in fact, more lively than in the previous altarpiece: more quick and finely probing of variety of form; and the lighting, somewhat deeper than in the *Harpies*, is equally more various and fine-faceted. Brisk and subtle both, the chiaroscuro and the drawing make an overcast of almost sparkling energy on the persons of this picture and on their order of design, as if thereby to compensate its severity of basic structure. This energy of small form is also the expression in visual terms of a relieving quality in the picture's content: as the affect of larger structure supports the actors' gravity of attitude and meaning, so the vitality of smaller form conveys their energy of converse.

One of Andrea's rare excursions into portraiture dates from this time in his career, at a moment which, apparently, is closer to the *Harpies* than the *Disputà*. This is the so-called *Portrait of a Sculptor* (London, National Gallery),[567] for which every external consideration suggests its identification with Jacopo Sansovino except that, unfortunately, the face is not his. It cannot be reconciled with the documented iconography of Sansovino unless we may assume that, on this one sitter only, Andrea exercised an idealizing process more drastic than that imposed on the invented actors of his altarpieces. Such liberties in portraiture seem to have occurred in Raphael — witness the various faces, all of them almost verifiable, of the Fornarina — but they are improbable in Andrea.

Very strongly, this image conveys that its mode of feeling and its sense of form emerge from the close context of the *Harpies* altar. The character of shapes and the touch in drawing of the portrait are almost interchangeable with passages in the larger picture (as for example, the sleeve of this sitter and that of St. Francis); and the pose in the portrait is an almost inevitable compound of the upper bodies of the two Saints. The quality of expression — much less merely romantical or sympathetic than the *sfumato* at first makes it seem — is actually sharper and more communicatively intense than in the Saints of the altarpiece. In the portrait there is not their veiling consciousness, as they look toward us, of other presences, but only the insistent private dialogue between sitter and the spectator.

In terms of Florentine precedent, accustomed to the portrait style of Ridolfo Ghirlandaio or of Franciabigio — or even from the point of view of contemporary Rome — this picture is of remarkable originality. Only Raphael achieves a like incisiveness of psychological characterization, but this in him has more sense of the separateness of the observing artist from the sitter; there is not the compelling intimacy of communication that Andrea effects here. This is not only a result of the expression of the face; in part it proceeds from the fineness and acuity that exist both in Andrea's psychological perception and in his way of perceiving form and light: not merely subtly objectively analytic but responsive, as if there were a degree of identification between the painter and the seen thing that is not in Raphael. The atmosphere — in literal and figurative senses both — of this portrait has been made intimate. The pose of the sitter, more relatively informal and movemented than in any Florentine portrait, or in any Roman portrait to this date, is manipulated into an almost perfect poise, only a little tensed, and in this exactly reflective of the subject's psychological situation.

Four drawings survive in which Andrea searches toward his idea of design (Uffizi 661 v and r, 301 r and v, in that order):[568] in them an alternation between turning complication and frontality is resolved finally into the complex equilibrium, in the painting, of a pose diagonally set, but referred to a controlling pattern of the picture plane. The physical presence is very close to us, but still evidently separate; it makes a self-contained aesthetic order, spatially projected on, and just behind, the sensible boundary of the picture plane. What verges on too strong an intimacy of psychological communication with the sitter is controlled, not quite with normative classical effect of distance, but still with classical discreteness, by the identity as an aesthetic construct of the image.

Shortly after the end of May 1518, Andrea left Florence for his visit to the court of Francis I where he stayed until, finding absence from his wife intolerable (according to Vasari, V, 30–31), he returned home before October of the following year. He intended, apparently, to return to France, but (again according to Vasari's account) carelessness, or worse, in the expenditure of money entrusted to him by the King for the purchase of works of art, but not so used, made Andrea's reappearance at the court impossible. Andrea's coming to France had been preceded, by more than a year, by the aged Leonardo — with his inseparable baggage of unfinished masterpieces — who had taken up residence at Amboise. The arrival of Andrea at Fontainebleau must have been followed shortly by that of two major imports from Raphael in Rome, the *St. Michael* and the *Holy Family of Francis I*, both sent on their way in July 1518.

The sole work that certainly survives from Andrea's stay in France, the *Caritas* (Paris, Louvre; dated 1518)[569] shows the marks of contact only with imported works by Andrea's fellow-countrymen, and no trace of any influence of past or present French art; there was no reason why Andrea should not have shared Francis' conviction of the superiority of the Italian product. The *Caritas* is also untouched, as far as we can determine, by influence of any art Andrea might have seen on his way to France — whatever his route from Florence might have been. He may, however, have carried with him the impress of a very recent and significant event of art in Florence: the first publication on major scale in the Mannerist style by his former pupil, Jacopo Pontormo, in the altar for S. Michele Visdomini, dated 1518.

The *Caritas* is altogether on the same extraordinary plateau of accomplishment to which Andrea had ascended in the year before with the *Madonna of the Harpies*, and is intimately related to it and to the *Disputà*, just antecedent to the trip to France. Yet the French picture is different in some respects from these two preceding works, and its particular effect of style is unique within Andrea's art. The *Caritas* is the product of a conjunction of extraordinary circumstances both within Andrea's personal development and external to it. There converge in it the consequences of his previous accomplishment of an apparent ultimate of classicism in his style, and his realization at their fullest of constructive powers and of private sensibilities; and into these circumstances outside stimuli were injected, of experience of other works of art. First among these were the paintings of Leonardo that Andrea had not seen since his youth (almost positively, but not provably, he had seen them then); then the imported Raphaels, in which he could observe the latest tendencies of style in Rome. Perhaps among the works that compelled Andrea's attention were also other "foreign" paintings, "di Venegia e di Lombardia" (Vasari V, 29), in the King's collection. Finally, remembered from Florence, there may have been the provoking image of what young Pontormo had just recently achieved. Generated at such a moment in Andrea's evolution, and out of such experiences, the *Caritas* became an unsurpassable climax and a crisis, simultaneously, in Andrea's classical style.

Part of the distinction between the *Caritas* and the two preceding major works is impelled, evidently, by the difference in its subject. It is a matter to be handled in a somewhat different mood than the two formal altarpieces, at least in the light of Andrea's own temperamental habits and his earlier experiences with this theme. Still more evidently, it is an unlike formal problem to that in the altars, but it is not unrelated to that in the central portion only of the *Madonna of the Harpies*. In the *Caritas*, the figures of the children are, with iconographic appropriateness, more closely integrated with the mother figure, and the integer of form they thus compose becomes the matter of design of a whole picture rather than a part.

Almost certainly, the adoption for the *Caritas* of a pyramidal design and a setting in a landscape was determined by the example of Leonardo's *St. Anne* altar.[39] However, Andrea's composition is not an imitation of the Leonardo, but an inspired paraphrase; almost annihilatingly impressive as it was (and is) the *Anne* altar would have seemed, in 1518, a little inflexible and old-fashioned. It is instructive of the different present stage of evolution of the classical style to observe Andrea's mode of paraphrase. The basis of design for the *Caritas* is, as in Leonardo's picture, a containing pyramid internally articulated in a complex equilibrium of turning rhythms, but Andrea's conception of how this scheme should work specifically is unlike Leonardo's. In her single shape the Caritas demonstrates the spatial evolution which, in the Louvre altar, is carried by the two main figures; her form rises in an arching spiral, and this finds its own equilibrium, gently tensed: the lesser forms of the putti only elaborate and comment on her simultaneity of energy and breadth. Her poise seems more resilient than that of Leonardo's group. As if to control and counter this effect of flexibility Andrea has given to the Caritas a compensating grandeur in her sense of scale and a canon of proportion that suggests the Michelangelesque: on one hand the Caritas recalls the dignity of the Sistine Sibyls; on the other she seems almost to anticipate the majesty, and the motive, of the as yet uninvented *Medici Madonna.*

In this single, magnificently dominating form there is a more evident effect of unity than in the Leonardo *St. Anne* and, at the same time, this unity is more continuously differentiated. Further, while in the Leonardo there is — in this comparison — a sense of juxtaposition between the generalization of large forms and the scale of detail, in the *Caritas* the distinctions between whole and part are more gradual and fluid. The relation of parts to the whole is by a process more continuous, and thus more indicative of unity. This applies not only to the figure group but to the relation of the group to landscape. The *Caritas* is more *sfumato* than in the painting of the inventor of *sfumato*; and while Andrea's figures are sufficiently affirmed in their identity within the light and air of landscape they are also, by means of a *sfumato,* in more affirmative connection with it. It is ultimately Leonardo's own instrument, the handling of light, that Andrea has so much more evolved to be a major agency of his higher unity of form. Andrea's light is more directly responsive to the optical complexity in nature, but not less carefully manipulated than by Leonardo for effects of art. The visual texture of Andrea's image is a more apparent, and also more complex and fluid, integer than in the Louvre *St. Anne.*

The use of light in the *Caritas* is only somewhat, but perceptibly, different from that in the *Madonna of the Harpies* or the *Disputà.* It could not be a more pervasive presence than in those two pictures, but it is a more assertive one. It is less accompanied by a draughtsmanship that defines larger shapes, or finally discriminates exact detail; still more evidently, this light does not contain those clarities of contrast which serve to make sure modelling of form. There is a resurgence, in the *Caritas,* of that chiaroscuro mode which had been most conspicuous before the *Harpies,* as in the *Holy Family* of Leningrad: obviously not as it had been there, but in a dialectic with the much more specifically manipulated light that since intervened. The visual and emotional tonality of *sfumato* that was in the Leningrad picture reappears, but with a more precise articulation of its affective role. There is also the reassertion in the *Caritas*, though by no means to the degree that was in the Leningrad picture, of the dominance of optical over plastic effect: this figure group is an integer of shape but not so much of substantial form. The complex light makes faceting distinctions in the form, but at the same time softens these distinctions into continuity; almost no plastic element remains unbroken and assertive.

Color works with similar effect: more than in the antecedent pictures color is sensible as a function of the light — almost, but not quite, in Venetian-wise (perhaps from influence of such Venetian works as Andrea would have seen in France; there is a strong Venetian accent in the figure episode within the distant landscape). Color is muted like the light and more subtly differentiated than before in hue: an interwoven tissue of bleached reds, dulled orange and paled red-violet is spun across the central surface of the group; above and below the browned-green strip of landscape there is a marvelous accord of blues, of the sky and of the Madonna's ample skirt, exactly equal, in attraction for the eye, to the area of reddish tones that they enclose. Color helps less to model form than to create a veiled prismatic variety of its surface. Beyond its wholly adequate but unassertive distinctions in plasticity and space, the image is more evidently presented to us as a highly differentiated unity of optical sensation, experienced at near distance to the eye. It is not altogether overcharacterized if we assert that, reversely to the differentiation of the image as if out of a chiaroscuro ground in the preceding works, in this one the image appears as if by differentiation of the optical texture of the picture's surface. More than in the *Harpies* or the *Disputà*, and despite the setting in a landscape, the formal substance of the *Caritas* is bound in tighter unity into the picture plane.

What is also different from the *Harpies* and the *Disputà* is the temper of expression of this form; and the difference in expression of the picture is created more by properties of form than by elements of illustration or by meaning in the countenances. There had been something much like this temper in the Leningrad *Holy Family*, but there less sophisticated and precise: a muted vibrance of sensation, almost febrile; and in the *Caritas* this feeling has assumed the fineness of articulation — and the exposition through an absolutely masterly technique — that had developed in Andrea's paintings since. Here there is a quick and complex definition of the shifting light and of nuances of color: and in handling of line there is an including range from bold decisiveness to almost morbid sensibility — there is no passage in Andrea's art before this so intensely, nervously refined as in the silhouette of Caritas. The febrility of form that was in the Leningrad picture is, furthermore, now compounded with a flexible controlling strength. An extreme, almost feminine, intimacy of sensation is communicated within monumentality; and a complexity of formal matter at once more various and more intense works within an infrangible entirety. And there is also, in the figures of the *Caritas*, a quality that was not in the *Harpies* or the *Disputà*: not only a subtler poise than in them, nor even only a more quick-tempered grace, but a refinement and attenuation of form to the point of elegance: the counterpart of the expression in her of the sense of grandeur.

Beyond the experience of Leonardo — as we have seen, an experience transcended — in Andrea's making of the *Caritas*, and discounting that of Venetian pictures that we do not know (though one, perhaps identifiable, may have been recalled by Andrea much later on), Andrea's vision of the two royal Raphaels must certainly have been important to him. There is no literal likeness between the *Caritas* and either of the two Raphaels; but it may be that the grandeur of form of the *Caritas* and the combination with it of extreme refinement, and the particular impressiveness of scale of silhouette against the landscape — this not in the Leonardo *Anne* — owes something to the example of Raphael's *St. Michael.*[437] The posture of the Caritas, with its spiral axis that is brought up out of depth at the figure's left and ascends in a diagonal, may also have resulted from a study of the *Michael.* It may be in part by inspiration from the Raphael that the *Caritas* comes closer to it than any other Florentine painting to fulfilling, as the *Michael* does, the most sophisticated compound of ambitions possible to the most developed moment of classical style. In Giulio's execution of the *Michael,* but still more in the *Holy Family of Francis I,* Andrea would have found encouragement for reassertion of his former chiaroscuro mode, and in the latter picture also — though in Giulio's peculiarly equivocal terms — a suggestion for the veiling of the figures' third dimension that is in the *Caritas.* More important, the temper of quick, precise, complex involvement of design in the *Holy Family* is similar to that in the *Caritas*: a phenomenon new to Andrea except for its appearance once before, in the Louvre painting of 1516 — there also under Raphael's, and Giulio's, stimulus.

It is Andrea's particular accent, in this temper of design, of a muted excitation, faceted and angular, that first suggests some likeness to Pontormo in the Visdomini altar, and this sense of a resemblance is increased by the postures of the putti and their rhythmic interplay; it is pressed farther by the attenuation of proportion, exceptional in Andrea, in the Caritas herself. Andrea's experience of Pontormo's painting prior to the trip to France is just chronologically possible: the dating 1518 on the Visdomini altar would not have been inscribed, according to the Florentine calendar, before the last days of March; not much more than two months might be supposed between the date of publication of the Pontormo and Andrea's leaving. It cannot be excluded that the resemblances we see are fortuitous, and that these similar qualities could have developed independently. There is, after all, a wide common basis between Andrea's and Pontormo's art; and it is a specifiable historical fact that a great part of what is in Pontormo's style in the Visdomini altar proceeds directly from an exploitation of Andrea's precedents. If the style of the Visdomini altar did affect the *Caritas*, it was no one-sided transaction but a return to Andrea of his coin, with unforeseen interest. It remains, however, that there is the possibility of Pontormo's chronological precedence in those effects which are similar in the *Caritas*, and while Andrea could have seen Pontormo's picture, Pontormo could not have seen his.

What is similar in these two works is so in part by likeness of motive, but it is more important that there is a measure of similarity in the expression that results from manipulation of the forms. In both pictures there is an optical and rhythmical excitement made with quick-shifting, somewhat eccentrically related shapes and lights; and there is a dynamic nervous sensibility in both works, more communicative of an intimate and private personality than in other works of Florentine provenience, and more so conspicuously than in works from Rome. The stimulus to this particular expressive temper in the *Caritas* may come, if our assumption is correct, from Andrea's vision of Pontormo, but this does not mean that what Andrea makes of the style of his picture is what Pontormo made in the Visdomini altar. The excitement of aesthetic and of illustrative sensation in the *Caritas* is, precisely, muted; and though sensibility in it is extreme, it is not exacerbated. What is in the *Caritas* is an ultimately complex diversification of the content of a synthesis — the most vibrant texture possible of a harmonious unity — but not its disruption. The distinction, more vital to observe even than the similarity of these contemporary objects, will emerge more clearly when, later, we examine the Visdomini altar in detail. Even touched, as we assume he may be here, by a first major assertion of the style of Mannerism, Andrea uses the experience toward a yet more elaborate and refined achievement of classical style. In its very complexity, however, and in the fineness of its equilibrium in synthesis, this is a precarious *summa*; and it is a developmental end. It is also a declaration of private personality as intimate, and as subtly shaded, as it is possible to make within the approximate restraints of a classical objectivity. Having reached this end in the *Caritas*, Andrea confronts, in this climax of his classical style, its necessary crisis also. For the next three years his art is involved with crisis, and with a probing of new possibilities of direction almost as urgently questioning, but not the same, as in the emerging Mannerists.

Andrea's return to Florence late in 1519 brought him back again to the contemplation of Pontormo's disturbing and radical accomplishment in the Visdomini altar. This time, Andrea's more meditated study took place in the context of his uncertainty, since the accomplishment of the *Caritas*, for the course his art might take. Hesitant himself, and impressed by Pontormo's bold new resolution, Andrea's response to the Visdomini altar was more explicit and affirmative than it had been in early 1518. In one work, and for its moment only, he becomes a pupil of his former pupil; he accepts Pontormo's vocabulary and almost succumbs to the proposition that he makes of a new style. This painting is the *Madonna and Child with St. John* (Rome, Galleria Borghese 334; late 1519, possibly early 1520).[570] There may be just an index in this picture of the route of Andrea's return journey, logically enough by way of Milan; the head of the Madonna seems to recall Leonardo's *Virgin of the Rocks*,[10] and for the first time there appears in one of Andrea's backgrounds what may be his own reduction of Leonardo's geology in that picture.

In the Borghese panel, more evidently than in the *Caritas*, Andrea borrows back from Pontormo the younger painter's highly surcharged variant of what had once been Andrea's theme of joyously inspired and energetic children. The relation of Andrea's Christ Child to the Child of the Pontormo altar is unmistakable, though as Andrea sees the motive it retains the accent of an earlier experience: the famous central figure of the Cascine Cartoon. There is no connection of the motive of St. John's posture with Pontormo's repertory; it is, obviously, an adaptation of Andrea's own invention in the Scalzo *Baptism* of 1517. But in St. John, as in the Christ Child, there is the visible difference from Andrea's earlier comparable forms that has been made by a Pontormesque reinterpretation. The children act with an immediate impulsiveness — almost drastically — with a force of movement more abrupt and an effect of pattern far more sharply angular than ever in Andrea's infants earlier; their emotion equally is more positive and pointed. Their sharpness of effect of form is emphasized by a decisive draughtsmanship, and by a modelling from which the almost excessive refinements of the *Caritas* have gone, and most of all by an urgency of contrast in chiaroscuro for which there is no precedent in Andrea's art, but which is explicit in the altar of the Visdomini. In certain passages of modelling, as in the face of the Madonna, or yet more specifically in that of St. John, the light — and the brush that indicates it — is handled in a manner that almost inverts Andrea's antecedent practice into that of the exactly corresponding passages in the Pontormo. Almost least expected, Andrea's composition accepts from the Pontormo a radical idea of composition, the intrusion into the figure structure of a V-shaped motive, very apparent, and quite abnormal to the classical system of design.

Color in this panel does not depend on the Pontormo, recessive and discreet in this respect alone. The hues are those of Andrea's customary palette, but the manner of their use is altered to accord with the new, Pontormo influenced effect intended by the forms. The color of the Borghese painting is dominated by a powdery blue (for which the only previous analogy is in the London portrait), which glows at once cool and intense in the contrasting light.

From the stimulus taken in Pontormo's altarpiece, Andrea retreats in the Borghese panel from the consummate subtlety of expression of the *Caritas*, and seeks instead a more urgent and more obvious expressive mode; and to this end Andrea uses means and motives of Pontormo's style: this is the nearest point in the orbit of Andrea's art to the new Mannerism. Not only Andrea's adopted devices but his motivations in their use resemble those of Pontormo, but they are not identical; the result in the Borghese picture is not Mannerist. Andrea's will to more pointed and assertive meaning is not a will either to eccentric psychological situation or to disruption of the rationality of form. The emotion that inspires Andrea's children is intense, but it is not, as in the Visdomini altar, a precarious ecstasy. Andrea's infants move with sharp energy, but not in the patterns of disjointed violence of Pontormo's. Even Pontormo's radical V of composition is transformed by Andrea into a device that does not unsettle, but rather more highly charges an equilibrium of composition. Andrea's own asymmetry of design — more daring than Pontormo's in his altar — is manipulated into a balanced integer in end effect. What Andrea makes in his exploitation of Pontormo's means is, finally, a still classical gestalt, of fresh vitality and welcome unconventionality of appearance. A potential new avenue for development of classical style, thus revitalized, is opened to Andrea in the Borghese picture, but it is one too nearly compromised by the use in it, to achieve this end, of Mannerizing means. The whole tonality of such an expression as this, and of its machinery of form in particular, was not native to Andrea's temperament: it was too highly charged; too bold, and without modulation — a mode of feeling and form to which he would not have come except by the momentary impress made on him, in this time of his own uncertainty, by Pontormo's indication of a new direction.

There is no necessary consistency in the happenings of these few years of continuing crisis in Andrea's art. Like Raphael after 1515 Andrea has at his disposal all the past resources of an accomplished classical style to rework and refine, or press — if he can — toward new expressive powers; and he is free as well to probe, obviously less intellectually and less forcefully than Raphael, new and in part unclassical ideas of style. If the *Madonna with St. John and Angels*(?) (London, Wallace Collection 9)[571] belongs, as is most likely, in this place (1520) in Andrea's evolution, probably after the Borghese picture, it seems a reaction from that work's unaccustomed forthrightness of mood and form. The Wallace painting returns toward the manner of the *Caritas*, and works a vein not deeper in the same direction but tangential to its unsurpassable whole demonstration of a style. This picture is a specialized development of what might be described as the feminine aspect of the synthesis that is in the *Caritas*: a development of subtleties at the expense of the power which, in the *Caritas*, wholly compensates them. There is largeness of form in the Wallace picture but — properly to its different size and household function — no such monumentality as in the *Caritas*; and there is a meditated order but not the complex and precise calculation of design that is in that work.

This structure is in its own way remarkable: it is a unity as cogent as that in the *Caritas*, but of very different temper and affect. The Madonna (asymmetrically placed much in the manner of the Borghese picture, and against a background not unlike) establishes a motive of a *serpentinata* that works, as in Andrea's mature designs, in three dimensions simultaneously. This serpentine ascends through the Christ Child, descends from the head of the Madonna toward the right and ascends again, coiling back upon itself, through the St. John and attendant angels; as it moves across the surface it warps as well through the placing of the figures in their space. This armature of the design is a deep, slow convolution, yielding and extremely suave. The forms that amplify it — of a warmer, darker consonance in color than the *Caritas* — are still more than in it *sfumato*-soft; their contours meld more subtly with the atmosphere. In the drawing with the brush there is an utmost fineness, in places a delicacy, that is quite in contrast with the handling of the Borghese panel.

This whole yielding form and what the figures demonstrate of feeling are inseparable reciprocal functions of one another. There is no comparable illustration of a quality of love that so softly permeates the countenance, either in Andrea or even in the pictures of the earlier Raphael. The cast of this emotion is feminine, or childish, as befits its bearers; only a shade less of continence in its expression would make it sentimental. The Madonna here is surely identifiable as a portrait of Andrea's wife, as she is not so identifiable in most of the instances Vasari takes care elsewhere to allege; she is the same person who earlier was portrayed as St. Catherine in the *Holy Family* of Leningrad.[558] Here she takes the primary role, and Andrea's private feeling for the actor is infused through her into what is enacted. More than any earlier one among Andrea's pictures, this one demonstrates his responsive sensibility (which is a creative projection at the same time) to the psychological situation of his actors, and the sense of his identification (at once as creator and spectator) with them. In the Borghese panel Andrea had attempted to intensify the immediacy both of emotional and physical presence by means, and in a key of urgency, that were not entirely his own; in the Wallace picture, exploiting and refining resources that were peculiarly his, he achieves this end far more effectively. There are no closer presences to us, nor any which we feel more compellingly in Andrea's art except in the picture which, by our reckoning, succeeds this one.

This intenser presence is in the *Pietà* (Vienna, Kunsthistorisches Museum; c. 1521),[572] in which occasion, in the form of subject matter, and intention coincide to make the most impassioned communication in Andrea's art. His treatment of the subject matter in this way would have been impossible in any other time than this one of crisis in his art: we know enough of the lost *Pietà* of 1515–16 to gauge its different character, and the Pitti *Pietà* of 1524 provides the contrast of a later, and more settled, term. This version of the theme was conceived in a context that was, now, not only of Andrea's private searching after new avenues of expression but of probable further stimulation by — or even, perhaps, rivalry with — the increased production of the younger Mannerists; not, however, with the effect their first impact had on him of imitation. With means significantly different, but almost as inventive as those of the Mannerists, Andrea creates an image in this *Pietà* of no less cogent kind.

The resource of feeling that, in the Wallace Madonna, had seemed to be inexhaustible of tenderness and subtleties now yields an opposite emotive power. Where, in the Wallace picture, the spectator is as if received into its yielding and diffused, feminine, personality, in the *Pietà* the form and content are assertive. The handling is of the sharpest brilliance, quicker than even in Andrea's work before, and brighter in its light; and feeling is precisely focused and, in the person of the Virgin, projected out toward us. There is no difference from the Wallace painting in the degree of emotional identification we are meant to make with this image, but the kind of emotion and the direction of its working are unlike. In the Madonna of the *Pietà* Andrea's powers of psychological characterization are employed to make a countenance of anguish as convincing as the Wallace Madonna's countenance of love; in the anguish there is also love, but in a different aspect. In both pictures feeling is, in its fullest possible sense, a sympathy.

Andrea sees this theme, now, not as a projection of diffused and gentle pathos (as it had been in the *Pietà* of 1516), nor as an *existenzbild* (as it would become in 1524), but as a concentration of emotion in its utmost poignancy: the Virgin's countenance is the entire climax for the form and human meaning of this work. The other figures, even that of the lamented Christ, are accessory in place to the Virgin; and the movement of design is gathered in her. To assure entirely her domination of the picture she is described in slightly but perceptibly enlarged scale. Her face is framed by a shape of sharpest visual pregnance in the white coif, which at once isolates and comments what it frames by the excitement of its bright-lit, shifting pattern. The Virgin leans only a little forward, yet she seems to loom toward us, certainly psychologically more imminent than the body of the Christ and seemingly almost physically as near. Beside and behind the Virgin the mourning angels are relatively recessive and discreet, contrastingly accenting her aggressive pathos. The psychological implications that might be in the head or even in the body of the Christ are deliberately minimized: there is no residue of agony in the countenance and only the least trace of it in the corpse. His body is the visible but mute cause of the emotion of the Virgin. However, the Christ is the most explicit and assertive physical presence in the whole art of Andrea. He is an utterly unidealized simulacrum of nature, an apparently objective fact as close to us as it is possible to be. This picture demands not only our identification with its intense actuality of psychological existence, reaching toward us in communication, but imposes our immediate acceptance of the near presence of its physical facts.

There is no difference from the Mannerists in the intensity of emotion that Andrea invents in this picture, nor in the energy or extreme immediacy of its communication, but there is a marked distinction in the ways in which Andrea has achieved these ends. Andrea's avenue to more urgent expressiveness, both of emotion and of form, is by intensification of the sense of actuality of what, in natural experience, we might feel and see. His alteration in this work from his former style is in a lessening of ideality and an increase of naturalism, not unlike what we have observed in aspects of the latest classical style in Rome. Also, in this same respect, the community of the Vienna *Pietà* is less with Florentine Mannerism as we shall come to know it in this moment than — as we have observed of other tendencies in Andrea's art before — with contemporary phenomena of style in North Italy. This direction of research, if it were investigated strongly, could lead to a style of protobaroque character resembling that of Correggio. There is in fact a discernible analogy of style between this *Pietà* and the *Pietà* (Parma, Galleria Nazionale) of Correggio, usually dated between 1522 and 1526. As in that picture, the new urgency of participation by the spectator is in an intenser naturalness and not, as in Mannerism, in a more assertive inward vision: the subjective identification of the spectator is with the life within a more convincing, realized, object. In this sense of presence that Andrea achieves in his *Pietà* his innate tendency toward naturalism and his inclination to transcribe optical experience find a use like that they have in a protobaroque style.

The direction of a protobaroque is implied in Andrea's painting, but not more: it is still more attached to the classical style than it is distinguishable from it, and even its new tendencies are communicated through finally controlling classical principles. It is not like contemporary Mannerism, or contemporary works of protobaroque cast, that emotion here, intensified as much as it may be, is neither eccentric nor irrationally possessed; furthermore, the passion of the Virgin is projected in the context of a moderating chord of feeling in the attendant figures. Nor are Andrea's actors moved by their emotion to such demonstrative excess in posture — inspired, tormented, or merely artificial — as in nonclassical works; their attitudes are deeply decorously contained. What communicates excitement is the movemented pattern, of drawing and light and, in part, of color, that overlays these forms;

but the forms themselves are essentially stable and their mode of arrangement in a composition is, if anything, more indicative of high classical principle than some of Andrea's previous designs. Beneath the tissue of activity of light and drawing there is a manifest clear order, synthesized from the favorite motives of the classical repertory of design: a whole containing rounding shape, a gathering and stabilizing triangle, and a rectilinear grid. All of this is articulated in plastic forms that fill a limited and planar space close to but still, despite its great imminence, discrete from us. The community of style in which Andrea's picture belongs is still much more that of Fra Bartolommeo's latest *Pietà* than that of the contemporary Correggio, or of Rosso and Pontormo.

There is one more major document of this time of critical research by Andrea: the fresco *Tribute to Caesar*,[573] in the great hall of the Medicean villa at Poggio a Cajano where in the same year, 1521, Franciabigio and Pontormo also painted. In Andrea's fresco, almost diametrically unlike Pontormo's exposition there of a new aspect of the new Mannerism, Andrea achieves a result that is like the Vienna *Pietà* in basic character of style but, in consequence of its utterly diverse subject matter and scale, different in its repertory of inventive means. The energy and unconventionality, once more of proto-baroque cast, of ordering this fresco's monumental matter is Andrea's farthest probing of a new direction for his style. He still does not effect a revolution in this fresco in his own art, nor does he make of it a precedent of sufficient novelty to influence the art of others. This effort at Poggio is Andrea's last — almost — radical experiment; in the next years he returns to a reaffirmed classical position.

For the remainder of the decade, until the end of his career in 1530, Andrea works the permutations and combinations of an accomplished classical style with consummate intelligence, in no sense a doctrinaire of opposition to the increasing eminence of Mannerism but content enough with a different, and continuing, validity of his classical ideas. Only toward the end of Andrea's life does his standard of achievement lessen. His principle of classicism does not then change but its vitality diminishes, surely from his own lessening personal vitality, but perhaps also — and this is a matter for profounder speculation than we can give it here — from circumstances inherent in the cumulative changes of Florentine culture in the 1520's. But through most of this decade in Florence, in a context of unclassical experiment still more restless than that in contemporary Rome, Andrea's works demonstrated the continuing efficacy as aesthetic expression, and as a personal if not a generic cultural attitude, of the classical style.

Franciabigio's style had matured toward 1514–1515 and to some extent had set, at that time, in a different mold from Andrea's or Fra Bartolommeo's. He had incorporated into his style much of the look and some, but by no means all, of the principles of their classicism: he had retained a resistant core of preclassical mentality of form and a disposition toward unclassically graceless, though effective, pathos of content. Franciabigio had approached, toward 1515, but not yet reached his limit of capacity to absorb yet more of the example of the greater masters of the Florentine classical style.

However, the hybrid mode he had achieved seemed not only adequate to his intentions of expression but positively proper to them, and strongly communicative of Franciabigio's individual artistic personality. In his more important works that come within this present phase Francesco continues more or less to work in such a mode, by no means untouched by the developments of art around him, but essentially along a private course. What happens in his art is only partly relevant, from this time on, to the central issue in the evolution of the greater Florentines, both of his and of the younger generation, of classical or unclassical intention. His own evolution had been arrested, as it were, at an antecedent point in the history of this issue. Nevertheless, his art continues to confront it even with a vocabulary that now seems old-fashioned; and that which in his style had never been synthesized in an effective classicism comes to look, in the context of the events of this time in Florentine painting, like what is in the current process of a dissolution of classical synthesis. Franciabigio's hybrid style thus acquires, in these years, a specious historical effect of a modernity.

His *Annunciation* (Turin, Galleria Sabauda; c. 1515)[574] is an index of his situation toward the beginning of this phase. The picture is compounded of observations not quite comprehendingly made in the works of other contemporary masters, all of them in most general sense adherents of Bartolommeo's school (as is the almost universal case at this moment in Florence) but each of them different in his measure of adoption of Bartolommesque classicism: to be interested at once in the models of Albertinelli, Sarto, and Ridolfo Ghirlandaio certainly evinces no single-minded attitude toward classical style. Albertinelli's *Annunciation* altar of 1510[259] provides Francesco with the motive and much of the actual surface cast of style of his God the Father; Ridolfo Ghirlandaio's wonderfully awkward angel of the Cappella Priori fresco of 1514[285] is adapted, with an only somewhat less literal-minded handling, in Francesco's angel; the painting for S. Gallo by Andrea of circa 1512[309] affords the idea for Francesco's setting. The character of style of each borrowed part retains a visible trace of that of the source from which it came.

Francesco is concerned, however, to approximate in general, a little more convincingly, some things that he had grasped of classicism since the — for him unhappy — episode in the courtyard of the Annunziata. He had, in the interval, returned to study Andrea's rival fresco more exactly. Where Francesco can paraphrase its figure style, as in his Virgin, he does so: her form is modelled in roundness and suavity after Andrea's women of the *Birth of the Virgin*, and more precisely on the kneeling handmaid of the fresco. The accent of Francesco's paraphrase is, in contrast with his example, monotonous and unyielding; the Virgin's figure is, most unlike Andrea's, plastically isolated by sharp line and even light. She does seem monumental, but Francesco's means to monumentality is not by classical coincidence of amplitude and ponderation in the form, but by amplitude alone. He also expands in breadth the idea of a setting that Andrea gave him in the S. Gallo altar, and extends its depth as well. What Francesco achieves thereby (in this literal portrait of the Villa at Poggio a Cajano) has a clarity and largeness like that of a mature classical space, but quite lacks the essential classical effect of unity with its content of figures. This is still an additive relation between space and solids — as it is, indeed, among all parts of the composition, more even than in the antecedent *Cena* of the Calza or the *Marriage of the Virgin*. Francesco has apparently misread the injunction to a higher clarity of order that he sees in classical example, and in Andrea's example in particular, transcribing from it an effect of isolation more than an effect of indissoluble relation of forms.

As much as the *Annunciation* is eclectic, the product of Francesco's effort to gather what was happening in art around him, so is the *St. Job Altar* (Florence, Uffizi; dated 1516)[576] contrastingly a deeply personal expression, of singular pathetic power — stark, gloomy, and quite unbeautiful. Against a darkened architecture, of Brunelleschian severity, the few figures are set out in apparently simplest relation, each as an almost isolated shape: the John (a self-portrait of the artist, according to Vasari [V, 191]) and Job in near symmetry to the left and right, and the Virgin and Child in the center, not in a contrapposto but in a chiasma of their two forms, each oppositely inclined. A set of repetitions and intersections of diagonal motives of direction, between the Madonna and Child and the Saints, creates a pattern of relation among their separate forms. This pattern is quite singular, unlike in affect to precedent Florentine schemes of classical — or even unclassical — design. It is baldly simple, strict in geometric order, movemented, and at the same time stiff; relieved as it is in exaggeratedly contrasting light it acquires an abstractness of effect as of a diagram.

The inorganic movement of the whole design is exactly that of the figures out of which it is composed; yet these forms convey, however awkwardly, an impressive actuality of presence and a thoroughly convincing content of emotion. Both of these are conditioned by the nature of the light in which they are described: a deep chiaroscuro, inspired, probably, by the example of Fra Bartolommeo's *Pitti Pala* of 1512,[264] but different in its mode of use and in effect. Francesco's light is a greyed chill gloom (the very atmosphere of a Florentine church interior in dark midwinter), harsh in force of contrasts; isolating smooth hardnesses of form and searching passages of literal detail. It is less a differentiating unity, as in Bartolommesque, or in contemporary Sartesque, chiaroscuro, than a *proto-tenebroso.* It is peculiarly expressive in its special melancholy way and its flavor is intrinsic to the pathos of the picture.

It is this work that especially suggests the simultaneous and contradictory effects, of modernity and of archaism, in Francesco's style. Its design has the look of an inadequately comprehended classicism; but at the same time its disjointedness, its rigidity in movement, and its effect as of abstractness suggests what is also in the Mannerists' disruption of classical methods of design. Its chiaroscuro is an insensitive forcing of a Bartolommesque mode; but the result, of schematically sharpened contrasts, resembles what Pontormo, for example, imminently is to do — but with an altogether different deliberation of aesthetic purpose. The harshness of form and precision of drawing of detail in this picture is a traceable archaism of Francesco's style; but it suggests a contemporary tendency, not so much in Florence as in the school of Raphael in Rome. The graceless urgency of feeling that is here had also been a constant since Francesco's earlier career; but in that the conviction of his pathos is more important than its beauty, there is common ground between this, unclassical, and the postclassical attitude toward emotion. It is in general in the elements of community that we may find between the not-yet and the no-longer classical that this altar makes its seeming forward reference; according to a logic most familiar to us in the world of fashion, Francesco's old clothes look, once again, almost new.

There is not only both archaism and specious, quasi-Mannerist novelty in this work but — to complete its interest as a symptomatic historical document, if not as a work of art — a strong analogue with the most significant exactly contemporary aspect of the classical style itself. It is not wholly certain that Francesco could have known Fra Bartolommeo's essay of the same year in his severest style of classicism, the *Salvator Mundi*[536] but the assumption should be made of such a knowledge; it accounts, more easily than a possible invention by Francesco would, for the plainness and rigor of design in the *St. Job* altar. That all these disparate references of style intersect in this picture is not an indication of its stylelessness — in the sense of "style" as a personal *maniera* this work is a very highly characterized expression of a personality — but a demonstration of a broad historical fact we are too much inclined to lose from sight: that the matrix of art in Florence at this moment is an interwoven texture of preclassical, classical, and already postclassical elements of style, and that discrete phenomena of style are differentiated from this matrix by acts of individual artistic will. To make this differentiation required a different order of consistency and power of aesthetic purpose than that which Franciabigio possessed.

A more sophisticated variant of the style of the *St. Job* altar is in the two panels, each with a boy-angel, which frame the statue (after a *modello* by Jacopo Sansovino) on the altar of the Chapel of S. Nicola di Tolentino in Sto. Spirito (c. 1517–18).[575] In these, the intention of precise actuality of presence is as strong as in the preceding altarpiece, but the means to it are not so harsh and probing. Both the drawing and the mode of lighting have been much refined: the drawing into more intimate and rhythmically responsive indication of the form, of drapery especially, and the light into a more finely differentiating modelling of surface. The tendency and manner of refinement are like those in Sarto's example of these very years, and (considering the subsequent events of Francesco's style) it is likely that their appearance here is in consequence of study of Andrea's art. The accent of style in the angels becomes thus more identifiably like that in the contemporary Sarto, and there is not the difficult coincidence in them of rude archaism and modernity that was in the *St. Job* altar. However, the effect of marked individuality of Francesco's expression is not diminished by this partial concession to Andrea. The shapes that he sets down are finer in articulation than before, but they retain their basic gracelessness — an inescapable function of Franciabigio's gestalt. The tonality of light also, despite its new Sartesque differentiation, remains like that of the *St. Job* altar, hard and of a darkling melancholy. This melancholy, now more complex in the manner of its expression in posture of the body and in countenance, still dominates the content of the angels: it is the almost ineradicable quality of *bigio*, both of vision and feeling, that is in Francesco's art as well as in his name.

When Andrea del Sarto left for France in the late spring or early summer of 1518, it was presumed for good, the Confraternity of the Scalzo turned for the further decoration of their cloister to Franciabigio, the next in reputation among the older painters in the city. On July 27, 1518, first payment was made to him for a fresco of the *Meeting of Christ and St. John Baptist,*[577] then still to be executed; on March 18, 1519, payment was made for this and for another painting, the *Benediction of St. John by Zachary,*[579] then both complete. These scenes (much damaged; their lower parts all but obliterated) take up the story of the Baptist on the long wall opposite that on which Andrea had so far painted. Again, Francesco was in the difficult position that had so discomforted him before, in the courtyard of the Annunziata, of inviting comparison with Andrea. This time, however, the disparity of their styles in respect of classical development was not quite so great; Francèsco had since profited by the lesson that had been taught him in the Annunziata.

In these paintings he takes up again, but with the benefit of his increased sophistication, the fresco mode he had first attempted in 1514, in the *Cena*[315] of the Calza. It had been there that he had first decided, after the impact on him of Andrea's *Birth of the Virgin*,[311] that the first requirement of the new monumentality was sheer bulk of form; now, for the Scalzo frescoes, he conceives figures of equal or still greater largeness of dimension. He models these shapes with a precision he did not command in 1514, so that they make a strong assertion of plasticity. Squarish in outline, heavy-set and massive, swathed in complex foldings of drapery (of the seeming density of a sculptor's gessoed *modello*), these forms have the highest specific gravity of any in Florentine art. In this sense they are an innovation, but not of classical style. They quite overwhelm Andrea's figures, but by bulk alone. They do achieve an awkwardly impressive dignity; and they act (more articulately than in the Calza *Cena*), or even are immobile, with a ponderousness that lends conviction to their meaning: this, as always in Francesco, is a genuine but graceless pathetic sincerity.

As much as in the Calza fresco and more than in the recent altarpieces there is an effort to make, in classicizing manner, cursive relations of connection among these forms. Each of them has so strong a plastic identity, however, that they resist connection. The style of composition at which Francesco arrives is not synthetic; it is rather, as in certain early works of Fra Bartolommeo, a conjunctive system of design. So also are the two separate compositions conjunctive with each other: invented at one time (unlike Andrea's constantly interrupted works in this place), neither fresco is intended to make a whole internal balance in its composition but to function in a balance with its neighbor. In each scene there is a diagonal direction — making some small effect of animation on the heaviness of forms — which is meant to lead to, and be compensated by, the opposite diagonal of the adjacent fresco. As in the *St. Job* altar an evident intellectual deliberation has gone into the making of design but, as there, this deliberation is curiously abstract in its results. There is an almost art-school air in these compositions, as of the seeking of "interesting," but inadequately motivated, device. Francesco's deliberation is of effects, but not sufficiently profoundly of principles.

Francesco's substitution for Andrea in the Scalzo decoration seems to have been only part of such a function of deputizing in Florence for the absent Andrea. The *Madonna and Child with St. John* (Vienna, Kunsthistorisches Museum 208; c. 1518–19),[578] clearly of Francesco's execution, is a partial paraphrase — a copy, almost — of Andrea's more elaborate composition of c. 1517–18 in the Louvre (no. 1516), to which a landscape (taken nearly literally from the early *Madonna del Pozzo* [87]) has been appended. The dependence on Andrea is not just of exact composition but of manner; Francesco has willfully attempted as much as is possible to him of a counterfeit of Andrea's painting style. The effort is of only dubious success; Francesco's native heaviness of hand does not permit a more than superficial approximation of Andrea. Such a surrender of identity is unexpected in an artist whose personality, as we have seen it manifest itself in recent years, is so strongly marked, yet its result is familiar: it recalls the close relation of Francesco and Andrea in earlier years, when they were partners. It is possible that this entire concession to Andrea is the consequence of some renewal of this ancient arrangement, perhaps for this painting only: a work commissioned from Andrea may have been left instead, on his departure, for execution by Francesco. Other suppositions come to mind, however, perhaps as valid; among them that this picture may have had no motivation of any economic kind to account for its appearance but may be a gratuitous admission by Francesco, in the form of imitation, of the superior interest of Andrea's style. Whatever the specific *raison d'être* of this painting, the Sartesque inclination that it demonstrates is not unique: *in a small *Leda* (Brussels, Museum; probably very close to Vienna 208 in time)[580] Franciabigio refurbishes the famous composition of Leonardo, but with an accent both in type and handling that is pronouncedly Sartesque.

The access of *Sartismo* seems to have been no more than an episode in this phase of Franciabigio's career, and it was an alternative rather than an exclusive tendency if we assume, as we do, that these two evidences for it are contemporaneous with the very personal manner that Francesco demonstrated in the Scalzo frescoes. Even as an alternative it was of no significant duration; it appears to have coincided more or less with the time when Andrea was not in Florence to represent his style for himself — or criticize its counterfeit by others. Toward 1520 Francesco seems to have resumed his own personality exclusively, continuing a development that, in panel painting, is consequent on the *St. Job* altar and, in fresco, on the Scalzo scenes of 1518–1519. A *Madonna* (Bologna, Pinacoteca 294; c. 1520)[581] represents the former category; in it Francesco employs a compositional type, of the Madonna in three-quarter length behind a parapet, which approximates one used by him in an earlier phase (Rome, Galleria Nazionale; dated 1509).[305] The effect of the compositional idea is altogether in Francesco's present vocabulary: this form has the largeness of dimension and the affirmation of plasticity of the figures in the Scalzo frescoes. In sharp silhouette against the landscape setting, the Madonna (and the shape of the Child, which hers includes) have a similar impact of gravity and — for more than a quantitative reason only — a higher unity. This unity proceeds not only from the continence of form in one large outline but from the manner of description of the form within. There is not the labored complication of large folds of drapery, as in the Scalzo style, nor the worrying particularism of detail that was in the Madonna of the *St. Job*;[576] instead there is a higher and simpler mode of generalization that permits — for the first time in Francesco's maturer style — the coherence of parts of form into the whole. Finally, Francesco's process of selection of the data of appearance works according to a recognizable classical principle.

The figures still act ponderously, but their relation in movement is far more responsively calculated than before: the two shapes of the Madonna and Child confront each other in an interlocking pattern of parallel rhythms, not of isolated repetitions as in the composition of the *St. Job* altar. This picture makes a unity of impressive, even rather grand form, heavily and still rather awkwardly movemented; and this quality of form is that also of its human content — a grave pathos, all the more convincing for the touch of awkwardness with which it is expressed.

As on occasion since the time of the Calza *Cena*, but nowhere so much as in this more developed work, Francesco suggests analogy in his heavy dignity of form and gravity of pathetic intent with an aspect of the classical style in Rome. For this picture the analogy is more nearly, but by no means exactly, specifiable: on a very differently ineloquent level of accomplishment, it is with the contemporary style of Sebastiano. No influence need be implied; the analogy arises from the working on similar data of resembling traits of personality. Yet there is the more than casual possibility that what Francesco was so slow to grasp of classicism from his betters in Florence was finally effectively impressed on him by a second experience of contemporary art in Rome, possibly in 1520. The plastic and dramatic temper that prevailed in Roman classicism was much more nearly sympathetic to the personality of Francesco than the fine and introspective temper of Sartesque style; like Sarto himself, Franciabigio was more likely to heed a lesson taught by Rome.

When, in 1521, Franciabigio joined Andrea and Pontormo in the decoration of the *Salone* at Poggio a Cajano, his *Triumph of Caesar* [582] was conceived* in a style that is a conceivable result of study of the Stanza dell' Incendio; not only the character of style but some specific motives in Francesco's fresco suggest the possibility of such connection. Now, there is small trace of the rudenesses (and at least among the principal figures, none of the archaisms) that had been so stubbornly persistent in Francesco's art. This is at last, and almost without equivocation, a sophisticated and explicitly "modern" accomplishment, as effective a probing of a new dimension for Florentine classical style as Andrea's companion, but different, research. Francesco comes abreast of Andrea's development of classicism at what is, in a sense, its apogee and — in the larger perspective of the history of Florentine painting — also its end. Whatever combination of personal effort and external influence carried Franciabigio to this point, it was a situation he did not exploit, and seemingly had not resource enough even to maintain; in the few works that come between this time and his death in January 1525, his art regresses, for the most part, toward its former stature.

What there was of pedestrian personality in Franciabigio emerges most in the portraits that he painted in this phase. In these, the momentary Leonardism of the portraits dated 1514, *sfumato* in form and expression, is replaced by a literalness still less interesting, if that is possible, than in the usual portrait style of Ridolfo Ghirlandaio. To explain this alteration in Francesco's portraiture may require the influence on him of Ridolfo's work; Ridolfo's portraits were still, toward 1515, the most popular demonstration in Florence of the genre. In the records of the faces of contemporaries that Franciabigio has left us, as in Ridolfo's, there may be a corrective to the tendency to generalize about a Florentine society pervaded, in these years, by a ferment of intellect and spirit — like that which is in a part only of the contemporary art, and to some degree is even in Francesco's art, when he is not confronted so directly with his fellow-citizens who are, prima facie, art patrons.

Francesco's own features have been set down in a self-portrait, in which he holds his tools of art, taken almost full-face to the mirror (New York, Hunter College, ex Kress Collection 1060; c. 1515?).[583] Granted the effect of a broken — or badly bent — nose seen at a different angle, this face compares sufficiently well to the self-portrait Vasari has identified for us in the Baptist of the *St. Job* altar. There is nothing here, however, of the shadowed emotionalism Francesco had painted into his impersonation of St. John. He has described himself with the same unbeautifying scrupulousness as in the altar, but in a clear and evenly revealing light. He does not permit any subjective factor to intrude into the form that might distort the truth of record of appearance; and there is as little as it seems could be possible in a self-portrait of psychological self-revelation. The look is the intent staring, sharp and somewhat stiffly fixed, of a man seeking the objective fact his mirror has arrested, and no more; yet it cannot help but tell us something of the personality, serious, laboring, and intense, that comes through elsewhere in Francesco's art. As an iconographic document this portrait has a double interest: as a record of appearance of the artist obviously, but more as a type of the self-portrait. There is no earlier known instance in which the painter shows himself to us with tools in hand, in the act of confrontation with the mirror. It is indicative of the temperament we already know that Francesco should attempt to tell us of himself so honestly. As the Mannerists will later do, he is searching for a truth of portraiture differently direct from that in a classical portrait image, but he seeks for it in an opposite, objective, direction.

There is more formality, but hardly less objectivity, in Francesco's portrait of the goldsmith Caradosso (London, art market, formerly Yarborough Collection; dated 1516).[584] There is a specious Raphaelesque reminiscence, in this portrait, of the recent *Fedra*, but only from the grossness of physique of the subject; actually its reference is to the older (and in Florence, accessible and persistently influential) model, the *Angelo Doni*.[52] Adapting a Flemish or, equally possibly, a Venetian device, the figure is posed behind a parapet. Like Francesco himself, this sitter willingly demonstrates the identifying symbols of his trade. The form of composition is of simple geometrical effect, unavoidably broad, and equally unavoidably massive. The aesthetic deliberation of the artist stops with the carefully restrained and heavily balanced posing of the figure; from there onward in the process of painting the effects of art are deliberately minimal. Surfaces are smooth, and there is no rein given whatsoever (as there is in the contemporary religious paintings) to any ornamental manipulation of effects of light or draughtsmanship. The intention is to make record of an actual appearance, in which art, by Franciabigio's apparent calculation, would interfere. This object is accurately and unbeautifully achieved, and with some worth of a pedestrian dignity.

There is a nearly Germanic accent in the unsparing realism with which Francesco seems to have transcribed the very different subject, spare and unshaven, of the portrait dated 1517 (Vienna, Liechtenstein Collection 157).[585] In this instance only among the portraits of this phase, Francesco has recalled the chiaroscuro he had used in his portraits of 1514, and something also of their introspection, but in this context of unhandsome actuality these factors make a most unlike effect. This light is not a *sfumato* veiling but a means of opposite hard revelation, stressed within the dark silhouette in *contre-jour*; and the expression is of an unattractive, timid melancholy. The nature of the subject seems to have been such as to demand some more direct involvement with his personality than in the other portraits of this time, and some commentary on it by effects of light and composition. But such subjective indicators as there are are reticent. We still feel mostly of this portrait that what we see is the truth of appearance and habitual expression of this man: we are reminded that there still were *piagnoni* in Florence at this late date.

The last important portrait of this phase, of the *Fattore* of Pier Francesco de' Medici (Hampton Court; c. 1518–20)[586] is again unequivocally an objective record; it employs much the same means, and achieves an effect, not dissimilar to that of the *Caradosso*. The accessories of occupation here are multiplied: in the background there are gardeners' tools, and across the sitter's forearm the keys of the property entrusted to his care; the parapet on which he leans serves him as a desk on which he is shown in the act of keeping his accounts. There is the wish, in this as in the self-portrait and in the *Caradosso*, to show more of the actuality of the sitter than his looks alone: what he is in a yet more objectifiable sense, in his function in the practical world, has been described. In the *Fattore*'s portrait Franciabigio makes not merely an identifying reference to this function but a catalogue. As a conception of a man shown in his social state it is without exact precedent in the portraiture of Florence: this is a bourgeois anticipation of the later idea, differently aristocratic, of the state portrait.

In all these portraits their pedestrian character of form and content is not merely a projection of a facet of Francesco's own personality; it is a result of a willed objectivity in point of view toward the character which, in this time, he believed the portrait should possess. Francesco's portraits are an evidence of his searching for a variety of truth more graspable than that of the "fine" art of his religious pictures, and a meaning more simple and immediate than that which he tried to find in those religious works by such effortful manipulation of feeling and aesthetic form. Unlike Andrea or the more gifted of the younger artists, Franciabigio could not wholly reconcile the requirements of actuality with those of art.

THE SECONDARY MASTERS

BUGIARDINI

In the closing years of the preceding phase of his development Giulio Bugiardini had evolved the style which, with some alteration, was to serve him for some time to come. This style represents his attainment, sufficiently tardily, of a personal maturity. After about 1512 he no longer found it necessary to experiment with new varieties of borrowed modes; the one he had adapted from Fra Bartolommeo about that date seemed basically adequate to Bugiardini's limited expressive needs. There is no indication in his art of this present phase of any interest in the more novel inventions of style in painting. His comprehension of the resources even of Bartolommeo's classical style was incomplete; and he could not respond, even in a superficial imitative sense, as did Franciabigio for one moment, to the more complex classicism of Andrea del Sarto. Still less, evidently, was he capable of response to the innovations of the younger generation. Bugiardini had his own conspicuous eccentricities and his unclassicisms, but they were not, as in the younger artists, aesthetically purposeful. In this situation of style Bugiardini reflects what is, in general, that of the secondary painters in Florence of his approximate generation.

Because in this period (and for almost a decade later) Bugiardini does not show the traceable succession of adopted manners that was apparent in his earlier works there is less possibility than before of a fairly definite chronology for his paintings; and there is no more external support than there was earlier for the dating of his works. It is only very loosely that we place his *Temptation in the Garden of Eden* (New York, private collection; on two canvases)[587] in the neighborhood of 1515; its time of production could as well be somewhat earlier or later: close in time to the *Leda* of the Treccani Collection or, alternatively, to the time of his execution for Fra Bartolommeo of the Pitti *Pietà*. There is no marked change in the *Temptation* from the conception of types or of human form that was in the *Leda*, but such differences as do exist are not altogether incidental. These figures are (unless this is an illusion of condition) less Quattrocento-harsh than the *Leda* in modelling and in contrast with the background, more flexible in movement of their contour and not quite so graceless in pose: they approximate, if only awkwardly, the look and logic of classical contrapposto. More evidently than in the *Leda* there is — beyond the obvious arrangement into near-symmetry of the Adam and the Eve — some care, in the adjustment of relations of composition, to make continuities of rhythm and responsive balances of form. This thinking of design, more classicizing than in the *Leda*, sees both the figures and their setting as parts of a coherent unity of pattern.

The shape of this composition and the design invented by Bugiardini for its subject matter are both exceptional and it may be that an exceptional circumstance accounts for them. The likeness of shape and (in each of the single canvases) approximate size to those paintings by Andrea and Pontormo presumed to be for the decoration made for Leo X, the similarities in posture of the figures, and the possible coincidence of date in 1515 make it a speculative possibility that Bugiardini's picture was some part of the apparatus of this same occasion. The resemblance to Piero di Cosimo (to whom this picture has been attributed; Douglas), in idea if not in handling, would then be not only an extension of a tendency observed in the prior panels of "Antique" nudes but a consequence of actual renewed association: the documents indicate that Bugiardini and Piero both "dipinsero ed abbigliarono le figure" (Vasari V, 25n3) on the arches set up for Leo's triumph.

The softer surfaces and more relaxed and flowing contours that we believe we discern in the *Temptation* are more clearly visible in the *St. Sebastian* (New York, Kress Collection 1172; c. 1517),[588] who is almost interchangeable in anatomy with the Adam. The *Sebastiano* is, however, more fluently, even — for Bugiardini — slickly drawn. The motive of Sebastiano's pose cannot but help recall the many instances of the same theme by Perugino; but still more clearly, Bugiardini's Saint shows the result of his exposure, even if only partly successfully, to the mature classicism of the intervening years. Bugiardini labors to achieve an almost modern sophistication of contrapposto, and more than in any earlier — and more also than in most succeeding works for a long time to come — he achieves, by sheer obvious insistence, some effect of cursive grace. With the awkward inventive intelligence of form that Bugiardini demonstrates sporadically he has treated the branches of Sebastiano's tree (of an eccentricity of shape he repeats often in succeeding years) as if they were an extension of the contrapposto of the Saint: an ingenious idea which, as Bugiardini works it out for us in visible form, at once becomes obvious and inept; but this is the unfortunate destiny of most of this painter's hard-found, and sometimes original ideas.

The *Sebastiano* is evidently closer to a sense of classical style than Bugiardini's paintings of the time preceding 1515, yet it still seems, in the context of achievement of the major masters of this present phase, most *arrière;* ten years before, perhaps, it would have worn the look of entire contemporaneity. There is an air of backward reference also in his *Madonna and Child with the Infant St. John* (Dunblane, Collection Stirling; only roughly datable c. 1517).[589] This work suggests Bugiardini's continued study, a decade or so after the fact, of Raphael's Madonnas of the *Prato* group, and what he has made of his study seems somewhat to resemble what Franciabigio accomplished in his Raphaelesque derivations long before, toward 1508 or 1509. The look of a stylistic archaism is, however, only one aspect of this painting. This striving and self-conscious, but only incomplete, intelligence has realized something of the changing atmosphere of Fra Bartolommeo's later style, and has tried to infuse what he understands of it into this work of his own. Bugiardini has tried to "modernize" the older Raphaelesque basis of composition, instilling in it a more vigorous and spatially complex action, and one which has more communicative pathos. The character of form as well as feeling is not like that in the youthful Raphaels but is more consonant with the ideals of severity and dignity of a more nearly contemporary classical style. As in the *Temptation* and the *St. Sebastian*, there is Bugiardini's accustomed discrepancy between the merit of idea and that of execution, but the gap here is perhaps less grave. The posture of the Virgin — a spatial contrapposto arranged around oppositely intersecting diagonals — is so decisively conceived, and the articulation of her feeling is so convincing, that these main facts all but override the painter's too conspicuous ineptitude in other matters.

The reference to Fra Bartolommeo's painting style is quite evident in the manner of handling of the Stirling Madonna; but in the picture of the same theme (Florence, Uffizi; signed and dated 1520)[590] the connection with Bartolommeo's vocabulary is no longer so clear. The chiaroscuro mode, which had conditioned Bugiardini's native harshness of handling in his works since 1512, has here receded somewhat. Light and dark are treated in sharply delineated contrasts, and pattern made by line assumes a new measure of importance. Surfaces are harder than ever before in Bugiardini's style (but matt, and not as they had once before seemed to be, metallic). In all likelihood this deviation from Bartolommeo's manner in the few years since his death was motivated more by personal impulse than by outside influence: these qualities are the reassertion, in more sophisticated terms, of tendencies present long before in Bugiardini's art. However, in their more precise and consciously articulate definition in the Uffizi picture they assume another value: no longer archaic-seeming but, inversely — in a process that we have observed before — suggestive of comparison with phenomena that are relatively modern in the experience of classical style. There is some resemblance in this handling of form to that in Franciabigio's *Madonna* (Bologna),[581] which we think closely contemporary; and perhaps yet more than Francesco's picture this one offers points of comparison with quite current phenomena of style in Rome. Hard-surfaced and sharp-drawn, stiff in articulation — of artificial and of rather statuary effect — Bugiardini's Madonna would, as a generalization, not be wholly out of place among the works that issued in this time, under Giulio Romano's direction, from the Raphael shop.

The design of the Uffizi picture is not wholly new. In the figures it nearly literally reuses the cartoon of a signed painting by Bugiardini of some years earlier (Allentown, Pennsylvania, Museum; from the Kress Collection),[591] in the artist's imitative Raphaelesque phase. The idea is, again, at once ingenious and obvious: it is the result of hard aesthetic deliberation apparently initially inspired by Raphael's unfinished *Madonna Esterhazy*, but of which the result is in the end original. In the early version of the design its articulation emphasizes, as much as this is possible to Bugiardini, the connective fluency within its rhythmic pattern; in the later version only relatively slight changes in the scheme produce a radically unlike effect. The postures, of the Madonna in particular, but also of the St. John, are so manipulated as to make more precisely rigid and rectilinear-seeming accents of design, and lighting and drapery are so used as to diminish, or mask wholly, the spatial implication of the forms. The design now makes an inarticulate, yet active, geometry aligned upon the picture's surface and, very differently from in the early version, largely sealed from space by setting. As Bugiardini reinterprets his old design it has assumed a character like that in contemporary exercises in the late classical style; and as we observed of the handling as well, the analogy is more to contemporary Rome than Florence.

The whole expressive personality of this work has Roman savor: in its intended intellectuality, in its emphasis of contrast and intended clarity, and in its somewhat stiff dignity. What is lacking is, of course, the sophistication and the qualities of hand of the generic Roman analogues. No direct experience of Rome is required to account for this apparent *Romanità* in Bugiardini's style in this work. A look, however tardy, at the *Madonna dell'Impannata* and a continued rumination on the post-Roman pictures of Fra Bartolommeo could have provoked this response in Bugiardini. A classicism that contained within it elements of its own disruption would have become, at this late date, more wholly comprehensible to him than a classicism in its maturity: Bugiardini intersects the classical style on its descending parabola. Having achieved this tardy contemporaneity, Bugiardini rigidified within this labored formula of later classical style; and soon again, as the arts developed all about him, was a visibly old-fashioned artist.

RIDOLFO GHIRLANDAIO

Ridolfo's staple merchandise of art remains, persistently, his own variant of Ghirlandaiesque realism, and even in this time there was still a substantial market for it in the Florentine community. Increasingly in this phase, however, Ridolfo inclines toward the model of style that had been established by Fra Bartolommeo, to which, like the majority of his colleagues in the school of Florence, he had made his first concession a few years before. For a while within this phase, Ridolfo's susceptibility to the Frate's style yields more than the merely superficial, archaistically awkward imitation of it he had shown before. Among Ridolfo's major efforts of this time there are examples in which he seems to compound, into his own formulae of realism, genuine elements of the monumentality and pathos that are in the mature art of the Frate. The result is a somewhat aberrant incident in the history of Florentine classical style, not altogether singular in character, but more explicit in its demonstration of this character than in other secondary masters. As is also to be seen, but less clearly, in the art of Bugiardini or Franciabigio, larger elements of form and the quality of expression in Ridolfo's pictures tend to conform to the canons of a mature classicism, but the surface and descriptive touch are but little altered from a persistently preclassical mode. More than Bugiardini, Ridolfo now appears to know what he intends of classical effects; and the intentions of a classical kind he entertains are simpler and less effortfully ambitious than are Franciabigio's. Ridolfo makes both his diverse points, of classicizing and of realist kind, more explicitly than most of his contemporaries of like artistic rank.

The same tenor of conservative, official taste that had found a proper agent in Ridolfo for the decoration of the Cappella dei Priori was responsible for his selection, in 1515, for a similar small, but important, fresco scheme. It was to Ridolfo that the commission fell for decoration of a chapel in S. M. Novella, intended for use by Pope Leo during his stay in Florence. Ridolfo himself did only a small part of the actual painting of what has been called, since then, the Cappella del Papa, and for the rest functioned in a supervisory role. With Andrea di Cosimo Feltrini, who had been his collaborator also in the Cappella dei Priori, he determined the system of partitioning of the spaces to be decorated — a system of geometrical divisions much like that in the former chapel — and probably generally prescribed, or communicated his patrons' prescription, for the matter that this layout would contain. The major work of figure painting was subcontracted to a younger artist whose association with Ridolfo Ghirlandaio seems, at first thought, to be a remarkable improbability: what is aesthetically and historically memorable in the Cappella del Papa is Jacopo Pontormo's contribution. We cannot now reconstruct Ridolfo's motives in engaging this particular deputy, but their conjunction in this moment is a less unlikely one than it would have seemed before or shortly afterwards. In 1515, these antithetic artistic personalities at least shared, despite their many and acute differences, a common denominator in their convergence — from separate directions and from distinct motives — on Bartolommesque classicism. What Ridolfo and Jacopo stood for was thus, in this moment, and in this very elementary respect, not so drastically unlike.

Ridolfo's only executed part in the painting of this chapel, the lunette with the

Coronation of the Virgin[592] (matching the more famous *Veronica* of Jacopo), is so much restored that it cannot be trusted in detail, but its larger form accurately indicates the comprehension, deeper than that in the figures of the Cappella dei Priori, which Ridolfo has acquired, in this brief time, of the classical example of Fra Bartolommeo. The two figures of the *Coronation* make an imposing, energized, and rhythmically interwoven silhouette, which nearly fills their space. Their proportion, as well as their effect of scale, is more impressive than in the population of the Priori decoration; and they no longer seem, as there, a merely wooden approximation, inorganic and uninhabited, of Bartolommesque types.

Of Ridolfo's two large panels of the history of St. Zenobius, *Resuscitation of a Youth by St. Zenobius* and the *Translation of the Body of St. Zenobius* (Florence, Academy),[593–4] only the latter shows clear evidence of an accentuation of classical intent like that in the *Coronation*, and it is likely that a difference in time of conception and execution of the two panels accounts for this. Both pictures were paid for in 1517; they were hung, when finished, as wings for Albertinelli's *Annunciation* altar of 1510 (then in S. Marco) which had been commissioned by a confraternity dedicated both to the Purification of the Madonna and to St. Zenobius. The *Resuscitation* is altogether in a style like that of Ridolfo's Prato altarpiece of circa 1514; as in it, forms are relatively sparse and still disjunctive in their manner of arrangement, and the effect of Bartolommesque example is evident mostly in a sharp accenting of chiaroscuro. The composition of this earlier of the Zenobius panels shows no clear organizing principle. The painter's chief concern has been to gather, within his topographical perspective stage, as many actors as he can, each of the most convincing possible portrait-like reality; and in fact the actors are for the most part portraits, presumably of members of the confraternity. Even Ridolfo's father had rarely managed to submerge the content of a religious scene into a context of portraiture, of persons and of place, more effectively than here. Normal for the late Quattrocento, or for that aspect of it that the older Ghirlandaio's art had dominated, such an approach to a problem of narrative painting seems in aggravated discord with the habits of the dominant contemporary style: a denial, certainly not made on any intellectually considered ground, of the whole classical proposition of reconciliation between fiction (or history) and current actuality.

The *Translation* scene, painted probably in 1517, is very differently conceived. Large forms, generalized in outline and rhythmically related in their shapes, make a plastically dense, closed structure in the foreground picture plane. The portrayed spectators are few and unobtrusive in their place, and the topographical setting is of limited perspective effect. The impressive bearers of the reliquary move with an appropriate slow processional dignity, and their quality of action and expression of countenance is full of the solemnity of their occasion; they are not merely artificial and conventional in their response to meaning, as are both protagonists and spectators of the *Resuscitation*. In this scene even the portrayed spectators make evident their sharing, with the principal actors, of their tonality of feeling. The somewhat unusual subject matter does not affect the fact that the design of the *Translation* and the larger forms of which it is composed, and its character of content also, are deliberately conceived according to the prescription of a developed Bartolommesque style, and approximate this model more successfully than in almost any other work by a secondary master.

For all this concession by Ridolfo to classical principle, there has been no more than a moderating, but no substantial sacrifice, of his descriptive literalness of mind. Now his characteristic laboring of detail operates, more evidently than it did before, within larger fields of form that have been generalized, but his surfaces are still of unrelenting hardness; and all the insistent, exact, physical existence he creates is projected in an evidently airless void. The design has the quality of classically measured movement, and so do the persons who act in it; but the hand that describes them has a fatal and contrary lifelessness.

The limit of Ridolfo's penetration into the Bartolommesque style is in his altarpiece of the *Madonna with Six Saints* for S. Pier Maggiore, Pistoia (Pistoia, Museum; c. 1518; commissioned, according to Milanesi [V, 536n2], in 1508, but not less than a decade later in execution, with assistance).[595] On larger scale, and in a context of feeling and form much more seriously meant, the Pistoia altar develops some of the motives that Ridolfo earlier had used, in 1515–1516, in the fresco tabernacle of his own country house, the present Villa Agostini (near Galuzzo). The figures of the Pistoia painting are of grander dimension even than in the *Translation of St. Zenobius,* but by their very exaggeration in this sense seem *gonflé*; they stand in attitudes that paraphrase, a little vacantly, the restrained dignity of Fra Bartolommeo's precedents. The arrangement of the figures and their setting are specifically imitative of the Frate's altar types.

Where the imitation is so close as here it relieves the insufficiencies of the imitator. The ineradicable literalness of Ridolfo's mind and hand stiffens these Bartolommesque forms and makes relations among them unresilient, and not even a transcription of the Frate's most complex mode of chiaroscuro (in the manner of the *Pitti Pala* of 1512) supplies the energies, or the sense of drama, that Ridolfo temperamentally lacks. The chiaroscuro does endow the picture with an atmosphere of murky, erratically shadowed gravity, and this, with the stiffness in design and the hard insistence on detail, suggest a likeness in ambition and achieved effect to Franciabigio's nearly contemporary *St. Job* altar of 1516, also incompletely classical and imperfectly Bartolommesque.

It was their common interest in descriptive truth, much more exactly indulged by Ridolfo than by Franciabigio, that inclined both these painters to the frequent practice of portraiture. By their ability to satisfy the stringent but unimaginative taste for fact, unaestheticized, of a bourgeois public they were able, as we have remarked before, to dominate commerce in the Florentine portrait field. Ridolfo's exercise in portraiture was, of course, not confined to the specific portrait form alone; his most noteworthy efforts of portraiture in the middle years of this decade are in the compilations of contemporary countenances in the Zenobius panels. Their almost wearisome insistence on descriptive precision is still more apparent, but also more tolerable, in the examples of Ridolfo's single portrait paintings of this phase. Of these, the most effective may be the so-called *Girolamo Benivieni* (London, National Gallery; c. 1515?),[596] a topographical document of extremest factual exactness, almost sculptural in its effect of presence. Here the harsh firmness of Ridolfo's drawing and the sharp modelling of light are reinforced by the clarity of silhouette. The unyielding character of form is also that of psychological expression; the inflexible severity of this characterization in portraiture is more — or less — than human. Its literalness seems and is an archaism, but there has been brought to bear, on the process of materialization of the image, the sophistication of resource of the Cinquecento. Domenico Ghirlandaio could not have seen so finely, nor recorded with such acid sharpness as his son has here. It is, ultimately, a facet of the experience of Leonardo, isolated from its whole context and dedicated to a Ghirlandaiesque end, that permits Ridolfo to accomplish his effects.

A portrait of a younger man (Florence, Galleria Corsini),[597] of about contemporary date, is less singular in subject than the *Benivieni,* and thus also in form and in expression; but it is not much less drastically assertive of the sitter's literal reality. This kind of probing after physiognomic fact is much more penetrating than in the portraiture of Franciabigio of the same time; his portraits, in comparison, tell a less unveiled truth, and the personalities of their sitters are less inaccessible. If Ridolfo is capable anywhere of passion it is in the intensity with which he observes and with which he makes record of his observation. It seems as if the harsh and even hostile fixity of his staring at the object he is asked to paint may have been given, as in a mirror image, to that object: the sitter comes to wear the look that Ridolfo may have worn when painting him.

There is hardly any precedent of portrait style in Fra Bartolommeo's art that could have left an impress on Ridolfo, but Ridolfo's efforts in his religious works toward a Bartolommesque classicism did affect, if only momentarily, his manner as a portraitist. A portrait of a man of middle age (Florence, Collection Marchesa Luisa Torrigiani; c. 1518–20)[598] would seem allied in handling and, more important, in its larger character of style with the Pistoia altar. Identical in formula of pose with the Corsini portrait, this figure is longer and more simply ample in dimension. An architecture seemingly adapted from an altar type supports the silhouette, and helps to make a sense of nearly monumental dignity. The posture of the sitter is no longer merely inorganically stiff but conveys the idea of a willed erectness; and the countenance makes, more than in the preceding portraits, a measure of communication. The assiduity of physical description is not less than it had been before but its effect of harshness is somewhat moderated by a more diffused and complex handling of light, like that in the Pistoia altar. As in the religious paintings of this most nearly Bartolommesque moment in his art, Ridolfo finally admits a part at least of the classical idea, that what the artist has been asked to represent may be more than a physical fact alone.

Ridolfo's partial and tardy approximation of a classical style, on Bartolommeo's example, does not persist beyond the limit of this decade. What for a few years had been — nearly — inspiration from the classical style soon became mere formula in him, of clear but utterly uninhabited structure. Content again became, as it had been before, at best conventional and null at worst, and the main concern for form was in its only literal reproduction. Even the quite evident dependence, still, on Bartolommeo in Ridolfo's *Pietà* (Colle di Val d'Elsa, S. Agostino; dated 1521)[599] cannot conceal its relapse from any valid classicizing standard. This work has almost come full circle; only its specific vocabulary of form and its inscribed date, but not its basic character of style, distinguish it from Ridolfo's pictures of a dozen or more years before. Ridolfo lived an unconscionable time into the sixteenth century, and through these years he was responsive, always in limited degree and in superficial facts alone, to the changing models of reigning artistic mode. Eventually, his art became vacant even of its former content of realism; and then the tradition of the Ghirlandaios of the Quattrocento, which had stubbornly persisted in Ridolfo's art throughout the years of classicism, vanished in entire inanition.

GRANACCI

Granacci's fidelity to the tradition of his Quattrocento master, Ridolfo's father, had been in some ways more than Ridolfo's own. As, in the preceding half-decade, Granacci made his slow and conservative adjustment toward the model of Bartolommesque classical style he preserved, almost alone among Florentine painters of some note, the quality of smooth and lucent surface, and the relatively high tonality of color, of a quattrocentesque Ghirlandaism. Unlike Ridolfo, Granacci was no more than slightly and occasionally touched by Bartolommeo's conception of a chiaroscuro mode. Granacci was never so descriptively literal as Ridolfo, but — as we have observed — neither in fact were the Quattrocento Ghirlandaios. In compositional types Granacci tended, at least in his more ambitious works, to a continuing dependence on models like those for which, in Domenico Ghirlandaio's shop, he had been an executant. Yet, despite this conservatism, Granacci's pictures of the years before 1515 do not make an altogether *retardataire* effect. His technique, unlike Ridolfo's, gives no impression of undue laboring but, instead, of suavity; and there is a pleasant blandness in his color. The psychological climate of his actors, who act but little, is temperate. In these respects there is an approximation to some of the effects at least of classicism, but of an early phase, as yet uninvolved and unproblematical.

In a major work, which must only shortly postdate the opening of this present phase, the *Madonna with Sts. Francis and Zenobius* (Florence, Academy; c. 1515–16),[600] the qualities of form and temper that suggest a classical style become differently explicit than they had been before. The motives of composition still refer to what, by now, are mostly conservative precepts: to Granacci's own altar at Villamagna, and through it to the Frate's painting in S. Marco of 1509 and to Ghirlandaiesque models older still; but there is also reference, in the architecture and in the drapery with its supporting angels, to Andrea del Sarto's Dresden altarpiece of recent date. The scheme is simple: not with a simplicity strenuously imposed, as in the Frate's *Salvator* altar of this same time, nor awkwardly deliberated, as in Franciabigio's *St. Job* of the same year, but genuinely unproblematical. It is different from Granacci's antecedent altars not in any new complexity of form, but by a new deliberation in it of a principle of composition. These forms are more evidently rhythmically related than before, effectively connected by cursive sequences, and by this they approximate a classical unity of pattern. What shortly before had been a rather recessive character of blandness, almost of inertia, in Granacci's manner of design has been transformed into a positive expressive motivation, seeking for effects of ease and of urbanity.

That he has in fact achieved these effects in this altarpiece, even in this relatively simple scheme and at this late date, is not a trifling accomplishment. Such a character of form was basic to a classical aesthetic, and more strenuous efforts by the other secondary masters to achieve it yielded no equivalent results. Further, this new character is evident not only in Granacci's scheme of larger form but in his handling of lesser surfaces and shapes. More subtly differentiated in their modelling and more cursive in their drawing than they were before, his figures no longer have their former air of a slight rhythmical incoherence.

As is the case with Ridolfo Ghirlandaio, the measure of Granacci's coincidence with a more or less mature classical style (equally on a Bartolommesque model, despite the avoidance of a chiaroscuro) is not profound, and its span in time is relatively brief. Granacci's new suavity of rhythmical organization and of handling of surfaces does not conceal his absence of the power, or will, to assimilate a deeper or more intellectually complex constructive sense of classical style. His habit of reference to older ideas of design, evident in the altar in the Academy, persists: in a picture close to this one in date, a *Holy Family* (Boughton House, Collection Duke of Buccleuch; c. 1516)[601] he reuses, fairly literally, a cartoon a decade old, for his painting of the same subject now in Dublin. The new aspect with which Granacci recreates the old design almost redeems its archaism, and gives it a specious appearance of modernity so that it resembles somewhat the Frate's contemporary Holy Family compositions. Another smaller painting of like date, a *Madonna and Child* (San Francisco, Palace of the Legion of Honor; c. 1515–16; improperly attributed to Fra Bartolommeo),[602] is an adaptation into Granacci's new vocabulary of a far older composition, recalled before this to contemporary art in Florence by Alonso Berruguete: a design traceable to Donatello. That, however, is a deliberate historicism, different in its motive from any mere reuse, as in the Buccleuch picture, of an old cartoon.

Probably in 1517–1518 an old connection of Granacci's was renewed, with

Michelangelo, now intermittently in Florence. According to Vasari (V, 344) it was Michelangelo who furnished to Granacci the design for a high altar for the Convent of S. Apollonia, as well as for the center panel of the painting to go on it, to which Granacci added "alcune storie di figurette piccole a olio ed alcune grandi." The main feature of the altarpiece, on Michelangelo's alleged design, is lost, but Granacci's own inventions still exist. The large figures: four standing Saints in half-life size on separate panels (Jerome, John Baptist, Apollonia, and the Magdalen),[603] apparently wings for the former altarpiece, are in Munich; of the "storie di figurette piccole," [604–6] evidently a predella, six are in the Academy in Florence and two in the Berenson Collection. The appearance of the large panels tends to confirm Vasari's report of Michelangelo's intervention close by, but not directly in, these figures: their breadth of dimension is much greater than in Granacci's other paintings of this phase, and it is achieved by a drapery style of unusual fullness and elaboration for which, in Florence at this time, only Michelangelo's art could supply a model. Granacci's paraphrase of Michelangelo, even in terms so general as here, is not of good effect; such busy amplitude of drapery is more than Granacci's limited power of synthetic order can command. The result is rhythmically discoordinate, of a hollow and pretentious-seeming largeness: the opposite of the effect which, surely, was intended, of a Michelangelesque charged monumentality. Perhaps now reinforced by Michelangelo's example of a canon, these figures of Granacci's seem, as they are enlarged in body, smaller still in the proportion of their heads, and the effect is of disjointed preciosity.

The style of these large figures differs from the "figurette piccole" only in degree, but it is precisely this degree that creates, in the predella panels, their effect not only of aesthetic, but of historical surprise. In the small figures the diminution of the size of head in relation to that of the body is markedly exaggerated; and the breadth of the body is, in general, diminished. Its whole contour is drawn with a quick cursive line. Not only the heads but the other bodily extremities are tapering and pointed. The figures are disarticulate and unreal in appearance, which seems to be determined more by arbitrary graphic impulse than by any law of structure. They assume the air of delicate and mannered puppets, in character entirely at variance with the episodes of cruelty and martyrdom the predella scenes describe.

Every characteristic of form in these predelle can be accounted for in terms of an exaggeration of qualities already present in the large figures of the same altar, or which occur sporadically in earlier examples of Granacci's works; and it is possible that the style of the predelle is essentially Granacci's personal invention. However it is striking that their kind of figure, and something also of their mode of composition, so much resemble ideas, closely contemporary or just prior in appearance, of the younger Mannerists. The stronger likelihood is that the new vocabulary of Granacci's predelle has been inspired by experience of their works; he was the collaborator, or competitor, of some among the younger men, and of Pontormo conspicuously, in a decoration (begun in 1516 and completed in 1518) for Pier Francesco Borgherini. The singular circumstance in Granacci's figures is that they are in some respects more mannered still than those of the younger artists, but in the sense of a personal mannerism rather than, as in them, a purposeful deviation from classical ideas of style. Granacci's net result is not distinguishable by much from theirs, but the distinctions that exist suffice to separate this phenomenon in him — even if it has happened as a consequence of influence from the younger Mannerists — from their early essays. Granacci shares, in these predelle, something of the Mannerists' novelty of style, but he does not share the kind or intensity of expressive purpose which, in them, is the motivation of new style.

If we are able for a moment, in our consideration of these predelle, to discount the apparently reflective Mannerizing imprint on their figure style their meaning as a happening within Granacci's art may come more clear. What has occurred in them is not a wholly new phenomenon, but it is one of recent date in the history of art in Florence. We have already had occasion to observe, in Fra Bartolommeo's small *Annunciation* (Louvre) of 1515,[535] how the painter saw fit to permit himself, in a small-scale work, a different mood and manner from that in exactly contemporary monumental works, as if the picture in small scale — like, but not quite as much as in a drawing — should invite a less structurally controlled and emotionally more spontaneous expression. The idea is not exclusive to the Frate: it occurs also, quite contemporaneously, in painters of the younger generation. Liberties that the younger men, and even the explicit Mannerists among them, may not presume to take in major works may appear initially in smaller ones.

Such a relation between the measure of a work and the measure of artistic license in it had been only dimly adumbrated earlier than this, in the painting of predelle and *cassoni*, but not before so explicitly admitted by Florentine painters. It may be significant that the first positive evidences of distinction between a monumental style and style on small scale appear at a time of crisis and search for redirection in Florentine painting. The freer essays in small scale have a double function: of an evasion of the disciplines of classical style, and of a channel for new experiment. This phenomenon in Florence is, as we have seen, related in its motives and in some part of its results of style to closely contemporary happenings in Rome, as in Peruzzi's frieze in the *Sala delle Prospettive*,[478-9] in the figure paintings of the Raphael Logge, and in the emergence into prominence of grotesquerie.

Among these Roman analogues there was, in Peruzzi's case, a likely element of recall of quattrocentesque disposition, though not of quattrocentesque models, among its motive sources. Among the Florentines, in more immediate contact with their Quattrocento art, it seems there may have been a demonstration of precise interest, in this moment of reassessment, in the early models of their own tradition. We have remarked Granacci's near-quotation of a Donatello motive (and Berruguete's also); in the figure and drapery style of the S. Apollonia predelle, and also in their setting, there are qualities that seem to recollect another early Quattrocento model: Ghiberti's doors, not only those of Paradise but, still more mediaevalizing, the older set. The resemblance may be quite fortuitous, for no provable likenesses can be deduced, but a study of such models by Granacci would accord with slight but more specific evidence of such an interest among contemporary Mannerists.

The liberty of small-scale style Granacci shows in the Apollonia predelle is somewhat less in other works of roughly comparable scale. It is only rather timidly exercised in a panel larger in its whole dimension, but in which the figures are of even smaller size: the *Entry of Charles VIII into Florence* (Florence, Museo Mediceo; c. 1518; perhaps painted in connection with the French marriage of Lorenzo de' Medici in that year).[607] Like the Apollonia predelle, this has a new transparency and lightness of handling and a flexibly informal, though generally less novel, drawing of the figures. Most casually composed — quite unlike a modern parade — Granacci depicts the royal procession as it advances from the depths of an airy (and slightly insubstantial) perspective down the Via Larga. The scene has a lively and engaging illustrative efficacy that belies its being, as it is, a reconstruction rather than an actual record of the event.

We remarked that the direct occasion for Granacci's contact with the artists of the younger generation had been in his employment with them in the decoration (with scenes from the life of Joseph) of a chamber for Pier Francesco Borgherini. The two panels done by Granacci for this set are in the Uffizi, and represent (in roughly similar size but rather different scale) *Joseph Presents his Father to Pharaoh* (No. 2152)[608] and the *Arrest of Joseph* (No. 2150).[609] There may be some small but appreciable difference in the time of execution of the two panels, and the *Presentation* in that case may be the earlier, about 1517. The *Arrest* is fairly certainly of 1518 or even shortly afterward: one motive in it (the statue on a column to the right) is a clear paraphrase from Pontormo's last contribution to this same commission, datable in 1518.

In the mode of composition of the *Presentation* — open, sparsely populated and diffuse — it seems like a recall of a long anterior cassone style of the later Quattrocento, of Botticelli or Bertoldo di Giovanni. The figure style, however, has the smoother ease that came into Granacci's art only at a relatively recent moment. These figures have the careful suavity of form of those in the Academy altarpiece, or in the Buccleuch *Holy Family*, and in their smaller scale they are yet more finely and deliberately worked. In drapery and posture they are more gracile than the monumental forms, and more pointed and precious in their drawing of extremities and countenances. As the figures diminish in scale toward the background they assume an increasing eccentricity of shape, according to Granacci's long evident private mannerism; and on smallest scale in the distance they become almost interchangeable with the mannequins of the Apollonia predelle. In the *Arrest of Joseph* these fragile and attenuated forms are more prominent in place, and their more apparent presence is enough to color, with their touch of freer fantasy, the whole character of content of the scene.

Otherwise, however, the *Arrest* is conceived with more evident, and on the whole classicizing, deliberation than its companion piece. The setting shows a mode of architecture and handling of space like that in the most conservative vein of Florentine classicism, resembling what Sarto had evolved toward 1512. Before this setting, carefully rectilinear and orthogonal, the protagonists are disposed almost as if in a frieze, close to the foremost plane. They are not markedly different from the actors of the *Presentation*, but projected in a larger scale, they are more conservative in their construction, more like the figures of Granacci's larger works. The evidence of a newer tendency of style is in the accentuation in the foreground figures, more than in the *Presentation*, of their gracility of pose and movement, and their union in a cursive ornamental pattern, consciously artificial in effect. Neither the appearance nor the content of these figures has to do with an unclassical example, but their principle of composition may be influenced by the latest of the companion panels in this series by Pontormo. But this element of resemblance to Mannerism makes no weight in the essential conservatism of Granacci's picture, nor does his incidental background population of smaller figures, more nearly comparable to Pontormo's style. Conspicuously unlike the Mannerists, Granacci does not carry over into major forms the inventive liberties of his small-scale style; the difference of his art from the contemporary efforts of the Mannerists is nowhere more explicitly demonstrated than it has been here.

Considering Granacci's prior history and the fact of his generation — he is the oldest of the wholly active Florentine painters at work in this phase — it is remarkable that the problem of a relation to the Mannerism of the younger generation should have to be raised at all, and that the problem is more relevant in his case than in those of the other secondary masters of the older group. In the pictures of Granacci we examined so far in this phase the positive effects of his connection with the new style seem of only minor consequence; but one work of his survives that indicates a closer interest in Mannerism than we might suppose, from the other evidence, could be possible to him. A *Madonna with St. John* by Granacci (formerly Munich, Drey Collection),[610] for which we can only hazard a dating around 1518 or slightly later, is as close a paraphrase of the earliest Mannerist style as a painter not himself a Mannerist could produce. This picture is a composite of motives of Granacci's own (related in the background to the *Arrest of Joseph*, and in the figure group to the old cartoon for the Buccleuch and Dublin paintings) and of a Madonna figure borrowed from a work of Rosso (perhaps from the *Holy Family* in the Galleria Borghese, but more likely from Rosso's still earlier Madonna in Arezzo). It is less Granacci's borrowing of this major motive from Rosso that is a matter for surprise than his imitation of the younger painter's eccentricities of drawing: the drapery and, still more conspicuously, the anatomy are almost as rhythmically captious and as warping of the normal data of appearance as in Rosso's painting. The imitation is confined to form, however; Granacci does not wish to emulate the singularity of feeling which, in the younger painter's work, is inextricably bound up with his novelty of form.

This picture seems to be a unique episode within Granacci's *oeuvre*; it has no certain consequence within this phase or, in the inadequate degree to which it can be precisely traced, in his work that follows. The freedom of form and the gift, minor but engaging, for visual fantasy that Granacci evidenced toward 1517–1518 are later exercised, as then, only in small scale; the larger, "serious," portions of his work remain conservative. A painting commissioned to him in 1521, an altar of the *Madonna with Four Saints* (Montemurlo, Pieve)[611] is mannered only in its preciosity of handling, still more accentuated than before, and in its elaboration, but in details only, of rhythmic ornament. In larger structure and in content the picture remains uninspiredly traditional. Granacci's accent in the surface character of style is enough, however, to give this painting a recognizable cast of contemporaneity. "Si diede pochi pensieri" says Vasari of Granacci as a painter (V, 345), but it is not so much the paucity of his thought as the absence of profundity in it that is his limitation. He was more in touch with, and more responsive to, the changes in the world of art around him than any of the masters of his class and generation, but this responsiveness was never matched by any power to make inventive change himself.

SOGLIANI

The fact of generation was obviously not in itself the determinant of an artistic style; and this is nowhere more clearly demonstrated than in the case of Giovanni Antonio Sogliani. Born in 1492, and thus younger by more than two decades than Granacci, Sogliani was no less conservative a painter than he. Sogliani had almost the most reactionary training that a sixteenth-century Florentine could find, in the *bottega* of Lorenzo di Credi — outmoded but still functioning — where for a long but unspecifiable term of years he was an assistant. Such an education would have left its inhibition on a stronger man.

Sogliani may not have set up independent practice until about 1515, and it is not certain if a painting still so strongly within Credi's manner (but in which Sogliani's own varieties of type and technical detail are visible) as the tondo *Madonna with St. John* (Baltimore, Walters Art Gallery)[612] is a product of the Credi shop or of the first moments of Sogliani's independence. With some justifiable lack of confidence in his facility of invention Sogliani reused the cartoon for the two main figures of this picture in two further, but not more certainly independent, variations of the same theme, in rectangular format, in the museums at Brussels[613] and Turin.[614] In each of these works there is a deviation from the previous near-exact fidelity to Credi's style, and more reference, as it were backward through the art of Credi, to its partial source in Leonardo. This reference is chronologically retrogressive, but it is to a style which, even at this date, was more relevant to "modern" practice of painting in Florence than the style of Credi. By this indirect and excessively cautious route, Sogliani approaches nearer than he had been earlier to a common basis with the dominant contemporary style. The change in model is not only a change from an old imitative dependence to a new; there is also, more evidently in the Brussels one of these two latter paintings, some emergence of Sogliani's own limited expressive personality. His tendency is to minimize the unaccented full plasticity of Credi's style and make form more complex, and, with the help of Leonardesque example, to make handling sharper and more various through chiaroscuro.

After Sogliani had been for some while outside the confines — and this they had been for him, literally — of the Credi shop he must have sloughed off most of his residue of Quattrocento habits fairly quickly, but no clearly datable evidence survives of his process of accommodation to a modern style until 1521, in his *S. Acasio Altar* (Florence, S. Lorenzo)[615] signed and dated in that year. There is no hint in this of Sogliani's former archaism, and there even may be some indication of relation to progressive tendencies. As the majority of Florentine painters had some years before, Sogliani has adopted the mature style of Fra Bartolommeo as his model, and in this work at least his following the Frate's style is closer, in typology, in chiaroscuro mode, and in intention of its content than any other independent Florentine's so far. But Sogliani's canon of proportion differs evidently from that of the Frate: his figures are more slight and attenuated, and partly on this account are much more insubstantial-seeming, in effect of content, as well as form. It may be that this different and less classical proportion is entirely a personal expression, and this would seem to be confirmed by the persistence of this canon in most of Sogliani's works of the later years of his career. At the same time, it somewhat recalls the canon earlier evolved in the first large-scale Mannerist painting of Pontormo, the Visdomini altar of 1518,[646] and Sogliani may have found in this work — also in important ways still Bartolommesque — if not the inspiration toward attenuated form, then some confirmation of a private tendency.

Despite its clarity and regularity of pattern (made by the repeated use of crosses in the composition) the *Acasio* altar does not have a properly classical coherence in design. There is a kind of order in this scheme, basically rectilinear, which in a way suggests the structure of Fra Bartolommeo's *Salvator Mundi*,[536] but conspicuously does not have the same motivation of purposeful severity of discipline. Sogliani's too-apparent order has the superficial look, but not the vital principle, that inhabits Bartolommesque structures. Each form in the design is, by comparison with Bartolommeo's work, inert both psychically and physically and seems, in its inertness, without power of communication or connection with the others. This is, even in its almost persuasive imitation of the Frate's mode, such an academicization — a transcription of an uninhabited formula — of classical style as we have seen before, but never in Florence in so clear a demonstration.

This *calque* of Bartolommeo's style in the *Acasio* altar is the closest approach — parallel, but not coincident — to classicism that Sogliani makes. Even in this same year another altarpiece by Sogliani, the *Madonna della Cintola* (Florence, Academy; dated 1521), shows a style less careful in its imitation of the surface qualities of Bartolommeo's art, and more wooden in its simulacra of Bartolommeo's types and design; and in 1522 Sogliani's *S. Brigitta Altar* (Florence, Academy)[616] quite completes the process of petrifaction of Bartolommeo's style. This dry shell of classicism has become, like the artist as Vasari describes him (V, 123), ". . . nell' aspetto freddo e malinconico . . .": this is a posthumous event in the history of Florentine classical style. It is a ghost that will not be laid, and for two more decades Sogliani continued to fabricate icons of this kind, enlivened sporadically and only in detail by graces and motives taken over from the vocabulary of Mannerism when, finally, it became fashionable, as classicism had been in former years. Sogliani enjoyed a good market till his latest age among those who (Vasari V, 132) ". . . senza dilettarsi delle fatiche dell' arte e di certe bravure, amano le cose oneste, facili, dolci e graziose." Vasari's adjectives speak more for his tolerance than for the qualities of Sogliani's art.

PULIGO

*Domenico Puligo had established a close working connection with Andrea del Sarto around 1513, and it continued on an occasional basis well into the later years of this decade. He painted at least three works of some importance for Andrea after 1515: he is the entire executant of a partial variant of the *Holy Family* of which the original exists in Leningrad (London, National Gallery; c. 1516; without the attendant Saint),[617] and the substantial executant of the two panels of the history of Joseph, which Andrea designed for Pier Francesco Borgherini (Florence, Pitti 87, 88; 1515–16 and c. 1517 respectively).[618–19] The London *Holy Family*, wholly Puligo apart from the cartoon, betrays his accustomed aberration from Andrea's style, discounting almost altogether its special virtue of optical and psychological communication. As we have seen in Domenico's earlier transcriptions of Andrea, he is responsive to the softness in Andrea's forms and contents, but not to their complex vitality. It may be understandable why Domenico should turn, in his independent work, from Andrea's to Fra Bartolommeo's example, of which the simpler formulae lend themselves more readily to generalization and to imitation. As is the case not only with Domenico's inferiors, like Sogliani, but with his artistic betters, Bartolommeo's is still the formative example of these years.

A *Madonna with St. John* by Puligo (Florence, Pitti 242; c. 1517–18)[620] is based on the vocabulary of form and on ideas of composition such as are in the Frate's Madonna pictures, circa 1515–1516; and not only the form but the tone of sentiment suggest, for example, that of the Frate's London version of his late Madonna themes. Domenico's style in his picture is in general derivative; yet it bears a marked, but by no means forceful, accent of his own personality. More than in Bartolommeo's models or in Puligo's own earlier independent paintings, the design in this one is precarious in balance. It contains an interesting and effectively articulated formal and affective motive: the mobile elegance, almost Tanagrene, of the form of the Madonna. Her shape is tenuous, and (with more traceable cause than in the case of Sogliani) there may be some evidence of a response to the example of Pontormo in this attenuation. But this reflection of a look as of contemporary Mannerism, if it is such, is out of order in Domenico; by around 1520 he had opted, in his works of larger scale, for a style which, in the context of this time's events, is unequivocally conservative. As in the *Madonna with St. John and Angels* (Florence, Galleria Corsini; c. 1520–22),[621] typical of the style to which he adhered for these few years, he has evolved a simple, unambitious and, finally, structurally clear reduction of the Bartolommesque mode. This result is post-classical only in a particular sense: in the fact of its evident congealing into a formula so smooth, inert, and unproblematical as this; and there is some pale relation (as there had always been in the content of Puligo's paintings) between his sentimental intimacy of emotion and an aspect of the disposition toward expression that is in the Mannerists.

The conservative and rather vapid formula of style to which Puligo develops in such larger pictures is more meaningful for his practice after 1520 than for his principal occupation — or what seems to have been such — in the immediately preceding years. His work as Andrea's executant in the pictures for the Borgherini decoration seems to have directed Puligo into a special métier, inextricably related — as the whole set of Borgherini paintings obviously is — to the tradition of furniture or, more loosely, cassone painting. Except for the increasingly rare works of this kind of Piero di Cosimo, this was a tradition that had almost lapsed by the middle of the second decade of the century, at least as a matter of traceable practice by named masters. Bacchiacca, similarly involved in the Borgherini decoration, seems also to have found the basis there for a career in such a métier, in his case much more nearly exclusive and enduring in the specialty than Puligo's. We have already had occasion to observe in Granacci's pictures of these years (including his paintings for Borgherini) how a considerable distinction may exist between the painter's small and large-scale work; with Puligo the degree of difference is apparent, but not quite so drastic. In Puligo's small-scale pictures he displays a liberty and variety of handling that we cannot document for him elsewhere and he comes to develop a rather fancifully eccentric novelty of small style that is unlike his vacant classicistic larger mode.

The two Borgherini panels in which Puligo worked as an assistant for Andrea are only in part and in a superficial sense determined in their style by him. Both pictures were specifically planned and carefully projected on the panel by Andrea to the point of underdrawing and in some parts painted by Andrea also; there is no other instance of so fine an approximation by Domenico, so precisely controlled by Andrea, of Andrea's painting style. Domenico's personal vocabulary emerges only in detail, and in the later panel in occasional incidents of drapery. There is no distinction worth remark between the style in general — in forms or even in the handling — of these pictures and that of Andrea's larger pictures of the date that corresponds to each.

What may be Puligo's first traceable independent essay in a small-scale narrative picture, an *Adoration of the Kings* (formerly Milan, Collection Crespi; only roughly datable c. 1518),[622] cannot be specifically related in its style with the Borgherini panels. The adjustment toward Bartolommesque models we have observed in a contemporary larger work (Pitti 242) also is apparent here: this composition is specifically dependent (Berenson) on an early drawing of Fra Bartolommeo's, full of Leonardesque reminiscences. Andrea's repertory has supplied one motive, of the group at lower right, adapted from his fresco of the same theme. In his painting, Puligo's handling is more sharply angular and more schematizing than it had been in his following Andrea, as in the execution of the Borgherini panels; and it is more brusquely accented with chiaroscuro. There is more fidelity directly to Bartolommesque prescriptions than to the transformations that had been worked on them by Andrea.

This particular (and as it proves, momentary) accent of Domenico's small style in the *Adoration* is less relevant than its general congruity of appearance with the pictures of the Borgherini series, and its sharing of some of the common denominator that exists, in their panels in the series, between Andrea and Pontormo. Beyond their example (which is in fact also his own in that there he is executant for Andrea) Puligo takes liberties in drawing of a more obvious and differently motivated kind. Certainly, the sharp-accented incorrectness of the drawing in the *Adoration* was in part intended, presumably for formally affective ends, but — unlike in Pontormo's perfectly controlled deviations — it is Domenico's ineptitude, more than his purpose, which distorts. On this small scale his eccentricity of form — like that in Granacci's contemporary *Apollonia* predelle — seems to have been permissible. We can only speculate that it might have been in accord with the nascent taste for deviation from normative form among the Mannerists that, wholly purposeful or not, such eccentricity should be considered aesthetically tolerable.

Puligo's *Deposition* (Venice, Seminario; c. 1518–20)[623] is, like the *Adoration*, almost altogether dependent on a borrowed composition; this time from a still more old-fashioned source, a Perugino of which a surviving version (but probably not the one from which Puligo's design is derived) exists in fresco, dated 1517, at Città della Pieve. The same design was twice used by Puligo's companion painter of small pictures, Bacchiacca, more nearly imitatively and almost surely slightly earlier than by him. Puligo's transcription is not so reminiscent of the model's archaic mode, either in design or in specific vocabulary of form. The handling is more confidently loose than in the *Adoration*, freer in detail but at the same time more conventional of whole effect. The manner of painting and the figure style make a fair mélange of Bartolommeo and Andrea, with some cast, in the nudes, of the older model in the Perugino.

In this case the presence of the model may have imposed a particular restraint, but Puligo's abandonment of the peculiar sharp-angled distorting eccentricity of drawing of the *Adoration* is deliberate. In a less dependent picture, close to the *Deposition* in its time, the *Preaching of St. John Baptist* (formerly London, Collection Henry Harris; c. 1518–20)[624] the drawing seems a compromise between that in the *Deposition* and the *Adoration*: weakly fluent, but using pointed accents in extremities and face. The figure types take on a somewhat singular appearance, of which the cause now seems to lie, in more nearly equal measure than in the *Adoration*, in intention as well as in the accidents of an awkward hand. It is as if the painter had determined, here still rather tentatively, to exploit purposely the singular effects of shape to which his hand inclines, and had begun to feel these tendencies of hand might register, expressively, peculiarities of vision and of sense in which he might not indulge in his more formal larger works. The inclination in portions of the *Preaching* toward a caricatural accent of form is quite opposite that which, in Puligo's larger pictures, becomes explicit around 1520, toward inert classical correctness.

As the one tendency matures, so does its antithesis. A highly idiosyncratic small-scale style, self-consciously stressful of its abnormalities of form, appears circa 1520 in Puligo's scenes from the *History of Joseph* (Rome, Galleria Borghese 463; there wrongly attributed to Bacchiacca).[625] The inspiration from the panel with, in part, the same scenes in the Borgherini histories is evident, but only general; a comparison is much more indicative of the departure Domenico has taken — even in his mode of handling — from Sartesque style. This present style in the Borghese panel makes what is of interest in it by its fine-worked singularities of type and shape; its sharp, slightly caricatural images take on a visual, and some expressive, piquancy that their counterparts in a more classically correct vocabulary do not possess. The scene becomes something other than straightforward narrative. It assumes, from the element of strangeness in its actors and in its description of milieu, a quality of unreal fancy. There is only doubtfully any specifiable dependence on preceding ideas of the Mannerist painters, but the climate of the narrative and some part of the means used to create it are not unlike those of contemporary Mannerism. In far less intellectually meditated and less consistently reforming terms Puligo has made, in small scale, a naïve approximation to the character of the new postclassical style.

A few small narrative pictures by Domenico can be traced which, in our reckoning, are from the early 1520's; in them, as in the *Apollo and Daphne* (Florence, Galleria Corsini;[626] a variant, London, Collection W. M. H. Pollen), the eccentricity of form is still more stressed and the atmosphere of fairy-tale unreality more pronounced. It is as if there were a willed approximation in these pictures, not of a contemporary Mannerism but of an opposite archaism, like that of a quattrocentesque primitive, and the sense of distance from us and of fantasy is in the work in part on this account.

Toward the middle 1520's the element of Mannerism in the small-scale subcurrent of Puligo's art emerged and made irruption into his larger works. By then the style of Mannerism had made a clear place for itself in Florence, competing with the continuity of classicism in the art of Puligo's old friend and employer, Sarto. Puligo had too soft a susceptibility and never enough independence of mind to resist the fashion, and because there were now two fashions he opted inconclusively for both. The painting of his last few years, until his death in 1527, is, in most of its vocabulary, Sartesque in basis but often Mannerist in accent of form, and of color in particular; and its expression often verges on morbidity as extreme as can be found in any of his Mannerist contemporaries. Puligo was an incomplete convert to the new style, but he was the earliest, among the painters of the generation to which Pontormo and Rosso belonged, to accept a measurable portion of their doctrine of art.

BACCHIACCA

Where Puligo practiced in small scale only secondarily, his slightly younger contemporary, Francesco Bacchiacca, was an almost exclusive specialist in it. More than any other painter of the school of Florence in these years it was Bacchiacca who remade the small-scale genre, giving new currency to an old tradition. Bacchiacca did not reinvent the genre, which had fallen into desuetude with Piero di Cosimo's decline; that was a collective action, precipitated in a group of artists by the program of a patron, Pier Francesco Borgherini. In this commission Bacchiacca was — in terms of quantity only — the principal participant. In the years that followed the Borgherini decoration he alone among its group of painters continued to work in its vein as his main business. We have remarked already that the small-scale picture, in the form in which it appears in the Borgherini histories, may have met a need peculiarly felt at this moment in the career of Florentine classical style, for kinds of expression more intimate and accessible than the canons of a monumental classicism readily allowed; that Bacchiacca made an exclusive business of this genre and found, apparently, a wide market for it, is a stronger quantitative support for this supposition than we can make from the production of any other contemporary artist.

There is, then, among the basic premises of Bacchiacca's genre, some element in common with the motivations behind Mannerism. However, despite his almost certain knowledge of the subsequent work on small scale of his colleagues in the Borgherini scheme, Puligo and Granacci, Bacchiacca does not, in the years before 1520, press his own case in a new direction even as tentatively as they do theirs. The scale of Bacchiacca's personality is that of his genre; his mind is not of a dimension that invents. In these years he demonstrates a limited ability to control form, but no power to dominate it synthetically, much less purposefully to revise it. To some extent (though not so much as in the case of Puligo) Bacchiacca's effects of form, occasionally singular, are determined partly by ineptitude of hand. His sensibility is more evident than his discipline, but neither is his sensibility a profound or forceful instrument. He has one special gift that is markedly individual, even in this early time, as he begins to use it: his sense for stimulating and complex, though discoordinate, effects of color, and occasionally for effects of light. His colorism is based eventually on Sartesque example, but is less controlled, more various and more incipiently eccentric in its working. More than in any other aspect of Bacchiacca's style within this phase there is a measure, in his color, of inventive novelty like that of a Mannerism, and a measure of analogy with — and perhaps suggestion from — the art of Rosso.

Bacchiacca's art from his discernible

beginnings up to 1520 is essentially conservative, in a way that is tangential to the history of contemporary Florentine classical style. Considering his education, it expects too much that it should be otherwise: he was, according to Vasari (III, 592), a pupil of the weary and immutable late Perugino. What may be as early a work as we know of Bacchiacca, a *Deposition* (Bassano, Museo Civico; only approximately datable c. 1515),[627] is a small-scale variant, perhaps a copy, of a Perugino composition we have also seen used (possibly through the intervening medium of this picture) by Puligo. Except for its Morellian details Bacchiacca's version does not deviate significantly from his master's style. This work has no intrinsic interest, but it serves as an example of the role in the early Cinquecento of such small devotional paintings as this, and of their difference from the special genre Bacchiacca shortly would help reestablish. This picture hardly lays claim to the status of a work of art. It is not that, in this particular case, the picture is more a reproduction than an invented work; the whole category of small picture to which this belongs was not intended to be more than ordinary household icons. They describe accustomed subjects in nearly impersonally conventional terms, or even in near-stereotypes. This class of painting had been in general, and now in Florence had especially become, craftsman's matter more than the affair of artists.

Bacchiacca's initial status was that of a craftsman-painter, and he never wholly lost the marks of this beginning (and Vasari never lost sight of this cast even in Bacchiacca's later art). But from the time of his involvement in the Borgherini decoration, and perhaps a little earlier, Bacchiacca's small pictures began to assume a distinguishable private personality, endowing even a conventional subject — or a borrowed one — with some accent of idiosyncratic perception and response, and with the evidence of individuality of hand. His *Adam and Eve* (Philadelphia, Museum, Johnson Collection; c. 1516?)[628] may predate the Borgherini series: based, with only inadequate disguise, on a Perugino drawing (for an Apollo and Marsyas! and betraying other, imperfectly assimilated sources also), and still archaically labored in technique, it nevertheless is individual in style. There is the mark of personality in the taut drawing of this picture's shapes and in its mode of stress of light; and it is not wholly neutral in psychological content.

Some evidence of Peruginesque inheritance is still present in the style of Bacchiacca's panels for the Borgherini series (two of cassone shape, London, National Gallery 1218, 1219; four of small rectangular format, Rome, Galleria Borghese 425, 426, 440, 442; all 1516–18).[629–32] The broad, full proportion of their figures and many of the formulae of drapery recognizably depend upon Perugino; much in the character of landscape and, in one panel, of architectural setting, is also Peruginesque. In both the larger panels the type of composition still resembles the predelle of the older master. However, Bacchiacca's compositions are much more flexibly conceived, with a variety of movement and a continuity of rhythm that assimilate them to a modern, rather than a Peruginesque, kind of classicism. The same relative flexibility (missing in the more cautious draughtsmanship of the *Adam and Eve*) distinguishes the figure style of the Borgherini panels: a fluid and continuous outline defines shapes smoothly and elliptically, and a polished modelling completes them. Bacchiacca's result is animate and ornamental as it never was in Perugino; but there is something still of Perugino's vacancy of form. The general intention is to approximate the appearance of a current classicizing style, and it is realized in almost the same degree as, among Bacchiacca's collaborators, it is in the paintings of Granacci.

While, in this project, Bacchiacca demonstrates his acquisition of an adequate, but imperfect, modern classicism his own idiosyncrasies emerge as well. But what, in them, does not conform to classicizing principles is not remotely comparable in power of motivation to the novelty created by his colleague in this task, Pontormo, and is distinct from it in kind. Bacchiacca's singularities are of curious facial types and costumes, some imagined and some observed in nature or in Northern prints, and of forms warped part by a pronounced ornamental will and part (as in Puligo) by inexpertness. There is no transmutation of form by intense spiritual and aesthetic purpose, as in Pontormo. Bacchiacca's unclassicisms give piquant accent to his forms, but do not disturb their basic conventionality.

It is the effect of Bacchiacca's color, taken in conjunction with that of his form, which more particularly heightens the accent of individuality that is in his style. In the Borgherini panels color is already more various, more sparkling and sharp, than in most contemporary painting in Florence; in a second version of the *Deposition* (Florence, Uffizi; c. 1518)[633] — no longer an imitation but a personal paraphrase of Perugino's old design — the interest of color dominates the picture. There is a remarkable variety of hues of drapery, tender and rather feminine in cast: pinkish reds, paled greens, lilacs, and golden yellows. The flesh of the figures is blue-shadowed; and in the landscape there is a slightly acid blue-green, which suggests the distances of Patinir. In this atmosphere the variety of color shimmers, a little dissonantly, and with something of the accidental order, or lack of it, of a kaleidoscope. Compared with the Sartesque colorism from which this mode eventually derives this is capricious; intended to be wayward, visually playful, and off-key. In intention and in some of its effects this color resembles Mannerist inventions, particularly those already published by Il Rosso; but in Bacchiacca there is nothing like the sharpness of motive and precision of means with which Rosso articulates what is comparable in his intention. Nevertheless, in the *Deposition* the archaic composition and its contents are transformed as if in their substance by their coloristic guise. The color of this picture has, in common with that in Rosso, the character of an evidently postclassical (and specifically a "post-Sartesque") event.

Even as this degree of novelty and individuality of color (but less likely, granted Rosso's precedent, of invention) emerge in Bacchiacca's style it is not accompanied by any corresponding change in other facets of his art. He is not competent to think in terms of the inventions of an intellectual *disegno*, making significant new shapes for appearance and new kinds of constructive form. It has only in part to do with the economy of Bacchiacca's genre that he continues to adopt old, borrowed schemes and often interprets them less personally than he last had Perugino's *Deposition*: of this kind is a close imitation of a design by Fra Bartolommeo, the *Creation of Eve* (Sweden, private collection; c. 1518–20; wrongly attributed to Raphael),[634] in which not much more than the Morellian detail of form is Bacchiacca's. A *Leda* (Rotterdam, Collection van Beuningen; c. 1518–20)[635] adapts Leonardo's well-known work, and does so with a care for classicizing correctness greater than in Franciabigio's contemporary version of the theme. However, the subject invites Bacchiacca's accent of piquant psychological expression; and he recalls, and here demonstrates more fluently, the special sensibility to effects of light he had shown since his early *Adam and Eve*. His predella (Florence, Uffizi)[636–7] for Sogliani's *S. Acasio* altar (of the same date, 1521) contains borrowings of the most diverse kind: to mention only some of them, of Nordic types and costumes from the prints of Lucas, of motives from the Raphael *Attila*[221] and, more evident, from the S. Romano battlepieces of Uccello. The latter are some index of an interest that Bacchiacca shares with other members of his generation, in the art of the older Quattrocento. Despite the multiplicity of borrowings the whole character of style in these predelle is more personal than in any antecedent piece. They are less observant of the classical conventions: their compositions are more open and more nearly informally dispersed than in the Borgherini panels of a comparable shape, and figures tend to become slighter, more rhythmically complex and, in places, pointed.

The Acasio predelle are transitional to the entire emergence of Bacchiacca's individuality of style, of which his panels (Dresden and Berlin) for a commission for Giovanni Benintendi (c. 1523)[638] are the explicit document. Certainly taking stimulus by now from the established practices of Rosso and Pontormo, Bacchiacca has assertively developed his own long-evident inclination to eccentricities of shape and sentiment; his preferences are now quite overtly unclassical. Only traces survive of his earlier imitative discipline of figure style; for the most part the forms of actors in these pictures are pointed and brittle, and disarticulate in the way of mannequins. Their order of design is equally loose-jointed, and their space is episodic; no principle of unity, even that of a narration, resists the dissolution of the image into parts. The interest of these pictures, for us as for the personality that made them, is in these parts: precious and eccentric facetings of shapes, of spaces and of psychological sensations.

The means that make this interest are only partly like those of contemporary Mannerism. More than in the rare pictures of comparable type by the Mannerists (for example, the *Adoration of the Kings* painted by Pontormo for this same series) Bacchiacca's panels recollect qualities — eccentrically fanciful, disjunctive and minute — that are in works of this kind from the later Quattrocento. His means and his effects are unintellectual and in part naïve; and they are in small, as befits the genre, and the temperament that chose it. This is a highly personal style, but it hardly has acquired the character of a phenomenon of historical style, as the new Mannerism is; conspicuously, there is almost nothing in it of Pontormo's or of Rosso's profound and consistent recreation of a whole aesthetic order. Nevertheless, the generic climate of this art of Bacchiacca's is, in naïve terms, like that of a Mannerism. Once thus established in this time this vocabulary persists with minor alterations only, and with no significant change in level of sophistication, through the rest of Bacchiacca's long specialist career.

PONTORMO

Even the earliest Pontormos are the evident creations of a markedly individual personality, and of a personality of which some traits do not conform with classical conventions. Yet there is no revolutionary intention in the beginnings of Pontormo's career. His earliest works we can identify are cast of necessity in a learned style, not an invented one, and the chief efforts of his development through 1516 are given to the assimilation of this style as his elders practice it and, in the same process, to a fuller realization than they had achieved of certain of its possibilities. The symptoms of a temperamental incompatibility with classicism decrease as this development proceeds: the special and intense expressiveness of the very earliest pictures turns, in the works of 1515, into — so to speak — authorized channels and becomes the motive power of a new level of accomplishment of Florentine classical style.

Jacopo's seeking and conquest of a classical discipline distinguishes him from his coinventor in the new style, Rosso; every unclassical innovation in

Pontormo is made with most precise awareness of the nature and the limits of the classical idea from which it has diverged. Pontormo's inventions are generated, much more intimately than Rosso's, from the very tissues of the classical style, and his revolution transforms more elements of classical inheritance more profoundly, though in the final result not more decisively, than Rosso's. Jacopo's Mannerism is integrated into the continuity of the history of style of Florentine painting as Rosso's is not, and for this reason, and not from any circumstantial accident, it is more potential to the shaping of the future. And the profundity of what had been a classicizing discipline persists as mental and spiritual habit into Jacopo's processes of new, unclassical invention and helps him in these searching years to depths and complexities of meaning, and to their exact articulation, that Rosso's equal genius does not reach.

Two major works, of which the time of execution must have intersected, are the documents of Jacopo's brief, but most important, moment of classical maturity. These are the monumental fresco *Visitation* in the cloister of the Annunziata (for which records of payment exist from December 1514 to June 1516)[639-40] and the fresco *Veronica* in the Cappella del Papa of S. M. Novella (late summer-autumn, 1515).[642] The design of the first must have been prepared close to the turn of 1514–1515, and substantially adhered to in the longish course of execution; the conception and painting of the *Veronica*, intended for the visit of Pope Leo in November 1515, intruded into the completion of the larger work.

There was no question of the classical identity of the *Visitation* in the older criticism; nor could there have been any question in Pontormo's mind of its close relation to the style and accomplishment of this moment in Andrea and Fra Bartolommeo. In Pontormo's history this is his emergence from the immaturity of style that still marked the closely precedent Ruffillo altar, and the resolution of its uncertainties of form and conflicting tensions of expression. Obviously, close as they are in time, there is clear relation in some respects between the new work and that for S. Ruffillo, but this is more of part than essence. The rough concentration of disproportionate and broken forms in the Ruffillo altar, of so drastically compressed an energy, has yielded in the *Visitation* to another kind of order: not less dense or energetic and no less emotionally charged but, now, differently articulate. The effect of physical proximity of Andrea's *Birth of the Virgin*[311] on Pontormo's change of style in the *Visitation* is quite clear, yet the deeper basis for the style of the *Visitation* is in Jacopo's earlier and more persistent loyalty, to Fra Bartolommeo; it is symptomatic that Pontormo's types and much of his handling of drapery are still recognizably those of a disciple of the Frate, more than of Andrea's.

Jacopo has adapted, even for this narrative scene, the precedent of structure of the Frate's great *pale* as, in particular, of the Pitti altarpiece of 1512 [264]: there is the Frate's theme of a curving architecture, fronted by steps, to serve as stage and monumental support for the figures, and an arrangement of the figures in a near-full circularity in plan. In the original forcefulness of color of the fresco (now partly recovered) the emphasis of this choral space must have been still more than it seems today. Into this basically Bartolommesque order Pontormo has infused a diversity and energy of form that is not the Frate's, at least of the moment when this fresco was designed. Bartolommeo himself was not stimulated to a comparable animation of his style until after his experience of Rome, and at the moment of Jacopo's design no results had come of this as yet.

The precedent to a fluidity and variety of forms like this is rather in Andrea's nearby fresco, and there also is authority for what, up to this time, the Frate had not presumed in monumental composition: an asymmetry of movement within the general stability of design. The model for such various and movemented composition is Andrea's, and its means are learned by Jacopo from him, but Jacopo's impetus toward it is wholly personal: with Andrea's means he learns to discharge, into exactly manipulable and coherent, classically articulated form, the intense and conflicting energies that were compressed in the S. Ruffillo altar. The urgency of these energies in Pontormo exceeds Andrea's; it is not the difference in the nature of the subject matter of their two frescoes that alone accounts for the different compositional force, so much more direct, of the *Visitation*.

The variety of forms in Pontormo's fresco is as much as in Andrea's, and in the *Visitation* these forms are more highly charged; at the same time the general structure of the *Visitation* retains much more than is in Andrea's fresco of Bartolommeo's formality of discipline. The two highest, and now somewhat divergently developed modes of classical composition in the Florentine school of this moment intersect in the design of the *Visitation*, not conjunctively but in a new synthesis; and this resynthesis is not merely of two modes of form but of their affects.

Another source, only newly locally available but of Roman origin, may have influenced the specific shape assumed by Pontormo's composition. The Raphael *Madonna dell' Impannata* [240] of 1514 (perhaps by now already in Florence; it would shortly influence Andrea) may have suggested the unusual relation in Pontormo's fresco of the two protagonists (Gamba), of which Pontormo makes a moving circumstance, literally and figuratively, that it was not in the Raphael.[640] The power of diagonal impulsion that is in this motive is the chief agent of vitality in composition, and is the armature of its intense human and dramatic sense. The fluency of movement in the secondary figures, like that of Andrea's actors, is only ancillary to this decisive impetus of form and of emotion. If there is in fact a dependence on the *Impannata* in Pontormo's central group, there is no conceivable connection between the two whole compositions; yet the essential character of design in the *Visitation* is like that of the *Impannata* (and by extension like that of Raphaelesque design of this time) more than are either Andrea's or Bartolommeo's designs of 1514. Like the *Impannata*, the *Visitation* is a synthesis of stringent discipline and powerful internal animation (in both cases exactly articulated in cursive and diagonal forms) for which there was, as of 1514, no other Florentine equivalent in precise kind or degree. In 1515, as Pontormo's design was in course of execution, there was an analogue of its style intended, but hardly successfully achieved, in Fra Bartolommeo's first great post-Roman exercise, the *Misericordia* altar;[532] and in 1515–1516, at least partly as the result of study of the *Impannata*, Andrea evolved designs — none, however, on monumental scale — of comparable simultaneous discipline and complexity.

The state of mind that determines Pontormo's new mold of synthetic form has its components in the immediate precedents of Florentine classical painting; but the result his synthesis of these components brings and, equally, his sense of an expressive urgency, have no earlier counterpart in Florence. The *Visitation* speaks the language of grandeur and of high decorum of Fra Bartolommeo, but through actors who, like Andrea's, are less inhumanly remote. Differently from in Andrea, however, the actors in the *Visitation* are not so finely distinguished in their feelings. They exist in a more generalized and serious climate of emotion — and this, again, is like the Frate — and even where the secondary figures attend on, more than they participate, in the urgency of the central action they reverberate with and share its tone. For the nobly impressive and compelling impulse in the two protagonists there is no antecedent in Florentine sources, nor is there one in Jacopo's possible specific single experience of a contemporary Raphael. So far, the Frate had made an ennobled but somewhat inert art, and Andrea an art of naturalness within ennobled form; but Jacopo's fresco is the first — and tardy — incident in Florence of an example, of the first artistic merit, of dramatic rhetoric which, for all its still evident limitations, approximates the art of recent Rome.

The limitations are evident: this is the first work of such dimension and complexity by an artist still not secure in his maturity (and who indeed reached his twenty-first year only while this fresco was in progress). There is a gap between idea and execution in the *Visitation*: the inventive power of mind and grasp of general ideas has outstripped the painter's evolution of a specific formal vocabulary. Pontormo as yet only partly commands his masters' sense of structure and proportion of a classical humanity, or more exactly only inconsistently demonstrates his interest in achieving this command. It is most apparent in the central figures, most nearly imitative of the manner of Andrea in the *Birth of the Virgin*, but in other figures there is a schematic handling of drapery and an insecure articulation of anatomy that even exaggerate the model of the Frate. This population has not yet been molded by Pontormo to a single shape, expressive of a consistent concept of expressive personality. Also, the role of persons in the drama that, in its main theme, Jacopo so strongly feels is not conceived with the singleness of purpose that is in, for example, the analogues of this dramatic art in Raphael. Jacopo knows no Roman precedent for stage management in the Grand Manner; his examples are in Andrea's frescoes and in their antecedents in the Florentine Quattrocento of discursive reportage. There is evidence in the *Visitation* that Pontormo had been interested in one of the most discursive examples of Quattrocento narrative, the Ghiberti doors: it has long been noticed that the burden-bearing woman at the left — one of the least integrated actors in Jacopo's Visitation scene — is borrowed from this source. There is some touch in the *Visitation* — encouraged, certainly, by the relation of space to subject — of the old Florentine pleasure in accessory incident, not quite wholly welded to the central theme. That the consequent distraction is so relatively small is due to the power, far more commanding, of the whole form in which these incidents appear.

There are, then, still the evidences within the remarkable classicism of idea of the *Visitation* of this idea's as yet imperfectly classical articulation. In one sense these "imperfections" are the mark of a maturity not yet achieved, both of the painter's personality and of his exact comprehension of the meanings of the classical style; as had been the more obvious case in the earlier Ruffillo altar, these indices of unclassicism are indices still of a preclassicism in Pontormo's evolution. But now, in this context, these disparities assume another meaning also. Where the artist has not only so well understood but given new development to essential propositions of the classical style it would seem that his points of continuing divergence indicate a temperamentally resistent, and aesthetically and expressively purposeful, difference from it. Now these differences can be viewed less as symptoms of an insufficient penetration into classicism than as the indices of the immediately imminent postclassical shape of things to come.

In part the unclassical elements within the *Visitation* are the same as those in the Ruffillo altar, but moderated toward classical example and not so awkwardly explicit: it is as if the painter's native disposition were, in these respects, not willingly more tractable. His inconsistent sense of human substance and his tendency to schematize its manner of description are, in nearer hindsight from the subsequent events of Mannerism, readable in an anticipatory way. So also is the tone of Jacopo's emotional expression. Like the bodies, the countenances too are typed and generalized, more even than in the style of Fra Bartolommeo, and the articulation of expression in them is correspondingly unindividual; we have already observed that Jacopo does not differentiate the responses of each actor so finely as Andrea. There is, in the *Visitation*, what might be described as a lesser emotional objectivity than in Andrea. Unlike Andrea, Jacopo does not suggest the sense that emotion, as we read it in the picture, originates genuinely within the actors: feeling seems a mold projected by the artist on them. There is less concern than in Andrea to effect a penetration into the feeling that the actors may be supposed to have, and to specify it in each particular personality. Emotion has not been separated out enough, not only among the actors but as between the creator and his creatures: it remains in this sense unobjectified. Yet the nature of this feeling, as we have seen, is more serious, and of a differently compelling intensity than in Andrea. In a shortly subsequent moment Jacopo's specificity of emotional description will grow to match Andrea's, and Jacopo's power of emotional communication will then wholly outstrip his.

There had already been, in the S. Ruffillo altar, a symptom of such a consuming energy of feeling, but there it had not yet found a classicizing channel of communication. Conceived and executed during the process of painting of the *Visitation*, Jacopo's fresco *St. Veronica* [642] (in the Cappella del Papa in part subcontracted to him by Ridolfo Ghirlandaio) effects the coincidence of a native, and developing, intensity of content with a classical form: the one more urgent than in the *Visitation*, and the other — in consequence not only of its subject but of the artist's experience — more concentrated and powerfully effective still. The *Veronica* occupies the second of the two lunettes in the papal chapel, facing Ridolfo's *Coronation of the Virgin*,[592] aesthetically dwarfing it and summarizing, in their contrast, the opposite contemporary poles of evolution within the Florentine classical style. The other figure decorations of the chapel, in the geometrical divisions of the ceiling between Andrea di Cosimo's grotesques, were also left to Jacopo. They consist of a central tondo of a blessing God the Father, and emblem-bearing putti in the lesser spaces,[641] now in dubious condition but even originally roughly and apparently quickly painted, and hardly very meditated in design; it would seem that Jacopo regarded his contribution to the ceiling as mere decorator's work.

Like the *Visitation*, the *Veronica* is an achievement of marked individuality, which at the same time affirms its close connection to the precedents of Florentine classical style. Fra Bartolommeo's tradition is as evidently in it as in the *Visitation*, and perhaps there is specific inspiration from his Besançon altar of three years before:[261] there is a similar dramatizing effectiveness of motive in the *Veronica*, cloud-borne within a monumental architecture, as in the Virgin in Glory of the Frate's altar. The reference to Andrea is also nearer and more precise than it is in the *Visitation*: the very influential altar now in Dresden has again (as in the S. Ruffillo fresco) much shaped Pontormo's conception here. He has adapted Andrea's sweeping baldacchino and its angelic supporters from the Dresden picture, and the postures of all of Jacopo's figures are, generically, in the mold of Andrea's in that work. But the relation of Andrea's model to the *Veronica* is no longer what it had been to the Ruffillo fresco: there is still the evident example of Andrea's emotionality for that of Jacopo, but now the whole of his image, not one head only (as in the S. Ruffillo altar) generates a force and fluency of feeling that exceed Andrea's. And even the borrowed Sartesque elements of form have acquired a different potency in the *Veronica,* and with it, the effect of an aggrandized physical and expressive scale.

There may be, in the *Veronica*, the first reflection in Pontormo of Michelangelo's world of forms and spiritual ambitions, from the Doni tondo[27] or the famous central turning figure of the Cascina Cartoon; and there may also be a symptom of contrary kind, a first evidence of interest in Dürer (though in a matter of iconography and costume, not of substance). Beyond the possible relation of motives, there is more in the *Veronica* than in anything in Florence of this date of a kind of expression and of form that are like Michelangelo: more than in the art, alternately — or at the same time — febrile and monumental of Andrea, or even than in the episodes of imitative Michelangelism of the Frate. There is an independent analogue of Michelangelo's heroic canon of the human form in the body of Veronica; and more important, that form is inhabited and moved, in its bold contrapposto, by a comparable force. *Veronica* makes an inspired and impassioned monumental presence by comparison with which everything in Florence but the relics of Michelangelo seem less in power and in spiritual dimension. Still more than the *Visitation,* the *Veronica* speaks with the declamatory force of contemporary Rome, but with a simpler and more instantly compelling emotional effectiveness — without the Roman apparatus or tonality of declamation. With these two works Pontormo carried the postulates of classical style that had been given him to a kind of fulfillment no other artist in the city had as yet attained and which, in this kind, no other artist would surpass. From this fulfillment Pontormo would proceed with the same intensity to its undoing.

Something of that latter process may have begun almost concurrently with the classical fulfillment, in Jacopo's contributions to the decorations for the *salotto* of Pier Francesco Borgherini. Far more apt than his collaborators to seek a possibility of new expression, Pontormo took more advantage than they of the liberty of design allowed by narrative composition, and of the freedom of forms permitted by small scale. There are four panels by him from the series, of which the sequence can be ascertained by internal evidence; they range in date from 1515–1516 to 1518. In the first three of them a development is evident of which the consequences, more decisively expressed on monumental scale, will contribute to the making of Mannerism; and the last of these panels is the most complex revolutionary document of its half-decade.

However, the earliest of the set, *Joseph Revealing Himself to his Brothers*[643] (Henfield, Collection Lady Salmond, as are the next two panels also; 1515–16) is not significantly to be distinguished in style from the *Visitation.* Despite its small scale and cassone shape it is composed with the exact deliberation of a monumental fresco, and in the vein of design of the *Visitation.* An extensive landscape space is ordered by its content of figures and by architecture into a classicizing structure, logically arranged almost to the entire exclusion of residual effects of accident. By comparison, Andrea's early, larger panel for this series, of contemporary date, is engagingly informal. On one side of Pontormo's panel a figure group is disposed in semicircular pattern, as in the *Visitation*; and also as in the *Visitation,* a diagonal stress within it carries the expressive point. This group of figures encloses a lucid content of space. In balance with it on the other side, more rearward, is a circular architecture with figures almost symmetrically arranged upon and near it — a unit of equal spatial lucidity. The curving profile in elevation of each group is precisely calculated to intersect the other in the center of the panel, and affirm their relation of balance. Pontormo's absorption of this moment in the problem of classical pictorial organization is such that he works at it as rigorously in this cassone-like shape and scale as in his contemporary monumental paintings.

The effect of scale is visible, however, in the character of shape and manner of drawing of Pontormo's figures. His tendency to angular accenting of drapery, preexistent to the *Visitation* but somewhat suppressed in it, is more indulged in these small forms. The pattern of drapery and of figure contour is more diverse and broken than in the *Visitation,* but it is also finely controlled, even delicate, in its management of sequences of rhythm. These figures are more fragile in their articulation and of a slighter grace. They recall some part of the character of the actors of the early *Ospedale,*[323] but not their ghostly indeterminateness; the expressive action of these figures, as well as their forms, has now been specified. The mood established by posture, gesture, and by faces has the seriousness of that of the actors in the larger works and the same conviction of intensity, but it is more intimately defined.

The second panel, usually titled *Joseph Sold to Potiphar,*[644] is more certainly of the year 1516. Different in shape and on larger scale than the first panel, this seems not to have invited so careful a refinement in its execution. The handling of the brush is less fine-pointed, broader in touch and quicker in temper than in the preceding scene. On this scale the freer handling of necessity affects the figure style: the movement of the brush brings out in the figures as a dominant a quality that, in the recent monumental frescoes, had been the lesser, deliberately restrained note. The figures are of swift-movemented angularity of contour, fined down in substance and hardly plastically articulate, and improbably pointed in their extremities. They move according to no norm, but in a variety of ways: some a brittle parody of classical grace, and others of a seeming accidental naturalness. Much more than in the first Borgherini panel there is a reemergence of the kind of temper — an emotion not too strong, but too disruptive, to be classically continent — that had been in the S. Ruffillo altar, and it is now far more self-consciously complex than it was there. There is small inspiration to intensity of feeling in the given theme: Pontormo has supplied it wholly, by absorbing the subject matter into a private sphere of excitant sensibility, of which the visual agencies are the temper of his handling and the pattern of his forms. At the same time he has enriched the given theme with unbeautiful incident, observed from actuality, of a kind that would not find place in a classically selective scene of narrative.

What is most conspicuously different from the first of Jacopo's *Joseph* panels is the absence in this one of clear geometric order in the composition — not in theory incompatible with this mode of handling — and of classicizing clarity of space. An order of arrangement, both of the figures and of space, may be perceived within this panel, but it is imperfectly defined; and what is defined of it seems less important to the meaning of the whole than are effects that are not comprehensible, in any classical sense, as order. The meaning of design is less in its discernable relations of balance of shape or counterpoise of direction than in its complex, unlogical sequences of angular movemented rhythm, which pervade the surface of the picture and dominate the relics in it of geometry; and the effects of this complex excitement of design are intensified by color. Neither does the handling of space intend logic or stability: in the foreground, figures — of diminished substance — are as busily related in their space as they are in superficial pattern; behind them is a gap of middle distance, unarticulated save for one disturbing figure, and high in a farther distance is a populated architecture seen from an unnormal perspective point of view. Interval is not clearly measurable in this space, nor is it, as interval, aesthetically sensible. The character of space has been determined not as it is classically, clearly circumscribed and apprehensible, but oppositely, in an unstable and uncertain shape and content. Like the pattern of design on the picture's surface the space, too, is illogically active. The relation between depth and foreground has become ambiguous or, perhaps still more positively even in this picture, ambivalent; and it is at once an agency of tension and cohesion between depth and picture surface that the pattern made by forms in space is so evidently knit into the pattern in the foreground.

Jacopo has taken the given liberty of small scale and manipulable subject in this Borgherini picture to make a far more radical essay of style than any of his collaborators in the series chose, or were impelled, to make. A disposition, which before its willed conformity with classical convention had shown strong symptoms of eccentricity to it in emotional kind and in mode of form, reemerges in this second *Joseph* panel with more mature and far more sophisticated means; and now its unclassical inclinations work directly and corruptively upon the classical conventions learned in the interval. What before had been, in the S. Ruffillo altar or the *Ospedale*, eccentric to classical style but also previous to it, is now, in this moment, unclassical but subsequent to classicism, and inclusive of its experience. The innate impulse to another order of expression now works with entire and exact awareness to reshape the vocabulary of classical style into a new speech.

We have encountered instances elsewhere, particularly among small-scale works, where more tentative departures from the norms of current classicism than Pontormo's in this panel seemingly sought inspiration, and perhaps an authority of precedent, in works of the Quattrocento. In Pontormo the evidence of interest in older art already had appeared in the Ghibertian figure of the *Visitation*. It has also been observed (McKillop) that there may be borrowings of motives in this panel from Ghiberti, from the same particular scene in the *Porta del Paradiso* from which the borrowed figure of the *Visitation* also comes. In this case, as in the other references noted to the Quattrocento, the artist's adaptation of a motive may be an index of sympathy to the style of the work of art from which the motive came. Pontormo's turning, at this moment, from current classical conventions is not provoked by study of Ghiberti or of any other outside source; but there may be a seeking, in this older, incompletely classical art, for precedent and suggestion for Pontormo's own, unclassical, direction. There also may be here, as we have suspected elsewhere, a deliberate archaistic accent, by a psychological response not wholly unexpected in a time of classical fulfillment, when the established style could seem, to some personalities, less interesting than its "imperfect" antecedents. There is, in Jacopo's second *Joseph* panel, little or nothing that is provably imitative of the style of Ghiberti (as distinguished from the possible adapted motives), but there are things in it that had not been in Pontormo's works before and that are, in a general sense, present in Ghiberti's models. Among these are the aberration of spatial order and the discursive multiplicity of persons and of incident; but both these factors in Pontormo are much more accentuated and more evidently the result of precise aesthetic purpose than they are in the *Porta del Paradiso*.

More than it suggests a native Quattrocento precedent, the complexity of contents and of pattern in the second *Joseph* panel suggests a frequent property of contemporary Northern prints. We can document the current popularity of such imported works in Florence, and know specifically of Jacopo's prior use of a Dürer motive at least in a detail of the *Veronica*; his later interest in Northern prints is of course notorious. Yet there is no provable relation between the style of this Borgherini panel and that of Dürer or of Lucas. The situation is like that of Pontormo's possible relation to Ghiberti: there are elements of general resemblance, and grounds for believing in the painter's sympathetic response to style; but there is no provable indication that North European prints had effective influence on his invention of the second *Joseph* panel. Its character is essentially derivable from what is present and potential in Jacopo's preceding art, and external influences have, in his process of invention, at most the value of suggestion.

Of the contributors to the Borgherini decoration only Pontormo and Andrea (and Andrea's executant Puligo) seem to have worked with such consideration of each other's ideas as collaborators in such a project should in theory show, and this is despite the standardized Vasarian report of their dissympathy. Certain common types appear, evidently by intention, in the panels of both artists; these seem to be more likely of Andrea's invention than Jacopo's, but not altogether so. There are also common motives, and for these it is more difficult to determine a priority. No clear evidence, external or internal, can establish precedence in time between Pontormo's third panel of the Borgherini series, *The Butler Restored and the Baker Led to Execution,*[645] and Andrea's second panel (larger in scale and more elaborate in contents) of the *Dream of Pharaoh* (Pitti 88).[619] Andrea's picture (with much of Puligo's execution in it, as we have observed) is almost surely of 1517; Jacopo's painting could, on grounds of style, be slightly earlier, but on the same grounds could be still more comfortably dated in this same year. Of the number of relations perceivable in these two pictures the most striking is that between the main motive of Pontormo's painting, the exit from prison of the butler and baker, and the motive in the background of Andrea's panel, of Joseph's release; the similarity of theme does not alone suffice to justify their close similarity of form. One, but which one cannot be determined, is a paraphrase of the other.

There is more to this resemblance than the common motive. In the background of Andrea's picture, and among the smaller figures so freely distributed against the stage-like setting toward the right (where there is more of Andrea's hand than Puligo's), there is a particular demonstration of Andrea's optical acuity. The movemented shapes of persons are described with subtlety and brilliance in silhouette against the architecture; there is a sensation of visual aliveness, in this area of the painting, which is that — to use the phrase in an unaccustomed context — of a *tranche de vie*. This vitality is not just of the spontaneous-seeming arrangement and action of the figures, but of the sharp quickness with which they have been seen, and of which the temper is preserved in their technique of description. There is the same sense in the Pontormo of an acuity of perception and description which, in his work so far, is new. But in his figures, also silhouetted against architecture, there is an energy of contour and a distinction within form still more incisive than in Andrea. Not only more pronounced accents of line but sharper differentiations of light and color have been made by Jacopo, so that his actors seem to be perceived, and to exist, with a more vital actuality than Andrea's.

The intensity of personality that, in Jacopo's preceding works, had been infused into a psychological communication, or discharged into a pattern made on forms, has now been turned — in all likelihood on the initial inspiration of Sartesque example of this moment — into the visual experience of nature. Jacopo's act of vision is altogether more highly charged than Andrea's and more penetrating, and yields an intenser conviction of existence, but it does not for this reason necessarily yield an equally objective truth. Andrea operates with a vital, but — by comparison — primarily receptive sensibility to record his objects; for Jacopo the act of vision is not only receptive but equally or more an active discharge of energy upon the seen thing. His hand records with the same intensity that is in his seeing: it is not enough for him to state the visual situation as Andrea has, with surpassingly refined sympathy; as Jacopo paints it, the object takes on the stresses and the pressures of his energy of seeing. This surcharge in Pontormo's seeing can result, at once, in an accentuated force of existence, in poignant fragments of visual truth, and in its distortion.

As in the second of Andrea's panels, Jacopo's acuity of vision is most strongly exercised in the middle distance and background of his picture; the draped figures of the closest foreground are, except in color, relatively conventionally seen. But in the Pontormo, middle distance and background are in another relation altogether to the foreground than in Andrea's work. It is hardly likely, given their quite separated narratives, that Jacopo's second and third panels were given their similar perspective system from consideration of a place intended for them in the decoration; the low perspective point of view and the raised distance in each were, apparently, aesthetically determined. That this is so may be indicated by the fact that the raising and closure of the space in the third panel is more distinct than in the second, and in the third panel certain consequences of this spatial situation have been more evidently drawn. Among these is an elongation of figures, which is in relation to the painter's point of view on them. This attenuation of the human shape extends the tendency Pontormo only symptomatically evinced before, toward occasional slender, pointing refinement of his forms. Here its consistent demonstration proceeds from, and is justified by, a perspective pretext. It also accords with, but exceeds, a closely contemporary inclination toward refined proportion that appears in Sarto.

More important, however, is the consequence for the whole character of design of such a perspective system, in this third panel still more than in the second unlike the system used by Andrea. Where the perspective structure of the *Dream of Pharaoh* makes comfortable intervals of space, Jacopo's perspective compels the spatial components of his painting into a condensed relation, and makes them more responsively and tensely dependent on each other. Further, this condensation of the forms in space makes a tighter interdependence among them in the pattern they project upon the picture surface. In its verbal expression, this proposition does not seem so different from one we had occasion to remark in demonstrations, both in Florence and in Rome, of a highest classical style; but as Pontormo articulates it, it could hardly be more different. In a Sartesque design such as the *Trinità* [566] each element, in its close relation to the others, is measurable, scanned, and stable; in Pontormo's panel the essence of the image is, instead, in its motility: each part depends at once precariously and insistently upon the others. The compression of relations between the elements of spatial order and the superficial design — the compression, indeed, of one into the other — is thus a dynamic, demanding, and involving, phenomenon for the spectator, not one he can assess objectively, in a discrete harmony. Though interval, in the sense of spatial interval, is no longer aesthetically meaningful in Jacopo's third panel, the intervals within the pattern made by spatial condensation have been highly charged, and with a life unlike that in the patterns of Andrea. Where Andrea's temper responds in this time to the finest differentiations of a harmony, Jacopo responds, with his more concentrated intensity, to the more poignant sensations that are in imminent or actual dissonance: not only do his individual shapes have a pointed and incipiently eccentric liveness; they have a tense and pointed pregnance of relationship in pattern to each other.

Jacopo's whole composition is based on an eccentric order; what is comparable in motive in Andrea's *Dream of Pharoah* [619] has no such effect. This has no precedent either in its configuration or its character of design. Far extending an old pretext of Andrea's, the forms are distributed in a manner that intends the effects of spontaneity of accident; but on this apparently accidental view of the event an arbitrary order has at once been imposed. It is an order that contains its own unconventional and thoroughly irregular geometry, drastically charged with the impulse of eccentric movement. A zigzag armature of pattern precisely binds the elements of narrative together, and at the same time laces into tighter unity the pattern on the surface and in the narrow planes of space. From any classical conception of an order there is small logic in this scheme, but it has its own aberrant kind of sense, and no less deliberate a discipline than is in a classical design. And despite its eccentricity of form and temper of motility, the composition finds a precarious, yet perceptible effect of balance.

Evidently, an expression so distinct as this from what is in the previous art of Florence, and one so articulate of its individuality, is the product of a high sophistication — even if, as we know of Pontormo from his biography, that sophistication was in aesthetic matters only. The extreme calculation of aesthetic artifice that came in the course of development of the classical style was itself the ground on which a painter so young as Pontormo at this time could find, as it were ready-made, the basis for his own artistic sophistication: not only as much as was in his masters but, by a process of historical accumulation, potentially still more. An individuality so self-aware as Jacopo's, and charged with his unsettling intensity of temperament, could not but express itself in forms of novel tendency and, beyond this, even seek the stimuli that are in experiment and in novelty for their own sake. Such an impulse to the excitements of new vision and new form is already identifiable in both this third Borgherini panel and in the preceding one, yet by no means to the degree that will very soon be manifest. In both pictures the substance of new formal and expressive principle is more novel than the appearance that has been given them. Pontormo's equally inventive but less profoundly disciplined contemporary, Rosso, is more and earlier a seeker after novelty.

It is in part the deliberate interest in what is not conventional that determines the kind of response that Pontormo has to Northern prints, so different from the response of Andrea which, at this moment, is more in demonstrable quantity than Jacopo's. Where, as in this panel (in the headdress of Pharaoh's wife or the type of one Germanic executioner), Jacopo adopts a Northern detail it is with stress on its effect of foreignness and piquancy; Andrea's far more liberal borrowings from Northern prints (the *Dream of Pharaoh* is larded with plagiarisms from Lucas van Leyden) are denatured to the point of near loss of recognizable identity, and submerged in their classicizing context.

The symptoms of novelty of style in this third one of Pontormo's *Joseph* panels are not uniform in character or in the direction of development they may imply; they could, indeed, be thought of as divergent. There is departure from classical norms in the sense of an intensified existence, and while this is in part a more optically penetrating objective truth, it is also in part an intensified subjective, emotional, truth. But these are not separable in their working, and their joint result is a dislocation from the controlled naturalism of classical style in character both of form and content. Also, as this more intense presence in the picture is achieved, it has been cast within an order of design more abstract than in the classical conventions: less reproductive of the environment of space, more arbitrarily compelling of connection in the pattern made of forms, and less reducible to a graspable gestalt of geometric shape. The inventive deviations from the classical style in Pontormo, still more evidently than in contemporary Rome, proceed in antithetic directions beyond the boundaries within which classical synthesis may function.

What in the small scale of the Borgherini panels had the value of experiment is developed, made explicit, and expanded into major form in Pontormo's altar for the Pucci Chapel in S. Michele Visdomini (Florence, *in situ*; dated and set up 1518).[646] It is this work that clearly indicates to Florence a new proposition of artistic style, no longer comprehensible within the limits — no matter how flexibly conceived — of classicism. As an event in the history of style (though not as an aesthetic or a human document) this is almost comparable in importance to Leonardo's long-previous *Adoration of the Magi*:[3] as that had marked the effective beginning of the history of High Renaissance classical style, this is the decisive monument for the beginning in Florence of the new postclassical style of Mannerism. The Visdomini altar had, no more than Leonardo's *Adoration*, the force of instant authoritative example: its appearance — as we realize from what we have observed so far — did not either quickly or drastically alter the artistic practice of the majority of Florentines. Also as with Leonardo's *Adoration*, this work, similarly decisive in all essential points of a new style, is not — and, in the nature of the process of artistic invention, cannot be — entirely separated from its antecedents. Pontormo's very acts of innovation in the Visdomini altar are performed upon the matter given him by his inheritance and education, and by his own partly classical career so far; part of what he chooses to invent, and part of its character as invention, is accounted for by these data, with which perforce he works. There is an inevitable element of resistance in this matter to his new intentions for it. It is because of this that while what he intends primarily is his new positive creation, what he achieves, in this first major effort of invention, also has the negative effect of a revolt against the past, as if it were a willed anticlassicism. This effect, the result of conflict between new and old, is a byproduct, and not the motivation, of Pontormo's making of this new event of style.

Part of the extraordinary force of meaning in the Visdomini altar proceeds from the conflict of art-historical situation that is apparent in it. There is dual reference in almost all of its important facts of style: to classical tradition, and to the almost invariably decisive alteration of it. In compositional and iconographic type the picture is clearly dependent on Fra Bartolommeo, as it is also, partly, in the handling of chiaroscuro; the obvious reference is to the Frate's impressive Pitti altarpiece of 1512.[264] Andrea's influence, too, is present in the form of the Visdomini altar, though it is less immediately clear. His complicating development of Bartolommeo's chiaroscuro, demonstrated at a height of power and subtlety in 1517, has made a quick impression on Pontormo's style; before this example in Andrea there was no variety and refinement comparable to that in the Visdomini altar in Jacopo's management of chiaroscuro. More than in matters of form, Andrea's precedent is important for Pontormo's mode of psychological sensation. It is more evident in the Visdomini altar even than in Jacopo's preceding works that the kind of psychological state he here records is related to one in Andrea's art, of which the Dresden altar [310] had been the most generalized expression, but which since then had been mostly confined to incidents in Andrea's paintings. Earlier than this, Jacopo had demonstrated that this kind of psychological description in Andrea was a springboard for his own far more intense psychological characterization; but until now he, no more than Andrea, had made it the prime matter of a whole monumental work.

It is a gross simplification to describe what has happened in the Visdomini altar, in reference to the antecedents that it still visibly resembles, as a (literally) eccentric dislocation under intensest expressive pressure of the elements of classical synthesis. This is not merely a negative process of anticlassical disruption but, as we have indicated, an avenue through which, in Pontormo's historical circumstances, it was necessary to proceed toward his own positive novelty of creation. The most apparent index of this — summarily characterized — dislocating process is in the compositional arrangement of the altar. The figures are disposed in a scheme that suggests a balance by their distribution in equal number around a vertical axis; and they conform approximately in whole pattern to the shape of a triangle. The supporting architecture is explicitly symmetrical, parallel to the picture plane and not unusual in type. These things are explicit references to classical ordnance, but each of them contains its own contradiction, of unclassical effect. The vertical axis is so strongly stressed, and all horizontal elements of structure are so masked, that the vertical direction quite dominates the whole design; its equilibrium of directions is upset and its reference to gravity is made unstable. The approximation of triangular order is more assertively disturbed, by the rightward displacement of some figures and the marking, almost with the emphasis of a gash, of a diagonal direction in the composition. The major rightward inclination of this part of the design is countered (more than it is, in the accepted implication of the word, balanced) by an opposite diagonal direction of the figures on the left; and to the effect of their inclination there is added the extraordinary energy in them of psychological impulse. Sharp fanwise movements project outward and upward in this composition, in clear contradiction of the reminiscence in it of a traditional triangular order. These fanwise movements make a shape inverse that of the triangle, which quite negates the remnant in it of stability.

The very temper of the forms that constitute the parts of this design is actively unstable. The charged outline and angular accenting of shapes that appeared in the Borgherini panels is much intensified: the pattern in which whole figures are now cast, in posture and in indication of their drapery, is of sharpest movement, with quick, unsettling, disconnective changes of direction. A dispersive as well as a disruptive energy emerges from these forms, and makes a complex fragmenting of the picture's surface. The color, much moderated by the chiaroscuro, does not contribute to this effect of design, but the chiaroscuro itself, so strongly differentiated (though not so much as it seems to be in photographs), in part determines and intensifies it. The contrasts of the light stress and isolate the active fragments of design, and tend to suppress — with a certain arbitrariness — the elements of form that are not part of the intended pattern. Chiaroscuro is no longer, as it had been even in Bartolommeo's or Andrea's most developed uses of it, an aesthetic and optical continuum, as much unifying as differentiating; it has become instead — more obviously even than in the contemporary art of Giulio Romano — a vehicle of disruption. As with the devices of composition, the mode of light has been subjected to too violent a charge to maintain its classical coherence of form or meaning.

The synthetic coherence of the classical image has been dispersed, in this picture, into fragments, but these fragments have been reconstituted in a new kind of aesthetic order. Its premises were already incipiently evident in the third Borgherini panel, and they are explicit here. It is not its remnants of classical geometric order that give this design its sensible effect of an aesthetic unity. Its order is basically not of classical kind; it is founded on an inversion of the relation in classical design between stable substance and energy. What in the classical system had been the vitalizing incident of form, or the ornament of an artistic sensibility on substance, here becomes the primary matter of design. Design now is essentially the making of relations among the kinetic virtues that reside in forms, rather than the disposition in an eventually stable order of their substances. The repertory of the classical style here still, however, much conditions the patterns in which this kinetic structure moves. There is a pseudo-logic of geometry in the relations among forms: near-balances, repetitions, and near-fluent rhythmical connections exist in this design; but no relation, even in terms of movement only, arrives at a semblance of classicizing counterpoint. Each shape contains a disequilibrium within it, and as one shape is related, with clear deliberation, to another it is simultaneously affirmed that their relation, too, is not in equilibrium. This simultaneity of affirmative and negative relation, of near-accord and dissonance in pattern, puts each shape in a state of tension in respect to others; the kinetic nature of design is both of the separate forms and their relation. However, in the whole picture structure this complex kinesis is finally manipulated into a difficult, restless, and precariously suspended equilibrium, so that the picture as a whole conveys the sense that it contains a complete aesthetic order and is, in form, an integer.

The effect of an aesthetic consistency within the picture is supported by two further, interrelated, circumstances of its structure. Still more evidently than in the third Borgherini panel, the projection of space has been minimized in the Visdomini altar, and the working of design within the narrow space is now explicitly indissoluble from, and quite dominated by, the working of pattern on the picture surface. The figures, too, have been arranged so that, despite their complicated postures, they are dominantly aligned with the picture plane. Their tight-woven and intensely energetic pattern, furthermore, occupies almost all the surface of the picture. As the space has been closed forward what would be its normal contents have been raised up in successive layers, as it were substituting a situation of height for one of depth, in a manner that recalls (as has often been remarked) a principle of mediaeval style. There are no effective spatial intervals — no caesuras made by space — in this design; there is only minimal relief from its intense, unsettling, overall activity.

We have observed that the idea of a planar discipline of structure, with higher cohesion between spatial and superficial order, is a phenomenon that appears in the highest development of classical style, and that its intention there is of a maximum concentration and integrity of form within the image. There were fewer precedents in Florence than in Rome of such structure, but one certainly, and more likely two, major examples of it were available to Pontormo when he conceived the Visdomini altar: Andrea's *Madonna of the Harpies*[565] and his *Trinity*.[566] If Pontormo observed this principle of structure in them it may well have clarified his own intention for the Visdomini design, and supported the idea already present in the second as well as in the third Borgherini panel. But Pontormo's variation of this classical principle is also dislocating: Andrea meant by it connection, not near-identification, of plane and space; and conspicuously he did not mean a disequilibrium between the force of an aesthetic principle and the reproduction of reality. The more drastic conclusion that is drawn by Jacopo is both from intention and necessity: his more urgent unity of dimensions in design is needed to control his differently kinetic and imminently unstable pattern.

As in the classical style in its ultimate development, Pontormo is concerned in the Visdomini altar only with persons; but his persons, related though they visibly still are to Andrea's and Fra Bartolommeo's, are still more visibly a mutation of the breed. The dislocative process that we have observed so far in terms of structure is apparent also in the terms of human organism and of state of mind. The physical dislocation is achieved in part by actual alteration of the canons of classical style, and in part by manipulation of optical devices. The proportion of the body itself extends only somewhat a tendency to increase height in respect to width, which had been evident in the third Borgherini panel, and of which the first Florentine evidences may have been in Andrea's works of 1516–1517 rather than in Jacopo's own. Unlike anything in Sarto, however, Jacopo makes a new effect of proportion of the whole figure by a significant diminution of the size of head in relation to that of the body. Some stimulus to this change may have come from the example of Michelangelo, and possibly from the observation of drawings by him of recent date; it must be remembered that Michelangelo was again intermittently in Florence.

The nature and result of this change in Pontormo's figures cannot, however, be accounted for by an external stimulus: to his actual alterations of physical type Jacopo adds the purely optical effects of his particular chiaroscuro mode in this altarpiece, and compounds with these the effects he makes by his whole temper of design. The darks mask or even altogether suppress part of the dimension in width of the figures, each of which is already so posed, flank to us or nearly so, as to present no more than a fraction of its breadth. The lights, which contrastingly reveal these fractions, almost suggest that these parts are all that effectively exist. The movement of these parts, quick, complex, and centrifugally disarticulate, tends to reinforce the visual sensation that we are dealing with an only partially substantial humanity. Substance is attenuated just as, in a more literal sense, proportion is. This effect of a new figure type is in obvious contradiction of almost every classical prescription for the human form, but the most drastic of its contradictions is of natural plausibility; this is (with Rosso's contemporary S. M. Nuova altar) the first instance on monumental scale in Florentine painting of the Cinquecento in which the record of human appearance is, on the face of it, not assimilable to a normal visual experience. Yet this group of eccentric, unsubstantial, beings has been evolved, in their painted form, after an observation of nature in preparatory drawings that exceeds Andrea's in responsive sensibility and in exactness. In these drawings there is not only a surpassing observation of physical fact; they have a subtlety and power of psychological description beyond even Andrea's genius of this time.

The nature of the emotions Jacopo describes, or projects, in these drawings (and in their less marvelously subtle translation into paint) is not within Andrea's region of spiritual experience. Jacopo's particular identity of feeling, of which the symptoms had been evident in occasional overt form before his episode of classicizing discipline, and covertly during it, is the ultimate motive force to new style in this picture. The kneeling Saint of the early S. Ruffillo fresco had been moved by an incontinent, devouring ecstasy; a state of psyche still basically like this, but more finely and variously articulated, inhabits the persons of the Visdomini altar. Such intense spiritual yearning drives the Joseph and St. John Evangelist (as they turn, following the pointing gesture of the Madonna and the gaze of the Christ toward the high altar) that they are, as no classical emotion would permit, as it were beyond themselves: they have surrendered the sense of self, of the self's bodily existence, and of environment. The Francis is in a different, but also extreme state of feeling: rapt, almost paralyzed, in his contemplation of the Christ.

The children are more nearly related to Andrea's breed, from whom they explicitly descend, but they are far more sharp and even violent in their discharge of emotion. Only the Madonna and St. James and, less, the Infant Baptist, retain some semblance of self-awareness and emotional control; they alone are not inspired or possessed to the point of evident irrationality.

Except in the St. Francis, all these states are of psyches utterly separate from one another. These intensities of feeling drive the beings who suffer them not into communion but into inward, subjective, isolation. Their passions not only animate their faces but compel their bodies into tense complexities of posture, but these are less expressive as empathic communications of a state of mind (as they would be in a classical system) than as symbols, in the temper of their pattern, of such psychic states. In these postures the classical conception of a contrapposto has been abstracted of its plastic and organic sense and syncopated in its rhythms of movement; and so different are the means and meanings of the postures in this picture that even their point of departure from classical precedent has been obscured. The affect that is in each bodily pattern, both representationally and aesthetically indicative of its straining spiritual unrest, is extended into the affect of the whole design, where it is at once compounded and (in the manner we have described before) exactly articulated and controlled: the whole form is by one stage more than its component parts a transmutation into an abstracting aesthetic symbol of the motivating state of mind. The affect of this structure is profoundly different from that of classical designs, but the fact of its achievement of a whole aesthetic order symbolizing content is not. This is, for this case as in classical designs, the indication of essential concord between form and content that demonstrates the presence of a decisive, rather than an only tentative, act of artistic style.

All that is in this object — in form, in affect, and in overt emotion — is in a different relation to the spectator than in works of classical style. We are not able to contemplate it, as we are, for example, a mature classical work of Fra Bartolommeo's, as a synthetic entity potential of complete existence separately from us; nor do we stand toward it in the somewhat different relation that we entertain toward current works of Sarto. In his developed paintings of near date we are in an active communion — which only shortly later than this can become intimate to the point of near-identification — with the object, but that object is still a complete and harmonious, though highly animate, existence; and our relation to it is an adding of another dimension to its synthesis: a reflecting of, and intersection with, its complex harmony. In the Visdomini altar no element is a function of a harmony (except in the most abstract sense of its precarious whole equilibrium of pattern), and each tension of form or an emotion inspires a like tension in the spectator. The picture's form, spatially compressed toward us, imposes itself without relief or interval, and the emotions that it comments or contains compel, in us, a sharing response. Such an image requires more of us than a communion; it demands our active participation in its tensions and irrationalities. And since the completeness of the image — in the sense of any integral harmony — has been lost, and its conviction of a plausible natural experience also, the picture is no longer an objectifiable aesthetic or representational fact. The boundary that was almost always sensible in the classical style, between the object of art and the spectator's subjective sensation of it, can no longer clearly be defined. The response to this work that is required of the spectator is as inextricably involved with it as the painter was in its creation.

So far, the observation seems not to have been made that the predella intended for the altar of S. Michele Visdomini was that of which the chief parts, a *Pietà* and attendant separate figures of saints, is in the gallery in Dublin (two further saints at Warwick Castle, Collection of the Earl of Warwick).[647-9] Drawings survive that attest exactly the connection, in one process of preparation, of the Dublin predella and this altar (Cox). Further, the width of all the extant parts of this predella and of the Visdomini altar piece sufficiently agree: the predella 182 cm, the altar 185; a loss of three centimeters is a probable result of cutting the predella into parts. When proper consideration is given to the different scale of predella and altarpiece their community of style is more striking than their differences, and they very reasonably may be placed in the same year. Iconographically there is no obstruction to their association. The association is explicit, but it is relevant to us only insofar as the parts of the Dublin-Warwick work are actually by Jacopo's own hand. He is the author of the *Pietà* and the *St. Lawrence* certainly, and fairly surely of the (presumed) *St. Francis*; and the *St. Apollonia* may * be his. The other saints have been contributed by an anonymous helper, or perhaps more than one, from the Sarto school, and may be later (the Warwick pieces even considerably) than 1518. That the predella may not have been completed with the altarpiece may help account for its separation from it.

Just as the gestation of the altarpiece is out of an accustomed formula of composition, so also is there reference in the predella *Pietà* to the tradition, and in this case the reference is at least outwardly more literal. Fra Bartolommeo's recent *Pietà* is less Pontormo's source than is the Raphael design that also, less exactly, served the Frate (that one preserved in painted form in the Gardner panel from the Pala Colonna). Though Jacopo's design is so clear a derivation it went through a process as of recreating it entirely anew. One of the most extensive series of preparatory drawings that we have from Jacopo is concerned with the remaking into his own terms of the borrowed basis for this minute picture; and as with the studies that survive for the altarpiece itself these show a most penetrating faculty of observation. The studies for the Christ include anatomical descriptions that are characterized with such emphasis as to suggest Michelangelo's influence, and the possibility of knowledge of the older man's designs, even of recent date. The basic motives of the composition are derived from Raphael, but in the group of the Virgin and the Christ there is a stronger sense of analogue in pose and drapery to the early *Pietà* of Michelangelo in St. Peter's, and a character of severe and isolated silhouette that suggests the *modello* Michelangelo prepared for Sebastiano's picture in Viterbo: not in its final but in some intermediate, self-recollective stage.

The meaning of this small *Pietà* is not in its derivations but, as in the main picture, in their transmutation into creative novelty. The scale of this piece most resembles, among Pontormo's preceding works, that of the first Borgherini panel, and their handling is alike in fineness; however, the personality that moves the brush is now inspired by the same decisive differences that are demonstrated in larger scale in the altar. The drawing with the brush does not now make, as in the early Borgherini panel, a sharpening of complex rhythmic grace but, instead, a minute fragmenting of form. Shapes are described in almost nervously vibrating, brittle sequences of small angularities: the sense of form is the counterpart, in terms of the miniscule and intimate sensations of this scale, of that in the figures of the altar. The change from classicizing canons of proportion is less immediately apparent — the mode of lighting here does not so much suppress effects of breadth of body as it does in the altarpiece — but the actual relative dimension of the parts of body is the same. The effect of alteration from a normative proportion results more evidently, as is perhaps appropriate for this scale, from caricatural aberrations of smaller details, as in the simultaneous pointing and flattening of the faces in particular. Aside from the careful anatomical demonstration in the Christ, the quality of appearance in these little figures is eccentric; and the kind of eccentricities that we perceive are, in the more free and private expression permitted on small scale, exaggerations of those in the altar's corresponding types. The emotional content of the figures of the *Pietà* is also the more private equivalent, no less intense and in some ways more compelling, of the sensations of the more obviously demonstrative actors of the altar.

An important part of the tonality of feeling in the *Pietà* depends upon its optical tonality: the vibration in it of a darkling light. Its affect is like that of the vibrant, broken draughtsmanship; both together are the context in which we read the subject and the description of emotion in the actors. The light is deeply differentiated, but not forced into major contrasts as in the altarpiece; again the distinction is appropriate to their difference in scale. Where the lighting in the altarpiece makes effects of bold activity in form and content, that in the predella makes subtle visual excitement, and its content is of a febrile, moving, and possessing melancholy.

This light makes half-visible a dark, barren, and almost altogether empty landscape, less meaningful as a record of a space than as a setting for a mood. Against this landscape the actors are disposed as if in despite of the notion that there is room in it for habitation. They are arranged within the narrowest plane of space, as close as possible to and in strict parallel with the picture plane; they are against the landscape rather than within it. And, exactly like the figures of the altarpiece, these are manipulated in posture so that their effect is, principally, of conformation with this frontal plane. This principle has no role in the first Borgherini panel, and is not so strictly demonstrated even in the third; only the Visdomini altar itself shows a comparable evolution of this formal idea. In spite of this stringency of arrangement there is no such sense in the *Pietà* as in the altarpiece of exactly intellectually deliberated aesthetic scheme; the meaning of the *Pietà* resides more nearly directly in its, of itself, more instantly communicative subject, and in other varieties of expressive form than those of a constructed pattern. The distinction again proceeds in part from a factor of scale, but it is also symptomatic of an alternate approach to the problems of artistic communication that Pontormo will explore in later works.

It is again in a work of lesser scale and narrative subject that Pontormo probes in new directions of experiment that proceed even beyond the decisive innovations of the Visdomini altar. His last panel for the Borgherini decoration, the so-called *Joseph in Egypt* (London, National Gallery; 1518)[650] is inspired by a still more acute consciousness than in the altar of a new individuality, and by a more explicitly defined will to search out means of style that are not in the classical repertory. The tonality of expression in this panel is unlike that in any of Jacopo's three prior panels for this set, and still less like that in the contributions of his colleagues. The actors of this diffuse narrative are inhabited by emotions which, though not the states of ecstasy of the Visdomini altar, are as compelled as the sense of the situation here will bear, and in places more. (Only the boy Bronzino, in Jacopo's portrait of him in the center foreground, seems a little numbed by the circumstances in which he finds himself.) These emotions are differentiated through a variety of types greater than in any earlier work of Jacopo's, of accented individuality of features that partakes of caricature. In some of these countenances there is the suggestion of a possible reference to the exercises in caricature of Leonardo; more certainly, some of this eccentricity of appearance takes inspiration from the example of North European prints. The particular proof of Pontormo's study of them in this moment is in the background, where the rustic architecture is adapted from the *Ecce Homo* of Lucas van Leyden (the same print from which Andrea had culled motives for one of his companion scenes). As in true caricature, the eccentricity of form in these faces, and in some parts of their bodily structure also, is arrived at by a warping of reality that has been studied with intense concentration. Jacopo's draughtsmanship, still here his principal artistic instrument, becomes more various than before in this dual function of description and distortion. In his handling of light, too, there is a simultaneous increase of what is arbitrary and what is, with quite Flemish subtlety, reproductive of precise visual experience.

In this *Joseph* panel there are no longer any norms to which the recreation of an image conforms, not even that of a consistent kind of abnormality, which had been evident in the Visdòmini altar. Pontormo works, here, for the first time in a sphere from which the conception not only of a classical canon, but of any canon, has been banished. He is free to seek emotional, aesthetic, or descriptive meaning in whatever direction his experimental impulse guides him. There is the utmost variety in this assembly of human forms: acceptable conventional appearance in some of them, a cursive distension in others, and in still others a pointed singular emaciation; and in both these latter diverse directions the distortion of the form in places exceeds credibility. In almost every shape of drapery or anatomy there is a particular stress of its complexities of rhythmic structure, warping of our normal expectation in it of appearance. Almost no part of human form remains merely descriptively inert; each is charged by the artist's intensification, through his draughtsmanship, of its activity of shape.

As in the Visdomini altar, but here yet more explicitly, this activity of shape is disequilibrating; it seeks the aesthetic and psychological excitements of eccentricity. Even aside from the states of mind and bodily action, already communicative of emotional unbalance, in the persons Jacopo describes, the patterns he imposes on them make for tensions. There is tension, also, between the kinetic surcharge laid in this way on the figures and the residue in them, still considerable, of plastic substance; there is a pervasive, but very variable tension between figures made so subjectively malleable as these and the incidents among them of most cogent visual actuality; and there is a tension induced by the disparate variety among themselves of this humanity. There is, as we observed, no longer any norm to which we can refer our experience within this picture; its levels of reality (and of unreality) are multiple, and in shifting relation to one another. This willed unsettling of our terms of reference in the pictorial world is even extended by Pontormo to the boundary between his "real" actors and his representations of statuary: the statues are imminently as animate as the actors.

Beyond its character in parts, the character of whole design in this picture differs — much more radically than in Jacopo's third *Joseph* panel — from any precedent of classicism. In the setting, Jacopo has given an unprecedented prominence to the exotic architecture borrowed from the print of

Lucas; and he has invented, on his own account, a construction which, though made up of elements of classical vocabulary, in its sum is both irrational and, as an architecture, quite implausible — perhaps the first architecture conceived in Florence according to Mannerist principle. More than by this fantasy of setting, however, the very pattern of distribution and relation of the picture's forms determines a character of compositional eccentricity in it which, unlike that in the third Borgherini panel, and more even than in the Visdomini altar, is instantly apparent. The armature of composition here discards the residues of a constructable geometry that had been in these two preceding works, and develops in a new and more movemented way an idea that was in the repertory of the altar. Not merely an element in this design (as it had been in the altar), but its basis, is a fanwise radiation of directions from a single point, which now is drastically asymmetrical in location, in the painting's rightmost lower group. Each of these directions is developed in a cursive sequence, which warps simultaneously across the picture's surface and within its space: forward to the group at the left of Pharaoh receiving Joseph and his family, rearward through the waiting figures in the landscape and those on the stairs; the two latter lines curve, conch-like, with the movement of the architecture and the last turns in upon itself, toward the topmost scene of Jacob's blessing, altogether like the spiraling of a shell. Each of these sequences is an armature not only of a part of the design but of a separate episode of the narration.

Much more than Jacopo's immediately precedent designs, this one functions in an apparent space. Within this space, however, there are almost none of the clarities of interval, or measurable relations among large forms, that are usual in works of classical style. There is no graspable unifying system of perspective and no consistent measure for the scale. The deviations from a normal visual experience of nature and the disparities in relations of size and place in space are not aggressive, but in the course of looking at the picture they become increasingly apparent. The scale and situation in particular of the group in the center, of Joseph's waiting relatives, admits no reasonable explanation. Behind them the landscape, quite disconnected, rises at least as much as it recedes into the space. The whole spatial order seems not only unclassical but even un-Renaissance, as if it had been conceived in despite of the mechanism, the sense, and, eventually, the implied philosophy of rational perspective.

As in other respects we have remarked before, there is a resemblance in this spatial order to the still partly mediaeval style of the early Quattrocento, as in the Ghibertian doors; and here as elsewhere these may have served Jacopo as a point of departure for his own invention. The resemblance is made closer by the way in which Jacopo, like Ghiberti in some of the panels of the *Porta del Paradiso*, sets out his episodes of narrative as if on a multiplicity of stages. In Pontormo's panel the relation of these stages to one another is, at the same time, less diffuse and more purposefully disconnective. The reference to what, in Ghiberti, is a still mediaeval unlogic of style has been made by an altogether differently sophisticated personality, whose dislocations of logic (and of reality) are made, in more complex way even than in the Visdomini altar, with the acutest sense of their relations — even illogical — to one another.

In the whole of this design, as in its parts, these relations are expressed in the kinetic terms of tensions (developing the system in the altar); among these tensions the positive connection of one form with others is quite as sensible as is their disparateness. The dislocations that exist in space and scale are all imbedded, as it were, in a continuous pictorial texture, which is initially created in the picture by the vertical, rather than horizontal, extension of its architectural and landscape setting. All the forms, regardless of their apparent place in space, are referred to an organization of design that is projected on, and in only limited degree through, the picture surface. Analogues of shape and implied or actual rhythmical continuities relate the forms that may be disparate from one another, as they do in the Visdomini altar; but much more than in the altar the connections among forms are made with cursive rhythms. With a compelling fluency these cursive sequences bind form to its adjacent form and group to its adjacent group, regardless of their different levels in the space. Within this unifying cursive net the tensional relations, both of distinction and connection, work more resiliently than in the altarpiece. This is a less sharply difficult, more flexible, but not less intensely energetic aesthetic organism.

As in the exactly contemporary Roman style in the Logge, the cursive mode of design assists in the unfolding of a narrative; but Pontormo's cursive mode, much more than its Roman counterpart, is urgent and complex as is the content of his narrative. Necessarily, the affect of Jacopo's taut, quick-driven cursive form is felt in the communication of his content. The intention of the cursive element in the design is more than this, however, and more also than its function of compelling an aesthetic unity of structure: it also has the constant implication of its value as an ornament. Different in temper of its movement and in its irregular, complex sequences of rhythm from the cursive forms in Jacopo's few authentically classicizing works — and in the same way different from the whole of classical usage of cursive rhythms — this mode is nevertheless a transmutation, to new purposes and into new personality, of a property of classical style. With its reappearance in Pontormo's work in this transmuted guise the function of the work of art as ornament is readmitted, and as in the classical style the nature of this ornament is one of rhythmic fluency. This makes yet another element of tension in this complex style: Jacopo's concern for such ornamental value may make open conflict with his searching after novel, dissonantal, qualities of form and content. This conflict between a will to new and eccentric sensation and a sense of ornamental beauty became one of Pontormo's most difficult and pressing problems. It was not easily resolved; and the history of its solution is central to the later process of maturing of Pontormo's Mannerism.

In 1518, in the close vicinity of both the Visdomini altar and the last panel of the Borgherini series, Pontormo received a portrait commission of unusual kind, for an image of the long-dead Cosimo de' Medici (Florence, Uffizi).[651] Apparently, Cosimo's portrait was meant to have been accompanied by a pendant portrait of his son Piero, for which Jacopo made drawings, of this same date, which survive in the Uffizi Cabinet (440F)[652] and in the Corsini Cabinet in Rome (124162, 130559). These drawings were exploited only much afterwards, by Pontormo or by a pupil, in a portrait last recorded in Bordeaux (Collection Chabanneau). These were by no means the first instances of recollections in portraiture of past historical personages, but the one that was executed, of Cosimo, is the first portrait of this kind in which the painter shows a recognizable historical sense of distinction between past and present.

The *Cosimo* intends an effect of archaism, not only in costume but in character of style, and this reference to the past pursues the interest Jacopo had displayed already in an art that was, in fact, of Cosimo's very time. Jacopo's intention in the portrait was, evidently, not merely of an archaizing reconstruction; his historicism in this instance is, from the character of the given subject, more obvious but no more literal or imitative than are the incidents of it we have seen in his preceding works. He has created, in the *Cosimo*, an image that — with clearly deliberate and most moving effect — seems suspended between past and present: between the archaic and modern, and the remembered and the actual; it occupies a disquieting, unstable plane between the regions of the quick and the dead. The head, imitated from an old medal, has been modelled with an insistence that suggests its plastic actuality, yet it is, as in the medal, only the abstracting profile half of a reality; and the insistent modelling, furthermore, is in the greyed tones of an unliving flesh. The drawing of Cosimo's head accentuates the peculiar identity of each shape to that degree which (as in the old men of the last *Joseph* story, and in a way still more reminiscent of Leonardo) verges on caricature. Because this highly characterized appearance is so close to caricature it simultaneously suggests the actual and the implausible. The gaze of Cosimo, unaltered from that in the profile medal, is veiled and distant; he is psychologically removed in another region than our own.

The body is at least as ambivalent in meaning: in part in a posture that accords with the profile of the face, and in part so turned, in three-quarter view, as to suggest the character of a more modern and more nearly vital pose. The turning is without organic sense, just as the body of the ghostly personage is without substance; the turning of the body mostly serves the end of making an abstracting oval shape of compositional pattern. Against this insubstantiality of body, and different from the ambivalent existence of the head, the hands — anonymous hands — stand out with a contradictory entire aliveness, physically and expressively intense and immediate. At the left side of the picture is the symbolic still life (the *Broncone*, with its allusion to the living and dead branches of the Medici house; Cox), in fact most unstill: nervously drawn, and complexly reflecting of an actual light.

To all this play of form between the affirmation and denial of aliveness the color adds a quotient more integral to the meaning of the picture than in any earlier work of Pontormo. Cosimo's drapery is wine-red, light-flooded, and particularly radiant in contrast with the dark background of the portrait. With almost irritant insistence the light and color suggest the texture of an actual material but will not define one, and between the claret of the dress and the muted vermilion of the sitter's hat there is such a tension, of simultaneous attraction and divergence, as we have elsewhere seen expressed in terms of form. But this activity of color, too, becomes melancholic and, appropriately, funereal, against the sombre background.

The problem of portraiture presented by the *Cosimo* was hardly ordinary, and it excited in Pontormo such imaginative reactions to its possibilities of content, and stimulated such devices of form, as he might have employed in a contemporary work of religious or of narrative subject matter, rather than in a true portrait. He was confronted, probably in the next year, by a more normal problem of portraiture, and his solution of it was considerably different. In his *Portrait of a Musician* (usually identified as Francesco dell' Ajolle; Florence, Uffizi; c. 1519)[653] Jacopo willingly constrains his inventive powers of imagination and of form, and devotes himself to the sensitive recording of the appearance and the quality of personality of this sitter, actual and present to him. The basic formula of the portrait does not differ much from those in current use in Florence or in Rome; the special quality of the *Ajolle* is in the accent in it of Pontormesque personality, rather than in Pontormesque invention.

Evidently, in the Florentine school of this time only Andrea's rare portraits can bear comparison with this one. The comparison indicates, in the *Ajolle,* a penetration of the sitter's personality that seems psychologically more profound than Andrea's, but not more finely sensitive. Ajolle's so direct, melancholy, look conveys less of his possible complexity of personality than is present in Andrea's *Sculptor,* for example,[567] but it also seems to give us access to a more poignant, more frankly self-revealing, and more nearly essential psychological truth.

The comparison with Andrea's portraiture also indicates a differently deliberated and more nearly abstracting discipline of form in Jacopo. Somewhat as in the *Cosimo*, but now with a continuity of cursive contour that recalls the mode developed in the London *Joseph*, the oblique posture of Ajolle is bound into a pattern that conforms essentially to the picture plane; except for the bright page of the open score no color, and little light, interrupts this consistency of plane. The pose, and in the face the lighting, unassertively diminish the apparent breadth of form, and the movement of the contour as it ascends accents the sitter's look of slender, somewhat attenuated refinement: Ajolle's plastic existence is adequately implied, but only within these formal limits. The character of rhythm, slow and musically fluid, and the dark tonality are inseparable from the quality of Ajolle's mood.

In the *Ajolle*, more consistently and more evidently than in the London *Joseph*, there is not only the admission but the stress of ornamental value in the cursive rhythm of the picture's pattern: something that resembles, though in different temper, the *grazia* of classical style. The same quality is far more freely expressed in another work of 1519 where there are not the self-imposed restraints of portraiture: the life-size *Sts. John Evangelist* and *Michael*,[655-6] painted as framing pieces for some older image in the church of S. Michele in Jacopo's own town of Pontorme (Empoli, Collegiata). In both figures the most apparent new element of style is the entire dominance in their design of cursive rhythms: the contour of each figure, the large pattern of its drapery and the drawing of almost all details are in this cursive mode. More than in any precedent — the left group of the London *Joseph*, or the *Ajolle* — these rhythms are elaborated and complex, and most precise in draughtsmanly articulation; their movement also is swift in tempo as it had not been before. In the principal rhythmic passages the fullness of the curves is less: the "wave-length," so to speak, of each curve is longer. The forms these curves enclose also are attenuated, it would seem almost less from any will to minimize their substance than from the effect on them of this impulse of long, quick, cursive rhythm. The quality of grace these images possess is, literally, thinned out by comparison with that in classical figures; what these convey is at a higher pitch and in faster tempo, more nervously precise, than the musicality, suave and sonorous, of classical forms. These lines and shapes compose an equilibrium, but one far more precarious than in classical style; their harmony is just imminently evasive. Yet, for all the unbridgeable distinction between these images and those of classicism, they manifest the intention to make ornamental beauty of form a dominant property of art, as it had been in the maturity of classical style.

These figures, then, in a differently positive way from what had intervened since Pontormo's own classical episode, are a transmutation of the forms and values of his classical inheritance; a dialectic resolution in them of what has been termed the "anticlassicism" of the Visdomini altar is evident by comparison with it. In the panels from Pontorme there is not the exasperation with classical ideals of form that was evident in the Visdomini altar, nor is there any comparably violent intention of expression. The Pontorme figures — even the rapt Evangelist — communicate more of preciosity and elegance than of authentic passion. Feeling in them is as precisely fine in its articulation as the drawing of their form, and like the form its fineness is of a new degree. The distinction from the Visdomini altar emerges so explicitly only in the actual paintings themselves; in the most complete of the surviving preparatory drawings (Uffizi 6571)[654] the Evangelist looks and feels more like his antecedent in the Visdomini altar. The decisive alteration in a new sense of the style of this figure, and of his expressive content in particular, occurred only in the act of execution of the painting. It was then only, in the process of giving final definition to the image, that Jacopo's preoccupation with its form as such — with its precise refinement and its value of ornament — emerged, and assumed the new character we have described; and in consequence in part submerged and altered a previous character of content.

There is a whole further region of difference in these panels from the Visdomini altar: in their mode of lighting and in the role that color plays in them. There is no trace here of the exaggeration of Bartolommesque chiaroscuro that had been used for, and with, such drastic effectiveness in the Visdomini altar. This light is high-keyed and clear; its contrasts are less of illumination than of color. A lighting like that of the earlier altar would literally obscure the fine draughtsmanship that is the chief means of defining form and determining its affective character in the Pontorme panels; and this affect, of ornamental elegance, would be ill-suited by the atmosphere of a dark chiaroscuro light. There is a most self-conscious manipulation of the brighter light used in the Pontorme altar, more variously and precisely indicative than in any work before of Jacopo's remarkable sensibility to actual optical effects. There are subtlest differentiations of luminosity in small passages, as in the modelling of faces, and in the larger areas of drapery there is a radiance more intensely brilliant than can be recalled in the whole repertory of classical painting. In one way the character of light subserves the new draughtsmanly and plastic manipulation of the form, but in another it is a function of a still more radically innovative use of color. Like the light, the color is in higher key, and in its way of working is the counterpart, still more positively characterized, of the unstable and accelerated rhythmic temper of the form. And in the color there is the sense, more acute than in the underlying forms, of artifice: surprising and naturally implausible but, as artifice, entirely compelling.

The principle on which this color works had already been indicated in the London *Joseph* and the *Cosimo*, but not expressed before in such complexity or scale as here. There is, in the Pontorme panels, a new variety of color, and equally important, new hues that are not in the repertory of classical style. They are so chosen that they are intrinsically unstable: off-colors, deviant from the accustomed primaries and eccentric to our ordinary experience; each hue is in itself a visual surprise. In part they are combined in a relation that develops what we remarked in the *Cosimo*: a tensional near-similarity, which suggests both connection and disparateness; but beyond this, each larger field of off-hue is related to a complementary off-hue, not necessarily less eccentric. In addition, there are small episodes of color that seem purely willful accents, not resolvable in any system of relations. There is an exploitation of the possibilities of color, which is not more subtle than that of the most developed colorism of the classical style — as in, for example, the contemporary art of Sarto — but which is of most unlike effect. Instead of the complex differentiation of a harmony, vibrantly low-pitched, there is a high-keyed visual excitement, made by a shifting, energized ambivalence between near-harmony and imminent or actual dissonance.

In both Pontorme figures the dominating hue, relating them assertively, is the cherry-red of the mantle each Saint wears; one mantle is a subtly dissonant variant of the color of the other, but both stand out with equal brilliance against their common neutral-brown backgrounds. Also repeated in both figures is a metallic grey-blue, of the Evangelist's robe and of Michael's armor; this hue is a near-complementary of both cherry-reds. These principal relations established within and between both figures, it is in the Michael — the less grave and more visually appealing personage — that the further play of color comes. From the red of his mantle there derives a range of differentiated oranges, from the peach of the buskins below to the dark russet of the shield above; the grey-blue of the armor bleaches into greyed white in the puff of Michael's sleeve and into pale lavender in his stockings. There is no earlier such play with coloristic sensation so finely calculated as this to skirt the edge of a disharmony; Rosso's coloristic innovations are earlier in the history of Mannerism, but they are not so intellectually conceived, nor so aesthetically disciplined, as those of the Pontorme altar.

It is doubtful that this altar ever had a further contribution made to it by Jacopo, but there is good evidence that one was planned. On the back of the panel with St. John there is a sketch of a *Pietà* by Pontormo, in his style of this same moment; this sketch relates closely to a more finished drawing in the Uffizi Cabinet (300F),[657] which is in lunette form, and seen in pronounced perspective, as if it were intended as a design for a crown-piece for an altar: evidently, in view of the correspondence with the drawing on the rear of the panel, this one. There is no indication that it was ever executed, but the design offers further evidence for Jacopo's intentions of this time.

Like the painted figures of the Saints, the drawing of the *Pietà* is organized in a quick cursive ornamental scheme; but unlike the Saints, aestheticized in expression as well as form, the *Pietà* has an intense pathos — so intense, and so remarkably integrated in exact meaning with its form that it is unlikely that it would have been, in course of a translation into painting, too much diminished. What the painting could not retain, of course, would have been the vibrant flexibility of Pontormo's draughtsmanship as he had come to use it only in this year.

Had it, then, been completed by this intended crown-piece of the *Pietà*, the altar at Pontorme would have worn a different whole aspect, more revealing of the artist's style in this next major step after the Visdomini altarpiece. Sufficiently remarkable though they are in themselves, St. John and St. Michael are two facets only, neither of them inconographically or contentually the primary one, of this intended whole. The ornamental organization that is in them, which dominates their formal and their human personality together, would not, beneath the *Pietà*, have seemed the chief matter of the altar. Though no less precisely — and even more elaborately — ornamental, the intention for the *Pietà* was, at the same time, one of most impassioned communication, even more urgent and direct than in the Visdomini altarpiece. Jacopo's concern with an unsettling power of emotional sensation had not diminished in any way (as the images of the two Saints alone would seem to indicate) or receded behind an emergent pure aestheticism — an aesthetic, admittedly, in itself of exceptional affective value. However, in the context of the new kind of form that is in the painted Saints, and which is indicated in the drawings for the *Pietà*, the character of emotional expression, though not less vital, changes. Its tonality is no longer so abrupt and nervously dislocative as in the Visdomini altar: the nature of emotion partakes of the nature of the cursive form in which it not only is expressed, but even initially felt. The intense pathos acquires a tensile fluency like that of the rhythm, and a quality of ornamental beauty, lyric in effect, which is that of the form. Again, as with the form, the character of the emotion is less drastically separate than it had been, in the first revolutionary step of the Visdomini altar, from the ideals of the classical style.

There is an only inadequate document in painting near to this moment in which the subject is inspired with an impulse of movement, emotional and physical, like that in the design for the *Pietà*, and from which we may gather something of the impress it would have made in paint: this is the single figure of *St. Anthony Abbot* (Florence, Uffizi; 1519–20),[658] in which the model is the same as that for the Evangelist of Pontorme. Here the aged Saint is in a state of almost fearful spiritual commotion, which he communicates in his intense, yet haunted glance and equally in the urgent inclination of his body. His form composes in a looming oblique oval curve, meant evidently (like the figures of the *Pietà*) to be seen from a low perspective. This curve makes a long, swift, fluently movemented line; its basic pattern, both in surface design and in space, appears as if it were continuous with the unrolling of the saint's lettered scroll. The quality of his impelling emotion is at once expressed in and tempered by the rhythmic line, and translated in it into an equivalent quality of aesthetic sensation. There is no such startling coloristic liberty here as in the saints of the Pontorme altar, but there is, in subtler terms, a more singular effect of color than is generally observed: intervening between the close, yet differentiated, concord of Anthony's brown robe and the dulled olive background of the painting is a luminous dark blue in his broad mantle. The color, like the light, is melancholy but unquiet, like one part of the saint's own psychological state.

There is an element of resemblance, in the bigness of Anthony's form and in his posture to precedents in Michelangelo: the analogy, though entirely personally transformed, is to the Prophets of the Sistine.[107-8] Such a model might have been made available (as we have observed already of an earlier case) in Michelangelo's drawings; from 1519 especially Michelangelo was almost continuously resident in Florence. Other evidence, however, and in particular that which can be deduced from a series of Jacopo's own drawings datable in 1519, indicates a strong likelihood that he actually undertook a Roman journey in that year (Cox). Its effects are ascertainable only with difficulty. They appear, when they do, in such transformed guise at least as in the *Anthony*; and very shortly the influence of Michelangelo in Rome was superseded by the example of the present Michelangelo in Florence. Not even then, however, did the art of Michelangelo have an essential influence on the formation of that which was of genuine historical novelty in Pontormo's style; the revolutionary component in Pontormo's Mannerism was his own invention. Only in the later and fuller maturity of his style, in the period of the Felicita decoration, does there come to be a profoundly meaningful relation of Jacopo's art to that of Michelangelo. Then, the component in Pontormo's Mannerism that depends on Michelangelo serves mostly as a classicizing counterweight to its component of unclassical innovation. This later moment of a fully mature Mannerism in Pontormo is, then, for its moment at least, not anticlassical, but a resolution of unclassical invention with transmuted residues of classical ideals, still powerfully exemplified in Michelangelo.

But this, without traceable Michelangelesque example, is already basically the solution Jacopo had reached in 1519, after hardly more than a year of drastically unclassical, and anticlassical, experiment. In its later form, in the full maturity of the Felicita phase, this dialectic is not only more apparent but far more profoundly thought and felt, but it had long since been adumbrated. The most precarious equilibrium of all in Pontormo's art is, however, not in any one of his aesthetic structures; it is this equilibrium, between the unclassical and classicizing components of this dialectic resolution, and its precariousness is of his very historical and cultural situation. Even the resolution achieved in the supreme accomplishments of the time of the Felicita decoration did not endure for more than a few years, and that which anticipated it in 1519 did not last that long. It was succeeded, until the brief moment of an equilibrium should come again, by a half-decade of research, far more extreme and more private than that we have described so far, for new and unclassical possibilities of art.

BERRUGUETE

The role of Alonso Berruguete in this phase of Florentine Mannerist invention was limited to its beginning only, for not later than mid-1518 he returned to Spain. In December 1518 a contract, written at Saragossa, records his presence in his native country: he had become court painter to Charles V who, in this time, was settled in Valladolid. A fairly continuous record exists of subsequent Spanish commissions, in which Berruguete was to establish himself as the chief sculptor of the century in Spain and as the most remarkable personality of sixteenth-century Spanish art before El Greco. From the works he left in Italy one would not expect the later measure of his genius, but in his few paintings that we know of the years from 1515–1518 his originality and unclassical inventiveness are quite apparent. His contribution to the formation of Florentine Mannerism should not, however, be overestimated: not only was his actual involvement with this process limited in time — though the moment at which he was involved was crucial — but few in its now traceable productions; and none of them is of the scale or complexity of the work of this time by Pontormo or Rosso, or of comparable exemplary importance. Berruguete did not work with anything like the intellectual awareness of aesthetic problems that is in Pontormo, nor with so innovative an expressive individuality as Rosso; his is a comparably powerful personality, but simpler in intention and in means. He is nevertheless the third in this creative company of three — the least of the inventors but, unlike other native Florentines, one of them.

Unlike Pontormo, and for cultural as well as temperamental reasons more than Rosso, Berruguete was impervious to the substantive character of Florentine High Renaissance classicism; and this was (as we have seen) despite his deliberate references to it in his earliest identifiable work. As he matured and came more nearly to have the courage of his own convictions he came to regard the authority of classical example less: this is already evident in his contributions, circa 1513–14, to Filippino's altar in the Louvre. We have observed that the more nearly convincing analogue of style there, still more than for the antecedent Borghese *Holy Family*, is with the latest, and unclassical, manner of Piero di Cosimo. What in the Louvre altar is an individual expressive accent and a novel, but not yet strongly characterized, mannered form assumes a different force in what, in our reckoning, is Alonso's next surviving work.

In his *Salome* (Florence, Uffizi; c. 1515)[659] there is again a resemblance to the style of Piero and, beyond it, to some Leonardesque precedents; but more apparent than these backward references is an absolutely innovative power of deformation. The unctuous or merely ornamental character of Alonso's earlier forms has gone and they are inhabited instead by an intense and eccentric rhythmic force which pulls against the norms of shape. Substance is much more positively defined than before, but the power that deforms substance is still more assertive: not only two-dimensional appearances of form, but almost every plastic relation is tormented out of its accustomed order. No axes in Salome's figure are normal to one another or in balance. The planes of her body, and even of her face, are as if twisted into disequilibrium; and the most acute tension among axes is in the aberrant perspective scheme. In these deformations, no consistent character of pattern is intended. This is not, as in Pontormo's structures, a precisely calculated disarticulation, and an equally calculated reformation, of the shapes made by appearances. A straining restlessness, at once psychological and aesthetic in its motivation, inhabits and warps substance, appearances and pattern: this is the first clear symptom, as yet more unquiet than passionate, of the extreme malleability of Berruguete's later sculpture.

The exact role of Berruguete in the formation of the Mannerist vocabulary cannot be determined because, in the case of his few extant works, unlike those of his fellow-innovators, there is no basis for precise chronology. It cannot certainly be ascertained if Berruguete's two Madonnas, that from the Loeser Collection, Florence (once generally attributed to Rosso; now Florence, Palazzo Vecchio)[661] and that recently recovered from the Uffizi deposit (Beccherucci)[660] precede the decisive Mannerist inventions of Pontormo and Rosso in their date. The Loeser *Madonna* is probably not earlier than 1517, and may be from the first half of 1518; the Uffizi *Madonna* is most likely of this later date. Both are, in some respects, more radically unclassical in style than the approximately contemporary work of Pontormo and Rosso, and in this they are like certain paintings of a still prior time by the Sienese, Beccafumi. Like Beccafumi, Alonso is less involved with the precedents of classical authority than his Florentine associates, and equally like Beccafumi, Alonso deals, in his assertion of new style, with less of the problem of transformation of the old. Though in part more radical, his accomplishment of this critical moment is thus a less aesthetically complete and less historically meaningful phenomenon than that in the two Mannerist Florentines.

There is some possibility that Berruguete's ideas in these two Madonna paintings are not without influence from Beccafumi: the Loeser tondo (and certain evidence in Berruguete's few Italian drawings also) indicates that he may have revisited Rome about 1516, and in the course of his journey may have come to know the not wholly dissimilar, and earlier, style of Beccafumi in, for example, the Cappella del Manto or the altar (Siena, Pinacoteca) of the *Trinity with Saints*. This unclassical direction is, however, compounded in the Loeser tondo with a new access of classical reference apparently inspired by Rome. This painting surely depends on Raphael's *Madonna della Sedia* [248] in some motives and in part of its compositional idea; and there is an accent of Michelangelism in the types and forms which, in Rome, would have been easier to come by. At the same time the composition — and still more evidently that of the Uffizi picture — makes a quite different reference, to the same Donatellesque model that had appeared in Alonso's art before.

The Loeser tondo is a much more sophisticated work than the *Salome*. What is, there, still mostly a disruptive energy of form and feeling has here assumed a purposeful identity of new style. The drawing and the handling in paint are self-consciously precise, almost as articulate of the new intention as in Pontormo in this same time. The powerful deforming pressures to which Alonso subjects shape now work toward a consistent end. Form is warped, in part quite beyond natural plausibility, by an insistent, yet flexible impulse of rhythm into an elongated and unstable oval scheme. In places, as in the fine attenuation of the head and hands of the Madonna, Alonso accepts the consequence of a consistent application of such patterning, as Pontormo at this time does not. These hands anticipate (in their artificial placing of the fingers as well as in their extreme pointing elegance) the later artifice of Parmigianino. In its own terms, the whole image makes not only an internal formal consistency but a kind of harmony, not less unstable than in the contemporary Pontormo but less calculatedly fine; and it anticipates the ornamentalism, and exaggerates the mannered *grazia*, of Pontormo's works of 1519. It is more as in Rosso than the current work of Jacopo that the Madonna of the tondo gives so much the effect of an eccentric fantasy, only partially embodied.

The Uffizi *Madonna* develops these ideas with more boldness and with still more consistency, and without trace of restraint by reminiscence in types or motives of the precedents of classicism. The reference to Donatello, now much more explicit, seems a calculated archaism; and even more than in this early Quattrocento model the abnormality of form in the Madonna suggests an abstracting ornamentalism, like that of a mediaeval style. The Madonna's profile pose is deliberately made to seem substanceless; her face has the precise effect, as in sculpture, of a low relief. The Christ Child is of more plausible appearance, but He is most summarily described: His contour is the rough summary only of a containing rhythm. His body is gathered against the Madonna into a single flattened oval pattern, woven in a serpentine around a leaning axis. The design is dynamically arbitrary. It intends no more than an unstable equilibrium, and makes only passing reference to substance; it is, indeed, so fluent as to make the substance in it seem ungraspable. It is at the same time of an almost sensible muscular energy and quite ornamentally abstract. In the human content of the painting there is also a duality, between the adequate effect of psychological and physical vitality of the Christ Child and the Madonna's abstractness, which is reflective not of actuality but of a chronologically distant other work of art.

What has emerged in such a work as this of Berruguete's is more radically unclassical than what is in the exactly contemporary Florentines, and it is disjoined, as the style of the Florentine Mannerists at least as yet is not, from the tradition of Florence. It has been generated out of Tuscany, but the style of the Uffizi picture is already recognizably that of the later Spanish sculptor.

ROSSO

As a native product — even in his extreme and eccentric individuality — of Florentine culture, Rosso was involved with its history and its current happenings as the Spaniard Berruguete was not. Rosso had at least a potential sensibility to aspects of the classical style deeper than those, of type and motive mainly, which had touched Berruguete. As the classical style reached its apogee in Florence and assumed its full dimension of impressiveness, Rosso, like Pontormo (but by no means in the same degree), in part accepted its authority. His earlier demonstration of innately unclassical personality became, in the years 1515–1517, less exclusive, and much less as if in despite of the existence in Florence of a classicism. Given Rosso's more marked eccentricity of temperament and its precocious, deliberate development, there could of course not be, in him, any question of such genuine coincidence with classical style as occurred in these same years in Pontormo. Rosso's response to the impressiveness of classicism was much more ambivalent than Pontormo's; very differently — indeed almost maniacally — possessed by the sense of his own singularity, and lacking Jacopo's flexibility and profundity of mind, Rosso was not amenable to any generalization of artistic law. For him authority meant, even as he might accept it, challenge.

The first instance in this phase of a significant response by Rosso to classical authority is in his *Madonna in Glory* (Leningrad, Hermitage; c. 1515;* hitherto incorrectly dated late, and sometimes as late as 1523).[662] The central motive of the picture is still related to that in the Arezzo and Borghese paintings of the just previous years, and the Madonna figure is immature in the same disproportionate way as in those paintings. This — as it were automorphic — juvenile immaturity of proportion does not occur again in any later work: the phenomenon is like that in the figures of the Ruffillo altar [324] of Pontormo. The motive of pose of the Child and Madonna has been revised into a less unstable balance than in the early pictures; this after an eclectic study of specifically classical examples. Drawings by, or after Michelangelo (like those which may have served the painter of the London Gallery's *Manchester Madonna)*[336] may account for the posture of the Child; and the engravings by (or attributed to) Marcantonio after the *Foligno* altar account, more surely, for much in the pose of Rosso's Virgin, and for some accessory motives. The Madonna in Glory of the Frate's Besançon altar [261] is a source as well, not only for the attitude of Rosso's Virgin but for the putti who support her. These are not mere references of motive: by contrast with his precedent Madonnas Rosso has intended, here, a discernible classicizing correction of his style. The manner of his drawing in the Virgin, firm and somewhat angular, means to approximate Bartolommeo's style, as does the broad, planar chiaroscuro modelling; in place of the literally superficial colorism of the early pictures, in Rome and in Arezzo, Rosso paints in a deliberately plastic mode — in the putti of more than Michelangelesque exaggeration. The whole character of this work is one, for Rosso, of new constructive discipline. Expression, too, if not genuinely more amiable, is at least more clearly articulated than in the preceding paintings, and there is more sense of its relation to the varieties of feeling that Fra Bartolommeo, and Andrea more, explore.

All this willing inclination toward classical style is of course not exclusive, nor enough to overbalance Rosso's still more willful eccentricity. The effect of classical example is not admitted to the point that might make any form seem normal or any shape entirely harmonious: in varying degree, each figure is warped to make formal, representational, and psychological disturbance. This is different from the caricatural stresses of form or expression that may occur in Jacopo, or from the disequilibrating rhythmical distortions of Berruguete. Rosso probes deliberately for the values of sensation that are in eccentricity of form and feeling as such: for him, queerness of appearance and of state of mind is, of itself, a primary artistic end. Where, as here, this end appears within a complex of classicizing ideas and references it cannot but be felt as in conflict with them: as willed perversion of the classical sense of harmony and beauty. Recalling the classical precedents, and at the same time perverting them, Rosso's image is not only a new kind of personal expression but a parody, perhaps more than a little consciously malicious, of the older style. In the same moment that Rosso recognizes the authority of classicism he denies it, in a spirit and intention which, more explicitly than that of his Mannerist contemporaries, can be identified as "anticlassical."

There is a less overt ambivalence in a portrait by Rosso of circa 1516, that of a young man (Berlin, Museums):[663] as is usual in a portrait, the genre itself tends to impose restraints on the painter's liberty of style. As in the Leningrad *Madonna*, Rosso here intends some recognizable conformity with classical example, in this case to the models of successful portraiture by Franciabigio (to whom this once was attributed); ultimately, the model Rosso may have had in mind may have been Raphael's *Angelo Doni*.[52] In general formula of composition, and even in its plastic modelling of form — much like that in the Leningrad picture — there is no drastic deviation from these conventional models of a portrait style, and the character of psychological expression also is not unlike that which can be found in Franciabigio. The actual effect of Rosso's picture is, however, eminently unclassical: he has made a few, highly disquieting, revisions of elements of form, and given a cast of almost dangerous abnormality to the expression of the sitter's countenance; and these things make it impossible to reconcile this image with any classical aesthetic of the portrait or with any classical conception of personality.

The sitter's body is altogether according to the usual conventions of High Renaissance portraiture; only the fine and somewhat pointing drawing of the hands and the brittle painting of the drapery give it a difference in accent from the ordinary. The head, however, has been strangely dislocated in respect both to the axis of the body and the vertical axis of the picture, and it has been even more abnormally displaced in space, thrust preternaturally forward to the foremost plane. It is framed squarely by the lank long hair and by the hat, a flat floating biomorphic shape. In the background landscape, the topmost level of the trees continues the straight line of the hat, already singular enough, in an irrational connection between near and distant. Thus imminently disjoined from its context and compelled toward us, the face is then subtly warped on its own axis (like, but far more subtly than in Berruguete's *Salome*), the far side pulled slightly toward the picture plane. The eyes turn still more toward us and stare, the pupils sharp against the white, with an unbearably insistent gaze. This unpleasant communication is all in one direction: there is no sense of a pacific and mutually interested inspection, as in Raphael's or Andrea's portraits, or of such deeply sympathetic interchange between sitter and spectator as is in Pontormo's. Rosso's sitter inverts the normal relation between spectator and the portrayed subject: he aggressively examines us, but does not permit that we examine him. We can look at him only with unease, and with the sense that association with him, even in this purely psychological domain of art, might be dangerous; he is a male and anticlassical inversion of the *Mona Lisa*. His insistent, unsharing stare is the antecedent, but in terms of an aggression rather than of cool reserve, of the psychological attitude of much later Mannerist portraits, of the second generation.

Rosso's *Assumption* (Florence, SS. Annunziata; 1517)[664] was his first work on monumental scale, and the last in the series of frescoes of the life of the Virgin that had been begun by Andrea six years before. Rosso's fresco is the final term in what, otherwise, is a classical complex, and this association serves to show still more clearly how in this painting, as in his two previous pictures of this phase, there is equivocation between classical precedent and personal unclassical assertion. The comparison of Rosso's fresco and the adjacent *Visitation* of Pontormo [639] specifies the difference in relation to the classical style of the two young men, in somewhat but not yet significantly separate moments, since the conversion to an explicit Mannerism would come, for both, only in 1518. In this context, almost the first impression that emerges from the Rosso is of its bizarre types and their expressions: snub-nosed, weak-chinned and shapelessly fat of face; the Apostles bemused or vacant, and the angels in a slightly maddened ecstasy, exaggerating just to the point of unreason the inspiration in the putti of Andrea's and Pontormo's scenes nearby. None of these persons is quite humanly believable, except for two among the Apostles who are real portraits. One of these, just left of the center of the group, is of quite agreeable expression, not unlike the actors in Andrea's fresco, but more sharp and momentary in psychological characterization; the other, at the far left (St. James; but according to old tradition a portrait of the poet Francesco Berni) [665] is very differently characterized. By comparison with him the subject of the Berlin portrait is subdued in temper; this develops a psychological eccentricity into open and extreme terms. So strange a grimace, evoking such an irrationality of spirit in an actually portrayed being, is without antecedent in the Renaissance, even in the most abnormal imaginings of Piero di Cosimo; this is one of Rosso's children grown mature, and maturely powerful, and given a countenance out of reality.

An influence of German prints may help account somewhat for the Apostles' types, but only for those who are types, not these portraits. The Apostles' draperies are more certainly of partly Germanic inspiration; Dürer's prints are the most likely model for their angular and disconnective energy of pattern. But not less apparent than the new, foreign accent of drapery style is the amplitude, extraordinary for Rosso, of the draped forms: he accepts and even exaggerates the breadth of dimension of Andrea's figures in the *Birth of the Virgin*,[311] and of Pontormo's in the *Visitation*. There is a similar compound of imported novelty and local classical tradition in the scheme of composition. There is at least a possible suggestion for this design in Dürer's *Pentecost* from the *Small Passion* (Kusenberg), but its more immediate references are nearby: among others, to Bartolommeo's fresco of the *Last Judgment* for S. M. Nuova,[21] to his more recent Pitti altarpiece and, in the posture of the Virgin, to the Lucca altar of the *Misericordia*. The composition intends a broad lateral stability and a balance — more than that, a near-symmetry — on both its vertical and horizontal axes, explicitly according to the Frate's prescription of a mature classical mode. Even the color scheme is, for Rosso, relatively contained; like Pontormo's adjacent fresco, it enlivens and sharpens (in this case with a dosage of oranges and greens) Sarto's nearby precedent, but is much related to it.

Much more than in the Leningrad *Madonna* Rosso has regarded and accepted classical authority in the *Assunta*: it has become a more substantial and sensible component of this fresco's style. The elements derived from classical style coexist with the bizarreness of description and of illustration in this work, and even manage partly to survive some fundamental alterations that Rosso has imposed on them. The most important of these is in the management of space and substance. More ample than the forms of the Leningrad *Madonna*, the figures of the *Assunta* are not for that reason more, or even as much, plastically complete: the broad color planes of movemented drapery obscure substance more than they define it. The figures are arranged in space, in both the upper and the lower spheres, in what we can perceive, intellectually, to be a variation on Fra Bartolommeo's ground plans. Among the Apostles, the inner group stands in a full circle, and from this circle tangent arcs extend, more or less symmetrically, through the figures to both sides; in the upper sphere, the Frate's idea of rotation of a chorale of angels around the Virgin is recalled, and developed with a greater boldness than in him. Between the two spheres there is such a keying-together, and some of the actual concordance in plan between them, as the Frate's works display.

All this spatial plotting is intellectually discernible, but it has almost no sensible effect. In the lower range the broad forms are close-pressed, leaving hardly any intervals among them by which we could see through to and appreciate their spatial order. The pattern of the draperies obscures the intervals still further, overriding them; the draperies make a kaleidoscopic continuity, differentiated in color, but not articulate of form. There are no measurable perspective distinctions among the figures of the Apostles, and they are aligned, despite differences of place in plan, into a flattening isocephaly. And, in the upper sphere, although there are quantities of ingenious foreshortening, there are also no measurable perspective differences of scale. The Bartolommesque circle around the Virgin is projected as if it were, rather, an oval on the picture plane. While, conceptually, this upper structure implies space, in actual visual effect that implication is denied; much more than in the sphere below there is a willed ambivalence between design in terms of surface and effects of space.

The vision — or the dogmatic actuality — of the Assumption hovers in an abstract and impalpable distance, but the Apostles seem almost exaggeratedly close to us. In the very center of the composition the bulking robe of one of their vast forms spills out over the picture frame in illusionistic projection toward us; but this is only the extreme indication of our sense, in all of the Apostles, of their imminent presence. The contrast in this respect with the Pontormo in the next bay is acute: there, there are figures that assist us into the picture's classically defined depth, but there is no compulsion toward us of the actors' forms. This, rather, is like the device to which Pontormo comes in the Visdomini altar,[646] of compression toward the spectator of the picture's contents; and Rosso's intention in his earlier and more aggressive use of it is much the same: to abolish the boundary between the spectator and the emotional experience described to him in the work of art.

This, in the Rosso, is an experience of different human temper, and of far less deliberated aesthetic effect, than in the Visdomini altar. Rosso's Apostles make an agitation — of drapery pattern, of color, and of broken, movemented silhouette against the sky — which is far more than that of their physical motion; more even than by their expressions of face or their bodily response, their colors and their rhythms serve to catch us at once into an atmosphere of clamorous, irrational excitement. Our participation in the picture is immediate, but it is more immediately in its abstract affects of excitement of its form than in the physical existence it describes.

The most unclassical idea possible inspires the subject of Rosso's *memento mori* drawing (Uffizi 6499;[666] less likely 1517, as the added *cartellino* indicates, than early 1518, and almost certainly expressly made as a *modello* for an engraving by Agostino Veneziano of that year). The theme is one of North European popular images of the time, and of a very few popular engravings of the Italian Quattrocento; this is a case where the persistence of mediaeval — in Italy, so to speak, Savonarolesque — conceptions in the popular mind coincides with the personal unclassicism of Rosso and with his fascination with the bizarre. Intended by distribution in engraving at least partly for popular consumption, Rosso's image is inevitably far more sophisticated than this market, and more sophisticated than any Italian precedent or German counterpart for such a theme. His strange and pitiful evocations of old age and death are, far more than in them, poignantly and precisely characterized, and his expressive differentiations are much more acute.

The drawing gives evidence, in spite of its expressive individuality, of much more careful consideration of past art than Rosso had ever shown before. The intensity with which he illustrates his subject, and the hyperrealism of its emaciated types, suggests that there may have been, as in other instances about this time, some study of examples of an earlier Quattrocento style in which there are unclassical elements: in this case of the late mode of Donatello and of the S. Lorenzo pulpits in particular. The wasted, already half-skeletal figures of old age, perhaps so inspired, that first appear in this drawing would have a long life in Rosso's succeeding work. Another backward reference is more explicit, and more complex in its meanings for Rosso's interests of this moment: to Leonardo's *Adoration of the Magi* (Carroll), a kind of reverse image, in its situation in respect to classical invention and unclassical residue, of Rosso's drawing. In the ghostly, half-defined actors of the *Adoration* [3] Rosso saw — as he would temperamentally have been disposed to see — the models of the impassioned faces of his old men, and of their gesticulation. His adaptation is not just of a type but of several quite specific motives, the most evident among them the prostrate figure in the left foreground and, above him, the man who holds one hand to his head and the other to his breast. Further, Rosso's idea of a copiously populated scene, within which there is elaborate differentiation of response, is inspired by Leonardo; so, also, is the basic geometry of Rosso's composition. This has been revised, however, according to more "modern" examples of a curving disposition into depth, like those in Fra Bartolommeo's monumental schemes. The perspective differentiation of the forms in space is more evident than among the Apostles of the *Assunta,* yet the effect of a classicizing spatiality is almost as little as it is there, for reasons which, color obviously aside, are much the same. The very differently spare forms of the drawing just as closely intersect to make a single net of movemented pattern, of which the rhythmic energy is not less than in the *Assunta,* and the temper of which is more complex and nervously acute.

Still more than the *Assunta,* the drawing has elements in it that not only refer to classical precedent but seem to intend classical effects, and at the same time it contains elements of form and content — beginning with the subject matter — that are more drastically unclassical; but, as in the fresco, there is no question of the character that dominates this work. It is more conservative and more radical, at the same time, than the contemporary production of Pontormo, but like it belongs to a new category of artistic style. The quotient of novelty, however, is rather differently motivated and differently achieved. It comes not so much by precisely self-conscious aesthetic manipulation as in Jacopo — indeed, the intellectuality that works, in this drawing, in terms of aesthetic order is most of all in it according to convention — as by an illustrative intent: the expressive character of forms is, before all else, a result of their bizarre (and in this case piteous) abnormality of appearance. The way that Pontormo finds in 1518 explores more complicated, and more difficult resources of art than this.

The persons of Rosso's altar for S. M. Nuova (Florence, Uffizi; 1518) [667-8] are only somewhat less extraordinary than those of the *memento mori* drawing. The effect of their apparition on the churchman who commissioned the picture is recounted by Vasari (V, 157): ". . . lo spedalingo . . . vedendole abbozzate, gli parvero, come colui ch'era poco intendente di quest'arte, tutti quei santi, diavoli . . ."; Vasari continues to explain, "avendo il Rosso costume nelle sue bozze a olio di far certi arie crudeli e disperate, e nel finirle poi addolciva l'arie e riducevale al buono." Rosso's first, uncensored, statements on the panel were, then, according to Vasari's report, more extravagant than those we see, and suggestive of more violent and disturbing associations of emotion. The present image is in the way of being a concession to convention.

These types still are more aberrant from normality than those of Pontormo in his exactly contemporary altar, and the quality of their expression is more queer; it is, however, less concentratedly intense. Rosso's characters wear an air of just perceptible genteel lunacy which, in a moment, could become hysteria or shapeless psychological collapse; from this only the two infants in the foreground are exempt. The faces parody, even in its refinement, the extreme sensibility of expression in Andrea's pictures of the just preceding years and make inhumane caricature of it. This teasing eccentricity of emotional sensation is very different from the transforming passion of Pontormo's actors in the Visdomini altarpiece; it is also differently less pervasive of the whole of Rosso's creatures. Their feeling inhabits countenances, but does not move their bodily forms; they stand in quite conventional attitudes drawn from the repertory of Fra Bartolommeo, and in an order that depends, still more evidently, on his models of design. But this residue of classical convention does nothing to redeem the eccentricity of content and appearance in Rosso's picture; the convention is so obviously only that, and not a symptom of a classical constructive meaning.

There is not now any trace, as there had been in varying degree in Rosso's other works since 1515, of an equivocation between classical and unclassical effects of style. In this compass, more restricted than the Annunziata fresco or the *modello* for the *memento mori*, Rosso's translation of the once-classical convention of design into a virtually spaceless pattern is more obvious, and the character of that pattern is also more articulately defined. The illustrative deformations are not in themselves more extreme, but they are made with a finer manipulation of artistic means — of drawing and of color in particular, and of light as well — that communicates the expressive quality of deformation in more precise terms of form.

Rosso begins, in this painting, to find an exact, rather than an approximate, aesthetic language for his image of humanity; more than just describing its eccentricities, this language also now translates its character into highly-articulate psychological and visual indices of sensation. Drawing assumes, in this altarpiece, a new responsive sharpness and complex fragility: the contours of the body and the patterning of drapery simultaneously express rhythmical continuity and a fine, faceting, angular disruption of it. Since his *Assunta*, Rosso has applied himself to the study of works by Sarto of more recent date than the *Birth of the Virgin*,[311] and it is Andrea's kind of sensitivity of rhythmical response, in drawing of anatomy, and still more of drapery, in such a painting as the *Harpies* [565] that is the precedent for Rosso's differently irritant sensibility here. This complex energy of smaller patterning is magnified in the effects of larger forms, in the agitation of contour around the silhouetted heads and in the stabbing angular convergence of the gestures. The whole effect of pattern is of a skein of excitant movement, woven almost entirely against the picture's surface: no opening into space interrupts the continuity of pattern and no resistance is opposed to it by any separating, plastic, integrity of forms. Implausible in appearance, the figures are also almost impalpable in substance.

Almost more than by any other means, the sense of an extraordinary, unsubstantial vision in this picture is made by color. Most unlike Pontormo's reticence of color in the Visdomini altar — but anticipating and in part perhaps suggesting to Pontormo the new intensities he finds in his two saints of 1519 — Rosso's color here goes radically beyond any mere descriptive function. He uses hues that are at least as abnormal to our ordinary experience as are his forms, and these hues are more excitant than his rhythmic patterning in draughtsmanship. In his combination of colors there is a tendency, only partly restrained, to dissonance, of more active and more acid temper than in Pontormo's altar of 1519, but not deliberated in the way that it is there. The Madonna, for example, wears a mauve headdress and a blue-green cloak, this framing a magenta, crossed by a vermilion girdle, in her dress. The magenta goes *changeant* to blue in shadow; one sleeve is curiously transformed by light to yellow-gold. The John Baptist is red-haired, clad in a mantle of pale rose, bleached white in highlights, which contrasts with the tones of blue-white, grey, and dark green of his other garments. The browned body of Jerome opposite is draped in matt blue, very dark in shadow and very cool in light. A full account of this complex and evidently irrational scheme of color is hardly possible, but these indications give the idea of its novelty. The color contains, obviously, an unprecedented, stimulant eccentricity of emotional effect.

The role and character that color takes on in the S. M. Nuova altar had been adumbrated in one of Rosso's *juvenilia*, the *Holy Family* of the Borghese.[327] What was already purposefully laid down there is now enunciated more precisely and with drastic emphasis: by its inherent energy and its descriptive unreality color assumes, as never in a classical work of art, an aesthetic value which seems separable from that of the drawn and modelled form — a value almost abstractly sensible in and for itself; color incandesces as if before the form. Indeed, in this picture there is hardly substance enough left, in its impalpable forms, for color to adhere to. This use of color extends Rosso's own earlier invention, but its present complex articulateness depends, no less than that of Rosso's present mode of drawing, on what he had discerned in Sarto's most recent precedents: Sarto's ultimately complex harmonies are the inspiration and the basis on which Rosso works his own complex dissonantal transformation. And it is as if, in this altarpiece, Rosso should have stripped the skin of color only from a Sarto, leaving its substances behind.

The S. M. Nuova altar is not so searching or so precisely articulate a *pronunciamento* of the new style as is the Visdomini altarpiece, yet almost all the essential new ideas that are in one are in the other. In character of content, and in liberty of transcription into art of nature, there is clear community between the two altarpieces, and a common dissimilarity from classical style. Where Pontormo's more important innovations in aesthetic language are in *disegno* — in the manipulation, with a remarkable coincidence of intellectual calculation and extreme sensibility, of form — Rosso's are in color, and they are not so calculated, nor so fine in sensibility. There is a modern analogy between Pontormo's kind of new investigation and the first development of cubism, and between Rosso's and that of our expressionism; but like all analogies of this kind, this one must not be pressed. The likeness of the two young Florentines' inventions is, in any case, more important than their dissimilarities. In part this likeness may have come through interchange of influence, which we can no longer document, between the two painters — and with Berruguete also; more of it may be accounted for by the similar working of creative personalities, resembling in kind and of the same generation, on the common data given to them both by the existing classical style: their essential innovation is predisposed, not however predetermined, in part by the matter historically given them to work upon.

In Florence, as in contemporary Rome, the style of classicism had reached its own apparent limit of fulfillment toward the years 1516–1518, but its greatest practitioners were none the less still concerned with the development of new resources and effects. Though, in Florence, this probing for the limits of classical expression was less dynamic than in Rome, and more cautious of experiment that strained classical sense, the researches of Sarto and Fra Bartolommeo still pointed in directions that could, with other and more urgent impulse than theirs, lead beyond classicism. In Rome the impetus of Raphael's and of Michelangelo's (still earlier and more radical) new research was stronger, but so also was the exemplary authority of the constant of classicism in their styles; in Florence the probings of the Frate and Andrea were more tentative, but to balance this, their classicism as such was nothing like so authoritative as that of Rome. Florentine classicism was also not so much as that of Rome a nearly autocratically exclusive style in its time; and in Florence, which had a history of modern art as Rome did not, the High Renaissance could be thought of as an episode of which the values were at least susceptible to challenge by those which could be perceived in the great art of the Quattrocento.

An increasing acuity of historical interest and sense, a consequence of the historical nature of the Renaissance itself so far, could encourage reference to the past; and this sense of history was corollary to a more intense sense of the distinctness of the individual self that observed its context of the present as well as the past. We have seen before that the young men who made Mannerism were the heirs of the whole accumulation of the Renaissance awareness of personal individuality. These individualities came to their first maturity — as the Roman Giulio did, more precociously — in the moment of fulfillment of the classical development of style and of critical research by the classical masters for new possibilities of art. The two authentically creative individualities of the younger Florentine generation, intersecting this critical moment, drew consequences from it that the older generation did not intend.

There was latent conflict in Pontormo and Rosso with the aspect of classical style that requires the acceptance by the individual of conventions and of generalization, and in the weakening in crisis of classical conventions this conflict became explicit. They proceeded to transform the data of the existing style, with remarkable quickness, into a more libertarian and private language. There were analogues for what they wished to do in the art, less conventionally ordered and sometimes irrationally inspired, of the Florentine Quattrocento and, in less degree, in that of Northern Europe, and in the first moments of their new exploration they found precedent in both. But more important by far than any older reference, and almost as historically significant as the novelty of invention in the new style, are the continuities between the recent style and the new. Even drastically distorted or transmuted into unlike meaning, and compounded in a new gestalt, there is hardly any factor of Rosso's or Pontormo's Mannerism, in their first decisive documents of its appearance — even the whole new gestalt — which does not take its point of departure in a happening, or in an implication, of the just prior moments of the classical development of style. There is not one cord alone between the classical matrix and its Mannerist offspring but a nexus of connections: a few simple and direct, but more strained and twisted, sometimes to the breaking point; the relation of the new style to its antecedent is like that of the new style's elements among themselves.

Beyond the impulse to originality of new statement that is so strong in both Pontormo's and Rosso's extreme individualities, it is much more in the latter that we can discern a will not only to transform the old style and invent a new, but to invent in its despite, in dissympathetic reaction against the values held by classicism. This response to classicism is not explicit until the S. M. Nuova altarpiece; we have seen how, until then — and even in that altarpiece, in traces — there was much ambivalence in the maturing Rosso's relation to classical style, more than there had been in his *juvenilia.* Even once defined, however, Rosso's willful anticlassicism is still conditioned by the nature of the style he reacts against. All of his eccentricity, so much more capricious and disquieting than Pontormo's, is an authentic function of his creative personality, but certain aspects of it are differently motivated — from different levels of that personality, so to speak — than others. There is an element of malice, of sardonic humor, and even of will to make human and artistic outrage, in Rosso's personality that works inextricably together with his most deeply serious expressive motives, and some of his ideas are certainly conceived with the perverse — but not for this reason, in him less emotionally genuine — intention of parody of the ideals of classical style. What he does of this kind still cannot be detached wholly from its classical precedent: one important aspect of its meaning is in its nature of a distorting mirror held up to classical art, and in it we may see the ruin of a whole realm of the aspirations of the Renaissance.

VII

EPILOGUE: THE ASCENDANCY OF MANNERISM

(SOME EVENTS OF 1521)

VII

EPILOGUE: THE ASCENDANCY OF MANNERISM

(SOME EVENTS OF 1521)

IT must not be forgotten how young the Florentines of the new generation were when they made their first explicit pronouncements of Mannerist style toward 1518, or how much younger still their counterparts in Rome were when they moved at the same time in the same direction. These youthful pronouncements were personally decisive, and in long retrospect they were historically decisive also, but they could not as yet have the authority of means and purpose that only fuller personal maturity, and time to ponder further and distill the meanings of those first ideas, could give.

In Rosso and Pontormo in Florence, and in Giulio and Perino del Vaga in Rome (in that forcing artistic climate more personally precocious), expressions of the new style that are compellingly authoritative appear only in 1521; in Rome, obviously, their emergence owed much to the removal from the scene of Raphael. With the appearance of these works the major destiny of painting in Central Italy was sealed for this generation and, as it proved, for two generations more to come. The profoundly creative personalities — always few — of the younger generation were committed to what we now call a Mannerist style, different for each personality, and different between the two schools as in all styles, but sharing of all essential common denominators. Inevitably, their example came to draw into its orbit of style lesser more or less contemporary personalities, and, in time, those of a generation younger still, and also to affect the art of older masters.

In Rome, with its more nearly autocratic artistic economy, by no means dissolved at Raphael's death, the process of consolidation of the new style was quicker and more general than in Florence. In Florence, always more libertarian, the Mannerist conversion was slower and much less inclusive, and (as we have sketched it out before for individual cases) by no means so complete.

Nevertheless, the decision for the future had been made there, too, by the events of 1521. Their essential consequences for the history of Florentine painting were not altered even by Michelangelo's presence through the twenties in the city. He had himself, long before, explored some directions of style similar to those in Mannerism, and now he came increasingly to adopt ideas of style which, if not as yet coincident with Mannerism, were in a region of classical thought that comes closest to it. What he gave to the Florentine development in these years in his models was read by the younger artists, all the more easily than earlier classical example, as matter apt for transmutation into Mannerism.

Rosso's works of 1521 were not executed for Florence, and had no immediate effect as models on the art of other painters there. They play no direct part in the process — in any case not yet of measurable dimension — of the dissemination of the new style to others, but they are the crucial events in the maturing of his own Mannerist style. Their consequences for the development of painting in the city would be indirectly felt through what he would build on them, in the next few years, for publication within Florence itself. His two surviving works of 1521 were for Volterra and for the village, near * by, of Villamagna: a monumental *Deposition* for the Cathedral [670-3] and, for the village *Pieve* (and seemingly beyond its pocket and its taste), a *pala* of the *Madonna with Sts. John Baptist and Bartholomew.*[669] The latter (probably the later picture also) is the most extreme evocation of an implausible humanity in Rosso's career, and by comparison with it his deformations in the S. M. Nuova altar [667] almost seem hesitant and mild. Rosso's means, in that picture, had still resembled those of caricature, with the sensible relation between the painted image and the expectation of usual experience that caricature implies. The creatures of the Villamagna altar are, in contrast, barely embodied images of fantasy: summoned ghosts present at the most in ectoplasm. It is as if, in this picture lost on the altar of a country church, Rosso had presumed to make openly the "cruel and desperate" commentary on humanity that, in his *abozzo* of the S. M. Nuova altar, had so distressed its patron; in this obscure place Rosso may have felt no responsibility for discourse with anyone other than himself. The picture inevitably recalls, and more than the S. M. Nuova altar quite perverts, a classical precedent, in this case Andrea's *Madonna of the Harpies,*[565] but there is no sense here of sardonic parody of classical style. No work could seem to be more anticlassical in the sum of its effects than this, but there is no trace of a destructive, "anti," motive in it. It is the affirmation of a wholly positive creative impulse, clear and self-knowing as it had not been in 1518; and this is projected with extraordinary purity, without inhibiting concern either for approval or the shocked dismay of any audience. Its content and its form are an unearthly lyric, of confessional sincerity.

Both the Villamagna altar, so nearly a private work of art, and the *Deposition* for the Cathedral, so oppositely aware and awaiting of the presence of the spectator, are markedly distinguished from Rosso's prior works by their consistency and explicitness of style, and by the matured force of personality and thought their styles contain. For the explicitness, and for much else as well that is important, it would seem that Rosso is in some debt to Pontormo's example as it was given him in the Visdomini altar in particular — too nearly contemporaneous, apparently, with the painting for S. M. Nuova to have been taken into much or any account in it. That picture, like Rosso's just preceding ones, had almost no discernible discipline of shapes: his intentions — of design, though not of color — had been, as we suggested, deformative and illustrative rather than constructive of a new aesthetic. In the *Deposition* Rosso has accepted Pontormo's canon of human form as it was first indicated in the Visdomini altar, and more important, he has accepted the aesthetic of shape that underlies that canon: of elongated rectangles, sharp angular conjunctions, and pointing extremities. These shapes are defined by Rosso with extreme distinctness, with a remarkable clarity of contour and of modelling in light and color; and they are combined in an articulate movemented geometry of whole design. Rosso has acquired, like Pontormo, the virtue of an exactly enunciated speech.

He has developed, probably with some Pontormesque stimulus, the incipient fineness of draughtsmanship of the S. M. Nuova altar into a most precisely controlled drawing with the brush, thin and brittle-seeming, yet as sharp and strong as wire. As a descriptive and expressive instrument the drawing does not have, and does not intend, the flexible empathic energies or the almost sensuous affects of ornament that are in Pontormo's line; Rosso's line is more abstracting in means and in result. Deliberately dry, with small residue in it of the hand's responsive sensibility, it delineates shape in such a way as to stress the quotient in it of geometry, however irregular, more than its meaning of description. This effect is reinforced, and still more obviously meant, by the character of modelling within the contour of the shapes: sharp-edged planes summarize the distinctions, in relief and in light and shadow, of anatomy and drapery. In the picture for S. M. Nuova there had been no more than the indistinct prognosis of such an insistent geometrical analysis, by modelling, of form; and what occurs of this kind in the *Deposition* goes far beyond the similar tendencies in the Visdomini altarpiece. To this conspicuous abstracting process in the form there is added the effect of color (already, in the S. M. Nuova altar, sufficiently an artifice), made to work now, in a precise conjunction with the geometry of form.

The force of abstraction that is in all these formal elements together gives to the record of appearance an effect of transformation greater than in fact it is; bizarre distortion is no longer needed to recast the look of actuality; nor is it sufficient now to Rosso's more sophisticated purpose. More important, this power of abstraction confers upon the picture's aesthetic structure, as such, the value of a stressed and separable function within the work of art: the aesthetic order of form and color provokes, of itself, fascination and astonishment. There had been only the symptoms of this in the Visdomini altar, nothing like so assertive or explicit in effect as here. More than this precedent, the *Deposition* disrupts the balance that is in classical images between aesthetic and descriptive meaning.

What is described in the *Deposition* is, in any event, not meant as a substantial actuality. There is no physical content in these shells of a humanity; they exist only by virtue of response of their geometry of surface to the light. This light is both pretext and cause for their character of form: cool and studied, yet intense, the light discerns the silhouette of each form sharply, and with equal sharpness fragments it in prismatic facets. The light makes paradox: by it our perception of the picture becomes an intense optical experience, but this optical experience is not of visual reality. A means of optical illusion is employed to convince us of an existence that is not illusion, but only allusion to an actuality; the world the light reveals is not an appearance but an apparition.

The light makes paradox and it is, further, of paradoxical nature in itself, quite without antecedent in any earlier painting (except perhaps, by stretched analogy, the later pictures of Uccello). The *Deposition* occurred, according to the Bible text, by night, and Rosso's is — at least to our knowledge — the first representation of the scene that takes this in account. This is night light, or moonlight, observed as a datum of visual experience; but this is an experience exceptional to record in painting at this time, and provocative of singular appearances of forms and singular effects of mood. What has been observed in this light, and with exceeding sensibility, is then not literally transcribed, but transmuted by a shift of its effects onto a more abstracting plane. The light shines, not through an atmosphere but in an airless space, cool, purified, and still: a stratosphere removed from earth. The vacant sky is like a sheet of ink-blue slate, opaque and flat; by no measurable gradation it lightens toward the horizon to reflect, palely, the shining of the moon. The color of the figures is suspended on this matt, abstracting tone of sky and is relieved against it. The color (thin and hard, just as the drawing is) is not so aggressive in its dissonances as in the S. M. Nuova altar, but, revealed and transmuted in this lunar light, the effects of color are more disquieting and strange — for example only, in the moon-struck, green-grey body of the Christ. The darker fields of color have a soured and metallic cast, the lighter fields a hard radiance; smaller accents of color, of the hair or in the draperies, seem to phosphoresce.

All this prismatic pattern of color and the form to which it is attached exist in a thin stratum only of this barely habitable world, close to or on the very surface of the painting. One figure in the foreground, of the younger Mary at the left, gazes at us with infantile directness, across a mass of drapery that seems to grow toward us even beyond the foremost plane; and to the right the grieving figure of the red-haired St. John, his white mantle shattering and reflecting the intensest light, bows his stricken head toward us quite out of the picture.[671] It is supposition, but also probability, that this *Giovanni rosso* who exists so passionately and actually in both the picture world and in our own stands for the artist; this figure is the symptom of his idea of the interpenetration of artistic vision and of actuality — or better — of the sense of actuality (that supplants and is more than a literal reality) that has been assumed by the artistic vision. The St. John is the symbol also of the new relation of the artist to his creation which, now, he more than makes; he inhabits it.

Both as aesthetic and emotional experience the picture is as near as possible to us. It is only as objective, formal, fact that we must describe the image in this picture as projected on its foremost plane; where the image works as an experiential fact is rather on the foremost plane of our subjective consciousness. There is no possible demarcation between this intense imminence and its creating mind, or our mind that apprehends it. The *Deposition* has the aspect of a vision, the force of a hallucination, and the acuity of most poignant actual experience. In it Rosso has attained a dimension of different meaning in the new style that is aesthetically and humanly not less than had been in the old.

Pontormo's emergence upon the same plane of authoritative statement in the Mannerist style — for him a lesser step than it had been, toward 1521, for Rosso — occurred in a context of surrounding circumstance that throws his accomplishment into strong historical relief. In his contribution to the decoration of the Grand Salon of the Villa at Poggio a Cajano, Pontormo was the collaborator, but as much the competitor, of the two chief painters of the antecedent generation: his own past master, Sarto, and Franciabigio. We have already briefly characterized the two frescoes which, in 1521, the older masters painted in the Poggio *Salone* — with Pontormo's lunette, all that was executed of an intendedly much grander scheme. Both Andrea and Franciabigio were involved, with obviously different intelligence and diverse results, with the exploration in their frescoes of new possibilities of style: an exploration provoked in Andrea by his own seeming fulfillment of the possibilities of classicism, and in Franciabigio by his perpetual sense, in his style, of its insufficiencies. Franciabigio's *Triumph of Caesar*[582] was, as we observed, a courageous and even moderately successful attempt to paint in a monumental and dramatic mode, exceptional for Florence, and suggestive of analogy with recent accomplishments of Rome, and like them fundamentally adherent to a classicism. Andrea, at the time of his work at Poggio, was *en plein crise*: for two years past or more he had been searching (with more inventiveness and will than he would ever in the future use) for new avenues of art, probing close to the limits of classical style prescribed to him by his temperament, his past accomplishment, and his education. In his *Tribute to Caesar* [573] he made his boldest experiment in monumental composition, seeking in it new liberty of form and power of impulse, which (as we have characterized it) could have become — but only with more decisive pressure than it was in Andrea to exercise — a first step in the revision of classical style into an incipient baroque. We have observed that the *Tribute* fresco remained symptom; it had no consequence in Andrea's later style or in other Florentine art in his time.

There was, thus, in the work at Poggio by Andrea and Francesco, already significant partial evidence of the situation of Florentine painting in 1521, which Pontormo completed with an authoritative affirmation of the new style of Mannerism. His *Vertumnus and Pomona* [678-80] is more important than the two frescoes of the still classical masters for the future history of style in Florence, and of higher status absolutely as a work of art. Pontormo's accomplishment in this lunette was not, as Rosso's *Deposition* seems to be — perhaps only for lack of the relevant evidence — a sudden, near-miraculous ascent into a new realm of the new style; it was the result, achieved in profound creative travail, of a process of gestation that began with his receipt of a commission for work at Poggio in 1520 (or, perhaps, even within 1519).

His assignment at that time included the painting of the end wall beneath the actually executed lunette, and his first thought of design was apparently for this wall space. His ideas for it are most fully indicated in a sheet in the British Museum (1860–6–16–106) of which the principal scene represents the *Anointing of an Athlete*,[674] not later than 1520 in its drawing style. The conception has a Roman accent, in part in consequence of its main subject (determined by the Romanized Paolo Giovio), but more the probable result of the artist's experiences in his likely recent trip to Rome. Nude male figures of what would have been, in execution, an overwhelming scale posture in rather rhetorical-seeming attitudes, on an architecture like that of a stage. Unlike Jacopo's preceding works, this design evidently intended an explicit decorator's illusionism: the painted scheme of architecture was meant to be taken as if real, and its painted inhabitants are shown as if they existed within it and, projecting in our space, before it. The upper structure of this fictive architecture has its own decoration, like the painted façade of a contemporary house: among other elements, the chief ones are a lunette with a *Leda* and smaller fields with putti bearing Medicean arms. Not only is the impact on Pontormo of Michelangelo's Roman, Sistine, style evident but that of Raphael also, in his later manner and in particular in his illusionistic vein. The drawing indicates a profound divergence in Pontormo from his ideas of the just preceding, first Mannerist, years; the presumed Roman experience seems to have quite disoriented him. His first notions for this decoration — the first in Florence of which the intention was comparable to the schemes of Rome in classical matter, secular destination and in size — are classicist in nudity and in rhetoric tenor, urgently assertive of physical illusion, and Sistine-like in scale.

Jacopo's first idea for the lunette he did execute (Uffizi 454F)[675] is differently but not less Romanized than the wall design: more than it, this project for the lunette depends on Michelangelo, and on the Ceiling specifically, for inspiration. In this drawing the anatomies, titanic in form and scale, and the postures are overt deductions from the Sistine, and their pretext of action — holding the branches of a coiled tree — is also, more tangentially, like the pretext of function Michelangelo has given the Ignudi. Jacopo's arrangement of design does not depend specifically on any precedent within the Sistine — it is too explicitly conceived out of the circumstances of his own decorative problem for that — but in it there was surely the recall of the weaving in circular pattern of gigantic nudes in the *Brazen Serpent*.[143] As there, Jacopo's design must have intended an enormous potency and weight of physical illusion. This borrowed Michelangelesque vocabulary of form has, however, almost no content of Michelangelesque meaning, or indeed of any important meaning of emotion, much less of an identifiable narrative. Utterly absorbed by his memory of Michelangelo in Rome, Jacopo has first seen in this wall space an opportunity to work with Michelangelo's apparatus — of form only, for there is no place in the subject matter assigned to Jacopo in this lunette for Michelangelo's kinds of content; and the Michelangelesque form has been intruded in despite of the subject's possibilities of meaning. This is the first major, though passing, instance of Jacopo's life-long recurrences of thraldom to the art of Michelangelo.

As virtually contentless forms, however, these anatomies and postures serve more readily an end, of design in terms of ornament, that is not Michelangelesque, but personal to Pontormo and to his development in Mannerism; and this design is of such a power and such consistency of aesthetic order as he had not attained before. Part of this consistency, and of the power of design also, comes from factors in it that have been classically influenced: the weight of forms and their density of pattern, and their disposition in a relatively simple, balanced counterpoint. But the scheme of rhythm that connects these forms is not classical; it makes, "Manneristically," a more involved, swifter and more variously accented tissue than in classical example, and works in a continuity woven not only close against the picture's surface but as if into it. The sense of the integrity of pattern, and of the abstract aesthetic value of the pattern this integrity supports, is more explicit than in any previous design by Pontormo, and more affirmative of a principle of Mannerism. A brilliant and fantastic conceit, of the tree-form wound around the *oeil-de-boeuf*, with branches lacing through the figures, supplies a visible armature for the continuity within one plane of rhythmic scheme. A device of form initially, this motive also is the pretext for what is in the figures of physical energy and action (as distinguished from their posing for the purposes of ornament); and the empathic and descriptive affect in the tree motive of a tension (quite sensible, and in part translated into anthropomorphic terms) charges both the formal temper and the illustrative content of the scene.

The drawing is a remarkable enough conception, in itself and in terms of its decorative purpose, and it is a significant document for Pontormo's new personal level of maturity and his maturing of a Mannerism. Yet it is also the evidence of a momentary aberration in Pontormo's evolution. Even more than his companions of the older generation, Jacopo was victim to the uncertainties and experimental deviations of this time of crisis, not always fruitful and certainly not conducive to development in a straight line. There is a clarification of his own new principles of style in this first lunette design, but at the same time more concession than in his just preceding works to classicism, to Michelangelo's example in particular. There is an obscuring, in the borrowed *pseudo-terribilità* of human shape and scale, of the private individuality not only of sensation but of an aesthetic that Pontormo in these years was still trying to define, but had not yet succeeded in defining altogether. Equally important, the preoccupation with Michelangelism of form had made, in this case, direct and drastic intervention between Jacopo and his given subject. The Medicean patrons may have been responsible for the dismissal of this first plan, but more likely it was set aside by Jacopo himself. He seems to have come to the realization that this imitative *terribilità* would be, in its painted scale, close to monstrous, and not only inappropriate to the subject he was meant to represent but, indeed, its antithesis of meaning. This realization put an end to Jacopo's abstracted intercourse, on this sheet of paper of the first design, with the world of Michelangelo.

We have the record of Jacopo's next idea for the lunette (Uffizi 445F),[676] intermediate between his first discarded thought and that he finally executed. The relation of the second idea to the first is still clear, in motives of posture and their arrangement into pattern especially, but it is most unlike in scale and, also, in consequent effect of density. The second scheme is far less physically substantial: lighter and more open (but of more open surface still, not opened into space), and not at all so propulsive or so muscular in its design in rhythm. The role as armature of the motive of the coiled tree is less, and its tension quite relaxed; the figures no longer literally depend from it. They are, now, not recognizably Michelangelesque in form, and with their changed appearance they have assumed a very different personality. These are no longer grandiose Roman nudities but, quite oppositely, Tuscan *villani*

— rustics in type and costume, comparatively casual in pose and homely in their actions and expression. Jacopo is still thinking of the assigned subject — as the Ovidian text itself might invite him to do, without need of suggestion from the inventor of the program — as an allegory of a situation rather than a narrative. Now, however, the personifications he conceives for the allegory are not unsuitably quasi-heroic, artificial beings, but the characters of the real bucolic experience that Jacopo and the dwellers in the Villa might encounter in this very countryside. It was not in the nature of Pontormo's temperament to confront a theme, even this one of classical literature, in the terms of a classical distance, personified by creatures of a Romanized Olympus; he begins, in this second design, to think and feel the pastorale of Vertumnus and Pomona in terms of place and persons that would make it actual to him. With a disregard that is not less than heroic for the whole prior Renaissance ethos of subject matter, he exactly de-heroizes the Ancient theme, and makes the *contadini* sole actors in a fresco of monumental size.

The change from this design to that used finally in the executed fresco was in great part motivated by Jacopo's will to experience, to the limits of his intensity and sensibility, the actuality he had begun to realize in his subject matter — literally to realize, putting classical prescript of idealization quite aside. Not only does he use the models of real pastoral experience (even the Antique undress he concedes to the lesser actors only more reveals their contemporaneity) but he recreates, with acutest responsiveness, the atmosphere in which they exist. With the sense, but not the word, of the Antique text he makes poignant poetic idyll of this whole presence, of humanity and nature. Jacopo has, as it were, lived himself into this bucolic actuality, but his profound apprehension of it is accompanied, at every moment of its functioning, by an apparently contrary purpose: to adjust the data of this actuality, which has been characterized with a penetration that goes beyond the limits of classical style, into an aesthetic order more abstract and artificial, and more subtle and irrationally complex, than the systems of design of classicism.

It is, here, as if the ideas of naturalism and of artificial order of the classical style should each have been exaggerated to a degree no longer comprehensible in classical experience: in the alteration toward realism of one and toward abstraction of the other, two properties which, in their former classical guise, had been expressed in compromise and close synthesis have been divergently developed in antithesis to one another. The genesis of the realism of record and the abstraction of design in Pontormo's fresco is, historically, precisely this; but this does not mean that its results remain antitheses. For Pontormo has achieved, finally, a new mode of relation among elements of style, which results, despite such nominal disparities, in artistic synthesis of another kind, based on different principle, than that of classicism.

Sarto had approached this new idea closely in his works since 1518, but not attained it; and Rosso came to it, contemporaneously with Jacopo, in 1521. The basis of this new principle of relation among properties of style is the same as that we have already seen in Jacopo's response to subject matter: its experience as an ultimate personal actuality — more than observed by the artist, lived by him: in systematic terms, the identification of the artist with the work of art and the elimination of distinctions of objective and subjective meanings between him and it; and in further consequence the elimination of distinctions of this kind within the work of art itself. There is no longer any comparably meditated sense of separate consideration, as there is in general in classical style, between the facts observed in nature — physical and psychological — and the artist's communication of their meaning for him, or between these facts and the requirements of aesthetic artifice; all together are not only synthesized in the end result of the work of art, but absolutely fused in the first moment of their apprehension. Furthermore, there is no such comparable intent as in works of classical style to endow the subjectively invented structure of the image with a verifiable and measurable, and thus objectified, value of geometry; the essence of Pontormo's order in this fresco is not in its relatively simple generalization of whole scheme but, quite oppositely, in its life of intimate and unrationalizable relations.

Still more than in the finished fresco, where the results of this fusion between subjective and objective have been finally exquisitely suspended, its nature is discernible in Jacopo's preparatory drawings — the largest group surviving to us of his studies for a single project, containing among them some of the highest accomplishments of draughtsmanship of the sixteenth century. As is the case with Sarto's preparatory studies, the bulk of Jacopo's drawings for his final scheme are from the model, and seek to specify, from nature, an appearance and a posture established generally in a grand design. In drawings of this kind by Andrea there is the constant evidence of his disposition to see and to set down what he sees, no matter how finely, in reference to norms and general conventions: even a fact of some pronounced visual or psychological individuality in Andrea's studies is transcribed with an effect as of objective record, and suggests connection with a category. In Jacopo's drawings [677] the experience of looking at the model, even without thought for his eventual role as actor in the composition, seems to generate a different, immediate and intense, communication. Often this results in a response to a psychological content in the model quite irrelevant to the final painting, but from which Jacopo cannot keep himself immune. He experiences the body of the model not as a discrete substance but as a vital fact whose life he shares, with such alertness and responsiveness as make it seem that, while he draws, he empathically inhabits it. The visual data, incisively searched by Pontormo as they are, do not suffice to register the whole of this experience. Each line must record more than an appearance; it must describe the energies which, more than they are seen, are felt; and what is felt is, furthermore, not just what is in the model but what is projected on him from the artist's passion in the act of seeing. Each contour and each shape must characterize a coincidence of objective and subjective sensation, intensified in the excitement of its apprehension, to make record not of a reality but of a more poignant actuality into which the natural datum has been thus transformed.

However, what Jacopo sets down on paper goes farther, even, than this notation of an empathically experienced actuality. The energies he perceives in and projects on human form are not only those of physical and psychological vitality; they are, in the same moment and indissolubly from them, the energies of sheer aesthetic response to a rhythm or to tensions and resiliencies of shape as such. Parts of the human structure yield to swift deforming pressures of which the evident main motive is to give pregnance, more than the observed form contains, to its character of shape or to relations of pattern. While Jacopo's line defines and denotes his visual and psychological experience it simultaneously invents, beyond that denotation, an abstracting, brilliantly eccentrically movemented aesthetic order; and the definition of the seen thing is ultimately subsumed, in part or whole, in this aesthetic order. But there is no sense of boundary between the two; the mind and eye are carried too swiftly by the energy of line to find or meditate the point where stress turns from actuality to abstraction — an abstraction which is, aesthetically, no less alive.

In the painting, more than in the preparatory drawings, the implication of abstracting aesthetic value is made finally precise, but there is still no means of perceiving the distinction between it and Jacopo's communication of actuality. The indissoluble fusion of aesthetic process with the characterization of what he sees and feels in what he represents extends, then, through the texture of the executed whole lunette. In this final image its higher actuality — its apparent greater realism, or immediacy, of human presence — and its higher abstraction of aesthetic order become as inextricable an artistic tissue as they are in the preparatory drawings. The vast difficulty of achievement of this interwoven texture — as unitary as any in the classical style — is documented not only in the long labor of Jacopo's preparatory studies but in the final reconciliation of their results into the whole design: Vasari (VI, 264–65) tells us that Jacopo ". . . guastando e rifacendo oggi quello che aveva fatto ieri, si travagliava di maniera il cervello che era una compassione; ma tuttavia andava facendo nuovi trovati . . . ." The fresco is in its entirety a *trovato*, of an originality more profound, though less sensational, than that of Rosso's contemporary *Deposition*.

In the fresco,[678–80] as distinguished from the surviving second plan, the effect of a believable presence of the actors has been increased by their reduction, once again, in scale, to that point where, as the spectator in the salon looks at them, they seem — though they are not — the size of an actual humanity. With this lessening of scale the last trace of artificial grandeur vanishes and content can assume, instead, its appropriate bucolic tone. By this same change in scale the scene is opened yet again, now to admit the air and light of nature: a muted shimmering of atmosphere, like that of a reality, exists behind and sifts among the figures. The scene takes on a formal sense of respiration, and its content a *respiro* of another kind — an illusion of the quality, almost breathable, of country air. The pastorale invites our access into it: to the front its setting, like a narrow stage, seems built upon the actual architecture of the room and gives the idea of a plausible extension of it. On this stage the nearer figures, with postures of a seemingly unmeditated grace — consummately artistic in the absence in them of the look of artifice — move a little toward and even in our space, suggesting that their existence is not separate from ours; the women, and three of the children also, seem to address us with an unassuming intimacy. There is no baroque cast of assertiveness in this connection with us; the tone of welcome to this company is as relaxed as the atmosphere around them of a summer day. The whole scene, like the single figures in it, makes an eminently believable existence, not only accessible to us but, more than that, inviting our participation. For all this, the fresco is no less a construct of pronounced abstractness.

In the fresco there is the visual and psychological sensation of open space but, convincing as it is, there is no sense that the space is also an extension. The background of a vapored sky is a more discreet, but not less effective, definition of a planar limit than a neutral ground or an opaque architecture (like that in the Visdomini altarpiece) would be. The low wall and the stage-like step define a minimum of habitable space — a panel not physically enclosed, but none the less defined — between the sensible aesthetic limits of the sky to the rear and the surface of the picture to the front. Every part of the configuration — the patterned branches laid across the sky, and each contour and each differentiation in foreshortening of human form — is contained within this tissue-thinness of a space, or better, differentiated out of it; even the gentle intrusion toward us of some forms is, as it were, laced back again into this planar continuity.

Within this plane, or panel, of a space the forms are set out in a relatively simple, almost flat pattern of responsive balances. This evident order is explicit, but it is also fragile; it works like a geometrical spider-web to catch and to connect the figures suspended in it. Within this gentle but precise constraint, each figure takes a pose of which the seeming naturalness is also the effective pretext of its pattern of movemented shape, and in this pattern its own complex of energies and tensions is adjusted in a fine, but barely stable equilibrium. Impulses of various direction emanate, through this equilibrium, beyond each figure: a skein of rhythmic suggestion, part quite explicit and part almost evanescent, relates each figure to the adjoining ones. Analogies of shape, not quite precise or graspable, press the effect of a relation still farther. Beyond this, however, there is a transformation to new importance and new personality of an old device of connection in design, not before so expressively articulated as here: this is the sense of tensions generated in the intervals among the forms. Here, the irregular contour of each figure makes, with those that adjoin it, a sensible pattern of eccentric shape that in itself is tensional: the "negative" areas between forms are charged with energies, as if an irrational magnetism infused the interval between one shape and the next. There are, on this account, no vacancies that we feel as such in the design; its openness is a fact of natural appearance, but not an aesthetic fact. These charged intervals complete the continuity of the planar tissue of design that is woven, in the figures, of their web of rhythmical connections and analogies of shape. The atmosphere, almost palpable in its vibrance of light and differentiated color, is the final element, subtle but pervasive, in this tapestry-like consistency of the whole tissue of design.

This discipline of a planar structure is not less severe or less intellectually made than the devices of design of the highest classical style, and it is not less dogmatically absolute. Yet, within this discipline, pattern works not in terms of rigor but of ultimate refinement of flexible sensibility: this pattern is felt and set down as if with the very nerve-ends, suspending sensations of flickering, accented, eccentric form within an equilibrium of supreme fineness.

In this, as in no image in the previous history of the Renaissance, there is the thought of the abstract integrity of the picture as a two-dimensional surface, and of its design as an articulation of this surface that shall leave this abstract, essentially pictorial, identity unmarred. There is analogy in this — but certainly no recollection, and partial analogy only — with a principle of early mediaeval style; however, the mediaeval style that observed this principle was in the beginning moved to it by representational (more precisely, by nonrepresentational) considerations, more than by aesthetic principle. Unlike the paintings of an early mediaeval style, Pontormo's image continues to deal with the illusion of reality — as we have described it, with an actuality still more poignant than is in his inheritance from the preceding Renaissance. The peculiar miracle of art that Jacopo achieves in the Poggio lunette is his reconciliation of this actuality, of light and substance, with the abstract integrity of a picture made upon a plane. Not until a much later and more drastic crisis of art, in the time of Post-Impressionism, would the problem of this reconciliation be so precisely understood again, but not again so comprehensively or so articulately solved.

No conflict of issues remains in Jacopo's lunette, but all the issues of art to which this questing and consummately refined intelligence fell heir are held within its fragile net in tensions that identify the vital meaning of each one of them. But this memorable accomplishment of a new synthesis was not an end for Pontormo; it was a threshold for a new research.

The last year of the Medicean papacy was, as usual, more generous of its sponsorship of art in Rome than in Florence. The death of Raphael made small difference in the demand in Rome for works of art: the output of his school remained considerable, and the school continued as before to dominate the Roman scene. In part at least, conceptions of style of Raphael's own invention, or ideas already developed by his pupils under him, remained the Roman currency of art. Three great decorative commissions were undertaken by the heirs of Raphael late in 1520 or in 1521: two of these are not distinguishable in basic character of style from like schemes of the just preceding years. Differences of new individuality are visible in parts of these, but not of such kind as might transform the effect of the whole: these two of the three major projects of the moment still belong, in sum, to a category of late Raphaelesque classicism.

The first of these is the great Loggia of the Villa Madama,[681-6] of which the decoration was begun for the Cardinal Giulio by Giulio Romano and Giovanni da Udine, jointly, late in 1520 and in part completed within 1521 (by Giovanni mostly, with help from Baldassare Peruzzi for the painting of the figured cameos within the vaults; Pouncey). Its scheme is, in substance, an extension of the grotesque decorative style evolved in the Logge of the Vatican. Here, the greater grandeur of the frame — Raphael's expression, in architectural form, of his highest classical style — makes it still more clear how the grotesquerie is, at once, an ornament and compensation for a monumental geometry of architecture, and of a unified aesthetic texture with it. The distinctions from the Logge at the Vatican are not in an intention of the decorative style, but in the consequence of different scale and shape of building; Giovanni, the responsible designer of this grotesque scheme, has no wish to change in any fundamental way what he developed in the Logge under Raphael's guidance. Indeed, the sense of the master's classical presence and controlling will is still here, in the architecture. It is only in the figure inserts into the grotesque scheme, in Peruzzi's small cameos,[685-6] and in the adjunct to it of Giulio's fresco on one end wall, of a *Polyphemus* — now quite ruined — that the accent of personality and style divergent from classical example is perceptible.

Nearly the same situation exists in the decoration of the *Sala dei Pontefici*[689-91] in the Vatican, begun in 1521 and substantially completed by the time of Leo's death. Its theme, an astrological constellation presided over by genii of victory, may be an illustrated horoscope of Leo, in the manner of that cast in the Farnesina for the banker Chigi. Reflecting the archaeological sophistication of the intervening years, this scheme is projected on the ceiling of the *Sala dei Pontefici* in deliberately imitative Antique, neoclassic, guise. Responsibility for the design here, as in the Loggia of the Madama, is Giovanni da Udine's, and his intention of design is again not one of change but of development of a previously established decorative mode: the precedent is his own and Raphael's prior *Stufetta* for the Cardinal Bibbiena. This, on larger scale, is a freer and lighter, less literally archaeological, adaptation of the antecedents within Ancient art but not, in sum, less recollective of Antiquity; much more than Giovanni's grotesque style, this is *calqué* after Ancient counterparts. The basic device of this design, of division of the surface into simple geometric shapes — nicely adjusted to each other in flat "Pompeian" color and proportions — is necessarily of more abstract effect than the grotesque mode, and more effacing still of the personality of art into that of decoration. This abstracting framework is interspersed, however, with some fields of grotesque in paint and stucco, of Giovanni's accustomed style and invention; and still more strongly given character by inserts — tondi, squares, and cameos — of rather larger scale, of figured scenes.

Of these, the main executant, and equally the designer, is the young Perino del Vaga;[689-90] and in most of the inserts he designs and paints with a self-conscious classicizing accent, which intends accord with the neoclassic character Giovanni has established for the whole. In consequence, Perino's Mannerism of the last bays of the Logge is sufficiently diminished so that there is no sense of disparity of style between these inserts and the (in any case somewhat recessive) personality of the geometrical decor. The sense of a divergence from a classicism in these episodes is negligible. This is not so, however, in the largest central field of the design, also left to Perino to invent and execute. In this roundel, where four *Nikes* (who are, apparently, also Christian angels)[691] supervise Pope Leo's destiny, Perino makes more positive assertion of a Mannerism than in any of his works so far, and achieves a clarity of personal statement in the new style as marked as that of his contemporaries in this same year.

The roundel is a daring exercise in illusionism: the four *Nikes* are seen as if through an *opaion*, hovering in silhouetted flight against the sky. Evidently there is recall of more than one precedent for this illusionist idea, among them the pre-Raphaelesque oculus of the Stanza della Segnatura[96] and, in Raphael's own repertory, the celestial images of the chapel in S. M. del Popolo.[386] Perino's illusion, however, is not like that either of its preclassical or Raphaelesque late-classical analogies; his *Nikes*, sharply characterized in light and extremely sharply drawn, seem more brilliant apparitions — more visually striking, if not more convincing in substantial presence — than those of illusionistic frescoes of the past. In part, his evident intention is to make, in this already startling construction, at least a first impression of more pungent actuality. He succeeds in this: the impact on us of this first optical conviction remains even when, in the moment that instantly succeeds, we begin to see that the *Nikes* are, individually, creatures of unlikely artifice, and that their anatomies and draperies are the matter of a sheerly ornamental patterning of form. The evolution of this pattern, richly involved and elaborately gracile, is more important than considerations of mere natural plausibility: draperies in particular behave according to the dictates not of gravity but of the painter's ornamental will. The effect of this calligraphy on grand scale is remarkably abstract, but even as we apprehend its measure of abstraction the virtue of illusion is not lost; its force reverberates as if within the pattern. What Perino seems finally to have revealed to us is not a merely natural but a preternatural truth, such as is accessible to art: he has evoked an angelic order, and there is no reason to believe that it might not be so ornamentally beautiful as this.

There is much in common in the creative basis of this amalgam of illusion and aesthetic abstraction with the contemporary ideas of Pontormo and of Rosso; specifically of course, Perino's vocabulary and effects are different. His Roman education in these last years, absolutely formative for him, makes it inescapable that he should speak a classicistic language, and that his idea of beauty should depend, even in its Mannerist transformation, on the forms of the Antique and Raphael. It is not a motive in his Roman education, however, that impels that this transformation be into so sensitive a draughtsman's grace; this is personal, but it recalls the sensibilities of Tuscan, not of Roman personality. Perino's strain of Mannerist style, ultimately still more influential for the Roman future than that of Giulio Romano, is in this sense another in the long series of affirmations of Florentine culture within Rome.

Perino's contribution to the *Sala dei Pontefici* is enough in quality and enough explicit in the Mannerism of its major piece to suffuse the framework laid down by his older, more conservative, collaborator with a Manneristic cast, but not more than this; it does not change the basic effect of affiliation with Raphaelesque classicism that is in the whole. It was Raphael's closest pupil, and his most gifted one, who conceived the first authoritative *entire statement on grand scale of a Mannerism in Rome, in the decoration of the Vatican's *Sala di Costantino*.[692-700] Giulio is phenomenally quick to affirm and to extend, in this decoration, the symptoms of unclassical individuality he had shown in Raphael's lifetime: we have suggested that the death of Raphael was taken by this difficult disciple as a liberation. The *Sala di Costantino* was the occasion, for Giulio, of a monumental assertion of his independence; but even in his decisive assertion of new style there was confession of a profound bondage to the old, which could not be loosed. The classical style by now was not a personal datum, but an inextinguishable datum of modern Roman culture. It could be compromised by the death of its principal protagonist but in no least way forgotten. Much more, and much more visibly, than in the new style in Florence, each of Giulio's innovations has been made upon the basis of a property or principle of classicism, and the relation to the classical style of the innovation, of extension or of contradiction of it, can clearly be discerned. The unclassicism — and even the anticlassicism — of the Roman Giulio is of ineradicably classicistic cast, and this is in far more than its obvious preoccupation with an archaeology.

By comparison with what happens in the art of Giulio, the results and process both of the Florentine invention of new style seem positively libertarian: in Giulio, despite his no less individual creative force, what he makes, and his mode of making it, appear of rigid, almost schematized deliberation, deduced by precise, yet daring, logic from the antecedent style. We have observed that these processes had been in part initiated by Raphael himself. Because of the strictness of relation to the classical style in Giulio's Mannerism, it contains, more poignantly than the Mannerism of Florence, the sense of contrast, and of ambivalence, between classical and unclassical values. His art is, as much as that of his Florentine contemporaries, a demonstration of this conflict as a phenomenon of personality; but still more than theirs, his is pregnant with the sense of this moment's cultural and historical situation.

The chronology of Giulio's work in the *Sala di Costantino* is expressly indicated in the documents, in part in letters written by Sebastiano and Sellaio to Michelangelo when Sebastiano hoped, even after painting had begun, to substitute the heirs of Raphael in this commission. From these letters — in effect the reports of eye-witnesses — and from other contemporary written evidence it emerges that the decoration was initiated with a trial figure barely three months after Raphael's death (Golzio, 129).[692] From the fact that this and another trial figure of close date (both in oil) were incorporated without change into actual executed frescoes it is sure that the basic mode of division of the walls (with the papal thrones,[697–8] accompanied by Virtues, flanking a space for a narrative subject at that time still to be determined) was fixed even at this very early date. Vasari (V, 528; whose reports are otherwise exceptionally unclear) tells us that the "partimento" of the room had been conceived by Raphael, and in view of the brief time that intervened between his death and the execution of the trials it may be that the assertion is correct. This does not, however, diminish Giulio's responsibility for the specific way in which he gave articulation to what may have been Raphael's no more than conditional idea.

Early in September 1520 two of the narrative subjects — the *Vision of Constantine* (the so-called "Allocutio")[695] and the *Battle of Constantine*[696] — had been determined (Golzio, 131–32), and by mid-October work in fresco had been in progress for at least a month (Golzio, 134–35). By this date a scaffolding, apparently sufficient for roughly half the extent of this room, was paid for (Golzio, 107; there only partly transcribed). By mid-December 1520 (Golzio, 140) some of the papal groups had been completed, probably those on the *Allocutio* and *Battle* walls. By mid-December a year later the decoration was already half or better done (letter of Castiglione, Golzio, 145–46): the *Allocutio* and *Battle* walls, with their attendant papal thrones, were thus completed and (on evidence of style rather than of document) the wall with the *Donation of Constantine* begun. The death of Leo and Adrian's succession brought work to a temporary halt, and it was not begun again till early 1524, after Clement's coming to the throne: payments were resumed from February of that year. By August 1524 the whole scheme must have been substantially complete: another letter of Castiglione (September 5, 1524 [Golzio, 151]) informs us that the room "è riuscita molto bella." The date 1524 is twice inscribed within the room: on a *cartella* in the scene of the *Baptism of Constantine* and again in the embrasure of a window, in such a place as might well have been the last to receive its decoration. There is no reason to assume that the work of painting accompanied our record of the — habitually tardy — discharge of payments into 1525 (Golzio, 125n1), after Giulio's transfer to the court of Mantua; and there is still less reason to propose (Hartt) that the frescoes done in 1521 were undone and remade in 1524.

The scheme of the whole decorative project was conceived, then, in the few months that succeeded Raphael's death (perhaps developing a notion of the "partimento" already generated in the Master's mind), and half or better executed by the end of the succeeding year. Responsibility of Giulio for design is not disputable and he seems, in place of Raphael's great but liberal authority, to have erected a near-tyranny over what, now, became in fact his school. His own role as executant, quite unlike the later Raphael, was considerable: virtually the whole wall with the *Allocutio* fresco and its papal groups is his, and a great deal in the vast extent of the *Battle* scene is also painted by his hand. During the campaign of 1521 (our concern here does not go beyond this) Penni was mostly engaged elsewhere, and Raffaellino del Colle became Giulio's principal aide. Other assistants are recorded (only imprecisely as for this decoration) by Vasari, but their names cannot be associated with specific portions of the execution. One assistant whom Vasari does not name, Polidoro da Caravaggio, may have been active, probably in part within this first campaign, in a subsidiary but distinct role in the design and much of the painting of a specialty of his, the *finti bronzi* on the basamenti [700] of the room.

The theme of the series of Popes installed on thrones and accompanied by Virtues (surely the ancestor of the Roman Baroque type of tomb), with which Giulio's decoration was begun in the summer of 1520, was predetermined for this place, perhaps also within Raphael's lifetime. It is to this room that contemporary exact reference is made (by Sebastiano, in his first letter which concerns it [Golzio, 125]) as the *Sala dei Pontefici*, rather than to the room (decorated by Giovanni da Udine and Perino) below it. The association of the history of Constantine, from which the *Sala* takes its present name, with the persons of the Papacy is of course generally sensible, and in the circumstances of this moment in the history of the Church it was evidently intended as a homily on the proper relation of the temporal, and especially of the Imperial, to the papal, spiritual, power: this room contains the admonition that was so drastically to be disobeyed in 1527.

The Constantinian scenes [695-6] have, at first sight, the appearance of conventional frescoes painted into the spaces left between the papal thrones. It is only in a second moment that we see that they intend to simulate tapestries, hung from the stuccoed entablature above and, at the sides, (as if the space allowed for them was just too small) furling against the architecture of the papal thrones. The general idea is not new: fictive tapestries had been used by Raphael and by Peruzzi in the ceilings of the Farnesina and the Stanza d'Eliodoro to suggest the reproduction, at the same time, of nature and of another work of art. There, however, the effect of the device was very different: a diminished space and muted color had suggested some accord with our usual expectation of a textile; and the idea was used in combination with a repertory of images that were themselves, in a rough sense, ideal. In Giulio's pseudo-tapestries there is, instead, aggressive excavation of a depth of space and, in the figures, a plasticity of nearly violent insistence. In contradiction of the look of tapestries, the figures here suggest an almost tangible existence; but this existence seems to be less of human than of statuary forms. The painting, which counterfeits one genre of art in its frame, counterfeits an antithetic genre, that of sculpture, in its contents; in its contents, further, there is pretense to counterfeit, simultaneously, of both art and actuality. The whole intellectual and visual situation given us to comprehend within these scenes is of more than an ambivalence; it is a calculated and emphatic multivalence.

This effect is compounded by that of the adjacent papal groups,[697-8] where the invasion is of yet another medium of art: that of an architecture, which works to excavate the wall and, even more strongly, to project out of it. The invasion is again not only of a boundary of art but of our actuality; there is no illusionist intrusion in our space so strongly urged as this in the whole prior history of Roman or Florentine art. The blocky juttings of the forms of architecture and the massive and movemented figures on them, hard as stone, leave no visual fact unstressed in this assault on the domain of the spectator. The general effect is powerfully immediate, but its specific working makes an equivocation, which is in its way as difficult and complex as that in the *soi-disant* tapestries. It is impossible, in these throne-structures, to find a plane that truly coincides with that of the actual wall, so that we are deprived of a term of reference by which to fix and measure the illusionistic functioning of these groups. Within them, further, there are wholly arbitrary differences of figure scale. Evidently, there is more than casual memory of the Sistine Seers, their attendant putti and the Ignudi in the combination of the figures of the papal groups, but on the Ceiling the images of different scale are separately compartmented, not brought together into necessary contrast as they are here. The lesser figures on the thrones can be approximately reconciled in scale with those of the adjacent narratives; neither, however, can be reconciled with the preternatural dimension of the Popes. The juxtaposition of the thrones and tapestries creates more pressing conflicts than this one of scale: a contrast of extruded mass in one with relative openness of space within the other is compounded by a tension between their systems of perspective, converging toward a relatively low vanishing point in the thrones and, in the narratives, toward a vanishing point deliberately rather high.

Within the thrones and tapestries separately, there is a constant shifting between the levels both of art and of reality, and a willed ambivalence is made between one level and the other; and in the juxtaposition of the thrones and tapestries a still more urgent set of tensions, even of contradictions, has been generated. There is no surviving trace of a classical controlling plane of reference for the whole work of art, which fixes a dominating and apparent mean of structure and establishes a constant of relation to reality. It is, here, as if the synthesis of classical style had been thrown into a centrifuge and its separated elements recombined, but into a system of unstable contrasts: the sense of this scheme is in its powers of stated or implicit conflict. The effect of the whole room, with its succession of contrasting episodes of dense and drastically movemented form, is of a vast organized commotion. Once, when the room was still of its original height (before the ceiling was considerably raised in 1585), this commotion must, even more than now, have imposed the sense of necessary involvement with it of the spectator.

The mode of composition within the *Allocutio* and *Battle* scenes of 1521 develops, in a different way from that of the design of the whole, the same essential principles. The stringency with which these principles are applied and their decisiveness of novelty of effect is more, incidentally, than in the scenes of 1524. The fullest energy of new style seems, in Giulio, to be in its initial affirmation; by comparison the later frescoes — not from difference of their kind of subject only — are more relaxed. Both the *Allocutio* and *Battle* scenes refer in compositional ideas to Raphaelesque antecedents: in both, the image of the *Ostia* (in part Giulio's own) has some authority; the *Paul at Lystra* helps to stage the *Allocutio*, and the *Attila* fresco is recalled somewhat in the *Battle of the Bridge.* These references determine nothing in the sense of style; they rather serve to illustrate Giulio's inescapable relation to a past which, nevertheless, he essentially transforms. In both frescoes an accumulation of movemented plastic forms is crowded in a rigid outline of geometric shape: this shape, of exceedingly precise severity, is as if clamped upon the forms, imprisoning their dense substance and their energies; beyond the limit of this dominating shape the contents of the scene, of figures or landscape, are only loosely organized, dispersed into contrasting openness.

The shape imposed on the main substance of design is almost abstractly clear; however, it is not rationalizable. It is irregular and asymmetrical and, despite its whole rigidity, is put together from movemented parts; its boundaries make sharp, unequal, and uncomfortable intersections. From its abstracting and containing force this shape acquires the sense as of a configuration projected on the picture surface, but this sense is opposed at once by a careful differentiation of the contents of the shape in depth. In this structural design, then, each element is, at once, rigid and in tension; and each device contains its own contradiction, or is the contradiction of another. Nothing is left of classical precepts of design except the clarity and force with which this system makes its opposite effects.

What is in this system of design is not a new invention in principle or in the means of its effects. What is in the *Allocutio* and the *Battle* scenes is the extension in extreme degree of symptoms Giulio had exhibited from his first precocious affirmation of maturity, and had developed since. Now, however, we are not dealing with symptoms, or with a development that classical authority has held in check, but with the most aggressive possible creative affirmation: the style of design is fused by the pressure of intense assertion into a new totality.

The same holds for the figure style of the frescoes done in 1521: again each factor has its antecedent symptom in the time of the first crisis of the classical style, which Giulio was so quick to exploit, as in his figures in the *Fire in the Borgo.*[376] Now, each former fact of Giulio's figure style has been so much accentuated in its degree as (by familiar principle) to resolve the whole effect into a different kind. The figures of the *Allocutio* and *Battle*, and most of those also of Giulio's execution in the papal groups, are beyond all precedents — Giulio's own, Raphael's, and even Michelangelo's — in the sheer insistence in them of their plastic definition. Giulio intends to affirm in them a more compelling conviction of substantial presence than had ever been achieved before: their forms are as if excavated by the brush, not merely modelled, and their surfaces are polished to a brilliant hardness, on which the most precise and even minute passages of detail are as if incised. The conviction of presence is in fact more than had ever been conveyed in paint, but to make it has required a literally vital sacrifice.

The entire preoccupation of the artist is with the facts of outward form: he sees, and desires to see, the shell only of this humanity, and not the energies and powers that the forms contain. The human substance is observed (somewhat as some preclassic painters, or even Flemings, of the fifteenth century had observed it) as still-life rather than as an inhabited organism, and the recording of this observation is of disjunctive, not of organically related parts. This is willed effect, not merely temperamental tendency; we have seen, in the figures of the narratives particularly, how Giulio expressly assimilates his image of humanity to that of an Ancient statuary, and with what ambivalent effect between their sense of actual presence and their recreation of an Ancient world of art.

These deliberately statuary figures only draw the extreme conclusion of Giulio's anticlassical conception of humanity, now finally clear in him and explicitly confessed (the trial figures, in deliberate Raphalesque disguise, had not yet been so frank). The human image, for Giulio, has no real content of vitality; it is essentially powerless to act of its own will. Its energy of psyche may be considerable, even violent or intense, but it is not purposeful; it cannot be translated into bodily action of convincing practical effect. Incapable of consequential action of their own — impeded, even were their energies of mind enough directed, by their own statuary, rigid mass — the movement of the figures is determined for them by Giulio as absolutely as if they were marionettes, or truly statuary. Giulio does not, like Raphael, interpret human will and translate it into terms of energy of form; he substitutes his will for that of the humanity he represents, making a tyranny within his own domain of art.

He disposes of the nearly inert mass of stony torsos and of limbs so as to illustrate the functions that the figures are, as subject matter, required to describe; but beyond that, with more positive intention and effect, he determines action that will suit his own will of aesthetic pattern. In the *Battle* he arranges the combatants — fierce of face, but in body of a lifeless violence — in a complex pattern of eccentric angular geometry, making endless interlocking combinations of the forms; in the *Allocutio* he compels the rank of soldiery into a vehement and broken patterning that is, at the same time, more rigid in its repetitions than any movement of a true parade ground. The way in which the figures act, locked thus into the sum of an abstracting scheme, cancels the individuality of action and makes it collective and anonymous. The pattern of each movement, furthermore, is such that it denies its own efficiency: if any vital current did exist within these parts of statuary form it would be paralysed within the rigid angles made of posture; and each action is opposed by the utter lifeless weight of the very part of the anatomy that makes it. These are not actions in more than the merest illustrative sense; they are displacements made by the artist of the inert form.

The figures are deprived of their vitality as human agents; and this is a sufficient, but not more than a negative evidence of the difference in Giulio's concept of them from that of the classical style. His new, positive, principle is to replace the human liveness that is lost by an urgent, even violent, life of art. These figures in fact communicate a drastic power, which is not that of an illustrated human energy. It derives from the force of characterization of each of the positive effects of figure style, but still more comes from the deliberate contrast of these effects with one another: the energy of art that is in these forms is in the power in them of antithesis. Paradox is a prime motive of this art; Giulio's figures affirm themselves so violently by virtue of their contradictions. One of the sharpest of these, and the most encompassing in its meaning and effects, is the contrast, which almost every figure of the *Allocutio* and *Battle* scenes contains, between its character of actuality and its guise not merely of sculpture but of an archaeological statuary. The effect of surface and the look of costume, and in instances a quotation of an

Ancient pose, combine, in the figures, to make the most literal possible reference to Antiquity. The intention of an archaeology goes much farther than the figures: it is in the impedimenta, in details of setting and, in the *Battle,* even in the topography of the scene. There, too, much in the character and style of composition is deliberately imitative of the battle sarcophagi of late Antique art.

It is Giulio's intention to recreate the Roman past in the terms of the evidence of its appearance that survived to him in Roman art; but by this archaeological exercise he recreates, not Ancient history, but Ancient art. He proceeds to endow this Ancient art with the existential force of a present actuality (of which the real effectiveness, again, is not in its reproduction of life but in its force of art). There is a profound contradiction in this intention to reconcile, on one hand, a reality more pressing, and on the other, an archaeological past more pervasive and exact, than were in Raphael's classical style. For Raphael, both archaeology and actuality were matter for mutual concession, to be harmoniously fused in a synthetic image of his own classicism; for Giulio, they are the matter of an irresolvable — and wilfully exploited — contrast.

Even as Giulio protests to us that he has revived, more truthfully than Raphael, the Ancient world, he demonstrates that the dream of its recreation is a fallacy. But the still profounder contradiction made by this archaeology, with its show of outward trappings of a classicizing art, is the assertion Giulio makes by it — to himself in part, as well as us — that the classical style to which he had just put an end is not yet dead. It was, in the very way in which Giulio may have felt it, a kind of truth: though the life of creation of the classical style was ended it had shaped the nature, even in its antithesis, of this succeeding style. In a still wider sense it was a whole truth: for centuries to come men would feel the accomplishment of High Renaissance classicism, as they had come to feel that of Ancient classicism, as living presence: as an inextinguishable illumination, but also as a defeating burden, for the later world of art.

Florence, Italy, April 16, 1959

INDEX RAISONNÉ

REGISTER OF PLACES

CORRIGENDA

INDEX

INDEX RAISONNÉ

This index contains a general bibliography, individual bibliographies by artists, and lists of the works of each artist discussed in this text with abbreviated references to the bibliographic items relevant to the individual work. The pages in this volume where the work is initially dealt with, followed by the illustration numbers for it (set off from the page numbers by a vertical bar), are also given.

The general bibliography contains selected items that concern the major topics discussed within this book. Our citation of a given item in either the general or individual bibliographies does not necessarily imply agreement with or dependence on its data; in fact, care has been taken to cite, where possible, items that present other conclusions and points of view than ours. The list of an individual artist's works is confined to the works with which this book has dealt. These are listed in the chronological order we assume for them. Where chronology is established by inscribed date or by document it is so indicated; otherwise, chronology depends on our assessment of the evidence of style.

In the individual bibliographies the selection of items is limited to those that contain the most useful references to the particular works, and to the portions of the artist's career, that are discussed by us; neither the bibliographies nor the lists of works intend completeness. Museum catalogues (but not necessarily catalogues of special exhibitions), catalogues of private collections, guides, lists, encyclopedia and dictionary articles are not cited, nor are the contemporary or near-contemporary source books (except in a few instances where their notes, in a modern critical edition, may be of special relevance). The abbreviated references to such standard sources as Vasari, Golzio, or Pastor, already given in the body of the text, are not repeated. Republished works are given, in the bibliographies, in not only their first, but in their most convenient subsequent edition. For the convenience of the reader, the reference to the principal section on each artist in Vasari's *Vite* has been noted. The bibliographic selections are complete through 1959, beyond the date of the completion of the text.

Indications of places of pictures are as they were known to the author at the close of 1959. For pictures in public collections museum numbers have been given where necessary to prevent confusion in identification.

The following abbreviations have been used in the individual bibliographies for works that appear frequently:

Berenson, *Drawings* [1938]	Berenson, B., *Drawings of the Florentine Painters* (1st ed., 2 vols., London, 1903; 2nd ed., 3 vols., Chicago, 1938)
Berti, *Pontormo* 1956	Berti, L., et al., *Mostra del Pontormo e del Primo Manierismo Fiorentino* (Florence, 1956)
Bodmer, *Leonardo KdK* (1931)	Bodmer, H., *Leonardo* in *Klassiker der Kunst* (Stuttgart, 1931)
Burckhardt, *Der Cicerone* [1855] or [1879]	Burckhardt, J., *Der Cicerone* (1st ed., Basel, 1855; 4th ed. [W. Bode], Leipzig, 1879)
Clapp, *Pontormo* 1916	Clapp, F., *Pontormo: His Life and Work* (New Haven, 1916)
C & C, *Painting*	Crowe, J. A., and Cavalcaselle, G. B., *A New History of Painting in Italy* (1st ed., 3 vols.,

	London, 1864–1866; 2nd ed., 6 vols., New York, 1903–1914 [vol. VI edited by T. Borenius, 1914])
Fischel, *RZ*	Fischel, O., *Raphaels Zeichnungen* (parts 1–8, Berlin, 1913–1941)
Friedlaender, "Anti-Classical Style" (1925)	Friedlaender, W., "Die Enstehung des antiklassischen Stiles in der italienischen Malerei um 1520," *Repertorium für Kunstwissenschaft* 46 (1925) 49–86; trans. as "The Anti-Classical Style," in *Mannerism and Anti-Mannerism in Italian Painting* (New York, 1957)
Gabelentz, *Fra Bartolommeo* 1922	Gabelentz, H. v., *Fra Bartolommeo und die Florentiner Renaissance* (Leipzig, 1922)
Golzio, *Raffaello* 1936	Golzio, V., *Raffaello nei documenti nelle testimonianze dei contemporanei e nella letteratura del suo secolo* (Città del Vaticano, 1936)
Knapp, *Fra Bartolommeo* 1903	Knapp, F., *Fra Bartolommeo und die Schule von S. Marco* (Halle a. S., 1903)
——— *Michelangelo KdK* (1912)	——— *Michelangelo* in *Klassiker der Kunst* (4th ed., Stuttgart and Leipzig, 1912)
Longhi, *Precisioni* (1927)	Longhi, R., "Precisioni nelle gallerie Italiane," *Vita Artistica* 1 (1926), 2 (1927); in book form (Rome, 1928)
Marazza, *Leonardo* 1954	Marazza, A., *Leonardo, Saggi e Ricerche* (Rome, 1954)
Rosenberg-Gronau, *Raffael KdK* (1909)	Rosenberg, A. [G. Gronau, ed.], *Raffael* in *Klassiker der Kunst* (4th ed., Stuttgart and Leipzig, 1909)
Scritti . . . L. Venturi 1956	*Scritti di Storia dell'arte in onore di L. Venturi*, M. Salmi, ed. (2 vols., Rome, 1956)
V-M, *Vite*	Vasari, G., *Le vite de' più eccellenti pittori, scultori ed architettori* [1568], G. Milanesi, ed. (9 vols., Florence, 1878–1885; repr. 1906)
Venezia e l'Europa	*Venezia e l'Europa, Atti del XVIII Congresso Internazionale di Storia dell'Arte* (Venice, 1956)
Venturi, *Storia*	Venturi, A., *Storia dell'Arte Italiana* (Milan, 1901–1939)

Boll. d'A.	*Bollettino d'Arte*
Burl.	*Burlington Magazine*
GBA	*Gazette des Beaux-Arts*
JKSW	*Jahrbuch der Kunstsammlungen in Wien*
JPK	*Jahrbuch der preuszischen Kunstsammlungen*
Mitt. KHIF	*Mitteilungen des Kunsthistorischen Institutes in Florenz*
MK	*Monatsheft für Kunstwissenschaft*
PARA Rend.	*Atti della Pontifica Accademia Romana di Archeologia, Rendiconti*
Rep. KW	*Repertorium für Kunstwissenschaft*
Riv. d'A.	*Rivista d'Arte*
ZBK	*Zeitschrift für Bildende Kunst*
ZK	*Zeitschrift für Kunstgeschichte*

GENERAL BIBLIOGRAPHY

Alazard, J., *Le Portrait Florentin de Botticelli à Bronzino* (Paris, 1924)

Battisti, E., "Il concetto d'imitazione nel Cinquecento da Raffaello a Michelangelo," *Commentari* 7 (1956) 86–104

Becherucci, L., *Manieristi Toscani* (Bergamo, 1944)

Berenson, B., *Italian Pictures of the Renaissance* (Oxford, 1932; Milan, 1936)

——— *Drawings of the Florentine Painters* (1st ed., 2 vols., London, 1903; 2nd ed., 3 vols., Chicago, 1938)

Berti, L., et al., *Mostra del Pontormo e del Primo Manierismo Fiorentino* (Florence, 1956)

Bruhns, L., *Die Kunst der Stadt Rom* (Vienna, 1951), esp. pp. 293–380

Burckhardt, J., *Der Cicerone* (1st ed., Basel, 1855; 4th ed. [W. Bode, ed.], Leipzig, 1879)

Crowe, J. A. and Cavalcaselle, G. B., *A New History of Painting in Italy* (1st ed., 3 vols., London, 1864–1866; 2nd ed., 6 vols., New York, 1903–1914), esp. vol. VI [T. Borenius, ed.]

Curtius, E. R., *Europäische Literatur und lateinisches Mittelalter* (Berne, 1948), Trans. as *European Literature and the Latin Middle Ages* (New York, 1953)

Dvorak, M., *Geschichte der italienischen Kunst im zeitalter der Renaissance* (Munich, 1927–1929)

Frey, D., *Gotik und Renaissance* (Augsburg, 1929), esp. ch. 3: "Das raumproblem des XVI. Jahrhunderts"

Friedlaender, W., "Die Entstehung des antiklassischen Stiles in der italienischen Malerei um 1520," *Repertorium für Kunstwissenschaft* 46 (1925), 49–86; trans. as "The Anti-Classical Style," in *Mannerism and Anti-Mannerism in Italian Painting* (New York, 1957)

Giovannoni, G., *Il Quartiere Romano del Rinascimento* (Rome, 1946)

Gnoli, D., *Facciate graffite e dipinti in Roma* (Arezzo, 1938)

Hagen, O., "Das Dürerische in der italienische Malerei," *Zeitschrift für Bildende Kunst* 53 (1918) 223 ff.

Hauser, A., *The Social History of Art* (2 vols., New York, 1951), esp. vol. I, ch. 4, "The Classicism of the Cinquecento," and ch. 5, "The Concept of Mannerism"

Hetzer, T., *Das Deutsche Element in der italienischen Malerei des 16. Jahrhunderts* (Berlin, 1929), esp. part I. ch. 3, "Der Wandel um 1500"

Hirschfeld, W., *Quellen zur Geschichte der Fassadenmalerei in Rom* (Halle a. S., 1911)

Hoffmann, H., *Hochrenaissance, Manierismus, Frühbarock* (Zurich-Leipzig, 1938)

Hübner, P., "Studien über die Benutzung der Antike in der Renaissance," *Monatsheft für Kunstwissenschaft* 2 (1909) 267–280

Jaeger, W., ed., *Das Problem des Klassischen und die Antike* (Leipzig-Berlin, 1931)

Kainz, F., "Vorarbeiten zu einer Philosophie des Stils," *Zeitschrift für Aesthetik und Allegemeine Kunstwissenschaft* 20 (1926) 21–63

Klaczko, J., *Rome and the Renaissance: The Pontificate of Julius II* (New York, 1913)

Lermolieff, J. [Morelli, G.], "Kunstkritische Studien über italienischen Meister der Renaissance," *Zeitschrift für Bildende Kunst* 9 (1874)

——— *Die Werke italienische Meister in den Galerien von Munchen, Dresden und Berlin* (Leipzig, 1880)

——— *Kunstkritische Studien über italienische Malerei* (3 vols., Leipzig, 1890–1893)

Longhi, R., "Precisioni nelle gallerie Italiane," *Vita Artistica* 1 (1926), 2 (1927), esp. 85–91, 168–173; in book form (Rome, 1928)

Maccari, E., *Saggi di architettura e decorazione dei secoli XV e XVI* (Milan, n.d.)

Müntz, E., *Histoire de l'art pendant la Renaissance* (3 vols., Paris, 1889–1895), esp. vol. II, "*Italie, L'Age d'Or*" (1891)

Paatz, W. and E., *Die Kirchen von Florenz* (6 vols., Frankfort a. M., 1952–1955)

Panofsky, E., *Idea* (Leipzig and Berlin, 1924)

Pevsner, N., "Die italienischen malerei vom ende der renaissance bis zum ausgehenden rokoko," in Pevsner, N. and Grautoff, O., *Barockmalerei in den Romanischen Länder* (Wildpark-Potsdam, 1928)

Rodocanachi, E., *Le Pontificat de Jules II* (Paris, 1928)

——— *Le Pontificat de Léon X* (Paris, 1931)

Rosenthal, E., "Wandlungen in der italienischen Malerei um 1500," *Cicerone* 22 (1930) 297–306

Salis, A. v., *Antike und Renaissance* (Erlenbach-Zurich, 1947)

Schmarsow, A., "Der Eintritt der grottesken in die Dekoration der italienischen Renaissance," *Jahrbuch der preuszischen Kunstsammlungen* 2 (1881) 131–144

Steinmann, E., *Die Sixtinische Kapelle* (2 vols., Munich, 1901 and 1905)

Strzygowski, J., *Das Werden der Barock in Raphael und Correggio* (Strasbourg, 1898)

Venturi, A., *Storia dell'Arte Italiana* (Milan, 1901–1939), esp. vol. IX, part 1 (1925), part 2 (1926), part 5 (1932)

Voss, H., *Die Malerei der Spätrenaissance in Rom und Florenz* (2 vols., Berlin, 1920)

Wackernagel, M., *Der Lebensraum des Künstlers in der Florentinischen Renaissance* (Leipzig, 1938)

Weixlgärtner, A., "Alberto Duro," in *Festchrift für Julius Schlosser* (Vienna, 1927), pp. 162–208

Wölfflin, H., *Die Klassische Kunst* (Munich, 1899), trans. by P. and L. Murray as *Classic Art* (London, 1952)

——— "Das Klassische," in *Gedanken zur Kunstgeschichte* (Basel, 1941)

——— *Kunstgeschichtliche Grundbegriffe* (Munich, 1915), trans. as *Principles of Art History* (New York, various eds.)

Zürcher, R., *Stilprobleme der italienische Baukunst des Cinquecento* (Basel, 1947)

INDIVIDUAL BIBLIOGRAPHIES

Mariotto ALBERTINELLI (1474–1515)

BIBLIOGRAPHY

Berenson, *Drawings* [1938] I, 161–163

Bodmer, H., "Opere giovanili e tarde di Mariotto Albertinelli," *Dedalo* 9 (1929) 599–620

Burckhardt, *Der Cicerone* [1879] II, 633

C&C, *Painting* VI (1914) 105–113

Knapp, *Fra Bartolommeo* 1903, 40, 212–213, 226–228

V-M, *Vite* IV (1880) 217–229

Venturi, *Storia* IX/1 (1925) 348–383

See also the bibliography for Fra Bartolommeo.

PAINTINGS

dated 1500 · *Madonna and Saints, Annunciation* [portable triptych] (Milan, Poldi-Pezzoli Museum) Knapp 1903, 40; Venturi (1925) 361–362. p. 55 | 40

dated 1503 · *Visitation* (Florence, Uffizi) Knapp 1903, 212–213; Venturi (1925) 364ff; Berenson [1938] I, 162. p. 55 | 42

dated 1505 · *Crucifixion* (Florence, Certosa di Val d'Ema) Venturi (1925) 371–372. p. 56 | 41

c. 1508 · *Annunciation with Sts. Sebastian and Lucy* (Munich, Pinakothek) Bodmer (1929) 612. pp. 59–60 | 47

c. 1510 · *Madonna with Four Saints* (Florence, Academy) Burckhardt [1879] II, 633; Knapp 1903, 227. p. 198 | 256

c. 1510 · *Trinity* (Florence, Academy) Knapp 1903, 226; Berenson [1938] I, 162. p. 198 | 257

dated 1510 · *Annunciation* (Florence, Academy) Knapp 1903, 228. pp. 199–200 | 259

ANDREA del Sarto (1486–1530)

BIBLIOGRAPHY

Berenson, *Drawings* [1938] I, 280–294

Burckhardt, *Der Cicerone* [1855] 884–889

Comandé, G. B., *Introduzione allo studio dell'arte di Andrea del Sarto*, Palermo, 1951

——— *L'Opera di Andrea del Sarto*, Palermo, 1952

C&C, *Painting* VI (1914) 161–204

Fraenckel, I., *Andrea del Sarto*, Strasbourg, 1935

Giglioli, O., "Chiaroscuri inediti del Andrea del Sarto, di un suo aiuto e del Pontormo," *L'Arte* 29 (1926) 261–266

Guinness, H., *Andrea del Sarto*, London, 1899

Janitscheck, H., "Andrea del Sarto," in Dohme, *Kunst und Künstler*, Leipzig, III (1879) 22–48

Knapp, F., *Andrea del Sarto*, Leipzig, 1907

Longhi, *Precisioni* (1927) 85ff

Mantz, P., "André del Sarto," *GBA* ser. 2 *14* (1876) 465–482; *15* (1877) 38–50, 261–280, 338–354

di Pietro, F., "I disegni di Andrea del Sarto negli Uffizi," *Vita d'Arte 6* (1910) 128–171, 173–232 (in book form, Siena, n.d.)

Reumont, A., *Andrea del Sarto*, Leipzig, 1835

Schaeffer, E., *Andrea del Sarto*, Berlin, 1904

Sinibaldi, G., "Le opere di Andrea del Sarto che si conservano a Firenze," *L'Arte* 28 (1925) 1–23

V-M, *Vite* V (1880) 5–60

Venturi, *Storia* IX/1 (1925) 513–626

Wagner, H., *Andrea del Sarto: Seine Stellung zu Renaissance und Manierismus*, Strasbourg, 1951

Andrea del Sarto (continued)

Wischnitzer, R., "Jacopo Pontormo's Joseph Series," *GBA* ser. 6 *41* (1953) 145ff

PAINTINGS

Andrea del Sarto (continued)

BACCHIACCA [Francesco Ubertini] (1494–1557)

BIBLIOGRAPHY

Fiocco, G., "Fra Bartolommeo e Raffaello," *Riv. d'A.* 29 (1954) 43–53

McComb, A., "Francesco Ubertini," *Art Bulletin* 8 (1926) 141–168

Middeldorf, U., "Sull'attività della bottega di Jacopo Sansovino," *Riv. d'A.* 18 (1936) 245–263

Scharf, A., "Bacchiacca: A New Contribution," *Burl.* 70 (1937) 60–70

Tinti, M., *Bacchiacca*, Florence, 1925

Venturi, *Storia* IX/1 (1925) 453–474

PAINTINGS

Fra BARTOLOMMEO [Baccio della Porta] (1472–1517)

BIBLIOGRAPHY

Berenson, *Drawings* [1938] I, 155–161

C&C, *Painting* VI (1914) 50–98

Fiocco, G., "Fra Bartolommeo e Raffaello," *Riv. d'A.* 29 (1954) 43–53

Gabelentz, *Fra Bartolommeo* 1922

Gamba, C., "Raffaello e Fra Bartolommeo," *Rassegna Marchigiana* 12 (1934) 169–173

Gruyer, G., *Fra Bartolommeo della Porta et Mariotto Albertinelli*, Paris, 1886

Knapp, *Fra Bartolommeo* 1903

Fra Bartolommeo (continued)

Venturi, *Storia* IX/1 (1925) 223–347
V-M, *Vite* IV (1880) 175–202

Bibliographical references up to the date of publication are given in Gabelentz 1922. The only earlier references given below are to the more accessible volume of Knapp 1903 (reissued 1928).

PAINTINGS

doc. 1499–1501 · *Last Judgment* [with Albertinelli] (Florence, Museo di S. Marco) Knapp 1903, 16; Gabelentz 1922, I, 125, 137, 139. pp. 32–34 | 21

1504–07 · *Vision of St. Bernard* (Florence, Academy) Gabelentz 1922, I, 140. pp. 57–58 | 43

c. 1506 · *Noli me Tangere* (Paris, Louvre) Gabelentz 1922, I, 141. p. 58 | 45

1507–08 · *Assumption of the Virgin* [with Albertinelli] (destroyed, formerly Berlin) Knapp 1903, 71–72; Gabelentz 1922, I, 43, 143–144. pp. 58–59 | 46

c. 1508–09 · *Holy Family* (London, National Gallery 3914) Gabelentz 1922, I, 151. pp. 193–194 | 252

dated 1509 · *God the Father with Sts. Mary Magdalen and Catherine of Siena* (Lucca, Pinacoteca) Knapp 1903, 78, 94; Gabelentz 1922, I, 147; Venturi (1925) 272–279. pp. 194–195 | 253

dated 1509 · *Madonna with Six Saints* [with Albertinelli] (Florence, S. Marco) Gabelentz 1922, I, 56–57, 199. p. 196 | 254

dated 1509 · *Madonna with Sts. Stephen and John Baptist* (Lucca, Cathedral) Gabelentz 1922, I, 146; Venturi (1925) 272, 350. pp. 196–197 | 255

dated 1511 · *Marriage of St. Catherine* (Paris, Louvre) Gabelentz 1922, I, 155. pp. 201–202 | 260

doc. 1511–12 · *Virgin in Glory with Saints* [with Albertinelli] (Besançon, Cathedral and Stuttgart, Gallery) Knapp 1903, 124; Gabelentz 1922, I, 69, 161, 164; Venturi (1925) 350. pp. 202–204 | 261–262

c. 1512 (doc. 1510–15) · *St. Anne Altar* (Florence, Museo di S. Marco) Gabelentz 1922, I, 159; Berenson [1938] I, 160. pp. 204–205 | 263

dated 1512 · *Marriage of St. Catherine* [the *Pitti Pala*; with assistants] (Florence, Academy, ex-Pitti) Gabelentz 1922, I, 157. pp. 204–205 | 264

doc. 1514 · *St. Paul, St. Peter* [the latter with Raphael] (Rome, Vatican Museum) Gabelentz 1922, I, 166; Venturi (1925) 309–312; Gamba (1934) 173; Fiocco (1954) 44. p. 206 | 265–267

doc. 1514 · *Virgin and Child* [fresco] (Florence, Convent of S. Marco) Gabelentz 1922, I, 168; Venturi (1925) 312. p. 428 | 529

c. 1514 · *St. Mark Evangelist* (Florence, Pitti) Gabelentz 1922, I, 167. pp. 429–430 | 530

dated 1515 · *Madonna della Misericordia* (Lucca, Pinacoteca) Knapp 1903, 155; Gabelentz 1922, I, 81, 170. pp. 430–432 | 532

doc. 1515 · *Annunciation* [fresco] (Le Caldine, Convento della Maddalena) Knapp 1903, 159; Gabelentz 1922, I, 174. pp. 430–433 | 533

dated 1515 · *Annunciation Altar* (Paris, Louvre) Gabelentz 1922, I, 172. pp. 433–435 | 535

dated 1516 · *Salvator Mundi* (Florence, Pitti) Knapp 1903, 162; Gabelentz 1922, I, 83, 177; Venturi (1925) 329–332. pp. 436–438 | 536

dated 1516 · *Presentation in the Temple* (Vienna, Kunsthistorisches Museum) Gabelentz 1922, I, 179. p. 438 | 539

c. 1516 · *Isaiah, Job* (Florence, Academy) Gabelentz 1922, I, 178. pp. 438–439 | 540–541

Fra Bartolommeo (continued)

dated 1516 · *Assumption of the Virgin* [with Fra Paolino] (Naples, Galleria Nazionale) Knapp 1903, 190, 261; Gabelentz 1922, I, 183; Berenson [1938] II, 249. p. 439 | 542

dated 1516 · *Holy Family* (Rome, Galleria Nazionale) Gabelentz 1922, I, 180. pp. 439–440 | 544

dated 1516 · *Madonna and Child with Elizabeth and John* (London, Kenwood, Iveagh Bequest, Trustees of the Cook Coll.) Gabelentz 1922, I, 181. pp. 439–440 | 545

c. 1516–17 · *Pietà* [with Bugiardini] (Florence, Pitti) Gabelentz 1922, I, 87–88, 175; Venturi (1925) 325–326. p. 440 | 546

dated 1517 · *Noli me Tangere* [fresco] (Le Caldine, Convento della Maddalena) Gabelentz 1922, I, 184. p. 440 | 547

Alonso BERRUGUETE (1486/90–1561)

BIBLIOGRAPHY

Barocchi, P., *Il Rosso Fiorentino*, Rome, 1950
Becherucci, L., "Note Brevi su inediti Toscani," *Boll. d'A.*, ser. 3 38 (1953) 168–169
Berti, *Pontormo* 1956
Gomez-Moreno, M., *Los Aguilas del Rinaciamento Español*, Madrid, 1941, part IV
Kusenberg, K., *Le Rosso*, Paris, 1931
Longhi, R., "Comprimarj spagnuoli della Maniera Italiana," *Paragone* 43 (1953) 3–15
Zeri, F., *Trenta Dipinti Antichi della Coll. Saibene*, Milan, 1955
——— "Una Madonna con S. Giovanni," *Paragone* 43 (1953) 49–51

PAINTINGS

c. 1512 · *Madonna and Elizabeth with the Two Holy Children* (Rome, Galleria Borghese 335) Longhi (1953) 7. pp. 252–253 | 328

c. 1512–13 · *Madonna* (Milan, Saibene Coll.) Zeri 1955, plate 27. p. 254 | 329

c. 1513–14 · *Coronation of the Virgin* [begun by Filippino Lippi; parts only] (Paris, Louvre) Longhi (1953) 6. pp. 255–256 | 331

c. 1515 · *Salome* (Florence, Uffizi) Longhi (1953) 8. p. 537 | 659

c. 1517–18 · *Madonna with St. John* (Florence, Palazzo Vecchio, Loeser Coll.) Kusenberg 1931, 128; Barocchi 1950, 45; Longhi (1953) 9. p. 537 | 661

c. 1518 · *Madonna* (Florence, Uffizi) Becherucci (1953) 168–169. p. 537 | 660

Giuliano BUGIARDINI (1475–1554)

BIBLIOGRAPHY

C&C, *Painting* VI (1914) 114–120
Dami, G., ed. [Vasari, G.] *Vita di Giuliano Bugiardini*, Florence, 1915
Douglas, R. L., "The Fall of Man by Piero di Cosimo," *Burl.* 86 (1945) 134–139
——— *Piero di Cosimo*, Chicago, 1946
Fischel, O., *Raphael*, London, 1948
Rosenberg-Gronau, *Raffael KdK* (1909)
Sirén, O., "Alcuni Quadri sconosciuti di Giuliano Bugiardini," *Dedalo* 3 (1926) 773–783
V-M, *Vite* VI (1881) 201–211
Venturi, *Storia* IX/1 (1925) 402–426

PAINTINGS

c. 1500 · *Madonna and Child with St. John* (New York, Metropolitan Museum) p. 76 | 71

c. 1505–08 · *Holy Family* (Turin, Galleria Sabauda) Venturi (1925) 408. pp. 76–77 | 72

c. 1508 · *Portrait of a Lady* (Urbino, Gal-

Giuliano Bugiardini (continued)

Francesco FRANCIABIGIO (1482/3–1525)

BIBLIOGRAPHY

Bodmer, H., "Ein unbekanntes werk des Franciabigio," *Pantheon* 12 (1933) 270–275

C&C, *Painting* VI (1914) 121–132

Fraenckel, I., *Andrea del Sarto*, Strasbourg, 1935

Giglioli, O., "Un' affresco inedito di Franciabigio," *Riv. d'A.* 11 (1929) 212–215

——— "Note su Franciabigio e Jacopo del Conte," *Riv. d'A.* 18 (1936) 191–194

V-M, *Vite* V (1880) 189–200

Venturi, *Storia* IX/1 (1925) 427–452

PAINTINGS

Francesco Franciabigio (continued)

1513–14 · *Marriage of the Virgin* (Florence, SS. Annunziata) C&C (1914) 124–125; Venturi (1925) 430. pp. 235–239 | 314

dated 1514 · *Last Supper* (Florence, Convento della Calza) C&C (1914) 129–130. pp. 238–239 | 315

dated 1514 · *Portrait of a Man* (Florence, Uffizi 8381) C&C (1914) 126; Venturi (1925) 432–435. pp. 239–240 | 317

dated 1514 · *Portrait of a Man* (London, National Gallery) C&C (1914) 126–128. pp. 239–240 | 318

c. 1515 · *Annunciation* (Turin, Galleria Sabauda) C&C (1914) 121–122; Venturi (1925) 428–429. pp. 475–476 | 574

c. 1515 [?] · *Self-Portrait* (New York, Hunter College, ex-Kress Coll.). p. 482 | 583

dated 1516 · *Portrait of Caradosso* (London, Art Market; formerly Yarborough Coll.) C&C (1914) 128. pp. 482–483 | 584

dated 1516 · *St. Job Altar* (Florence, Uffizi). pp. 476–478 | 576

dated 1517 · *Portrait of a Man* (Vienna, Liechtenstein Coll.) Venturi (1925) 442. p. 483 | 585

c. 1517–18 · *Angels* (Florence, Sto. Spirito). p. 478 | 575

1518–19 · *Meeting of Christ and St. John Baptist; Benediction of St. John by Zachary* (Florence, Scalzo) C&C (1914) 130–131; V-M V (1880) 194–195n3; Venturi (1925) 436–437. pp. 478–479 | 577, 579

c. 1518–19 · *Madonna and Child with St. John* (Vienna, Kunsthistorisches Museum 208) Venturi (1925) 441. pp. 479–480 | 578

c. 1518–19 · *Leda* (Brussels, Museum) Venturi (1925) 429. p. 480 | 580

c. 1518–20 · *Portrait of a Fattore* (Hampton Court) C&C (1914) 128–129. p. 483 | 586

c. 1520 · *Madonna* (Bologna, Pinacoteca 294). p. 480–481 | 581

doc. 1521 · *Triumph of Caesar* (Poggio a Cajano) Fraenckel 1935, 166ff. pp. 481–482 | 582

Ridolfo GHIRLANDAIO (1483–1561)

BIBLIOGRAPHY

Clapp, *Pontormo* 1916

C&C, *Painting* VI (1914) 138–152

Gamba, C., "Ridolfo e Michele di Ridolfo del Ghirlandaio," *Dedalo* 9 (1928/9) 463–490, 544–561

Gronau, G., "Ridolfo del Ghirlandaio, Ritratto di Donna," *Riv. d'A.* 8 (1914) 55

Longhi, *Precisioni* (1927) 168–173

Poggi, G., "Della Serie dei 'Miracoli di S. Zenobi' . . .," *Riv. d'A.* 9 (1916/18) 62–67

Rajne, G. M., "Un nuovo affresco di Ridolfo Ghirlandaio," *Riv. d'A.* 28 (1953) 137–144

V-M, *Vite* VI (1881) 535–547

Venturi, *Storia* IX/1 (1925) 491–512

PAINTINGS

dated 1503 · *Madonna with Sts. Francis and Mary Magdalen* (Florence, Academy) Gamba (1928/9) 474. p. 77 | 74

1504 · *Coronation of the Virgin* (Paris, Louvre) C&C (1914) 142; Gamba (1928/9) 471. p. 77 | 75

c. 1506 · *Road to Calvary* (London, National Gallery) C&C (1914) 140–141; Venturi (1925) 493. pp. 77–78 | 76

c. 1505–06 · *Portrait of a Man* (Chicago, Art Institute) Gamba (1928/9) 465. p. 78 | 80

c. 1507–08 · *Marriage of St. Catherine*

Ridolfo Ghirlandaio (continued)

(Florence, Istituto delle Quiete) C&C (1914) 151; Gamba (1928/9) 484. p. 78 | 77

c. 1507–08 · *Lady with a Rabbit* (New Haven, Yale University Art Gallery) Gamba (1928/9) 488. pp. 78–79 | 81

c. 1508 · *Altar Wings with Angels* (Florence, Academy) C&C (1914) 152n3; Gamba (1928/9) 487. p. 78 | 78, 79

c. 1508–09 · *Girl with a Unicorn* (Rome, Borghese) Venturi (1925) 507; Longhi (1927) 168–173. p. 79 | 82

dated 1509 · *Portrait of a Lady* (Florence, Pitti) C&C (1914) 144; Gronau (1914) 55; Gamba (1928) 481. p. 209 | 277

c. 1509 · *Adoration of the Child* (destroyed; formerly Berlin, Museums) C&C (1914) 144. p. 209 | 278

dated 1510 · *Adoration of the Shepherds* (Budapest, Museum) C&C (1914) 144. pp. 209–210 | 279

1512–15 · *Nativity with Six Saints* (New York, Metropolitan Museum; formerly Milan, Crespi Coll.). p. 210 | 280

1512–15 · *Adoration of the Shepherds* [shop assistant] (formerly London, Henry Harris Coll.). p. 210 | 281

1512–15 · *Portrait of a Goldsmith* (Florence, Pitti) C&C (1914) 142n1; Gamba (1928/9) 481. p. 210 | 283

doc. 1514 · *Cappella dei Priori* (Florence, Palazzo Vecchio) C&C (1914) 145; Venturi (1925) 497–498. pp. 210–211 | 284, 285

1514–15 · *Madonna della Cintola* (Prato, Cathedral) C&C (1914) 145. p. 210 | 282

doc. 1515 · *Coronation of the Virgin* (Florence, S. M. Novella; Cappella del Papa) Clapp 1916, 123. p. 488 | 592

c. 1515 · *Resuscitation of a Youth by St. Zenobius* (Florence, Academy) C&C (1914) 146; Poggi (1916/18) 62ff; Gamba (1928/9) 488. p. 488 | 593

c. 1515 [?] · *Girolamo Benevieni* [?] (London, National Gallery). p. 489 | 596

c. 1515 [?] · *Portrait of a Man* (Florence, Galleria Corsini) Venturi (1925) 500. pp. 489–490 | 597

c. 1517 · *Translation of the Body of St. Zenobius* (Florence, Academy) see *Resuscitation of a Youth.* p. 488 | 594

c. 1518 · *Madonna with Six Saints* (Pistoia, Museum) V-M VI (1881) 536n2; C&C (1914) 147; Gamba (1928/9) 488. p. 489 | 595

c. 1518–20 · *Portrait of a Man* (Florence, Marchesa Luisa Torrigiani). p. 490 | 598

dated 1521 · *Pietà* (Colle di Val d'Elsa, S. Agostino) C&C (1914) 148–149. p. 490 | 599

Francesco GRANACCI (1469/70–1543)

BIBLIOGRAPHY

Berenson, *Drawings* [1938] I, 143–145
Clapp, *Pontormo* 1916
C&C, *Painting* VI (1914) 153–160
Fiocco, G., "La data di nascita di Francesco Granacci e un'ipotesi Michelangelesca," *Riv. d'A.* 12 (1930) 193–220; 13 (1931) 109–131
Longhi, *Precisioni* (1927) 87–88
Scharf, A., "The Robinson Collection," *Burl.* 100 (1958) 299–304
V-M, *Vite* V (1880) 339–345
Venturi, *Storia* IX/1 (1925) 475–489
Zeri, F., "Il Maestro della Madonna di Manchester," *Paragone* 43 (1953) 15–27

PAINTINGS

c. 1500 · *Holy Family* (Washington, National Gallery, Kress Coll. 573). p. 75 | 67

c. 1500 · *Madonna with Two Saints* (Berlin, Museums; formerly Halle) C&C (1914) 155. p. 75 | 68

Francesco Granacci (continued)

c. 1505–06 · *Holy Family with St. John* (Dublin, National Gallery) Fiocco (1931) 110 ff; Zeri (1953) 20. pp. 75–76 | 69

1508–09 · *Madonna della Cintola* (Florence, Academy) Venturi (1925) 484–485. p. 76 | 70

c. 1511 · *Madonna with Two Saints* (Villamagna [near Florence], S. Donnino). p. 211 | 286

c. 1510–12 · *Madonna della Cintola* (Sarasota, Ringling Museum) C&C (1914) 156–157. p. 211 | 287

c. 1512 · *Trinity* (Berlin, Museums) C&C (1914) 156. p. 211 | 288

c. 1512 · *Pietà* (Quintole, S. Pietro). p. 211 | 289

c. 1512–14 · *Madonna in Glory with Four Saints* (Florence, Academy). p.212 | 290

c. 1512–14 · *Holy Family with St. John* (Florence, Pitti) Fiocco (1931) 130. p. 212 | 291

c. 1515–16 · *Madonna with Sts. Francis and Zenobius* (Florence, Academy) Fiocco (1930) 208. p. 491 | 600

c. 1515–16 · *Madonna and Child* (San Francisco, Palace of the Legion of Honor). p. 491 | 602

c. 1516 · *Holy Family* (Boughton House, Duke of Buccleuch). p. 491 | 601

c. 1517 · *Joseph Presents His Father to Pharaoh* [from the Borgherini series] (Florence, Uffizi) Clapp 1916, 208; Venturi (1925) 487–488. p. 494 | 608

c. 1517–18 · *S. Apollonia Altar* (Munich, Pinakothek) and predella (Florence, Academy, and Berenson Coll.) C&C (1914) 156. pp. 492–493 | 603–606

c. 1518 · *Arrest of Joseph* (Florence, Uffizi) see *Joseph Presents His Father to Pharaoh.* p. 494 | 609

c. 1518 · *Entry of Charles VIII into Florence* (Florence, Museo Mediceo) Venturi (1925) 488. p. 493 | 607

c. 1518–20 · *Madonna with St. John* (formerly Munich, A. S. Drey) Longhi (1927) 87–88. p. 495 | 610

(after) 1521 · *Madonna with Four Saints* (Montemurlo, Pieve) V-M V (1880) 345n1. p. 495 | 611

LEONARDO da Vinci (1452–1519)

BIBLIOGRAPHY

Bibliography to 1930 is compiled in Varga, E., *Bibliografia Vinciana*, Bologna, 1931 (*reviewed* in Calvi, G., *Archivio Storico Lombardo* 59 [1933] 500, and Heydenreich, L., *ZK* 4 [1935] 340). Bibliography from 1930 to 1939 is compiled in *Raccolta Vinciana* 14 (1930/4); 15/16 (1935/9). Bibliography from 1939 to 1952 is compiled in Heydenreich, L., "Leonardo-Bibliographie," *ZK* 15 (1952) 195–200.

Altena, J. Q. v. R., "Rubens as a Draughtsman: I. Relations to Italian Art," *Burl.* 76 (1940) 194–200

d'Ancona, M., "La Vergine delle Rocce di Leonardo," *Arte Lombarda* 1 (1955) 98–104

Beenken, H., "Zur Entstehungsgeschichte der Felsgrottenmadonna in der Londoner National Gallery," in *Festschrift für Hans Jantzen*, Berlin, 1951, 132–140

Beltrami, L., *Documenti e Memorie riguardanti la vita e le opere di Leonardo da Vinci*, Milan, 1919

Berenson, *Drawings* [1938] I, 49–68

Bodmer, *Leonardo KdK* (1931).

——— "Leonardos zeichnerische Vorarbeiten zur Anghiarischlacht," *Mitt. KHIF* 3 (1932) 463–491

Brizio, A., "Il Trattato della Pittura di Leonardo," in *Scritti . . . L. Venturi* 1956, I, 309–320

Cassirer, E., *Individuo e Cosmo nella Filo-*

Leonardo da Vinci (continued)

sofia del Rinascimento (tr. F. Federici), Florence, 1935, esp. ch. iv

Castelfranco, G., "Il concetto di Forza in Leonardo da Vinci," *Proporzioni* 3 (1950) 117–122

——— "Momenti della Recente Critica Vinciana," in Marazza, *Leonardo* 1954, 417–477

——— *La Pittura di Leonardo da Vinci*, Milan, 1956

Clark, K., *Leonardo da Vinci*, Cambridge, 1939

Fasola, G. N., "La Nuova Spazialità," in Marazza, *Leonardo* 1954, 293–311

Florisoone, M., et al., *Hommage à Léonard de Vinci*, Paris, 1952

Gould, C., "Leonardo's Great Battle-Piece: A Conjectural Reconstruction," *Art Bulletin* 36 (1954) 117–129

Heydenreich, L., "La Ste. Anne de Leonardo da Vinci," *GBA* ser. 6 10 (1933), 205–219

——— *Leonardo da Vinci*, Berlin, 1943 (ed. 2, rev. Basel, 1953; tr. Basel, 1954)

Hours, M., "La Peinture de Léonard vue au laboratoire," *L'Amour de l'Art* 31 (1952/3) 17–33

Lessing, M., *Die Anghiarischlacht des Leonardo da Vinci*, Bonn, 1935

MacCurdy, E., *The Notebooks of Leonardo da Vinci*, London, 1938

McMahon, A. P., tr. and ed., *Treatise on Painting*, Princeton, 1956

Marazza, *Leonardo* 1954

Möller, E., *Das Abendmahl des Leonardo da Vinci*, Baden-Baden, 1952

Neufeld, G., "Lonardo da Vinci's Battle of Anghiari: A Genetic Reconstruction," *Art Bulletin* 31 (1949) 170–183

Passavant, G., *Andrea del Verrocchio als Maler*, Düsseldorf, 1959, 38–94

Pedretti, C., *Studi Vinciani*, Geneva, 1957, 132–138

Popham, A., *The Drawings of Leonardo da Vinci*, London, 1946

Richter, J. P., *The Literary Works of Leonardo da Vinci*, London and New York, 1939

de Rinaldis, A., *Storia dell'Opera Pittorica di Leonardo da Vinci*, Bologna, 1926

Rudel, J., "Le métier du peintre," *L'Amour de l'Art* 31 (1952/3) 35–45

Sanpaolesi, P., "I Dipinti di Leonardo agli Uffizi," in Marazza, *Leonardo* 1954, 29–46

von Seidlitz, W., *Leonardo da Vinci, der Wendepunkt der Renaissance*, Berlin, 1909

Sirén, O., *Leonardo da Vinci*, New Haven, 1916

Suida, W., *Leonardo und sein Kreis*, Munich, 1929

Suter, K. F., "The Earliest Copy of Leonardo da Vinci's Battle of Anghiari," *Burl.* 55 (1929) 181–188

Thiis, J., *The Florentine Years of Leonardo and Verrocchio*, London, 1913

Tolnay, C., "Les conceptions artistiques de Léonard et leur origine," *Etudes d'Art* 8–10 (1952) 375–396

Venturi, L., "Imagination et pensée dans l'art de Léonard de Vinci," in *Actes du XVIIeme Congrès International d'Histoire de l'Art*, The Hague (1955) 31–40

Wilde, J., "The Hall of the Great Council of Florence," *Warburg Journal* 7 (1944) 65ff

——— "Michelangelo and Leonardo," *Burl.* 95 (1953) 65–77

References to the principal literature to 1952 may be found in Heydenreich 1954, 179–184, 188–189. Only later references of particular interest are given here.

PAINTINGS

c. 1476 · Portions of Verrocchio's *Baptism of Christ* (Florence, Uffizi) Heydenreich 1954, 26; Sanpaolesi (1954) 29–46; Passavant 1959, 38–94, 236–237.

pp. 3–5 | 1, 2

doc. 1481 · *Adoration of the Magi* (Florence, Uffizi) Heydenreich 1954, 28–29;

Leonardo da Vinci (continued)

Rudel (1952/3) 35ff; Sanpaolesi (1954) 40–46. pp. 5–9 | 3

doc. 1483 · *Virgin of the Rocks* (Paris, Louvre) Heydenreich 1954, 32–35; d'Ancona (1955) 98ff. pp. 18–21 | 10

c. 1495–7 · *Last Supper* (Milan, S. M. delle Grazie) Möller 1952, *passim*; Heydenreich 1954, 37–41. pp. 21–23 | 12

c. 1499 · *St. Anne Cartoon* (London, Royal Academy) Heydenreich 1954, 41–43. pp. 38–40 | 22

doc. 1501 · *St. Anne Cartoon* (2) [lost] Heydenreich 1954, 41–43. p. 38 | *cf.* 23

doc. 1503–04 · *Battle of Anghiari* [lost] Heydenreich 1954, 44–48; Gould (1954) 117–124. pp. 44–46 | *cf.* 28–29

1503–06 · *Mona Lisa* (Paris, Louvre) Heydenrich 1954, 48–52. pp. 50–51 | 37

c. 1507 and later · *St. Anne, Virgin, and Child* (Paris, Louvre) Wilde (1953) 69; Heydenreich 1954, 43. pp. 51–53 | 39

c. 1513 [?] · *St. John Baptist* [assisted ?] (Paris, Louvre) Heydenreich 1954, 55–56. pp. 186–187 | 250

MASTER OF THE MANCHESTER MADONNA

BIBLIOGRAPHY

Berenson, *Drawings* [1938] I, 195–196

Bertini, A., *Michelangelo fino alla Sistina*, Turin, 1942 (ed. 2, rev. 1945), 48–49

Carli, E., *Michelangelo*, Bergamo, 1946, 33

Fiocco, G., "Sull'inizio pittorico di Michelangelo," *Le Arti* 4 (1941/2) 5–10

——— "Primizie di Michelangelo," *Riv. d'A.* 26 (1950) 149–155

Knapp, *Michelangelo KdK* (1912)

Longhi, R., "A proposito dell'inizio pittorico di Michelangelo," *Le Arti* 4 (1941/2) 136

Popp, A., "Garzoni Michelangelos," *Belvedere* 8 (1925) 6–28

Tolnay, K., *Michelangelo*, Princeton, I (1943) 236–237, 242

Wölfflin, H., *Die Jugendwerke des Michelangelo*, Munich, 1891, 82ff

Zeri, F., "Il Maestro della Madonna di Manchester," *Paragone* 43 (1953) 15–27

PAINTINGS

c. 1500 · *Madonna and Child with St. John* (Vienna, Academy) Popp (1925) 6ff; Zeri (1953) 21. p. 256 | 332

c. 1500 · *Virgin Reading with the Christ Child and St. John* (New York, Kress Coll.) Tolnay (1943) 242; Zeri (1953) 20. p. 256 | 333

c. 1500–05 · *Pietà* (Rome, Galleria Nazionale) Zeri (1953) 15–18. p. 256 | 334

c. 1505 [?] · *Madonna* (Baden bei Zürich, Private Coll.) Zeri (1953) 22. p. 256 | 335

c. 1510–12 · *Madonna with St. John and Four Angels* ["The Manchester Madonna"] (London, National Gallery) Carli 1946, 23; Zeri (1953) 22–23. pp. 256–257 | 336

c. 1512–15 · [completion of] Michelangelo's *Entombment* (London, National Gallery) Zeri (1953) 20; Wölfflin 1891, 82ff; *KdK* (1912) no. 87; Berenson [1938] I, 195–196; Carli 1946, 33; Tolnay (1943) 236–237; Bertini 1945, 48–49. pp. 257–258 | 338

c. 1515 · *Madonna* (Florence, Art Market) Zeri (1953) 22. p. 258 | 337

MICHELANGELO (1475–1564)

BIBLIOGRAPHY

Bibliography to 1926 is compiled in Steinmann and Wittkower, *Michelangelo Bibliographie, 1510–1926*, Leipzig, 1927; for 1927–1930 in Steinmann, E., *Michelangelo im Spiegel seiner Zeit*, Leipzig, 1930;

Michelangelo (continued)

for 1931–1942 in Cherubelli, P., "Supplemento alla Bibliografia Michelangiolesca (1931–42)," in *Michelangiolo Buonarroti nel IV Centenario del Giudizio Universale,* Florence, 1942, 270 ff.

[Anon] *Michelangiolo nel IV Centenario del Giudizio Universale,* Florence, 1942

Battisti, E., "Note su alcuni Biografi di Michelangelo," in *Scritti . . . L. Venturi* 1956, I, 321–339

——— "Il significato simbolico della Cappella Sistina," *Commentari* 8 (1957) 96–104

Baumgart, F., "Jugendzeichnungen Michelangelos bis 1506," *Marburger Jahrbuch für Kunstwissenschaft* 10 (1937) 209–262

Benkard, E., *Michelangelos Madonna an der Treppe,* 1933

Berenson, *Drawings* [1938] I, 184–237, 346–354

Bertini, A., *Michelangelo fino alla Sistina,* Turin, 1942 (ed. 2, rev. 1945)

de Campos, R., *Raffaelo e Michelangelo,* Rome, 1946

Carli, E., *Michelangelo,* Bergamo, 1946

Dussler, L., *Die Zeichnungen des Michelangelo,* Berlin, 1959

von Einem, H., "Michelangelos Juliusgrab im Entwurf v. 1505," in *Festschrift für Hans Jantzen,* Berlin, 1951, 152ff

Fiocco, G., "La data di nascita di Francesco Granacci e un'ipotesi Michelangelesca," *Riv. d'A.* 2 (1930) 193–220; 3 (1931) 109–131

——— "Sull'inizio pittorico di Michelangelo," *Le Arti* 4 (1941/2) 5–10

——— "Primizie di Michelangelo," *Riv. d'A.* 26 (1950) 149–155

Frey, K., ed., *Le Vite di Michelangelo Buonarroti scritte da Giorgio Vasari e da Ascanio Condivi . . .* Berlin, 1887

Frey, K., *Die Dichtungen des Michelagniolo Buonarroti,* Berlin, 1897

——— *Die Handzeichnungen Michelagniolos Buonarroti,* I, II, Berlin, 1909/11; III (by F. Knapp) Berlin, 1925

Gotti, A., *Vita di Michelangelo Buonarroti,* Florence, 1875

Hartt, F., "Lignum Vitae in Medio Paradisi: The Stanza d'Eliodoro and the Sistine Ceiling," *Art Bulletin* 32 (1950) 115–145, 181–218

Justi, C., *Michelangelo,* Leipzig, 1900 (ed. 2, Berlin, 1922)

——— *Michelangelo, Neue Beiträge zur Erklärung seiner Werke,* Berlin, 1909

Kauffmann, H., "Bewegungsformen an Michelangelostatuen," in *Festschrift für Hans Jantzen,* Berlin, 1951, 141–151

Knapp, *Michelangelo KdK* (1912)

Koehler, W., "Michelangelos Schlachtkarton," *Kunstgeschichtlichen Jahrbuch der K. K. Zentral-Kommission für Kunst- und Historische Denkmale* 4 (1907) 115–172

Panofsky, E., "The First Projects of Michelangelo's Tomb of Julius II," *Art Bulletin* 19 (1937) 561–579

Poggi, G., "Note Michelangiolesche," in *Michelangiolo Buonarroti nel IV Centenario del Giudizio Universale,* Florence, 1942, 113ff

Sobotta, R., *Michelangelo und der Barockstil,* Berlin, 1933

Springer, A., *Raffael und Michelangelo,* Leipzig, 1878

——— *Michelangelo in Rom, 1508–1512,* Leipzig, 1895

Steinmann, E., *Die Sixtinische Kapelle,* Munich, I (1901), II (1905)

Thode, H., *Michelangelo und das Ende der Renaissance,* Berlin, 1902–1912

——— *Michelangelo, Kritische Untersuchungen,* Berlin, 1908–1913

Tolnay, K., "La Théorie de l'Art et Michel-Ange," in *Deuxième Congrès International d'Esthétique et de Science de l'Art,* Paris, 1937, III, 25ff

——— *Michelangelo,* Princeton, I (1943), II (1945), III (1948), IV (1954)

——— *Michelangiolo,* Florence, 1951 (and in French, *Michel-Ange,* Paris, 1951)

V-M *Vite* VII (1881) 135–317

Michelangelo (continued)

Venturi, A., "Raffaello e Michelangelo nel 1513," *L'Arte* 21 (1918) 279–284
——— *Storia* IX/1 (1925) 627–914
Wilde, J., *Italian Drawings . . . in the British Museum: Michelangelo and His Studio*, London, 1953
——— "Michelangelo and Leonardo," *Burl.* 95 (1953) 65–77
Wind, E., "The Ark of Noah," *Measure* 1 (1950) 411–421
Wölfflin, "Die Sixtinische Decke," *Rep. KW* 13 (1890) 264ff
——— *Die Jugendwerke des Michelangelo*, Munich, 1891

References to the principal literature may be found in Tolnay (1943), Tolnay (1945), and in Tolnay 1951, 231–262, 270–275. Further references are given only to items of particular interest since the latter date.

WORKS

c. 1490–2 · *Madonna of the Steps* (Florence, Casa Buonarroti) Tolnay (1943) 75–77, 125ff. p. 30 | 17

c. 1492 · *Battle of the Centaurs* (Florence, Casa Buonarroti) Tolnay (1943) 77–79, 133ff. p. 30 | 18

1496–7 · *Bacchus* (Florence, Bargello) Tolnay (1943) 89–90, 142ff. pp. 30–31 | 20

doc. 1498–9 · *Pietà* (Rome, St. Peter's) Tolnay (1943) 90–92, 145ff. pp. 31–32 | 19

c. 1501 · *Bruges Madonna* (Bruges, Notre Dame) Tolnay (1943) 99–100, 156ff. p. 41 | 25

doc. 1501–04 · *David* (Florence, Academy) Tolnay (1943) 93–98, 150ff. pp. 41–42 | 26

c. 1504 · *Doni Holy Family* (Florence, Uffizi) Tolnay (1943) 109–11, 163ff; Wilde (1953) 69. pp. 42–43 | 27

doc. 1504 · *Battle of the Cascine* [lost] Tolnay (1943) 105–109, 209ff; Wilde (1953) 73–74. pp. 46–47 | *cf.* 36

1505–06 · *First Project for the Julius Tomb* Tolnay (1943) 32ff, 167ff; von Einem (1951) 152ff; Tolnay (1954) *passim.* pp. 47–49 | *cf.* 35

c. 1505–07 · *Entombment* [in part, finished by the Master of the Manchester Madonna] (London, National Gallery). See Master of the Manchester Madonna. pp. 257–258 | 338

c. 1506 · *St. Matthew* (Florence, Academy) Tolnay (1943) 113–115, 168ff. pp. 49–50 | 34

doc. 1508–12 · *Ceiling of the Sistine Chapel* (Rome, Vatican) Tolnay (1945) *passim*; Battisti (1956) 96ff. pp. 92–112 | 97–148

Fra PAOLINO da Pistoia (c. 1490–1547)

BIBLIOGRAPHY

C&C, *Painting* VI (1914) 99–103
Gabelentz, *Fra Bartolommeo* 1922, I, 164
Knapp, *Fra Bartolommeo* 1903
Venturi, *Storia* IX/1 (1925) 386–392

PAINTINGS

dated 1516 · *Crucifixion* (Siena, Sto. Spirito) C&C (1914) 100. p. 441 | 548

c. 1516–17 · *Holy Family with St. John and Angels* (Rome, Galleria Doria) Knapp 1903, 238; Venturi (1925) 386–388. p. 441 | 549

doc. 1519 · *Pietà* (Florence, Museo S. Marco) Knapp 1903, 239; Gabelentz 1922, I, 164; Venturi (1925) 388–389. p. 441 | 550

Baldassare PERUZZI (1481–1536)

BIBLIOGRAPHY

d'Ancona, P., *Gli Affreschi della Farnesina in Roma*, Milan, 1955

Baumgart, F., "Beiträge zu Raffael und seiner Werkstatt," *Münchner Jahrbuch der Bildenden Künste*, ns 8 (1931) 49–68

Bertini, A., "Contribuito al Peruzzi," in *Scritti . . . L. Venturi* 1956, I, 341–347

Brizio, A. M., "Lorenzo Lotto e i Primi avvii del Manierismo in Roma," in *Venezia e l'Europa* (1956) 262–265

de Campos, R., *Le Stanze di Raffaello*, Rome, 1952, 54

C&C, *Painting* VI (1914) 12–29

Dollmayr, H., "Die Zeichnungen zur Decke der Stanza d'Eliodoro," *ZBK* nf *1* (1890) 292–299

——— "Raffaels Werkstätte," *JKSW 16* (1895) 232–363

Dussler, L., *Sebastiano del Piombo*, Basel, 1942, 143

Fischel, O., "Group of Sybils," *Old Master Drawings* 5 (1930) 33–34

——— *Raphael*, London, 1948, 362

Förster, R., *Farnesina-Studien*, Rostock, 1880

Frizzoni, G., "Baldassare Peruzzi considerato come pittore," in *Arte Italiana del Rinascimento*, Milan, 1891

Gerlini, E., "To Whom Should the Monochrome Lunette in the Galatea Hall of the Farnesina be Attributed?", *GBA* ser. 6 39 (1952) 173–184

Gombosi, G., "Sodomas und Peruzzis Anteil an den Deckenmalereien der Stanza della Segnatura," *Jahrbuch für Kunstwissenschaft* 23 (1930) 14–24

Griseri, A., "Perino, Machuca, Campaña," *Paragone* 87 (1957) 13–21

Hartt, F., "Lignum Vitae in Medio Paradisi: The Stanza d'Eliodoro and the Sistine Ceiling," *Art Bulletin* 32 (1950) 124–129

Hermanin, F., *La Farnesina*, Rome, 1927

Hirschfeld, W., *Quellenstudien zur Geschichte der Fassadenmalerei in Rom*, Halle a. S., 1911

Longhi, R., "Ampliamenti nell'Officina Ferrarese," *La Critica d'Arte 4* (1940) 20

Mariani, V., "La Romanità nell'arte di Baldassare Peruzzi," *Roma 1* (1923) 276–281

——— "Dal Taccuino di Baldassare Peruzzi," *Arte* 32 (1929) 256–265

Martini, L., "Le Fonti storiche per la vita e le opere di Baldassare Peruzzi," *La Diana 4* (1929) 127–158

Ortolani, S., *Raffaello*, Bergamo, 1942, 40

Pallucchini, R., *Sebastiano Viniziano*, Milan, 1944, 40, 160

Pope-Hennessy, J., "A Painting by Peruzzi," *Burl. 88* (1946) 237–241

Pouncey, P., "Early Italian Engraving," *Burl. 91* (1949) 235

Rosenberg-Gronau, *Raffael KdK* (1909)

von Salis, A. v., *Antike und Renaissance*, Erlenbach-Zürich, 1947, 207ff

Saxl, F., *La Fede Astrologica di Agostino Chigi*, Rome, 1934

Steinmann, E., *Die Sixtinische Kapelle*, II (1905), Munich, 116–119

V-M, *Vite* IV (1880) 589–611

Venturi, *Storia* IX/5 (1932) 375–421

Weese, A., *Baldassare Peruzzis Anteil an dem malerischen schmucke der Villa Farnesina*, Leipzig, 1894

Wickhoff, F., "Marcantons Eintritt in den Kreis Römischer Künstler," *JKSW* 20 (1899) 180ff

PAINTINGS

c. 1504 · *Choir Decoration* [parts] (Rome, S. Onofrio) C&C (1914) 13; Fischel (1930) 33–34; Venturi (1932) 377–382; Longhi (1940) 20. p. 83 | 91, 92

c. 1508 · *Three Graces* [fresco fragment] (San Francisco, Zellerbach Coll.) p. 135 | 182

1510–11 · *Decoration of the ground-floor rooms, Villa Farnesina* (Rome) Hermanin 1927, *passim*; d'Ancona 1955, *passim*

Sala di Galatea C&C (1914) 16–19; Venturi (1932) 384–388; Saxl 1934, *passim*; Brizio (1956) 264. pp. 136–138 | 183–190

Baldassare Peruzzi (continued)

Sala del Fregio C&C (1914) 20; Förster 1880, 86ff pp. 139–140 | 191–193

Giant Head, Sala di Galatea Gerlini (1952) 173–184. p. 142 | 204

1511 · *Ceiling of the Stanza d'Eliodoro* (Rome, Vatican) Dollmayr (1890) 292–299; Weese 1894, 73; Dollmayr (1895) 244–245; Steinmann (1905) II, 116–119; Rosenberg-Gronau, *Raffael KdK* (1909) no. 81; C&C (1914) 14–15; Venturi (1926) 236; Baumgart (1931) 49–52; Ortolani 1942, 40; Fischel 1948, 362; Hartt (1950) 124–129; de Campos 1952, 54. pp. 147–150 | 205

c. 1512 · *Adoration of the Child* (Rome, S. Rocco) p. 150 | 211

c. 1513–14 · *Holy Family in a Landscape* (London, Pouncey Coll.) Pope-Hennessy (1946) 237ff. pp. 150–151 | 212

c. 1514–15 · *Portait of a Carmelite* (Rome, Art Market) Dussler 1942, 143; Pallucchini 1944, 40, 160. p. 408 | 493

c. 1515 · *Sala delle Prospettive* [or *delle Colonne*] (Rome, Villa Farnesina) Förster 1880, 88; Weese 1894, 73; C&C (1914) 19–20; Hermanin 1927, 81ff; Venturi (1932) 388–391; von Salis 1947, 207ff; Brizio (1956) 265. pp. 399–404 | 478–485

dated 1516 · *Ponzetti Chapel* (Rome, S. M. della Pace) C&C (1914) 21–23; Venturi (1932) 394–406. pp. 406–408 | 490–492

c. 1516 · *Apollo and the Muses* (Florence, Pitti). p. 405 | 488

c. 1517–18 · *Presentation of the Virgin* (Rome, S. M. della Pace) Venturi (1932) 391–393. pp. 408–411 | 494

c. 1520 · *Decoration* (Rome, Palazzo della Cancelleria, apartment of the Cardinal-Vicar) Griseri (1957) 13–21. pp. 411–412 | 495–496

PIERO DI COSIMO (1462–1521)

BIBLIOGRAPHY

Berenson, *Drawings* [1938] I, 150–154

C&C, *Painting* VI (1914) 42–49

Douglas, R. L., *Piero di Cosimo*, Chicago, 1946

Gamba, C., "Ridolfo e Michele di Ridolfo del Ghirlandaio," *Dedalo* 9 (1928/9) 465

——— "Piero di Cosimo e i suoi quadri mitologici," *Boll. d'A.* ser. 3 30 (1936) 45–57

Knapp, F., *Piero di Cosimo*, Halle a. S., 1899

van Marle, R., *The Development of the Italian Schools of Painting*, XIII (1931) The Hague, 335–390

Morselli, P., "Piero di Cosimo, saggio di un catalogo delle opere," *L'Arte* 23 (1958) 67–92

Panofsky, E., "The Early History of Man in Two Cycles of Paintings by Piero di Cosimo," in *Studies in Iconology*, New York, 1939, 33–67

V-M, *Vite* IV (1880) 131–144

Zeri, F., "Rivedendo Piero di Cosimo," *Paragone 115* (1959) 36–50

Full bibliographical references are given in Morselli (1958).

PAINTINGS

c. 1503 · *Madonna with Saints* [the *Innocenti Altar*] (Florence, Ospedale degli Innocenti) Knapp 1899, 46–49; van Marle (1931) 357; Douglas 1946, 107; Morselli (1958) 78. p. 73 | 63

c. 1505–06 · *Immaculate Conception* (Florence, Uffizi) Knapp 1899, 74–79; van Marle (1931) 361; Douglas 1946, 107; Morselli (1958) 77. p. 73 | 64

c. 1505–08 · *Madonna with St. John* (Vienna, Liechtenstein Coll.) Knapp 1899, 83–85; van Marle (1931) 356; Douglas 1946, 119; Morselli (1958) 85. p. 74 | 65

c. 1508 · *Liberation of Andromeda* [from

Piero di Cosimo (continued)

the *Legend of Perseus*] (Florence, Uffizi 1536) V-M IV (1880) 140n; Knapp 1899, 89–91; van Marle (1931) 370–371; Douglas 1946, 108; Morselli (1958) 79; Zeri (1959) 41–42. pp. 74–75 | 66

(after) 1510 · *Doctrine of the Immaculate Conception* [with assistants] (Fiesole, S. Francesco) Knapp 1899, 12–18; C&C (1914) 48; van Marle (1931) 374; Douglas 1946, 106–107; Morselli (1958) 78; Zeri (1959) 41. p. 213 | 292

c. 1512–15 · *Legend of Prometheus* (Munich, Pinakothek and Strasbourg, Museum) Knapp 1899, 87–89; van Marle (1931) 371–374; Panofsky (1939) 43–56; Douglas 1946, 112, 118; Morselli (1958) 81; Zeri (1959) 43–44. p. 213 | 293–294

c. 1515 · *Adoration of the Child* (Rome, Borghese) Knapp 1899, 53–54; Gamba (1928/9) 465; van Marle (1931) 367–368; Gamba (1936) 57; Douglas 1946, 123; Morselli (1958) 91; Zeri (1959) 40, 44. pp. 213–214 | 295

Jacopo PONTORMO (1494–1557)

BIBLIOGRAPHY

Becherucci, L., *Manieristi Toscani*, Bergamo, 1944

Berenson, *Drawings* [1938] I, 300–321

Berti, *Pontormo*, 1956

Bologna, F., et al., *Fontainebleau e la maniera Italiana*, Florence, 1952

Clapp, F., *Les Dessins de Pontormo*, Paris, 1914

——— *Pontormo*, 1916

Cox, J., "The Drawings of Pontormo" (unpub. diss., Radcliffe College, Cambridge) 1957

Fasola, G. N., "Pontormo e Dürer," *Arti figurative* 2 (1946) 37–48

——— *Pontormo o del Cinquecento*, Florence, 1947

Fraenckel, I., "Jugendwerke Pontormos," in "Festschrift für Walter Friedlaender," (unpub. ms. in the Kunsthistorisches Institut Florenz, 1933) 145–179

——— *Andrea del Sarto*, Strasbourg, 1935

Friedlaender, "The Anti-Classical Style" (1925) [tr. 1957]

Gamba, C., *Il Pontormo*, Florence, 1921

——— *Contribuito alla conoscenza del Pontormo*, Florence, 1956

Giglioli, O., "Chiaroscuri inediti del Andrea del Sarto, di un suo aiuto e del Pontormo," *L'Arte* 29 (1926) 261–266

Goldschmidt, F., *Pontormo, Rosso, Bronzino*, Leipzig, 1911

Grassi, L., "Appunti sul Pontormo e i suoi Disegni," *Emporium* 103 (1946) 29–44

Lavin, I., "Observations on 'Medievalism' in Early Sixteenth Century Style," *GBA* ser. 6 50 (1957) 113–187

McKillop, S., "Pontormo's Development to 1520" (unpub. paper, Dept. of Fine Arts, Harvard Univ., Cambridge) 1958

Sinibaldi, G., "Una predella del Pontormo," *L'Arte* 28 (1925) 153ff

Steinbart, K., "Der Gotiker Jacopo Carucci aus Pontormo," *Pantheon* 23 (1939) 3–12

Toesca, E., *Il Pontormo*, Rome, 1947

V-M, *Vite* VI (1881) 245–291

Venturi, *Storia* IX/5 (1932) 83–192

Voss, H., *Die Malerei der Spätrenaissance in Rom und Florenz*, Berlin, 1920, I, 163–181

Wischnitzer, R., "Jacopo Pontormo's Joseph Series," *GBA* ser. 6 *41* (1953) 145–166

Additional references may be found in Berti 1956.

PAINTINGS

1513–1st half 1514 · *Faith and Charity* [ruined] (Florence, SS. Annunziata) Clapp 1916, 9–10, 116; Gamba 1956, 8; Berti 1956, no. 1. p. 243 | —

1514 · *Ospedale di S. Matteo* (Florence, Academy) Clapp 1916, 115; Fraenckel (1933) 150ff; Berti 1956, no. 13. pp. 244–245 | 323

Jacopo Pontormo (continued)

1514 · *Madonna with Four Saints* [fresco altar, from S. Ruffillo] (Florence, SS. Annunziata) Clapp 1916, 7–9, 117. pp. 245–247 | 324

doc. 1515–1st half 1516 · *Visitation* (Florence, SS. Annunziata) Clapp 1916, 15, 117; Voss 1920, I, 164; Venturi (1932) 94–96; Fraenckel (1933) 160ff; Gamba 1956, 9; Friedlaender (1957) 20. pp. 504–508 | 639

2nd half 1515 · *St. Veronica* [and other fresco decorations in the Cappella del Papa] (Florence, S. M. Novella) Clapp 1916, 11, 123; Venturi (1932) 98; Fraenckel (1933) 156ff; Becherucci 1944, 12. pp. 508–509 | 641–642

1515–16 · *Joseph Revealing Himself to His Brothers* [Borgherini series (1)] (Henfield, Lady Salmond). pp. 510–512 | 643

1516 · *Joseph Sold to Potiphar* [Borgherini series (2)] (*ibid.*). pp. 512–513 | 644

c. 1517 · *The Butler Restored and the Baker Led to Execution* [Borgherini series (3)] (*ibid.*) Goldschmidt 1911, 5; Clapp 1916, 21–23, 156–157, 162ff; Venturi (1932) 116–120; Fraenckel 1935, 208n29; Becherucci 1944, 13; Wischnitzer (1953) 145ff; Gamba 1956, 10; Berti 1956, nos. 24–26. pp. 513–516 | 645

dated 1518 · *Madonna and Saints* [the *Visdomini Altar*] (Florence, S. Michele Visdomini, Cappella Pucci) Clapp 1916, 19, 126; Venturi (1932) 100; Becherucci 1944, 14; Fasola 1947, 29; Friedlaender (1957) 20–21. pp. 517–523 | 646

Predella for the Visdomini Altar (Dublin, National Gallery; Warwick Castle) Sinibaldi (1925) 153–158; Venturi (1932) 109–112; Fraenckel (1933) 161ff, 173n3; Becherucci 1944, 12. pp. 523–525 | 647–649

1518 · *Joseph in Egypt* [Borgherini series (4)] (London, National Gallery) see Borgherini series (1–3). pp. 525–529 | 650

1518 · *Cosimo de' Medici* (Florence, Uffizi) Clapp 1916, 21, 147ff; Venturi (1932) 122–126; Becherucci 1944, 14; Fasola 1947, 57; Berti 1956, no. 37. pp. 529–530 | 651

c. 1519 · *Portrait of a Musician* [Francesco dell'Ajolle ?] (Florence, Uffizi) Gamba 1921, 6; Venturi (1932) 100; Berti 1956, no. 36. pp. 530–531 | 653

c. 1519 · *Sts. John Evangelist and Michael* (Empoli, Collegiata, on deposit from Pontorme, S. Michele) Clapp 1916, 177–178; Becherucci 1944, 14; Berti 1956, nos. 31–32. pp. 531–533 | 655, 656

1519–20 · *St. Anthony Abbot* (Florence, Uffizi) Clapp 1916, 132–133; Venturi (1932) 181–182; Berti 1956, no. 72. pp. 534–536 | 658

1520–21 · *Vertumnus and Pomona* (Poggio a Cajano) Clapp 1916, 28–36, 173–177; Venturi (1932) 128–132; Berenson [1938] I, 304–308; Becherucci 1944, 15–16; Friedlaender (1957) 22–23. pp. 563–566 | 678–679

Domenico PULIGO (1492–1527)

BIBLIOGRAPHY

Berenson, *Drawings* [1938] I, 296–297
C&C, *Painting* VI (1914) 194, 200
Gamba, C., "Di alcune pitture poco conosciute in Toscana," *Riv. d'A.* 4 (1906) 47
Guinness, H., *Andrea del Sarto*, London, 1899, 67–68
V-M, *Vite* IV (1880) 461–468
Venturi, *Storia* IX/5 (1932) 233–249

PAINTINGS

c. 1512–13 · *Madonna and Child with St. John* (Rome, Palazzo Venezia). p. 242 | 319

c. 1514 · *Madonna with St. John Approaching in a Landscape* (Rome, Borghese 338). p. 242 | 322

Domenico Puligo (continued)

c. 1516 · *Holy Family* [on Sarto's cartoon] (London, National Gallery) C&C (1914) 200; Guinness 1899, 67–68. p. 497 | 617

c. 1517–18 · *Madonna with St. John* (Florence, Pitti 242) Venturi (1932) 235. p. 497 | 620

c. 1518 · *Adoration of the Kings* (formerly Milan, Crespi Coll.) Berenson [1938] II, 26. p. 498 | 622

c. 1518–20 · *Deposition* (Venice, Seminario). p. 499 | 623

c. 1518–20 · *Preaching of St. John Baptist* (formerly London, Henry Harris Coll.). p. 499 | 624

c. 1520 · *History of Joseph* (Rome, Borghese 463). p. 499 | 625

(after) 1520 · *Apollo and Daphne* (Florence, Galleria Corsini) C&C (1914) 194. pp. 499–500 | 626

c. 1520–22 · *Madonna with St. John and Angels* (Florence, Galleria Corsini) Venturi (1922) 235–236. p. 497 | 621

RAPHAEL (1483–1520) AND HIS SHOP

BIBLIOGRAPHY

Older bibliography, to 1883, is given in Müntz, E., *Les historiens et les critiques de Raphael*, Paris, 1883. Documents and literary sources are compiled in Golzio, *Raffaello* 1936

Alpatov, M., "La Madonna di S. Sisto," *L'Arte* ns 21 (1957) 25–72

d'Ancona, P., *La Stanza della Segnatura*, Bergamo, 1937

——— *Gli Affreschi della Farnesina in Roma*, Milan, 1955

Arslan, W., "Intorno al Sodoma, a Raffaello e alla Stanza della Segnatura," *Dedalo* 9 (1929) 525–544

Baumgart, F., "Beiträge zu Raffael und seiner Werkstatt," *Münchner Jahrbuch der Bildenden Künste* ns 8 (1931) 49–68

Brizio, A. M., "Lorenzo Lotto e i primi avvii del Manierismo in Roma," in *Venezia e l'Europa* (1956) 262–265

Burckhalter, M., *Die Bildnisse Rafaels*, Laupen bei Bern, 1932

de Campos, R., *Raffaello e Michelangelo*, Rome, 1946

——— "Dei ritratti di Antonio Tebaldeo e di altri nel 'Parnaso' di Raffaello," *Archivio della Società Romana di Storia Patria* 75 (1952) 51–58

——— *Le Stanze di Raffaello*, Rome, 1952

——— "Cromatismo Veneziano di Raffaello nella 'Messa di Bolsena,'" in *Venezia e l'Europa* (1956) 259–262

Coppier, C., *L'enigme de la Segnatura: Etude Historique sur le collaboration de Raphael et du Sodoma*, Paris, 1928

C&C, *Raphael*, London, 1882 (ed. 2, 1885)

Cugnoni, G., *Agostino Chigi il Magnifico*, Rome, 1878

Dollmayr, H., "Die Zeichnungen zur Decke der Stanza d'Eliodoro," *ZBK* nf 1 (1890) 292–299

——— "Raffaels Werkstätte," *JKSW* 16 (1895) 232–363

Donati, M., "Dell'Attività di Guglielmo di Marcillat nel Palazzo Vaticano," in *PARA Rend.* 25/6 (1950/1) 267–276

Escher, K., *Malerei der Renaissance in Italien*, Potsdam, 1922, 249–283

Fiocco, G., "Fra Bartolommeo e Raffaello," *Riv. d'A.* 29 (1954) 43–53

Fischel, O., *Raphaels Zeichnungen, Versuch einer Kritik*, Strasbourg, 1898

——— *RZ*, parts 1–8, Berlin, 1913–1941

——— "Zeichnungen der Umbrer," *JPK* 38 (1917) 1–72 and suppl. 1–188

——— "Raphael's Auxiliary Cartoons," *Burl.* 71 (1937) 166–168

——— "Raphael's Pink Sketch Book," *Burl.* 74 (1939) 181–187

——— *Raphael*, London, 1948

Förster, R., *Farnesina-Studien*, Rostock, 1880

Raphael and His Shop (continued)

Frey, K., "Zur Baugeschichte des St. Peter," *JPK* 31 (1910) suppl. 9–32

Gamba, C., "Raffaello e i suoi veri maestri," in *Mélanges Bertaux*, Paris, 1924, 93ff

——— *Raphael*, Paris, 1932

——— "Raffaello e Fra Bartolommeo," *Rassegna Marchigiana* 12 (1934) 169–173

Gere, J., "Drawings in the Ashmolean Museum," *Burl.* 99 (1957) 159–162

Gerlini, E., *La Villa Farnesina in Roma*, Rome, 1949

Ghidiglia, A., "Di alcune opere di Giovanni da Udine," *L'Arte* 30 (1927) 150–170

Glück, G., "Ein wenig Beachtetes Werk Raffaels," *JKSW* nf 10 (1936) 97–104

Gombosi, G., "Sodomas und Peruzzis Anteil an den deckenmalerien der Stanza della Segnatura," *Jahrbuch für Kunstwissenschaft* 23 (1930) 14–24

Gombrich, E., *Raphael: Madonna della Sedia*, London, 1956

Gould, C., "Leonardo's Great Battle-Piece: A Conjectural Reconstruction," *Art Bulletin* 36 (1954) 126–127

Grimme, H., "Das Rätsel der Sixtinische Madonna," *ZBK* 33 (1922) 41–49

Gronau, G., "Some Portraits by Titian and Raphael," *Art in America* 25 (1937) 93–104

Gruyer, A., *Les Fresques de Raphael provenant de la Magliana*, Paris, 1873

Hartt, F., "Lignum Vitae in Medio Paradisi: The Stanza d'Eliodoro and the Sistine Ceiling," *Art Bulletin* 32 (1950) 115–145, 181–218

Hauptmann, M., *Der Tondo*, Munich, 1936

Hermanin, F., *La Farnesina*, Rome, 1927

Hetzer, T., *Gedanken um Raffaels Form*, Frankfort a. M., 1932

——— *Die Sixtinische Madonna*, Frankfort a. M., 1947

Hofmann, T., *Raffael in seiner Bedeutung als Architekt*, Zittau, 1908–1911, esp. vol. IV (1911)

Hoogewerff, G., "Die Deutung der Grisaillen unter Raffaels Parnass," *MK* 8 (1915) 10–16

——— "Raffaello nella Villa Farnesina," *Capitolium* 20 (1945) 9–15

——— "Documenti . . . che riguardano Raffaello ed altri artisti contemporanei," *PARA Rend.* 21 (1945/6) 254–268

——— "La Stanza della Segnatura," *PARA Rend.* 23/4 (1947/9) 317–356

——— "Leonardo e Raffaello," *Commentari* 3 (1952) 172–183)

Hübner, P., "Studien über die Benutzung der Antike in der Renaissance," *MK* 2 (1909) 278ff

Knackfuss, J., *Raffael*, Leipzig, 1897

Labò, M., ed. [Vasari] *Vita di Perino del Vaga*, Florence, 1912

Lanckoranska, K., *Zu Raffaels Loggien*, *JKSW* ns 9 (1935) 111–120

Lermolieff, J. [Morelli, G.] "Raffaels Jugendentwicklung," *Rep. KW* 5 (1882) 147ff

Luetgens, H., *Raffaels 'Transfiguration' in der Kritik der letzten vier Jahrhunderten*, Göttingen, 1929

Middeldorf, U., *Raphael's Drawings*, New York, 1945

Müntz, E., *Raphael: Sa vie, son oeuvre, et son temps*, Paris, 1881 (tr. W. Armstrong, London, 1882)

——— *Les Tapisseries de Raphael au Vatican*, Paris, 1897

Oppé, A., "Right and Left in Raphael's Cartoons," *Warburg Journal* 7 (1944) 82–94

Ortolani, S., *Raffaello*, Bergamo, 1942

Pallucchini, R., *Sebastiano Viniziano*, Milan, 1944

Parker, K., "Some Observations on Oxford Raphaels," *Old Master Drawings* 14 (1939/40) 34–43

Passavant, J., *Raffael v. Urbino und sein Vater Giovanni Santi*, Leipzig, 1839 and 1858 (French ed., Paris, 1860)

Pope-Hennessy, J., *The Raphael Cartoons*, London, 1950

Putscher, M., *Raffaels Sixtinische Madonna*, Tübingen, 1955

de Quincy, Q., *Histoire de la vie et des ouvrages de Raphael*, Paris, 1835

Raphael and His Shop (continued)

Ragghianti, C. L., "Dalle Riviste," *Critica d'Arte* 3 (1938) xxxii
Ricci, C., *Raffaello*, Milan, 1920
Riedl, P., "Raffaels 'Madonna del Baldacchino,'" *Mitt. KHIF* 8 (1959) 223–246
Rocca, E. N., "Note sulle vicende della 'Madonna di S. Sisto,'" *L'Arte* 56 (1957) 73–76
Rosenberg-Gronau, *Raffael KdK* (1909)
von Rumohr, C., "Uber Raffael von Urbino und dessen nähere Zeitgenossen," in *Italienische Forschungen* III (1831)
von Salis, A., *Antike und Renaissance*, Erlenbach-Zürich, 1947
Sanpaolesi, P., "Due Esami Radiografici di Dipinti," *Boll. d'A.* ser. 3 31 (1938) 495–505
Saxl, F., *La Fede Astrologica di Agostino Chigi*, Rome, 1934, 53ff
Springer, A., *Raffael und Michelangelo*, Leipzig, 1878
Steinmann, E., "Chiaroscuri in den Stanzen Raffaels," *ZBK* nf 10 (1899) 169–178
——— "Die Anordnung der Teppiche Raffaels in der Sixtinischen Kapelle," *JPK* 23 (1902) 186–195
——— *Die Sixtinische Kapelle*, Munich, I (1901), II (1905)
Suida, W., *Raphael*, New York, 1941
Tozzi, M., "La volta della Stanza della Segnatura," *L'Arte* 30 (1927) 171–186
V-M, *Vite* IV (1880) 315–386
Venturi, A., "Raffaello e Michelangelo nel 1513," *L'Arte* 21 (1918) 279–284
——— *Storia* IX/2 (1926) 1–336
——— *Raffaello*, Milan, 1935
Vogel, J., *Bramante und Raffael*, Leipzig, 1910
——— "Zu Raffaels 'Transfiguration,'" *MK* 13 (1920) 298–305
Wanscher, V., *Raffaello Santi da Urbino*, London, 1921
White, J., and Shearman, J., "Raphael's Tapestries and Their Cartoons," *Art Bulletin* 40 (1958) 193–221; 299–323
Wickhoff, F., "Die Bibliothek Julius II," *JPK* 14 (1893) 49ff
Wind, E., "Platonic Justice Designed by Raphael: The Four Elements in Raphael's Stanza della Segnatura," *Warburg Journal* 1 (1937/8) 69–70; 2 (1938/9) 75–79
Wölfflin, H., "Das Problem der Umkehrung in Raffaels Teppichkartons," *Belvedere* 9 (1930) 63–65
von Wülfingen, O. B., *Die Verklärung Christi von Raffael*, Berlin, 1946
Zocca, E., "La decorazione della Stanza dell'Eliodoro e l'opera di L. Lotto a Roma," *Rivista dell'Istituto Nazionale d'Archeologia e Storia dell'Arte* ns 2 (1953) 329ff
Zubow, V., "Zur Komposition von Raffaels 'Sposalizio,' 1504," *ZK* 16 (1953) 145–153

INDIVIDUAL ASSISTANTS

GIOVANNI da Udine (1487–1564)

Battaglia, S., "La Stufetta del Cardinal Bibbiena," *L'Arte* 29 (1926) 30ff
Ghidiglia, A., "Di alcune opere di Giovanni da Udine," *L'Arte* 30 (1927) 150–170
V-M, *Vite* VI (1881) 549–567
Venturi, *Storia* IX/2 (1926) 399–404

GIULIO Romano (1499[?]–1546)

Boudot-Lamotte, M., "Histoire d'un tableau de Raphael," *Revue de l'Art* 65 (1934) 49–60
Fischel, O., "Un cartone per il ritratto di Leone X nella Sala di Costantino," *Boll. d'Arte* ser. 3 28 (1934/5) 484–486
Gombrich, E., "Zum Werke Giulio Romanos," *JKSW* nf 8 (1934) 79–104; 9 (1935) 121–150
Hartt, F., "Raphael and Giulio Romano, with Notes on the Raphael School," *Art Bulletin* 26 (1944) 67–94
——— "The Chronology of the Sala di Costantino," *GBA* ser. 6 36 (1949) 301–308
——— *Giulio Romano*, New Haven, 1958
Hess, J., "On Raphael and Giulio Romano," *GBA* ser. 6 32 (1947) 73–106

Raphael and His Shop (continued)

——— "The Chronology of the Sala di Costantino," *GBA* ser. 6 37 (1950) 130–132

Shearman, J., "Giulio Romano" [review of Hartt 1958], *Burl.* *101* (1959) 456–460

V-M, *Vite* V (1880) 523–557

Venturi, *Storia* IX/2 (1926) 338–387

Vogel, J., "Giulio Romanos Jugend und Lehrzeit," *MK* *13* (1920) 52–66

Guglielmo (Guillaume) MARCILLAT (c. 1470–1529)

Donati, M., "Dell'attività di Guglielmo di Marcillat nel Palazzo Vaticano," *PARA Rend.* 25/6 (1950/1) 267–276

V-M, *Vite* IV (1880) 417–430

PELLEGRINO da Modena (1460/5–1523 [?])

Fiocco, G., "Pellegrino da Modena," *L'Arte* 20 (1917) 199–210

V-M, *Vite* IV (1880) 649–651

Venturi, *Storia* IX/2 (1926) 448–452

Gianfrancesco PENNI (c. 1488–c. 1528)

Venturi, *Storia* IX/2 (1926) 387–398

PERINO del Vaga (1500/1–1547)

Labò, M., ed., [Vasari] *Vita di Perino del Vaga*, Florence, 1912

Poggi, G., "Due Affreschi di Perino del Vaga nella Galleria degli Uffizi," *Boll. d'A.* ser. 3 3 (1909) 270–273

Popham, A., "On some works by Perino del Vaga," *Burl.* *86* (1945) 56–66

V-M, *Vite* V (1880) 587–632

Venturi, *Storia* IX/2 (1926) 404–434

POLIDORO da Caravaggio (c. 1500–1543)

Pacchiotti, C., "Nuove attribuzioni a Polidoro da Caravaggio in Roma," *L'Arte* 30 (1927) 188–213

V-M, *Vite* V (1880) 141–154

Venturi, *Storia* IX/2 (1926) 434–446

Citations of important literature to 1909 are given for most works in Rosenberg-Gronau, *Raffael KdK* (1909), hereafter referred to, in this section, as *KdK* (1909). References given below are restricted to later items of particular interest.

PAINTINGS

dated 1504 · *Marriage of the Virgin* (Milan, Brera) *KdK* (1909) no. 15; Zubow (1953) 145–153. p. 62 | 49

1505 · *Madonna del Granduca* (Florence, Pitti) *KdK* (1909) no. 22; Venturi (1926) 138; Fischel 1948, 47–48, 358. pp. 63–64 | 50

dated 1505 · *Madonna del Prato* (Vienna, Kunsthistorisches Museum) *KdK* (1909) no. 28; Fischel 1948, 358. p. 65 | 53

c. 1506 · *Portraits of Angelo and Maddalena Doni* (Florence, Pitti) *KdK* (1909) nos. 32–33; Burckhalter 1932, 23; Fischel 1948, 57–59. pp. 65–66 | 51, 52

1505–06 · *Madonna del Cardellino* (Florence, Uffizi) *KdK* (1909) no. 29; Fischel 1948, 49–51, 359. pp. 66–67 | 54

dated 1507 · *La Belle Jardinière* (Paris, Louvre) *KdK* (1909) no. 36; Fischel 1948, 51, 359. pp. 67–68 | 55

c. 1507 · *Bridgewater House Madonna* (Edinburgh, National Gallery, Ellesmere Loan) *KdK* (1909) no. 43; Fischel (1939) 187; Fischel 1948, 359. p. 69 | 56

c. 1507 · *Holy Family of the Casa Canigiani* (Munich, Pinakothek) *KdK* (1909) no. 40; Fischel 1948, 359. p. 69 | 58

dated 1507 · *Entombment* (Rome, Borghese) *KdK* (1909) no. 41; Fischel *RZ* IV (1923) nos. 164–186; Fischel 1948, 62–64, 359. pp. 69–70 | 59

1507–08 · *Madonna del Baldacchino* (Florence, Pitti) *KdK* (1909) no. 46; Fischel *RZ* III (1922) nos. 140–148; Fischel 1948, 67–68, 359; Riedl (1959) 223–246. pp. 70–71 | 60

doc. 1508–11 · *Decoration of the Stanza della Segnatura* (Rome, Vatican) *ceiling*, late 1508–early 1509; *Disputà*, 1509; *Par-*

Raphael and His Shop (continued)

Raphael and His Shop (continued)

Oppé (1944) 82–94; Fischel 1948, 250–272, 365; Pope-Hennessy 1950, *passim*; Hartt 1958, 17–21; White and Shearman (1958) *passim*; Shearman (1959) 457. pp. 273–293 | 355–371

c. 1515–1st half 1517 · *Stanza dell'Incendio* [with Giulio and Penni] (Rome, Vatican) *Battle of Ostia*, 1515; *Fire in the Borgo*, c. 1516; *Coronation of Charlemagne*, c. 1516; *Oath of Leo*, early 1517; basamenti with *Royal Protectors of the Church*, late 1516–1st half 1517. *KdK* (1909) nos. 110–116; Ortolani 1942, 55; Hartt (1944) 68–73; Fischel 1948, 365; de Campos 1952, 55–66; Hartt 1958, 21–24; Shearman (1959) 457. pp. 293–312 | 374–385

1515(–16) · *Cappella Chigi* [with Alvise de Pace] (Rome, S. M. del Popolo) *KdK* (1909) no. 144; Saxl 1934, 53ff; Fischel 1948, 149–152, 365. pp. 314–316 | 386

2nd half 1515–1516 · *Baldassare Castiglione* (Paris, Louvre) *KdK* (1909) no. 119; Fischel 1948, 115–117, 365. pp. 333–336 | 423

doc. 1st half 1516 · *Apartment for Cardinal Bibbiena* [with Giovanni da Udine] (Rome, Vatican) Dollmayr (1895) 269–271; Hofmann IV (1911) 141–228; Battaglia (1926) 203–212; de Campos 1946, 31–59; von Salis 1947, 203ff; Hartt 1958, 31–32. p. 316 | 389–393

1st half 1516 · *Antonio Tebaldeo* [lost] de Campos (1952) 51–58. p. 336 | *cf* 425

1st half 1516 · *Andrea Navagero and Agostino Beazzano* (Rome, Galleria Doria) *KdK* (1909) no. 143; Gronau (1937) 93–104; Fischel 1948, 117, 365. pp. 336–338 | 426

c. 1516 · *Bindo Altoviti* [Giulio] (Washington, National Gallery) *KdK* (1909) no. 117; Hartt (1944) 90; Fischel 1948, 122, 365; Hartt 1958, 51–53. pp. 338–339 | 427

1516–17 · *Madonna della Tenda* (Munich, Pinakothek) *KdK* (1909) no. 124; Fischel 1948, 132–133, 365. pp. 347–348 | 432

1516–17 · *Spasimo di Sicilia* [with Penni] (Madrid, Prado) *KdK* (1909) no. 146; Venturi (1926) 392; Fischel 1948, 276–278; Hartt 1958, 25–26. pp. 348–351 | 433

1517 · *Sala dei Palafrenieri* [*dei Chiaroscuri*; reconstruction by Taddeo Zuccaro and others] (Rome, Vatican) Müntz 1881, 465ff; Dollmayr (1895) 317–318; Hess (1947) 76, 105. pp. 320–321 | 394

2nd half 1517–18 · *Leo X with the Cardinals Giulio de' Medici and Luigi Rossi* (Florence, Pitti) *KdK* (1909) no. 148; Fischel 1948, 120–121, 366. pp. 340–343 | 429

(late 1517–1518) · *Sala di Psiche* [with Giulio and others] (Rome, Villa Farnesina) *KdK* (1909) nos. 150–156; Hübner (1909) 279; Venturi (1926) 394ff; Hermanin 1927, 55ff; Hartt (1944) 75ff; Hoogewerff (1945) 9–15; Hess (1947) 78; von Salis 1947, 198ff; Fischel 1948, 166–168, 183–186, 366; Hartt 1958, 32–33. pp. 322–327 | 397–409

c. 1517 · *Cardinal Bernardo Bibbiena* [copy] (Florence, Pitti) *KdK* (1909) no. 203; Fischel 1948, 113–114. pp. 339–340 | 428

c. 1517–1st half 1520 · *Transfiguration* [with assistants] (Rome, Vatican Museum) *KdK* (1909) no. 194; Vogel (1920) *passim*; Hartt (1944) 86–88; von Wülfingen 1946, *passim*; Fischel 1948, 278–288, 367; Hartt 1958, 33–35. pp. 356–362 | 438

dated 1518 · *St. Michael* [with Giulio] (Paris, Louvre) *KdK* (1909) no. 158; Venturi (1926) 38; Hartt (1944) 85; Fischel 1948, 275, 366; Hartt 1958, 27. pp. 354–356 | 437

dated 1518 · *Holy Family of Francis I* [with Giulio] (Paris, Louvre) *KdK* (1909) no. 157; Fischel *RZ* VIII (1941) 385; Hartt (1944) 84–85; Fischel 1948, 366; Hartt 1958, 26–28. pp. 351–353 | 436

1518 · *Giovanna d'Aragona* [Giulio] (Paris,

ROSSO (1495–1540)

BIBLIOGRAPHY

Alazard, J., *Le Portrait Florentin de Botticelli à Bronzino*, Paris, 1924, 136ff

Barocchi, P., *Il Rosso Fiorentino*, Rome, 1950

Becherucci, L., *Manieristi Toscani*, Bergamo, 1944

Berti, *Pontormo* 1956

Bologna, F., et al., *Fontainebleau e la Maniera Italiana*, Florence, 1952

Carroll, E., "Rosso" (unpub. paper, Dept. of Fine Arts, Harvard Univ., Cambridge) 1957

Ciaranfi, A. M., "Alcune Opere del Beccafumi," *Bollettino Senese di Storia Patria* 5 (1934) 1–12

Gamba, C., "Antonio di Donnino," *L'Arte* ns 21 (1957) 7–9

Goldschmidt, F., *Pontormo, Rosso, Bronzino*, Leipzig, 1911

Hartt, F. [review of Barocchi 1950] *Art Bulletin* 34 (1952) 63–69

Kusenberg, K., *Le Rosso*, Paris, 1931

——— "Autour du Rosso," *GBA* ser. 6 *10* (1933) 158–172

Longhi, *Precisioni* (1927) 87

——— [review of Barocchi 1950] *Paragone 13* (1951) 58–62

——— "Comprimarj spagnuoli della Maniera Italiana," *Paragone* 43 (1953) 3–15

Phillips, C., "Il Rosso (Fiorentino) by Himself?" *Burl.* 20 (1911/12) 140–146

Sabatini, A., "Il Rosso Fiorentino," *La Rinascita* 4 (1941) 422

V-M, *Vite* V (1880) 155–174

Venturi, *Storia* IX/5 (1932) 193–231

PAINTINGS

c. 1512 · *Madonna and Child* (New York, Finch College, Kress Coll. 485). pp. 248–249 | 325

c. 1513 · *Madonna in a Landscape* (Florence, Uffizi 8309, on deposit Arezzo, Museum) Ciaranfi (1934) 1–12; Longhi (1951) 59; Bologna 1952, no. 1; Longhi (1953) 8; Berti 1956, no. 155; Gamba (1957) 7–9. p. 248 | 326

c. 1513–14 · *Holy Family* (Rome, Borghese) Longhi (1927) 87; Becherucci 1944, 24; Barocchi 1950, 20; Longhi (1953) 8; Berti 1956, no. 156; Gamba (1957) 7–9. p. 248 | 327

c. 1515 · *Madonna in Glory* (Leningrad, Hermitage) Kusenberg 1931, 14, 128; Becherucci 1944, 27; Barocchi 1950, 45; Longhi (1951) 61. pp. 539–540 | 662

c. 1516 · *Portrait of a Young Man* (Berlin, Museums) Phillips (1911/12) 140; Alazard 1924, 136ff; Venturi (1925) 442–443; Becherucci 1944, 24; Barocchi 1950, 88–89; Hartt (1952) 64–65; Berti 1956, no. 158. p. 541 | 663

doc. 1517 · *Assumption* (Florence, SS. Annunziata) Kusenberg 1931, 8ff; Venturi (1932) 194; Becherucci 1944, 25; Barocchi 1950, 27. pp. 541–544 | 664

doc. 1518 · *Madonna and Saints* [S. M. Nuova Altar] (Florence, Uffizi) Kusenberg 1931, 11, 128; Venturi (1932) 194; Becherucci 1944, 26–27; Barocchi 1950, 32. pp. 545–548 | 667

dated 1521 · *Deposition* (Volterra, Museum) Kusenberg 1931, 14–18, 184n32–35; Becherucci 1944, 27; Barocchi 1950, 35. pp. 554–557 | 670

dated 1521 · *Madonna with Sts. John Baptist and Bartholomew* (Villamagna [near Volterra] Pieve) Sabatini (1941) 422; Becherucci 1944, 27; Barocchi 1950, 39–40; Berti 1956, no. 162. p. 554 | 669

SEBASTIANO del Piombo [Veneziano] (c. 1485–1547)

BIBLIOGRAPHY

d'Ancona, P., *Gli Affreschi della Farnesina in Roma*, Milan, 1955

d'Achiardi, P., *Sebastiano del Piombo*, Rome, 1908

Berenson, *Drawings* [1938] I, 238–250

Sebastiano del Piombo (continued)

Bernardini, G., *Sebastiano del Piombo*, Bergamo, 1908
Dussler, L., *Sebastiano del Piombo*, Basel, 1942
——— *Die Zeichnungen des Michelangelo*, Berlin, 1959
Fischel, O., "A New Approach to Sebastiano del Piombo as a Draughtsman," *Old Master Drawings 14* (1939–1940) 21–33
Gombosi, G., "Sebastiano del Piombo," *Pantheon* 13 (1934), 161–167
Hermanin, F., *La Farnesina*, Rome, 1927
Pallucchini, R., *Sebastiano Viniziano*, Milan, 1944
Pouncey, P., "A Study by Sebastiano del Piombo for the 'Martyrdom of St. Agatha,'" *Burl.* 94 (1952) 116
von Salis, A., *Antike und Renaissance*, Erlenbach-Zürich, 1947, 196
Tietze, H. [review of Dussler 1942] *Art Bulletin* 26 (1944) 129
Tolnay, K., *Michelangelo*, Princeton, III (1948) 15ff
V-M, *Vite* V (1880) 565–586
Venturi, *Storia* IX/5 (1932) 1–82
Wilde, J., *Italian Drawings . . . in the British Museum: Michelangelo and His Studio*, London, 1953, 27ff

References to the literature through 1942 are given in Pallucchini 1944; only later references of interest or references not there cited are given below.

PAINTINGS

2nd half 1511 · *Lunettes, Sala di Galatea* (Rome, Villa Farnesina) Pallucchini 1944, 31–34, 157–158; von Salis 1947, 196. p. 142 | 196–197

1511–12 · *Adoration of the Shepherds* (Cambridge, Fitzwilliam Museum) Pallucchini 1944, 29, 157. pp. 143–144 | 199

1512 · *Polyphemus* (Rome, Villa Farnesina, Sala di Galatea) Pallucchini 1944, 31ff, 158. p. 136 | 198

dated 1512 · *Portrait of a Girl* [called "La Fornarina"] (Florence, Uffizi) Pallucchini 1944, 38, 158. pp. 145–146 | 202

c. 1512 · *Death of Adonis* (Florence, Uffizi) Pallucchini 1944, 29–30, 157. pp. 144–145 | 200

c. 1513 · *Portrait of a Girl* [called "Dorothea"] (Berlin, Museums) Pallucchini 1944, 38, 158. p. 146 | 203

1513–14 · *Madonna and Child* (London, Pouncey Coll.). p. 145 | 201

c. 1514 · *Man in Armor* (Hartford, Atheneum, formerly London, Sebright Coll.) Pallucchini 1944, 40, 160. p. 370 | 455

c. 1515 · *Young Violinist* (Paris, Baron G. de Rothschild) Pallucchini 1944, 38–39, 159. pp. 370–372 | 456

c. 1515 · *Pietà* (Viterbo, Museum) Pallucchini 1944, 47–49, 162; Tolnay (1948) 20. pp. 376–380 | 461

c. 1515–16 · *Portrait of a Young Man* (Budapest, Museum) Pallucchini 1944, 40, 160. p. 372 | 457

dated 1516 · *Cardinal Bandinello Sauli and Suite* (Washington, National Gallery, Kress Coll.) Pallucchini 1944, 41–42, 161. p. 374 | 460

dated 1516 · *Pietà* (Leningrad, Hermitage) Pallucchini 1944, 47, 161; Tolnay (1948) 19. pp. 380–382 | 462

doc. 2nd half 1516–1524 · *Decoration of the Cappella Borgherini* (Rome, S. Pietro in Montorio) *Prophets*, 2nd half 1516; *Flagellation* [on Michelangelo's design] 1516–24; *Transfiguration*, 1st half 1521. Berenson [1938] I, 240; Pallucchini 1944, 52ff, 162; Wilde 1953, 27ff; Tolnay (1948) 15ff. pp. 389–392 | 467–473

c. 1517 · *Cardinal Antonio Ciocchi del Monte Sansovino* (Dublin, National Gallery) Pallucchini 1944, 41, 160. pp. 372–374 | 458

doc. 1517–1st half 1519 · *Resurrection of Lazarus* (London, National Gallery) Pal-

Sebastiano del Piombo (continued)

lucchini 1944, 49–51, 163; Wilde 1953, 29–30; Tolnay (1948) III, 20; Dussler 1959, nos. 371, 561–562. pp. 382–387 | 463

c. 1519(1517–25) · *Holy Family with St. John Baptist and Donor* [P. F. Borgherini (?)] (London, National Gallery) Pallucchini 1944, 51–52, 162. pp. 387–389 | 466

1519–(dated) 1521 · *Visitation* (Paris, Louvre) Pallucchini 1944, 56, 164. pp. 393–395 | 474

dated 1520 · *Martyrdom of St. Agatha* (Florence, Pitti) Pallucchini 1944, 57, 164; Pouncey (1952) 116. pp. 395–396 | 475

Giovanni Antonio SOGLIANI (1492–1544)

BIBLIOGRAPHY

C&C, *Painting* VI (1914) 132–137

Degenhart, B., "Die Schüler des Lorenzo di Credi," *Münchner Jahrbuch* ns 9 (1932) 95–161

Knapp, *Fra Bartolommeo* 1903

Scharf, A., "Bacchiacca: A New Contribution," *Burl.* 70 (1937) 60

V-M, *Vite* V (1880) 123–132

Venturi, *Storia* IX/1 (1925) 392–402

PAINTINGS

c. 1512–15 · *Madonna with St. John* (Baltimore, Walters Art Gallery). pp. 495–496 | 612

c. 1512–15 · *Madonna with St. John* (Brussels, Museum); *Madonna with St. John* (Turin, Galleria Sabauda) C&C (1914) 133; Venturi (1925) 396. pp. 495–496 | 613, 614

dated 1521 · *S. Acasio Altar* (Florence, S. Lorenzo) C&C (1914) 133; Scharf (1937) 60. p. 496 | 615

dated 1521 · *Madonna della Cintola* (Florence, Academy) C&C (1914) 136; Knapp 1903, 248. p. 496 | —

date 1522 · *S. Brigitta Altar* (Florence, Academy) C&C (1914) 137; Knapp 1903, 247. p. 496 | 616

REGISTER OF PLACES

This register lists by location all the works discussed in the text. It indicates further the page or pages on which a given work is discussed initially, followed by the illustration number or numbers for it. As in the Index Raisonné, illustration numbers are set off from page numbers by a vertical bar. When a work is discussed, but not illustrated, the vertical bar is followed by a dash.

CORRIGENDA

page 18.

My characterization of the London version of the *Virgin of the Rocks* as "not by Leonardo" is much too abrupt, and it was not meant to read so harshly even when it was written (in 1954). There is no question that the London picture is the one that was finally delivered, only in 1508, to the patrons who had commissioned the first (Paris) version from Leonardo a full quarter of a century before. It could be argued that the changes in design from the first to the second version, when the latter was begun (in the middle or later 1490s) were instigated by Leonardo. However, as I read the evidence, the main labor of execution was then left to Ambrogio de Predis, Leonardo's documented helper, while Leonardo's intervention at this time was very limited. (It is visible, probably, in the Virgin's head and in that of the angel.) About a decade later, after 1506, when the contract for this painting had to be renegotiated (again with Ambrogio's participation), Leonardo intervened more substantially, and in a later style, leaving his touch in the Christ Child, in the head of the St. John, and in the Virgin's foreshortened hand.

page 34.

More recent investigations into Fra Bartolommeo's beginnings (see especially E. Fahy, *Burl.* 108 [1966] 450–63) indicate that Leonardo had a more considerable and more decisive role in the formation of Bartolommeo's Cinquecento style than my account allows. Fahy's reattribution (from Bugiardini) to Fra Bartolommeo of the Metropolitan Museum's *Madonna and Child with St. John* (our fig. 71) is evidence of Bartolommeo's relatively early concern with Leonardesque example.

page 44.

Information in a recently discovered manuscript of Leonardo's (Codex Madrid II, see *Burl.* 101 [1968] 18) gives us the date on which Leonardo began the actual painting of the *Battle*: June 6, 1505.

page 62.

This account of the chronology of Raphael's pre-Florentine years conforms to the critical view widely held when it was writtten. But it now seems to me and to others who have recently turned their attention to this time of Raphael's career that the order of events is somewhat different. Raphael's time of study with Perugino is better taken as preceding 1500; in that year Raphael is described as *magister,* and was presumably by then an independent painter. Despite this, it remains true that his style does become (as the text asserts) in some important respects more rather than less Peruginesque in the course of these first few "independent" years: the extreme of this process is in the Oddi *Coronation of the Virgin* (Vatican Museum; painted, it should be noticed, for Perugia and most likely in the year 1503, contrary to the supposition of a date c. 1500 R. Wittkower has made in *Bulletin of the Allen Art Museum,* 20 [1963] 150–68). *The Three Graces* and its companion *Dream of the Knight* (London), as well as the other small panels in similar style which the older view assigned to c. 1500, are better shifted to the latest moments of Raphael's Umbrian career or, with still greater likelihood, to the beginning of his residence in Florence. For a good account of the important evidence for the course of Raphael's earliest career see C. Gilbert, *Bulletin of the North Carolina Museum of Art,* 6, no. 1 (1965) 3–35.

page 76.

For the reattribution, from Bugiardini to Fra Bartolommeo, of the Metropolitan Museum's *Madonna with St. John,* see my note to page 34.

page 77.

I am no longer convinced that Bugiardini is the author of the *Lady* ("La Muta") of the Urbino Gallery. Though the Morellian elements in this picture still seem to me like him, the quality in general of execution, and in some passages the command of form also, are more than our experience of Bugiardini's painting may allow us to expect. In these latter respects there is much in the Urbino portrait that comes close to Raphael, and most critical opinion of recent years believes that it is his. I still find serious impediments to this opinion.

page 80.

Franciabigio's *Holy Family* in Vienna and his *Madonna del Pozzo* are, in my present opinion, a few years later in date than the text here indicates: probably c. 1512, following a trip to Rome I have hypothesized near that time (see p. 237).

page 109.

What is referred to here as the "first" unveiling, in August 1511, was very likely not the first actual uncovering of the ceiling to view. A letter of Michelangelo, written at the end of August 1510 (see K. Tolnay, *Michelangelo,* Princeton, 1945, II, no. 36), states that he has uncovered a portion of the vault; this is likely to have occurred at about its middle point.

pages 110–111.

J. Wilde, in "The Decoration of the Sistine Chapel," *Proceedings of the British Academy,* 44 (1958) 61–81, has made more concrete an idea (originally put forth by Steinmann) that the lunettes of the Sistine Ceiling were painted along with the bays above them on the vault, not in a separate campaign of work (October 1511–October 1512) as is put forth here (and in somewhat different form by Tolnay, *op. cit.,* 108–9). I now consider that Wilde's idea is correct; this requires that the chronology I have given in the text for the completion of the ceiling as if exclusive of the lunettes be taken instead as including them. My working out of the internal chronology of the ceiling differs from Wilde's (as it is specified, not by Wilde himself but by J. Schulz, *Art Bulletin,* 45 [1963] 162–3) in some important respects. I have calculated that the average rate of work was about 3 months per bay, including the relevant lunettes. My *Painting in Italy 1500–1600* (Pelican *History of Art*), Harmondsworth and Baltimore, 1971, 468, note 17, offers a more extended explanation.

pages 112 and 117.

I now exclude the possibility that either Sodoma or Peruzzi may have collaborated with Raphael on the Segnatura ceiling or that they may have assisted him in the execution of either the *Theology* or *Philosophy* tondi.

page 134.

While confirming the community in style between the frescoes in the Palazzo dei Conservatori and the group of drawings that includes the *Triumph of Titus,* P. Pouncey and J. Gere (*Raphael and His Circle,* London 1962, I, 135–137), have revived the older attribution of the drawings to Peruzzi, rather than to Ripanda.

page 140.

The dating 1512, given here for Sodoma's *Marriage of Alexander and Roxane,* previously generally taken as correct, has been advanced by A. Hayum (*Art Bulletin,* 48 [1966] 215–217), I believe correctly, to 1516–17, on grounds that have to do in the main with a later dating than has usually been assumed for the Raphael drawing from which the Sodoma fresco is derived. In this light, Sodoma's relationship to Raphael's example becomes yet more retarded and provincial than my text suggests.

pages 147-150.

Evidence gathered by J. Shearman ("Raphael's Unexecuted Projects for the Stanze," in Walter Friedlaender zum 90. Geburtstag, Berlin, 1965, 158–80) and K. Oberhuber (*Mitt. KHIM* 12 [1966] 225–44), including the rediscovery of two preparatory studies by Raphael, seems to have settled in Raphael's favor the long controversy concerning the first design for the wall that now contains the *Bolsena* fresco, and the designs for the Old Testament scenes in the *tende* of the Stanza d'Eliodoro ceiling. Shearman gives good grounds to believe that whatever Peruzzi may have painted in the *tende* spaces was broken up by Raphael about 1514 and replaced with the present scenes on his design. I concede Raphael's invention of the *tende* frescoes, but I still cannot altogether reconcile their execution with what I know of Raphael's own hand (and shaping mind, as well) as a *frescante,* and I do not believe that my doubts are caused entirely by the condition of the frescoes, now rather reduced. Is it possible that Peruzzi might have been recalled to work on the ceiling as executant for Raphael's new designs? It is suggestive that his authorship of the Oxford drawing (our fig. 207) seems to be unequivocal, and it is not after the finished painting.

Shearman proposes that the drawing illustrated in our fig. 206 copies a project by Raphael, pre-dating mid-1510, for the *Law* wall of the della Segnatura, rather than for the Eliodoro room.

page 150.

C. Frommel, *Die Farnesina und Peruzzis architektonisches Frühwerk,* Berlin, 1961, 121–122, has found a document which dates the *Adoration of the Child* in S. Rocco in 1515.

page 151.

Shearman, *op. cit.,* has advanced good arguments to indicate that Raphael's inventions for the walls of the Stanza d'Eliodoro were all contemporary, and precedent to the beginning of his painting in the room. Rather than justify the iconography of the frescoes by connection with "current" events that precede the presumed date of the designs (probably still within 1511), Shearman prefers to consider that their subjects are "prophetic," and have no contemporary reference. By his account, the painting of the ceiling post-dates the wall frescoes and the concord between the subjects on the ceiling and on the walls is *post-facto.*

page 167.

M. Hirst (*Journal of the Warburg and Courtauld Institutes,* 24 [1961] 171 ff.) has satisfactorily established that the *Resurrection* studies were intended by Raphael for an altarpiece, which he did not execute, for the Chigi Chapel in S. Maria della Pace. Hirst proposes that the correct date for the studies would be c. 1514.

page 172.

I now believe that the *Madonna dell'Impannata* shows Raphael's execution substantially, and that there has been no major intervention by Giulio.

page 179.

The Czartoryski "Fornarina": it was the apparently rather abraded condition of this portrait (which I have not seen in the original), and the effect of thinness (and occasional weakness in drawing) that resulted mostly from it, that caused my disbelief in Raphael's authorship. I am now disposed to think it is mainly by Raphael himself and about contemporaneous with the *Donna Velata.* It is worth observing that the Czartoryski picture is yet more *Mona Lisa*–like than the *Donna Velata.*

page 188.

My speculation of so early a date as 1514 for Correggio's visit to Rome is too radical. The Raphaelisms that appear in Correggio's painting from c. 1515 onwards are sufficiently explained by the presence in North Italy of the *St. Cecilia Altar* and the *Sistine Madonna.* See my *Painting in Italy 1500–1600,* chapter IV.

page 199.

It is now more widely held that the larger role in the execution of the early *Annunciation* of Volterra is the Frate's rather than Albertinelli's.

page 200.

It has been proven correct that, as Vasari reported (IV, 223), Albertinelli's retirement from painting at the termination of his partnership with Fra Bartolommeo (in January 1513) was only an interlude. At least two pictures which post-date 1512 have been brought to public notice in recent years: an altarpiece at Volognano near Florence, signed and dated 1514, and a *Coronation of the Virgin* in S. Maria della Quercia, Viterbo, begun probably in 1514 but completed only in 1523 by Fra Paolino. See especially V. Borgo, *Burl.* 108 (1966) 468.

page 213.

I should now date Piero's *Prometheus* panels somewhat earlier, towards 1512, and place the Borghese tondo *Adoration of the Child* slightly earlier still. At the date I proposed in the text for that work, c. 1515, I believe that we should place the *Holy Family* in the Cini collection, Venice, and the *Madonna with Angels* in Tulsa (Kress Collection). To these, however, no more than the general point of the characterization that we have made for the Borghese *Adoration,* of the special and personal character of content, may apply: they demonstrate a decline in Piero's control over the matter of his art. See M. Bacci, *Piero di Cosimo,* Milan, 1966, for illustrations.

page 214.

The results of further study of Andrea's career were presented in my *Andrea del Sarto* (Cambridge, Mass., 1963). The subsequent publication on Andrea by J. Shearman (Oxford, 1965) contains, among other valuable contributions, a probing into Andrea's origins farther back than I had been able to go, establishing that Raffaellino del Garbo had been Andrea's teacher more recently than Piero di Cosimo, and indicating the survival of a few pictures of Raffaellino-like mold, of earlier date than I could find. My *Sarto* will supply the reader with the opinions I now hold that may be in contrast with this text.

page 222.

My unwillingness to credit the date 1509 inscribed on Franciabigio's Borghese *Madonna and Child* has, in retrospect, no justifiable ground. My former discomfort with this date is quite resolved by the dating, later than 1509, I am now prepared to assign to Franciabigio's *Madonna del Pozzo.* See my note to p. 80 above.

page 228.

Sarto's *Marriage of St. Catherine* in Dresden is wholly autograph; the supposition of Puligo's assistance in execution I made for this and for certain other pictures by Andrea of somewhat later date (*Madonna with the Infant St. John,* Borghese, no. 336, p. 242; *Tobias Altar,* Vienna, p. 242; *Story of Joseph* 1 and 2, p. 497) should be discounted.

page 235.

Shearman, *Burl.* 102 (1960) 152–6, publishes documentary information that Franciabigio's *Marriage of the Virgin* was finished by September 1513. Thus, Vasari's famous account of Franciabigio's rage at the "premature" comparison of his fresco with

Andrea's *Birth of the Virgin* must be incorrect. It nevertheless remains that Franciabigio (also according to document) *did* damage his own fresco.

page 242.

See my remarks to p. 228. Qualities I took as demonstrating Puligo's hand and temper, especially in the *Tobias Altar,* are, in fact, idiosyncrasies of Andrea's artistic behavior about 1511–13. I now regard the date of the *Tobias Altar* as being 1511.

pages 248–251.

The route that Longhi had indicated as an avenue to the identification of Rosso's early work, through the *Holy Family* of the Borghese, seemed at the time logical and persuasive to most students of the field. But the investigations by Frederico Zeri of what he has baptized the Florentine "Eccentrics" (*Boll. d'A.*, 47 [1962] 216–36, 314–26; see especially 216 ff.) have established clearly that the works we thought Rosso's "juvenilia" are in fact part of a much larger body of paintings by another and so far still anonymous artist, of much less merit, whom Zeri has christened "Master of the Kress Landscapes." The same painter is responsible for the *Madonna with St. John* formerly in the Drey Collection (my fig. 610, where Longhi's proposition that it is by Granacci, working in dependence upon "Rosso's" Borghese *Holy Family,* can no longer hold).

page 257.

I would not now assert the presence of Michelangelo's hand in the London *Entombment* with any comparable certainty to that which I formerly entertained.

page 274.

The study in the Louvre for the whole of the *Pasce Oves* composition now seems to me (cf. J. Shearman, *Burl.*, 101 [1959] 457 and Oberhuber *JKSW* 58 [1962] 29) to be by Raphael himself.

page 294.

The accumulation of critical opinion in favor of Raphael's entire authorship of the preparatory study (Albertina) of two standing nudes for the *Ostia* is sufficient to make me put aside my former reservations about it. The study for the *Miraculous Draught of Fishes,* also in the Albertina, which I assigned to Penni, has been shown convincingly by Oberhuber (*loc. cit.*) to be characteristic of Giulio's manner at this moment.

My placing of the *Ostia* earlier in time than the *Fire in the Borgo* does not now seem to me correct, and I prefer the traditional view that puts the *Fire* first—probably antecedent in invention to the Tapestry Cartoons, but mostly subsequent to them in execution. Oberhuber, *op. cit.*, 42 ff., and Shearman even more (e.g., in Walter Friedlaender zum 90. Geburtstag, 1965, 175) argue for Raphael's substantial role in the execution of the *Fire* fresco, a case I now accept in part.

page 316.

The altarpiece originally intended for the Chigi Chapel in S. M. del Popolo was, as Shearman (*Journal of the Warburg and Courtauld Institutes,* 24 [1961] 129 ff.) has determined, an *Assunta:* the attitude of God the Father and, in general, the representation of a "heaven" in the dome is thus more precisely explained.

page 323.

The degree to which the presumed contribution of Raffaellino del Colle is "identifiable" is more speculative than the phrasing of this sentence makes clear.

page 326.

A more generous view than this should be taken of Raphael's authorship of the surviving studies for the Farnesina. Chatsworth and Cologne also possess studies that may be for this project.

page 331.

The lower loggia is on the first floor (by non-U.S. nomenclature), not the ground floor, of the Cortile.

page 332.

The problem of Raphael's supply of first ideas in drawing for the biblical stories of the Logge can now be differently assessed, admitting more likelihood of his responsibility for them, though in what form and what measure remains uncertain.

page 338.

If we concede a larger role for Raphael in the execution of the *Fire in the Borgo* (see my note to p. 294), then we should be more flexible about the possibility of his execution of the *Bindo Altoviti;* however, this latter is a consequence of the former position that I find myself reluctant to accept.

page 348.

The completion of the *Spasimo* should more likely be taken as within 1516 rather than into 1517. The North European elements in the *Spasimo* include references to Dürer's *Large Passion* and to a Lucas van Leyden of 1515.

page 351.

I should now concede a more extensive participation by Raphael himself in the execution of the *St. Michael.*

page 365.

It is not clear from my presentation of the *Madonna della Perla* that I believe it started with an idea of some kind, however small or merely suggestive, supplied by Raphael.

page 369.

Among this group of "studio" works, recent criticism tends to regard the *Madonna della Rosa* as possibly of Raphael's own execution.

page 383.

The attribution to Sebastiano of these drawings (and of a number of others such as those for the *Flagellation of S. Pietro in Montorio,* p. 391 and figs. 470 and 472) is a matter of serious contest. Since J. Wilde's publication of the Michelangelo drawings in the British Museum (*Michelangelo and his Studio,* London, 1953) many critics subscribe to the view that they are Michelangelo's. I have put the question up for further debate in a note in *Art Bulletin* 45 (1963) 253–258, articulating in some detail the arguments for Sebastiano's authorship of this disputed group.

page 411.

It should be noted that C. Frommel, *Baldassare Peruzzi als Maler und Zeichner* (Beiheft zur Romischen Jahrbuch für Kunstgeschichte XI), Vienna and Munich, 1967–8, 125, prefers, on the basis of his consideration of the style of Peruzzi's *Presentation of the Virgin,* to put it forward in time, into the early years of the following decade (i.e., shortly after 1523, following Peruzzi's absence of 1521–3 in Bologna). I see no compelling reason to date the painting so late as this, but it well may be that my dating in 1517 or in 1518 is a couple of years too early. I should like to indicate that the dating of Peruzzi's room in the Cancelleria now puzzles me. Could the lunettes and ceiling be of different dates? The ceiling would, in such a case, seem to be the later. That hands other than Peruzzi's were involved in the execution of this room is evident.

page 415.

See my note to page 332. Pouncey and Gere, *op. cit.,* 53–55, assigned to Penni not only the surviving preparatory studies for vaults 1 through 9 but those for the last vaults, which I have given to Perino. However, Pouncey and Gere affirm that the ultimate responsibility for invention of the Logge stories must rest with Raphael.

CORRIGENDA

page 417.

Recent cleaning of the Sto. Stefano *Pietà* has altered its appearance significantly. The landscape has proved to be an addition of the later 16th century, while the style revealed in the figures shows the date of the fresco to be nearer 1520 than I supposed; this later dating is confirmed by the evidence of a newly discovered preparatory study (Oberhuber, *Master Drawings* 4 [1966] 175). The *Pietà* is reproduced in its cleaned state by Brugnoli in *Boll. d'A.* 47 (1962) 340, fig. 23.

My assumption of Perino's authorship for the Louvre drawing in my fig. 526 no longer seems valid. For the while it must return to its former indefinite attribution: "Raphael School."

page 440.

V. Borgo (*Burl.* 108 [1966] 463–68) has proposed, and I think correctly, that the *Pietà* of the Pitti is a picture begun in 1511 on commission from the Certosa di Pavia, that it was handed over to Albertinelli (to whom the commission originally had come) on the dissolution of the joint shop with Fra Bartolommeo in January 1513, and subsequently given by Albertinelli to Bugiardini for completion. According to Borgo, the older literature has made a confusion between the Pitti *Pietà* and one painted by Fra Paolino for the Convent of the Maddalena at Le Caldine (see p. 441 and fig. 500); the latter picture seems to have been laid out in Bartolommeo's studio and left unfinished at his death.

page 442.

The vaulting of the loggia of the Scalzo cortile is an 18th century alteration of what had been, originally, a flat roofing; the painted lunettes which "match" the vaults are an addition of the same time. Andrea's painted fields stop at the upper line of the *atticae* which crown the frescoes. See J. Shearman's carefully researched and documented demonstration in *Mitt. KHIF* 11 (1960) 206–20. Since this writing, the Scalzo frescoes have been detached and cleaned.

pages 442–471.

See my *Andrea del Sarto* for my later ideas on several of Andrea's works discussed in this section, especially in respect to datings. I summarize the differences: (p. 442) the *Caritas,* for which there is no documented date, should be of 1513–14 rather than 1515. (p. 446) The same dating should apply to the stylistically similar decorations in grisaille, for which I have suggested a connection with the entry of Leo X. This connection is speculative, and Shearman (*Burl.* 104 [1962] 478–83) has suggested they should be associated rather with a festival of 1513. (p. 447) The Leningrad *Holy Family with St. Catherine,* a part of this same stylistic group, must be dated with it. (p. 450) For the *Redeemer* of the Annunziata I prefer c. 1515 to c. 1516. (p. 469) The Borghese *Madonna and Child with St. John* should precede Andrea's French trip, not follow it; I have redated it to c. 1517, and consider that the painting is indicative of Andrea's influence on Pontormo's Visdomini altarpiece, not vice-versa. (p. 470) For the Wallace *Madonna,* c. 1519 works better than 1520, and (p. 471) for the Vienna *Pietà* 1520 better than 1521.

page 479.

I am no longer certain that the version in Vienna of Sarto's *Madonna and Child with St. John* (Louvre no. 1516) must be by Franciabigio, but I cannot satisfactorily identify another author. See my *Sarto* II, 85 for the critical history of this painting.

page 480.

Shearman, *Andrea del Sarto* II, 216, attributes the Brussels *Leda* to Sarto, c. 1513–14. A recent opportunity to re-study this picture has convinced me that it is at least from Andrea's shop.

page 481.

Franciabigio's fresco would seem to represent the *Triumph of Cicero* rather than the *Triumph of Caesar.*

page 483.

I now find the attribution to Franciabigio of the Liechtenstein portrait of 1517 unsatisfactory. The *Fattore* at Hampton Court carries the date 1523 inscribed on the sitter's book.

page 495.

See my note to pp. 248–51.

page 497.

For my more recent views on Puligo's part in Sarto's works of c. 1513–17 see my note to p. 228.

pages 498–500.

Zeri's clarification of the personality of Antonio di Donnino in his "Eccentrici fiorentini" (*op. cit.*, 231–36) has made clear that the whole group of small pictures here assigned to Puligo is instead by that lesser painter, or in the case of the ex-Crespi *Adoration* (fig. 622) at least closer to him than to Puligo. This considerable shift of evidence leads me now to question also my attribution of the larger Pitti *Madonna* no. 242 to Puligo: might this too be Antonio di Donnino?

page 523.

J. Cox-Rearick, *The Drawings of Pontormo*, Cambridge (Mass.) 1964, I, 137–145, considers that while the essential elements of design in the predella are Pontormo's the painted execution is wholly by another hand, rather later in date than the designs.

page 539.

See my note to pp. 248–51. Our knowledge of Rosso's beginnings does not antedate c. 1516. The Leningrad *Madonna in Glory*, which I here dated c. 1516, I should now think later, probably of c. 1519. I should like to indicate that I have a slight but ineradicable discomfort about the certainty of the attribution to Rosso of the *Portrait of a Young Man* in Berlin, fig. 663.

page 554.

Rosso's *Deposition* was commissioned originally for the Compagnia della Croce of Volterra and only subsequently exhibited in the Cathedral.

page 568.

Recent research has established that Raphael himself was in some still unspecified measure involved with the project to decorate the Sala di Costantino. See especially Shearman, *op. cit.*, 1965, 177–80, and a summary of the evidence in L. Dussler, *Raffael*, Munich, 1966, 96–97. Vasari's affirmation that the basic mode of division of the walls was Raphael's is almost certainly correct, and there is a fair presumption that Raphael, rather than Giulio, may be the author of at least two of the preparatory studies for this Sala that survive. My insistence that the style in which the room was actually executed is essentially Giulio's, and not a reflection of an intention that may have been in Raphael, remains, in my view, correct.

INDEX

In this index, as in the preceding material, the illustration number of the work mentioned is set off from the text page number or numbers by a vertical bar. When a given work is discussed but not illustrated, the vertical bar is followed by a dash.

Raphael and his Shop (continued)

Raphael and his Shop (continued)

Raphael and his Shop (continued)

Sebastiano del Piombo [Veneziano] (continued)

72 73 74 12 11 10 9 8 7 6 5 4 3 2 1